ENGLISH SPIRITU

For Anne

ENGLISH SPIRITUALITY

From 1700 to the Present Day

Gordon Mursell

First published in hardback in Great Britain in 2001

Society for Promoting Christian Knowledge
36 Causton Street
London SW1P 4ST

This paperback edition published 2008

The author and publisher acknowledge with thanks permission to use extracts
from the following in Volumes 1 and 2:
Philip Larkin, 'Faith Healing', in *Collected Poems*, Marvell and Faber, 1988.
T. S. Eliot, 'Murder in the Cathedral' and 'Choruses from *The Rock*',
in *Poems and Plays*, Faber and Faber, 1936.
R. Hamer, ed. and trans., 'The Seafarer' and 'The Dream of the Rood',
in *A Choice of Anglo-Saxon Verse*, Faber and Faber, 1970.
T. Shippey, trans., *Poems of Wisdom and Learning in Old English*, D. S. Brewer, 1976.

British Library Cataloguing-in-Publication Data
A catalogue record for this book is available from the British Library

ISBN 978–0–281–05992–8

1 3 5 7 9 10 8 6 4 2

Typeset by Kenneth Burnley, Wirral, Cheshire
Printed in Great Britain by Ashford Colour Press

Produced on paper from sustainable forests

Contents

Introduction

This book forms the second part of a two-volume study of English spirituality. The methodology, and the way in which 'spirituality' is understood, are considered in the first chapter of the first volume, and are not repeated here. Nonetheless, because after much reflection I decided to adhere to a straightforwardly chronological approach, it is hoped that this book, which covers the subject from 1700 until 2000, can in most respects stand alone.

One or two preliminary remarks need to be made. The sheer quantity of material which might be thought relevant to the subject inevitably increases in more recent centuries, and the need for some judicious abridgements becomes unavoidable. I am deeply indebted to SPCK for their willingness to publish a work which in its final form was nearly twice as long as the one they originally asked for; but even so, large amounts had to be left out. In the final chapter in particular, it was impossible to explore some aspects of the burgeoning contemporary interest in spirituality in any detail, though it may be hoped that the bibliographies will help to direct people looking for more extended treatment of this or that area. The responsibility for deciding what to include and what not is of course mine alone.

The sensitive issue of gender-inclusive language is unavoidable in a book of this kind. I have tried to ensure that the language of the book is as inclusive as possible: where translating from other languages, I have done so inclusively where the original permitted; when drawing on others' translations, I have emended them (in each case indicating any changes in the notes) where it seemed appropriate to do so. I have sought to avoid the use of the masculine gender in relation to God wherever possible. I have used the NRSV whenever citing a text from the Bible. However, when citing extracts from historical texts written at a time when 'man' was understood to cover female as well as male, I have not presumed to interfere – except in a number of twentieth-century instances where my own judgement is that the author would have used inclusive language were she or he alive today (all such cases are of course indicated in the notes).

Finally, reference was made (in the Acknowledgements in Volume One) to my indebtedness to the Revd Gordon Wakefield in the years of research preparatory to the writing of these books. Gordon died in September 1999, just before this volume was to go to the press. Like many others, I have lost a dear friend and a wise mentor:

re-reading the pages of this volume in particular makes me aware of how much I owe him. It is a great sadness for me that he did not live to see it published. May he rest in peace.

GORDON MURSELL

Note

The New Revised Standard Version of the Bible is used throughout for biblical texts. Where translations are made from other languages into English, the translator is always acknowledged: where no such acknowledgement is made, the translations are my own.

In writing this book, every effort has been made to offer a coherent and continuous narrative for each chapter. The footnotes are not just references: they are intended to amplify, to comment upon, or suggest ways of exploring further, themes mentioned in the main text.

Each chapter has its own bibliography. All works cited in the bibliographies are works which have been drawn on in the writing of this book, or which enlarge upon some aspect of its contents. Books and articles of specific and very limited relevance to a particular point are cited in the footnotes only.

1

Enthusiasts and Philosophers

English Spirituality in the Eighteenth Century

Upon one Account the Libertine seems to be a much less formidable Enemy than the Enthusiast, as there are more Hopes of a Reformation from him than from the other. As he generally acts upon no Principles at all, or else upon very unsettled ones, and such as have been but very slightly examin'd by him, he may, as the Heat of Youth goes off, and after a Fatigue of sensual Pleasures, arrive at his right Mind, and true Notion of Things. But we can have no room to think so of the Enthusiast. He acts upon Notions, wild as they are, which to him appear as certain as Revelations from the Deity, nay, which he oftentimes is positively persuaded in himself are Revelations. How then can we expect a Change in this Man, who shelters his Errors under the Pretext of Infallibility, and pretends to act by the immediate Influence of Heaven?

That there are now such a Set of Men in the World, who would endeavour to persuade us that they are actuated by an extraordinary Influence from above, that they openly aver their Principles, and are continually striving to gain Proselytes to them, can be no Mystery to any one who has well consider'd the Tenets and Dispositions of our Modern Methodists.

What an unhappy Influence their Notions may have upon the Young and Unwary, I shall prove to you, by an Account of a Visit I lately made to a Gentleman of my Acquaintance, unaccountably possess'd by them. I had formerly a very particular Intimacy with him at School, where I had observ'd in him an amiable Simplicity of Manners, with a wonderful Quickness and Vivacity of Parts. In short, his Capacity and Accomplishments were such as, I have often thought, could not but one Day make him a Delight to his Friends, an Honour to his Country, and an Ornament to whatever Profession he should think proper to engage in.

I was surpriz'd to find myself receiv'd by him with a wonderful Coldness. Instead of warm Expressions of Friendship, and Proposals for the Continuance of it, I immediately perceiv'd the Marks of Dissatisfaction upon his Countenance. His demure Look and Reservedness of Behaviour, quickly told me that I was no welcome Guest. However, I was resolv'd to stay some Time, in order to examine into the Reasons of this Change of Disposition towards me. It was not long before the Discourse turn'd upon Religion.

I now began to perceive the Cause of his Distemper. He descanted to me on the stupendous Subjects of Free Grace, Holy Influences, Regeneration, Election, Reprobation, and gave some shrewd Hints that I had the Tokens of the last upon me. The many wild Inconsistencies he ran himself into in half an Hour's Talk, together with the natural Aversion I have to any thing of Moroseness in Religion, threw me into the utmost Concern for him. Besides the utter Impossibility of persuading those People by plain Reason and Argument, there appear'd some thing so ridiculous in the whole Tenor of his Discourse, as intirely forbad me to making a serious Reply. What could I do? To have laugh'd would have been as great a Breach of good Manners in me, as it would have been thought by him, irreligious and profane. I remember'd likewise, the Advice of old *Osborn* to his Son, *viz.* 'Despise not a Profession of Holiness, because it may be true. But have a Care how you trust it, for fear it should be false.'

This is an extract from an article which appeared anonymously in *The Gentleman's Magazine* in 1739.[1] The author is dismayed to find a friend whom he had hitherto prized for his 'amiable Simplicity of Manners' and fluent social skills to have embraced the 'enthusiasm' of the Methodists: as a result, it appears, his friend has become morose, unsociable and possessed of a highly subjective religious credulity. A sunny and well-mannered piety, which sat easily with the culture of polite society, has (it appears) been transmogrified into a dark and narrow exclusivism.

The author was by no means alone in his attack on enthusiasts: Horace Walpole said to Hannah More that he would 'shave their heads and take away some blood'.[2] Laurence Sterne, author of *Tristram Shandy* and rector of Sutton-on-the-Forest in Yorkshire, declared in one of his sermons that

the great and unedifying rout made about sanctification and regeneration in the middle of the last century, and the enthusiastic extravagances into which the communications of the spirit have been carried by so many deluded or deluding people in this, are two of the great causes which have driven many a sober man into the opposite extreme.[3]

And Oliver Goldsmith, though acknowledging that Methodist preachers could speak with more feeling than their Anglican counterparts, regretted their lack of common sense:

I have attended most of our pulpit orators, who, it must be owned, write extremely well upon the text they assume. To give them their due also, they read their sermons with elegance and propriety; but this goes but a very short way in true eloquence. The speaker must be moved. In this, in this alone, our English divines are deficient . . . When I think of the Methodist preachers among us, how seldom they are endued with common sense, and yet how often and how justly they affect their hearers; I cannot avoid saying within myself, had these been bred gentlemen and been endued with even the meanest share of understanding, what might they not effect![4]

'Enthusiasm in religion,' he concluded, 'which prevails only among the vulgar, should be the chief object of politics,' where it may be kept firmly under the government of reason.[5]

INTRODUCTION:
THE SOCIAL AND INTELLECTUAL CONTEXT OF EIGHTEENTH-CENTURY ENGLISH SPIRITUALITY

The growth of urban society

This tension, between reason and emotion, between the 'enthusiast' and the 'philosopher', goes to the heart of English spirituality in the eighteenth century; but before examining both in more detail we need to consider the context in which this tension developed. It is no surprise to find substantial differences in culture and context between the England of (say) the mid-seventeenth century and that of a hundred years later; and a few are worth noting. First, the eighteenth century was relatively more settled than its predecessor: though we should not underestimate the alarm felt by many during the Jacobite rebellions of 1715 and 1745, and the cost of foreign wars, the century witnessed a growth in stability and (in its second half) a growth in parliamentary power. Even so, contemporaries believed it to be a period of change: the poet William Cowper declared in 1780 that

> when we Look back upon our Forefathers, we seem to Look back upon the
> People of another Nation, almost upon Creatures of another Species.[6]

Secondly, during the century Britain became an imperial power: Canada (1763), large tracts of what would later become the United States (1763–83), and Madras (1748) were established as British colonies. The 1713 Treaty of Utrecht granted Britain more than land: it won the contract to import slaves to the Spanish Indies, making the eighteenth century the golden age for the slave trade and Great Britain one of its largest beneficiaries.[7]

Thirdly (and, for our purposes, most significantly of all), the eighteenth century witnessed the rapid growth of the major towns, a growth that not all contemporaries approved of:[8] William Cowper speaks of

> Suburban villas, highway-side retreats,
> That dread th'encroachment of our growing streets[9]

and (in the same poem) of the growing popularity of seaside expeditions.[10] And he also warns of the moral dangers of towns:

> Such London is, by taste and wealth proclaim'd
> The fairest capital of all the world,
> By riot and incontinence the worst . . .
> God made the country, and man made the town.[11]

The growth of towns helped to foster an increasingly sophisticated urban society: the arts of conversation, as a means of acquiring right principles, became extremely important,[12] as did the provision of social meeting-places. Daniel Defoe believed there to be more than 200,000 alehouses in England in his day;[13] and one of the most striking features of eighteenth-century social life was the replacement of older forms of collective organization with new ones: London coffee-houses and Methodist 'class meetings' alike reflect a new interest in developing different forms of identity, both personal and communal, in which freedom of expression and personal choice became increasingly important.[14] Again, not everyone approved: the great Independent clergyman Isaac Watts spoke of those who 'waste [their] days in coffee-houses'.[15] And the growth of towns also led to increasing rootlessness and widespread urban poverty, together with the breakdown of some of the social and moral conventions which the Evangelicals would be prominent in attempting to restore.[16] Yet this fissiparous socializing benefited religion too: many important religious societies were formed during the eighteenth century, with an important role to play in fostering lay piety;[17] the growth of towns inevitably led to an increased privatization of religious practice, as people chose their own church to worship in; and a new emphasis on Christian education developed, exemplified by publication of vast amounts of morally improving literature for children.[18]

With the growth of towns came a number of other changes or developments. Travel became easier, albeit only for those who could afford it; and a striking number of spiritual as well as other books reflect its growing popularity.[19] Yet, as so often, this improvement could be perceived as a two-edged sword: the introduction of exotic ideas and artefacts from India, China, and North America might appear to subvert established beliefs and customs; and the follies and garden ornaments beloved of eighteenth-century English artists and landowners served not only to *reflect* foreign themes but also to *domesticate* them, stripping them of any undesirable spiritual significance.[20] Literacy increased, as did the availability of books in general, though there may still have been more men than women who benefited by this.[21]

The dissemination of ideas was further fostered, not least in provincial society, by the rapid growth of the publishing industry.[22] And the growth of towns helped to produce a new variety of outlooks on nature: the gradual separation of increasing numbers of people from the harsh realities of a rural economy led both to an idealizing of landscape (which will be explored more fully below) and also to a new interest in studying and understanding the world around us, an interest which in itself presupposes a certain leisure and detachment from what is being studied.[23]

This leads to another significant feature of eighteenth-century English life. The period saw a massive increase in human knowledge, in a vast range of subjects, which in turn led to a fondness for ordering, classifying and harmonizing that knowledge. This of itself was not new: medieval thinkers loved to produce *summae* of all that was known in this or that branch of learning. But the presuppositions of (say) Diderot's *Encyclopédie*, or the first edition of the *Encyclopaedia Britannica* (in 1768–71), or of Thomas Bewick's popular *A general history of quadrupeds* (1790),[24] were significantly different from that of their medieval forebears (who, formally at least, saw all knowledge as under the umbrella of theology): there is a new interest in learning for its own sake, and not simply as an extension of theology.[25] We must beware of exaggerating the difference: Bewick's work, for example, was underpinned not only by a proud provincialism and a love of nature and landscape but also by a concern for education in enduring moral and spiritual values.[26] What is new is a willingness where necessary to pit revealed truth against scientific or rational truth: for the 'enthusiast' the former remained primary (sometimes as a bastion against unwelcome insights from abroad), but for the 'philosopher' the long age of its dominance was over at last. And this passion for ordering and arranging had fearful consequences for some: the eighteenth century saw a massive increase in the enclosure of land, tilting the balance yet further from common to private ownership of England's countryside.[27]

One of the positive effects of these developments was a growth in religious tolera-tion (though, as will be seen, the Roman Catholics continued to suffer from discriminatory legislation).[28] In the early 1730s Voltaire visited London and wrote admiringly of what he had seen:

> Take a view of the *Royal-Exchange* in *London*, a place more venerable than many courts of justice, where the representatives of all nations meet for the benefit of mankind. There the Jew, the Mahometan, and the Christian transact together as tho' they all profess'd the same religion, and give the name of Infidel to none but bankrupts . . . If one religion only were allowed in England, the government would very possibly become arbi-trary; if there were but two, the people wou'd cut one another's throats; but as there are such a multitude, they all live happy and in peace.[29]

This kind of toleration is a new feature of the eighteenth-century spiritual landscape. But we should not exaggerate its influence: John Locke's classic *Letter concerning toler-ation* of 1689 did not extend the principle to non-Christians, and was in any case furiously attacked by High Churchmen as poisonous heresy and betrayal of truth;[30] and some, like Hannah More, warned against a toleration so indulgent that it 'ends in an indifference to all'.[31]

The nature of 'enthusiasm' and 'philosophy'

And this anxiety about indifference on issues such as moral and religious truth returns us to the tension with which we began. Where the enthusiast laid emphasis on the primacy of revealed truth, to be apprehended and indeed experienced by every believer, the philosopher sought instead an Olympian and rational detachment.[32] The term 'enthusiasm' itself was not new: indeed it can be traced back to Plato, and was fre-quently used during the seventeenth century.[33] In his influential *The gospel-mystery of sanctification*, published in 1692, Walter Marshall uses the word in its literal Greek sense to denote a spiritual experience wrought by outright supernatural means, and thus vulnerable to the charge of being dangerously subjective;[34] and it is precisely this charge which is taken up by eighteenth-century critics of any piety which appeared to them to be irrational or superstitious, not least by the author of our opening text.

The term 'philosopher' was of course not new either; but the new intellectual context in which it found expression in this period, which was later to be known as the

Enlightenment, certainly was. Recent studies of the Enlightenment have warned against too absolute a distinction between the principles associated with it and those of revealed religion: indeed it was, in England, precisely a *Protestant* 'Enlightenment' that called for freedom of religious and intellectual enquiry in the face of the perceived threat of Roman Catholic 'superstition', a threat which concentrated innumerable minds when Bonnie Prince Charlie arrived at the gates of Derby in December 1745.[35] That threat, together with the more thoroughly secular thinking of the French Enlightenment, could lead to some surprising coalitions of Evangelicals and anti-dogmatists, enthusiasts and philosophers against a perceived common enemy.[36]

Furthermore, as we shall see, some of the greatest artists and writers of this period appeared to find no difficulty in moving easily from what we might regard as scientific rationalism to esoteric mysticism: Sir Isaac Newton's fascination with alchemy and the prophecies of Daniel, Law's fondness for the thought of Boehme, and Coleridge's love of the German Romantics, should warn us against too sharp a distinction between Enlightenment philosopher and religious enthusiast.[37]

Even so, the challenge to Christian spirituality represented by eighteenth-century philosophy was a formidable one. Broadly speaking, the Latitudinarian thought of the later seventeenth century exalted reason alongside, and eventually above, revelation: Greek thought was preferred to Hebrew, light to darkness:[38] James Wyatt's tidied-up interior of Salisbury Cathedral made for clarity and order (though also, as Pevsner justly notes, to 'a certain coolness'[39]); and the great writers of the Augustan age sought to imitate pre-Christian classical exemplars.[40] The implications can be seen in divergent eighteenth-century views about the workings of providence: on the one hand John Wesley continues to defend the traditional notion of an interventionist God, who can cause an earthquake and protect those who trust in him.[41] And Laurence Sterne also defends divine providence against those who

> have atheistically inferred, – that because there was so much of lottery in this life, – and mere casualty seemed to have such a share in the disposal of our affairs, – that the providence of God stood neuter and unconcerned in their several workings, leaving them to the mercy of time and chance to be furthered or disappointed as such blind agents directed.[42]

On the other hand the Scottish philosopher David Hume argues that, even if the argument from design requires belief in a Deity, such a God is absolutely unknowable; and thus mysticism (maintaining that God is mystery) is virtually indistinguishable from atheism.[43] 'A total suspense of judgment is here [with regard to religion and religious systems] our only reasonable resource.'[44] And for him the sheer quantity of suffering in the world argued against any kind of supreme being:

> Look round this universe. What an immense profusion of beings, animated and organized, sensible and active! You admire this prodigious variety and fecundity. But inspect a little more narrowly these living existences, the only beings worth regarding. How hostile and destructive to each other! How insufficient all of them for their own happiness! How contemptible or odious to the spectator! The whole presents nothing but

the idea of a blind Nature, impregnated by a great vivifying principle, and pouring forth from her lap, without discernment or parental care, her maimed and abortive children![45]

Hume argues that the behaviour of most priests or practitioners of religion does not in any case encourage adherence to their beliefs; and the wise magistrate will 'preserve a very philosophical indifference' to all religious groups, and 'carefully restrain the pretensions of the prevailing sect; otherwise he can expect nothing but endless disputes, quarrels, factions, persecutions, and civil commotions'.[46] In his important essay *Of suicide*, Hume sets out the position of the eighteenth-century deist with clarity:

> The providence of the Deity appears not immediately in any operation, but governs everything by those general and immutable laws, which have been established from the beginning of time . . . There is no event, however important to us, which he has exempted from the general laws that govern the universe, or which he has reserved for his own immediate action and operation.[47]

The relevance of this to Christian spirituality is clear. On Hume's view, there is no room for miracles, or for answers to prayer, just as there is no possibility of incurring God's wrath by taking one's life: God will not intervene whatever happens.

The challenge to Christian spirituality: Edward Gibbon

But perhaps the most significant critique of revealed religion in England in this period, and thus implicitly the most powerful challenge to Christian spirituality, was that of the great historian Edward Gibbon. For Gibbon, history was not a record of God's providential dealings with humanity but a dispassionate endeavour to discern the underlying causes of events, whilst recognizing the blind nature of much of what happens. In studying history, he sought an objectivity which led him to criticize the atheism of Voltaire as much as the piety of the Christians.[48] 'I am still more offended', he wrote of Voltaire, 'at the haughtiness of his unbelief, than at his unbelief itself';[49] and he wrote in what he describes as 'the full light and freedom of the eighteenth century'.[50] He rejoiced at having been born 'in an age of science and philosophy'.[51]

Here at once is a strong challenge to a religious tradition which had always believed, and would often continue to maintain, that the road to holiness led back to the supposed purity of the primitive apostolic church. For the eighteenth-century philosopher, the best was neither in past nor future, but here and now.[52] In order to see the force of this challenge, we need briefly to consider what Gibbon believed 'philosophy' to be.

Earlier in English usage, 'philosophy' had come to signify the patient endurance of suffering, as Sterne points out;[53] and Jeremy Taylor could speak approvingly of 'the charity of christian philosophy'.[54] But Taylor had in mind a tradition of Christian thought rooted in the past, in patristic scholarship, whereas by the eighteenth century this use of the term had been supplanted by the notion of the philosopher as an objective and rational seeker after truth.[55] In one of his earliest works Gibbon uses the term 'philosophical' to describe an approach which goes beyond simple definitions and facts to deducing underlying theories:[56] in another, he says simply that 'The end of Philosophy is Truth; the end of Poetry is Pleasure';[57] and in *The history of the decline and fall of the Roman Empire* he describes himself as 'a mere philosopher'.[58] But he is as usual being ironic: 'Our philosophy is not of the dogmatic kind' is a point he makes in his *Vindication* against his ecclesiastical critics;[59] rather it is rooted in a search for what most conduces to human happiness, a search which must begin with religious tolerance. He writes thus of pre-Christian Roman religion:

> The various modes of worship, which prevailed in the Roman world, were all considered by the people, as equally true; by the philosopher, as equally false; and by the magistrate, as equally useful. And thus toleration produced not only mutual indulgence, but even religious concord.[60]

Philosophy is unashamedly élitist, in the sense that only those with learning and taste can indulge in it; but if it is indifferent, it is so only with respect to the (from Gibbon's viewpoint) ludicrously trivial arguments of Christian theology, not with respect to the sufferings of humanity.[61] From the point of view of Christian spirituality, Gibbon touches the heart of the matter in his famous study of the emperor Julian, at once prince and philosopher.[62] Julian

> possessed such flexibility of thought, and such firmness of attention, that he could employ his hand to write, his ear to listen, and his voice to dictate; and to pursue at once three several trains of ideas, without hesitation, and without error.[63]

Gibbon compares this balanced rationality with the ridiculous credulity of the early Christian monks: Julian could commune with the gods and experience their guidance in dreams and visions, but only as a means to an end; whilst

> the useless lives of Antony or Pachomius were consumed in these vain occupations. Julian could break from the dream of superstition to arm himself for battle; and after vanquishing in the field the enemies of Rome, he calmly retired into his tent, to dictate the wise and salutary laws of an empire, or to indulge his genius in the elegant pursuits of literature and philosophy.[64]

For Gibbon, then, philosophy is at once contemplative and practical, demanding reflection and the calm pursuit of wisdom, but only in order to go out and seek to bring about a greater measure of human happiness; and he thus offered his age a new kind of piety, albeit of a refined and exclusive kind: an ordered, rational contemplation of human life and history, and of the great spiritual principles of truth, justice and freedom, which was directed towards actions that would improve the lot of contemporary society. There was little room for God in such a programme, and even less for 'enthusiasm': 'My temper', wrote Gibbon, 'is not very susceptible of enthusiasm, and the enthusiasm which I do not feel I have ever scorned to affect.'[65] His famous critique of Christianity in the *Decline and fall* is carefully nuanced: in his description of the apostolic era his principal point is that both pagans and Christians themselves were seduced by the 'wild enthusiasm' and 'airy speculations' of some new Christian converts, who caused the primal simplicity of the new faith to be lost in a welter of enthusiastic and superstitious accretions.[66]

For Gibbon, the problem with enthusiasm is that it is so close to prejudice, and hence to intolerance too.[67] The enthusiast who entered the Byzantine emperor Justinian's newly-completed Sancta Sophia 'might be tempted to suppose that it was the residence, or even the workmanship of the Deity'; while the 'philosophic eye' could see through Justinian's grandiloquent restoration programmes to the Empire's real and continuing weakness.[68] At best, 'enthusiasm' was a youthful or romantic exuberance:[69] at worst it led to the terrible fanaticism of the monasteries[70] and the medieval Crusades.[71]

Much of the remainder of this chapter will be taken up in exploring how English Christianity sought, directly or indirectly, to address the challenge represented by Hume, Gibbon, and others. We may conclude this section with four responses to that challenge from contemporaries. The Anglican layman John Byrom, writing in 1729 after having purchased, but not yet read, William Law's *A serious call*, noted that people like Law, and the Christianity they represented, were 'mightily out of fashion at present', because people 'are, and love to be, all of a hurry, and to talk their philosophy . . . in which they agree with one another in nothing but rejecting many received opinions'.[72]

The Evangelical poet William Cowper argued that reason may *illuminate* the human condition: what it lacks is any power to *change* that condition for the better:

> But reason still unless divinely taught,
> Whate'er she learns, learns nothing as she ought;
> The lamp of revelation only, shows,
> What human wisdom cannot but oppose,
> That man in nature's richest mantle clad,
> And graced with all philosophy can add,
> Though fair without, and luminous within,
> Is still the progeny and heir of sin.[73]

He agreed with Gibbon that religious discord had caused wars, but argued that the remedy was not the replacement of religion by philosophy, but the replacement of false Christianity by the true one:

> Angels descend from Heaven to publish Peace between Man and his Maker, the Prince of Peace himself comes to confirm and establish it, and War, hatred, and desolation are the consequence. Thousands quarrel about the Interpretation of a Book which none of them understand. He that is slain dies firmly persuaded that the Crown of Martyrdom expects him, and He that slew him is equally convinced that he has done God service . . . they have exchanged a Zeal that was no better than madness, for an Indifference equally pitiable and absurd . . . The exercise of Reason enlighten'd by Philosophy has cured them indeed of the misery of an abused understanding, but together with the delusion they have lost the

substance . . . The wise of this world, with all their wisdom, have not been able to distinguish between the blessing and the abuse of it. Voltaire was offended, and Gibbon has turned his back, but the flock of Christ is still nourished, and still encreases, notwithstanding the unbelief of a philosopher is able to convert bread into a stone, and a fish into a serpent.[74]

Finally, Oliver Goldsmith's Vicar of Wakefield is in no doubt that 'philosophy' fails to offer any adequate meaning to human beings in the face of the terrible certainty of death:

The consolations of philosophy are very amusing, but often fallacious. It tells us that life is filled with comforts, if we will but enjoy them; and on the other hand, that though we unavoidably have miseries here, life is short, and they will soon be over. Thus do these consolations destroy each other; for if life is a place of comfort, its shortness must be misery, and if it be long, our griefs are protracted. Thus philosophy is weak; but religion comforts in an higher strain. Man is here, it tells us, fitting up his mind, and preparing it for another abode . . . Thus to the fortunate religion holds out a continuance of bliss, to the wretched a change from pain.[75]

And his suffering wife tells her husband to 'Open [the Bible], my love, and read our anguish into patience'.[76]

ANGLICAN SPIRITUALITY IN THE EIGHTEENTH CENTURY

Spirituality and the Church of England

Introduction

The long-held assumption that the eighteenth century represented, if not a trough, then certainly a dull plateau, in the history of the Church of England has recently been effectively challenged.[77] At the very least, the established church ministered to the needs of far more English people during this century than all other denominations or faiths put together and, even allowing for some laxity and neglect, was actively involved at every level in the life of individual and nation.[78] There is also some evidence for a high degree of active piety throughout society during the eighteenth century, though especially among the gentry and aristocracy; and, as the demands of urban life and industry drew men further, or for longer periods, away from home, it was often left to women to maintain an ordered family piety.[79]

We should not, however, be too optimistic about the state of the eighteenth-century church. The ecclesiastical canons of William III (1695) sought to 'suppress the great abuses occasioned by pluralities' (the holding by a single parish priest of multiple benefices), insist that the parish clergy shall live exemplary lives, shall say public prayers in church 'not only on holy days and litany days, but as often as may be', shall celebrate the Eucharist frequently, visit the sick and catechize their flocks;[80] and there is evidence to suggest that such problems persisted, notwithstanding this legislation.[81]

Certainly it was not an easy time for the established church. William Cowper felt obliged to defend the ordered piety of cathedral worship against its detractors:

> There are . . . well-meaning people who dislike cathedral service because they cannot understand it when they hear it; that is, for want of being accustomed to it, for a little use would soon render it intelligible to them; and notwithstanding the constant repetition of the same sounds, those who are truly devout, will, instead of being tired with such repetitions be better pleased with, and find their devotions more and more warmed and enlivened thereby.[82]

And Oliver Goldsmith's *The deserted village* paints a vivid portrait of the village priest, threatened by depopulation and mercantilist greed:

> Thus to relieve the wretched was his pride,
> And e'en his failings leaned to virtue's side;
> But in his duty prompt at every call,
> He watched and wept, he prayed and felt for all;
> And, as a bird each fond endearment tries
> To tempt its new-fledged offspring to the skies,
> He tried each art, reproved each dull delay,
> Allured to brighter worlds, and led the way.
> Beside the bed where parting life was laid,
> And sorrow, guilt, and pain, by turns dismayed,
> The reverend champion stood. At his control
> Despair and anguish fled the struggling soul;
> Comfort came down the trembling wretch to raise,
> And his last faltering accents whispered praise.[83]

But there were more hopeful signs. The eighteenth century saw the origins of the Sunday Schools, and a new interest in Christian education which will be considered more fully below.[84] It was also a notable period for church architecture;[85] and the tradition of Anglican scholarship flourished: Joseph Bingham's *Origines ecclesiasticae* (1702–22) was a massive study of Christian antiquity, and exemplifies the extensive interest in patristic theology long before the Oxford Movement, an interest by no means restricted to high churchmen.[86]

High and Low Church movements

There were a number of different movements or groupings within the Church of England, of which the Evangelicals merit separate consideration.[87] The term 'Latitudinarian' was used (albeit infrequently) during the eighteenth century to denote those who stressed the need for 'comprehension' (that is, Anglican comprehensiveness) in ecclesial theory and practice: they also stressed reason and morality in Christian theology rather than more controversial and less 'practical' doctrines, doubtless in part at least in reaction to the ferociously divisive disputes of the previous century.[88] The term was used pejoratively by adherents of the High Church movement, who were generally Tory and whose roots lay in the clergy and the country gentry.[89]

The High Church movement was itself divided by the 'non-juring' controversy: those who refused to swear allegiance to William III on the grounds that they had already sworn inviolable oaths to James II came to be known as the Nonjurors: their principal concern was to protect the church both from too much state intervention and from what they perceived to be the dangerously subversive 'toleration' of dissent;[90] and some of their more prominent members, notably William Law (1686–1761) and Thomas Ken (1637–1711), exerted an important influence on Anglican spirituality. Like many Nonjurors, Ken, an eirenic and scholarly man, was extruded from his see (Bath and Wells) in 1689, and refused it even when it was offered back to him late in his life.[91] The Low Church movement comprised those who gave a 'low' place to Catholic principles such as episcopacy and sacraments, and thus tended towards Protestant theology: Gilbert Burnet (1643–1715), Bishop of Salisbury, and his wife Elizabeth Burnet (1661–1709), are prominent exemplars of this grouping.[92]

Joseph Butler (1692–1752)

The contributions made by representatives of these movements to English spirituality will be explored in what follows (though William Law will be considered separately), together with that of several other prominent eighteenth-century Anglicans who were not aligned with any of them. Joseph Butler was one of the finest theologians of the period: born at Wantage, he was educated by Dissenters, but insisted on joining the established church, and, as well as becoming successively Bachelor and Doctor of Law at Oxford, became in 1740 Dean of St Paul's Cathedral and in 1750 Bishop of Durham, 'wafted to that see in a cloud of metaphysics', as Horace Walpole put it.[93] His most important work, which appeared in 1736, exerted an immense influence both on his own time and on later scholars like Newman: its full title (*The analogy of religion, natural and revealed, to the constitution and course of nature*) reflects Butler's concern to show, against the Deists, that Christian theology is thoroughly compatible with both reason and science.

John Byrom (1691–1763)

John Byrom is important as a layperson at a time when spirituality was still predominantly clerical in tone and influence, though he can hardly be said to be typical: a Manchester-born, Cambridge-educated scholar and man about town, he comes across in his writings as a deeply attractive, ecumenical, and unselfconsciously devout man.[94] He invented a form of shorthand, was a brilliant linguist, and was immensely well read in classical literature: he had a particular interest in continental mystical theology, and was deeply (though not uncritically) influenced by William Law. One of his best biographers comments that he was 'too firmly rooted to the earth' to be a mystic himself, as though that were *ipso facto* a weakness:[95] but when Byrom himself notes in his journal, after yet another learned theological conversation, that 'I was edified by his talking, [but] there always seems to be something which through the affairs of worldly life escapes me too much again', he reveals exactly why he matters;[96] for a spirituality that cannot be tested against 'the affairs of worldly life' will, even at best, elude the experience of large numbers of Christians.[97]

Laurence Sterne (1713–68) and Christopher Smart (1722–71)

Two other eighteenth-century Anglicans will be considered in what follows, though they are too well known in other disciplines to merit much comment here: Laurence Sterne, born in Ireland, was ordained in 1738 and presented to the living of Sutton-on-the-Forest near York in the same year: apart from famous literary works like *Tristram Shandy* (1761–6) and *A sentimental journey* (1768), he published a number of sermons under the title *Sermons of Mr Yorick* which include some observations that are important for an understanding of contemporary English piety.[98] The poet and hymn-writer Christopher Smart was born in Kent, and spent four years in an asylum for the insane: his hymns, with their often rapt celebration of the goodness of creation, also contribute significantly to contemporary spirituality.

The Church of England and 'enthusiasm'

We may begin by seeing how these varying strands of Anglicanism responded to the challenge of 'enthusiasm' outlined above. Joseph Butler, perhaps not surprisingly, was not keen on it: he preferred 'serious persons, the most free from enthusiasm, and of the greatest strength of mind'.[99] William Warburton (1698–1779), Bishop of Gloucester and one of the finest Anglican theologians of the period, was even less keen: in a letter to John Byrom, he wrote

> You suppose enthusiasm consists in the mind's being carried with eager-
> ness and violence towards its object. I imagine this alone does not
> constitute the passion, and that justly to charge the mind with this
> weakness you should add, that, in its progress for the establishment of the
> supposed truth which it makes its object, *the conviction of its conclusions
> exceed the evidence of its principles.* From this time truth begins to be
> betrayed, and the inquirer after it justly incurs the character of an enthusi-
> ast.[100]

But John Byrom holds to a more nuanced view: 'there is', he declares, 'a right *Enthusiasm* as well as a wrong one, and a Man is free to admit which he pleases';[101] and he continues

> Think not that you are no Enthusiast, then!
> All Men are such, as sure as they are Men.
> The Thing itself is not at all to blame;
> 'Tis in each State of human Life the same,
> The fiery Bent, the driving of the Will,
> That gives the Prevalence to Good or Ill . . .
> Blame not *Enthusiasm*, if rightly bent,
> Or blame of Saints the holiest Intent,
> The strong Persuasion, the confirm'd Belief,
> Of all the Comforts of a Soul the Chief,
> That God's Continual Will and Work to save,
> Teach and inspire, attend us to the Grave;
> That they who in His Faith and Love abide,
> Find in His Spirit an Immediate Guide.

> This is no more a *Fancy* or a *Whim*,
> Than that 'we live, and move, and are in Him.'
> Let Nature, or let Scripture, be the *Ground*,
> Here is the *Seat* of true Religion found.[102]

Spirituality and reason

The question, then, is not whether enthusiasm of itself is either good or bad: rightly directed by the Spirit, and rooted in both nature and scripture, 'the fiery Bent, the driving of the Will' is unquestionably a good thing, provided it is firmly founded upon reason and truth. For Butler, it was the nature of that foundation which was primary; and his greatest achievement was to challenge the scepticism of a Gibbon or a Hume by demonstrating the reasonable nature of the Christian life and faith. The 'analogy' of religion that he wrote about was a notion derived from Origen:[103] Butler uses it to argue that much of what we conclude is true in life is based on what is *likely* on the basis of our past experience. Hence we may look at the natural world, recognize its intelligibility, and conclude by analogy that it must have had an intelligent Creator: so sophisticated a design requires a Designer.[104] This is not to deny the importance of what is revealed, supremely in scripture; but it is to say that the existence of God is manifest to anyone who chooses to look at the rich complexity of the world around us.[105] Butler thus concludes that Christianity has both an internal and an external component: the former, which is what concerns spirituality, is 'an inward principle' that leads us to give 'reverence, honour, love, trust, gratitude, fear and hope' both to God the Father (whose existence we can deduce by analogy from our understanding of the world around us), and to God the Son and God the Holy Spirit (whose existence is revealed to us through scripture and tradition).[106]

Creation and progress

This approach leads eighteenth-century Anglicans to celebrate the goodness of the created world more positively than most of their immediate predecessors. The poet Christopher Smart does this by following the *Benedicite* in exhorting animals to praise God and pray to him:

> Come, ye creatures of thanksgiving,
> Which are harmoniz'd to bless,
> Birds that warble for your living,
> Beasts with ways of love express.[107]
>
> The raven urgent in his pray'r . . .[108]

It also leads them to stress the capacity of creatures, especially human beings, to be changed and make progress, a view in happy conformity with the more optimistic eighteenth-century views of landscape and design. Butler wrote:

> The constitution of human creatures, and indeed of all creatures which come under our notice, is such, as that they are capable of naturally becoming qualified for states of life for which they were once wholly unqualified . . . We are plainly made for improvement of all kinds.[109]

Attaining the fullest state of life in this world of which we are capable is what we call 'maturity'.[110] And we are assisted towards attaining this by the guidance of God, who governs the world and instructs his creatures according both to certain laws or rules evident in nature and known by reason and experience, and to what divine Providence has revealed to us.[111]

All this might seem too optimistic, too easy a process. And Laurence Sterne is well aware that true contentment is far more elusive a goal than the restoration of country mansions and the creation of landscapes: we set ourselves goals, and attain them, only to find they make us no happier.[112] Only religion allows us to distinguish between happiness and pleasure: for the former is attainable only through the consciousness of virtue 'and the sure and certain hope of a better life, which brightens all our prospects, and leaves no room to dread disappointments'.[113] And we cannot attain this happiness unaided. John Byrom wrote that

> Every man, by the unbounded love of God in Christ Jesus, has the princi-
> ple of eternal life planted in him, and is therefore as much designed for life
> as every acorn is prepared to be an oak; but if any acorn had free will, and
> should . . . pretend to erect itself into an oak without either soil or sunshine
> (as Deists, who trust to their reason without grounding it in God's word
> and promise . . . pretend to grow good and happy) . . . would it not be
> mistaken?[114]

The crucial point, as Butler, Sterne and Byrom all note, is that this interior principle is profoundly *attractive*, drawing us towards itself.[115] Why? Because its essential nature is divine love: 'it is', as Thomas Ken declares, 'love that most naturally attracts love';[116] and elsewhere he defines this divine love as

> a grace rather to be felt than defined, so that I can do no more than rudely
> describe it: it is the general inclination and tendency of the whole man, of
> all his heart, and soul, and strength, of all his powers and affections, and of
> the utmost strength of them all, to God, as his chief, and only, and perfect
> and infinite good.[117]

And we may experience this divine love not only within ourselves, but outside too: Ken describes the kingdom of God as 'the catholic seminary of divine love'.[118]

Walking with God

In eighteenth-century Anglican piety, then, our rational understanding of ourselves and the world around us leads us to conclude that there is indeed a Creator, a conclusion enriched and strengthened by what is revealed to us in scripture and tradition. We come to experience the reality of an inward principle, a truth at once intelligible and attractive, which is the love of God for all that God has made. For Butler, this brings us to the heart of the matter:

> Resignation to the will of God is the whole of piety . . . Thus we might
> *acquaint ourselves with God, and be at peace.* This is piety and religion in the
> strictest sense, considered as an habit of mind; an habitual sense of God's

> presence with us; being affected towards him, as present, in the manner his
> superior nature requires from such a creature as man: this is to *walk with
> God.*[119]

And he sets out the heart of his understanding of the spiritual life in a manner that is
intensely Augustinian, and none the worse for it:

> Let us, then, suppose a man entirely disengaged from business and
> pleasure, sitting down alone and at leisure, to reflect upon himself and his
> own condition of being. He would immediately feel that he was by no
> means complete of himself, but totally insufficient for his own happiness
> . . . It is feeling this deficiency, that they are unsatisfied with themselves,
> which makes men look out for assistance from abroad . . . It is plain that
> there is a capacity in the nature of man, which neither riches, nor honours,
> nor sensual gratifications, nor anything in this world can perfectly fill up,
> or satisfy; there is a deeper and more essential want, than any of these
> things can be the supply of. Yet surely there is a possibility of somewhat,
> which may fill up all our capacities of happiness; somewhat, in which our
> souls may find rest; somewhat, which may be to us that satisfactory good
> we are inquiring after. But it cannot be anything which is valuable only as
> it tends to some further end . . . If you can lay aside that general, confused
> undeterminate notion of happiness, as consisting in . . . possessions; and
> fix in your thoughts, that it really can consist in nothing but in a faculty's
> having its proper object; you will clearly see that in the coolest way of con-
> sideration, without either the heat of fanciful enthusiasm, or the warmth
> of real devotion, nothing is more certain, than that an infinite Being may
> himself be, if he please, the supply to all the capacities of our nature.[120]

Some (as we shall see) would still find this account too lofty and cerebral to be truly
capable of transforming people. But Butler is battling to defend the essence of the
Christian life against those who want to set God firmly on the sidelines for ever. And
this elevated, optimistic view has some important implications for Christian spirituality.

First, there is evidence of a rich historical perspective, a concern to encourage people
to draw deeply from the wells of tradition and history in fashioning their spiritual
lives. John Byrom was one of a number of learned men who studied and conversed
about mystical writers both ancient and contemporary.[121] Sometimes this manifests
itself in a quasi-monastic piety: thus Thomas Ken constantly uses images drawn from
the cloister in evoking a medieval intimacy between the soul and God;[122] and in his
devotion to the Virgin Mary he presents her as an exemplar of monastic spirituality:
'When *Mary* rose to Lauds, and humbly pray'd . . .'[123] More generally, Sterne laments
our lack of reflective self-knowledge;[124] and integral to this is a historical perspective of
Gibbonian scope but drawing a very different lesson:

> we are to take our account from a close survey of human life, and the real
> face of things, stript of everything that can palliate or gild it over. We must
> hear the general complaint of all ages, and read the histories of mankind . . .

Consider the dreadful succession of wars in one part or other of the earth, perpetuated from one century to another with so little intermission, that mankind have scarce had time to breathe from them, since ambition first came into the world; consider the horrid effects of them in all those bar-barous devastations we read of, where whole nations have been put to the sword, or have been driven out to nakedness and famine to make room for new-comers. – Consider how great a part of our species, in all ages down to this, have been trod under the feet of cruel and capricious tyrants, who would neither hear their cries, nor pity their distresses.[125]

Secondly, there is a clear concern for an integrated piety which will hold prayer and daily life firmly together, the church's 'seemly course of practic pray'r and laud' cele-brated by Christopher Smart.[126] The Sussex grocer Thomas Turner left a diary which not only suggests a high level of theological literacy among laypeople,[127] but also reflects precisely this concern. Turner notes an observation recorded in the *Universal Magazine*: 'We should not measure men by Sundays without regarding what they do all the week after, for devotion does not necessarily make men virtuous.'[128] He did not always practise what he preached: this village merchant and churchwarden was both a deeply religious man and a deeply serious drinker; and although he notes principles of repentance and discipline, and national fast days, in his diary, it is not always clear that he observes them himself.[129] Elizabeth Burnet insists that the best preparation for receiving Holy Communion is 'a holy life'.[130]

The whole duty of man

Most interesting of all in this connection is Richard Allestree's *The whole duty of man*. It was first published anonymously in 1657, but became extremely influential in the eighteenth century, reaching its twenty-eighth edition in 1790 (though William Cowper dismissed it as 'that repository of self-righteous and pharisaical lumber'[131]). Its title is significant: this is a characteristically Anglican concern for the whole person, and for every person (it is 'for the *use* of *all*, but especially the *meanest reader*';[132] and the preface ('Of the necessity of caring for the soul') warns of the perils incurred by neglecting our spiritual natures). Though written well before the natural theology of Joseph Butler, the book stresses the light of reason as well as that of revelation.[133] It also reminds readers that the spiritual cannot be divorced from the practical: if prayer is not answered, it could be that the person praying is unwilling to *do* anything that will contribute towards the outcome desired;[134] and parents are to bless their children, not only by their prayers but by their piety: 'they are to be such persons themselves, as that a blessing may descend from them upon their posterity'.[135] By the same token, prayer for others is an integral part of charity:

> We are of ourselves impotent, feeble creatures, unable to bestow blessings, where we most wish them; therefore if we do indeed desire the good of others, we must seek it on their behalf from him, whence *every good and perfect gift cometh* (James 1.17). This is so necessary a part of charity, that without it our kindness is but an insignificant thing, a kind of empty com-pliment: For how can he be believed to wish well in earnest, who will not

thus put life and efficacy into his wishes by forming them into prayers, which will otherwise be vain and fruitless?[136]

Spirituality and society

In more general terms, this kind of approach leads to a spirituality centred upon order, structure, balance, and prudence. Positively, this can offer rich spiritual resource for people to call on in times of crisis. Thus Christopher Smart celebrates the 'Forms of prayer to be used at sea' in the Book of Common Prayer:

> Thanks to God we have a form
> Of sound words aboard the ship,
> In the calm, or in the storm,
> To exalt him heart and lip.
>
> There Jehovah's dove may perch
> On the topmast as she swims –
> Ev'ry vessel is a church
> Meet for praise, for pray'r, and hymns.[137]

Less positively, this approach can give Anglican piety in the eighteenth century a sense of being written *de haut en bas*. Thomas Broughton's *Serious advice and warning to servants* (1746) was written to encourage gentlefolk and other 'governors of families' to 'set up the worship of GOD in your Families'.[138] It contains much moralizing advice for servants; and the author has little sympathy with those servants whose long hours leave little space for prayer:

> if there be any such *Egyptian Task-Masters*, yet still your hearts may be disengaged, though your hands are full; and you may send up holy ejaculations towards heaven, in the midst of your most busy hours.[139]

They should observe the Lord's Day, attending family worship, and meditate on the word of God day and night.[140] They should be constant in their morning and evening devotions, and suitable prayers for these are included.[141]

The theology and practice of prayer

But it can also reveal a spiritual life whose theological depth offers firm foundation. Sterne locates prayer thus in human beings' grateful recognition of their existence as creatures lovingly sustained by God and dependent upon him.[142] Seen in this light, prayer is an utterly *natural* duty:

> this duty of prayer and thanksgiving to GOD . . . takes no bullock out of thy field, no horse out of thy stable, nor he-goat out of thy fold; it costeth no weariness of bones, no untimely watchings; it requireth no strength of parts, or painful study, but just to know and have a true sense of our dependence, and of the mercies by which we are upheld: and with this, in every place and posture of body, a good man may lift up his soul unto the Lord his GOD.[143]

And it is also a duty involving the whole person, again for ontological reasons: 'in the present state we are in, we find such a strong sympathy and union between our souls and bodies, that the one cannot be touched or sensibly affected, without producing some corresponding emotion in the other'.[144] Hence good actions are more precious than prayers, for to obey is better than sacrifice; nevertheless, both are needed.[145] Thus he notes that Elijah's 'urgent' prayer on behalf of the widow of Zarephath caused him to be 'involved in the success of his prayer himself'.[146] The whole of us, then, is to be involved in our prayer, though this is no excuse for show:

> When the true heat and spirit of devotion is . . . lost and extinguished under a cloud of ostentatious ceremonies and gestures, as is remarkable in the Roman Church – where the celebration of high mass, when set off to the best advantage with all its scenical decorations and finery, looks more like a theatrical performance, than that humble and solemn appeal which dust and ashes are offering up to the throne of God; – when religion, I say, is thus clogged and borne down by such a weight of ceremonies – it is much easier to put in pretensions to holiness upon such a mechanical system as is left of it, than where the character is only to be got and maintained by a painful conflict and perpetual war against the passions.[147]

True piety, in short, is hard work. Richard Hurd, Fellow of Emmanuel College Cambridge and later Bishop of Coventry and Lichfield, argues strongly for the continuing importance of sacrifice as a vital element in an authentic Christian life;[148] and Thomas Ken notes that 'it is an usual method with God to lay the foundation of a great sanctity in affliction', as with the prophet Daniel.[149] Ken encourages beginners to learn some prayers by heart, above all those of the Psalms:

> You cannot imagine the great benefit of learning psalms by heart; for when you are under any temptation, or are in any affliction, or when you lie waking in the night, or when sick, these psalms will come into your mind; and the devout repeating them, will yield you most seasonable consolations.[150]

Conclusion

If eighteenth-century Anglican piety can on occasions seem too composed and ordered, we should remember Byrom's insistence that the principle of eternal life implanted in each human being is there because of the love of God for us revealed in Jesus Christ; and all prayer is therefore life in Christ. Christopher Smart wrote

> Take ye therefore what ye give him,
> Of his fulness grace for grace,
> Strive to think him, speak him, live him,
> Till you find him face to face.[151]

And Thomas Ken stresses the value of regular meditation, not simply as some rational and ordered spiritual exercise, but precisely because true meditation prolongs Christ's presence in the human heart; and if Christ appears to desert the person praying, he or she must draw Christ back down:

> If up to Heav'n Thou wilt ascend,
> Though Heav'n I cannot open rend,
> Though I want Wings to soar,
> Where Seraphs Thee adore,
> I'll draw Thee down from Heav'n by violent Pray'r,
> To visit me, and re-assume my Care.[152]

Above all, this kind of piety emphasizes the freedom of individual human beings, who may choose either to co-operate with the divine grace that longs to draw them into a deeper relationship with God in Christ, or to reject it. There is no hint of Calvinist predestination in these words of John Byrom, whose rational and ecumenical spirituality evokes much of what is best in the Church of England of his day:

> True religion . . . is not a word, but a thing; not a matter of dispute, but of practice. Let men lay aside their proud lust and avarice, and all they have imagined, fancied; let them grant only these two [propositions], that we were born, and that we shall die; and consequences are plainly deducible by any means whatsoever. There are but the three systems that all others fall into, chance, necessity, Providence; and there is no possible room [or] employment for sense or reason, virtue or vice, in the two first. Chance supposes ignorance only in us; and necessity makes understanding void. They are the idols of thoughtless minds; but Providence solves everything, and all is darkness and confusion without It. Every man may be happy, if he will; if he will not, there is the true origin of evil. Freedom is the free gift of Heaven; if we will use it to choose good, to worship Real Power, and to obey Supreme Wisdom, to love Infinite Goodness, we are wise and happy for ever. If we choose to be fools, we have a right to our follies, and none can or will hinder us from them. What we ask we shall have, and what we sow we shall reap. Now is the time to make a good choice.[153]

Evangelical Spirituality

Introduction: the roots of English Evangelicalism

The pattern of spirituality just described did not satisfy everyone, and perhaps could not have been expected to: its broadly optimistic view of human life and the natural world, its stress on integration, rationality and order, and its corresponding suspicion of 'enthusiasm', may have represented a vigorous attempt to respond to the challenges of Enlightenment thought and Augustan culture; but for many it must have appeared as an anodyne, bloodless piety, doing scant justice both to the Gospel and to the perceived need for a religion that would address the darkest depths of the human condition and seek to transform them. Those who felt like this found what they were looking for in what came to be known as the Evangelical Revival.

If Butler and Byrom represent a response to secular thought, the Evangelical movement represents both a response and a reaction to it.[154] Rooted in the Gospel and thus setting revelation above reason, personal spiritual experience above natural theology, this movement was far from being a purely English phenomenon:[155] indeed it underlines the increasing inseparability of English piety from what was happening across both the Channel and the Atlantic. The Moravian *émigré* communities established first in Saxony by Count Nicholas von Zinzendorf (1700–60), but later in England and America as well;[156] the religious societies that flowered both in England and overseas;[157] the legacy of seventeenth-century English Puritan piety; the Evangelical revival in North American Christianity, and especially the influence of Jonathan Edwards;[158] and the work of the itinerant evangelists John and Charles Wesley and George Whitefield – all these exerted a profound impact on eighteenth-century English spirituality. The epicentre of that impact was within the established church; but its shockwaves were felt far beyond.

But although Evangelicalism helped to foster much intense theological debate, its impact was not only an inward one: its adherents came to be passionate advocates of social reform and philanthropy; and even if some 'Augustan' values (such as refinement and classical restraint) were of no interest to them, others (such as public truth and moral integrity) certainly were. It is important to emphasize this, for Evangelicalism was not only a reaction to Enlightenment principles: it was also an application of some of them to the sphere of religion, not least the emphasis on seeking to establish the authentic truth of any given discipline. Evangelicals rejected Enlightenment scepticism; but they did not reject Enlightenment rationality and optimism.[159]

George Whitefield (1714–70), William Cowper (1731–1800) and John Newton (1725–1807)

Apart from the Wesleys, who will be considered separately, three figures dominated eighteenth-century Anglican Evangelicalism. George Whitefield was the youngest son of Gloucester innkeepers:[160] educated at Oxford, he joined the Wesleys' 'Holy Club' and experienced a Christian conversion in 1735. In 1736 he was ordained deacon at Gloucester, and soon became known as an outstanding preacher, attracting huge numbers.[161] In 1737 he went to Georgia as a missionary, and spent the rest of his life as a itinerant evangelist on both sides of the Atlantic, dying in America in 1770. A less gifted organizer than John Wesley, he separated from him over theology, remaining a lifelong Calvinist as well as (like Wesley) a lifelong Anglican.[162]

William Cowper was brought up in the gentle landscapes of Hertfordshire, which helped foster his love of nature; after leaving Westminster School he became a lawyer; but in 1763 he suffered a complete mental and physical breakdown, which was followed a year later by a dramatic conversion experience when he came upon Romans 3.25.[163] He moved to Huntingdon in 1765, and (at the invitation of John Newton) to Olney in Buckinghamshire two years later.[164] In 1773 he suffered another mental collapse, believing that God had abandoned him utterly and attempting suicide:[165] his recovery from this was slow and fitful; and he died at East Dereham in 1800.

John Newton had in effect three careers: as merchant sailor, surveyor, and cleric. His *Authentic narrative*, in the tradition of Puritan spiritual autobiographies, describes his life as an ill-disciplined sailor following the early death of his mother.[166] Shipwrecked off the African coast, he became a slave for 15 months to a planter's black mistress: later he returned home, married Mary Catlett in 1750, became master of his own ship, and engaged in the slave trade, though he was forced to abandon the sea because of

ill-health in 1754 (the same year that he accepted Calvinism). He became an enthusiastic follower of Whitefield while a tide surveyor at Liverpool, where he heard him
preach in 1755. In 1758 he was refused ordination by the archbishop of York because
of his (still then unfashionable) Evangelical views; but he was at last ordained in 1764
and became incumbent of Olney. Much of his best work was written here: thereafter
(in 1779) he was appointed incumbent of St Mary Woolnoth in the city of London,
where he remained until he died: he sustained there an outstanding Evangelical
ministry and supported Wilberforce's endeavours towards the abolition of slavery.[167]

In addition to his *Authentic narrative* (1764), Newton wrote an extended personal
diary, contributed extensively to an Evangelical journal (*The Gospel Magazine*) and
was a prolific correspondent (many of his letters on the spiritual life were collected and
published together), as well as preaching a series of fifty sermons in 1784–5 on the
texts which Handel had used for his oratorio *Messiah*.[168] But much of his finest work is
in his hymns; and many of the best of these appear in the *Olney hymns* (1779), a joint
collection of hymns by Newton and Cowper.[169]

What is interesting and original about *Olney hymns* is their arrangement: the third
part is based 'on the rise, progress, changes, and comforts of the spiritual life' and thus
constitutes a kind of manual of Evangelical spiritual formation. Each subdivision represents a stage of the Christian's spiritual journey: first, 'Conflict', beginning with
Cowper's famous 'God moves in a mysterious way';[170] then 'Comfort', whose first
hymn is entitled *Faith a new and comprehensive sense*, to be prized above our physical
senses.[171] Then follows 'Dedication and surrender', including Cowper's *Love con-
straining to obedience*, which ends

> To see the Law by Christ fulfill'd,
> And hear his pard'ning voice;
> Changes a slave into a child,
> And duty into choice.[172]

The last two sections are entitled 'Cautions' and 'Praise'.[173]

The sources of English Evangelicalism

Eighteenth-century Evangelicals were widely read and travelled, even though their
theology owed as much if not more to personal spiritual experience as to intellectual
study.[174] Cowper translated some of the semi-mystical works of the French quietist
Jeanne-Marie Guyon (1648–1717), whose autobiography (as well as some works of
Fénelon, Bossuet, Pascal and Boehme) was also read by Newton.[175] The
Cambridge-educated Francis Okely (1719–94) came under the influence of Boehme
via William Law and the Moravians (from whom, on the continent, he gained an
excellent knowledge of German – he eventually became a Moravian himself); like
Law, he sought to collect the best mystical writings and propagate them, seeking an
eirenic synthesis of all that was best in Christianity, and one which would elide the difference between Evangelicalism and mysticism.[176]

John Fletcher, vicar of Madeley in Shropshire, was born Jean Guillaume de la
Fléchère, at Nyon in Switzerland, where he was educated: he settled at Madeley in
1760 and became a kind of English *curé d'Ars*:[177] Southey describes him as 'a man of

rare talents, and rarer virtue. No age or country has ever produced a man of more fervent piety, or more perfect charity; no church has ever possessed a more apostolic minister.'[178] Yet this gentle and holy man was also a combustible preacher: John Wesley records his first sermon, in the village of Atcham, on 19 June 1777:

> His text was, (a very bold beginning!) 'Ye adulterers and adulteresses, know ye not that the friendship of this world is enmity with God?' (James 6.4). The congregation stood amazed, and gazed upon him as if he had been a monster.[179]

Spirituality and conversion

Evangelicals were well aware that the sobriquet 'enthusiast' was no compliment. Newton told his congregation at St Mary Woolnoth that

> A consistent christian, whose integrity, humility, and philanthropy mark his character and adorn his profession, will in time command respect; but his attachment to unfashionable truths, and his separation from the maxims and pursuits of the many, will render him, in their eyes, singular and precise, weak and enthusiastic.[180]

The 'attachment to unfashionable truths' and 'separation from the maxims and pursuits of the many' was characteristic of Evangelicalism, and like much of its spirituality derived from the two sources already noted: an unqualified commitment to the Gospel, and a recognition of human beings' radical need for conversion.[181] Newton's own conversion experience was to prove immensely influential: in *An authentic narrative* he describes himself on board ship in 1748 picking up Stanhope's version of Thomas à Kempis and wondering whether what it said was true.[182] This immediately preceded what he regarded as his own conversion experience, when praying on board the *Greyhound* during a ferocious storm:

> when I saw, beyond all probability, there was still hope of respite, and heard, about six in the evening, that the ship was freed from water, there arose a gleam of hope. I thought I saw the hand of God displayed in our favour; I began to pray; I could not utter the prayer of faith; I could not draw near to a reconciled God, and call him father; my prayer was like the cry of the ravens, which yet the Lord does not disdain to hear.[183]

Later that year, he was in Derry, in Ireland; and one day 'I arose very early, was very particular and earnest in my private devotion; and, with the greatest solemnity, engaged myself to be the Lord's for ever, and only his. This was not a formal, but a sincere surrender . . .' though he was soon to abandon it.[184] Conversion for Evangelicals was more often than not a gradual process, even if marked by periodic moments of disclosure; Wesley notes, in his biography of John Fletcher, how the latter's conversion took some time, involved much wrestling with the Lord, and depended as much on a clear-eyed awareness of his own sin and helplessness as on any emotions that might be kindled.[185]

In some of his spiritual letters Newton explores the process more systematically. He defines it as a process of *awakening*[186] – 'the general characteristics of young converts are zeal and love'[187] – like the Israelites after the crossing of the Red Sea. He notes that 'they who are in this state of their first love, are seldom free from something of a censorious spirit' – often also self-righteous and wilful:

> However, with all their faults, methinks there is something very beautiful and engaging in the honest vehemence of a young convert. Some cold and rigid judges are ready to reject these promising appearances on account of incidental blemishes. But would a gardener throw away a fine nectarine, because it is green, and has not yet attained all that beauty and flavour which a few more showers and suns will impart? Perhaps it will hold, for the most part, in grace as in nature; some exceptions there are; if there is not some fire in youth, we can hardly expect a proper warmth in old age.[188]

What normally happens is that, once the novelty of the experience wears off, the convert will 'experimentally learn and feel' his or her own weakness, become aware of sin, and learn to live by grace.[189] In practice, though, growth into a mature faith is often accompanied both by the loss of that initial fervour and by a general lackadaisicality:

> He takes up the Bible, conscious that it is the fountain of life and true comfort; yet, perhaps, while he is making the reflection, he feels a secret distaste, which prompts him to lay it down, and give his preference to a newspaper.[190]

Nonetheless something real and profound has begun to take root in the life of the convert: 'all that is good or gracious, is the effect of a new creation, a supernatural principle, wrought in the heart by the gospel of Christ, and the agency of his Spirit'.[191]

Newton goes on to emphasize that, though conversion and faith are gifts of God, the person can do something: she or he can wait upon God. . . .

> You ask, If a man can do nothing without an extraordinary impulse from on high, is he to sit still and careless? By no means – I am far from saying man can do nothing, though I believe he cannot open his own eyes, or give himself faith. I wish every man to abstain carefully from sinful company, and sinful actions, to read the Bible, to pray to God for his heavenly teaching. For this waiting upon God he has a moral ability; and if he persevere thus in seeking, the promise is sure, that he shall not seek in vain.[192]

The work of grace: 'Glorious things of thee are spoken'

This approach is compatible with all but the most extreme Calvinism; and it does not mitigate the decisive importance of election and grace in Evangelical spirituality. We may explore it best by using one of Newton's most famous hymns as a point of entry. He gave it the title 'Zion; or the City of God', basing it on a passage from Isaiah (33.20–1):

Glorious things of thee are spoken,
Zion, city of our God!
He, whose word cannot be broken,
Form'd thee for his own abode:
On the Rock of Ages founded,
What can shake thy sure repose?
With salvation's walls surrounded,
Thou may'st smile at all thy foes.

See! the streams of living waters
Springing from eternal love,
Well supply thy sons and daughters,
And all fear of want remove:
Who can faint while such a river
Ever flows their thirst t'assuage?
Grace, which, like the Lord, the giver,
Never fails from age to age.

Round each habitation hovering,
See the cloud and fire appear!
For a glory and a covering,
Showing that the Lord is near:
Thus deriving from their banner[193]
Light by night, and shade by day;
Safe they feed upon the manna[194]
Which He gives them when they pray.

Bless'd inhabitants of Zion,
Wash'd in the Redeemer's blood!
Jesus, whom their souls rely on,
Makes them kings and priests to God:
'Tis his love his people raises
Over self to reign as kings,
And as priests his solemn praises
Each for a thank-offering brings.

Saviour, if of Zion's city
I through grace a member am;
Let the world deride or pity,
I will glory in thy Name:
Fading is the worldling's pleasure,
All his boasted pomp and show;
Solid joys and lasting treasure,
None but Zion's children know.

Newton begins with a conflation of a verse from Psalm 87 with his Isaiah text:[195] he cites the Psalms elsewhere in describing the state of his own soul as being 'like a besieged city', but maintains that

my Lord will at length raise the siege, and cause me to shout deliverance
and victory. Pray for me, that my walls may be strengthened.[196]

This seamless movement back and forth from biblical text to personal experience,
from the corporate situation of the people of God to the personal predicament of the
sinner, is characteristic: elsewhere Newton explicitly notes that 'Zion and Jerusalem
are indifferently used as emblems of the church, or professing people of God'.[197] No
less characteristic is the use of images from the Psalms, particularly those that carry
overtones of protection, security and shelter: hence Newton speaks, in the second half
of the first verse, of the 'Rock of Ages', an image which his near-contemporary
Augustus Toplady was to popularize in a no less famous hymn of his own.[198] There is
little interest, here or anywhere else in Evangelical piety, in the natural world for its
own sake: although Newton has a series of hymns on the seasons in *Olney hymns*,[199] he
uses nature very much as a source of religious instruction:

> The book of nature open lies,
> With much instruction stor'd:
> But till the Lord anoints our eyes,
> We cannot read a word.[200]

Far more important here is the sense of assurance Newton seeks to convey ('What can
shake thy sure repose?'), a Reformed doctrine of primary importance in Evangelical
piety. On some occasions, such as this, it can suggest a serene, even defiant trust in the
face of enemies.[201] Elsewhere, however, Evangelicals articulate the heart of the struggle
involved in seeking assurance: the seemingly calm and childlike trust is won only at
great cost.[202] Its positive fruit is a boldness before God which we have already seen to
be characteristic of much Calvinist piety.[203]

The second verse of Newton's hymn is a reflection on grace, a subject with which he
has become especially associated through the popularity of his hymn 'Amazing
grace'.[204] It is worth noting the strong visual sense in Newton's writing here ('See! the
streams of living waters'): both this and the imagery of water are found in the Isaiah
text on which he is reflecting; but his use of images in this way is carefully calculated.
He noted in a letter that the powers of the imagination are extensive but transient,
while those of the understanding are both more enduring and more limited.[205]

Like Jesus, to whose service he believed himself called, Newton never stopped
preaching and teaching: his piety is rooted in the Evangelical longing to convey the
power of the living Word by whatever means are close at hand; and his awareness of his
own 'desultory, ungovernable imagination' did not prevent him from using images
judiciously in order to communicate the truth that had seized him.[206]

And with good reason. For Newton, grace, like faith, affects the whole person, not
just the intellect: 'the grace of God influences both the understanding and the affections'.[207] And it brings about a profound personal transformation:

> When cast in the spring of the soul,
> A wonderful change will produce,
> Diffusing new life through the whole.[208]

In the third verse Newton stretches the static image of the city on a rock by introducing imagery from Exodus: like the Puritans before them, the eighteenth-century Evangelicals loved to stress the nature of life as a spiritual journey towards home.[209] This too is no accident: the understanding of Christian life as a process of deliverance by grace from exile and bondage in Egypt to freedom in the Promised Land underpins not only Evangelicals' own experiences, but their hatred of the very trade in which Newton had himself been involved as both slave and slaver.[210] Many Evangelical texts of this period emphasize the priority of social justice for Christians; and Wesley notes John Fletcher's reputation as one who cared for the poor whilst at the same time being 'dead to the things of the world'.[211]

In the fourth verse Newton moves from Old to New Testament imagery as he approaches his climax. The reference to the Redeemer's blood is characteristic of piety of this kind, rooted as it is in atonement theology (though it is worth noting in passing that Evangelical piety shows much interest too in the historical events of Jesus' life).[212] The reference to the text from Revelation about Christians as kings and priests before God is even more telling: for Evangelicals, it is precisely through raising the love of God above ourselves, as Newton puts it here, that we become kings; and precisely in our offering of praise and thanksgiving that our status as priests is made manifest.[213]

But it is the final verse which brings Newton to the heart of the matter: for here, in characteristic Evangelical fashion, he seeks to appropriate for the life and experience of the person singing what is being reflected on.[214] We should note at once an important textual point: Newton's 'Saviour, *if* of Zion's city' had been altered, by the time of the publication of *Hymns ancient and modern*, to 'Saviour, *since* of Zion's city', replacing Newton's original and nuanced conditional with a certainty admitting of no doubt whatever.[215] More generally, we can see at this point how Newton clothes the whole Isaiah passage in the Evangelical theology of grace, at the same time broadening the biblical allusions to encompass scripture from Exodus to Revelation. His hymn begins and ends with references to the fortress-like security the city of Zion offers its inhabitants: in the final verse the 'foes' of verse 1 are brought on stage: they turn out to be the 'worldling's pleasure', pomp and show, and empty or evil secular power. But notice too how in this closing verse the hymn becomes explicitly a prayer ('Saviour, if of Zion's city . . .'): instead of talking to Zion, Newton ends by talking to God.

Prayer plays a vital role in Evangelical piety. It is itself a gift of grace, as this verse and many other texts make explicitly clear.[216] But it demands things of us too: above all, a willingness to *persevere* and to wait upon God.[217] In one of his letters Newton says that the true Christian's time 'is divided between serving his country in public, and wrestling for it in private'; there can hardly be a clearer illustration of the seriousness with which Evangelicals took participation in public life.[218] Nor was their view of prayer or the spiritual life narrowly introspective: John Fletcher once 'wandered into a wood, musing on the importance of the office [he] was going to undertake', when 'such a feeling sense of the justice of God fell upon me, and such a sense of his displeasure at sin, as absorbed all my powers, and filled my soul with the agony of prayer for poor, lost sinners'.[219] And Newton told a correspondent:

I look upon prayer-meetings as the most profitable exercises (excepting the public preaching) in which christians can engage: they have a direct tendency to kill a worldly, trifling spirit, to draw down a divine blessing upon all our concerns, compose differences, and enkindle (at least to maintain) the flame of divine love amongst brethren.[220]

The theology and practice of prayer

But other qualities essential to the Evangelical view of prayer are evident in the stirring last verse of Newton's great hymn. First, prayer is an adventure: a defiant challenge to the powers of evil that is rooted in the Christian hope. Newton is determined that prayer should not be *boring*:

> When my prayers are a burden and task,
> No wonder I little receive;
> O Lord, make me willing to ask,
> Since Thou art so ready to give.[221]

And elsewhere he noted that 'the prayers of some good men are more like preaching than praying. They rather express the Lord's mind to the people, than the desires of the people to the Lord.'[222] Nor do we pray alone: it may seem surprising to hear an Evangelical penning these lines:

> When Satan and his host appear,
> Like him of old, I faint and fear;
> Like him, by faith, with joy I see
> A greater host engag'd for me.
>
> The saints espouse my cause by prayer,
> The angels make my soul their care;
> Mine is the promise seal'd with blood,
> And Jesus lives to make it good.[223]

But Newton has in mind here the story of Elisha and the Aramaeans in 2 Kings chapter 6, rather than Catholic belief in the saints' intercession. Secondly, prayer is rooted in our status as children ('None but Zion's children know'):

The spirit of prayer is the truth and token of the spirit of adoption. The studied addresses with which some approach the throne of grace, remind us of a stranger's coming to a great man's door; he knocks and waits, sends in his name, and goes through a course of ceremony before he gains admittance; while a child of the family uses no ceremony at all, but enters freely when he pleases, because he knows he is at home. It is true, we ought always to draw near the Lord with great humiliation of spirit, and a sense of our unworthiness. But this spirit is not always best expressed or promoted by a pompous enumeration of the names and titles of the God with whom we have to do, or by fixing in our minds before hand, the exact order in which we propose to arrange the several parts of our prayer.[224]

So our defiance of the world is not some easy bravado but the fruit of childlike trust:

> To be humble, and like a little child, afraid of taking a step alone, and so conscious of snares and dangers around us, as to cry to him continually to hold us up, that we may be safe, is the sure, infallible, the only secret of walking closely with him.[225]

This childlikeness is in itself a gift: we are adopted as children. Newton was aware of darker passions present in human beings:

> Last week we had a lion in town. I went to see him. He was wonderfully tame; as familiar with his keeper, as docile and obedient, as a spaniel. Yet the man told me he had his surly fits, when they durst not touch him. No looking-glass could express my face more justly than this lion did my heart. I could trace every feature: as wild and fierce by nature, yea, much more so; but grace has in some measure tamed me. I know and love my Keeper, and sometimes watch his looks that I may learn his will. But, oh! I have my surly fits too; seasons when I relapse into the savage again, as though I had forgotten all.[226]

And both Newton and Cowper are aware that any prayer worthy of the name will have to engage with the harsh realities of life: indeed we are most likely to pray only after having exhausted all other sources of help:

> Could the creatures help or ease us,
> Seldom should we think of prayer;
> Few, if any, come to Jesus,
> Till reduc'd to self-despair.[227]

And this is Cowper, agonizing in his personal diary about the attractiveness of suicide in 1795:

> Why didst Thou ever say –
> Woe to Him that is *alone* when he falleth [Ecclesiastes 4.10].
> What opportunities of Suicide had I, while there was any Hope, except a miserable, a most miserable moment, in '73? that moment lost, all that follow'd was as sure as necessity itself could make it. How are such opportunities to be found where the intention is known, watch'd and guarded against? O monstrous dispensation! I cannot bear the least part of what is coming upon me, yet am forced to meet it with my eyes open'd wide to see its approach, and destitute of all means to escape it.[228]

Much prayer is therefore a costly struggle, a wrestling with God;[229] but its fruit is profoundly therapeutic, imbuing us as it does with a spirit of gratitude that is part of the Christian's spiritual armoury:

> Have you no words? ah, think again,
> Words flow apace when you complain;
> And fill your fellow-creature's ear
> With the sad tale of all your care.

> Were half the breath thus vainly spent,
> To heav'n in supplication sent;
> Your cheerful song would oft'ner be,
> 'Hear what the LORD has done for me!'[230]

And this spirit is beneficial for others as well as for the person praying. Wesley records someone as saying that John Fletcher would pray quietly but particularly for each person present whenever he was with others, and that the effect of the 'life and energy' which flowed from his words was enriching to everyone.[231]

Evangelicals had little doubt that prayer would be answered. Consider this extract from Wesley's *Life of John Fletcher*:

> From hence [Fletcher and his party] went to an inn [having arrived in England from Europe]; but here they were under another difficulty. As they spoke no English, they could not tell how to exchange their foreign into English money; till Mr Fletcher, going to the door, heard a well-dressed Jew talking French. [Fletcher] told him the difficulty they were under, with regard to the exchange of money. The Jew replied, 'Give me your money, and I will get it changed in five minutes.' Mr Fletcher without delay gave him his purse, in which were ninety pounds. As soon as he came back to his company, he told them what he had done. They all cried out with one voice, 'Then your money is gone . . . Men are constantly waiting about the doors of these inns, on purpose to take in young strangers.' Seeing no remedy, no way to help himself, he could only commend his cause to God. And that was enough; before they had done breakfast, in came the Jew, and brought him the whole money.[232]

What are we to make of such stories? Beneath the sunny confidence of the closing verse of Newton's hymn lies, as we have seen, a recognition of darker ambiguities. Newton speaks of how God often deliberately refuses to answer our prayers as we had hoped, so as to inculcate in us a deeper dependence on his grace rather than an easy assumption that we somehow achieved the results ourselves.[233] And he unequivocally rejects the idea that 'rational assent', 'such as we give to a proposition in Euclid', can possibly be the same thing as faith;[234] for he knows that the life of faith is often a hard struggle:

> Notwithstanding all my complaints, it is still true that Jesus died and rose again, that he ever liveth to make intercession, and is able to save to the uttermost. But, on the other hand, to think of that joy of heart in which some of his people live, and to compare it with that apparent deadness and want of spirituality which I feel, this makes me mourn. However, I think there is a scriptural distinction between faith and feeling, grace and comfort; they are not inseparable, and perhaps when together, the degree of the one is not often the just measure of the other. But though I pray that I may be ever longing and panting for the light of his countenance, yet I would be so far satisfied, as to believe the Lord has wise and merciful reasons for keeping me so short of the comforts which he has taught me to desire and value more than the light of the sun.[235]

He used to devote Saturday evenings from about six o'clock onwards to a review of the past week's mercies and sins in preparation for the following sabbath: he called it 'my weekly confession and acknowledgement'.[236] For Evangelicals, human nature is pervasively flawed through sin; and only a radical transformation wrought through grace, the fruit of faith in Christ's redeeming sacrifice at Calvary, can transform it.[237] And this transformation must be *felt* if it is to be authentic. Newton believed that man, despite the effects of the Fall,

> by nature, is still capable of great things. His understanding, reason, memory, imagination, &c. sufficiently proclaim that the hand that made him is divine. He is, as Milton says of Beelzebub, majestic, though in ruins. He can reason, invent, and, by application, attain a considerable knowledge in natural things. The exertions of human genius, as specified in the characters of some philosophers, poets, orators, &c. are wonderful. But man cannot know, love, trust, or serve his Maker, unless he be renewed in the spirit of his mind.[238]

Conclusion

This theme recurs regularly in Evangelical spirituality, and gives it a strong interior dynamic.[239] The weakness is that piety of this kind can become self-regarding, irretrievably inward looking and to some extent world-renouncing – a tendency apparent even in Newton's 'Glorious things of thee are spoken'. Perhaps 'world-defying' would be more accurate, for all the Evangelicals stressed family piety and moral education, and many (as we have seen) were passionately committed to social reform.[240] Like monasticism, they envisaged the Christian life as a total commitment, and a spiritual struggle against apathy and evil.[241] Unlike monasticism, Evangelicals envisaged a transformation of this world that is rooted precisely in the uniqueness of each individual, and his or her potential eternal inheritance. Cowper dreamed of the day when 'the Partition Wall between Christians of different Denominations would every where fall down flat';[242] and here he is, frail and often mentally unstable, but hammering slavery with all the force at his command in 'The negro's complaint':

> Forc'd from home, and all its pleasures,
>   Afric's coast I left forlorn;
> To increase a stranger's treasures,
>   O'er the raging billows borne,
> Men from England bought and sold me,
>   Paid my price in paltry gold;
> But, though theirs they have enroll'd me,
>   Minds are never to be sold.[243]

CATHOLIC SPIRITUALITY

Introduction

Until fairly recently it was customary to see eighteenth-century English Catholicism as a rather thin and dull prelude to the far more exciting events that followed. Yet on

the continent it was a period of significant developments, some of which impinged on
the life of the English Catholic community: if the Evangelicals were deeply influenced
by the Moravians and Americans, the Catholics were no less open to what was taking
place across the Channel. The preaching and work of St Alphonsus Liguori (founder
of the Redemptorists) among the poor of Naples;[244] the enormous influence of spiritual texts such as St François de Sales' *Introduction to the devout life*;[245] and the spread
of devotion to the Sacred Heart of Jesus, stimulated in part by James II's exiled queen –
all these features of continental Catholicism had their impact in England. And the
flamboyant characteristics of baroque piety and art quietly inveigled themselves into
the cool empirical world of the English eighteenth century: the chapels in London's
Catholic embassies offered baroque splendour for grandiose liturgy;[246] and, although
Handel was a Protestant, the rhetorical artifice of his Italianate operas and oratorios,
paralleled in sculpture by the work of Louis François Roubiliac (both at Westminster
and in the Northamptonshire countryside) must have exerted a powerful effect on all
who experienced them.[247]

   None of this is to say that life was easy for Roman Catholics in eighteenth-century
England: the reverse was often the case. The law invoked severe penalties against them
throughout the century; and although, as Horace Walpole notes, George II, 'persuaded that his indulgence to and toleration of the Catholics would secure him from
their plotting, was constantly averse to every proposition of rigour towards them,' the
1715 and 1745 rebellions did nothing to ease their situation.[248] This did not prevent
active proselytizing from taking place, albeit more in some areas than others: the
Catholic historian Joseph Berington (1743–1827) estimates that in 1780 there were
around 60,000 of them in the country (though many of these will have been members
of, or attached to, long-established recusant families).[249] In the mid-1770s an Act of
Parliament, supported by Edmund Burke, significantly eased the discrimination
against Catholics, though this in turn led to a backlash in the form of the Gordon riots
of 1780. In 1791 a further Act allowed Catholics to worship openly; and thereafter the
Catholic community expanded rapidly, not only in its traditional heartlands (such as
Lancashire and the west Midlands) but also in London and the burgeoning industrial
towns.[250]

Eighteenth-century monastic spirituality

With the intriguing exception of the short-lived Trappist community of St Susan at
Lulworth in Dorset at the end of the century, English monastic spirituality during this
period was very much an *émigré* affair:[251] the evidence suggests that monastic observance was generally very strict, among both English *émigrés* and indigenous
continental houses, as part of another period in which a longing to return to primitive
observances was dominant.[252] Monastic life remained little esteemed by many
eighteenth-century English folk: Laurence Sterne derides, albeit ambivalently,
the 'crack-brain'd order of Carthusian monks' who prefer sorrow to laughter, the
house of mourning to the house of feasting.[253] But others were far more discriminat-
ing: John Byrom wrote a moving description of the life profession of a French
Ursuline sister he attended in a letter from Montpellier in 1718.[254]

Richard Challoner (1691–1781) and John Gother (1654–1704)

Joseph Berington argued that his fellow Catholics in the eighteenth century were 'more carefully instructed in their youth' than their Protestant neighbours.[255] But he is less positive about the Catholic clergy of the period:

> Our priests, in their general character, are upright and sincere: But narrowed by a bad education, they contract early prejudices, which they very seldom afterwards deposite [sic]. The theological lumber of the schools supplies, in their minds, the place of more useful furniture.[256]

The priests, formed in rigorous continental seminaries like Douai, nonetheless became active catechists as well as pastors: indeed arguably the greatest of them, Richard Challoner, like other Catholic bishops, was a medical as well as a spiritual practitioner.[257] Challoner was born at Chiddingly in Sussex in 1691; went to Douai in 1705 and returned to join the English mission in London in 1730. Ordained bishop in 1741, he became vicar apostolic of the London district in 1758, assisted by about 60 secular priests and perhaps 100 religious – a formidable force. He was received into the Roman Catholic Church by a significant figure from the previous generation: Fr John Gother, a prominent controversialist and catechist among the London poor during the reign of James II.[258] This concern for the poor profoundly influenced Challoner; and both men produced an immense quantity of devotional and catechetical material for the use of those among whom they lived and worked.

Much of this material is not very original: Challoner in particular adapted and borrowed from earlier authors where he thought pastoral circumstances merited it; and as Eamon Duffy argues, his written work is best seen as an extension of his pastoral concern.[259] What is striking is a gradual movement away from a firmly world-denying, monastic pattern of piety towards one more concerned to equip Catholics for life in this world, and not simply in the next.

Liturgical spirituality

One of Gother's most influential works was his *Instructions and devotions for hearing Mass*:[260] these include guidance for beginners as well as for more experienced Catholics, and are based on the traditional assumption that both observing and imitating the priest offers the surest road to holiness. The Mass was of course central to eighteenth-century Catholic piety; and Challoner includes some similar instructions in his popular *Garden of the soul*,[261] beginning with a theological exposition of what the Mass is: the unbloody sacrifice, daily applying to souls the benefits of Christ's sacrifice on the cross. It concludes

> Hence the best devotion for hearing mass, is that which has for its object the passion of *Christ*, and which tends to unite the soul to *Christ*, and through him to his Father; and which most perfectly answers all the other ends of this sacrifice, *viz.* the adoration of God, thanksgiving for all his benefits, the obtaining pardon for all our sins, and grace in all our necessities.[262]

Gother's spirituality is unequivocally rooted in that of the cloister. He stresses the virtue of punctuality in prayer ('it is by the strict observance of this, religious houses have one great advantage above those in the world').[263] Posture is important too:

> hence . . . must be reproved that hasty, huddling way of running over prayers, in which the words are so much chopt or lost, that whosoever should speak so, even to a companion, would be esteemed either a fool, or mad.[264]

Yet posture and punctuality are not enough; and prayers will 'be nothing better than hypocrysy, or a useless formality, if it be not the effect of a heart seeking God, and sensible of being unworthy of obtaining what it asks'.[265]

One of the ways in which Gother sought to help the faithful to grow spiritually was by producing practical and useful short spiritual reflections for each saint's day.[266] Here is what he wrote about St Sabbas, whose feast day was 5 December:

> 1. He retired into a desert, where, free from the distractions of the world, he might attend with greater application to the business of eternity: Lament the many dissipations of mind to which thou hast voluntarily exposed thyself; resolve to withdraw from whatever is dangerous, unprofitable, or not becoming thy state: Pray for constancy amidst all unavoidable distractions; remember God and eternity in the midst of thy business; learn to be an hermit in the world, by taking off thy affections from all thou possessest: Thou art one day to leave all; practise something of this every day: It is a difficult work, and is best done by degrees. 2. He was an abbot: Pray for all those who have this charge, that in their zeal for virtue and religion they may follow this great example.[267]

Note the firmly other-worldly, monastic tone, balanced only by a tacit recognition of what is practical for a lay Catholic. Here is what Gother wrote about St Valentine:

> It is thought, the charity of this Saint, has given a beginning to the custom of chusing valentines for an encouragement to christians of giving a mutual help to one another in prayer and other good works. If thou observest this custom, perform the charity, but see no abuse or sensuality be promoted under this cover, for there can be no greater provocation than to prostitute holy things . . . Trust not then the fairest pretext of piety, when it is for the improving of a more than ordinary familiarity.[268]

English Salesian spirituality

Challoner produced an extensive quantity of material designed to help the faithful with the practice of meditation, much of which is derived from St François de Sales:[269] like St François's *Introduction to the devout life*, it is designed to help Catholics to live and pray in the world, and hence has a much less markedly monastic tone than Gother's work. The pattern of evening prayer varies between the different editions, suggesting some uncertainty as to whether this should be recited corporately or individually:[270] apart from the Catholic gentry, with their private chapels, the English

Catholic community in the eighteenth century included many poor people as well as tradesmen and professionals and their families (though these were still largely restricted to the Catholic heartlands mentioned above);[271] and Challoner tried to produce material suitable for all of these.[272]

His *Garden of the soul* begins with 'A summary of Christian faith and morality' – what every Christian must believe and what every Christian must do.[273] The latter section begins by setting out the primary obligations of every Christian: to *worship*, to *hope*, to practise *charity*; and 'by the virtue of *religion*, the chief acts of which are *adoration*, *praise*, *thanksgiving*, *oblation* of ourselves to God, *sacrifice* and *prayer*'.[274] There follows a series of biblical texts, a table of feasts and fasts to be observed by Catholics, and vernacular material adapted from the breviary and elsewhere to provide daily morning, evening, and night prayer.[275]

More interesting are the signs of a developing lay spirituality. Challoner includes prayer for use at work;[276] an examination of conscience (which includes some extremely searching and particular questions about sexual behaviour);[277] and devotions for sacramental confession. The book also includes prayers for the sick and the dead, as well as 'A prayer that may be daily said by a woman with child'.[278] In his *Think well on't* (1728), a set of reflections for every day of the month, the subjects for meditation include the dignity and obligations of a Christian (day 4), the presence of God ('He is every where infinitely Good to his Children; his Love and Kindness to them surpasses that of the most tender Mother'[279]), and a series of reflections on the passion of Christ.

Above all, though, Challoner sought to help Catholics fashion a method of prayer that would embrace the whole of their lives, conforming all that they did to the faith they professed:

> in order to pray well, our heart and mind must go always along with what we are about, or, which is the best attention of all, and most conducing to bring us to the love of God . . . for how can we expect that God should hear or regard our supplications when we present them with so much indolence and indifference, as if we told the Almighty we did not care whether he heard us or not?[280]

The Lives of the saints

Another approach to fostering lay piety by seeking to hold together mind and heart, the sacred and the secular, can be found in Fr Alban Butler's massive *Lives of the saints* (1756–9). Butler was sent by his mother to the English college at Douai at the age of eight, returning to England to work as a priest in Staffordshire, where he completed his immense compendium of hagiography. It was directly intended to foster not just scholarship, but devotion:

> But some may say, What edification can persons in the world reap from the lives of apostles, bishops, or recluses? To this it may be answered, that though the functions of their state differ from ours, yet patience, humility, penance, zeal, and charity, which all their actions breathe, are necessary virtues in every person. Christian perfection is in its spirit and essence every where the same, how much soever the means or exercises may vary.[281]

Butler's hope was that his work would provide devotional nourishment, Catholic instruction, and entertainment, whilst also giving English Catholics a deeper perspective of the universal communion to which they belonged.[282] The brief homilies which Butler himself inserted in the life of the first saint for each day of the year give hints of his own spiritual life, which is further revealed in his own (posthumously published) meditations and discourses: the stress on habitual prayer and an ascetic manner of life reflects the spirituality of St François de Sales:

> Perfection consists not in raptures and lofty contemplation; nor in great austerities, or any extraordinary actions: for thus, it would have been above the reach of many. But God has placed it in what is easy, and in every one's power. The rich and poor, the learned and unlearned may equally aim at perfection: for it requires only that we perform our daily actions in a spirit of true Christian virtue . . . we must be holy not by fits, but by habit . . . it is then our ordinary actions performed in a true spirit of virtue, our sleeping, our eating, our recreations, &c., which must sanctify our lives.[283]

SPIRITUALITY AND DISSENT:
PHILIP DODDRIDGE AND DANIEL DEFOE

Introduction
Before the separation of Methodism from the Church of England, the overall proportion of Dissenters to the total population of the country in the eighteenth century was not large: perhaps a little over 5%.[284] Yet the world of Dissent during this period was both diverse and immensely creative, not least in responding to the challenges of rationalism and 'philosophy': thus (to give one example) the great Unitarian scholar Joseph Priestley (1733–1804) argued forcefully against contemporary French atheists, in the process maintaining that doctrines such as transubstantiation and the Trinity are precisely what made it hard for thinking people to accept belief in the God and Father of Jesus Christ.[285] A few of the salient movements and figures are worth mentioning now before exploring their spirituality.

The Society of Friends in the eighteenth century
Eighteenth-century Quakerism retained an emphasis on simplicity of life and a pervasive concern for the poor: the two were articulated in the contemporary spiritual virtue of 'plainness'.[286] Thus in 1742 this question was asked of members at the Quaker Yearly Meeting:

> Is it your Care by Example and Precept to Train up your Children in all Godly Conversation, and in the frequent reading the Holy Scriptures, as also in Plainness of Speech, Behaviour and Apparell?[287]

In 1757 'Servants and those under their care' was added after 'Children', doubtless reflecting a rise in social status among Friends. They were to avoid extravagance of speech, dress, or behaviour in order to avoid being conformed to the way of the world: plainness thus became a characteristic mark of the true Quaker.[288] Their ministers remained basically itinerant; many were relatively unlettered, intense and fervent, and they undoubtedly encouraged a certain anti-rational, even quietist strain in eighteenth-century Quakerism.[289] It is important to note that this did not reduce the movement to an introspective or individualist affair: it did mean that prayer, whether alone or during a meeting, had to be 'divinely moved', and that until that happened it was better to wait in silence for the Spirit to begin its work.[290] But spiritual progress for Quakers was inseparable from a concern for the common good: eighteenth-century Friends believed that their spiritual welfare depended on both their unity in the truth and their willingness to encourage one another to live what they professed.[291] Later in the eighteenth century English Quakers, in most cases influenced by their American co-religionists, became more actively involved in social reform: the minute book of a women's Friends meeting in Somerset in 1785 records that 'the epistle from our Womon [sic] friends of America . . . was read at this meeting which being the first of the kind we have had rather cheerd some druping spirits that was almost ready to faint for want of bread'.[292]

The Countess of Huntingdon (1717–91)

Selina, Countess of Huntingdon was a remarkable person: she was widowed in 1746 and thereafter devoted her life to the service of God: both her sons also predeceased her. The congregations who came to worship in her proprietary chapels and hear men like Whitefield preach were very diverse; and her contacts with gentry, wealthy merchants, and especially with William Wilberforce (1759–1833) extended Evangelical influence significantly. For most of her life a devoted member of the Church of England, she was eventually obliged to choose between the closure of her chapels and departure from the Church: in 1783 she chose the latter;[293] but, lacking Wesley's organizational ability, her fledgeling movement (the Countess of Huntingdon's Connexion) did not long survive her.[294] Her vision for the short-lived college she established reflects a concern to instil in her students a rigorous spiritual discipline: they were

> to rise at the Sound of the Bell; which is to be rung at 5 O'Clock – to appear in the Study at a quarter after 5, before the Master, to sing a Hymn. From this time 'till 6 they are to retire for private prayer and meditation; and to make their Beds, and clean themselves. At 6 O'Clock, the Morning [spiritual] exercise begins. Breakfast at 7. NB to be over in a quarter of an hour. At eight, the Academical Studies begin.[295]

Her longing to see what she believed to be the pristine simplicity of the apostolic Church restored in her own day is palpable, precisely when her own spiritual vision for her chapels was being disappointed: 'the more apostolic we are, the better; and I must say, as a most remarkable blessing, I know of none [in the Connexion] anxious or discontented among us, even when it might justly have been excused, seeing myself unable to do what my heart so much desired'.[296]

Philip Doddridge (1702–51)

Philip Doddridge was one of the greatest figures in eighteenth-century Dissent. Born in London, of devout parents, he was (like all Dissenters) prohibited from attending university at Oxford or Cambridge, and so was educated at dissenting schools and academies, showing great intellectual ability and becoming minister of the Independent church at Kibworth in 1723, aged only 20. Two years later he moved to Market Harborough, and in 1729 became minister of Castle Hill Independent church at Northampton, where he remained for the rest of his life; he died of tuberculosis in Lisbon in 1751, having gone there in the hope of convalescing.[297]

Doddridge's writings were influential during his own lifetime as well as later.[298] His greatest published work was perhaps his *The rise and progress of religion in the soul* (1745), described by his contemporary biographer as 'a body of practical divinity and christian experience'.[299] It is in effect an extended work of Evangelical spiritual direction, with prayers provided at the end of each chapter in order to allow the reader to appropriate the advice given. He also wrote a massive six-volume work entitled *The family expositor* (1738–50), designed for Christian family use: the contents of the New Testament are paraphrased but with the actual text included in italics; and each section concludes with an 'Improvement': these are

> entirely of a practical nature, and generally consist of pressing exhortations, and devout meditations, grounded on the general design, or on some particular passages, of the *section* to which they are annexed. They are all in an *evangelical strain*, and they could not with any propriety have been otherwise.[300]

Daniel Defoe (1660–1731)

One other major figure in the world of English Dissent deserves inclusion. Daniel Defoe was an active Dissenting Christian throughout his long life; but he was also a tradesperson, at one point a wine and tobacco importer and at another a brick merchant; above all, a journalist, and a political journalist at that, frequently causing controversy. He was also frequently in debt, and at least twice imprisoned for bankruptcy; and he is certainly the only person mentioned in this book who was convicted of seditious libel by the government and sentenced to stand in the pillory. He died in penury in 1731, after having spent all the money his (vastly popular) books had earned him. These attributes are in themselves almost a perverse justification for including him, since he is so unlike all the other characters treated. But there are other reasons too; and we may begin this exploration of Dissenting spirituality by reflecting on his attitude to providence.

Spirituality and Robinson Crusoe

Defoe's most famous work, whose full title was *The life and strange surprizing adventures of Robinson Crusoe of York, mariner* (1719), stands with *The pilgrim's progress* in the tradition of Puritan conversion narratives;[301] but there are important differences between Defoe's masterpiece and Bunyan's. Where Christian has virtually no option but to flee from the wrath to come and thus embark on his spiritual pilgrimage,

Crusoe declares that 'I would be satisfied with nothing but going to Sea,' thereby rejecting his father's recommendation of a safe legal career.[302] He can, and does, choose what to do with his life; and he thus represents increasing numbers of eighteenth-century townspeople in a position to do the same.

Crusoe is also someone who flouts the warnings of providence, and the counsels of prudence or convention. The most striking parallel is with the story of the Prodigal Son: like him, what Crusoe does is done voluntarily;[303] like him, Crusoe soon finds himself rapidly losing his control over events;[304] and, again like the Prodigal, he finds himself at his lowest ebb not at his original act of sin but just before his conversion.[305] Defoe himself quotes the Prodigal in his book, when near the beginning Crusoe reflects on being offered the chance to return home:

> Had I now had the Sense to have gone back to *Hull*, and have gone home, I had been happy, and my Father, an Emblem of our Blessed Saviour's Parable, had even kill'd the fatted Calf for me.[306]

There are other differences from Bunyan too: thus it is hard to imagine Bunyan's pilgrim agreeing with Crusoe in wondering why God has chosen to conceal the knowledge of salvation from millions like Friday who 'would make a much better use of it than we did'.[307] And Crusoe reflects the age of Gibbon as much as that of Bunyan when he roundly declares to himself that

> As to all the Disputes, Wranglings, Strife and Contention, which has happen'd in the World about Religion, whether Niceties in Doctrines, or Schemes of Church Government, they were all perfectly useless to us [i.e. for him and Friday]; as for ought I can yet see, they have been to all the rest of the World.[308]

The problems for Crusoe occur when, as he himself puts it, we submit to the 'secret overruling Decree that hurries us on to be the Instruments of our own Destruction, even tho' it be before us, and . . . we rush upon it with our Eyes open'.[309] Later he notes that

> there are some secret moving Springs in the Affections, which when they are set a going by some Object in view; or be it some Object, though not in view, yet rendered present to the Mind by the Power of Imagination, that Motion carries out to the Soul by its Impetuosity to such violent eager embracings of the Object, that the Absence of it is insupportable.[310]

Human desires and longings are at once dangerous and creatively risky, opening up for us new frontiers beyond Eden.[311]

Against this 'secret overruling Decree' of fate stands God's firm, wise but not authoritarian providence, though this is often unclear to us: thus when Crusoe is marooned he says:

> I had great Reason to consider it as a Determination of Heaven, that in this desolate Place, and in this desolate Manner I should end my Life; the Tears would run plentifully down my Face when I made these Reflections, and

> sometimes I would expostulate with my self, Why providence should thus
> compleatly ruine its Creatures, and render them so absolutely miserable,
> so without Help abandon'd, so entirely depress'd, that it could hardly be
> rational to be thankful for such a Life.[312]

Crusoe's discovery of the ears of green barley growing, apparently spontaneously, in
the back of his cave-dwelling, leads him at first to give thanks to divine providence;
but the wonder and gratitude abate when he realizes that 'all this was nothing but what
was common'.[313] Defoe appears here implicitly to be warning against too naïve a trust
in divine providence: later he makes Crusoe reflect that 'all our Discontents about
what we want, appear'd to me, to spring from the Want of Thankfulness for what we
have'.[314] He comes to see that true providence is a hidden source of personal guidance:

> 'tis never too late to be wise; and I cannot but advise all considering Men,
> whose Lives are attended with such extraordinary Incidents as mine, or
> even though not so extraordinary, not to slight such secret Intimations of
> providence, let them come from what invisible Intelligence they will, that
> I shall not discuss, and perhaps cannot account for; but certainly they are a
> Proof of the Converse of Spirits, and the secret Communication between
> those embody'd, and those unembody'd.[315]

He also comes to recognize that those very events which appear to be catastrophic may
be precisely the means by which providence can lead us forward:

> How frequently in the Course of our Lives, the Evil which in it self we seek
> most to shun, and which when we are fallen into it, is the most dreadful to
> us, is oftentimes the very Means or Door of our Deliverance.[316]

This forms a key part of Defoe's emphasis, in *Robinson Crusoe*, on how the individual Christian copes with his or her own experience of shipwreck.[317] And what he
constantly stresses is the need for an awareness of, and sensitivity to, the 'invisible
World' and its gentle but insistent solicitations: an awareness, that is, of the world of
the spirit.[318] And what Crusoe learns to do in his lonely adventure, the rest of us by
implication may do also, by seeking to become transparent to the spiritual dimension
of all life.[319]

Defoe's great achievement here is to offer a view of providence which manages to
leave plenty of scope for individual initiative and choice, and yet which, through
gentle promptings and hints which are constantly offered but never forced upon us,
reflects the divine longing to be a partner in our lives, not an overmastering or inflexible lord; and hence he shows us how we may make something enduringly creative out
of all life, both what we ourselves choose and that over which we have no control at
all.[320] And, more important still, such a view of providence offers the person who
acknowledges it a degree of mature trust that is rooted in the conviction that God will
never leave him to face even desert islands all alone, as a result of which Crusoe not
only survives his long ordeal but becomes the agent for others' transformation and
rescue – above all of course for Friday's.[321]

Doddridge's covenant spirituality

Philip Doddridge also invokes the image of the Prodigal Son in his treatment of the spiritual life, as we shall see. He takes a more conventional approach to the nature of our relationship with, and apprehension of, God than does Defoe; but he was writing catechetical and pastoral, rather than fictional, works. In *The rise and progress* he says that each person is to ask him or herself:

> Am I truly religious? Is the love of God the governing principle of my life? Do I walk under a sense of his presence? Do I converse with him from day to day, in the exercise of prayer and praise? And am I, on the whole, making his service my business and my delight, regarding him as my master and my father?[322]

He is addressing himself here to those who believe in God, but take little or no notice of him:

> Common sense will tell you that it is not your own wisdom, and power, and attention, that causes your heart to beat, and your blood to circulate . . . These things are done when you sleep as well as in those waking moments, when you think not of the circulation of blood, or of the necessity of breathing . . . Now what is this, but the hand of God?[323]

Reason as well as revelation testifies to creation's dependence on God.[324] And death should concentrate the minds of people to awaken from bondage to sin.[325] Having been thus awakened, the sinner can accept the free gift of God's justifying grace, and make the journey of the Prodigal towards the Father. Doddridge uses the Calvinist imagery of the covenant to express this process, and, in the original version of one of his most famous hymns, he uses the story of Jacob's covenant with God at Bethel to articulate what happens:

> O God of Jacob, by whose hand
>   Thine Israel still is fed,
> Who through this weary pilgrimage
>   Hast all our fathers led.
>
> To thee our humble vows we raise,
>   To thee address our prayer,
> And in thy kind and faithful breast
>   Deposit all our care.
>
> If thou, through each perplexing path,
>   Wilt be our constant guide;
> If thou wilt daily bread supply,
>   And raiment wilt provide;
>
> If thou wilt spread thy shield around,
>   Till these our wand'rings cease,
> And at our Father's lov'd abode
>   Our souls arrive in peace:

> To thee, as to our Covenant-God,
>   We'll our whole selves resign;
> And count, that not our tenth alone,
>   But all we have is thine.[326]

Doddridge encourages the person to make such an act alone, and to review this 'covenant' regularly, providing the reader with an extended form of such an act, of which this is an extract:

> Receive, O heavenly Father, thy returning prodigal! Wash me in the blood of thy dear Son: clothe me with his perfect righteousness; and sanctify me throughout by the power of thy Spirit! Destroy, I beseech thee, more and more the power of sin in mine heart! Transform me more into thine own image, and fashion me to the resemblance of Jesus, whom henceforward I would acknowledge as my teacher and sacrifice, my intercessor and my Lord![327]

By such an act the person becomes a member of 'God's covenant people', worthy to share in the ordinance of Holy Communion.[328] By such an act, too, a fundamental change takes place in the life of the believer:

> The change must be great and universal. Enquire then whether you have entertained new apprehensions of things, have formed a practical judgment different from what you formerly did; whether the ends you propose, the affections which you feel working in your heart, and the course of action to which, by those affections, you are directed, be on the whole new or old? . . . Enquire . . . whether God hath implanted a principle in your heart, which tends to him, and which makes you like him. Search your soul attentively, to see if you have really the image there of God's moral perfections, of his holiness and righteousness, his goodness and fidelity.[329]

Spirituality and the world of work

Dissenters showed a pervasive interest in every aspect of people's lives, not simply their religion: indeed the educational concerns of ministers like Doddridge are vital for an understanding of their piety.[330] Doddridge formed his own Dissenting academy at Market Harborough, and later moved it to Northampton, where in 1738 he also established a charity school in his own house: this attracted vicious opposition from some local Anglicans.[331] Undeterred, Doddridge remained wholeheartedly committed to social reform, preaching strongly and effectively in favour of the opening of a county infirmary for the poor at Northampton.[332] It is worth giving an indication of the wide-ranging syllabus and spiritual formation he offered students at his academy:

> I have at present [1740/1] a greater proportion of pious & ingenious Youths under my care than I ever before had . . . I think it of Vast Importance to instruct them carefully in the Scriptures, & not only endeavour to establish them in the great truths of Christianity, but to labour to promote

their practical influence on their hearts; for which purpose I frequently converse with each of them alone, and conclude the conversation with prayer... Most of the Lectures I read are such as I myself draw up, specially in Algebra; Jewish Antiquities; Pneumatology, Ethicks, Divinity, & the Manner of Preaching, & the Pastoral care in its Several branches. Whistons Euclid Dr Watts Logick & Ontology, Clares Fluids, Jennings Astronomy. Keils Anatomy. Gravesends or Desaguliers Philosophy. Buddeus Account of the Antient Philosophers. and Lampes Ecclesiastical History. are books which I Lecture thro' & Explain besides.[333]

Defoe contributes significantly towards what might be described as a spirituality of work. Robinson Crusoe is no skilled workman: 'I had never handled a Tool in my Life, and yet in time by Labour, Application, and Contrivance, I found at last that I wanted nothing but I could have made it.'[334] Some have argued that *Robinson Crusoe* represents an idealization of a primitivist back-to-nature philosophy, after the manner of Rousseau; others that it represents exactly the opposite, and that Defoe is commending work as therapy for all who find themselves in the loneliness of appalling predicaments, which would make the book into a celebration of what is now known as the Protestant work ethic.[335] Neither seems convincing: the likeliest interpretation is to see the book as encouraging a collaboration between human beings and their Creator, as Crusoe first struggles to survive and then attempts to develop a rudimentary cultural life on his desert island. In *The complete English tradesman* Defoe argues for a proper balance between secular and spiritual life for the worker:

> The duties of life, which are either spiritual or secular, must not interfere with, nor jostle one another out of its place. It is the duty of every Christian to worship God, to pay his homage morning and evening to his Maker, and at all other proper seasons to behave as becomes a sincere worshipper of God; nor must any avocation, however necessary, interfere with this duty, either in public or in private. Nor, on the other hand, must a man be so intent upon religious duties, as to neglect the proper times and seasons of business. There is a medium to be observed in everything.[336]

For all his own ill-fortune in business, some of it doubtless his own fault, Defoe remains very positive about the life of the tradesperson: significantly, he argues that such people can reflect on profound spiritual truths no less than the scholar and the aristocrat:

> I know no state of life, I mean in that we call the middle station of it, and among the sensible part of mankind, which is more suited to make men perfectly easy and comfortable to themselves, than that of a thriving tradesman ... and though he is not incapable of a disaster, yet he is in the best manner fenced against it of any man whatever. His life is perfectly easy, surrounded with delights; every way his prospect is good; if he is a man of sense he has the best philosophic retreats that any station of life offers him; he is able to retire from hurry, to contemplate his own felicity, and to see it the least encumbered of any state of the middle part of life.[337]

Yet this robustly affirmative attitude does not blind him to the terrible consequences of business failure. Almost all Defoe's heroes and heroines encounter catastrophe in one form or another; and Defoe's own experience undoubtedly helps him to probe acutely how they cope with it. He is sharply aware that poverty breeds immorality: 'as to honesty', says Amy to her mistress Roxana, 'I think honesty is out of the question when starving is the case';[338] and a little later Roxana herself admits that 'my circumstances were my temptation'.[339] Yet he is also aware that we can try to turn our own adversities to good effect by becoming more compassionate to others similarly afflicted.[340] Here too the gentle promptings of Providence can offer us wise counsel *in extremis*: if we reject them, we are apt to become enslaved to vice; and the person who does this 'defaces the image of God in his soul; dethrones his reason, causes conscience to abdicate the possession, and exalts sense into the vacant throne.'[341]

The theology and practice of prayer

What kind of spirituality can sustain us when things go wrong? Defoe is too experienced in the way of the world to have any naïve belief in prayer as providing instant solutions:

> A fallen tradesman should . . . always hope, and his hope will always keep him alive. A man that will lie still should never hope to rise; he that will lie in a ditch and pray, may depend upon it he shall lie in the ditch and die. This has determined diligence to be absolutely necessary to deliverance, as legs are to progression.[342]

This reads like stout Protestant piety: God helps those who help themselves. Doddridge warns his readers to expect times when God hides his face: 'you may lose your lively views of the divine perfection and glories'.[343] When this happens

> You may pour out your soul in private, and then come to public worship, and find little satisfaction in either; but be forced to take up the Psalmist's complaint; *My God, I cry in the day-time, but thou hearest not.*[344]

At such times Doddridge encourages the Christian to consider whether this spiritual distress may in reality have a physical or material cause, or be the result of sin.[345] The Christian should therefore engage in a strict examination of conscience whilst waiting patiently on the Lord.[346] Doddridge provides a magnificent hymn, based on two verses from the powerful thirty-eighth Psalm, for prayer in times of suffering or despair:

> My soul, the awful hour will come,
>   Apace it passeth on,
> To bear this body to the tomb,
>   And thee to scenes unknown . . .
>
> Whence in that hour shall I receive
>   A cordial for my pain,
> When, if earth's monarchs were my friends,
>   Those friends would weep in vain?

> Great King of nature, and of grace,
>   To thee my spirit flies,
> And opens all its deep distress
>   Before thy pitying eyes.
>
> All its desires to thee are known,
>   And every secret fear,
> The meaning of each broken groan
>   Well-noticed by thine ear.
> O fix me by that mighty power,
>   Which to such love belongs,
> Where darkness veils the eyes no more,
>   And groans are chang'd to songs.[347]

The development of a spirituality for use in adversity is explored by Defoe in *Robinson Crusoe*. Crusoe's spiritual sense develops slowly: he concedes that he had had little religious sensibility hitherto; and even when a sudden earthquake threatens his solitary dwelling,

> all this while I had not the least serious religious Thought, nothing but the common, *Lord ha' Mercy upon me*; and when it was over, that went away too.[348]

He prays to God when he is stricken with fever ('pray'd to GOD for the first Time since the Storm off of *Hull*, but scarce knew what I said, or why; my Thoughts being all confused'[349]). Once he has had time to reflect, and 'a leisurely View of the Miseries of Death came to place itself before me', he begins to make the move from trusting entirely in his own skill, or passively accepting his lot, to a deeper religious faith: this begins with a fearful experience of his own past sins – had he deserved all that had happened to him ('*Why has God done this to me/ What have I don to be thus us'd?*'[350])? Was *this* divine providence?[351]

> I refus'd their [his parents'] Help and Assistance who wou'd have lifted me into the World, and wou'd have made every Thing easy for me, and now I have Difficulties to struggle with, too great even for Nature itself to support, and no Assistance, no Help, no Comfort, no Advice; then I cry'd out, *Lord be my Help, for I am in great Distress*. This was the first Prayer, if I may call it so, that I had made for many Years.[352]

Then he ponders scripture, and in particular God's capacity to work seemingly impossible events: he recalls the Israelites' scornful scepticism in Psalm 78 ('Can God spread a table in the wilderness?'), which leads him to an unprecedented act:

> I did what I never had done in all my Life, I kneel'd down and pray'd to God to fulfil the Promise to me, that if I call'd upon him in the Day of Trouble, he would deliver me; after my broken and imperfect Prayer was over, I drunk the Rum in which I had steep'd the Tobacco, which was so strong and rank of the Tobacco, that indeed I could scarce get it down; immediately upon this I went to Bed.[353]

This is no mystical experience. But it does lead Crusoe to regular Bible reading and prayer, which give him great comfort.[354] Later, after his famous discovery of 'the Print of a Man's naked Foot', he says 'I was guided and encourag'd to pray earnestly to God for Deliverance', which gives him confidence to investigate rather than cower fearfully in his fortress-dwelling.[355] Certainly the naked footprint discovery is a crucial moment: Crusoe's briefly attained happiness is abruptly dispelled by an alien intrusion; as so often, paradise (or at least contentment) is spoiled at the very moment of its attainment.[356] But the seed is sown: Crusoe has discovered, in a very ordinary and down-to-earth way, the means to keep in contact with God in the midst of the random uncertainties of life.

Both Defoe and Doddridge explore the nature of prayer at length; but since much of Doddridge's fine treatment of the subject is similar to that of Isaac Watts, who will be considered below, we may conclude this section by a brief examination of how Defoe approaches it.[357] In *Religious courtship*, he describes a young gentleman from Hampshire who visits William, one of his humblest ploughmen, to find out how he may come to true religion: the gentleman is astonished when William tells his landlord that he is already praying, if he only knew it:

> *Landlord.* You must explain yourself, William, I do not understand you.
>
> *William.* Why, sir, those earnest desires you have after the knowledge of God, and after the true worship of God, which is the sum of religion, I say, those earnest desires are really prayers in their own nature; sincere wishes of the heart for grace, are prayers to God for grace; prayer itself is nothing but those wishes and desires put into words, and the first is the essential part; for there may be words used without the desire, and that is no prayer, but a mockery of God; but the desires of the heart may be prayers, even without the words.
>
> *Landlord.* You surprise me a little, William.
>
> *William.* Besides, sir, and't please you, those earnest desires you have after religion, and after the knowledge of God, will force you to pray, first or last, in a verbal prayer; they will break out like a flame that cannot be withheld; your heart will pray when you know not of it: praying to God, sir, is the first thing a sense of religion dictates, as a child crieth as soon as it is born.[358]

This is classic Protestant teaching on prayer, set out in a manner designed to make it accessible to anyone. God himself creates the desire within us:[359] human nature is in itself hopelessly fallen; yet, though God has to implant the desire in us, to pray is as natural to us as crying is for a child.[360] There is no need for ministers or spiritual directors to teach us all this.[361] Prayer with mere words but with no heart is worthless.[362]

Family piety
And, like many Protestants before him, Defoe is aware that it is within the family that true piety must be nurtured, just as it is there that 'religion grows unfashionable'.[363]

The family instructor considers this subject at some length, starting with an extended dialogue between parents and children once the parents realize they have been lax and decide to reinstate a firm spiritual discipline. Defoe's moral is patent:

> Religious children of profane or negligent parents are a double testimony to powerful invincible grace, but a dreadful reproach to the parents.[364]

Husband and wife reproach themselves not only for not having taught their child to pray but for not having prayed together themselves.[365] But Defoe goes further: true family piety requires that husband and wife 'communicate to one another their griefs, and most inward afflictions of mind, as well as their common disasters and troubles of the world'.[366] It also means that masters must 'reckon [their servants] under their care as well as under their government'.[367] None of this is easy: 'My dear,' says the mother, 'a religious conversation is not the easiest thing in the world.'[368] What is crucial is for everyone, perhaps especially those with power over others, to recall their own status as children of God, and thus under God's authority. 'To treat a child with passion and rage, is the same thing as other men treat slaves.'[369] For we are ourselves children of 'the great Parent of the world'.[370] And religion is easily counterfeited:

> Wherever God erects a house of prayer,
> The Devil always builds a chapel there,
> And 'twill be found upon examination
> The latter has the largest congregation.[371]

Conclusion

Philip Doddridge knew that last truth too. His piety, though serious, was not gloomy, and was often intensely joyful:[372] like Defoe, he reminded his readers that the Pauline teaching on our adoption as children is central to how we live spiritually. And his work gives the lie to the stereotyped picture of Dissent as narrow or world-denying. He may not have Isaac Watts' power or eloquence; but his legacy to English spirituality is substantial and enduring:

> There is a certain anxiety and servitude of spirit, which is beneath the genius of christianity; a gloomy and ungenerous conception of the Deity, which is a kind of heavy chain upon the mind; which makes all its operations unwieldy, and painful. This the gentle encouraging constitution of the gospel was intended to cure, by inspiring us with sentiments of gratitude, hope and love ... *For we have not received the spirit of bondage, but of adoption*; and full of filial affection and confidence, under the influences of that spirit, *we cry abba, Father.*[373]

Daniel Defoe is important for English spirituality, not only because he writes as a layperson whose piety is rooted in the soil of secular and mercantile life, nor simply because he had the ability to create characters of enduring and universal appeal. He matters because he is able to use his own life and experience – which, though unusual, are far more representative of eighteenth-century England than the lives of (say) Blake, Wesley, or Doddridge – and fashion a spiritual response to them.[374] Robinson

Crusoe is no saint, any more than his creator was. A good deal of what happens to him is his own fault. His spirituality grows fitfully, prayer and drinking rum forming uncomfortable (but doubtless not uncommon) cohabitants: acquiring a sense of God and of divine providence provides no insurance against further disaster, any more than it did for Defoe. What matters is how we respond to the hand that life deals us: just as Crusoe gets all he can out of the wrecked ship before it finally disappears, so we must seek with God's guidance to do the same with our lives. Defoe made of that simple but enduring truth a dazzling series of stories whose best characters must have spoken directly to the real world around them – and do so still. One of Defoe's very early *Meditations* may be allowed the last word:

> Did But My Meditacons More Enclyne
> To View What Tis I am
> From What & Whence I came
> Lord I should Never Then Repyne
> I am Not This Or That
> Or Have Not This or That Thats great
> If I remaine
> Life Does So Many Gifts Containe
> Alive I can have No sufficent [sic] Reason To Complaine.[375]

SPIRITUALITY AND BEAUTY:
BLAKE, COLERIDGE, AND EIGHTEENTH-CENTURY ART

Spirituality and the arts in the eighteenth century

Oliver Goldsmith argued that the reign of Queen Anne, the apogee of what came to be known as the 'Augustan' age because its principal poets sought to imitate the glories of their Roman imperial forebears, was the time when 'taste was united to genius'.[376] A preoccupation with taste, with seeking to separate the 'tasteful' from the everyday, was characteristic of England in the eighteenth century – and not only of its courtly élite.[377] Thus Goldsmith says of the Vicar of Wakefield's family that

> the whole conversation ran upon high life, and high-lived company, with pictures, taste, Shakespeare, and the musical glasses.[378]

The arts became more commercial and less courtly as they became more urban, linked to the technical improvements and commercial practices of the modern world.[379] The coffee house and the pleasure garden brought 'culture', however defined, to a far wider public than hitherto. Not everyone approved: William Law described going to the theatre as

> a Contradiction to all Christian Holiness, and to the Methods of arriving at it . . . If you are only for the *Form* of Religion, you may take the Diversion of the Stage along with it. But if you desire the *Spirit* of Religion, if you desire to be truly religious in Heart and Mind, it is as necessary to renounce and abhor the Stage, as to seek God, and pray for the Guidance of his Holy Spirit.[380]

Law, though by no means a lone voice, did not prevail. But arguments about the role of art in what might be called the spiritual life of the nation continued nonetheless. Handel was a regular and devout worshipper at St George's Hanover Square in London; and his music was heard and enjoyed by immense audiences.[381] Within the churches, Evangelicals wanted choirs to *lead* congregations, while those of the High Church tradition wanted organists and choirs to *perform* for congregations;[382] but Hannah More was by no means alone in disapproving of both:

> It is pleaded by the advocates for church music, that the organ and its vocal accompaniments assist devotion, by enlisting the senses on the side of religion; and it is justly pleaded as an argument in favour of both, because the affections may fairly and properly derive every honest aid from any thing which helps to draw them off from the world to God. But is it not equally true, that the same species of assistance, in a wrong direction, will produce an equally forcible effect in its way, and at least equally contribute in drawing off the soul from God to the world?[383]

Sense and sensibility

'Taste' was closely connected with sentiment and 'sensibility'. If the Augustan age of the early eighteenth century could be said to be characterized by an imitative classicism celebrating sobriety and simplicity, the middle decades of the century came to be known as the 'Age of Sensibility'.[384] Poetry and literature sought to cultivate the feelings by appealing to the senses, albeit with careful restraint: sensibility, like enthusiasm, needed careful scrutiny.[385] But it had a vital role to play in the life of the spirit. Thus Anna Barbauld, citing an earlier writer, notes that religion is not only a matter of *truth* and *habit* but may also be seen

> as a taste, an affair of sentiment and feeling, and in this sense it is properly called devotion. Its seat is in the imagination and the passions, and it has its source in that relish for the sublime, the vast, and the beautiful, by which we taste the charms of poetry and other compositions that address our finer feelings; rendered more lively and interesting by a sense of gratitude for personal benefits.[386]

Barbauld goes on to condemn contemporary criticism of 'sentiment': 'it is the character of the present age to allow little to sentiment, and all the warm and generous emotions are treated as romantic by the supercilious brow of a cold-hearted philosophy'.[387] She continues:

> Yet there is a devotion, generous, liberal, and humane, the child of more exalted feelings than base minds can enter into, which assimilates man to higher natures, and lifts him 'above this visible diurnal sphere.' Its pleasures are ultimate, and, when early cultivated, continue vivid even in that uncomfortable season of life when some of the passions are extinct, when imagination is dead, and the heart begins to contract within itself. Those who want this taste, want a sense, a part of their nature, and should not presume to judge of feelings to which they must ever be strangers.[388]

This is not to regard philosophy or the intellect as inimical to piety, though Barbauld does distinguish between 'the spirit of inquiry' and 'the spirit of disputation'.[389] Indeed philosophy is a vital dimension of religion: the trouble is that it 'represents the Deity in too abstracted a manner to engage our affections . . . We require some common nature, or at least the appearance of it, on which to build our intercourse.'[390] Thus

> the philosopher offers up general praises on the altar of universal nature;
> the devout man, on the altar of his heart, presents his own sighs, his own thanksgivings, his own earnest desires: the former worship is more sublime, the latter more personal and affecting.[391]

Hence too 'a prayer strictly philosophical must ever be a cold and dry composition'.[392] Prayer must find space not only for wonder, but also for feelings: 'In our creeds let us be guarded; let us there weigh every syllable; but in compositions addressed to the heart, let us give freer scope to the language of the affections, and the overflowing of a warm and generous disposition.'[393] The fact that devotion can run into superstition is no justification for avoiding it altogether.[394]

Others too saw a close relationship between prayer and sensibility. Cowper wrote:

> Let no low thought suggest the pray'r,
> Oh! grant, kind Heav'n, to me,
> Long as I draw ethereal air,
> Sweet Sensibility.[395]

Elsewhere Cowper criticized the country gentlefolk who put the pursuit of pleasure and cultivation of landscape before prayer, so that their estates were in perfect order but their minds 'a wilderness'. Note the reference to 'insensibility':

> Peace be to those (such peace as earth can give)
> Who live in pleasure, dead ev'n while they live;
> Born capable, indeed, of heav'nly truth;
> But down to latest age, from earliest youth,
> Their mind a wilderness, through want of care,
> The plough of wisdom never ent'ring there.
> Peace (if insensibility may claim
> A right to the meek honours of her name)
> To men of pedigree, their noble race
> Emulous always of the nearest place
> To any throne except the throne of grace.
> (Let cottagers and unenlighten'd swains
> Revere the laws they dream that heav'n ordains;
> Resort on Sundays to the house of pray'r,
> And ask, and fancy they find, blessings there.)
> Themselves, perhaps, when weary they retreat
> T'enjoy cool nature in a country seat,
> T'exchange the centre of a thousand trades,

> For clumps, and lawns, and temples, and cascades,
> May now and then their velvet cushions take.
> And seem to pray, for good example sake;
> Judging, in charity, no doubt, the town
> Pious enough, and having need of none.
> Kind souls! to teach their tenantry to prize
> What they themselves, without remorse, despise.[396]

More generally, and especially in *The task*, Cowper celebrates the beauties of nature, but from the point of neither sentiment nor pleasure: rather, country life both avoids the perils and unwholesomeness of towns and also allows human beings to live in the presence of God.[397]

Spirituality and landscape

Cowper's attitude is of course affected by his dislike of towns and industry. But it touches on another aspect of eighteenth-century cultural and spiritual life: their approach to landscape and nature. As increasing numbers of people became separated from the immediate processes of agriculture, so their attitude to nature changed: no longer need it be seen exclusively as oriented to production.[398] The very interest in ordering, classifying and understanding things referred to earlier in this chapter presupposed a certain distance, a standing-back from direct participation in natural processes.

Nature was thus something to be *observed*, even manipulated, by those with time and resources to spare: indeed it could be idealized, as an idyllic and even a holy place. In the later eighteenth century this became somewhat self-conscious: thus Coleridge, tramping the Lake District fells, is (like the German Romantics) contemplating not nature in itself, but its personal and spiritual effect on *him*.[399] The invention of the ha-ha is significant here: it enabled the wealthy to see what appeared to be a natural landscape (in fact subtly engineered by, say, 'Capability' Brown or Humphry Repton), but with the unattractive sight of sheep and cow droppings hygienically removed.[400] Samuel Johnson, visiting the Scottish Highlands, was acutely aware of the difference between artificial and natural landscapes:

> The imaginations excited by the view of an unknown and untravelled wilderness are not such as arise in the artificial solitude of parks and gardens, a flattering notion of self-sufficiency, a placid indulgence of voluntary delusions, a secure expansion of the fancy, or a cool concentration of the mental powers. The phantoms which haunt a desert are want, and misery, and danger; the evils of dereliction rush upon the thoughts; man is made unwillingly acquainted with his own weakness, and meditation shews him only how little he can sustain, and how little he can perform.[401]

And Cowper, bewailing the ruinous condition of rural churches, 'could not help wishing, that the honest vicar, instead of indulging his genius for improvements, by inclosing his gooseberry bushes with a *Chinese* rail . . . would have applied part of his income to the more laudable purpose of sheltering his parishioners from the weather during their attendance on divine service'.[402]

Spirituality and beauty

This brings us to the more general question of the relationship between spirituality and aesthetics. It might be supposed that a century fascinated by classicism, science and reason might have a chillingly formal view of beauty; but the truth is more subtle. In his treatise on beauty, Edmund Burke stressed that it is not simply a matter of proportion: deformity is the opposite, not of beauty, but of completeness; and 'the true opposite to beauty is not disproportion or deformity, but *ugliness*'.[403] Nor is perfection the same as beauty: 'beauty in distress is much the most affecting beauty', wrote Burke, though one wonders anxiously what he had in mind here.[404]

One of the qualities that connects aesthetics with spirituality is wonder, a subject explored by the philosopher Descartes a century earlier. In his *Les passions de l'âme* (1649), Descartes makes 'l'admiration' one of his six 'primary emotions', indeed the first and most important of all, because it is our immediate response to the reality we experience. The trouble is that mere wonder or astonishment is not necessarily creative: it can immobilize us fatally, as with the rabbit caught in a bright light.[405] Descartes thus concluded that wonder is best directed towards the one object which can never have this effect on us – God – and thus wanted to restrict wonder to philosophy, where it can be properly and safely exercised.[406] David Hume went further and insisted that wonder and religion should be kept separate, since he believed that the latter deliberately fostered wonder in order to serve its irrational ends.[407]

Burke explores the same theme, but takes a different view. He too is aware that astonishment of itself is not necessarily good: it is 'the effect of the sublime in its highest degree; the inferiour effects are admiration, reverence, and respect'.[408] But it is closely linked with terror, especially in the face of power;[409] hence when we contemplate God, it is his power more than his justice or mercy which strikes us most.[410] Cowper reserves wonder for the deepest mysteries of life, such as premature death:

> These are Mysteries, my Dear, that we cannot contemplate without astonishment, but which will nevertheless be explained hereafter, and must in the mean time be revered in silence.[411]

Beauty and wonder, then, may enrich our spiritual lives; but they may also be dangerous distractions from it. In an exquisite little prayer he wrote for a young girl, the poet Christopher Smart articulated the heart of a genuinely spiritual beauty:

> Christ, keep me from the self-survey
>   Of beauties all thine own;
> If there is beauty let me pray,
>   And praise the Lord alone.
>
> Pray – that I may the fiend withstand,
>   Where'er his serpents be;
> Praise – that the Lord's almighty hand
>   Is manifest in me.
>
> It is not so – my features are
>   Much meaner than the rest;

A glow-worm cannot be a star,
    And I am plain at best.

Then come, my love, thy grace impart,
    Great Saviour of mankind;
O come, and purify my heart,
    And beautify my mind.

Then will I thy carnations nurse,
    And cherish every rose;
And empty to the poor my purse,
    Till grace to glory grows.[412]

William Blake (1757–1827)

Burke had a contemporary, no less interested in the nature of beauty and its relationship to the things of the spirit, but arriving at sharply different conclusions. William Blake was a Londoner, a tradesman, an engraver, and a mystic:[413] sometimes curmudgeonly, certainly not clubbable, at home as much in the world of commerce as in the further speculative reaches of occult philosophy.[414] He was self-taught: he distrusted the sophistries of the cultural establishment. In the annotations he made to the *Discourses* of Sir Joshua Reynolds, he said what he thought about Burke:

> Burke's Treatise on the Sublime & Beautiful is founded on the Opinions of Newton & Locke; on this Treatise Reynolds has grounded many of his assertions in all his Discourses. I read Burke's Treatise when very Young; at the same time I read Locke on Human Understanding & Bacon's Advancement of Learning; on Every one of these Books I wrote my Opinions, & on looking them over find that my Notes on Reynolds in this Book are exactly similar. I felt the Same Contempt & Abhorrence then that I do now. They mock Inspiration & Vision. Inspiration & Vision was then, & now is, & I hope will always Remain, my Element, my Eternal Dwelling place; how can I then hear it Contemned without returning Scorn for Scorn?[415]

For Blake, inspiration and vision are not to be learned: they can only be received. You either have them or you do not. He distrusted learning, artifice, the acquisition of skills, the attainments of reason. He did not suffer fools gladly, or indeed at all: 'I love laughing . . . I hate crawlers,' he wrote once.[416] But he knew his Bible intimately, and professed himself a Christian.[417]

Samuel Taylor Coleridge (1772–1834)

We may explore his spirituality in tandem with that of another remarkable contemporary, Samuel Taylor Coleridge, who was if anything even more versatile: literary critic and teacher, philosopher, politician, playwright, travel-writer, naturalist and fell-walker, he was above all a poet with a childlike love of adventure stories: an enthusiast *par excellence*.[418] Communication was his lifeblood:

'Have you ever heard me preach, Charles?' he once asked his friend
[Charles] Lamb. 'N-n-never heard you d-d-do anything else, C-c-coleridge'
was the reply.[419]

For Coleridge, religion was 'a total act of the soul . . . the science of Being, the Being
and the Life of all genuine Science'.[420] Heart as well as mind needed to be addressed
and transformed. He agreed with Robert Leighton, the seventeenth-century archbishop of Glasgow (who profoundly influenced him) in maintaining that

> Religion doth not destroy the life of nature, but adds to it a life more excel-
> lent; yea, it doth not only permit, but requires some feeling of afflictions.[421]

Yet his enthusiasm did not shade off into superstition: indeed he carefully distinguished the two.[422] And, for all his emphasis on feeling and perception, he insists on a
firmly intellectual and rational foundation for 'spirituality', however defined. In his
comments on Isaac Taylor's *Natural history of enthusiasm*, he argues, *contra* Taylor, that
Christian and scriptural prayer, far from implying a hopelessly inadequate conception
of the nature of God on the part of human beings, is in fact

> perfectly conformable to the highest and clearest convictions of my *Reason*
> (I use the word in its most comprehensive sense, and comprising both the
> *practical* and the intellective, not only as the Light but likewise as the Life
> which *is* the Light of Man. John i.3).[423]

A few words about Blake's and Coleridge's principal sources with regard to spirituality may be useful. Both were intimately familiar with scripture, Blake perhaps
supremely with the Book of Job.[424] Coleridge, characteristically, embraced the Bible
with no holds barred; and in a footnote to Southey's *Life of John Wesley* he declared that
the person who could read the entire Bible meditatively and at leisure would be
someone for Christianity to be proud of.[425]

The influence of Plato

The influence of Plato and the Platonic tradition is primary for both men; and it may
well be true that for both this represented in part a reaction against the changing
nature of English life, and the new industrial landscape. On the face of it, Blake's
reaction was the same as Cowper's: 'those dark satanic mills' was his response to the
grim new factories burgeoning around him in south London.[426] He took little interest
in politics, loved to invoke the lore of ancient and arcane myths, or the lost splendour
of medieval Gothic, and responded to what he saw around him with Platonic bravura
– matter mattered, but spirit mattered more:

> This world of Imagination is the world of Eternity; it is the divine bosom
> into which we shall all go after the death of the Vegetated body. This World
> of Imagination is Infinite & Eternal, whereas the world of Generation, or
> Vegetation, is Finite & Temporal. There Exist in that Eternal World the
> Permanent Realities of Every Thing which we see reflected in this Veg-
> etable Glass of Nature. All Things are comprehended in their Eternal
> Forms in the divine body of the Saviour, the True Vine of Eternity.[427]

Yet, as we shall see, Blake's rich Platonized universe is shot through with a piercing compassion for those whose experiences in the world of matter are far from happy or easy. Platonism is only one element in Blake's spiritual worldview: another is a vigorous and visionary enthusiasm, rooted in a longing to recapture the primitive energy and purity that alone (in the view of many contemporary thinkers) made for human wholeness.[428] Coleridge's Platonism is different, and paradoxical: at one point he declares that 'the writings of Plato are smoke and flash from the witch's cauldron of a disturbed imagination!'[429] – only to speak of 'the divine Plato' a page or two further on.[430] Yet there is no doubt that Neoplatonism, as well as German idealism, are at the heart of his thought, and give it a metaphysical (and sometimes frankly obscure) tone which was not always well received even at the time.

Swedenborg and Boehme

Two other influences on Blake and Coleridge are worth briefly noting here. The first was the extraordinary Emanuel Swedenborg, the eighteenth-century Swedish miner-turned-mystic. Blake studied his writings closely:[431] in particular, Swedenborg's insistence on seeing the material in the light of the spiritual, his stress on 'correspondences' between the two, and on the incarnation of God ('the human form divine'), deeply influenced Blake.[432] The second was the German cobbler mystic Jakob Boehme, whose influence on seventeenth-century English spirituality has already been noted:[433] both he and Swedenborg heightened Blake's overriding emphasis on the imagination.[434] Coleridge explicitly acknowledged his indebtedness to Boehme;[435] and his year in Germany exposed him both to Boehme's thought and to the rich flowering of Romantic metaphysics then in vogue.[436]

The holiness of creation

Blake and Coleridge may be said to occupy a particular niche in the spectrum between enthusiasm and philosophy: they embraced both, unhesitatingly accepting metaphysics and revealed truth as well as the insights of reason and experience. This profoundly affected their attitude to the world around them. 'Every thing that lives is Holy' is the concluding line of Blake's *The marriage of heaven and hell*.[437] For him, God was in everything, from the lowest to the highest;[438] and everyone, however lowly, could receive divine inspiration.[439] Indeed it could be argued that Blake's sense of the holiness of creation was such that it led him to depreciate the value of individual holiness:

> Men are admitted into heaven not because they have curbed & govern'd their Passions or have No Passions, but because they have Cultivated their Understandings. The Treasures of Heaven are not Negations of Passion, but Realities of Intellect . . . The Fool shall not enter into Heaven let him be ever so Holy. Holiness is not The Price of Enterance into Heaven.[440]

This view too is firmly Platonic. In the early *Contemplation*, Blake describes man as 'slave of each moment, lord of eternity'.[441] Through the fall of humanity, we lose our spiritual sight (and hence our imagination) and become enslaved to the senses, able to recognize only the narrowly material dimensions of reality.[442] Later he went further and declared that

> Man has no Body distinct from his Soul; for that call'd Body is a portion of
> Soul discern'd by the five Senses, the chief inlets of Soul in this age. Energy
> is the only life, and is from the Body; and Reason is the bound or outward
> circumference of Energy. Energy is Eternal Delight.[443]

And later still, in *Jerusalem*, he advanced a view of humanity that reads like a combustible cocktail of Plato and Swedenborg:

> Man is born a Spectre of Satan & is altogether an Evil, & requires a New
> Selfhood continually, & must continually be changed into his direct
> Contrary.[444]

How is this to happen? How may our lost spiritual energies and vision be restored to us? Blake has in effect two responses, the second of which we shall consider later. The first is contemplation, which 'reinstates knowledge on his throne, once lost'.[445] Or, in a phrase which was to endure, he wrote:

> If the doors of perception were cleansed every thing would appear to man
> as it is, infinite. For man has closed himself up, till he sees all things thro'
> narrow chinks of his cavern.[446]

Coleridge had a similar view. He envisaged the starting-point of Christianity as an avoidance of evil; but this is 'but a preparatory awakening of the soul: a means of dispersing those gross films which render the eye of the spirit incapable of any religion, much less of such a faith as that of the love of Christ'.[447] He too celebrated the holiness of creation, and like Blake espoused a spirituality that is world-embracing:

> Religion is the sun whose warmth indeed swells, and stirs, and actuates the
> life of nature, but who at the same time beholds all the growth of life with a
> master-eye, makes all objects glorious on which he looks, and by that glory
> visible to others.[448]

We must learn to see the spiritual through the everyday, the presence of God in our midst. In an interesting footnote to his *On the constitution of church and state* Coleridge comments on Christ's words 'Where two or three are gathered together in my name, there am I in the midst of them' (Matthew 18.20): he argues that this has too often been understood as a kind of causal statement – that is, that Christ turns up to support his faithful when they gather together – rather than a spiritual indwelling:

> it is at least difficult not to infer, that they had interpreted the promise, as of
> a corporal co-presence, instead of a spiritual *immanence* . . . as of an individ-
> ual coming in or down, and taking a *place*, as soon as the required number
> of petitioners was completed! As if . . . this presence, this actuation of the 'I
> AM' . . . were an after-consequence, an accidental and separate result and
> reward of the contemporaneous and contiguous worshipping – and not the
> total act itself, of which the spiritual Christ, one and the same in all the
> faithful, is the originating and perfective focal unity. Even as the physical
> life *is* in each limb and organ of the body, 'all in every part;' but is *manifested*
> as life, by being one in all and thus making all *one*; even so with Christ, our

Spiritual Life! He *is* in each true believer, in his solitary prayer and during his silent communion in the watches of the night, no less than in the congregation of the faithful; but he *manifests* his indwelling presence more characteristically, with especial evidence, when many, convened in his name, whether for prayer or for council, do through him become ONE.[449]

Spirituality and pity

And this stress on our mutual indwelling in Christ is the key to the primacy of compassion in the spiritual vision of William Blake. His moving poem 'The chimney sweeper' (in *Songs of innocence*, 1789) reflects his concern about the conditions under which child sweepers had to live and work:

> A little black thing among the snow,
> Crying 'weep! weep!' in notes of woe!
> 'Where are thy father & mother? say?'
> 'They are both gone up to the church to pray.'
>
> 'Because I was happy upon the heath,
> And smil'd among the winter's snow,
> They clothed me in the clothes of death,
> And taught me to sing the notes of woe.
>
> 'And because I am happy & dance & sing,
> They think they have done me no injury,
> And are gone to praise God & his Priest & King,
> Who make up a heaven of our misery.'[450]

Constantly one is aware of Blake's deep sense of compassion and pity: thus Enion in *Vala or the four Zoas* powerfully declares:

It is an easy thing to triumph in the summer's sun
And in the vintage & to sing on the waggon loaded with corn.
It is an easy thing to talk of patience to the afflicted,
To speak the laws of prudence to the houseless wanderer,
To listen to the hungry raven's cry in wintry season
When the red blood is fill'd with wine & with the marrow of lambs.
It is an easy thing to laugh at wrathful elements,
To hear the dog howl at the wintry door, the ox in the slaughter house moan;
To see a god on every wind & a blessing on every blast;
To hear sounds of love in the thunder storm that destroys our enemies' house;
To rejoice in the blight that covers his field, & the sickness that cuts off his children,
While our olive & vine sing & laugh round our door,
    & our children bring fruits and flowers.
Then the groan & the dolor are quite forgotten, & the slave grinding at the mill,
And the captive in chains, & the poor in the prison, & the soldier in the field
When the shatter'd bone hath laid him groaning among the happier dead.
It is an easy thing to rejoice in the tents of prosperity.[451]

Doubtless Blake's own experience of poverty and insecurity is being evoked here; but so also is his opposition to a Church which he felt had accommodated itself too comfortably to the structures of an acquisitive society.[452] Pity is in his view a universal energy and love which unites all human beings.[453] He has no time for chastity, spiritual discipline, narrowly intellectual study: all these fetter the creative imagination and energy at the heart of human beings.[454] And this is why he had little time for organized religion, which is for him a thin, homogenized affair, lacking the imaginative depth and vision which would allow it to engage compassionately with the world outside:

> I went to the Garden of Love,
> And saw what I never had seen:
> A Chapel was built in the midst,
> Where I used to play on the green.
>
> And the gates of this Chapel were shut,
> And 'Thou shalt not' writ over the door;
> So I turn'd to the Garden of Love
> That so many sweet flowers bore;
>
> And I saw it was filled with graves,
> And tomb-stones where flowers should be;
> And Priests in black gowns were walking their rounds,
> And binding with briars my joys & desires.[455]

It is striking to see how, in his illustrations for Thomas Gray's 'Elegy written in a country churchyard', Blake's depiction of the parson at the interment is in black and white, with the parson an elegant but vapid figure – whereas by contrast his depiction, on the following page, of the agricultural worker harvesting is full of life, colour and physical vigour.[456]

Spirituality and forgiveness

This is not to say that Blake's vision of the spiritual life had no room for Christ. On the contrary; and this brings us to the second of his two responses to the predicament of fallen humanity. If the first is the 'cleansing of our perceptions', the second is something attainable only through Christ: the forgiveness of our sins:

> There is not one Moral Virtue that Jesus Inculcated but Plato & Cicero
> did Inculcate before him; what then did Christ Inculcate? Forgiveness of
> Sins. This alone is the Gospel.[457]

Only through the forgiveness offered to us by Christ can the effects of the Fall be undone. But the effects of this forgiveness are not some arid religiosity or sinless purity or static legalistic perfection, but the releasing of our latent spiritual energies which in turn allow us to see God in everything, not only (or even primarily) in church. It is fascinating to note how in his longer poems Blake moves effortlessly from (say) Urizen and Albion (representing common humanity) to Lambeth and Salisbury in a mere line or two.[458] And this sense of the pervasive interrelationship between the divine and the human finds expression in one of his most famous poems, and one which introduces us finally to Blake's and Coleridge's understanding of prayer. In *The divine image*, Blake wrote

> To Mercy, Pity, Peace, and Love
> All pray in their distress;
> And to these virtues of delight
> Return their thankfulness.
>
> For Mercy, Pity, Peace, and Love
> is God, our father dear,
> And Mercy, Pity, Peace, and Love
> Is Man, his child and care.
>
> For Mercy has a human heart,
> Pity a human face,
> And Love, the human form divine,
> And Peace, the human dress.
>
> Then every man, of every clime,
> That prays in his distress,
> Prays to the human form divine,
> Love, Mercy, Pity, Peace.
>
> And all must love the human form,
> In heathen, turk, or jew;
> Where Mercy, Love, & Pity dwell
> There God is dwelling too.[459]

The theology and practice of prayer

For Blake, all prayer is prayer to Christ; and nothing less than all humanity is to be the scope of our love.[460] For Coleridge too, 'prayer is *Faith* passing into act . . . It is the *whole* man that prays.'[461] And thus prayer is a *transforming* activity:

> But what the plant *is*, by an act not its own and unconsciously – *that* must thou *make* thyself to *become!* must by prayer and by a watchful and unre-sisting spirit, *join* at least with the preventive and assisting grace to *make* thyself.[462]

Coleridge looks for no 'outward or sensible Miracles from Prayer – it's [sic] effects and it's fruitions are spiritual'.[463] It is a gift of God to the elect, the reward of faith.[464] Hence the prayer of the Ancient Mariner is not heard ('I looked to Heaven, and tried to pray'), until he blesses the creatures he sees, and 'The selfsame moment I could pray'.[465] Hence too the Mariner's own simple but eloquent conclusion:

> 'He prayeth best, who loveth best
> All things both great and small;
> For the dear God who loveth us,
> He made and loveth all.'[466]

Conclusion

William Blake is the mirror-opposite of the rationalist thinkers, the Gibbons and the Humes, whom unsurprisingly he excoriates. 'Deism is the Worship of the God of this World . . . This was the Religion of the Pharisees who murder'd Jesus.'[467] His writing, like that of Coleridge, is often dense, obscure, rhetorical, and rarely consistent. Yet both are an antidote, on the one hand to a detached empiricism, on the other to a narrow and insular religiosity, each of which can be found among contemporaries. Both espoused a rich, full-blooded, Christ-centred spirituality that could transform human lives by empowering us not only to discern the divine in the heart of the secular, but to reach out in love and compassion to those that a rapidly-changing, industrializing society had managed to ignore. Unlike Coleridge, Blake took no interest in politics, did not travel far, and cared little for European philosophy or Romantic poetry (though he did take a great interest in the seismic events that accompanied the French Revolution). But his vision of a new Jerusalem builded here was no less enduring; and he would unquestionably have assented to Coleridge's vigorous insistence on the fact that Christianity 'is not a Theory, or a Speculation; but a *Life* . . . TRY IT'.[468]

CASE STUDIES

Isaac Watts (1674–1748) and the Independent tradition

One of Isaac Watts' hymns runs as follows:

> Nature with open volume stands
> To spread her Maker's praise abroad;
> And every labour of his hands
> Shews something worthy of a God.
>
> But in the grace that rescu'd man
> His brightest form of glory shines;
> Here on the cross 'tis fairest drawn
> In precious blood and crimson lines . . .
>
> O the sweet wonders of that cross
> Where God the Saviour lov'd and dy'd!
> Her noblest life my spirit draws
> From his dear wounds and bleeding side.[469]

It offers a useful corrective to the often-held assumption that Protestants of the seventeenth and eighteenth centuries were essentially unconcerned about the world outside the church (or, if they were concerned, exhibited only a narrow moralism). For Watts, everything created can teach us something about God. He was deeply interested in creation, science, animal life, and (perhaps above all) education. His choice of the word 'survey' in the first line of his most famous hymn, which will be explored in more detail below, is significant: in an age of innumerable surveys of landscape, flora and fauna, and other branches of knowledge, he happily applied to them the same careful and reverent scrutiny and reflection that he applied to his God. But his God came first.

Isaac Watts was born in 1674 in Southampton: he was a bright, precocious child, the son of a prosperous schoolmaster and clothier. Like Philip Doddridge, he was educated at Dissenting schools and academies: like him, he probably received an education that was more imaginative and flexible than he would have received had Dissenters been permitted to study at Oxford or Cambridge. After some years as a private tutor, he became in 1702 Minister of Mark Lane (Independent) Church in London, a post he held until his death in 1748. He left behind him a considerable body of written work, a good deal of it concerned with education and social reform (he wrote *The art of reading and writing English* (1720), which he dedicated to the three daughters of his patron Sir Thomas Abney;[470] and *An essay towards the encouragement of charity schools* (1728)). He wrote a book on logic (he was no narrow enthusiast) and another on ontology.

In addition to all this he published sermons, theological treatises, catechetical texts, and 697 hymns.[471] His *Hymns and spiritual songs* (first edition 1707) was extremely popular: until the Toleration Act of 1689, singing in Protestant churches had been restricted to psalmody and metrical psalms.[472] He wanted his hymns to be understood, not just sung, deliberately pitching the words towards 'plain country people . . . poor people who work for their living'.[473] He drew widely from other authorities, Protestant and otherwise (among them the philosopher John Locke);[474] but both content and style were all his own.

Watts began his first published sermon by warning his fellow Christians that they take for granted the fact that their religion is divine and true:

> There are two points of great and solemn importance, which it becomes every man to inquire into: First, Whether the religion he professes be true and divine; and then, Whether he has so far complied with the rules of this religion, as to stand entitled to the blessings thereof. The christians of our age and nation, have been nursed up amongst the forms of christianity from their childhood; they take it for granted their religion is divine and true, and therefore seldom enter into the *first* inquiry: but when they come to think in good earnest about religious affairs, their great concern is with the *second*.[475]

He goes on to warn them that they live in an age in which they can no longer take the first inquiry for granted.[476] 'Infidelity is a growing mischief of the present age, even in our own land. It seems to be a spreading infection.'[477] He frequently returns to the challenges put to Christianity by deists, such as that the behaviour of Christians and their disunity argues against the truth of their Gospel.[478] Watts argues against the first charge

> that if we take a nearer view, we shall see that no doctrine ought to fare the worse, because some wicked men are professors of it. It was not counted a discredit to philosophy, that some of the professors of it, who hated the gospel, were vicious in their lives. I would ask the deist now, is there any

ground to disbelieve natural religion, because there are some that make profession of it are fallen into great sins?[479]

What is noteworthy here is Watts' urgent concern to address the contemporary challenges to Christianity. Like the Lord he worshipped, his teaching was rooted in the immediate and the everyday, though often rising above it. His theology is rooted in Calvinism;[480] and sometimes his view of predestination is unattractive to twenty-first-century minds:

> Lord, I ascribe it to thy grace,
> And not to chance, as others do,
> That I was born of christian race,
> And not a heathen or a Jew.[481]

He guards himself against accusations of 'enthusiasm': in his first published sermon he tells his congregation

> I shall not lead you, nor myself, into the land of blind enthusiasm, that region of clouds and darkness, that pretends to divine light.[482]

The Christian faith is no 'bold fit of enthusiasm';[483] and to speak of the 'extraordinary witness of the Spirit' is 'not the language of wild enthusiasm'.[484] But if he avoids the Scylla of enthusiasm, he is even more determined to circumnavigate the Charybdis of philosophy: the problem with even 'the best of philosophers' is that they have no power to assure us whether or not our sins are forgiven:[485] their learning has no capacity to change them or warm their hearts:[486]

> The light of nature indeed would dictate thus much, that God is, in his own nature, gracious, and compassionate, and kind; but whether God would be gracious to you or me, compassionate to such ill-deserving sinners as we are, the light of nature could never determine.[487]

This is pure grace, revealed, not discernible by reason or natural religion alone. Nor can philosophy or reason tell us that we are loved for all eternity.[488] 'All the wisdom and learning of the philosophers could never do such miracles as this gospel has done, could never work such a divine life and temper in my heart.'[489] And those who criticize Christianity for having 'much of enthusiasm' should recognize the inadequacy of reason alone to discover truth:

> When a poor penitent creature, distressed under a sense of the power of sin dwelling in him, who has long and often toiled and laboured to bring his heart near to God, and to suppress the irregular and exorbitant appetites of his nature, addresses himself to the throne of God, and cries earnestly for divine help, it is a glorious provision that is made in the gospel of Christ, that the Spirit of God is promised for our assistance. Nor is it at all unworthy of a person of the greatest reason and the best understanding, humbly to wait and hope for the accomplishment of this promise. Thus the charge of enthusiasm vanishes, and the gospel maintains its honour.[490]

Even more importantly, philosophy cannot help us learn how best to face death: 'The religion of the ancient patriarchs, the religion of Moses and the Jews, as well as the religion of the philosophers, all come vastly short of christianity, in the important business of dying.'[491] Watts argues well: he knows his adversaries; and he wants to proclaim a faith that changes people, particularly those unlikely to be drawn to philosophy. So he tells his congregation:

> Your souls are form'd by wisdom's rules,
>   Your joys and graces shine;
> You need no learning of the schools,
>   To prove your faith divine.[492]

And elsewhere he declares with the preacher's rhetoric: 'Let all the sects of philosophy hide their heads, and lie silent; give me the Bible.'[493]

As with Newton and Charles Wesley, we may best explore the spirituality of Isaac Watts by looking in more detail at one of his hymns:

> When I survey the wondrous cross,
> Where the young Prince of Glory dy'd,[494]
> My richest gain I count but loss,
> And pour contempt on all my pride.
>
> Forbid it, Lord, that I should boast,
> Save in the death of Christ my God;
> All the vain things that charm me most,
> I sacrifice them to his blood.
>
> See from his head, his hands, his feet,
> Sorrow and love flow mingled down;
> Did e'er such love and sorrow meet?
> Or thorns compose so rich a crown?
>
> His dying crimson like a robe
> Spreads o'er his body on the tree,
> Then am I dead to all the globe,
> And all the globe is dead to me.
>
> Were the whole realm of nature mine
> That were a present far too small;
> Love so amazing, so divine
> Demands my soul, my life, my all.

Watts gave this hymn the title 'Crucifixion to the World by the Cross of Christ, Gal.vi.14.'[495] It is the seventh hymn in Part III of his *Hymns and spiritual songs* (1707): this third part consisted of hymns intended for the Lord's Supper.[496]

As already suggested, the use of the word 'survey' in the first line is instructive.[497] Watts himself uses the word frequently, and often in a quite straightforward way, meaning to look over, as if from above, comprehensively and dispassionately: 'Let us survey a few instances of this kind.'[498] He uses the word in this sense in theological contexts: 'When I cast my eyes around, and survey the present frame of things . . . my faith assures me they are all employed in rolling the months and hours away, that stand between me and immortal happiness.'[499] In addition, he uses the word in the context of self-examination, or with God as the subject: 'It is worth while for us now to take a survey of ourselves, to look back upon our lives, and ask, "What testimonies have we given to the glory of this gospel . . . ?"'[500] or 'God surveys himself, he is pleased with his own glories, delights in himself as the highest and noblest object.'[501] This reflection on the Cross, then, is a careful and contemplative paying-attention to the heart of the Christian faith, with an eye to what its implications will be for me.

And the cross that is being surveyed is *wondrous*. References to wonder abound in Watts' work; and he explores the subject in *The doctrine of the passions*, where he describes admiration, or wonder, as ranking with love and hatred as 'the most primitive and original passions, or those of the first rank'.[502] The trouble is that admiration 'has no regard to the agreeableness or disagreeableness of the object, but only the rarity of it'.[503] So it is important to seek out suitable objects for it,

> and continually dive deeper into the philosophy of nature, into the natural history of things, in the heavens, and on the earth; and especially, if we contemplate the nature and perfections of God, the amazing instances of his providence and grace, which he has manifested in his word.[504]

The most suitable object of all is of course God, 'an immense ocean of glories and wonder';[505] and a sense of wonder in the face of God animates our attitude to all creation:

> The soul that loves God is ready to see and take notice of God in every thing: He walks through the fields, he observes the wonders of divine workmanship in every different tree on his right hand and on his left, in the herbs and flowers that he treads with his feet, in the rich diversity of shapes and colours and ornaments of nature: He beholds and admires his God in them all. He sees the birds in their airy flight, or perched upon the branches, and sending forth their various melody: He observes the grazing flocks, and the larger cattle in their different forms and manners of life; he looks down upon little insects, and takes notice of their vigorous and busy life and motions, their shining bodies, and their golden or painted wings, he beholds and he admires his God in them all: In the least things of nature, he can read the greatness of God, and it is what of God he finds in the creature that renders creatures more delightful to him. Creatures are but his steps to help him to rise toward God.[506]

This magnificent passage is Augustinian in tone; and the resonances with the teaching of Descartes on the subject of wonder are manifest.[507] But Watts has more to say on the subject of wonder than this:

> There is yet still another world of wonders to employ the lover of God, and that is, the person of his Son Jesus Christ our Saviour. There God discovers himself in his fullest grace and wisdom, in his highest power and perfection.[508]

And the mainspring of such wonder is a recognition of the spiritual state you once experienced:

> Enter into yourselves, think what once you were, corrupt, abominable, unclean, unholy . . . Survey the promises that are big with blessings . . . and let the pious affections of hope and love break out and diffuse themselves with sweet delight. Read the history of the life and death of our blessed Lord, which is made up of love and wonders.[509]

Once you can do this, 'this world will be as a dead thing in your eyes; it will have very little power to work on your passions, and to draw you aside from God: He will be your love and your all. The strength of faith and the views of death will command your fears, and hopes, and desires.'[510]

We are very close here to the heart of the spirituality of Watts' hymn, as well as to the text from Galatians which inspired it. What is fascinating about Watts is his capacity, like Augustine, *both* to celebrate the wonder of the creation *and* to go far beyond that creation in order to reverence the wonder of its Creator: the point, for both writers, is that the creation has no value *except* insofar as it points beyond itself to its Creator. Thus he declares that

> this world is a fair theatre of the wisdom and power of God, but it is hung round and replenished with temptations to fallen man.[511]

So it is deserving of wonder only if we look through and beyond it, not for some intrinsic empirical or scientific value of its own. And thus the 'wondrous Cross' transcends it infinitely: for it is there that we see the 'love so amazing, so divine' made manifest. The wonder with which Watts' hymn begins and ends is our first response to the unfathomable mystery of the divine love.

But it is only our first response. In the second verse of the hymn, following St Paul's text in Galatians, Watts responds more directly to the mystery of the Cross, and does so by turning to prayer: 'Forbid it, Lord, that I should boast . . .'[512] From wonder we move to sacrifice, and a costly one at that: we are to surrender 'all the vain things that charm me most' as our own response to the self-giving love of God.

It is important to stress at this point that Watts is not offering in this hymn a purely subjectivist theology of atonement. Elsewhere he makes clear his belief in the objective efficacy of Christ's death;[513] though he rejects the notion of atonement as

> any such thing as shall in a proper and literal sense appease the wrath of God, the offended Governor, which is supposed to be kindled against his sinful creatures . . . [for] this is an idea or supposition in many respects inconsistent with the attributes and actions of the blessed God, and with the doctrine of the New Testament.[514]

What matters for our purposes is the *response* expected of the believer in the face of Christ's unique act of self-sacrifice; and that response will be costly.[515] For Watts, the process of sanctification presupposes 'a contempt of the present world, in comparison of the future'. He is thinking here not of an utter rejection of this world, but rather a recognition that much of what preoccupies us here is trivial, and will appear wretchedly so from the perspective of heaven.[516] Indeed he stresses that

Christianity does not abridge us of the common comforts of flesh and
blood, nor lay an unreasonable restraint upon any natural appetite; but it
teaches us to live like men, and not like brutes; to regulate and manage our
animal nature with its desires and inclinations, so as to enjoy life in the
most proper and becoming manner; to eat and drink, and taste the
bounties of providence, to the honour of our Creator, and to the best
interest of our souls.[517]

There is nothing wrong with mirth and merriment, as long as they are confined
'within the limits of virtue'.[518] But underlying this moderate view of asceticism is a
deeper sense of costly change as we respond to God's saving initiative in the Cross of
Christ. Nowhere is this more eloquently put than in Watts' nineteenth Sermon:

The grace of the gospel, which was typified by the ark of Noah, takes in all
manner of animals, clean and unclean, and saves them from the deluge of
divine wrath that shall come upon an ungodly world. But there is this
blessed difference, that the brutes went out of the ark with the same nature
they brought in; but those who come under the protection and power of
this gospel by faith, they are in some measure changed, they are refined,
they are sanctified. The wolf that came in, is turning into a lamb, and the
raven by degrees becomes a dove; surely, the gospel has begun to make
them so, for it has begun their salvation.[519]

This change will be difficult:

Reformation of all kinds, whether in families or churches, in cities, or
nations, demands a good degree of resolution and courage. It is a brave and
daring enterprize, to stem the torrent of the age we live in, and to attempt
to change the vicious customs of a city or nation.[520]

Ultimately, of course, Christ changes us, as he was himself transformed at the Ascension.[521] And this change takes place as we respond to God's call to 'look unto me and
be saved' (the visual element here is the same as that in 'When I survey the wondrous
cross'): our contemplation of the dying Christ involves us in a process of costly but
total transformation into his image:

It must be such a look as changes the soul and temper into another image,
even the image of Christ. 2 Cor.iii.18. *We, beholding as in a glass the glory of
the Lord, are changed into the same image from glory to glory.* In the glass of
the gospel beholding the glorious holiness of our Lord Jesus Christ, our
very tempers are changed into his holy likeness, from one degree of grace
to another, till it advance to complete glory; and then we shall be made
more perfectly like him by seeing him as he is, or face to face; *1 John* iii.2.
There will be a shine of holiness on our conversation in this world, as
reflected from the glory and holiness of Christ, whom we have seen, even
as the face of Moses shone he had *seen God*; Exodus xxxiv.29,30. That is,
when he had seen the Son of God conversing with him in a visible glory.[522]

So what has begun as a calm 'survey' of the 'wondrous cross' has already been insensibly transmuted into a radical transformation. *This* is the heart of Watts' spirituality: you can gaze on nature's landscapes, or works of art, for as long as you like; but they will not change you: 'many lovely accomplishments, joined together, will not carry a natural man to heaven'.[523] But surveying the cross of Christ is an altogether different enterprise, obliging you to abandon your cool objectivity and be transformed by what you see.

In the third verse ('See from his head, his hands, his feet') the visual element becomes explicit; and the language is close to that of medieval devotion to the suffering Jesus. And yet, although Watts does not eschew the physical manifestations of Jesus' sacrifice, his real interest is in getting us to gaze upon something completed, a victory won precisely through a seeming defeat, thorns composing the richest of crowns. Elsewhere he says:

> Look up to this blessed emblem, and you shall find this salvation complete and perfect, and your consciences pacified, under the agonies of your own guilty reflections, through the blood of Jesus, who died. This emblem of a dying sacrifice is also a refuge, a support, and a hope for saints.[524]

He wants to underline the fact that the Cross, though agonizing and horrendous to undergo, is in a profound and spiritual sense *beautiful* too, for in it we find 'a refuge, a support, and a hope for saints'. One of Watts' most enduring concerns is to present a deeply *attractive* Christianity;[525] and he insists that those grasped by it will want to experience more and more of it:

> We see christians, searching after God in ordinances and seeking for the Lord Jesus Christ in sermons, in prayers, in the closet, and in the sanctuary; for they live upon him. A holy soul pursues after the presence of his God, and his Saviour, with the same zeal of affection and fervent desire, that the men of this world indulge in their pursuit of created good.[526]

Watts expects clergy in particular to do all they can to portray it in this way.[527] He warns them to avoid 'the pomp and magnificence of the theatre' in their pulpit oratory; but to recall also that 'a dull preacher makes a drowsy church'.[528] Ultimately, however, it is the Gospel they preach which will draw people to Christ; and it will do so when they see the glory in the Cross. For Watts, crucifixion, resurrection and ascension are inseparable: with the latter,

> The scandal ceases from Christ, and it ceases from his people too: It is no longer a matter of shame or folly to be a believer or follower of such a Jesus. The power and grandeur of the Son of God, sitting on so illustrious a throne, takes away and annihilates all the scandal of a man hanging on a tree.[529]

So to the fourth verse of Watts' great hymn ('His dying crimson like a robe') and his depiction of the epicentre of St Paul's text. At the very moment of Christ's death, we die too: *then* am I 'dead to all the globe'. We die with him, and are raised with him. And our death, inasmuch as it demands the offering of ourselves, is scarcely less comprehensively demanding than his was. Watts is clear that Christian faith is an unconditional entrusting of the self into the hands of Christ, 'that he may be our Saviour': for faith, in the New Testament, means not only 'the *believing of a truth* but the *trusting in a person*'.[530] Understood in this sense, 'faith and practice make up the whole of our religion'.[531] So

> Saving faith is not a feeble belief of the words, or works, of power of Christ, upon a short hearsay and slight notice, but it is built upon knowledge and just evidence. It is not a mere doctrinal and historical assent to the truths which our Saviour spoke; nor is it a mere rational conviction by the best arguments, that Christ is furnished with such abilities to save: It is not a sudden fit of desire, or hope, or well-wishing to our souls to be saved by Christ; nor is it a rash and bold presumption that Christ will save me, and make me happy. But it is a solemn betrusting of my soul into his hands for salvation, built upon a deep sense of my own sin and danger; a solid knowledge of his sufficient furniture for such an undertaking; and an earnest desire to be made partaker of this salvation, in the full nature of it, both the holiness and the joy.[532]

By handing over ourselves without reservation to Christ, we become partakers in his salvation: we die to the world as he did, and share his risen life. Faith changes us; and Watts' view of it is immensely important, because it reflects his concern to offer, like Wesley, a piety that is neither narrowly rational nor narrowly emotional: neither philosophy nor enthusiasm is enough.[533] Hence the primacy of love, especially the love of God, which both integrates mind and heart and also inspires us to live the full Christian life – through wonder, love of neighbour, service of the poor, and so on. This is what happens when we have faith of this kind:

> I find my conscience, that was disturbed with the guilt of sin, established in peace, upon solid hopes of pardon. I have an interest in the love of God, and lively sensations of that love; I have a hatred of all sin, I live above the world, and have a holy contempt of the trifles, businesses, and cares of this life; I delight in the company of him that dwells in heaven; I find in my soul that I love him, and love those who are like him; I walk, as seeing him, who is invisible; I have a zeal for his glory, and with active diligence I am employed for the honour of his name in the world.[534]

Like many other great Protestant theologians, he conceives of the consequence of our being justified by faith as being the implanting within us of 'an active principle', the principle of eternal life; and this principle is

> no vain, fanciful, and enthusiastic business; for while every believer feels the argument working strong in his heart and soul, he finds also the convincing force of it upon his understanding.[535]

This rational dimension has, in Watts' view, been neglected by Protestants; and the neglect has tempted the prophane world to call our devout efforts of christian piety mere enthusiasm and wild imagination, the flashes of a kindled blood and vapours, that are puffed about with every wind: but when the testimony of the spirit is explained in the manner I have described, it must approve itself to all the sober and reasonable part of mankind.[536]

The workings of this inner principle do not happen all at once: it is a 'growing and improving' thing. Watts again has recourse to the visionary words of St Paul in 2 Corinthians chapter 3:

The testimony increases as the divine love increases; the greater the degree of holiness we arrive at, the more are we confirmed in the truth of christianity, the testimony grows stronger, 2 *Cor*.iii.18 . . . The image of Christ is transcribed upon our natures, we go on from one degree of it to another; we are changed *from glory to glory*, from one degree of glorious holiness to another: thereby the gospel appears to have a fairer, a brighter, and a stronger evidence.[537]

Nor is this process purely an inward one. It must be manifested in outward action and service:

We must feed the hungry, we must clothe the naked, we must love all men, even our enemies, and discover to the world that we are christians, by noble and sublime practices of every virtue and every duty, as far as it is possible, even by the best works, to discover inward religion.[538]

So to be dead to 'all the globe' is to entrust ourselves in faith into Christ's hands, to be changed – not at once, but nonetheless comprehensively – as the image of Christ is 'transcribed upon our natures'. Precisely because this change begins inwardly, it tends to be deeply unattractive to those who are prominent in worldly affairs;[539] but in heaven it will be gloriously made manifest, and those who have sought to live by it will themselves be astounded at how far it exceeds their wildest expectations.[540] Even here, however, it will lead us to a more thoroughgoing compassion and concern for the poor. And it is subversive in another way too:

What a glorious person is the poorest, meanest christian! He lives by communion with God the Father and the Son; for his life is hid with Christ in God.[541]

And so to Watts' magnificent closing verse ('Were the whole realm of nature mine . . .'). We have already seen that the 'realm of nature' matters deeply to him – and not only to him, for God does not manage 'all his providential kingdom, merely for the sake of his own people without any other view'.[542] But even the whole of creation, precious as it is, is 'a present far too small'. Only the total offering of ourselves even begins to be a response commensurate with what God has offered us. It is important at this point to recall that this hymn was intended for use at the Lord's Supper: elsewhere Watts says that

[Christ's] holy supper is provided for the exercise and establishment of your faith on a crucified Christ.

And he goes on to ask those who partake of it regularly: 'Is your love kindled into a higher flame to him *who died for you*?'[543]

The theology and practice of worship and prayer

We offer ourselves to God, then, first and foremost in our worship; and it is not surprising to find that for Watts worship and prayer are demanding exercises, yet worth every ounce of effort we devote to them. 'What a dull and uncomfortable thing is religion, without drawing near to God! for this is the very business for which religion is designed.'[544] Worship and prayer are rooted in the atoning sacrifice of Christ: 'the Spirit flows down to us in the blood of Christ'.[545] Hence we plead with God through the name and mediation of Christ;[546] and Watts prays:

> Must we indulge a long despair?
> Shall our petitions die;
> Our mournings never reach thine ear,
> Nor tears affect thine eye?

> If thou despise a mortal groan
> Yet hear a Saviour's blood;
> An advocate so near the throne
> Pleads and prevails with God.[547]

Watts makes the same point in a passage of transcendental eloquence, at once deeply pastoral and profoundly theological:

> If you find your heart so very dry and unaffected with the things of religion, that you can say nothing at all to God in prayer, . . . go and fall down humble before God, and tell him with a grievous complaint, that you can say nothing to him, that you can do nothing but groan and cry before him; go and tell him, that without his Spirit you cannot speak one expression, that without immediate assistances from his grace, you cannot proceed in this worship; tell him humbly, that he must lose a morning or evening sacrifice, if he condescend not to send down fire from heaven upon the altar. Plead with him earnestly for his own Spirit, if it be but in the language of sighs and tears . . . there hath been glorious communion maintained with God before the end of that season of worship, when at the beginning of it the saint could say nothing else but, *Lord, I cannot pray*.[548]

Our prayer is caught up in the prayer of the Holy Spirit, in the pleading of Christ before the Father. Hence the loneliest cry of despair can lead to 'glorious communion'. This is precisely the paradox of the great psalms of lament; and it is not surprising to find Watts drawing upon their spiritual resources. One of his most important works was *The Psalms of David imitated in the language of the New Testament* (1719), a work which has received a mixed reception.[549] It is true that Watts spiritualizes many of the psalmist's 'enemies' and adds 'faith and love' where the psalmist refers only to 'fear'.[550] But Watts himself writes:

> I have chosen rather to imitate than to translate; and thus to compose a psalm-book for christians, after the manner of the jewish psalter.[551]

And he justifies himself thus:

> As the greatest number of the psalms are devotional, and there the psalmists express their own personal or national concerns; so we are taught by their example, what is the chief design of psalmody, namely, that we should represent our own sense of things in singing, and address ourselves to God expressing our own case; therefore the words should be so far adapted to the general state of the worshippers.[552]

Here, as so often elsewhere, Watts' concern is with helping his fellow Christians to appropriate scripture for their own spiritual lives. With the Psalms this can cause problems, as he points out succinctly:

> Have you not felt a new joy spring within you, when you could speak your own desires and hopes, your own faith, love, and zeal, in the language of the holy psalmist? . . . But on a sudden, the clerk has proposed the next line to your lips, with dark sayings and prophecies, with burnt-offerings or hyssop, with new moons and trumpets, and timbrels in it, with confessions of sins which you never committed, with complaints of sorrows which you never felt; cursing such enemies as you never had; giving thanks for such victories as you never obtained; or leading you to speak, in your own persons, of things, places, and actions, that you never knew. And how have all your souls been discomposed at once, and the strings of harmony all untuned![553]

But better this than a narrowly subjective piety which never collided with our moods or stretched our self-absorbed imaginations. What concerns Watts is the kind of response we make to God's astonishing act of self-giving love manifested on Calvary:

> when this SPIRIT OF PRAYER has brought the soul near, when God has been pleased to turn aside the veil, to remove the mountain, and to discover himself in all his glory, beauty, and love, then there will be generally the gift of prayer also in exercise by the assistance of the promised Spirit; and such persons many times are able to address themselves to God with much freedom, and to pour out the soul before God in proper words, notwithstanding at other times they appear to have but weak capacities. When they have such affecting sights of their own sin and guilt, and such surprising views of the mercy of God manifested to them in particular, and at the same time when they look upon all things round them with a design for the glory of God; they are both naturally and divinely taught to pour out their souls before God, and represent their cares and circumstances to him in affecting language.[554]

The Spirit assists us in doing this, even though we are not always aware of it at the time.[555] But the response itself, as we have already seen, is unconditional: nothing less than 'my soul, my life, my all'. How can we possibly make such a response? Two points are worth making in conclusion. First, for Christians this God has become, not a distant master, but an intimate friend, with whom we can share everything, even if all our other friends were to desert us:[556]

> This is the noblest and highest friendship; all condescension and compassion on the one side, and all infirmity and dependence on the other, and yet both joined in mutual satisfaction. Amazing grace of God to man![557]

The threshold of paradise

Secondly, we offer ourselves in love to God and in hope and expectation of eternity. Watts' view of heaven is an utter delight, though some of his theories may surprise.[558] Watts cannot believe we shall be idle: worship, and supremely praise, will fill our time. But the souls in heaven will continue also to pray for and with the souls on earth:

> May not the church above join with the churches below in this language, Father, *thy kingdom come, thy will be done on earth as it is in heaven?* Are not the souls of the martyrs that were slain represented to us as under the altar, crying with a loud voice, *how long, O Lord, holy and true?* Rev.vi.9,10. This looks like the voice of prayer in heaven.[559]

He imagines that there will be 'lectures of divine wisdom and grace given to the younger spirits there, by spirits of a more exalted station', and perhaps Christ himself will,

> at solemn seasons, summon all heaven to hear him publish some new and surprising discoveries, which have never yet been made known to the ages of nature or of grace, and are reserved to entertain the attention, and exalt the pleasure of spirits advanced to glory.[560]

We shall continue to be instructed and encouraged, not just by God directly, but through the medium of the patriarchs, apostles, saints and angels.[561] Adam will tell us what went wrong in Eden; St Paul will still be giving lectures, in collaboration with Moses, illuminating 'the *dark* places of his own writings, better than he himself once understood them'.[562] He also, delightfully, imagines souls lightened by the absence of their bodies making frequent journeys to other planets, 'and bring back from thence new lectures of divine wisdom, or tidings of the affairs of those provinces, to entertain [their] fellow-spirits and to give new honours to God the Creator and the Sovereign'.[563] Best of all, souls in heaven will delight in observing the spiritual progress of their descendants.[564] And this is no speculative folly: the 'I' who 'surveys the wondrous Cross' and seeks to offer an appropriate response is in fact one with the whole company of saints who have already made that response their own.

Conclusion

Nothing speaks more eloquently about the vitality of eighteenth-century English

Dissent than the vigour and energy of its greatest apologists, and supremely of Isaac Watts and Philip Doddridge, perhaps Watts' greatest disciple. Nothing concerned Watts more than to recapture the transforming power of the original Gospel:

> They went to hear the gospel, poor, lame, blind, senseless and thoughtless of God and eternity; and they were awakened, convinced of sin and of righteousness; they learnt their ruin and their recovery at once, through the atonement and grace of Christ: the poor came home enriched with various graces: the blind see wonders, and the lame return leaping and rejoicing in the hope of glory. This gives plain proof of a divine doctrine, and a divine attending spirit and power.[565]

The manner in which he sought to do this undoubtedly raises questions. His Calvinist predestinarianism, as we have seen, is uncompromising. His strident patriotism may grate today: thus he celebrates Queen Anne with a hyperbole that one hopes even she found embarrassing: 'Blessed be God, we have a Moses in the midst of us on the top of the hill, a queen of a manly soul upon the throne of our British Israel.'[566] But his passionate commitment to education and social justice for the poor is heartwarming, as is his longing to enlarge the spiritual perspective and world-view of children.[567] And, like John Wesley, he combined an active pastoral ministry with a vast output of written works on an immense range of subjects, all designed, whether directly or indirectly, to meet the challenges of his day with a presentation of the Christian Gospel that could still stir spirits and change hearts. It is an extraordinary achievement:

> The christian life is no fantastic and visionary matter, that consists in warm imagination, and pretences to inward light and rapture; it is a real change of heart and practice, from sin to holiness, and a turn of soul from earth toward heaven.[568]

William Law (1686–1761) and the ascetic tradition

Introduction

On 25 April 1761 Thomas Patten wrote a letter to John Byrom in which the subject of William Law arose:

> Whilst Mr Law is in sight, I must remember to tell you that Lord Lyttleton having lately taken up the *Serious Call* about bedtime at a friend's house was fascinated to read it quite through before he could go to rest, and was not a little astonished to find that one of the finest books that ever were written had been penned by a *crack-brained enthusiast!*[569]

Of all the writers treated in this chapter, no one was more dismissively accused of 'enthusiasm' than William Law. And, if the term is taken to mean someone who stresses revealed truth and the primacy of subjective experience over a more empirical rationalism, then it is unquestionably an accurate description. Yet Law produced some superlative spiritual writing, leaving Mr Patten with the paradox recorded above. What needs to be remembered, as we have already seen, is that the challenge of 'philosophy', whether a supposed Newtonian empiricism or a historical scepticism, was perceived as threatening the very basis of revealed religion.[570] If the Wesleys offered one response to this situation, William Law offered another: his motives were as impressive as theirs, even if his chosen response was to prove less ultimately convincing.

Certainly Law was aware of the charge of 'enthusiasm'; and, though doubtless unhappy with the term itself, he vigorously rebutted the attack:

> What a Mistake is it . . . to confine Inspiration to *particular* Times and Occasions, to Prophets and Apostles, and extraordinary Messengers of God, and to call it *Enthusiasm*, when the common Christian looks, and trusts to be *continually led* and inspired by the Spirit of God![571]

William Law was born in 1686, in King's Cliffe, Northamptonshire, an area (as we have seen) noted for its Dissenters.[572] He was educated at Cambridge, and became a Fellow of Emmanuel College in 1711, only to resign in 1716 because of his convictions as a Nonjuror: he was a high-churchman who remained loyal to the Jacobite cause.[573] In 1723 he became tutor to Edward Gibbon, father of the great historian, and remained with the Gibbon household until 1739, whereupon he withdrew to King's Cliffe for the rest of his life.[574] In his *Memoirs*, Gibbon the historian (who possessed a copy of Law's *Serious call* in his library) wrote of Law:

> In our family he had left the reputation of a worthy and pious man, who believed all that he professed, and practised all that he enjoined . . . His last compositions are darkly tinctured by the incomprehensible visions of Jacob Behmen; and his discourse on the absolute unlawfulness of stage entertainments is sometimes quoted for a ridiculous intemperance of sentiment and language . . . But these sallies of religious frenzy must not extinguish the praise which is due to Mr. William Law as a wit and a scholar . . . had not his vigorous mind been clouded by enthusiasm, he might be ranked with the most agreeable and ingenious writers of the times . . . If he finds a spark of piety in his reader's mind, he will soon kindle it to a flame; and a philosopher must allow that he exposes, with equal severity and truth, the strange contradiction between the faith and practice of the Christian world.[575]

Gibbon was close to the mark. Law's attacks on theatre-going were indeed vitriolic: he described it as

> a Contradiction to all Christian Holiness, and to the Methods of arriving at it . . . If you are only for the *Form* of Religion, you may take the Diversion of the Stage along with it. But if you desire the *Spirit* of Religion, if you desire to be truly religious in Heart and Mind, it is as necessary to renounce and abhor the Stage, as to seek God, and pray for the Guidance of his Holy Spirit.[576]

We shall see later how this relates to the rest of his spirituality. His indebtedness to the 'incomprehensible visions' of Jakob Boehme is undoubted, though Boehme was only one of his 'mystical' sources: in *The spirit of prayer* he cites 'the apostolical [Pseudo-]*Dionysius*', 'the illuminated *Guion* and celebrated *Fenelon* of *Cambray*' – 'the truly spiritual Writers';[577] he celebrates the virtues of Thomas à Kempis' *Imitation of Christ* ('the best devotional book that I know of');[578] and he may well have been indebted to the Quakers (even though he describes them as 'a subtle, worldly minded people').[579] He was very widely read, and almost certainly drew from medieval mystical writers like Suso, Tauler, and Ruusbroec.[580] He may even have explored the further reaches of Jewish mysticism.[581]

But it was undoubtedly Jakob Boehme who most pervasively influenced Law, even though it is likely that he did not encounter his work in any detail until around 1733. Although this means that everything he wrote before then (including *A serious call*) was free from Behmenist influence, we should beware of drawing too absolute a distinction: there are good grounds for supposing that Law was attracted to Boehme because he found in his writings a fresh presentation of ideas he had already come to accept for himself.[582] The attraction of Boehme's esoteric mysticism in the English seventeenth and eighteenth centuries has already been noted, and should not surprise us: in an increasingly sceptical age, the search for a more 'spiritual' meaning in life is a natural reaction – as with the preference for 'spirituality' in developed consumerist countries at the end of the twentieth century. Law himself justified his indebtedness to Boehme

> because, above every Writer in the World, he has made all that is found in the Kingdom of Grace, and the Kingdom of Nature, to be one continual Demonstration, that *Dying* to self, to be *born again* of Christ, is the one only possible Salvation of the Sons of fallen *Adam*.[583]

Certainly he was pilloried for his Behmenist reverence, but remained undeterred. Coleridge spoke of Law having 'lost his senses, poor Man! in brooding over the Visions of a delirious German Cobbler, Jacob Behmen';[584] but Law may well have had Coleridge's criticism as well as that of Bishop Warburton in mind when he wrote that

> to call the blessed Man [Boehme], a *possessed Cobbler*, will be doing something; to call his Writings, *senseless Jargon*, may stand his learned Adversary in great stead; but if he tries to overcome him any other Way, his Success will be like his, who knocks his Head against a Post.[585]

The nature of Law's spirituality

The important point is to see Law in the context of his age. He was passionately concerned about what he believed to be the dangerous scepticism and moral degeneracy of his age, and doggedly opposed both with all the resources he could lay to hand. He told young clergy:

> You are entered into *Holy Orders* in degenerate Times, where *Trade* and *Traffic* have seized upon all holy Things; and it will be easy for you, without Fear, to swim along with the corrupt Stream, and to look upon him as an Enemy, or *Enthusiast*, that would save you from being lost in it.[586]

His response, though, was at its heart a deeply otherworldly one. He articulates the central principle of his spirituality in the opening statement of his *The spirit of prayer*:

> The greatest part of Mankind, nay of Christians, may be said to be asleep; and that particular Way of Life, which takes up each Man's Mind, Thoughts, and Actions, may be very well called his particular Dream. This Degree of Vanity is equally visible in every Form and Order of Life. The Learned and the Ignorant, the Rich and the Poor, are all in the same State of Slumber, only passing away a short Life in a different kind of Dream. But why so? It is because Man has an Eternity within him, is born into this World, not for the Sake of living here, not for any Thing this World can give him, but only to have Time and Place, to become either an eternal partaker of a Divine Life with God, or to have an hellish Eternity among fallen Angels.[587]

In other words: this world is in itself supremely unimportant; yet it is precisely in this world that a decision which affects our future for all eternity is to be made. Law therefore argues that a life devoted to the enjoyment of this world misses the entire and only reason for our being here, i.e. to make this decision: hence his description of it as dreamlike. This does not lead him to advocate a withdrawal from the world (though that was in effect his own response): he argues that

> he that renounces humble, charitable, and painful labour that he may advance in devotion, seems to mistake the point, and to renounce the very best preservatives of true devotion.[588]

But it does mean that his spirituality is deeply Platonic in content: what is spiritual endures, what is material is utterly transient and ultimately worthless. In respect of our spiritual natures we are created for union with God; and religion is the means by which growth towards this union is fostered.[589]

We should not be surprised, then, to find in Law a strong depreciation of human reason in favour of the truth that is revealed to us, in scripture and mystical experience. In *Christian perfection* (1726), he says:

> What are these Principles of Reason and Religion?
> They are such as these:
> First, That God is our *only Good*, that we cannot possibly be happy, but in such Enjoyment of him, as he is pleased to communicate to us.
> Secondly, That our Souls, are immortal Spirits, that are here only in a *State of Trial* and *Probation*.
> Thirdly, That we must all appear before the Judgment-Seat of God, to receive the Sentence of eternal Life, or eternal Death.[590]

No concessions to rationalism here: rather an unyielding adherence to the most ascetic teaching of the Gospel, as Law proceeds to make unflinchingly clear:

> It is therefore altogether impossible for any Man to enter into the Spirit of Religion, but by *denying himself*.[591]

Later he will stress that our natural reason must be set aside if we are to progress in religion, quoting Boehme:

> 'I *write not to Reason*', says the blessed *Jacob Behmen* . . . for without the New Birth, or which is the same Thing, without immediate and continual Divine Inspiration, the Difference between the Christian and the Infidel is quite lost.[592]

This 'immediate inspiration' means recognizing and co-operating with all good impulses and rejecting all evil ones.[593] The evil ones include almost anything that smacks of worldliness: even marriage was a poor second-best to chastity.[594]

This does not mean that Law saw himself as taking refuge in irrational speculation: quite the reverse. He has little difficulty in controverting Bernard de Mandeville's argument that human beings are fundamentally irrational:

> *Truth* and *Reason* is the Law by which God acts; Man is, in some degree, made a Partaker of that Truth and Reason; therefore it is a Law to him also. The more we act according to order, Truth and Reason, the more we make ourselves like God, who is Truth and Reason itself.[595]

Rather he believed that 'there is no Wisdom or Reason in anything but Religion';[596] and elsewhere he went so far as to argue that purely human reason is effectively the source of our sin.[597]

Law's deprecation of all things physical is underpinned by his view of 'nature'. The trouble with material realities is that they are fickle:

> it is the Business . . . of Religion, to put an end to these States of Slavery, to deliver Man from these blind Laws of *Flesh* and *Blood*, and give him a Wisdom and Constancy, a Taste and Judgment suitable to the Reason and Wisdom of the Laws of God. To fill our Souls with such Principles of Peace, as may give us Habits of Tranquillity, superior to the changeable Tempers of our Bodies.[598]

The point is that our true nature is our spiritual one, not our physical one: 'we are all of us, by Birth, the Offspring of God, more nearly related to him than we are to one another'.[599] And, following Boehme, he sees nature as

> in itself nothing, but an *hungry wrathful Fire* of Life, a tormenting Darkness, unless the Light and Spirit of God kindle it into a Kingdom of Heaven.[600]

This is an intriguing idea, because it gives Law a dynamic view of nature; but the dynamism is of the wrong kind – nature 'is at first only *spiritual*: it has in itself nothing but the spiritual Properties of the *Desire*, which is the very Being and Ground of Nature'.[601] This 'desire', in some respects not all that distant from modern Freudian teaching on psychology, is certain to lead us astray: hence it is only the presence and activity of the Holy Spirit within a person that makes that person good. Law leaves no room for a 'natural' goodness or virtue: you are either inspired by the Spirit, or you are evil.[602]

Mortification

It is not surprising, therefore, to find Law stressing the value of sacrifice and the virtue of mortification. He makes the point that the importance of sacrifice in the practice of worship could scarcely be proved by rational means: 'yet considered as a *Divine Institution*, it would be the greatest folly not to receive it as a reasonable service'.[603] Indeed, rational objections to the cruelty of pagan sacrifices are no argument against the sacrifice of Christ.[604]

Mortification is similarly commended. Law compares self-denial to having to forget a much-loved and familiar language in order to give ourselves entirely to learning a completely new one, and one which he concedes is difficult.[605] Hence he proscribes virtually everything connected with this life: 'poor *Amusements*, vain *Arts*, useless *Sciences*, impertinent *Learning*, false *Satisfactions*, a wrong *Turn of Mind*, a State of *Idleness*, or any of the vainest *Trifles* of Life, may keep Men at as great a Distance from the true Impressions of Religion, and from living by the Spirit of God, as the *Ignorance* of Childhood, or the *Debaucheries* of Intemperance'.[606] He proceeds to caricature those who prefer mathematics, literature, architecture or music: indeed he is so relentlessly negative about this world that it is all too easy to believe him when he eventually declares:

> This is the great and happy Work of Self-denial, which is to fill us with a Spirit of Wisdom, to awaken us into a true Knowledge of ourselves, and show us who, and where, and what we are.[607]

It is true that he does warn against a false mortification which is practised for its own sake and has the effect of making its practitioners 'self-sufficient, morose, severe Judges of all those that fall short of their Mortifications'.[608] Even so, it may well be that he goes even further than Boehme, who at least declares that renunciation of the world 'is not meant that one should run from house and home, from wife, children, and kindred, and fly out of the world, or so to forsake his goods as not to regard them; but [one's] own self-will, which possesses all this for a propriety, that he must kill, and annihilate'.[609]

Yet there are positive aspects to mortification: 'charity to the Poor is founded in the Necessities and Infirmities of this Life, yet it is as real a Degree of Holiness, and as much to be performed for its own Sake, as that Charity which will never have an End'.[610] Mortification is a voluntary action, arising out of an awareness of our own need for repentance, 'a Fellowship in the Sufferings of Christ'.[611] Law goes so far as to describe it as a state of mourning for the pitiable condition of humanity.[612]

Christian perfection

If we are to discover the real riches which Law has to offer, we need to look at two areas in particular: the nature of Christian perfection; and the practice of a holy life. On the very first page of his treatise on perfection, Law stresses the fact that there is only one kind of Christianity and Christian perfection: not a 'higher' kind for cloistered or expert Christians and a 'lower' kind for the rest.[613] Hence he defines such perfection as 'such a right Performance of all the Duties of Life, as is according to the Laws of Christ . . . a living in such holy Tempers, and acting with such Dispositions as Christianity requires'.[614] It is, in his view, better to aim for this and fail to achieve it than not to aim for it at all;[615] and he criticizes those who deliberately opt for 'a low Estate of Piety' rather than accept that degree to which God has called them.[616]

And the crucial point for Law is that the search for true Christian perfection demands nothing less than a total personal transformation: hence the need for radical self-denial.[617] In his attack on the theatre, Law addresses an imaginary opponent thus:

> You are for a Religion that consists in Modes and Forms of Worship, that is tied to *Times* and *Places*, that only takes up a little of your time on *Sundays*, and leaves you all the Week to do as you please. But all this, *Jucunda*, is nothing. The Scripture has not said in vain, *He that is in Christ is a new Creature*. All the Law and the Gospel are in vain to you: all Sacraments, Devotions, Doctrines, and Ordinances, are to no purpose, unless they make you this *new Creature* in all the Actions of your Life.[618]

Law is aware that, for most people, 'it is not gross Sins, it is not *Murder*, or *Adultery*, but it is their *Gentility* and *Politeness* that destroys them: It fills them with such Passions and Pleasures, as quite extinguish the gentle Light of Reason and Religion.'[619] Law's strictures on an easy, undemanding, but ultimately ineffectual religion are understandable; but his approach raises the question of whether it is possible to combine a genuinely transforming spirituality with a willingness on some level to engage with the world. He sees the two as utterly incompatible: the sheer *seriousness* of spiritual transformation excludes, in his view, the pursuit of any kind of worldly pleasure, and of most kinds of worldly activity.

And what really interests Law is the nature of Christianity as an agent for *change*, a point he makes again and again, and which applies to all Christians, lay and ordained alike:

> Christianity is not a *School*, for the teaching of moral Virtue, the polishing our Manners, or forming us to live a Life of this World with Decency and Gentility. It is deeper and more divine in its Designs, and has much nobler Ends than these, it implies an *entire Change* of Life, a Dedication of ourselves, our Souls and Bodies unto God, in the strictest and highest Sense of the Words.[620]

Note the use of words like 'strictest' and 'highest', and the lofty disapproval of the social ethics of politeness: this is a uncompromisingly ascetic spirituality. He insists that 'we must either leave this World, to become Sons of God, or by enjoying it, take our Portion amongst Devils and damned Spirits'.[621] There is an absolutist, near-dualist emphasis here:[622] Law is constantly attacking a superficial Christianity which conforms easily to worldly interests and makes no real demands on those who practise it.[623] This also leads him vigorously to condemn wealthy Christians, citing Dives and Lazarus, not because they are corrupt but simply because they are rich, though he draws only limited social implications: 'he sufficiently selleth all, who parteth with the Self-enjoyment of it, and maketh it the Support of those that want it'.[624]

Yet at the heart of this stern and unrelenting piety is something deeply attractive.

The mainspring of this 'entire Change' is 'a new Principle of Life, an entire Change of Temper'.[625] And the key to this principle is *childlikeness*:

> One peculiar Condition of Infants is this, that they have everything to learn . . . It is in this Sense, that we are chiefly to become as Infants, to be as though that we had everything to learn . . . to pretend to no Wisdom of our own, but be ready to pursue that Happiness which God in Christ proposes to us, and to accept it with such Simplicity of Mind, as Children, that have nothing of our own to oppose to it.[626]

For him, childlikeness means a willingness to be taught, to be utterly obedient and docile to the teachings of Christ:[627] in *An address to the clergy* he goes further: to 'be converted, and become as little Children' means denying our own reason, self and will equally.[628] This process begins with baptism, which he describes as an introduction into a 'State of Death', precipitating a war with our corrupt natures.[629] Each human person

> has a *Seed* of the Divine Life given into the Birth of his Soul, a Seed that has all the *Riches of Eternity* in it, and is always wanting to come to the Birth in him, and be alive in God. Outwardly he has Jesus Christ, who as a *Sun* of Righteousness, is always casting forth his enlivening Beams on this *inward Seed*, to kindle and call it forth to the Birth, doing that to this Seed of Heaven in Man, which the Sun in the Firmament is always doing to the vegetable Seeds in the Earth.[630]

And true faith proceeds from this '*Seed* of the *Divine* Nature in us', drawing us towards its likeness, which is Christ.[631] Law is heavily indebted here both to Boehme and, beyond him, to Plato – and even more so in *An appeal to all who doubt*, where Law argues that the desire which subsists in every individual thing is a form of participation in, or emanation of, the divine desire:

> In *Vegetables*, it is that Attraction, or Desire, which brings every growing Thing to its highest Perfection: In Angels, it is that blessed Hunger, by which they are filled with the Divine Nature: In Devils, it is turned into that Serpentine Selfishness, or crooked Desire, which makes them a Hell and Torment to themselves.[632] . . . Take away *Attraction*, or *Desire* from the Creature of this World, and you annihilate the Creature; for where there is no Attraction or Desire, there can be no Nature or Being.[633]

Positively, this gives Christian spirituality a dynamic quality:

> The Doctrine of the Holy Trinity is wholly practical; it is revealed to us, to discover our high Original, and the Greatness of our Fall, to show us the deep and profound Operation of the triune God in the Recovery of the Divine Life in our Souls; that by the Means of this Mystery thus discovered, our Piety may be rightly directed, our *Faith* and *Prayer* have their proper Objects, that the Workings and Aspirings of our own Hearts may co-operate, and correspond with that triune Life in the Deity, which is always desiring to manifest itself in us.[634]

The holy life

The way Law *appropriates* the doctrine of the Trinity here for our own personal experience is impressive.[635] And it brings us to his understanding of the holy life, the subject of his most famous book, *A serious call to a devout and holy life, adapted to the state and condition of all orders of Christians* (1729).[636] At the very start of it, he defines devotion as 'a life given, or *devoted* to God'.[637] Note the stress on an entire life, not a narrowly religious part of it: 'we can no more be said to live unto God, unless we live unto him in all the *ordinary* actions of our life'.[638] For it is a *total* life vowed to God that he wants to encourage: indeed he points out that the New Testament says far more about this than about the obligation of Christians to attend public worship, which is hardly mentioned there:

> The short of the matter is this, either Reason and Religion prescribe *rules* and *ends* to all the ordinary actions of our life, or they do not: If they do, then it is as necessary to govern all our actions by those rules, as it is necessary to worship God . . . Is it not therefore exceeding strange, that People should place so much piety in the attendance upon public worship, concerning which there is not one precept of our Lord's to be found, and yet neglect these common duties of our *ordinary* life, which are commanded in every Page of the Gospel?[639]

The failure to recognize this has important consequences:

> But yet though it is thus plain, that this, and this alone is Christianity, an uniform open and visible practice of all these virtues, yet it is as plain, that there is little or nothing of this to be found, even amongst the better sort of People. You see them often at Church, and pleased with fine preachers, but look into their lives, and you see them just the same sort of People as others are, that make no pretences to devotion.[640]

Law goes on to make the perceptive point that the reason for this state of affairs is simply that people don't sufficiently *want* to be Christians in the full-hearted sense of the word:[641] it is our intentions that matter: 'that we have not that perfection, which our present state of grace makes us capable of, [is] because we do not so much as *intend* to have it'.[642] It is one thing to fail to attain the high ideals of Christianity: it is quite another not even to want to, which means spurning the divinely-given desire referred to above.[643] And it is the stark reality of death and the looming experience of judgement that adds an urgency to this.[644] He cites Matthew 25, on the last judgement, and goes on to ask: 'what is there in the lives of Christians, that looks as if their salvation *depended* upon these good works?'[645] *Occasional* acts of charity are not enough: we must make charity the rule of all our actions.[646]

Thus the practice of a holy life is not the attainment of high ideals so much as the intention of aiming at them, with a consequent scriptural prudence and generosity in everything one does:

> Miranda's [the exemplar of the godly and generous woman] perfection does not consist in this, that she spends *so much* time, or *so much* money in

> such a manner, but that she is careful to make the best use of all that time, and all that fortune, which God has put into her hands.[647]

By contrast, this is what Law has to say about many contemporary business people:

> You see them all the week buried in business, unable to think of anything else; and then spending the *Sunday* in idleness and refreshment, in wandering into the country, in such visits and jovial meetings, as make it often the worst day of the week.[648]

They do this because their primary intention is not to be devoted to God, but to make money, or succeed. Law is concerned with a total integrity of life; but this is attainable, in his view, only by a radical world-denying lifestyle.[649] And it is only those who live thus who discover true happiness:

> If religion only restrains the *excesses* of revenge, but lets the spirit still live within you, in lesser instances your religion may have made your life a little more outwardly decent, but not made you at all happier, or easier in yourself. But if you have once sacrificed all thoughts of revenge, in obedience to God, and are resolved to return good for evil at all times, that you may render yourself more like to God, and fitter for his mercy in the kingdom of love and glory; this is a height of virtue, that will make you feel its happiness.[650]

Hence Law is led to conclude:

> I cannot see why every *Gentleman, Merchant,* or *Soldier,* should not put these questions seriously to himself: *What is the best thing for me to intend and drive at in all my actions? How shall I do to make the most of human life? What ways shall I wish that I had taken, when I am leaving the world?*[651]

The theology and practice of prayer

Law's emphasis on a total transformation of the person, and of devotion as an entire way of life devoted to God, means that 'it is as great an absurdity to suppose holy Prayers, and divine Petitions without an holiness of life suitable to them, as to suppose an holy and divine life without Prayers'.[652] He defines prayer, significantly, as 'an *earnest Application or Ascent of the Heart to God, as to the sole Cause of all Happiness*' – note the 'earnest'.[653] It presupposes, as might by now be expected, not only an accurate self-knowledge but also a radical awareness of our misery and weakness, together with thoroughgoing self-denial and renunciation of this world.[654] Ultimately this cannot be done by the person alone: you must *feel* the want of God before you can properly or adequately desire him.[655] Hence true devotion, or devoutness, consists not in formal prayers or intellectual study but in this fundamental reorientation towards God and away from the world . . . Law is, however, conscious that only a few will achieve this:

> The *Bulk* of Mankind are so dull and tasteless, so illiterate, as to set their Hearts upon *current Coin,* large *Fields,* and Flocks and Herds of Cattle.[656]

In his first Letter to the Bishop of Bangor, Law attacks the Bishop's insistence on prayer being a 'Calm, and Undisturbed Address to God': Law criticizes this since such a definition excludes the passions altogether: 'why,' Law asks, 'must *Prayer* have nothing to do with *Heat* and *Fervency?*' Instead he defines prayer as 'an *Address to Heaven, enlivened with such Degrees* of Fervour *and* Intenseness, *as our* Natural Temper, *influenced* with a true Sense *of God, could beget in us*'.[657] Law continues:

> Your Lordship says, you only desire to strike at the Root of *superstitious Folly*, and *establish* Prayer *in its room*; and this is to be effected by making our Addresses *calm and undisturbed*: By which we are to understand, a *Freedom* from *Heat and Passion*, as your Lordship explains it, by an Application to yourself.
>
> If therefore anyone should happen to be so *disturbed* at his Sins, as to offer a *broken* and *contrite Heart* to God, instead of one *calm* and *undisturbed*; or, like holy *David*, his Soul should be athirst for God, or pant after him, as the *Hart panteth after the Water-brooks*, this would not be Prayer, but *superstitious Folly*.
>
> My Lord, *Calmness* of *Temper*, as it signifies a Power over our *Passions*, is a *happy Circumstance* of a *Rational Nature*, but no farther: When the Object is well chosen, there is no Danger in the Pursuit.[658]

Law warns Christians of the dangers of implicitly praying for our own material advantage, and he also makes clear that 'the same Things which make an unchristian Prayer, make an unchristian Life':[659] the two are inseparably connected.[660] Hence true prayer is rooted in a right disposition of the heart, just as a habitual taste for music draws people to concerts.[661]

Unsurprisingly, therefore, Law criticizes brief or hurried prayers without devotion.[662] He suggests that we should recall how we felt and thought on those occasions when we were in a state of fervent devotion, and then try to 'put [ourselves] in the same State, recall the same Thoughts' at times when we feel ill-disposed towards prayer.[663] Better still, create a prayer journal:

> If you were then to put down in *Writing*, some short Remembrances of the *chief Things*, that ever raised your Heart to Fervency of Prayer, so that you might have Recourse to a full View of them, as often as your Mind wanted such Assistance, you would soon find a Benefit, that would well Reward your Labour.[664]

And he commends doing the same thing when feeling indisposed for prayer: examining your state, reflecting upon why it came about, pondering the causes of it. His point is that a state suitable for prayer doesn't simply happen: it has to be created, or prepared for, preferably by meditation and regular recourse to prayer.[665] Above all, though, what concerns Law is not the practice of prayer so much as the practice of a holy life:[666] he bewails the human propensity for devoting great time and skill to some activities but virtually none to the art of prayer.[667]

Law has some sharp insights into the nature of intercessory prayer. He devotes two sections of *A serious call* to this, and sees it as rooted in the 'nature and necessity of *universal love*': intercession is 'the most proper exercise to raise and preserve that love'.[668] Our capacity physically to relieve the world's sorrows is limited:

> You cannot heal all the *sick*, relieve all the *poor*; you cannot comfort all in distress, nor be a father to all the fatherless. You cannot, it may be, deliver many from their misfortunes, or teach them to find comfort in God.
>
> But if there is a love and tenderness in your heart, that *delights* in these good works, and *excites* you to do *all* that you can: If your love has *no bounds*, but continually *wishes* and *prays* for the relief and happiness of all that are in distress, you will be received by God as a benefactor to those, who have had nothing from you but your *goodwill*, and tender affections.[669]

Note, here as so often in Law, the emphasis on desire, and on the use of the emotions: this is both part of his Platonic and Behmenist inheritance and also part of his concern to stress prayer as part of a whole, integrated (hence *serious*) holiness of life. Intercession thus unites us with all those who do good, and also with God, for 'the love . . . of our neighbour, is only a branch of our love to God'.[670] And we love our neighbour, just as God loves us, not *because* we or our neighbour are good, but in order that we might be:[671]

> The *actions* which you are to *love, esteem,* and *admire,* are the actions of good and pious men; but the *persons* to whom you are to do all the good you can, in all sorts of kindness and compassion, are all persons, whether good or bad.[672]

Intercession 'was the *ancient friendship* of Christians, uniting and cementing their hearts, not by worldly considerations, or human passions, but by the mutual communication of spiritual blessings, by prayers and thanksgivings to God for one another'.[673] Furthermore, intercession is the surest route to our own happiness:

> He that daily prays to God, that all men may be happy in heaven, takes the likeliest way to make him wish for, and delight in their happiness on earth . . . When therefore you have once habituated your heart to a serious performance of this holy intercession, you have done a great deal, to render it incapable of *spite* and *envy*, and to make it *naturally* delight in the happiness of all mankind.[674]

Particular and specific intercession for those around us increases our love: 'there is nothing that makes us love a man so much, as praying for him'.[675] Hence priests should pray devotedly and daily for their parishioners, masters for their servants, parents for their children; and all of us should pray for those we are tempted to dislike or resent, or with whom we have had some misunderstanding:[676]

> The greatest resentments amongst friends and neighbours, most often arise from poor *punctilios*, and *little mistakes* in conduct. A certain sign that their friendship is *merely human*, not founded upon religious considerations, or supported by such a course of mutual prayer for one another, as

the first Christians used. For such devotion must necessarily either destroy such tempers, or be itself destroyed by them. You cannot possibly have any ill-temper, or show any unkind behaviour to a man, for whose welfare you are so much concerned, as to be his advocate with God in private.[677]

Furthermore, intercession reveals the state of our own hearts to us, correcting our capacity for gossip.[678]

Conclusion

The strengths of Law's view of the spiritual life are real and enduring ones. He gives a positive value to the feelings in prayer, and also to the imagination: for example, he encourages every individual to pause before singing a psalm in his or her private prayers, and imagine himself to be a part of the heavenly choirs: 'think upon this till your imagination has carried you above the clouds, till it has placed you amongst those heavenly beings, and made you long to bear a part in their eternal music'.[679] He is determined not to separate prayer from the rest of a holy life; and he wants to underline the potential for human beings to participate in the life of God by giving expression to the divine desires that dwell within them. Yet it is hard to avoid, with or without the influence of Boehme, a sense of *déjà-vu* in reading him: his disapproval of everything connected with this world, even scientific and theological learning (and that notwithstanding his own massive erudition)[680] makes his work old-fashioned to the point of obduracy.

This archaism is heightened by the form of many of Law's works: cast as Platonic dialogues, they are not likely to have been easily accessible to many of the people he doubtless would have most wanted to read them. The stern moralism and sweeping dismissals of so much of contemporary life (one of his Platonic-style characters contrives to dismiss gaming, balls, drink, hunting, architectural fashion, horses, foreign travel and opera in a single rhetorical *tour-de-force*) may have been a vigorous attempt to address the real moral dangers present at the time;[681] but it is just too unrelenting to persuade, let alone to appeal.

Yet Law remains an important figure in eighteenth-century spirituality, and not only for negative reasons. His piety (perhaps especially in the works influenced by Boehme) is firmly Christ-centred: he argues both for the crucial importance of Christ's historical life and death, and for the fact that this means nothing unless Christ is born in each individual: indeed he goes so far as to say that 'though God be everywhere present, yet He is only present to Thee in the deepest and most central part of thy Soul'.[682] He does not, however, mention one's neighbour. And ultimately, for all the attractiveness of his integrated approach to the spiritual life, the failure to give real seriousness to attempts to reform and improve the world, rather than to reject it, must be accounted a substantial weakness. True, he reproves those who seek to live as 'private persons', extolling the value of what is held in common;[683] and he passionately denounces internecine religious bigotry.[684] What seems to have been missing, as he sat and wrote in his lonely Northamptonshire fastness, was a genuine ability to *understand* this world before resolving unequivocally to *abandon* it. Which is tragic: for his work contains enough spiritual ordnance to ignite many lives in the service of Christ, had it only been more generously and humanely directed:

This is Christianity, a spiritual Society, not because it has no worldly
Concerns, but because all its Members, as such, are born of the Spirit, kept
alive, animated and governed by the Spirit of God.[685]

John and Charles Wesley and the Methodist tradition

Introduction

If anyone gives the lie to the notion that English Christianity in the eighteenth
century was a cool and dispassionate affair rooted in common-rooms and landscaped
gardens, it was John Wesley (1703–91). He was a man of superlatives: he travelled far
and wide, across both Channel and Atlantic (this in itself testifies to the international
context of English piety in the period); he wrote prodigious quantities of books and
letters, and read even more; he lived to a great age, and spent much of his life as an itinerant evangelist, an eighteenth-century St Paul, criss-crossing the British Isles on
horseback, preaching in fair weather and foul, to friend and foe alike.[686] He was endlessly busy; and his busyness was scrupulously and minutely recorded. Here, drawn
more or less at random from the voluminous pages of his private diaries, is the record
of one day in his life (Tuesday 4 May 1736):

> TUESDAY, May 4. 4 [a.m.] Private prayer; prayed with Delamotte. 5
> Read Prayers, expounded (twenty-five there); writ German. 6 German.
> 6.15 Breakfast. 6.45 With Germans. 7 Germans. 11 Trustees' Garden;
> *Ecclesiastical History*, Hebrew Psalm. 12 Fleury's *History*. 12.30 Dinner. 1
> German. 1.45 Slept. 2 German. 3.30 Mrs Musgrove and Miss Fawset,
> mostly religious talk. 4 Garden with Miss Fawset, religious talk. 4.30 Tea,
> religious talk (necessary). 5 Religious talk with Miss Fawset (she seemed
> affected). 5.45 Mostly religious talk. 6.30 Supper. 7 Read Greek Testa-
> ment with them. 7.45 Read Prayers. 8 Expounded. 8.20 With Germans,
> sang. 9.30 Prayed.
> Providence: Well. Miss Fawset seemed affected.
> Grace: 7 rating once [4 to 5 a.m.]; 6 nine times [5 to 11 a.m., 4 to 5, 7 to 9
> p.m.]; 5 six times [11 a.m. to 1 p.m., 2 to 4, 5 to 7 p.m.]; 4 once [1 to 2
> p.m.].
> Mercy: Preserved from w4 [2 to 3 p.m.].[687]

The 'grace' rating refers to a personal scale of evaluation for his 'temper of devotion',
measured from 1 to 9, 6 or more being regarded as the higher levels. 'Mercy' represents
those occasions when he felt himself preserved from impure thoughts.

What does all this tell us? It suggests someone ruthlessly driven, self-organized
almost to a fault, inflicting upon himself the severely *methodical* structure which was
to give his followers their name.[688] It suggests someone with phenomenal energy, and
energy that needed careful channelling if it were to be rightly directed, and thus of
someone who had to be in control of everything.[689] It suggests someone who knew
himself well, and was able to integrate extroverted activity and concentrated study.
Above all, though, it suggests someone deeply, perhaps obsessively, serious about his
faith, whole-heartedly committed to learning and growing, pastoring and preaching

and praying, and to using every hour of the day to its best advantage. 'Though I am always in haste,' he wrote of the long days he spent travelling, 'I am never in a hurry.'[690]

John Wesley averred that the sole aim of his life was to promote 'so far as I am able, vital, practical religion'.[691] He has no time for those who are orthodox but 'have no religion', such as drunkards or evil-livers.[692] It is not surprising to find that he was accused of 'enthusiasm', many times.[693] When George Lavington, Bishop of Exeter, published his *The enthusiasm of Methodists and Papists compared*, Wesley replied in 1750 with this splendid riposte:

> Though I did not design to meddle with them, yet I must here take notice of three of your instances of popish enthusiasm. The first is: 'that Mechtildis tortured herself for having spoken an idle word.' (The point of comparison lies not in torturing herself, but in her doing it on such an occasion). The second: 'that not a word fell from St Catherine of Siena that was not religious and holy.' The third, 'that the lips of Magdalen di Pazzi were never opened but to chant the praises of God.' I would to God the comparison between the Methodists and Papists would hold in this respect! Yea, that you, and all the clergy in England, were guilty of just such enthusiasm![694]

Eleven years earlier, he defended George Whitefield against another critic, saying that 'whatever is spoke of the religion of the heart and of the inward workings of the Spirit of God *must* appear enthusiasm to those who have not felt them'.[695] And this is the point: Wesley himself vigorously criticized those who embraced an uncritical, irrational piety, or made special claims to exclusive revelations from above;[696] and he was well aware that the term 'enthusiasm' was a slippery one, not easily defined and the reality thus not easily avoided;[697] but he passionately wanted to convey a Christianity that would have a perceptible, experiential, transforming impact on the believer, for no other Christianity would be worthy of the name:

> We are at length come to the real state of the question between the Methodists (so called) and their opponents. 'Is there perceptible inspiration, or is there not? Is there such a thing (if we divide the question into its parts) as faith producing peace, and joy, and love, and inward (as well as outward) holiness? Is that faith which is productive of these fruits wrought in us by the Holy Ghost, or not? And is he in whom they are wrought necessarily conscious of them, or is he not?' These are the points on which I am ready to join issue with any serious and candid man.[698]

He recognized that this involved him in the risk of being accused of 'zeal', and frankly admitted: 'I detest all zeal which is any other than the flame of love. Yet I find it is not easy to avoid it.'[699] And in any case the opposite is a far more serious sin: 'A lifeless, unconverting minister is the murderer-general of his parish.'[700] And he vigorously controverted the arguments of his correspondent 'John Smith' to the effect that real inward experience of God unsupported by miracles or other external testimony ceased with the early Church. The crucial point for Wesley is that any such experiences must be 'subjected to the examination of the Scriptures as to a touchstone'.[701]

The lives of John and Charles Wesley

John, Charles, and Samuel Wesley, together with seven sisters, were the survivors of the nineteen children born to Susanna and Samuel Wesley: the latter was Rector of Epworth in Lincolnshire, where the children were brought up.[702] Susanna and Samuel were Anglicans of the high church tradition; and both were strong characters.[703] Charles was sent to Westminster School, while John was educated at Charterhouse (where he suffered from bullying[704]): both went to Christ Church, Oxford. While there John was ordained, and divided his time between assisting his father in his parochial duties and enjoying a hectic social life at Oxford.[705]

In 1729 the two brothers, together with some fellow-students, formed a loose-knit circle which became known as the 'Holy Club', with a more demanding rule than those of the religious societies.[706] In 1734 John published his first work, *A collection of forms of prayer*; and in the following year, having rejected his father's request that he succeed him as rector of Epworth, he sailed with Charles for Georgia as missionaries;[707] en route, they met some of the German Christians who were to exert so great an influence on them later.[708] Both brothers were to return to England within two years, disappointed and disillusioned yet having achieved a significant amount while there.

In early 1738, under the influence of the Moravian Peter Böhler, John Wesley with others founded a new 'society' in London, at Fetter Lane.[709] Pentecost 1738 was the crucial conversion experience for both Charles and John: the latter, influenced by reading Thomas à Kempis' *Imitation of Christ* and William Law's *Christian perfection* and *A serious call*, began 'to aim at and pray for inward holiness'.[710] Early in the morning of Wednesday 24 May 1738, he opened his Bible at 2 Peter 1.4:

> There are given unto us exceeding great and precious promises, even that ye should be partakers of the divine nature.[711]

In the afternoon he went to St Paul's in London, where the anthem was a setting of Psalm 130 ('Out of the deep have I called unto thee, O Lord . . .'). Then

> in the evening I went very unwillingly to a society in Aldersgate Street, where one was reading Luther's Preface to the Epistle to the Romans. About a quarter before nine, while he was describing the change which God works in the heart through faith in Christ, I felt my heart strangely warmed. I felt I did trust in Christ, Christ alone for salvation, and an assurance was given me that he had taken away *my* sins, even *mine*, and saved *me* from the law of sin and death.[712]

He acknowledges that temptations assailed him immediately thereafter; but

> herein found I the difference between this and my former state chiefly consisted. I was striving, yea fighting with all my might under the law, as well as under grace. But then I was sometimes, if not often, conquered; now, I was always conqueror.[713]

The significance of this dramatic event has been much debated.[714] At the very least it can safely be affirmed that the event had a profound effect on the rest of Wesley's spiritual life, but that the word 'conversion', a term he himself rarely used, would be inappropriate: it was more a vital staging-post on a long and eventful journey.[715] Another occurred on 1 January 1739, when he seems to have experienced a second Pentecost: at Fetter Lane, while they were singing at 3 a.m., 'the power of God came mightily upon us, insomuch that many cried out from exceeding joy, and many fell to the ground'.[716]

After this, John travelled to Germany to meet Count von Zinzendorf:[717] he was profoundly impressed with the nature of Moravian Christian piety, not least their singing.[718] From his return to England his life was centred on a rhythm of preaching, meeting societies and visiting, which would remain its mainspring until his death: Charles shared this itinerant ministry until 1756, after which he became increasingly centred on his family.[719] The preaching effectively began with the famous sermon delivered by George Whitefield, also recently returned from America, to (largely unchurched) miners, on 17 February 1739 on a hillside outside Bristol – famous because it is often seen as the flame which kindled the fire of evangelical revival in England. Thereafter Wesley followed his example: the whole world, as he memorably described it, became his parish.[720]

In 1741 Wesley and Whitefield disagreed, Wesley affirming Arminian views on predestination (i.e. that everyone had a chance of salvation, if they accepted Christian faith) and Whitefield Calvinist ones (i.e. that some were predestined to salvation and others to damnation).[721] By this time local 'bands' of believers were beginning to form in Bristol as well as London: the Methodist 'society', still within the Church of England, was beginning to emerge.[722] Charles Wesley married in 1749, and his marriage was deeply happy. John was less fortunate: in 1751 he married a rich widow, Mrs Mary (Molly) Vazeille; but the marriage was effectively a disaster.[723] She hated the endless travelling, and was jealous of John's relations with godly women.[724]

Unperturbed, John threw himself into yet more energetic and distant travelling, and in 1784 began to precipitate a potential split with the Church of England by ordaining three men for ministry in America (in the same year the Methodist Conference was legally established).[725] In 1788 John produced his *Thoughts on separation from the Church*, effectively acknowledging that a process of separation was taking place, although in the following year he declared that he would never leave the Church of England. He never did: two years later, on 2 March 1791, he was dead, aged 88.[726]

The spirituality of early Methodism

Something needs to be said about the spirituality of the fledgeling Methodist movement before John's and Charles' own teaching on the spiritual life is explored.[727] Their Oxford emphasis on small groups of Christians meeting and praying together left its permanent mark on the structure of Methodism in the form of the society, class and band meetings, which were designed to complement the local parish church as a focus for spiritual growth. The rules for the local 'societies' were drawn up originally by Wesley himself.[728] He defines the society as:

> a company of men having the form and seeking the power of godliness, united in order to pray together, to receive the word of exhortation, and to watch over one another in love, that they may help each other to work out their salvation.[729]

The emphasis on mutual spiritual guidance, and the echoes of the early apostolic community described in Acts 2, are obvious and impressive.[730] Each local 'society' was subdivided into classes of about twelve people each, who would normally meet together weekly under a leader responsible for ensuring that their souls prosper.[731] The leader (who was a lay member of the class) acted as a form of spiritual director and pastor.[732] Prayer at the meetings was extemporary; and members (whose only qualification was 'the desire to flee from the wrath to come, to be saved from their sins'[733]) were expected to worship regularly at the local church and receive the sacraments there.[734]

But the class meeting was only the beginning. Those who had experienced the 'new birth' and were advancing towards Christian perfection were gathered into 'bands', smaller groups, also led by laymen, and confidential in nature. Members of bands were expected to remain in their class meetings as well. The chief end of the band was to fulfil James 5.16: 'confess your faults to one another, and pray for one another, that ye may be healed'.[735] Members committed themselves to attend at least once each week, beginning with singing or prayer, and then reflecting honestly together about the state of their souls and their sins and temptations.[736] They were expected to abstain from alcohol, to keep the sabbath, 'to be patterns of diligence and frugality, of self-denial, and taking up the cross daily'.[737]

Finally, there were the 'select societies' for those regarded as being furthest advanced on the road towards Christian perfection. In addition to the guidelines informing the lives of the band meetings, the select societies had three others:

> 1. Let nothing spoken in this Society be spoken again; no, not even to the members of it. 2. Every member agrees absolutely to submit to his minister in all indifferent things. 3. Every member, till we can have all things common, will bring once a week, *bona fide*, all he can spare towards a common stock.[738]

These small tightly-knit groups were effectively an *ecclesiola in ecclesia*, a miniature church within the larger one, small enough to foster real spiritual growth and mutual trust. There is nothing particularly new about the idea;[739] and Wesley himself stressed that Methodists must avoid 'laying the whole stress of religion on any single part of it'.[740] But this neither stopped the movement from acquiring a momentum of its own, nor prevented the established church from viewing it from the start with profound and growing suspicion.

The spirituality of John Wesley

The theology that underpinned this vision was above all that of John and Charles Wesley themselves, though the roots of that theology were many and eclectic.[741] John's reading was vast and discursive: he took what he sought when he found it, adapting to suit his purposes. His primary written source was of course scripture;[742] and after it patristic theology: Wesley absorbed the wisdom of eastern as well as western fathers.[743] He sought consciously to recover the pristine purity of primitive Christianity, and said so in his famous 'Letter to a Roman Catholic', after summarizing the essence of the Christian faith:

This, and this alone, is the old religion. This is true, primitive Christianity. Oh, when shall it spread over all the earth? when shall it be found both in us and you?[744]

The other principal sources of the Wesleys' spirituality are too numerous to mention; but among them were William Law, with whom John corresponded at length, and Jeremy Taylor;[745] the Moravians he encountered both abroad and at home;[746] and Jonathan Edwards, whose *Treatise on religious affections* is a classic example of spiritual autobiography.[747] Wesley's relationship with continental mystical writers is complex: here too he adapted and appropriated different insights; but his overall attitude was ambivalent.[748] In an early letter he describes 'mystics' as 'all, and only those, who slight any of the means of grace'.[749] But this did not prevent him from translating German hymns of a mystical character by Tersteegen and Scheffler;[750] and he clearly felt drawn to those 'whose noble descriptions of union with God and internal religion made everything else appear mean, flat, and insipid'.[751] Yet (as he goes on to say)

> in truth [the mystics] made good works appear so too; yea, and faith itself, and what not? These gave me an entire new view of religion, nothing like any I had had before. But alas! It was nothing like that religion which Christ and his apostles lived and taught. I had a plenary dispensation from all the commands of God. The form ran thus: 'Love is all; all the commands beside are only means of love; you must choose those which you feel are means to you, and use them as long as they are so.' . . . All the other enemies of Christianity are triflers; the mystics are the most dangerous of all its enemies. They stab it in the vitals.[752]

His real difficulties with them were: first, that 'each of them makes his own experience the standard of religion';[753] secondly, that they were essentially interested in a *solitary*, not a corporate, Christianity;[754] and thirdly, and crucially, that their faith lacked power really to change things, or deal with the reality of evil.[755]

In an early letter (1734) John Wesley defines 'religion' thus:

> I take religion to be, not the bare saying over so many prayers, morning and evening, in public or in private; not anything superadded now and then to a careless or worldly life; but a constant ruling habit of soul, a renewal of our minds in the image of God, a recovery of the divine likeness, a still-increasing conformity of heart and life to the pattern of our most holy Redeemer.[756]

This remained the heart of his faith for the rest of his long life.[757] We may take each of its four ingredients as the basis for an exploration of John's spirituality. 'A constant ruling habit of soul' presupposes, first, a turning-away from old habits: 'our being contemned', he wrote in the same year, 'is absolutely necessary to our doing good in the world'.[758] This conviction of sin, essential as a precondition to faith, must both be experienced inwardly ('when men feel in themselves the heavy burthen of sin . . . they tremble, they quake, and are inwardly touched with sorrowfulness of heart'[759]), and lead to 'real desires and sincere resolutions of amendment'.[760]

But conviction of sin is only a beginning. If a new 'ruling habit of soul' is to be introduced, we must believe; and our faith must be 'not barely a speculative, rational thing, a cold, lifeless assent, a train of ideas in the head; but also a disposition of the heart'[761] – it is characteristic of Wesley that heart as well as head must constantly be involved. Through faith we are justified; and with our justification, our journey towards perfection and holiness begins. We have made a covenant with God: or rather, God has made one with us, for the initiative lies with God rather than with us, even though as an Arminian Wesley always believed that 'some may be saved who were not always of the number of the elected'.[762] In his journal, he exhorts his fellow Methodists to renew their covenant with God jointly, telling them to begin by setting apart a day for 'solemn fasting and prayer'.[763]

Yet justification too is only a beginning:

> Justification implies only a relative, the new birth a real, change. God in justifying us does something *for* us; in begetting us again, He does the work *in us*. The former changes our outward relation to God, so that of enemies we become children; by the latter our inmost souls are changed, so that of sinners we become saints. The one restores us to the favour, the other to the image, of God. The one is the taking away the guilt, the other the taking away the power, of sin: so that, although they are joined together in point of time, yet are they of wholly distinct natures.[764]

How are we to know we have undergone this new birth (which introduces the second ingredient of true 'religion', the renewal of our minds in the image of God)? Wesley says we shall *feel* it, just as the newborn child feels a total difference in his life.[765] Our spiritual eyes are opened; the whole manner of our existence is changed; and our whole soul is sensible of God:

> The spirit or breath of God is immediately inspired, breathed into the new-born soul; and the same breath which comes from, returns to, God: as it is continually received by faith, so it is continually rendered back by love, by prayer, and praise, and thanksgiving; love, and praise, and prayer being the breath of every soul which is truly born of God. And by this new kind of spiritual respiration, spiritual life is not only sustained, but increased day by day.[766]

New birth is not the same as baptism:[767] a person may be born of water and yet not of the Spirit, though the two clearly belong together. Rather new birth is *regeneration*, the beginning of sanctification.[768] Wesley stresses the essentially *inward* nature of true holiness: it is 'the life of God in the soul; the image of God fresh stamped on the heart; an entire renewal of the mind in every temper and thought, after the likeness of him that created it'.[769] This state of renewal does not prevent inappropriate desires from *arising*, nor does it persist all the time (for feelings are, after all, transient): it does prevent such desires from *reigning*.[770] He quotes his father on his deathbed saying 'The inward witness, son, the inward witness . . . that is the proof, the strongest proof, of Christianity.'[771]

Yet that inward witness, vital as it is, must be manifested in an outward holiness of life: the tree is known by its fruits.[772] Holiness, *imputed* in justification, must become *inherent*, integral to our lives.[773] And without it we will bear no fruit: Wesley spells out its implications for ministerial work:

> If a single parish takes up your whole time and care, and you spend and are spent upon it, well. And yet I will be bold to say that no blessing from God will accompany your ministry, but the drunkard will be a drunkard still (and so the covetous, the brawler, the adulterer), unless you both believe and teach what you love to call my 'new notions of inspiration' . . . You will all the day long stretch out your hands in vain, unless you teach them to pray that the Spirit of God may inwardly witness with their spirits that they are the children of God.[774]

So we have a new 'ruling habit' in our souls, in virtue of our conviction of sin and justification by faith; we have had our minds renewed in the image of God in virtue of our new birth and progress towards inward holiness. But Wesley is not yet finished. For him religion includes also 'a recovery of the divine likeness, a still-increasing conformity of heart and life to the pattern of our most holy Redeemer'. We must become like God: here Wesley approaches a little nearer the teaching of eastern patristic writers, for whom participation in the life of God was fundamental to the spiritual life (though he is still some distance from them).[775] And this brings us to Wesley's teaching on perfection, which brought him into frequent controversy.[776]

Wesley himself says that his understanding of perfection derived from his reading of Jeremy Taylor's *Holy living* and *Holy dying* in 1725, as a result of which he felt

> a fixed intention to *give myself to God*. In this I was much confirmed soon after by the *Christian Pattern*, and longed to *give God all my heart*. This is just what I mean by Perfection now: I sought after it from that hour. In 1727 I read Mr Law's *Christian Perfection* and *Serious Call*, and more explicitly resolved to be *all devoted to God* in body, soul, and spirit.[777]

Perfection, then, is total self-giving. The difficulty is that the term can also imply a static state of sinlessness, which is what upset many contemporaries:[778] Wesley insisted that he did not much like the term, maintaining that it was his opponents who thrust it upon him continually.[779] He also insisted that it was possible to fall from the state of perfection;[780] and that it was a growing state, always susceptible of further growth in grace.[781] It did not take place instantly:

> Neither dare we affirm, as some have done, that all this salvation is given at once. There is indeed an instantaneous, as well as a gradual, work of God in his children; and there wants not, we know, a cloud of witnesses, who have received, in one moment, either a clear sense of the forgiveness of their sins, or the abiding witness of the Holy Spirit. But we do not know a single instance, in any place, of a person's receiving, in one and the same moment, remission of sins, the abiding witness of the Spirit, and a new, clean heart.[782]

Yet perfection was more than self-giving. It was true love: in a letter Wesley describes it as meaning 'neither more nor less than "loving God with all our heart,"' or having the mind that was in Christ and walking as Christ walked'.[783] Robert Southey describes Wesley's doctrine of perfection as 'a constant communion with God, which fills the heart with humble love'.[784] We become Christlike: this is the 'still-increasing conformity of heart and life to the pattern of our most holy Redeemer' about which Wesley wrote at the start of his ministry. This is still a long way from any deification, or ontological union between human beings and God, though Charles Wesley went further than his brother here, and did indeed come very close to implying that the state of perfection implied sinlessness: 'we cannot sin', he wrote, 'when pure in heart'.[785]

In developing his understanding of the spiritual life, John Wesley gave a prominent place to the work of the Holy Spirit; and this too caused controversy, some of his critics believing that he is claiming for his followers those 'extraordinary' gifts of the Spirit which were given only to the first Christians, and others maintaining that the Spirit was only present when you could feel or experience it. Nonsense, said Wesley;[786] and here, defending himself against Quakers on the one hand and Anglicans on the other, Wesley appears at his most invigoratingly persuasive:

> You are as really 'moved by the Spirit' when He convinces you you ought to feed him that is hungry, as when He gives you ever so strong an impulse, desire, or inclination so to do. In like manner, you are as really moved by the Spirit to pray, whether it be in public or private, when you have a conviction it is the will of God you should, as when you have the strongest impulse upon your heart.[787]

Hence also he can say, against quietists and others, that 'religion was designed not to extinguish, but to perfect [reason]'.[788] Rather it is the Holy Spirit who is

> the immediate cause of all holiness in us; enlightening our understandings, rectifying our wills and affections, renewing our natures, uniting our persons to Christ, assuring us of the adoption of sons, leading us in our actions, purifying and sanctifying our souls and bodies, to a full and eternal enjoyment of God.[789]

And we shall know if we have received the Spirit, partly by our own inner experience of it and partly by having 'a loving heart toward God, and toward all mankind'.[790] We will have been adopted as God's children; and the difference this makes will be so profound that the Christian 'can no more doubt the reality of his sonship, than he can doubt of the shining of the sun, while he stands in the full blaze of his beams'.[791] But (and this is crucial) such an awareness leads, not to presumption, but precisely to humility, to a deep recognition of how little you deserve so great a gift.[792]

This awareness is what Protestant Christians have habitually described as assurance, a word that Wesley also dislikes because of its lack of scriptural warrant.[793] He stresses that the conviction that we have been justified and adopted as God's children does not insure us against doubt;[794] nor does it in any way permit us to do whatever we want (contrary to the activities of some antinomian Methodists).[795] Rather it sets us free from fear of damnation, free to live as children of God, free to speak and live the truth in love.[796] There is a tremendous sense of joy in the spirituality of Wesley which is all too often forgotten by those (including our opening correspondent to *The Gentleman's Magazine*) inclined to assume that Methodism is world-denying and grim. In an early letter he wrote:

> I can't think that when God sent us into the world He had irreversibly decreed that we should be perpetually miserable in it. If it be so, the very endeavour after happiness in this life is a sin; as it is acting in direct contradiction to the very design of our creation. What are become of all the innocent comforts and pleasures of life, if it is the intent of our Creator that we should never taste them?[797]

And (in another early letter):

> I was made to be happy; to be happy I must love God; in proportion to my love of whom my happiness must increase. To love God I must be like Him, holy as He is holy; which implies both the being pure from vicious and foolish passions and the being confirmed in those virtuous and rational affections which God comprises in the word charity.[798]

Wesley longs to communicate a religion that will be *attractive*; and he cannot see the point of one that has little or no effect on people's lives. Writing to sceptics, he argues passionately for the faith to which he has dedicated his life:

> And when you thus love God and all mankind, and are transformed into his likeness, then the commandments of God will not be grievous; you will no more complain that they destroy the comforts of life: So far from it, that they will be the very joy of your heart; ways of pleasantness, paths of peace! You will experience here that solid happiness which you had elsewhere sought in vain. Without servile fear or anxious care, so long as you continue on earth, you will gladly do the will of God here as the angels do it in heaven; and when the time is come that you should depart hence, when God says, 'Arise, and come away,' you will pass with joy unspeakable out of the body, into all the fullness of God.[799]

There is no room in his spirituality 'for a stern, austere manner of conversing . . . let all the cheerfulness of faith be there; all the joyfulness of hope; all the amiable sweetness, the winning easiness, of love'.[800] This is not a *natural* joy, or a transient one:[801] it is a spiritual joy, one that abides; and its effect is a clear vision, an ability to see both the state of one's soul and the truth that transforms and endures.[802]

It remains to consider his understanding of prayer. Wesley took very seriously the biblical injunction to pray without ceasing, and makes this a key element (and manifestation) of Christian perfection:[803]

> Not that [the Methodist] is always in the house of prayer; though he neglects no opportunity of being there. Neither is he always on his knees, although he often is, or on his face, before the Lord his God. Nor yet is he always crying aloud to God, or calling upon him in words: For many times

'the Spirit maketh intercession for him with groans that cannot be uttered.' But at all times the language of his heart is this: 'Thou brightness of the eternal glory, unto thee is my heart, though without a voice, and my silence speaketh unto thee.' And this is true prayer, and this alone.[804]

This magnificent passage takes us to the heart of Wesley's spirituality. Prayer is not only a matter of words: it is silence, groans, adoration, and a constant sense of the presence of God. Wesley's high-church inclinations lead him to commend formal liturgical prayer and psalmody.[805] But prayer is more than these: it is 'the lifting up of the heart to God';[806] the living of the Christian life; for 'in souls filled with love, the desire to please God is a continual prayer'.[807] The focus of prayer is petition, and Wesley has some fine reflections on this. In an early letter he says, of someone experiencing doubt:

if she ceases not to cry unto Him to deliver her from her weakness, then let her be assured it shall not be in vain: for 'God is in the cry, but not in the weakness.'[808]

And elsewhere, in a superb sermon:

The end of your praying is not to inform God, as though He knew not your wants already; but rather to inform yourselves; to fix the sense of those wants more deeply in your hearts, and the sense of your continual dependence on Him who only is able to supply all your wants. It is not so much to move God, who is always more ready to give than you to ask, as to move yourselves, that you may be willing and ready to receive the good things He has prepared for you.[809]

The emotions have a major part to play in prayer; but they must be controlled.[810] Sometimes huge numbers of worshippers at one of Wesley's services could become very excited, shouting and roaring:

The church was quite filled, and hundreds were without. And now the arrows of God flew abroad. The inexpressible groans, the lamenting, praying, roaring, were so loud, almost without intermission, that we who stood without could scarce help thinking, all in the church were cut to the heart. But upon inquiry we found about two hundred persons, chiefly men, cried aloud for mercy; but many more were affected, perhaps as deeply, though in a calmer way.[811]

Later Wesley reflected on the phenomenon:

The danger *was* to regard *extraordinary* circumstances too much, such as outcries, convulsions, visions, trances, as if these were *essential* to the inward work, so that it *could not* go on without them. Perhaps the danger *is* to regard them too little, to condemn them altogether, to imagine they had nothing of God in them and were an hindrance to his work . . . Let us even suppose that in some few cases there was a mixture of *dissimulation*; that persons *pretended* to see or feel what they did not and *imitated* the cries or convulsive motions of those who were really overpowered by the Spirit of God. Yet even this should not make us either deny or undervalue the real work of the Spirit. The shadow is no disparagement of the substance, nor the counterfeit of the real diamond.[812]

In the final analysis, here as elsewhere, the test is simple, the touchstone scripture: 'You are not to judge by your own *feelings*, but by the word of God.'[813]

The spirituality of Charles Wesley

Although he wrote a good deal else besides, it is undoubtedly Charles Wesley's hymns that form the heart of his contribution to Methodist (and English) spirituality: he is estimated to have written over 7,000, of which 3,000 survive.[814] They were, and to some extent had to be, *the* primary means whereby Methodists might absorb and appropriate for themselves the teaching they heard. Hymns won their way first among Dissenters, and were not officially sanctioned in the Church of England until the early nineteenth century; and Isaac Watts' *Hymns and spiritual songs* of 1707 enlarged for Dissenters what had hitherto been a musical diet of Psalms, either biblical or metrical. Among his vast output, Charles Wesley's *Hymns on sacred scripture* can take pride of place: this immense collection of tiny (usually one-verse) hymns allows believers to do three things at once: to reflect on scripture, albeit scripture refracted through Wesley's own careful theological exposition; to absorb into their spiritual bloodstream the truths on which they are reflecting; and to offer some kind of response to the particular aspect of the Gospel treated in the hymn.

The singing of hymns was thus a distinctive feature of Methodist worship and piety from the beginning.[815] John Wesley told his followers to 'sing *lustily*, and with a good courage . . . Be no more afraid of your voice now, nor more ashamed of its being heard, than when you sung the songs of Satan.'[816] The writing of hymns and religious poetry was ingrained in the Wesley family; but it is difficult to estimate the relative contributions of the two brothers: certainly John could be critical of his brother's hymns, describing some of them once as 'namby-pambical'.[817]

As with John Newton, it may be easiest to explore the spiritual world of Charles Wesley's hymns by examining a single example in detail. Here is one of his most enduring productions, originally entitled 'Hymn for Christmas-Day', and in the form he first wrote it:

> 1. Hark how all the welkin rings,
> 'Glory to the King of kings,
> Peace on earth, and mercy mild,
> God and sinners reconciled!'

> 2. Joyful, all ye nations, rise,
> Join the triumph of the skies;
> Universal Nature, say,
> 'Christ the Lord is born to-day!'

3. Christ, by highest heaven adored,
Christ, the everlasting Lord,
Late in time behold Him come,
Offspring of a virgin's womb.

4. Veil'd in flesh, the Godhead see,
Hail th'Incarnate Deity!
Pleased as man with men to'appear
Jesus, our *Immanuel* here!

5. Hail the heavenly Prince of Peace!
Hail the Sun of Righteousness!
Light and life to all He brings,
Risen with healing in His wings.

6. Mild He lays His glory by,
Born – that man no more may die,
Born – to raise the sons of earth,
Born – to give them second birth.

7. Come, Desire of Nations, come
Fix in us Thy humble home;
Rise, the woman's conquering Seed,
Bruise in us the serpent's head.

8. Now display Thy saving power.
Ruin'd nature now restore;
Now in mystic union join
Thine to ours, and ours to Thine.

9. *Adam's* likeness, Lord, efface.
Stamp Thy image in its place;
Second *Adam* from above,
Reinstate us in Thy love.

10. Let us Thee, though lost, regain,
Thee, the Life, the Inner Man:
Oh! to all Thyself impart,
Form'd in each believing heart.[818]

The hymn is Charles' exposition of the Christmas story as told by St Luke. The first six verses are theological reflection; and the last four are the appropriation of that reflection for the believer. It is significant that these four are normally omitted from modern hymnals, allowing the person singing to contemplate Christmas without any need whatever to respond to the truth at its heart, and turning the worshipper from a participant into a spectator. Charles would have been horrified. Note too the pervasively corporate tone of the closing verses, essential to Charles' view of the spiritual life.[819]

Wesley begins by citing the song of the angels to the shepherds (Luke 2.14); but he adds to it a phrase from Pauline thought: 'God and sinner reconciled'. He wants to convey the whole Christian Gospel through the medium of a single Christmas hymn. The second verse ('Joyful, all ye nations, rise') alludes to Psalm 117, calling on all nations to acclaim the God who became flesh for the whole of humanity.[820] The third verse is, like so much of Charles Wesley's piety, firmly Christ-centred: he elaborates the text from Luke with an implicit reference to Hebrews 1.2 ('God . . . hath in these last days spoken unto us by his Son'). The use of exclamation marks and the reference to adoration in these opening verses are not rhetorical gestures: they underline the profound sense of *wonder* which should characterize our approach to the living and universal God: 'no local Deity/ We worship, Lord, in Thee'.[821] Doctrine must be incarnated in worship just as God's love was made flesh in Christ.[822] It is worth noting too the references to heaven and to glory in these verses: both are frequent themes for Wesley, and both may be experienced, even if transiently, here and now, as we like the shepherds 'hearken' to the herald-angels singing.[823]

But it is with verse 4 that we approach the heart of the matter. Wesley again alludes to the Letter to the Hebrews, whose rich theological reflection on the divinity of Christ suits his purposes admirably.[824] But he goes even further than its writer does in referring to 'the incarnate Deity'; and here we do sense something of eastern patristic theology, rooted as it is in the belief that humanity may participate in the divine nature because God in Christ first participated in ours (as 'Immanuel', God with us[825]).

The fifth verse is a typical Wesleyan *tour-de-force* of scriptural allusion and reflection, worthy of the medieval Cistercians. The 'heaven-born Prince of Peace' is a New Testament extension of Isaiah's prophecy about the coming Messiah.[826] The image of Christ as 'Sun of Righteousness' (drawn from texts in Malachi and St Matthew's Gospel[827]) is very common in Wesley's hymns, and, again like much eastern patristic theology, underlines his fondness for imagery of light.[828] 'Risen with healing in his wings', again from Malachi, occurs very frequently in Wesley's hymns.[829] The emphasis here is not just on the *fact* of Christ's coming or of his divinity, but on their *effects*: he brings healing, light and life to all – not only to the elect (the Wesleys' Arminian theology is implicit here too).

In the sixth verse Wesley completes the expository section of his hymn. The term 'mild', appearing for the second time in the hymn, means 'compassionate' or 'gracious' rather than 'gentle'.[830] The dashes present in Wesley's original rendering of this verse heighten the extraordinary contrast he wants to emphasize: Christ is *born* in order to give us second birth; and in his birth are the seeds of our immortality. The notion of a new birth is of course a key ingredient of the Wesleys' spirituality; and the notion of a second birth is found in other writers, notably in Zinzendorf, and also in Jakob Boehme.[831]

In the seventh verse (which, together with those that follow, is normally omitted in modern hymnals) Wesley begins, like all good preachers, to apply what has hitherto been expounded to the life of the believer. He still cites or refers to scripture;[832] but now he is praying, not preaching ('Come, Desire of nations'). In 'Fix in us thy humble home', he uses a verb which in the Authorized Version of the Psalms implies permanence;[833] but, as in his famous hymn *Love divine, all loves excelling*, he wants to apply the great Johannine saying of Jesus ('If a man love me, he will keep my words; and my Father will love him, and we will come unto him, and make our abode with him', John 14.23 AV) to every believer: Jesus is to be born in us as he was born in Mary. The reference to Christ as the 'woman's conquering seed', called upon to 'bruise the serpent's head', is to the Pauline doctrine of Christ as the second Adam undoing the sin of the first: Wesley returns to it two verses later, and elsewhere uses it constantly.[834] It is the only moment in this splendid hymn in which theological subtlety takes precedence over evangelical clarity.

But the effect is momentary: in the following verse (and note the insistent opening 'Now') he plunges us into union with God, and himself into considerable controversy. What does he mean by 'Now in mystic union join' our natures with Christ's? We should first note Wesley's other uses of the term 'mystic': he uses it fairly widely, and it is clear that for him its primary meaning is simply 'hidden': thus, in his rendering of Psalm 137, he writes 'Happy the man that sees in Thee/ The mystic Babylon within'.[835] But the matter is not that simple. In another hymn he writes:

> Fill me with all the life of love;
> In mystic union join
> Me to Thyself, and let me prove
> The fellowship Divine.[836]

The Wesleys can speak of being 'mystically one' with God;[837] and they can pray 'Steadfast let us cleave to Thee; Love the mystic union be'.[838]

The fact is that Charles Wesley frequently uses language which, although drawing back from eastern patristic teaching on deification, follows that teaching closely in emphasizing the ontological intimacy of our union with God through Christ, even though the fullness of that union is to be experienced only after death. At first sight his writing contains little that could not be found in any western Christian spiritual writer. Thus his great hymn 'Thou shepherd of *Israel* and mine', a meditation on Song of Songs 1.7, is a passionate prayer for intimate union with Christ:

> Ah, show me that happiest place,
> That place of Thy people's abode,
> Where saints in an ecstasy gaze,
> And hang on a crucified God:
> Thy love for a sinner declare,
> Thy passion and death on the tree,
> My spirit to *Calvary* bear,
> To suffer, and triumph, with Thee.[839]

The language is medieval in his intensely affective devotion to the crucified Christ; but it stops well short of any hint of deification. However, elsewhere Wesley goes further than almost any Protestant writer in using the language of merging to denote our union with God in Christ: 'lost in wonder, love, and praise' (in 'Love divine, all loves excelling') is scriptural and thoroughly orthodox; but 'swallowed up and lost in

God' or 'Resorb'd into perfection's sea,/ And lost, for ever lost in Thee!' is not really either; and similar phrases frequently recur.[840] There is, for example, this extraordinary concluding verse of his hymn on the story of the burning fiery furnace:

> Sin in me, the inbred foe,
> Awhile subsists in chains;
> But Thou all Thy power shalt show,
> And slay its last remains:
> Thou hast conquer'd my desire;
> Thou shalt quench it with Thy blood,
> Fill me with a purer fire,
> And change me into God.

Even so, we should recall that Wesley's primary concerns are twofold, *and both are pastoral*: first, to emphasize that the goal of this life is intimate personal union with God: it is the *personal* union that matters, even if in heaven we shall lose our identities and be lost in God's infinite love: 'Heaven itself could not suffice:/ I seek not Thine, but Thee', is how Charles himself puts it elsewhere.[841] Secondly, he wants to underline that our own union with Christ is no narrowly individual affair but a means to a greater love for all humanity – a point hinted at by the use of the plural in these closing verses of 'Hark how all the welkin rings', and made explicit elsewhere.[842]

What he has in mind becomes clearer as the hymn progresses. The prayer (in the ninth verse) for God to 'stamp' his image in us in the place of that of Adam is a very common one in Wesley's hymns. For him the image of God is love;[843] we are to be restored in it and awaken in it in heaven,[844] where 'all our glorious foreheads [shall bear]/ The glorious stamp Divine'.[845] By 'image' he means the character, the identity of God; and what he wants to underline, here as so often, is the necessity of a funda-mental *change* in the believer, a change that must take place if we are to become the people God longs for us to be. Again, that change is not just for us: we are to learn to discern that image in other Christians too.[846] A dramatic antithesizing of the two polar-opposite destinies open to humanity runs right through Charles Wesley's spiri-tuality: ruined, we are lost for all eternity; redeemed, we become Godlike: 'Standing as at first we stood [i.e. like Adam and Eve in Eden],/ Made a little less than God!'[847]

And so to the closing verse. The language of formation ('Form'd in each believing heart') also appears frequently in the Wesleys' hymns;[848] and it is perfectly compatible with scripture, underlining again Wesley's longing for the miracle of Christmas to become a reality in the life of each believer (a point completely lost if these verses are omitted). But even more important is the preceding line ('Oh! to *all* Thyself impart'): here again Wesley controverts the Calvinist view that only an elect few are predestined to salvation. The Incarnation is for everyone.[849]

It is time for some conclusions. Charles Wesley's spirituality is rooted in his longing to see Christ really present in the lives of believers: hence his many eucharistic hymns, which locate the presence of Christ in the believer rather than in the bread and wine.[850] In those hymns, even more than in his famous Christmas hymn discussed here, the *cost* to God of our redemption is again and again made clear:

'Tis not a dead external sign
Which here my hopes require,
The living power of love Divine
In Jesus I desire.

I want the dear Redeemer's grace,
I seek the Crucified,
The Man that suffer'd in my place,
The God that groan'd and died.[851]

But the whole point of that cost, and of the importance of Christ's presence, 'form'd in each believing heart', is to allow us to be changed utterly from sinners destined to despair and destruction to believers destined for heaven. This is what gives Charles' eucharistic hymns their power, because this is their purpose:

Rise, ye worms, to priests and kings,
Rise in Christ, and reign with God.

Now, Lord, on us Thy flesh bestow,
And let us drink Thy blood,
Till all our souls are fill'd below
With all the life of God.[852]

For that transformation we are to pray with all our strength: Charles Wesley constantly emphasizes that prayer is hard work – images of wrestling, agonizing and struggling abound in his hymns on the subject.[853] But it is also an essentially corporate activity, plunging us into the life of the whole church:

Hear, O Lord, the ceaseless prayer
The suffering members groan,
Lo! We all the burden bear,
And grieve the grief of one.[854]

And if our prayer disturbs the powerful, it is only one more sign of its enduring power:

On Saturday September 9th [1744] I rode, in heavy rain, to Church-hill, with Mr. Sh—. The Justice threatened him with terrible things, in case I preached. Many poor people ventured to hear, while . . . out of the abundance of my heart my mouth spake. When I had ended, Mr Justice called out, and bade them pull me down. He had stood at a distance, striving to raise a mob; but not a man would stir at his bidding. Only one behind struck me with a stone. While I was in my prayer, he cried again, 'Pull him down.' I told him, I had nothing now to do but to pray for him. He answered, 'I have nothing to do with prayer.' 'So I suppose, Sir,' said I; 'but we have.'[855]

Conclusion

There are many inconsistencies in the work of these two brothers; but that should not surprise us. They wrote not systematic but open-air theology, on horseback and in market-places: it was incarnated not in textbooks but in letters and hymns, born of specific controversies and directed to particular people or groups. In so doing, they shook the Church of England to its heart, and bequeathed it an enduring dilemma: can comprehensiveness and rationalism only be achieved at the cost of excluding 'enthusiasm'? And, if so, is the Church left with a religion that refines intellects but has no power to change people? The Wesleys threw everything they had into the struggle to present a faith that really could change lives, and had already changed theirs: they really were like twin St Pauls, hammering out in pulpit and by post the heart of what they believed Christ meant for humanity. No one went further in trying to hold together head and heart, 'philosophy' and 'enthusiasm', in a single convincing synthesis at the very time when powerful forces were prising them apart: no one came nearer to succeeding. On 17 September 1745, John Wesley visited the ruined Carthusian monastery at Mount Grace in Yorkshire:

> The walls of the church, of the cloister, and some of the cells, are tolerably entire. And one may still discern the partitions between the little gardens, one of which belonged to every cell. Who knows but some of the poor, superstitious monks who once served God here, according to the light they had, may meet us by and by, in that house of God, not made with hands, eternal in the heavens?[856]

The language may appear patronizing two centuries later. But in his day it was astonishingly ecumenical, prophetic even. Four years later he wrote to a Roman Catholic: 'O brethren, let us not still fall out by the way! I hope to see you in heaven. And if I practise the religion above described, you dare not say I shall go to hell.'[857] Dare not, indeed: English spirituality has had few, if any, more generous champions.

Samuel Johnson (1709–84) and the literary tradition

One of the qualities most often associated with Samuel Johnson (in addition to his massive erudition) is wit. A better description, however, might be a spirit of play. Here are two examples. The Revd Mr Parker recalled an incident when a party had been

> invited to meet the Doctor at Stow Hill: the dinner waited far beyond the usual hour, and the company were about to sit down, when Johnson appeared at the great gate; he stood for some time in deep contemplation, and at length began to climb it, and, having succeeded in clearing it, advanced with hasty strides towards the house. On his arrival Mrs Gastrel asked him, 'if he had forgotten that there was a small gate for foot passengers by the side of the carriage entrance.' 'No, my dear lady, by no means,' replied the Doctor; 'but I had a mind to try whether I could climb a gate now as I used to do when I was a lad.'[858]

In January 1764 Johnson visited his friend Bennet Langton's family seat in Lincolnshire. Later, Langton recalled what happened while Johnson was walking at the top of a very steep hill with Langton and his parents:

Poor, dear Dr Johnson, when he came to this spot, turned to look down the hill, and said he was determined 'to take a roll down.' When we understood what he meant to do, we endeavoured to dissuade him; but he was resolute, saying, he had not had a roll for a long time; and taking out of his lesser pockets whatever might be in them – keys, pencil, purse, or pen-knife, and laying himself parallel with the edge of the hill, he actually descended, turning himself over and over till he came to the bottom.[859]

This childlike sense of play remained a part of Johnson's life right to the end;[860] but it is not to be taken as a sign that his life was easy. His beloved wife Tetty died in 1752: their relationship was difficult, and Johnson's sociability and energy in founding clubs and enjoying conversation was more a desperate search for companionship and acceptance than an easy extroversion. But he missed her terribly; and melancholy dogged him for the rest of his life.[861] In 1783 he wrote to Hester Thrale:

The black Dog I hope always to resist, and in time to drive though I am deprived of almost all those that used to help me . . . When I rise my breakfast is solitary, the black dog waits to share it, from breakfast to dinner he continues barking.[862]

Many of his late letters reflect a deep loneliness, an acute self-knowledge and a painfully accurate realism about life:

A sick Man is a very perverse being, he gives much trouble, he receives many favours, yet is never pleased and not often thankful.[863]

Samuel Johnson's lifelong devotion to the Christian religion, and to the Church of England, is well attested.[864] His faith was at once rational and deeply personal, rooted in a thoroughgoing Arminianism that embraced the importance of good works as well as faith.[865] He began writing prayers when a young man, and planned a handbook of devotions;[866] but abandoned the idea, maintaining in any case that the Book of Common Prayer contained the only prayers worth praying.[867] But it was particularly in later life, when he was in his sixties, that Johnson came to seek real comfort in religious faith; and he was far too intelligent and self-aware to find it in any anodyne piety. His spirituality is in large measure private, not easily laid bare; and the fact that he felt unable to write much of a religious nature under his own name attests to the doubts and struggles that went on beneath the surface, partly about what would happen after death and partly about the essential uncertainty of any kind of religious belief at all.[868]

Thus Johnson advocated a balanced, ordered, 'over-ruling piety', but not from any Gibbonian detachment: rather it was because he was acutely aware of how easily human beings become distracted by transient concerns, or obsessive self-pity, or addiction to alcohol, or driven by some overmastering ambition. Hence we must

engage in a frequent, and intense meditation on those important and eternal rules, which are to regulate our conduct, and rectify our minds; [so] that the power of habit may be added to that of truth, that the most useful ideas may be the most familiar, and that every action of our lives may be carried on under the superintendence of an over-ruling piety.[869]

This alone will provide us with a sustaining and well-rooted spiritual life. Johnson was wary of any religious 'enthusiasm'; and this is what he wrote about Scottish Presbyterianism:

> The change of religion in Scotland, eager and vehement as it was, raised an epidemical enthusiasm, compounded of sullen scrupulousness and warlike ferocity, which, in a people whom idleness resigned to their own thoughts, and who, conversing only with each other, suffered no dilution of their zeal from the gradual influx of new opinions, was long transmitted in its full strength from the old to the young, but by trade and intercourse with England, is now visibly abating, and giving way too fast to that laxity of practice and indifference of opinion, in which men, not sufficiently instructed to find the middle point, too easily shelter themselves from rigour and constraint.[870]

This statement, Cranmerian in length, is a key statement of the rational and spiritual *via media* to which Johnson subscribed throughout his long life. Note the contrast between the extremes of 'enthusiasm' on the one hand and 'indifference of opinion' on the other. The 'middle point' is what matters; and instruction, coupled with openness to new opinions, is what aids us in charting a course to it.[871] But it would not be easy: 'To be strictly religious', wrote Johnson, 'is difficult; but we may be zealously religious at little expence.'[872]

There is another, equally significant, reason why Johnson is critical of 'enthusiasm': because it narrows the perspectives of charity:

> Enthusiasm has dictated another limitation of benevolence, which it has confined to those of the same religion, having taught, with a fatal confidence, that all other sects are to be considered, as the enemies of God; that error, however involuntary, is entitled to no compassion even from fallible beings; and that those, whom God hath cursed with ignorance, are to be excluded from the general charter of humanity.[873]

Thus he notes how the twin extremes of nonconformist and papist 'enthusiasm' cancel each other out. This is what he says of the ruined chapel on the isle of Raasay (off Skye), in his *A journey to the western islands of Scotland*:

> The malignant influence of Calvinism has blasted ceremony and decency together; and if the remembrance of papal superstition is obliterated, the monuments of papal piety are likewise effaced.[874]

We shall find the search for the 'middle point' between extremes of enthusiasm and ideological indifference a common factor in all that follows; but we should beware of any assumption that this will produce a spirituality that is detached or passionless. His sermons are crammed with perceptive observations and asides on the follies of the human condition, such as our easy proneness to criticize others.[875] He is constantly concerned with benevolence, with altruism in the best sense: 'To deserve the exalted character of humanity and good-nature, a man must mean *well*; it is not sufficient to mean *nothing*.'[876] He is acutely aware of the private nature of people's real thoughts and character:

We see only the superficies of men, without knowing what passes within. Splendour, equipage, and luxury, are not always accompanied by happiness; but are more frequently the wretched solaces of a mind distracted with perplexities, and harrassed [sic] with terrours. Men are often driven, by reflection and remorse, into the hurries of business, or of pleasure, and fly from the terrifying suggestions of their own thoughts to banquets and to courts.[877]

And, in any case,

if men would spend more time in examining their own lives, and inspecting their own characters, they would have less leisure, and less inclination, to remark with severity upon others. They would easily discover, that it will not be for their advantage to exasperate their neighbour, and that a scandalous falsehood may be easily revenged by a reproachful truth.[878]

This is a memorable encapsulation of Jesus' teaching about motes and beams. More important, though, it underlines the robustly realistic and practical dimension to his piety: thus our first and best response to the terrible poverty of the world must be to alleviate it;[879] for poverty is not the unalterable dictate of Providence, nor is it morally ennobling.[880] Rather the reverse: 'He who *begs* in the street in his *infancy*, learns only how to *rob* there in his *manhood*.'[881]

We may already, then, identify three elements in his piety: a sharp self-awareness; a concern to hold together the mid-point between heart and head; and a pervasive sense of compassion. Underlying all these is his emphatic stress on what is *common*:

The true state of every nation is the state of common life. The manners of a people are not to be found in the schools of learning, or the palaces of greatness, where the national character is obscured or obliterated by travel or instruction, by philosophy or vanity; nor is public happiness to be estimated by the assemblies of the gay, or the banquets of the rich. The great mass of nations is neither rich nor gay: they whose aggregate constitutes the people, are found in the streets, and the villages, in the shops and farms; and from them collectively considered, must the measure of general prosperity be taken.[882]

So he criticizes those for whom 'all regard to the welfare of others [has been] overborne by a perpetual attention to immediate advantage and contracted views of present interest'.[883] We should be compassionate because life is uncertain and short;[884] and, although suffering is not *fair*, it can be therapeutic if we use it well.[885] But he is acutely aware that it is easy to be philanthropic and disinterested if life has treated you comfortably. This is what he noted on the island of Mull on the subject of tree-planting:

There is a frightful interval between the seed and the timber. He that calculates the growth of trees, has the unwelcome remembrance of the shortness of life driven hard upon him. He knows that he is doing what will never benefit himself; and when he rejoices to see the stem rise, is disposed to repine that another shall cut it down. Plantation is naturally the employment of a mind unburdened with care, and vacant to futurity, saturated with present good, and at leisure to derive gratification from the prospect of posterity. He that pines with hunger, is in little care how others shall be fed.[886]

Yet being 'vacant to futurity', and living entirely in the present, is dangerous. Procrastination of amendment is our besetting sin: we live exclusively in the present at our peril.[887] He records in his diary the first occasion on which he was told by his mother about life after death.[888] He bewails the current indifference on the subject:

> if we visit the most cool and regular parts of the community, if we turn our eye to the farm, or to the shop, where one year glides uniformly after another, and nothing new or important is either expected or dreaded; yet still the same indifference about eternity will be found . . . They have no care of futurity.[889]

Terrible adversity taught him to ponder the randomness of life, and the ineluctability of death, with real seriousness. He had no time for predestination: sinners 'cannot perish everlastingly but by their own choice'.[890] God cannot be held responsible for all acts of human wickedness, nor could he reasonably prevent them, for

> if God should, by a particular exertion of his omnipotence, hinder murder or oppression, no man could then be a murderer or an oppressor, because he would be withheld from it by an irresistible power; but then that power, which prevented crimes, would destroy virtue; for virtue is the consequence of choice.[891]

On the other hand, he did stress the value of repentance, provided that this too was incarnated in action: 'reformation is the chief part of repentance; not he that only bewails and confesses, but he that forsakes his sins, repents acceptably to God'.[892] He spoke here in no superior spirit: it was a desperate struggle to forsake his own sins, and he was far more aware of them than anyone else could ever be. Towards the end of his life he recalled an occasion in his youth when he had selfishly refused to abandon his studies to stand in for his father at the Uttoxeter market:

> Pride was the source of that refusal, and the remembrance of it was painful. A few years ago I desired to atone for this fault. I went to Uttoxeter in very bad weather, and stood for a considerable time bare-headed in the rain, on the spot where my father's stall used to stand. In contrition I stood, and I hope the penance was expiatory.[893]

So he spoke a truth he knew only too well when he said:

> He is esteemed by the prudent and the diligent to be no good regulator of his private affairs, who defers till to-morrow what is necessary to be done, and what it is in his power to do, to-day. The obligation would still be stronger, if we suppose that the present is the only day in which he knows it will be in his power. This is the case of every man, who delays to reform his life, and lulls himself in the supineness of iniquity.[894]

It is utterly characteristic of Johnson to refuse to take refuge in any kind of withdrawal from reality; and it is this which lies behind his criticism of the monastic life:

> A man whose conscience accuses him of having perverted others seems under some obligation to continue in the world, and to practise virtue in publick, that those who have been seduced by his example, may by his example be reclaimed.[895]

Or, as he elsewhere put it: 'it cannot be allowed, that flight is victory; or that he fills his place in the creation laudably, who does no ill, *only* because he does *nothing*'.[896]

And yet there *is* a withdrawal we need to make: a withdrawal from a narrowly sensual, self-centred view of life; and a withdrawal too from a perspective which excludes, not only the uncertainties of the future, but the wisdom of the past. Here is Johnson movingly pondering his visit to the monastic island of Iona:

> Whatever withdraws us from the power of our senses; whatever makes the past, the distant, or the future predominate over the present, advances us in the dignity of thinking beings. Far from me and from my friends, be such frigid philosophy as may conduct us indifferent and unmoved over any ground which has been dignified by wisdom, bravery, or virtue. That man is little to be envied, whose patriotism would not gain force upon the plain of Marathon, or whose piety would not grow warmer among the ruins of Iona![897]

That is well said; and it underlines the way in which Johnson's learning, his sense of history and culture, touches his personal spirituality as well. And this brings us to the subject of prayer, which he describes as 'the great efficient of union between the soul and its Creator . . . No man can pray, with ardour of devotion, but he must excite in himself a reverential idea of that Power, to whom he addresses his petitions.' We must seek to preserve in the mind 'a constant apprehension of the divine presence'.[898]

But how do we do that? Periodic times of retirement from the world for reflection and forming new resolutions for the future, as well as occasional fasts (so long as they are not accompanied by 'wild enthusiasm'), are recommended by Johnson.[899] But there is more to prayer than that; and someone of his enormous and unflinching integrity might be expected to find it hard work. He had no illusions about the way prayer is answered: 'no human understanding can pray for any thing temporal otherwise than conditionally', he wrote to Hill Boothby in 1755.[900] And he knew how easily prayer could become simply the projection of impure human wishes.[901] He insisted that we must pray with understanding, not by the suspension of our intellect: in one letter, on experiencing the onset of a stroke, Johnson

> was alarmed and prayed God, that however he might afflict my body he would spare my understanding.[902]

Ultimately, of course, we learn to pray by praying; and we may learn it best when circumstance compels us to it. Johnson wrote several prayers on the death of his wife Tetty on 17 March 1752. One (dated 8 May 1752) is headed *Deus exaudi. – Heu!* (Hear, O Lord – alas!). Another (dated 25 April 1752) asks God to help him 'remember with thankfulness the blessings so long enjoyed by me in the society of my departed wife; make me so to think on her precepts and example, that I may imitate whatever was in her life acceptable in thy sight, and avoid all by which she offended thee'.[903] It continues:

> Forgive me, O merciful Lord, all my sins, and enable me to begin and perfect that reformation which I promised her, and to persevere in that resolution, which she implored Thee to continue, in the purposes which I recorded in thy sight, when she lay dead before me, in obedience to thy laws, and faith in thy word. And now, O Lord, release me from my sorrow.[904]

He continues with a prayer (26 April 1752) in which he asks 'that I may enjoy the good effects of her attention and ministration, whether exercised by appearance, impulses, dreams, or in any other manner agreeable to thy government; forgive me my presumption'.[905]

He was unsure as to the legitimacy of prayer for the dead; but it felt so natural a duty that he did it anyway: on the first anniversary of Tetty's death, he recorded that 'I prayed for her conditionally if it were lawful'.[906] And much later, in March 1782, he wrote sadly:

> This is the day on which in 1752 dear Tetty died. On what we did amiss, and our faults were great, I have thought of late with more regret than at any former time. She was I think very penitent. May God have accepted her repentance: may he accept mine . . . Perhaps Tetty is now praying for me. God, help me. We were married almost seventeen years, and have now been parted thirty.[907]

It is typical of Johnson that he faced the anguish of his own bereavement with a steadfast refusal to accept any kind of easy panacea or spurious illusion. In 1758 he wrote to his friend Bennet Langton criticizing him gently for lamenting the death in action of an English general:

> The only reason why we lament a soldier's death is that we think he might have lived longer, yet this cause of grief is common to many other kinds of death which are not so passionately bewailed. The truth is that every death is violent which is the effect of accident, every death which is not gradually brought on by the miseries of age, or when life is extinguished for any other reason [than] that it is burnt out . . . Let us endeavour to see things as they are, and then enquire whether we ought to complain. Whether to see life as it is will give us much consolation I know not, but the consolation which is drawn from truth, if any there be, is solid and durable, that which may be derived from errour [sic] must be like its original fallacious and fugitive.[908]

The unhappiness that marred so much of Johnson's life did not destroy his Christian hope: on the contrary, as he said to Boswell on Easter Day 1778, you cannot answer all objections. You have demonstration for a first cause: you see [God] must be good as well as powerful, because there is nothing to make him otherwise, and goodness of itself is preferable. Yet you have against this, what is very certain, the unhappiness of human life. This, however, gives us reason to hope for a future state of compensation, that there may be a perfect system. But of that we were not sure, till we had a positive revelation.[909]

Yet that hope remained precisely that: hope. He had no illusions: 'No rational man can die without uneasy apprehension,' he told Mrs Knowles earlier in the same year. The fear that death might issue in annihilation was a sufficient reason to remain alive, even if in pain.[910] So when Mr Edwards declared to him 'I am grown old: I am sixty-five,' Johnson retorted:

I shall be sixty-eight next birth-day. Come, Sir, drink water, and put in for a hundred.[911]

Hope, 'the cordial of life', must be founded on reason, not simply on desire.[912] For Johnson, who almost certainly regarded himself as a failure, that hope was both a lifeline and an elusive, hard-won acquaintance: his faith always trembled on the edge of terrible doubt. And that is exactly why he matters.

Women and spirituality in the Eighteenth Century

To bring together the principal women writers on the spiritual life, irrespective of their denominational allegiances, is fraught with hazard; but there are two compelling reasons for doing so. The first is that there is a larger and more coherent group of such writers in this century than in any previous one: the second, that, although they wrote for a wide public, they shared some common perspectives and in some cases very clearly wrote with other women in mind. Hannah More, by no means a radical even in her own day, maintained that in many respects women were more susceptible of religious instruction and practice than men.[913]

Much has been written about the position of women in eighteenth-century England.[914] They were unquestionably more prominent than ever before in cultural activities, not least in writing novels, plays and poems.[915] And, although for most of them the home remained their primary centre of operations, the houses of gentlefolk were not simply private domestic enclosures but places where people were entertained, business transacted, and power wielded. Women were at the heart of this, able to use the customs and etiquettes of contemporary life to their advantage.[916] The mushrooming of cultural institutions – circulating libraries, pleasure gardens, charitable institutions, clubs, theatre and concert seasons, assembly rooms and so on – opened up a whole new world in which women could do this.[917] And many were immensely active in social life and philanthropy: Sarah Trimmer's *The oeconomy of charity* contains extensive lists of practical advice for organizing soup shops for the poor and numerous similar activities.

There is a sense, then, in which even the famously radical Mary Wollstonecraft

(1759–97), one of four women writers to be considered here, was concerned more with a *cultural* than *political* emancipation; and many of her ideas appear not to be very different from the much more apparently conservative Hannah More.[918] Even so, we should not unduly soften the force of her appeal on behalf of women: as one of her characters enquires, 'was not the world a vast prison, and women born slaves?'[919]

Sarah Trimmer (1741–1810) was born in Ipswich, married at the age of 21 and had twelve children.[920] She was, as one author puts it, 'determinedly, even aggressively attached to the Church of England'.[921] She wrote a number of works in addition to *The oeconomy of charity* (1787), which was explicitly addressed to ladies 'with a particular view to the cultivation of religious principles, among the lower orders of people'. We should not sneer: Mrs Trimmer was a formidably active person long before the welfare state made such individual compassion less necessary. She also wrote a *Sacred history, selected from the scriptures* (1782–4) in six volumes; and *The history of the robins, for the instruction of children on the treatment of animals* (1786).

Anna Letitia Barbauld (1743–1825) was born of a prominent Dissenting family: she married a Protestant clergyman, Rochemont (or Rougemont) Barbauld (in 1774), who was mentally unstable and eventually committed suicide. Having no children of their own, they adopted one; and her *Hymns in prose for children* (perhaps her most famous work) reflects her lifelong love of children. In 1785 they settled in Hampstead, where Rochemont became pastor to a small Dissenting congregation; and in 1802 they moved to Newington Green where he took up a similar appointment. He died in 1808; but she lived on to the age of 82. As well as some writings for children, Anna Barbauld wrote an *Epistle to William Wilberforce* in 1791 (she was strongly opposed to slavery[922]), *Reasons for national penitence* in 1794, and a six-volume edition of Samuel Richardson's correspondence together with a biographical account.[923] Her extant work reflects someone with a good sense of humour as well as considerable intellectual ability and strength of personality.[924]

Hannah More (1745–1833) was for our purposes perhaps the most important of the four. The fourth of five daughters of a schoolmaster (all of whom were apparently lively and intelligent), she was born in Stapleton, north of Bristol: she seems to have longed to follow her father and be a teacher all her life; and in 1766 she and her sisters established a school in Bristol.[925] Education (both for children and moral education for adults) remained her overriding concern;[926] and she is most famous as one of the key figure in the foundation of Sunday Schools.[927] She never married but was intensely sociable: she was a regular guest at the Blue Stocking Club in London; and David Garrick, Joshua Reynolds, Samuel Johnson, and Horace Walpole were among her many friends.[928]

More was very active in social work among the poor, and was closely associated with the Evangelical Clapham Sect: John Newton was an important influence on her life and work.[929] She was no campaigner for women's rights (she told Horace Walpole that 'so many women are fond of government, I suppose, because they are not fit for it'[930]). She produced a series of *Repository Tracts* aimed at poorer people: these sold in enormous quantities, and propounded a basically conservative philosophy, though one that was frequently critical of the rich; and More, like Barbauld, was fiercely opposed to the slave trade.[931] She once described herself as 'most sincerely attached to the Establishment . . . not . . . from prejudice, but from a fixed and settled conviction at once affectionate and rational'.[932] She wrote poems, plays, sacred dramas, essays, educational works, and (for our purposes most significantly) *Practical piety; or, the influence of the religion of the heart on the conduct of the life* (1811): this was designed for a broad lay audience, but perhaps especially for women.[933] She became a national figure: Coleridge praised her as 'indisputably the *first* literary female, I ever met with – In part, no doubt, because she is a Christian'.[934] Horace Walpole praised her 'sweet piety',[935] and went so far as to call her 'a bishop *ex partibus infidelium*'.[936]

Hannah More had little time for 'enthusiasm', declaring it to be 'an evil to which the more religious of the lower classes are peculiarly exposed'.[937] At the same time she has little time either for 'an enlightened philosophy' which drains Christianity of its vitals, causing her to remark sadly that

> There is so little of the Author of Christianity left in his own religion, that an apprehensive believer is ready to exclaim, with the woman at the sepulchre, 'They have taken away my Lord, and I know not where they have laid him'.[938]

And, in 'The history of Mr Fantom' (one of her *Stories for persons of the middle ranks*) the eponymous philosopher is criticised by Mr Trueman:

> Well, Mr Fantom, you are a wonderful man to keep up such a stock of benevolence at so small an expense. To love mankind so dearly, and yet avoid all opportunities of doing them good; to have such a noble zeal for the millions, and to feel so little compassion for the units; to long to free empires and enlighten kingdoms, and yet deny instruction to your own village, and comfort to your own family. Surely none but a philosopher could indulge so much philanthropy and so much frugality at the same time.[939]

In fact, however, More's attitude to enthusiasm was more nuanced than this early work might suggest. In *Hints towards forming the character of a young princess* (1805) she begins her discussion on the subject by commenting that the 'holiness' and 'practical piety' encouraged by many since the Reformation had often become debased: but when, more recently,

> decency resumed her reign, and virtue was countenanced, and religion respected; yet mere decorum was too often substituted for religious energy.[940]

She goes on to point out that, in such a context, 'enthusiasm' is used as a football: it can and should be opposed if it implies irrationality, but is often opposed simply by those who seek an undemanding religion.[941] She criticizes Addison's definition of enthusiasm as 'a kind of excess in devotion', asking whether there can be such a thing as an excess in devotion or religion, in the proper sense of these terms:[942] she suggests a definition of the latter two words in terms of the Prayer Book collect:

What is religion, or devotion . . . but the 'so loving what God has commanded, and desiring what he has promised, as that, among the sundry
and manifold changes of the world, our hearts may surely there be fixed,
where true joys are to be found?' [943]

And what God has commanded is the love of God and neighbour.[944] More is usually
regarded as conservative; but her 'Christmas Hymn' has a vigorous message for the
wealthy:

> Come, ye rich, survey the stable
> Where your infant Saviour lies
> From your full o'erflowing table
> Send the hungry good supplies.[945]

The problem comes when this is no longer the aim of religion:

if, instead of cultivating and advancing in this love of God and man, –
instead of loving what God has really commanded, and desiring what he
has clearly promised in his holy word, – this word be neglected, and the
suggestions of an ardent or of a gloomy fancy be substituted in its room,
then the person becomes, in the strictest and truest sense, a fanatic.[946]

She therefore concludes that both enthusiasm and superstition are the result, not of an
excess of devotion or religion, but of 'a radical misconception of religion':

Each alike implies a compound of ignorance and passion; and as the
person is disposed to hope or fear, he becomes enthusiastical on the one
hand, or superstitious on the other.[947]

What both lack is *judgement*.[948] 'it is absolutely impossible for an intelligent votary of
scriptural Christianity to be in any respect fanatical':[949] for More, the Roman church
sank into superstition because it neglected the scriptures. The problem is that other
terms too can be abused: thus 'candour' can come to mean 'a latitudinarian indifference
as to the comparative merits of all religious systems'.[950] Her central argument is that

He . . . who studies the scriptures, and draws from thence his ideas and sentiments of religion, takes the best method to escape both enthusiasm and
superstition . . . In a word, Christianity is eternal truth, and they who soar
above truth, as well as they who sink below it, equally overlook the
standard by which rational action is to be regulated; whereas, to adhere
steadily to this, is to avoid all extremes, and escape, not only the tendency
toward pernicious excess, but any danger of falling into it.[951]

Like Samuel Johnson, Hannah More sought determinedly to cling to a mid-point
between various extremes, and yet not to succumb to a toothless piety that would
neither offend nor change anyone. There is a true and a false zeal: the former must
include love of neighbour; the latter is what, in her view, led St Dominic to institute
the Inquisition. Yet true zeal remains indispensable: 'he whose piety is most sincere
will be likely to be the most zealous'.[952]

Mary Wollstonecraft adopts a slightly different approach. She effectively presents the eponymous heroine in *Mary* as a 'dear enthusiastic creature'.[953] She speaks of the characters in the story being 'lost in a pleasing enthusiasm', which allows them to 'live in the scenes they represent' and not to be restricted by convention or dull reality.[954] Thus Mary herself, the principal character in this story, is described in her youth as being actuated by 'enthusiastic sentiments of devotion':

> her Creator was almost apparent to her senses in his works; but they were mostly the grand or solemn features of Nature which she delighted to contemplate.[955]

Mary 'thought that only an infinite being could fill the human soul', though passion and affection would later lead her to forget this.[956] But her capacity to sense the spiritual realities in life, both the transcendent in nature and the beauty in human beings who suffer, is quite incomprehensible to her materialist father:

> this was a language he did not understand, expressive of occult qualities he never thought of, as they could not be seen or felt.[957]

It is worth noting here Wollstonecraft's contrast between the spiritual person and the narrowly material one – precisely St Paul's contrast between 'flesh' and 'spirit'. So 'enthusiasm' for Wollstonecraft represents a capacity to be attuned to spiritual realities of every kind, from harmless daydreaming fantasies to enduring spiritual truths. At the very end of her life 'an enthusiastic devotion' overcomes the dictates of Mary's despair.[958] Wollstonecraft is aware that enthusiasm of this kind can be easily misdirected: in *Maria*, her principal character concludes that enthusiasm, when

> turned adrift, like some rich stream overflowing its banks, rushes forward with destructive velocity inspiring a sublime concentration of thought.[959]

Anna Barbauld is if anything even more interesting on the subject of enthusiasm and philosophy. In *Thoughts on the devotional taste*, she cites an earlier writer in arguing that religion may be considered not only as *truth* and *habit*, but also

> as a taste, an affair of sentiment and feeling, and in this sense it is properly called devotion. Its seat is in the imagination and the passions, and it has its source in that relish for the sublime, the vast, and the beautiful, by which we taste the charms of poetry and other compositions that address our finer feelings; rendered more lively and interesting by a sense of gratitude for personal benefits.[960]

This aesthetic approach is an important dimension of women's piety in the eighteenth century: it is not all robust moralism. Barbauld condemns contemporary criticism of 'sentiment': 'it is the character of the present age to allow little to sentiment, and all the warm and generous emotions are treated as romantic by the supercilious brow of a cold-hearted philosophy'.[961] She continues

> Yet there is a devotion, generous, liberal, and humane, the child of more exalted feelings than base minds can enter into, which assimilates man to

higher natures, and lifts him 'above this visible diurnal sphere.' Its pleasures are ultimate, and, when early cultivated, continue vivid even in that
uncomfortable season of life when some of the passions are extinct, when
imagination is dead, and the heart begins to contract within itself. Those
who want this taste, want a sense, a part of their nature, and should not
presume to judge of feelings to which they must ever be strangers.[962]

This is not at all to regard philosophy as inimical to religion: rather it is to distinguish between 'the spirit of inquiry' and 'the spirit of disputation'.[963] Philosophy is a
vital dimension of religion: the trouble is that it 'represents the Deity in too abstracted
a manner to engage our affections . . . We require some common nature, or at least the
appearance of it, on which to build our intercourse.'[964] Thus

> the philosopher offers up general praises on the altar of universal nature;
> the devout man, on the altar of his heart, presents his own sighs, his own
> thanksgivings, his own earnest desires: the former worship is more
> sublime, the latter more personal and affecting.[965]

Hence too 'a prayer strictly philosophical must ever be a cold and dry composition'.[966]
True, prayer must find space for wonder, but scripture argues that it must also find
space for feelings: 'In our creeds let us be guarded; let us there weigh every syllable; but
in compositions addressed to the heart, let us give freer scope to the language of the
affections, and the overflowing of a warm and generous disposition.'[967] The fact that
devotion can run into superstition is no justification for avoiding it altogether.[968]

If all these writers have a common theme, it is a concern to foster a 'practical piety'
that is translated into action. In her novella *Mary*, Wollstonecraft criticizes the conventional piety of the person who 'had a good opinion of her own merit – truly, she
said long prayers' but was in reality 'a gentle, fashionable girl, with a kind of indolence
in her temper, which might be termed negative nature'.[969] Later the principal character

> visited several convents, and found that solitude only eradicates some
> passions, to give strength to others; the most baneful ones. She saw that
> religion does not consist in ceremonies; and that many prayers may fall
> from the lips without purifying the heart.[970]

She touches the heart of the matter when she goes on to note that 'it is the office of
Religion to reconcile us to the seemingly hard dispensations of providence' and to
remind us both that virtue should be an active principle, 'and that the most desirable
station, is the one that exercises our faculties, refines our affections, and enables us to
be useful'.[971] This notion of religion as centred on an internal principle is also the heart
of Hannah More's *Practical piety*:

> Genuine religion demands not merely an external profession of our alle-
> giance to God, but an inward devotedness of ourselves to his service. It is
> not a recognition, but a dedication. It puts the Christian into a new state of
> things, a new condition of being . . . The happiness of a Christian does not
> consist in mere feelings which may deceive, nor in frames which can only

be occasional; but in a settled, calm conviction that God and eternal things have the predominance in his heart.[972]

More defines 'practical Christianity' as 'the actual operation of Christian principles';[973] and her piety is rooted in the practical challenge of doing good. 'It is by our conformity to Christ, that we must prove ourselves Christians,' says one of her characters in *Stories for persons in the middle ranks*, going on to cite Jesus's parable of the sheep and the goats as his proof text for a religion founded upon doing good.[974] She insisted that 'reformation must begin with the GREAT, or it will never be effectual':[975] it is no good expecting the poor to observe Sundays when they see the rich disporting themselves.[976] And even the most radical male freethinker will want his wife to be religious for the same reason as Voltaire wanted his butler to be devout: both are more likely to be trustworthy.[977]

Practical piety, then, involves active concern for the poor. Sarah Trimmer expresses in stronger language than More the failure of Christians to achieve this:

> This is the manner in which Christians have long lived together in this divided country, instead of maintaining, as the Divine Author of our Religion enjoins, a mutual interchange of good offices – instead of striving with one heart and one soul to advance the Glory of God, promote the interest of the whole body, and spread the belief and practice of Christianity through the land! It really is a scandal to the nation, to see such numbers of the common people in extreme indigence, while the plenty and riches of the land, enable the higher ranks to indulge in all the conveniencies and luxuries of life. Every Parish is a large family, and it behoves the heads of it to see that each individual in it, has food and raiment, or the means of procuring them at least; and that provision is made for their instruction in such things as concern their temporal and spiritual interests.[978]

At the same time, piety of this kind offers no insurance against personal suffering. In *Stories for persons of the middle ranks*, More has another character declare

> 'I do not see . . . that your religion has been of any use to you. It has been so far from preserving you from trouble, that I think you have had more than the usual share.' 'No,' [replies the other], 'nor did Christianity ever pretend to exempt its followers from trouble; this is no part of the promise. Nay, the contrary is rather stipulated; "in the world ye shall have tribulation." But if it has not taught me to escape sorrow, I humbly hope it has taught me how to bear it.'[979]

At the heart of 'practical piety' is the home, and the religion practised within it. Sarah Trimmer acknowledges that 'many people are deterred from an attempt to introduce the practice of *Family Religion*, from the fear of being censured for *Hypocrisy* or *Fanaticism*'.[980] Nonetheless she goes on to insist that it

> is a duty incumbent upon heads of families to collect the members of their households daily; to join together with one heart and one voice, in offering

up petitions, intercessions, and thanksgivings to the Giver of all good things; and the fear of being ranked with enthusiasts should not be suffered to operate to the neglect of it. Household blessings are promised only to those who keep up religion in their families – not to those who are ashamed to pay homage to the *universal Lord*.[981]

The emphasis on a piety practised *de haut en bas* is evident here too, as it is in Trimmer's and More's teaching on Sunday observance. Hannah More is unimpressed by the argument that attendance at Sunday concerts is morally acceptable if the texts be scriptural and the music be by 'the divine Handel':

> I am persuaded that the very hallelujahs of heaven would make no moral music to the ears of a conscientious person, while he reflected that multitudes of servants are, through his means, waiting in the street, exposed to every temptation; engaged perhaps in profane swearing, and idle if not dissolute conversation; and the very cattle are deprived of that rest which the tender mercy of God was graciously pleased, by an astonishing condescension, to include in the [fourth] commandment.[982]

And Sarah Trimmer argues that it is neglect of the sabbath by families that leads to 'domestic evil'.[983] Servants should not be allowed to devote Sundays to their own devices; they should be encouraged to be cheerful, but kept away from cards and novels.[984]

One other aspect of 'practical piety' deserves notice here: the emphasis on toleration, on judging religious beliefs by their fruits. More stresses religious intolerance as explicitly hindering a growth in piety:

> Every man who is sincerely in earnest to advance the interests of religion, will have acquired such a degree of candour, as to become indifferent by whom good is done, or who has the reputation of doing it, provided it be actually done.[985]

This strikingly modern-sounding statement does not, however, lead her to devalue religious beliefs altogether. Elsewhere she notes that 'the strong and generous bias in favour of universal toleration, noble as the principle is, has engendered a dangerous notion, that all error is innocent'.[986] And she firmly emphasizes the theological basis of holiness.[987] Even so, it underlines the crucial importance, for all these women, of a piety that is incarnated in active love and service of neighbour, rather than one measured only (or even primarily) by doctrinal orthodoxy.

It is, therefore, unsurprising to find that prayer is understood in terms that are rooted in practical and physical situations. Hannah More describes prayer as

> the application of want to him who only can relieve it; the voice of sin to him who alone can pardon it. It is the urgency of poverty, the prostration of humility, the fervency of penitence, the confidence of trust. It is not eloquence, but earnestness, not the definition of helplessness, but the feeling of it; not figures of speech, but compunction of soul. It is the 'Lord, save us, we perish' of drowning Peter; the cry of faith to the ear of mercy.[988]

For More, 'prayer is desire . . . an elevation of the soul towards its Maker'. It is 'not an emotion produced in the senses, nor an effect wrought by the imagination; but a determination of the will, an effusion of the heart', an act of both the understanding and the heart:

> It would not be *reasonable* service, if the mind was excluded. It must be rational worship, or the human worshipper would not bring to the service the distinguishing faculty of his nature, which is reason. It must be spiritual worship or it would want the distinctive quality to make it acceptable to Him who is a spirit.[989]

Prayer is supremely petition: 'we do not pray to inform God of our wants, but to express our sense of the wants which he already knows'.[990] We ask with penitence and humility; but we are still right to ask. More argues against an utterly disinterested, quietist-type prayer that asks nothing of God: 'to disconnect our interests from his goodness, is at once to detract from his perfections, and to obscure the brightness of our own hopes'.[991] Indeed 'we . . . acknowledge his liberality most when we request the highest favours'.[992] Thus

> there is a simple, solid, pious strain of prayer in which the supplicant is so filled and occupied with a sense of his own dependence, and of the importance of the things for which he asks, and so persuaded of the power and grace of God through Christ to give him those things, that while he is engaged in it, he does not merely imagine, but feels assured that God is nigh to him as a reconciled father, so that every burden and doubt are taken off from his mind. 'He knows,' as St John expresses it, 'that he has the petitions he desired of God,' and feels the truth of that promise, 'while they are yet speaking I will hear.' This is the perfection of prayer.[993]

True prayer, then, elicits assurance: theologically, this is what Hannah More means when she says elsewhere that sanctification and redemption are inseparably linked.[994] But 'the *act* of prayer is not sufficient, we must cultivate a *spirit* of prayer'.[995] More's whole point is that prayer and the practice of the virtues are inseparable: 'Prayer is designed for a perpetual renovation of the motives to virtue.'[996] Hence there should be a harmony between our prayers and our practice; 'for the beauty of the Christian scheme consists not in parts . . . which tend to separate views, and lead to different ends; but arises from its being one entire, uniform, connected plan'.[997] Hence

> The design of Prayer . . . is not merely to make us devout while we are engaged in it, but that its odour may be diffused through all the intermediate spaces of the day, enter into all its occupations, duties, and tempers.[998]

For the truth is that 'it is not easy, rather it is not possible, to graft genuine devotion on a life of an opposite tendency'.[999] Thus

> we should . . . endeavour to believe as we pray, to think as we pray, to feel as we pray, and to act as we pray . . . Prayer must not be a solitary, independent exercise; but an exercise interwoven with many, and inseparably

connected with that golden chain of Christian duties, of which, when so connected, it forms one of the most important links.[1000]

And the more we persevere, the more prayer will become a pleasure rather than simply a duty.[1001] The more you do it, the better you become.

In her early work *An estimate of the religion of the fashionable world*, Hannah More celebrates the high quality of Anglican liturgy in her day:

> Perhaps there has not been, since the age of the apostles, a church upon earth in which the public worship was so solemn, and so cheerful; so simple, yet so sublime; so full of fervour, at the same time so free from enthusiasm; so rich in the gold of Christian antiquity, yet so astonishingly exempt from its dross.[1002]

It is a fascinating remark: in part, this is because it celebrates the beauty of worship in an age which many think saw the Church of England in indolent decline, awaiting the spiritual renaissance to be introduced by the Oxford Movement in the following century. But it is also fascinating because it sets out precisely More's yardstick for holding fast to that middle ground which she advocated so single-mindedly: between enthusiasm and philosophy, between piety and philanthropy, between solemnity and joy. It is clear from this extract that More did not see this as anything new: the 'gold of Christian antiquity' was being mined, with energy but also with discrimination.

Hannah More is that rare specimen, a full-blooded Anglican; and she, Trimmer and Barbauld, albeit of different traditions, all espoused a piety that really could change people's lives. Charles Wesley would have been impressed:

> Women we own the foremost still
> Where stated prayer is made to'appear,
> They first the place of worship fill,
> They first the joyful tidings hear,
> The welcome messengers receive,
> And patterns to the faithful live.[1003]

The risk here was of a narrow moralism; but it was a risk of which they were sharply aware.[1004] And they were even more aware of the perils involved in a religion that failed to practise what it preached. In More's play *Percy*, Elwina hears that the king has conquered on a crusade to the Holy Land; when her father exclaims 'It is religion's cause, the cause of heav'n!', she responds:

> When policy assumes religion's name,
> And wears the sanctimonious garb of faith,
> Only to colour fraud and license murder,
> War then is tenfold guilt . . .
> 'Tis not the crosier, nor the pontiff's robe,
> Nor outward show, or form of sanctity,
> Nor Palestine destroy'd, nor Jordan's banks
> Delug'd with blood of slaughter'd infidels,
> No, nor th'extinction of the Eastern world,

Nor all the wild, pernicious, bigot rage
Of mad crusades, can bribe that Pow'r, who sees
The motive with the act. O, blind to think
Fanatic wars can please the Prince of peace!
He who erects his altar in the heart,
Abhors the sacrifice of human blood,
And hates the false devotion of that zeal
Which massacres the world he died to save.[1005]

CONCLUSION: THE BRIDGE AT SALTASH

In his monumental *Tour through the whole island of Great Britain* (1724–6), Daniel Defoe recalled crossing the 'very wide' Tamar river by ferry from Plymouth, and arriving at Saltash: 'a little poor shattered town'. He recalled a local tale told by the antiquarian writer Richard Carew:

> Mr Carew tells us a strange story of a dog in this town, of whom it was observed, that if they gave him any large bone, or piece of meat, he immediately went out of doors with it, and after having disappeared for some time, would return again, upon which after some time they watched him, when to their great surprise they found that the poor charitable creature carried what he so got to an old decrepit mastiff, which lay in a nest that he had made among the brakes a little way out of the town, and was blind; so that he could not help himself, and there this creature fed him. He adds, also, that on Sundays, or holidays, when he found they made good cheer in the house, where he lived, he would go out, and bring this old blind dog to the door, and feed him there till he had enough, and then go with him back to his habitation in the country again, and see him safe in.[1006]

Defoe, as we have seen, was no stranger either to poverty or to the spirit of charity; and he tells this story, with its hint of sabbatarian piety, in a manner as characteristic of the eighteenth century as are many other features of Saltash: the houses in Fore Street Hill, or the classical Town Hall of 1780 with its Tuscan columns, or the monuments to naval officers drowned at sea in 1798–9 in the parish church.[1007]

But if Defoe had lived to visit Saltash a century later, he would have encountered a wonder far greater that the compassionate dog: Brunel's bridge, vaulting over the 1,100-foot-wide Tamar and bringing the broad gauge railway into Cornwall. Like Defoe, Isambard Kingdom Brunel was a practical man; but, living a century later, he was to go much further than Defoe had done in limiting the action of divine providence in response to our prayers.[1008] This is what he wrote to his son:

> I am not prepared to say that the prayers of individuals can be separately and individually granted, that would seem to be incompatible with the regular movements of the mechanism of the Universe, and it would seem impossible to explain why prayer should now be granted, now refused; but

this I can assure you, that I have ever, in my difficulties, prayed fervently, and that – in the end – my prayers have been, or have *appeared* to me to be, granted, and I have received great comfort.[1009]

The gulf that separates Brunel's scientific approach to prayer from Defoe's is as striking as that which separates the design of his great bridge from the architecture of the little town nestling immediately beneath it. Poor Brunel was dying when Prince Albert came to Saltash, on 3 May 1859, to open the bridge that still bears his name; and the great engineer saw his completed bridge only once. But even then, as he lay on a specially prepared platform truck, while a steam locomotive drew him slowly beneath the pier arches and over the huge girders, he was looking out on a world vastly different from that which Defoe had seen when he travelled by ferry over the Tamar.[1010] The wonders of the eighteenth century that Defoe described – the elegant classicism, the sweeping landscapes, the foreign sights, the stories of canine (or even human) compassion – would be as nothing to those of the Industrial Revolution. And yet the latter, no less than the former, was born of the desire to make a better world.[1011] The enthusiasts and philosophers of the eighteenth century sought to find ways to fashion a piety suited to a rapidly changing society; and the legacy they bequeathed was no less enduring than that of Brunel's bridge, and perhaps scarcely less beneficial for those who came after them.

NOTES

1. Vol. 9 (1739) p. 256. The writer could be Joseph Trapp, whose sermons against 'enthusiasm' Dr Samuel Johnson popularized by abridging them for the magazine in 1739 (pp. 288–92). Was it Johnson himself? Unlikely: it is not listed by Boswell among the contributions Johnson himself wrote during that year: Boswell, *Life of Johnson* chapter 6, p. 40.
2. Letter to Hannah More, 22 September 1788, *Correspondence* vol. 31, p. 284.
3. Sermon 38, vol. 2, p. 280.
4. 'Of eloquence', in *The Bee* 7 (Saturday 17 November 1759), in *Miscellaneous works,* pp. 402–3.
5. p. 403. Cf. the remark of the French materialist Baron d'Holbach in 1767: 'Religion is the art of making men drunk with enthusiasm, to prevent them thinking about the oppressions committed by their rulers' (*Le Christianisme dévoilé,* quoted in Owen Chadwick, *The secularization of the European mind in the nineteenth century* (Cambridge UP, 1975) p. 49).
6. Letter of 6 August 1780, *Letters and prose writings* vol. 1, p. 375.
7. See the harrowing thirteenth chapter ('No Nation Has Plunged So Deeply into This Guilt As Great Britain') of Hugh Thomas' *The slave trade* (Basingstoke: Macmillan, 1997; repr. with corrections 1998) pp. 237–61).
8. Brewer (1997, p. 493) points out that during the century England became the most rapidly urbanizing part of Europe, provincial towns growing even more quickly than did London, whose population increased from 490,000 in 1700 to about 675,000 in 1750.
9. *Retirement* ll. 481–2, in *Poems,* p. 299.
10. *Retirement* ll. 515–26, in *Poems,* p. 300. Brighton was the fastest growing town in late Georgian England: Brewer (1997) pp. 493–4.
11. *The task* I, ll. 697–9 and 749, in *Poems,* pp. 323–4.
12. Ackroyd (1996) p. 85.

13. Defoe, *The complete English tradesman* 48, in *Works* vol. 18, p. 217: a survey of 1739 records 551 coffee houses, 207 inns and 447 taverns in London alone; see Brewer (1997) p. 35.

14. For the importance of choice in relation to spirituality see, e.g., William Law, *The case of religion*, in *Works* vol. 2, p. 137.

15. Sermon 52, in *Works* vol. 1, p. 569.

16. Hence the success of Methodism among the rootless urban classes rather than with more stable rural society: see the good summary in Jacob (1996) pp. 1–19.

17. For the religious societies in general see Duffy (1977), Rupp (1986) pp. 327–30, and Jacob (1996) pp. 77–92; for the SPCK, see Lowther Clarke (1944), Ward (1992) pp. 302–7, and Craig Rose ('The origins and ideals of the SPCK 1699–1716') in Walsh (1993) pp. 172–90.

18. This emphasis was in many ways conservative, seeking to minimize the risk of a violent underclass and keep the lower classes in their place: see Rose (1972) pp. 57–65.

19. See below, on Defoe; and the works of writers like Johnson, Sterne and Coleridge (for whom on this subject see Holmes (1989) pp. 10 and 60). In general, see Brewer (1997) pp. 631–8.

20. I am most grateful to Alison Corden for pointing this out.

21. Brewer (1997) pp. 167–90.

22. See Jacob (1996) pp. 107–9 and Brewer (1997) chapter 3.

23. See Brewer (1997), esp. pp. 624 and 654.

24. For this see Brewer (1997) pp. 514–18.

25. One of Edward Gibbon's characteristics was his *encyclopaedic* range of interests: thus he discusses the history of trowsers [sic] (*Decline and fall* chapter 11, vol. 1, p. 321 n. 79); and other interests reflected in the *Decline and fall* range from honey, gunpowder, whales, etymology of paradise, the prevalence of arthritis in seventh-century Constantinople (chapter 46, vol. 2, p. 901 n. 45), the difference between the camel and the dromedary (chapter 46, vol. 2, p. 911 n. 66), the effects of tarantula-bites on human propensity to break wind (chapter 56, vol. 3, p. 493 n. 55), and the history of windmills (chapter 61, vol. 3, p. 726 n. 65).

26. Brewer (1997, p. 527) points out that in Bewick's work the animals become moral exemplars, and nature has a freedom and 'natural law' written into it which is far superior to the shackles of aristocracy and church.

27. See Brewer (1997) p. 625. At the beginning of the century as much as 70% of land was already enclosed: but the process increased rapidly during the century – between 1750 and 1830 a further 21% was enclosed.

28. Voltaire was impressed with England as a centre of freethought because of the passing in 1727 of the first of the indemnity acts, relieving non-Anglicans of many of their civil disabilities; see Besterman (1970) p. 110.

29. Voltaire, *Letters concerning the English nation*, 1733 edn, pp. 44–5; quoted in Besterman (1970) p. 119. Addison saw the Royal Exchange as reflecting the new Anglocentric internationalism achieved by world trade (essay of 1711, repr. in J. Gross (ed.), *The Oxford book of essays* (Oxford UP, 1991) pp. 43–6.

30. For Locke's letter (or rather four letters dating from 1689 to 1704), see Mark Goldie, 'John Locke, Jonas Proast and religious toleration 1688–1692', in Walsh (1993) pp. 143–71; Young (1998) pp. 24–8; and Rivers (2000) chapter 1, esp. p. 10.

31. *Hints towards forming the character* 34, in *Works* vol. 4, p. 328.

32. Horace Walpole believed both to be equally useless: 'extremes meet: enthusiasm and philosophy are those extremes', Letter to Lady Ossory, 10 September 1792 (*Letters* vol. 34, p. 161; cf. his letter to the same person of 16 July 1793, vol. 34, p. 182).

33. See Sugden, ed. cit. of Wesley's *Sermons*, vol. 2, p. 86, for Plato's understanding of the word, which seems to have influenced its meaning in English during the seventeenth century. For its use during that period see also Anne Coppins, *Religious enthusiasm from Robert Browne to George Fox: a study of its meaning and the reactions against it in the seventeenth century* (Oxford University DPhil thesis, 1983); and Heyd (1995).

34. 'Let us enquire now whether the Spirit beareth witness that we are the Children of God, and enables us to cry Abba, Father, by the direct Act, or by that which they call the Reflect Act of Faith;

for we must not think that it is done by an Enthusiasm, without any ordinary means; nor can we reasonably imagine, that no true Believers can call God Father, by the Guidance of the Spirit, but only those few that are so sure of their own Sincerity' (Marshall, *The gospel-mystery of sanctification* (London: T. Parkhurst, 1692) p. 185).

35. For this subject, see esp. Young (1998), and Roy Porter, 'The Enlightenment in England', in R. Porter and M. Teich (eds), *The Enlightenment in national context* (Cambridge UP, 1981) pp. 1–18. It is worth noting that William Cowper uses the term 'enlightened' to refer to England on the grounds that it enjoys the blessings of evangelical religion (Letter of 8 March 1784, *Letters and prose writings* vol. 2, p. 222; cf. 'an enlighten'd Minister of the Gospel', Letter of 11 April 1784, vol. 2, p. 234).

36. Young (1998) pp. 61–2.

37. For the influence of Boehme on Isaac Newton, see Byrom's *Remains* vol. 2, p. 364 and n. 2. Hoyles (1972) shrewdly points out the way in which spiritual writers like Law sought (and looked for allies to help them) to distinguish 'Light and Enlightenment, real and nominal Christianity' (p. 111), and as a result identified 'enthusiasm' or divine illumination as the fulfilment of human nature, not some aberrant form of it (p. 123).

38. See Rupp (1986) p. 260.

39. Nikolaus Pevsner (revised by Bridget Cherry), *Wiltshire* (Buildings of England) (Harmondsworth: Penguin, 1975) p. 401.

40. For the importance of imitation in this period, see the remarks of Edmund Burke: 'it is by imitation far more than by precept, that we learn every thing; and what we learn thus, we acquire not only more effectually, but more pleasantly. This forms our manners, our opinions, our lives. It is one of the strongest links of society' (*Of the sublime and beautiful* 1.16, in *Works* vol. 1, p. 147).

41. Wesley, *Journal* vol. 21, pp. 2–3, 16 February 1755, in which a devout Christian and his son alone survive an accident. Wesley comments: 'Doth not God save those that trust in him?' See also vol. 21, pp. 13–16, where God works an earthquake.

42. Sterne, Sermon 8, vol. 1, pp. 131–2; cf. Sermon 12, vol. 1, p. 204. In Sermon 8 he goes on to argue that
    if a superior intelligent Power did not sometimes cross and overrule events in this world, – then our policies and designs in it would always answer according to the wisdom and stratagem in which they were laid, and every cause, in the course of things, would produce its natural effect without variation. Now as this is not the case, it necessarily follows . . . that there is some other cause which mingles itself in human affairs, and governs and turns them as it pleases; which cause can be no other than the First Cause of all things, and the secret and overruling providence of . . . Almighty God.

43. Hume, *Dialogues concerning natural religion* IV, pp. 406–7.

44. p. 430.

45. XI, p. 452; and see pp. 434ff.

46. p. 463.

47. Hume, *Of suicide,* p. 408.

48. For this subject, see David Womersley's excellent introduction to the ed. cit. of Gibbon's *Decline and fall*; also F. E. Manuel, 'Edward Gibbon: *Historien-philosophe*', in Bowersock et al. (1977), esp. p. 167; and Burrow (1985), esp. pp. 17 and 22. Robert Shackleton ('The impact of French literature on Gibbon', in Bowersock et al. (1977) p. 216) argues that, of all contemporary French writers, Montesquieu exerted the greatest influence on Gibbon. In one of his celebrated footnotes, he reprimands Voltaire, saying that 'the prejudice of a philosopher is less excusable than that of a Jesuit', chapter 58, vol. 3, p. 583 n. 65. Cf. also chapter 67, vol. 3, pp. 916–17 n. 13, where he calls Voltaire 'an intolerant bigot'.

49. Gibbon, *Index expurgatorius*, in Craddock (1972) p. 117.

50. *A vindication*, vol. 3, p. 1169 (and cf. 1182). In one of his last works, *An Address &c* (1793), Gibbon speaks of tracing the history of England 'from the lowest ebb of primitive barbarism to the full tide of modern civilization' (in Craddock (1972) p. 534) – he clearly regarded his present age as the best yet, and his own country as arguably the best in the world ('the only powerful and

wealthy state, which has ever possessed the inestimable secret of uniting the benefits of order with the blessings of freedom', p. 535).

51. *Memoirs of my life and writings*, p. 19.

52. See *Decline and fall* chapter 31, vol. 2, p. 207, where Gibbon criticizes the 'strong propensity' within human nature 'to depreciate the advantages, and to magnify the evils, of the present times' (cf. chapter 2, vol. 1, p. 82). The question whether Gibbon believed in progress is controverted: he appears unambiguously to adopt the notion of progress, arguing that 'every age of the world has increased, and still increases, the real wealth, the happiness, the knowledge, and perhaps the virtue, of the human race' ('General Observations on the Fall of the Roman Empire in the West', *Decline and fall* vol. 2, p. 516; but note that J. G. A. Pocock ('Between Machiavelli and Hume: Gibbon as civic humanist and philosophical historian', in Bowersock et al. (1977) p. 105) argues that Gibbon did *not* believe in progress, sharing the Enlightenment's basically static, sceptical view of human nature. For other views, see S. R. Graubard ('*Contraria sunt complementa*', in Bowersock et al. (1977) p. 135; and Burrow (1985) p. 19.

53. Sermon 15, vol. 1, p. 245. He went on to point out that too many of the classical philosophers spoke too much from the head rather than from the heart. 'And therefore however subtle and ingenious their arguments might appear in the reading, 'tis to be feared they lost much of their efficacy, when tried in the application' (pp. 245–6).

54. *Holy living* 2.6.

55. Burrow (1985, pp. 18–19) points out that the learned classical scholarship of the antiquarian *érudits* was under suspicion in the eighteenth century, with the rise of the new 'natural philosophy' exemplified by Newton's mathematics ('natural philosophy' in this period denotes what we mean by 'science': see Laurence Sterne, Sermon 20, vol. 1, p. 331). For Voltaire, who produced in 1764 a *Dictionnaire philosophique*, 'philosophy' meant something like 'freethought' or 'rationalism': seeking the truth about any given subject (see Besterman (1970) pp. 433–9).

56. Gibbon, review of Hurd on Horace, in Craddock (1972) p. 40.

57. 'Critical observations on the design of the sixth book of the Æneid', in Craddock (1972) p. 152.

58. *Decline and fall* chapter 70, vol. 3, p. 1045 n. 65.

59. *A vindication* vol. 3, p. 1157.

60. *Decline and fall* chapter 2, vol. 1, p. 56. It is worth noting Gibbon's unexpected interest in Genghis Khan as a model of religious tolerance (*Decline and fall* chapter 64, vol. 3, p. 793, and n. 6, where Gibbon compares Genghis' religious policy favourably with that of Locke). Note too Owen Chadwick's point ('Gibbon and the church historians', in Bowersock et al. (1977) p. 228) that toleration as a principle remained very insecure in the eighteenth century, far less secure than later generations were to assume.

61. Gibbon makes this point explicitly in *Decline and fall* chapter 10, vol. 1, p. 291.

62. On the connection between the two, note Gibbon's approving citation of the wise observation of the Byzantine emperor John Vataces: 'a prince and a philosopher are the two most eminent characters of human society' (chapter 62, vol. 3, p. 738).

63. *Decline and fall* chapter 22, vol. 1, p. 851.

64. *Decline and fall* chapter 23, vol. 1, p. 873.

65. *Memoirs of my life and writing* (ed. cit. pp. 156–7), though elsewhere in the *Memoirs* he acknowledges 'the first sallies of my enthusiasm' which at one point led him seriously to consider a military career (ed. cit. p. 106; cf. also p. 164: 'My judgment, as well as my enthusiasm, was satisfied with the glorious theme [for a projected history of Switzerland]').

66. *Decline and fall* chapter 16, vol. 1, p. 519. Cf. Richard Payne Knight (*An analytical inquiry into the principles of taste* (1805) 3.1, p. 366): 'The superstitious man sees, in his God, a severe and relentless judge; before whom he shrinks and trembles: the enthusiast sees a beneficent patron and protector; by whose favour he is preserved and exalted: the one images himself the object of perpetual anger, which it is the business of his life to avert or propitiate: the other conceives himself to be the object of special love and regard; the exhilarating idea of which expands and invigorates every faculty of his soul, and causes him to mistake its improved energies for supernatural inspirations.'

67. Cf. *Decline and fall* chapter 33, vol. 2, p. 283, where Gibbon, writing of the loss of Africa to the Vandals, concludes that 'the intolerant spirit, which disgraced the triumph of Christianity, contributed to the loss of the most important province of the West'.

68. *Decline and fall* chapter 40, vol. 2, pp. 597–8 and 599–600.

69. Gibbon is uncertain whether to describe Mohammed as an enthusiast or an impostor, noting that the step between the two is 'perilous and slippery' (*Decline and fall* chapter 50, vol. 3, pp. 212–13; cf. chapter 68, vol. 3, p. 964). He concludes that the mature Mohammed may well secretly have 'smiled . . . at the enthusiasm of his youth' (chapter 50, vol. 3, p. 214).

70. See *Decline and fall* chapter 37, vol. 2, p. 411: 'the Ascetics, who obeyed and abused the rigid precepts of the gospel, were inspired by the savage enthusiasm, which represents man as a criminal, and God as a tyrant'. He condemns the early Christian preachers who 'exalted the perfection of monastic virtue, which is painful to the individual and useless to mankind' (chapter 20, vol. 1, p. 763). He disapproves of St Bernard's indifference to worldly beauty, saying that before anyone is tempted to follow him, he or she, 'like myself, should have before the windows of his library the beauties of that incomparable landskip [of Lausanne]' (chapter 59, vol. 3, p. 625 n. 30). He says that Athanasius' 'expressions have an uncommon energy; and as he was writing to Monks, there could not be any occasion for him to *affect* a rational language' (chapter 21, vol. 1, p. 775 n. 32). He often speaks of monks in 'swarms' (chapter 27, vol. 2, p. 55) or 'swarming' ('on his return to Greece, [Barlaam, Petrarch's assistant] rashly provoked the swarms of fanatic monks, by attempting to substitute the light of reason to that of their navel', chapter 66, vol. 3, p. 898), or even 'vermin' (*Outlines of the history of the world*, in Craddock (1972) p. 181). (Coleridge notes the etymological point that the German word for fanaticism (*Schwärmerei*) is derived from the swarming of bees; see *Biographia literaria* 2, in *Works* vol. 7/1, p. 30 and n. 4).

    In one footnote Gibbon writes:

    I have somewhere heard or read the frank confession of a Benedictine abbot: 'My vow of poverty has given me an hundred thousand crowns a year; my vow of obedience has raised me to the rank of a sovereign prince.' – I forget the consequences of his vow of chastity (chapter 37, vol. 2, p. 424 n. 57).

    His most vigorous diatribe against the monastic and ascetic life appears in chapter 37 (vol. 2, p. 426), where he declares that those called to it

    aspired to reduce themselves to the rude and miserable state in which the human brute is scarcely distinguished above his kindred animals: and a numerous sect of Anachorets derived their name from their humble practice of grazing in the fields of Mesopotamia with the common herd (chapter 37, vol. 2, p. 426).

71. 'Never did the flame of enthusiasm burn with fiercer and more destructive rage' (*Decline and fall* chapter 59, vol. 3, p. 639). Louis IX's vow to embark on the sixth crusade 'was the result of enthusiasm and sickness' (chapter 59, vol. 3, p. 649).

72. Byrom, Letter in shorthand to Phoebe Byrom, 18 February 1729, cited in Talon (1950) p. 105.

73. 'Charity' ll. 337–44, in *Poems*, vol. 1, p. 345. Cf. *The task* II, ll. 161–5 and 174–8, p. 329. Cf. also *The task* III, ll. 221–4, pp. 349–50; and V, ll. 779ff.: 'Acquaint thyself with God, if thou woldst taste/ His works', pp. 401–2.

74. Letter of 6 October 1783 (to John Newton), in *Letters and prose writings* vol. 2, pp. 167–8.

75. *The vicar of Wakefield*, p. 183.

76. p. 96.

77. Notably by the contributors to Walsh (1993), and by Jacob (1996); but see also the wide-ranging survey in Rupp (1986) and Yates (1991) p. 55. It is interested how pervasive was the assumption that the eighteenth century was a period of decline: writing in 1905, an Anglican priest, Charles Bodington, unequivocally declares that 'the Church of God in England was in evil case in the eighteenth century . . . The history of her devotional life and work in the eighteenth century is a sad and depressing one' (*Devotional life in the nineteenth century* (London: SPCK, 1905) p. 26).

78. Jacob (1996, p. 12) argues that 'most people, or at least representatives of most households, went to church' in the eighteenth century; though he later acknowledges that the evidence for this is mostly circumstantial (p. 54). Rupp suggests that a slow decline in attendance probably

continued throughout the century: absentees tended to be from the poorer classes (1986, p. 510).

79. For this subject see Jacob (1996), esp. pp. 93–123.

80. Cited in *The Anglican canons 1529–1947*, ed. G. Bray (Woodbridge: Boydell, 1998) pp. 831–2.

81. Thus in 1809 there were 11,194 incumbents in the Church of England; of these, 7,358 were non-resident (L. W. Cowie, *Hanoverian England* (London: Bell, 1967) p. 71). See also Walsh (1993), esp. pp. 7–9. Bishop Gilbert Burnet of Salisbury produced his *Discourse of the pastoral care* in 1682 with the aim of improving the low standards of clerical behaviour and education; but twenty years later, writing the preface to the third edition of his *Discourse* in his seventieth year, Burnet looks out with sorrow on a state of affairs that was if anything getting worse: those seeking ordination were ignorant of even the 'plainest parts of the Scriptures', defending themselves by saying that their university tutors never taught these to them (Preface to the 3rd edn, *Discourse of the pastoral care*, pp. xxxix–xli). Nonetheless William Jones can boast, in 1803, of having spent only three Sundays out of his parish (Broxbourne, Herts) in over twenty-two years' ministry there (*Diary*, p. 154).

82. Cowper, article in the *Gentleman's Magazine*, September 1758 (repr. in *Letters and prose writings* vol. 5, pp. 31–2).

83. Goldsmith, *The deserted village*, in *Miscellaneous works*, p. 584.

84. The key figure in the origins of the Sunday Schools was Robert Raikes (1735–1811): see Rupp (1986) p. 526.

85. The Church did not, however, always succeed in building new, or restoring old, churches where they were most needed: in towns and cities. See Walsh (1993) p. 10.

86. For this see Barnard (1988): he argues (p. 201 and n. 68) that, whereas the Church of England in the late seventeenth and early eighteenth centuries was 'a natural home of learning', interest in historical study waned after c.1730. See also Jacob (1996). It is noteworthy that Gilbert Burnet, as a Protestant, commends to clergy the study not only of scripture but of patristic authors like Basil and John Chrysostom (*A discourse* 8, p. 184) and of classical authors ('the Greek and Roman authors have a spirit in them, a force both of thought and expression, that later ages have not been able to imitate', p. 185). Elizabeth Elstob (b.1683) was a considerable Anglo-Saxon scholar (see Gill (1994) p. 43).

87. These movements were often fluid and overlapping rather than sharply distinct: see the essays in Walsh (1993).

88. See Rupp (1986) pp. 33–5; Rack (1992), esp. pp. 25 and 29; Walsh and Taylor's article 'The Church and Anglicanism in the "long" eighteenth century' in Walsh (1993) pp. 1–66, esp. pp. 35–43; and M. Fitzpatrick ('Latitudinarianism at the parting of the ways: a suggestion') in Walsh (1993) pp. 209–27.

89. Rupp (1986) p. 55. The term came into use during the last decades of the seventeenth century (p. 53). See also G. W. O. Addleshaw, *The High Church tradition* (1941), and P. B. Nockles, *The Oxford Movement in context* (Cambridge UP, 1994).

90. See Mark Goldie's vivid portrayal of Jonas Proast for an exemplification of this (in Walsh (1993) pp. 145–8).

91. For Law, see below. For Ken, see esp. the excellent study by Hoyles (1972).

92. For Gilbert see Mark Goldie ('Locke, Proast and religious toleration') in Walsh (1993), pp. 143–71; and Young (1998) pp. 28–9; for Elizabeth see Clare Kirchberger, 'Elizabeth Burnet', in *Church Quarterly Review* 168 (1949). She was first married to Robert Berkeley (d.1693) and after seven years as a widow married Gilbert.

93. Walpole, *Memoirs of King George II* vol. 1, p. 98. For Butler's thought in its context, see Rivers (2000).

94. His interest in French Catholicism is reflected in his writings (see e.g. his description of a French Ursuline sister making her life profession, in a letter to Edward Byrom (Montpellier, 1718) (Talon (1950) p. 435; *Remains* vol. 1, pp. 37–8).

95. Talon (1950) p. 11. Talon goes on to say (p. 12) that Byrom's 'religion mainly assumed the form of sedate conformity to the Established Church'.

96. Journal entry for 18 February 1739, in *Remains* vol. 2, p. 237.

97. For Byrom see, as well as Talon (1950), Hobhouse (1927), Hoyles (1972) and Davie (1993) pp. 11–25. For his famous hymn 'Christians awake!' see Talon (1950) pp. 296–7 and Davie (1993) p. 16. Byrom purchased William Law's *Serious call* in 1729 (Byrom, *Remains* vol. 1, p. 327), and was widely read in the writings of near-contemporary spiritual and quietist authors like Antoinette Bourignon, Madame Guyon, François Fénelon and Pascal, as well as in the works of Boehme, Pseudo-Dionysius, Suso, Tauler, and Ruusbroec. References to Bourignon recur frequently in Byrom's work; and at one point (*Remains* vol. 2, p. 230) he admits that she was 'my favourite'; see also the letter Byrom received from his friend Mr Garden (*Remains* vol. 1, pp. 519–20), and the short poem Byrom wrote about Bourignon to his wife Phoebe (*Poems* vol. 3, p. 66). For Byrom on Guyon, see esp. *Remains* vol. 1, p. 557, vol. 2, pp. 112 and 302; for Fénelon, see esp. *Remains* vol. 2, p. 49 and vol. 2, p. 279; for Pascal, see *Remains* vol. 2, p. 96. This interest led Bishop William Warburton to describe Byrom as 'certainly a man of genius, plunged deep into the rankest fanaticism' (letter cited in notes to Byrom, *Remains* vol. 2, p. 522, n. 1).

98. The sermons were published in 1760, 1766, and posthumously in 1769. Some contemporaries thought them better described as essays, designed to amuse, than as sermons (see the Revd William Jones' *Diary*, ed. cit. pp. 20–1).

99. *The analogy of religion* 1.2, p. 108. Later in the same work he acknowledges that 'religion is supposed peculiarly liable to enthusiasm', but (in his view) no more than any other aspect of life (2.7, p. 283).

100. Letter to John Byrom, 12 December 1751, in Byrom, *Remains* vol. 2, p. 524. Both Warburton and Byrom agree that 'enthusiasm' extends to matters other than religion, 'seeing that it extends itself throughout the whole commerce of life' (Byrom, letter to Warburton, 22 February 1752, in *Remains* vol. 2, p. 527). Warburton distinguishes an innocent from a harmful enthusiasm: 'the first of which is chiefly employed in drawing pictures from the imagination; the other, in advancing opinions as the result of the judgment' (letter to Byrom, 3 April 1752, in *Remains* vol. 2, p. 533; cf. Byrom's reply, pp. 537 and 541).

101. *Poems* vol. 2/1, p. 169.

102. 'Enthusiasm: a poetical essay', in *Poems* vol. 2/1, pp. 190 and 193. The reference to the Spirit as 'an Immediate Guide' appears in other contemporary Anglican writers (see, e.g., Ken, 'Christophil', in *Poems* vol. 1, p. 427.

103. *The analogy of religion*, Introd., p. 75.

104. See *Analogy* 1: Conclusion, p. 187.

105. *Analogy* 2.6, p. 271. For the importance of revelation, see *Analogy* 2.1, p. 201.

106. 2.1, pp. 202–3.

107. *Hymns and spiritual songs* 4, p. 38.

108. *Hymns and spiritual songs* 14, p. 60.

109. *Analogy* 1.5, p. 141; 1: Conclusion, p. 190.

110. p. 145; cf. 2.5, p. 238.

111. 2.3, pp. 219–20.

112. Sermon 1, vol. 1, p. 14.

113. p. 16.

114. *Remains* vol. 2, p. 303. For the use of tree imagery to denote organic growth and ordered change in this period, see Tim Fulford, 'Wordsworth, Cowper and the language of eighteenth-century politics', in T. Woodman (ed.), *Early Romantics: perspectives in British poetry from Pope to Wordsworth* (Basingstoke: Macmillan, 1998), pp. 117–33.

115. See esp. Byrom's poem *The soul's tendency towards its true centre*, in *Poems* vol. 2/2, pp. 421–2. For Sterne, the essential principles of the Christian religion – above all, compassion for others – are rooted in our souls in virtue of our creation in God's image: 'as little appearance as there is of religion in the world, there is a great deal of its influence felt in its affairs – nor can one so root out the principles of it, but like nature they will return again, and give checks and interruptions to guilty pursuits' (Sermon 7, vol. 1, p. 124; cf. Sermon 10, vol. 1, p. 162).

116. *A sermon preached at Whitehall, 1685*, in *The prose works*, p. 83.

117. *An exposition of the church catechism*, in *The prose works*, p. 118.

118. p. 175.

119. Butler, Sermon 14, On the Love of God, in *Fifteen Sermons,* pp. 522–3.

120. Butler, Sermon 14, On the Love of God, in *Fifteen Sermons,* pp. 525–7.

121. See, among many references, Dr Cheyne's letter to Byrom in August 1742, in which he refers to '*Taulerus, Johannes à Cruce, Bernier, Bertôt* and *M. Guyon,* and all the most approved ancient and modern interior Christians called mystics' (*Remains* vol. 2, p. 330).

122. E.g., in 'Christophil', references to Jesus coming to the believer so that 'we two only fill the Cell', vol. 1, p. 430) – the whole of this 'Meditation on Jesus' (vol. 1, pp. 428–31) could have been written by a medieval monastic writer. Note Ken's reference to 'devout retreats', on Christ being 'solitary, not alone' (vol. 1, p. 435); and other references here to cell, closet (vol. 1, p. 436), as well as

> May I midst Objects foul or vain,
> Internal Solitude retain;
> And like the Angels, who here ply,
>   Keep Heav'n in eye
> (vol. 1, p. 438; cf. pp. 482 and 522).

123. 'On the Annunciation' (in *Poems* vol. 1, p. 20). He goes so far as to suggest that Gabriel, 'fearing to interrupt her Pray'r', waits 'Till her return from Heav'n her Height abates' (p. 21)! Later in the same poem he describes her as exceeding all other human beings 'in Glory, as in Grace' (p. 22). In *The Christian year* he describes Mary as praying seven times daily in accordance with Psalm 119, and being able to recite the entire Psalter from memory before she was fourteen (p. 59; see also p. 64). Later Ken describes her as far excelling all others (Hymn for Lent III, p. 101), comparing her heart (the ark of Jesus) to the Shekinah or presence of God (pp. 102–3). More generally, Mary appears prominently in many of his other hymns (notably of course that for the Annunciation, pp. 345–51).

124. Sermon 10, vol. 1, p. 165; cf. also Sermon 4, p. 54; Sermon 14, p. 228.

125. Sermon 10, vol. 1, pp. 168–70.

126. *Hymns and spiritual songs* 17, in *Poetical works* vol. 2, p. 67.

127. Turner regularly read Tillotson's sermons (p. 65), and works like Allestree's *The whole duty of man* (p. 137), and owned a large number of books (see Vaizey's Appendix D to ed. cit. of the *Diary,* pp. 347–53.

128. Turner, *Diary,* Saturday 11 January 1755, p. 4.

129. See e.g. p. 32.

130. *A method of devotion,* p. 233; and see her encouragement for Christians to reflect seriously on their baptismal vows on working weekdays, pp. 292–305.

131. Cowper, *Adelphi* (in *Letters and prose writings* 1.17).

132. Frontispiece, 1771 edition.

133. 'Now tho' Christ hath brought greater light into the world, yet he never meant by it to put out any of that natural Light, which God hath set up in our Souls' (*The whole duty of man,* Sunday 1, p. 2).

134. *The whole duty of man,* Sunday 5, p. 107.

135. *The whole duty of man,* Sunday 14, pp. 294–5. Cf. Sunday 16, p. 339: the vengeful person who prays '*Forgive us our trespasses, as we forgive them that trespass against us* . . . shall be forgiven just as he forgives, that is, not at all'.

136. *The whole duty of man,* Sunday 16, p. 324. Cf. Sunday 17, pp. 350–1, where the author underlines the scriptural teaching that almsgiving, as a voluntary sacrifice, is an integral part of worship.

137. *Hymns and spiritual songs,* in *The poetical works* vol. 2, p. 73 (from the Hymn to St Peter).

138. *Serious advice,* p. iv.

139. *Serious advice,* p. 26.

140. *Serious advice,* pp. 29 and 31.

141. *Serious advice,* pp. 34 and 39–44.

142. Sterne, Sermon 43 (On worship), vol. 2, p. 340.

143. pp. 341–2.

144. p. 344.

145. p. 345.

146. Sermon 5, vol. 1, p. 78.

147. Sermon 6, pp. 106–7 (on the Pharisee and the Publican).

148. Letter 77 (1746), in *The early letters*, pp. 162–4.

149. *A sermon preached at Whitehall, 1685*, in *The prose works*, p. 83.

150. *Directions for prayer for the diocese of Bath and Wells*, in *The prose works*, p. 201; cf. also p. 194. William Cowper, writing in 1756, notes that 'the good old practice of psalm-singing is . . . wonderfully improved in many country churches' (article in *The Connoisseur* 134, 19 August 1756, in *Letters and prose writings* vol. 5, p. 20).

151. Hymn 1, 'New Year', in *Hymns and spiritual songs*, p. 34.

152. 'Christophil', in *Poems* vol. 1, p. 427.

153. Byrom, Letter to Ralph Leycester (1730), quoted in Talon (1950) p. 123. Byrom was striking in the breadth of his sympathies: as well as Roman Catholic worship in France, he attended Quakers' and Anabaptists' worship in London (*Journal*, 18 April 1725, in *Remains* vol. 1, p. 120).

154. See the nuanced discussion in Walsh (1966).

155. Hindmarsh (1996, p. 1) points out that Newton only rarely used the term 'evangelical', preferring the term 'Gospel' (usually capitalized thus) with similar meaning. For the Evangelical Revival's European and American manifestations, see Watts (1978), Ward (1992), and Rack (1992) pp. 158–80.

156. See Podmore (1998), esp. pp. 5–28; Rupp (1986) pp. 330–8; Ward (1992) pp. 116–59.

157. See above, p. 4 and Rack (1992) p. 162.

158. See Ward (1992) pp. 241–95.

159. See Bebbington (1989), esp. pp. 48 and 50–63.

160. Whitefield, *Journals,* ed. Murray, p. 37. For a brief summary of his life, see Watts (1978) pp. 398–9.

161. For a vivid account of the electrifying effect of his preaching, see Southey, *Life of Wesley*, vol. 1, pp. 126–7; for a description of Whitefield himself, see p. 126. For the influence of continental, esp. Moravian, piety on Whitefield, see Ward (1992) pp. 314–16.

162. 'I am, and profess myself, a member of the Church of England,' wrote Whitefield firmly in 1739 (*Journals*, ed. Murray, p. 249). For Whitefield's close but uneasy relationship with the English Moravians, see Podmore (1998) pp. 80–96.

163. For Cowper's life, see Baird's and Ryskamp's introduction to *Poems* vol. 1, and his own (posthumously published) autobiographical narrative *Adelphi*. His proneness to mental illness began when he was still at school: see *Adelphi* (in *Letters and prose writings* vol. 1, pp. 6 and 8). In 1792 he wrote of 'a disorder of mind that unfitted me for all society' which had afflicted him nearly thirty years earlier (*Letters and prose writings* vol. 4, p. 51).

164. See the description of the death of Cowper's patron Morley Unwin in Cowper's letters of 1767 (*Letters and prose writings* vol. 1, pp. 169–76).

165. For Cowper's contemplation of suicide, see below. Cowper's reflections during his long periods of depression suggest that he identified himself with Job (see, e.g., his letter to Samuel Teedon, 25 January 1793, on p. 279; to the same writer, 16 May 1793, on p. 338, and esp. to the same writer, 13 September 1793: 'the night is become so habitually a season of dread to me, that I never lie down on my bed with comfort, and am in this respect a greater sufferer than Job', p. 396).

166. *Authentic narrative* 2, p. 4.

167. For an excellent account of his life and thought, see Hindmarsh (1996).

168. For the diary see Hindmarsh (1996) pp. 221–2. Among his letters are the important collection *Cardiphonia, or, the utterance of the heart* (1780).

169. For the circumstances surrounding *The Olney hymns*, see Hindmarsh (1996) pp. 258–62; for Newton as hymn writer see esp. pp. 268–9 and 279–80; for the hymns themselves see Watson (1997) pp. 282–99.

170. entitled 'Light shining out of darkness'; in *Olney hymns* 3:15–42, pp. 262–87.

171. *Olney Hymns* 3:43–58, pp. 287–300.

172. Cowper, *Poems*, vol. 1 p. 195; *Olney hymns* 3:62, p. 303; for this stress on childlikeness, see also

Newton's 'The child', in *Olney hymns* 3:65, p. 305. 'Dedication and surrender' comprises *Olney hymns* 3:59–67, pp. 300–7.

173. *Olney hymns* 3:68–79, pp. 307–17; and 3:80–8, pp. 317–24.

174. Bebbington (1989, p. 12) notes the relatively low value attached to learning by many Evangelicals.

175. See Cowper, Letters of 14 August 1782, in *Letters and prose writings* vol. 2, p. 73; also 27 October 1782, p. 84, and 3 August 1783, p. 153 (cf. vol. 2 pp. 70 and 157–8). In a letter of 21 June 1789 he describes her as 'a woman of a most heavenly mind and of very uncommon talents, but there is, sometimes, in her spiritual effusions a strain of familiarity, and sometimes of aenigmatical obscurity, which would render most of her compositions useless at least, if not disgusting, to the generality of her readers' (*Letters and prose writings* vol. 3, p. 300). For Newton's intellectual sources, see Hindmarsh (1996), esp. pp 238 and 332–6. Newton pays generous though not uncritical tribute to Baxter ('one of the greatest men of his age', *Letters to the Rev. Mr. P—* 4, in *Cardiphonia*, p. 206) and calls John Owen's Exposition of Psalm 130 'one of the closest and most moving addresses to sinners I ever met with' (*Letters to Mr. —* 3, in *Cardiphonia*, p. 238). He praises Owen, together with Robert Leighton, in *Letters to the Rev. Mr. B—* 3, in *Cardiphonia*, p. 256).

176. For Okely see Walsh (1975) and Young (1998) pp 158ff.; for his Moravian connection, see Podmore (1998) pp. 107 and 287–9. He produced an English version of von Franckenberg's *Memoirs of the life . . . of Jacob Behmen* in 1780.

177. See G. Lawton, *Shropshire saint: a study in the ministry and spirituality of Fletcher of Madeley* (London: Epworth, 1960); Whaling, introduction to *John and Charles Wesley: selected writings and hymns*, pp. 40–2; Hirst (1964) pp. 263–5.

178. *Life of Wesley*, vol. 2, p. 239; cf. also p. 397.

179. Wesley, *Life of John Fletcher* 3.6, in *Works* vol. 11, p. 342. Wesley's *Life* appeared in 1786: Cowper described it as 'that valuable little tract on the life and death of the excellent Mr Fletcher' (Letter of 21 June 1789, in *Letters and prose writings* vol. 3, p. 299). See also Schmidt (1962–73) vol. 2/2, pp. 108–10.

180. *Messiah* 45, ed. cit. p. 796. Cf. Cowper (Letter of 12 July 1765, in *Letters and prose writings* vol. 1, p. 105), acknowledging that his recently renewed faith 'is called enthusiasm by many, but they forget this passage in St Paul, "We are saved by grace through faith . . . "'

181. Bebbington (1989, pp. 2–3) suggests four central emphases in Evangelicalism: on the need for conversion, on the authority of the Bible, on an active concern to live by the Gospel, and on the centrality of the Cross.

182. *Authentic narrative* 7, p. 17.

183. *Authentic narrative* 8, p. 19. Cf. Cowper's reflection, in a letter to Newton during a period of deep depression in 1793: 'prayer, I know, is made for me, and sometimes with great enlargement of heart by those who offer it; and in this circumstance consists the only evidence I can find that God is still favourably mindful of me and has not cast me off for ever' (*Letters and prose writings* vol. 4, p. 325).

184. *Authentic narrative* 9, p. 21.

185. Wesley, *Life of John Fletcher* 2.4–5, in *Works* vol. 11, p. 336.

186. See *Twenty-six letters to a nobleman* 1, in *Cardiphonia*, p. 129; cf. *Letters to Mr. B—* 5, in *Cardiphonia*, p. 192; *Letters to Mrs. G—* 1, in *Cardiphonia* p. 211; *Messiah* 8, p. 673.

187. *Twenty-six letters to a nobleman* 1, in *Cardiphonia*, p. 129.

188. p. 130; cf. *Letters to Mrs. G—* 1, in *Cardiphonia* p. 211, where Newton says the Christian is 'not of hasty growth, like a mushroom, but rather like the oak, the progress of which is hardly perceptible, but which in time becomes a great deep-rooted tree'; cf. *Letters to the Rev. Mr. B—* 3, in *Cardiphonia*, p. 303.

189. p. 130.

190. *Twenty-six letters to a nobleman* 2, in *Cardiphonia* p. 131.

191. *Letters to the Rev. Mr. S—* 8, in *Cardiphonia*, p. 186.

192. *Letters to the Rev. Mr. S—* 8, in *Cardiphonia*, p. 186.

193. Later versions read 'Thus they march, the pillar leading'.

194. Later versions read 'Daily on the manna feeding'.

195. Psalm 87.3. Newton adapts his own first two lines elsewhere: 'Glorious things are spoken of the city of God, or (as I suppose) the state of glory, in Rev. xxi. from verse 10 *ad finem*' (*Twenty-six letters to a nobleman* 3, in *Cardiphonia*, p. 132).

196. *Letters to the Rev. Mr. R—* 6, in *Cardiphonia*, p. 263.

197. *Messiah* 11, p. 682. For an excellent introduction to the way in which Evangelicals approached scripture, see David K. Gillett, *Trust and obey: explorations in Evangelical spirituality* (London: DLT, 1993), pp. 129–57.

198. Toplady's 'Rock of ages, cleft for me' was first published in *The Gospel Magazine* for October 1775 and appeared again, slightly altered, in his *Psalms and hymns* of 1776. In Newton's case the phrase may well allude to Isaiah 33.16 (i.e. just before the stated text): 'He shall dwell on high: his place of defence shall be the munitions of rocks: bread shall be given him; his waters shall be sure.' (KJV) The notion of the Lord as Rock is of course very common in the Psalms (e.g. Psalm 62, where 'rock' and 'salvation' are twice combined in reference to the Lord). Newton frequently refers to the rock from which water flowed: see, e.g., *Olney hymns* 1:128, pp. 140–1. He refers to the Rock of Ages in *Twenty-six letters to a nobleman* 14, in *Cardiphonia*, p. 146 (and cf. Hannah More's 'the Rock of Ages is my friend' (*Here and there*, in *Works* vol. 6, p. 45).

199. 2:30–6.

200. *The book of creation*, in *Olney hymns* 2:81, p. 227.

201. See, e.g., Cowper's famous hymn 'Light shining out of darkness' or 'God moves in a mysterious way', *Poems* vol. 1 p. 175, *Olney hymns* 3:15, pp. 262–3, whose fourth verse runs:

> Judge not the Lord by feeble sense,
> But trust him for his Grace;
> Behind a frowning Providence,
> He hides a Smiling face.

The assurance here is all the more striking since this hymn was almost certainly written when Cowper was approaching or entering his mental collapse of 1773 (Baird and Ryskamp (eds), *Poems* vol. 1, p. 484). Cowper expressed his 'firm persuasion of the superintendence of Providence over all our concerns' in a letter of 4 September 1765 (*Letters and prose writings* vol. 1, p. 114). Later in his life, however, this view led him to conceive of God much as Job had: as an inscrutable and omnipotent sovereign from whose wrath there was no escape: see further below, and note 165 above.

202. See especially Cowper's fine *Olney hymn* (1:64, p. 80; *Poems* vol. 1, p. 148):

> The LORD will happiness divine
> On contrite hearts bestow:
> Then tell me, gracious GOD, is mine
> A contrite heart, or no?
>
> I hear, but seem to hear in vain,
> Insensible as steel;
> If ought is felt, 'tis only pain,
> To find I cannot feel.
>
> I sometimes think myself inclin'd
> To love thee, if I could;
> But often feel another mind,
> Averse to all that's good.
>
> My best desires are faint and few,
> I fain would strive for more;
> But when I cry, 'My strength renew,'
> Seem weaker than before.

Thy saints are comforted I know
And love thy house of pray'r;
I therefore go where others go,
But find no comfort there.

O make this heart rejoice, or ach [sic];
Decide this doubt for me;
And if it be not broken, break,
And heal it, if it be.

203. For Newton on this subject see, e.g., *Olney hymns* 2:79, p. 226; *Letters on religious subjects* 14, p. 68; *Messiah* 28, p. 739. Whitefield records in his diary that God 'gave me great boldness of speech' in preaching (*Journals*, ed. Murray, 1739, p. 221).

204. *Olney hymns* 1:41, pp. 58–9.

205. *Twenty-six letters to a nobleman* 3, in *Cardiphonia,* p. 132.

206. p. 132; see also 5, p. 134.

207. *Letters on religious subjects* 10, p. 58. Cf. 'As grace prevails, self is renounced' (*Twenty-six letters to a nobleman* 7, in *Cardiphonia,* p. 138).

208. Newton, *Olney hymns* 1:37, p. 55; cf. 'Saviour, shine, and cheer my soul', *Olney hymns* 1:44, pp. 61–2; and the comments of Hindmarsh (1996) p. 275.

209. The imagery here is from Exodus 13.20–1: cf. Newton's 'Supplies in the wilderness' (*Olney hymns* 2:58, pp. 206–7). The reference to a 'covering' is from Psalm 105.39 ('He spread a cloud for a covering: and fire to give light in the night').

210. See the moving letter from Cowper to Newton (19 February 1788, in *Letters and prose writings* vol. 3, pp. 105–7) in which Cowper wrestles with the theological implications of the slave trade. See also Cowper's 'Sonnet to William Wilberforce Esq.', ll. 1–4, in *Poems* p. 159; his passionate attack on slavery at the beginning of Book II of *The task* (in *Poems,* pp. 325–6). On the general subject of exile and homecoming, Adey (1988, p. 27) notes the prominence of exile and home-coming in the *Olney hymns,* not least in 'Amazing grace'. See also Cowper's 'R.S.S.' ll. 16–17, in *Poems* vol. 1, p. 42; 'Hope, like the short-lived ray', ll. 29–32, in *Poems* vol. 1, p. 41, which reflects Cowper's agony at being forbidden to marry his cousin Theadora; 'Doom'd as I am, in solitude to waste', ll. 15–18, in *Poems* vol. 1, p. 62; and 'On a mischievous bull', v. 4, in *Poems* vol. 1, p. 127; cf. Newton's 'The waiting soul', v. 6, *Olney hymns* 3:10, p. 259, a hymn wrongly attributed to Cowper in some editions. 'Human frailty' vv. 5–6, in *Poems* vol. 1, p. 407; 'The castaway', in *Poems,* pp. 175–7; and 'Retirement' ll. 767–70, where Cowper cites David 'driv'n out an exile from the face of Saul', *Poems* vol. 1, p. 397.

211. Wesley, *Life of John Fletcher* 9.10, in *Works* vol. 11, p. 404. See also Newton, *Olney hymns* 1:81, pp. 94–5, in which Newton insists that all Christians approach God like beggars approaching passers-by, except that God hears and responds when passers-by don't. In 'Death and war' (*Olney hymns* 2:5, pp. 159–60) Newton reflects on the terrible destructiveness of war. See also Cowper's 'For the poor' (*Poems* vol. 1 pp. 192–3, *Olney hymns* 3:57, p. 299), which ends 'Supply is sure while He is King,/You shall not be forgot.'

212. See, e.g., the large number of *Olney hymns* based on Gospel texts by comparison with those based on Pauline texts.

213. The text is Revelation 1.6 (KJV): 'And hath made us kings and priests unto God and his Father; to him be glory and dominion for ever and ever. Amen.' Cowper makes a similar point in 'The Christian', *Poems* vol. 1, p. 190, *Olney hymns* 3:50, p. 293. For Newton's stress on holding praise and repentance, 'miserere' and 'hallelujah' together, see his *Letters to Mr B—* 7, in *Cardiphonia,* p. 193. There is a powerful exposition of the role of Christ as high priest and intercessor, taking away our guilt and compensating for 'the poverty and narrowness of our prayers', in *Messiah* 47, p. 802.

214. Constantly Evangelicals sought to *appropriate* scripture for their own lives and experience: thus John Newton adapts John 9 ('one thing I know, that whereas I was blind, now I see') in 'Amazing grace' (see also *Diary 1751–6,* 9 August 1752, and Hindmarsh (1996) p. 43).

215. *New English hymnal* has replaced the original wording here but omits vv. 3–4, as do most modern hymnbooks. *Mission praise* and the *Redemption hymnal* both have the original 'if' instead of

'since'. Newton had little interest in ecclesiology if understood in terms of the visible church; but 'the conviction that believers shared in an invisible, transhistorical church was at the centre' of Evangelical self-understanding (Hindmarsh (1996) p. 329). The replacement in some modern hymnals of Newton's 'worldling' with 'world's best' is feeble: 'worldling' also appears in Newton's *Olney* hymn 1:69, p. 84; *Olney* hymn 1:102 ('The worldling'), p. 115, where the worldling is the rich fool of Luke 12.6–21, giving the term a rich scriptural association; and see also *Olney hymns* 1:105, p. 118, and 2:47, p. 197: 'They would not change their gospel-bread/For all the worldling's store'. *Olney hymns* 3:3 ('We were once as you are') includes a reference to 'the worldling's treasure' (p. 250).

216. ' . . . your whole hearts shall seek the LORD,/I'll put a praying spirit there', 'The covenant' ('The Lord proclaims his grace abroad'), *Poems* vol. 1, p. 152, *Olney hymns* 1:71, p. 86), an affair of the heart (God 'is enthroned in heaven, but prayer will bring him down to the heart', Newton, *Letters to Miss M— B—* 8, in *Cardiphonia* p. 194).

217. See above, and also: 'Yet we must wait till he appear,/And pray, and pray again', Newton, 'The importunate widow' or 'Our Lord, who knows full well', *Olney hymns* 1:106, p. 119; *Letters to Mrs. P—* 1, in *Cardiphonia*, p. 248; cf. Newton, *Olney hymns* 1:122, p. 134: 'Fervent, persevering prayers/Are faith's assur'd resource'; cf. Newton, *Twenty-six letters to a nobleman* 4, in *Cardiphonia*, p. 133; also, *Olney hymns* 2:61, p. 209: 'Wrestling prayer can wonders do'; 2:64, p. 212 'Ye saints, unite in wrestling prayer', (from 'On the commencement of hostilities in America'); and 3:25, p. 271 'Why may I not wrestle and plead?' Newton frequently cites Moses raising his hands to enable Israel to defeat Amalek (Exodus 17.9; see, e.g., *Olney hymns* 2:66, p. 214). Cowper ('Prayer for patience', *Poems* vol. 1, pp. 183–4, *Olney hymns* 3:28, pp. 273–4) argues that this capacity to persevere and to wait on God is itself a gift.

218. *Twenty-six letters to a nobleman* 9, in *Cardiphonia*, p. 140.

219. Wesley, *Life of John Fletcher* 5.16, in *Works* vol. 11, p. 362.

220. *Letters to the Rev. Mr. —* 8, in *Cardiphonia* p. 246.

221. From 'Rejoice the soul of thy servant,' *Olney hymns* 3:25, p. 270. Cf. also his *Letters on religious subjects* 18, p. 77, where he warns against the dangers of 'social prayer' – i.e. shared prayer – being too long: 'long prayers should in general be avoided, especially where several persons are to pray successively'.

222. *Letters on religious subjects* 18, p. 77.

223. From 'More with us than with them', *Olney hymns* 1:40, p. 58.

224. *Letters on religious subjects* 18, pp. 77–8; for Newton on our nature as children, see also *Letters to Miss M— B—* 11, in *Cardiphonia,* p. 197.

225. *Letters to Miss F—* 1, in *Cardiphonia*, p. 215. He tells his Olney parishioners 'to pray for a simple, child-like temper' (*Olney sermons* 3, p. 356; cf. 4, p. 360). See also Newton's *Letters on religious subjects* 24, which is a reflection on the subject of communion with God in the light of our status as God's children; and 27, p. 95.

226. *Letters to the Rev. Mr. B—* 3, in *Cardiphonia* p. 303. Cf. *Olney sermons* 19, p. 410.

227. *Olney hymns* 1:93, p. 106.

228. Cowper's spiritual diary, June–July 1795, repr. in *Letters and prose writings* vol. 4, p. 467.

229. 'None who plead and wrestle thus/Shall be empty sent away', as Newton puts it (*Olney hymns* 1:88, p. 101). See also *Olney hymns* 1:46, pp. 63–4, where Newton paraphrases part of Psalm 73, reversing the order of the original so that the lament comes at the end rather than the beginning. Elsewhere Newton maintains that heaven will rectify the cruel unfairnesses of this life ('Dwelling in Mesech', or 'What a mournful life is mine', *Olney hymns* 1:51, pp. 67–8, based on Psalm 120.5–7). And he says, 'I think David never appears in a more lively frame of mind than when he wrote the 42d, 63d, and 84th Psalms, which were all penned in a dry land, and at a distance from the public ordinances' (*Letters to Mrs. —* 5, in *Cardiphonia*, p. 288). Cf. Whitefield: 'My bowels yearned towards [fellow Christians in Wales]; I wrestled with God in prayer for them' (*Journals*, ed. Murray (1739) p. 231, cf. p. 273).

230. Cowper, 'Exhortation to prayer' vv. 5–6, in *Poems* vol. 1, p. 169; *Olney hymns* 2:60, p. 208. Cf. Newton's exhortation to his parishioners to 'raise your hearts and breathe forth your complaints to him' (*Olney sermons* 10, p. 378).

231. *Life* 6.2, in *Works* vol. 11, p. 366.

232. *Life* 1.12, in *Works* vol. 11, pp. 332–3.

233. *Letters to the Rev. Mr. R—* 7, in *Cardiphonia*, p. 264; cf. *Letters to Mrs. —* 5, in *Cardiphonia*, p. 287.

234. *Letters to the Rev. Mr. S—* 7, in *Cardiphonia*, p. 181.

235. *Letters to the Rev. Mr. B—* 6, in *Cardiphonia*, p. 259; cf. many other passages, e.g. *Letters to Mrs. —* 4, in *Cardiphonia*, p. 285.

236. Hindmarsh (1996) p. 224. In addition he engaged in a number of annual devotional reflections involving looking back over his life: the twin focus on mercies and sins remained (p. 227). He used key annual occasions like New Year's Day, his and his wife's birthdays, their wedding anniversary, and the anniversary of the North Atlantic storm which signalled his return to God (p. 228).

237. See Whitefield's sermon 'A penitent heart' (1904 edn, Sermon 3, pp. 60–93).

238. *Letters to the Rev. Mr. S—* 3, in *Cardiphonia*, p. 175.

239. Cf. Newton, *Letters on religious subjects* 12, p. 62; *Twenty-six letters to a nobleman* 7, in *Cardiphonia*, p. 137; and his vivid application of Psalm 137 to his own contemporary ministry ('Hoping for a revival', *Olney hymns* 2:52, p. 202).

240. Fletcher is recorded by Wesley as declaring that 'our national depravity turns greatly on these two hinges, the profanation of the Lord's day, and the neglect of the education of children' (*Life of John Fletcher* 8.5, in *Works* vol. 11, p. 393). Newton warns of the serious neglect of 'family-prayer' (*Letters on religious subjects* 4, p. 43): 'it was Abraham's commendation, that he not only served the Lord himself, but was solicitous that his children and household might serve him likewise'. In his letter Newton resists excessive categorization, but says that 'family-prayer cannot be said to be stated, unless it be performed at least daily, and, when unavoidable hinderances [sic] do not prevent, twice a-day' (p. 44). It must be 'a spiritual service', not a formal exercise. He encourages husband and wife to pray together, each taking it in turns to pray for the other (p. 45).

    And Cowper speaks of

> Domestic happiness, thou only bliss
> Of Paradise that has surviv'd the fall!
> (*The task* III, ll. 41–2, in *Poems* p. 345).

241. Adey (1988, p. 28) makes this point well. But monasticism itself is not appealing to Evangelicals: 'we were not designed to be mere recluses, but have all a part to act in life' (Newton, *Letters to Miss D—* 4, in *Cardiphonia*, p. 295).

242. Letter of 18 June 1768, in *Letters and prose writings* vol. 1, p. 197.

243. 'The negro's complaint' v. 1, in *Poems*, pp. 111–12; also in *Letters and prose writings* vol. 3, pp. 146–8. On 5 April 1792 Cowper wrote to Lady Hesketh to say: 'The slave-trade is now at last, I hope, in a fair way to be abolish'd. This day's paper has brought us the news, and now I begin to feel some pride again at the thought that I am an Englishman' (*Letters and prose writings* vol. 4, p. 49).

244. See Chadwick (1981), esp. pp. 160–2 and 231–2. Ronald Knox (1950, p. 446), compares St Alphonsus with Wesley as combining incessant missionary and organizational activity with a vast literary output.

245. Eamon Duffy suggests that the mainstream of eighteenth-century English Catholic spirituality was an 'Anglicized Salesianism' (quoted in Rupp (1986) p. 193).

246. Duffy (1981) p. 7.

247. For Handel in London, see M. F. Bukofzer, *Music in the baroque era* (London: Dent, 1948) pp. 324–45. *Rinaldo* was first produced in London in 1711. Roubiliac, together with artists like Hogarth, could be found chatting in London coffee houses (Brewer (1997) p. 35). His life-size statue of Handel was unveiled in 1738 in the Vauxhall pleasure gardens (pp. 375–6); and two of his grandest funerary monuments can be seen in the parish church of Warkton, near Kettering in Northamptonshire.

248. Walpole, *Memoirs of George II* vol. 3, pp. 55–6; see also Rupp (1986) p. 185.

249. Berington, *The state and behaviour*, p. 111. Recent scholars like Bossy and Butler suggest a figure nearer 80,000 (Butler (1995) p. 11).

250. Between 1770 and 1850 the Catholic community in England multiplied tenfold (Bossy (1975) p. 298).

251. For the Lulworth experiment, see D. A. Bellenger, 'A standing miracle: La Trappe at Lulworth, 1794–1817', in W. J. Sheils (ed.), *Monks, hermits and the ascetic tradition* (Studies in Church history 22) (Blackwell, 1985), pp. 343–50.

252. For English monastic spirituality in the eighteenth century (at Douai and Paris, for Benedictines, and Nieuport, for Carthusians), see the excellent article by J. C. H. Aveling, 'The eighteenth-century English Benedictines', in Duffy (ed.) (1981) pp. 152–73. For the Trappists, see Alban J. Krailsheimer, 'Armand-Jean de Rancé: convert and reformer', in *Cistercian Studies* 1983:1 (pp. 24–41), 1984:1 (pp. 43–61), and 1985:1 (pp. 44–51).

253. Sermon 2, vol. 1, p. 19.

254. *Remains* vol. 1, pp. 37–8.

255. *The state and behaviour*, p. 126.

256. *The state and behaviour*, p. 162.

257. For Challoner see esp. Duffy (1981). There were of course no Catholic schools during this century: hence the concern with catechesis.

258. Butler (1995) p. 147; Duffy (1981) pp. 1–3. For Gother see also Bossy (1975).

259. Duffy (1981) p. 21. Luckett (1981, p. 81) says 'it is never safe to assume that any passage in Challoner is original'.

260. *Works* vol. 10, pp. 1–160. See also Bossy (1975) p. 131.

261. pp. 58–100.

262. *The garden of the soul*, p. 63.

263. *Afternoon instructions for Sundays, holy-days and other feasts*, in *Works* vol. 6, p. 45.

264. *Works* vol. 6, pp. 47–8.

265. p. 48.

266. *Works* vols. 4–5.

267. *Works* vol. 4, p. 23. Sabbas was a priest from Cappadocia who died in 531.

268. *Works* vol. 4, pp. 241–2.

269. See his *Garden of the soul*, pp. 31–58; *Meditations for every day in the year* (1754); and *Think well on't*.

270. Bossy (1975) pp. 367–8. Bossy argues that the increasing availability of Catholic worship made the recitation of corporate evening prayer, in families or households, less necessary (p. 369). It also led individual priests to produce their own devotional material for the use of congregations locally (pp. 370ff.).

271. Bossy (1975) p. 298.

272. Thus, e.g., the Litany in his *Garden of the soul* is entitled 'Evening devotions for families, or for Particulars' (p. 151).

273. *Garden of the soul*, pp. 3–10.

274. p. 9.

275. pp. 19–136.

276. 'Make a closet in your heart for *Jesus Christ*, invite him in thither, and there entertain him as well as you can: feast yourself with *Magdalen* at his feet, and make frequent aspirations of love to him', (p. 167).

277. pp. 208–9.

278. pp. 282–4.

279. *Think well on't*, p. 137.

280. *Meditations for every day in the year*, pp. 153 and 157.

281. Butler, *Meditations and discourses*, p. 471.

282. See esp. Hilton (1980). A new revised edition of Butler's *Lives* has been produced (published by the Liturgical Press, Collegeville, Minnesota, 1995, under the editorship of Paul Burns and David Hugh Farmer), omitting much of Butler's devotional material and adding more recent saints.

283. Butler, *Meditations and discourses*, p. 471.

284. Jacob (1996, p. 6) estimates 5.6% in the early eighteenth century.

285. See Priestley's *Sermon for the National Fast* (28 February 1794) in *A farewell sermon* (Revolution and Romanticism, 1789–1834: facsimile reprints) (Oxford: Woodstock, 1989), esp. pp. 23–4. For an introduction to eighteenth-century dissent, see Watts (1978) and Davie (1978).

286. See Hall (1985).

287. *Christian and brotherly advices*, 1738, cited in Hall (1985) p. 310.

288. p. 316.

289. See Jones (1921) vol. 1, pp. 57–103; Hobhouse (1927), esp. pp. 191–6; and Hall (1985).

290. Jones (1921) vol. 1, pp. 79 and 85.

291. Stephen C. Morland, 'Mid-Somerset Friends in the 18th century', in *Journal of the Friends Historical Society* 52 (1968–71), p. 253.

292. Morland, p. 275; see also Jones (1921) vol. 1, pp. 320ff.

293. Schlenther (1997, pp. 154–5) describes the moment when the 'Countess of Huntingdon Connexion' was born.

294. See Rupp (1986) pp. 462–71; Rack (1992) pp. 284–6; Schlenther (1997) and Welch (1995).

295. Cited in Welch (1995) p. 185. Students also had to spend half an hour in family prayer each evening.

296. Letter to the Committee of Spafields Chapel (undated); text in Johnson (1983) p. 99.

297. For Doddridge see esp. Nuttall (1951), Nuttall (1967) pp. 146–69, Deacon (1980), and Everitt (1985), and the contemporary life by Orton (in *Works* vol. 1). There is an excellent biography by Nuttall in his introduction to Doddridge's letters (see Bibliography).

298. Cowper (Letter of 19 July 1765, in *Letters and prose writings* vol. 1, pp. 107–8) acknowledges his indebtedness to Doddridge, esp. to his *Rise and progress*.

299. Orton, *Life* 7, in *Works* vol. 1, p. 89.

300. *The family expositor*, Preface, in *Works, vol.* 6, p. 12. Scholarly footnotes are included, to be used at the leader's discretion (see Preface, p. 14). Everitt (1985, pp. 229–34) notes the wide social and geographical range, and predominantly lay character, of those who subscribed to the first edition.

301. For *Robinson Crusoe* as Puritan spiritual narrative, see especially Starr (1965) (tracing many of the fundamental elements in Puritan spiritual autobiography through Defoe's work). J. Paul Hunter (*The reluctant pilgrim* (1966) quoted in Shinagel (1975) p. 246) stresses the tradition of Puritan texts of spiritual guidance, including Defoe's own *The family instructor*. In this context what *Robinson Crusoe* does is to 'concretize in dramatic, symbolic particulars the saga of life as seen by the Puritan mind' (p. 248).

302. *Robinson Crusoe*, p. 4.

303. Starr (1965) pp. 56 and 84. The story of the Prodigal Son was popular in Puritan spiritual autobiography: see L. Damrosch Jr., 'Myth and fiction in *Robinson Crusoe*', repr. in Shinagel (1994), pp. 374–5.

304. Starr (1965) pp. 84 and 87.

305. Starr (1965) p. 99.

306. *Robinson Crusoe*, p. 12. Starr's suggested comparison with Balaam is much less convincing (1965, pp. 100–1 and 102), when he ridiculously (in an otherwise excellent book) suggests that Balaam 'goes mulishly on' – it is precisely *not* like the mule that Balaam travels!

307. *Robinson Crusoe*, p. 151.

308. *Robinson Crusoe*, p. 160. See Starr (1965) p. 124. This is a favourite theme of Defoe's: see his *Serious reflections* chapter 4, pp. 128–9 ('How do Christians, taking that venerable name for a general appellation, doom one another to the devil for a few disagreeing clauses of the same religion, while all profess to worship the same Deity, and to expect the same salvation?'), and further pp. 147–58 ('Of differences in religion'). Defoe viewed the matter empirically: '[what] to me is the greatest grievance among Christians, is the want of religious practice even when there are right principles at bottom, and where there is a profession of the orthodox faith' (p. 136). He looks forward to a heaven where 'we shall see that there have been other flocks than those of our fold, other paths to heaven than those we shut men out from; that those we have excommunicated have been taken into that superior communion; and those we have placed at our left hand have been there summoned to the right hand' (p. 155).

309. *Robinson Crusoe*, p. 12.

310. *Robinson Crusoe*, p. 136.

311. See *Robinson Crusoe*, p. 141.

312. *Robinson Crusoe*, p. 47.

313. *Robinson Crusoe*, p. 58.

314. *Robinson Crusoe*, p. 95.

315. *Robinson Crusoe*, p. 127. Defoe explores the matter further in his *Serious reflections . . . of Robinson Crusoe* chapter 5 ('Of Listening to the Voice of Providence'): see, e.g., p. 183 ('there are intimations given us, by which a prudent man may sometimes foresee evil and hide himself'), and p. 188 ('would we carefully listen to the concurrence of Providence in the several parts of our lives, we should stand less in need of the more dangerous helps of visions, dreams, and voices from less certain intelligences'). What matters is to combine thoughtful trust in (rather than an unthinking resignation to) Providence with 'all diligence in our callings' (p. 191): we are, as he summarizes it, to 'look up, and acknowledge the goodness of God in sparing us . . . , to look out, and take the needful caution and warning given of evil approaching . . . , [and] to look in, and reflect upon what we find Heaven animadverting upon' (p. 206).

316. *Robinson Crusoe*, p. 131. The same point is made on p. 182 as a further proof of providence: God sometimes makes the causes of our dereliction into precisely the means of our escape.

317. See Starr (1965) p. 29; and cf. Roxana's plight after the disappearance of her husband.

318. See p. 180: 'Let no Man despise the secret Hints and Notices of Danger, which sometimes are given him, when he may think there is no Possibility of its being real. That such Hints and Notices are given us, I believe few that have made any Observations of things, can deny; that they are certain Discoveries of an invisible World, and a Converse of Spirits, we cannot doubt' (pp. 180–1). Defoe explores the significance of dreams and the imagination as sources of providential wisdom further in his 'A Vision of the Angelic World' (in *Serious reflections*, pp. 237–314).

319. Virginia Woolf (*The second common reader*, quoted in Shinagel (1975) p. 287) surely misses this point, when she celebrates, understandably enough, Defoe's reverence for material things. *Robinson Crusoe* is not a canonization of a back-to-basics simplicity.

320. 'The splendid thing about providence, in the eyes of such writers [contemporary English Protestants like Defoe], is not that it simply "provides" for man, but rather that it affords him – if he is attentive and obedient to its dictates – the means of providing for himself' (Starr (1965) p. 189).

321. See Starr (1965) pp. 119 and 121. Michael McKeon ('Defoe and the naturalization of desire', in Shinagel (1975) pp. 408–9) makes the perceptive point that Crusoe, working with his new-found awareness of divine providence, not only finds that he can cope with the absence of human society: he is also able to redirect his desires and longings ('my very Desires alter'd, my Affections chang'd their Gusts, and my Delights were perfectly new . . . ', quoted on p. 409).

322. *The rise and progress* 2, in *Works* vol. 1, pp. 226ff.

323. *The rise and progress* 2, in *Works* vol. 1, pp. 229–30.

324. *The rise and progress* 15, in *Works* vol. 1, p. 331.

325. *The rise and progress* 3, in *Works* vol. 1, pp. 235–6.

326. *Works* vol. 3, p. 435. The hymn is entitled 'Jacob's vow' and based on Genesis 28.20–2. The biblical theme of covenant is the subject of many of Doddridge's hymns (e.g. nos.21–3, in *Works* vol. 3, pp. 444–5).

327. *The rise and progress* 17, in *Works* vol. 1, p. 347 (and see, more generally, pp. 343–9).

328. *The rise and progress* 18, in *Works* vol. 1, p. 350.

329. *The rise and progress* 14, in *Works* vol. 1, p. 317.

330. On the remarkable range and depth of the academic syllabus at his Northampton academy (much more intensive than that of Oxbridge), see Young (1998) pp. 8–9 and Deacon (1980) pp. 25–6. Glen (1983, p. 57), in her study of Blake and Wordsworth, stresses the Dissenters' 'unwavering confidence in the possibility of enlightenment through education' – an informed mind and a virtuous heart belong together (pp. 57–8).

331. Rupp comments sadly on the snobbish hatred of Dissenters on the part of Anglicans (1986, pp. 166–7; see also Orton, *Life* 8, in *Works* vol. 1, pp. 148–9).

332. See Deacon (1980) pp. 122–3.

333. Letter to Daniel Wadsworth, in *Calendar of the Correspondence*, pp. 131–2.

334. *Robinson Crusoe*, p. 51. West (1997, p. 244) says that 'Defoe's advice on planting corn, making a spade from iron wood, baking bread, fortifying one's home and building a dug-out canoe could serve as a manual for pioneers or mountain men in any part of America'.

335. See the nuanced discussion by Ian Watt, 'Robinson Crusoe as a myth', in Shinagel (1975) pp. 288–306.

336. *The complete English tradesman* 5, in *Works* vol. 17, pp. 33–4.

337. *The complete English tradesman* 36, in *Works*, vol. 18, p. 89.

338. *Roxana*, p. 26. Cf. the moving passage in *The complete English tradesman* (7, in *Works* vol. 17, p. 55) about how a tradesman responds to disaster.

339. *Roxana*, p. 43.

340. See *The complete English tradesman* 17, in *Works* vol. 17, p. 150; cf. 39, in *Works* vol. 18, p. 115; and 42, in *Works* vol. 18, p. 146.

341. *Roxana*, pp. 77–8.

342. *The complete English tradesman* 40, in *Works*, vol. 18, p. 126.

343. *The rise and progress* 24, in *Works* vol. 1, p. 406.

344. p. 407.

345. pp. 408–9.

346. pp. 410–11. He provides a prayer which quotes from some of the Psalms of lament (pp. 412–15).

347. *Hymns* 39, in *Works* vol. 3, p. 454.

348. *Robinson Crusoe*, p. 60.

349. *Robinson Crusoe*, p. 64.

350. *Robinson Crusoe*, p. 68.

351. *Robinson Crusoe*, pp. 66–7.

352. *Robinson Crusoe*, p. 67.

353. *Robinson Crusoe*, pp. 69–70.

354. *Robinson Crusoe*, p. 71.

355. *Robinson Crusoe*, p. 114.

356. Eric Berne ('The psychological structure of space with some remarks on *Robinson Crusoe*', in Shinagel (1975) p. 308) acutely points out the psychological implications of the famous naked foot discovery:

> When you think you are secure, having possession of everything on the body of land and no one to dispute your sovereignty, along comes somebody who wants to eat you, somebody who has been lurking in the background all along and who now must be dealt with face to face. It seems that after Crusoe had incorporated his island as far as he dared through exploration and exploitation, he felt guilty; he thought the devil should surely come after him and sure enough he did.

357. See especially *The rise and progress* 19, in *Works* vol. 1, pp. 356–69; 20, pp. 373–4; and 26, pp. 423–8.

358. *Religious courtship* 1.2, in *Works* vol. 14, p. 69.

359. p. 70; cf. *The family instructor* 1.1, in *Works* vol. 15, p. 29.

360. *Religious courtship* 1.2, in *Works* vol. 14, p. 72.

361. p. 77; *The family instructor* 1.1, in *Works* vol. 15, p. 30.

362. *The family instructor* 1.1, in *Works* vol. 15, p. 13; cf. 1.2, p. 207; 2.1, vol. 16, pp. 54, 59.

363. *The family instructor* 2.1, in *Works* vol. 16, p. 31.

364. *The family instructor* 1.1, in *Works* vol. 15, p. 53.

365. p. 61.

366. *The family instructor* 1.1, in *Works* vol. 15, p. 69.

367. *The family instructor* 1.2, in *Works* vol. 15, p. 237.

368. *The family instructor* 1.1, in *Works* vol. 15, p. 107.

369. *The family instructor* 2.2, in *Works* vol. 15, p. 194. Defoe may have been compassionate towards individual slaves, but he did little to condemn the slave trade itself: see West (1997) p. 407, and

Hugh Thomas, *The slave trade* (Basingstoke: Macmillan, 1997; repr. with corrections 1998), pp. 236 and 453–4).

370. *The family instructor* 2.2, in *Works* vol. 15, p. 196.

371. From *The true-born Englishman*; quoted in West (1997) pp. 59–60.

372. See Nuttall (1967) pp. 163–4 and his Introd. to Doddridge, *Letters* (1979 edn) p. xvii.

373. Sermon on the flight of the rebels from Stirling, no.7 of *Sermons on public occasions*, in *Works* vol. 3, p. 161.

374. Defoe was also more than capable of allowing his rich imagination to supply what his own experience lacked: many of his books are filled with exotic descriptions of places, both local and distant, which he had never seen.

375. *Meditations,* pp. 18–19.

376. 'An account of the Augustan age in England', in *The Bee* 8 (Saturday 24 November 1759), in *Miscellaneous works,* p. 411.

377. For this subject see esp. Brewer (1997).

378. *The vicar of Wakefield*, ed. cit. p. 50.

379. Brewer (1997) p. xviii; 'the culture of the courtly prince in England was killed by the same stroke' as decapitated Charles I (p. 6); 'money rather than privilege became the chief currency of culture' (p. 92).

380. *The absolute unlawfulness*, in *Works* vol. 2, pp. 143 and 145; cf. *Christian perfection* 10, in *Works* vol. 3, pp. 150–70 and pp. 11, 170–95 – the evil of theatre-going is clearly an obsession of Law's (see *A serious call* 7, in *Works* vol. 4, p. 60, &c.; and Brewer (1997) p. 333).

381. See Jacob (1996) p. 97. For the reasons (both musical and commercial) for Handel's immense popularity among church and theatre audiences at the time, see Charles Rosen, *The classical style* (London: Faber, 1972) pp. 171–2. For the popularity of music in general at this time, see Brewer (1997), esp. pp. 62–3 and 365.

382. Brewer (1997) p. 556.

383. Author's preface to her Tragedies, in *Works* vol. 5, p. xvii.

384. See Hindmarsh (1996) pp. 284–5. The phrase was originally coined by Northrop Frye in 1956.

385. Hence Sterne: 'l'amour n'est *rien* sans sentiment. Et le sentiment est encore *moins* sans amour' (*A sentimental journey*, World's Classics edn (Oxford UP, 1984) p. 47).

386. *Thoughts on the devotional taste*, in *Works* vol. 2, p. 232. For the influence of Romanticism on Barbauld, see W. Keach, 'Barbauld, Romanticism, and the survival of Dissent', in A. Janowitz (ed.), *Romanticism and gender* (English Association essays and studies, 1998) (Cambridge: D. S. Brewer, 1998), pp. 44–61.

387. p. 233.

388. p. 234.

389. p. 236.

390. p. 238.

391. p. 239.

392. p. 239

393. p. 241.

394. p. 245. Mrs Barbauld's critique of 'philosophy' here is closely linked with her defence of everyday things and realities as subjects suitable both for poetry and for spiritual reflection; for the way women poets challenged accepted canons of taste in this way, see Karina Williamson, 'The tenth muse: women writers and the poetry of common life', in T. Woodman (ed.), *Early Romantics: perspectives in British poetry from Pope to Wordsworth* (Basingstoke: Macmillan, 1998), pp. 185–99.

395. 'Addressed to Miss —' ll.65–8, in *Poems* vol. 1, p. 76; the context here affects its sense: see Baird and Ryskamp (eds), *Poems* vol. 1, pp. 476–7. Cf. 'sweet Music is sure to find a corresponding faculty in the soul, a sensibility that lives to the last, which even Religion itself does not extinguish' (Letter of 27 April 1782, in *Letters and prose writings* vol. 2, p. 45).

396. 'Hope', ll. 229–53, in *Poems*, p. 239; cf. Goldsmith's *The deserted village.*

397. See, e.g., *The task* I, ll. 420–44, in *Poems*, pp. 316–17 – 'Lovely indeed the mimic works of art;/ But Nature's work far lovelier', ll. 420–1. See also *The task* III, ll. 746–80 passim, in *Poems*, p. 362,

with its ferocious criticism of 'Capability' Brown. For Cowper's view of landscape, and its spiritual as well as political overtones, see further Tim Fulford, 'Wordsworth, Cowper and the language of eighteenth-century politics', in T. Woodman (ed.), *Early Romantics: perspectives in British poetry from Pope to Wordsworth* (Basingstoke: Macmillan, 1998), pp. 117–33.

398. See Brewer (1997), esp. pp. 618–24; and W. Howard Adams, *Nature perfected: gardens through history* (New York: Abbeville, 1991), pp. 158–93.

399. Holmes (1989, p. 183) argues that Coleridge really did perceive the presence of the Creator in the midst of the creation, and hence the holiness of creation, to an extent and in a way that Wordsworth never did. He argues (1989, p. 290) that the whole thrust of Coleridge's new Lakeland writings in his *Notebooks* (after he moved there in 1800) was 'towards self-consciousness, achieved through observation of the natural world and his responses to it. He was seizing upon the outward landscapes, analysing them, and internalising their effects.' See Coleridge's late poem 'To nature' (cited in Holmes (1998) p. 494) as a good example of this.

400. 'The ha-ha permitted Arcadia indeed – but Arcadia at a safe distance' (John Cannon, 'Georgian landscape', in *The Historian* 57 (1998) p. 6). See also W. Howard Adams (cited in note 398), pp. 163–6. I am grateful to Alison Corden for pointing out that the ha-ha allowed eighteenth-century landowners to continue the profitable management of their livestock whilst preserving the Arcadian illusion that their grounds were boundless.

401. From 'Anoch', in *A journey to the western islands*, pp. 40–1. Cowper criticizes 'our modern improvers of parks and pleasure grounds' for displacing the formal effect (in this case a lime tree walk) in favour of the pseudo-natural.

402. Cowper, *Letters and prose writings* vol. 5, p. 18 (article in *The Connoisseur* 134 (19 August 1756)).

403. Burke, *Philosophical inquiry into the origin of our ideas of the sublime and beautiful* (1757) 3.5, *Works* vol. 1, pp. 220 and 223. Cf. Blake: 'Variety does not necessarily suppose deformity, for a rose & a lilly are various & both beautiful. Beauty is exuberant' (*Annotations to Lavater* (c.1788), in *Complete works,* p. 81). Like Burke, Blake seems to have seen beauty in diversity, not simply in order or proportion. In his treatise, Burke defines beauty as 'that quality, or those qualities in bodies, by which they cause love, or some passion similar to it' (3.1, in *Works* vol. 1, pp. 203–4).

404. 3.9, in *Works* vol. 1, p. 231.

405. One of Coleridge's English colleagues during his stay in Germany remembers him making 'the profound, although seemingly trivial, remark that no animal but man appears ever to be struck with wonder' (quoted in Holmes (1989) p. 228), though like Descartes he was careful to distinguish a right wonder from a wrong one: 'in Wonder all Philosophy began: in Wonder it ends: and Admiration fills up the interspace. But the first Wonder is the Offspring of Ignorance: the last is the Parent of Adoration. The First is the birth-throe of our knowledge: the Last is its euthanasy [= 'a gentle and easy death'] and apotheosis (*Aids to reflection*, in *Works* vol. 9, p. 236).

406. See the illuminating discussion in T. G. Bishop, *Shakespeare and the theatre of wonder* (Cambridge UP, 1996), esp. pp. 6–8.

407. *The natural history of religion* 11, in *Essays moral, political, and literary by David Hume*, ed. T. H. Green and T. H. Grose (London: Longmans, Green, 1875; repr. 1912), vol. 2, p. 341). See also Hume's 'Of miracles', in *An enquiry concerning human understanding*, in vol. 2, p. 95: 'if the spirit of religion join itself to the love of wonder, there is an end of common sense; and human testimony, in these circumstances, loses all pretensions to authority'.

408. *Of the sublime and beautiful* 2.1, in *Works* vol. 1, p. 157–8.

409. 2.5.

410. 2.5, in *Works* vol. 1, p. 174; cf. also p. 177.

411. Letter of 4 December 1786 (on the death of his dear friend William Unwin), in *Letters and prose writings* vol. 2, p. 606; cf. Letter of 16 December 1786, p. 618.

412. *Hymns for the amusement of children* 11, p. 336.

413. For the influence of London on Blake, see Ackroyd (1996), esp. pp. 3, 20, and 253. References to parts of London recur constantly in *Jerusalem*.

414. Ackroyd (1996) pp. 32–3; Gibbons (1996) p. 191.

415. *Annotations to Reynolds*, in CW (= Complete Works, ed. cit.) pp. 476–7.

416. *Annotations to Lavater* (c.1788), in CW p. 67.

417. *Annotations to Watson* (1798), in CW p. 387. In an important study, Ryan (1997, p. 33) argues that Blake was committed to a prophetic renewal of Christianity, following Milton in conceiving of the English Reformation as unfinished business (see also chapter 2, esp. p. 46).

418. See Holmes (1989), esp. pp. xiv–xv and 6. Hazlitt described his 'mass of full black glossy hair' as 'peculiar to enthusiasts' (quoted on p. 180). With regard to Coleridge's childlikeness, note his remark that 'to carry on the feelings of childhood into the powers of manhood; to combine the child's sense of wonder and novelty with the appearances, which every day for perhaps forty years had rendered familiar . . . this is the character and privilege of genius' (*Biographia literaria* 4, in *Works* vol. 7/1, pp. 80–1).

419. Quoted in White, Introd. to ed. cit. of *Lay sermons*, p. xxxv.

420. *The statesman's manual,* pp. 90, 93.

421. *Aids to reflection*, in *Works* vol. 9, pp. 95–6. Cf. Prickett (1976, p. 19): '"Nature" was, for Coleridge, neither "out there" objectively independent of the mind perceiving it, nor the mere subjective creation of the individual, but something that is simultaneously *both* objective *and* subjective – or, rather, the . . . meeting-point of the two.'

422. Coleridge distinguishes between 'superstition' and 'enthusiasm' when he argues in favour of treating key Christian doctrines realistically rather than purely symbolically. Such truths are not primarily addressed to the Intellect, 'but are substantiated *for us* by their correspondence to the wants, cravings, and interests, of the Moral Being, for which they were given, and without which they would be devoid of all meaning' – he is distinguishing between such truths as can be mediated either by image ('the seeking after which is *Superstition*') or by sensation ('the watching for which is *Enthusiasm*'). Rather, he seems to be saying that what matters is to know the truth of a doctrine by living it, absorbing and experiencing its truth for yourself (see Beer, ed. cit. of *Aids*, pp. lxxiv–lxxv; texts cited from Coleridge's *Marginalia* in *Collected Works* vol. 3. See also Beer's note in ed. cit. of *Aids*, pp. 567–8, where he cites another observation of Coleridge on the subject: 'Fanaticism is the *fever* of *superstition*. Enthusiasm, on the contrary, implies an undue (or when used in a good sense, an unusual) vividness of ideas, as opposed to perceptions, or of the obscure inward feelings.' Cf. also *Biographia literaria* 2, vol. 7/1, pp. 30–1).

423. *Works* vol. 10, p. 171.

424. For Blake and the Bible, see Mee (1992) pp. 69–74, 80–3, and 161–213; and Ackroyd (1996) pp. 13 and 141. He seems to have conceived of Job's own life as a key source for his art (p. 111), eventually producing more than 70 paintings and engravings to expound the book (p. 277; see also p. 365).

425. Southey, *Life* vol. 1, pp. 429–30n.

426. For this see also Ackroyd (1996) pp. 133 and 156.

427. *A vision of the last judgment* (1810), in CW pp. 605–6; hence Chesterton's conclusion that 'Blake's philosophy, in brief, was primarily the assertion that the ideal is more actual than the real' (1910, p. 160) – hence too the *precision* of the mystic in describing the mystery she or he experiences. Cf. Paracelsus: 'Imagination is Creative Power . . . He who is born in imagination discovers the latent forces of Nature' (*Interpretatio alia totius astronomiae*, cited in Hirst (1964) pp. 65–6). There is much more Platonism in Blake: see, e.g., the supplementary passages to *The everlasting Gospel* (CW, p. 757), where he says 'There is not one Moral Virtue that Jesus Inculcated but Plato & Cicero did Inculcate before him; what then did Christ Inculcate? Forgiveness of Sins. This alone is the Gospel' (and cf. p. 758). For the antinomian implications of this, see E. P. Thompson (1993, esp. p. 165). For Blake's love of medieval and earlier culture, see Ackroyd (1996) pp. 51–2 and 316.

428. For this aspect of Blake's thought and its relationship with the Ossian poems, Rousseau, and others, see especially Mee (1992). For Blake's Platonism, see Edward Larrissy, 'Blake and Platonism', in A. Baldwin and S. Hutton (eds.), *Platonism and the English imagination* (Cambridge UP, 1994) pp. 186–98.

429. *The statesman's manual*, in *Works* vol. 6, p. 94.

430. p. 98. See Cunliffe (1994).

431. 'He was the philosopher who could give substance to Blake's visions' (Ackroyd (1996) p. 99). For Swedenborg see the texts cited in the Bibliography, and also Ward (1972); for his influence on Coleridge, see Beer (1959) pp. 56–9.

432. Ackroyd (1996) pp. 102–3; Ryan (1997) pp. 50–2; and see E. P. Thompson (1993, esp. pp. 43–5) for a contrary view. The phrase 'the human form divine' appears in Blake's *The everlasting Gospel* (CW p. 755). Swedenborg's theory of correspondences can be summarized in this extract from his *Arcana coelestia* (2993; ET as *The universal human*, ed. cit. p. 39):

> As long as we live in this body, we sense and perceive very little of the spiritual, since for us heavenly and spiritual realities drop down into the natural concerns in our outer person, where we lose any sensation or perception of them. Further, the representative and responsive things in our outer person are of such nature that they do not seem to resemble the things in the inner person to which they are responsive. So they cannot get through to our thinking until we have shed these outer things. Then blessed is the person who is 'in correspondence' – that is, whose outer person is completely responsive to the inner (2993, p. 39).

But Blake could be highly critical of Swedenborg – see e.g. some of his *Annotations to Swedenborg's 'Divine Providence'* (CW, pp. 131–3); and *The marriage of heaven and hell*, in CW p. 157. 'Swedenborg's writings are a recapitulation of all superficial opinions, and an analysis of the more sublime – but no further' (*The marriage of heaven and hell*, in CW p. 158). See also Mee (1992) pp. 49–55. Coleridge himself described Blake as 'a man of Genius – and I apprehend, a Swedenborgian' (quoted in Holmes (1998) p. 474).

433. See vol. 1 of this work, pp. 387–89. White points out (1964, p. 151) that Boehme's origins as a craftsman, and his lack of intellectual pretension, commended him to Blake. The same may well be true of Swedenborg. For Boehme's influence on Blake, see Ackroyd (1996) pp. 149–50.

434. Hirst (1964) pp. 64–5; Ackroyd (1996) pp. 151–2.

435. 'I owe him [Boehme] a debt of gratitude' (*Biographia literaria* 9, 7/1, p. 161). See also Beer (1959) pp. 60–3 and Gibbons (1996) pp. 190–1.

436. See Holmes (1989) p. 221; and the Introduction to ed. cit. of Coleridge's *Biographia literaria*, p.lxix.

437. CW p. 160.

438. *Annotations to Lavater* (c.1788) in CW p. 87). Note the importance of diversity and opposites too: 'Without Contraries is no progression. Attraction and Repulsion, Reason and Energy, Love and Hate, are necessary to Human existence' (*The marriage of heaven and hell*, in CW p. 149; cf. 'There is a place where Contrarieties are equally True', the first line of Book 2 of *Milton*, in CW p. 518). Blake was close to Boehme and Swedenborg in seeking to discern the presence of God and the spiritual in the heart of the material.

439. See Mee (1992) p. 20.

440. *A vision of the last judgment* (1810), in CW p. 615.

441. *Contemplation* (from *Poetical sketches*, 1769–78), in CW p. 37.

442. This fall is, in White's view (1964, p. 190) primarily intellectual, not ethical: it is our minds that lose their vision.

443. *The marriage of heaven and hell*, in CW p. 149.

444. *Jerusalem*, in CW p. 682. Hence his stress on rebirth or regeneration, a notion fundamental to Swedenborg (White (1964) p. 149).

445. *Then she bore pale desire*, in CW p. 42.

446. *The marriage of heaven and hell*, in CW p. 154.

447. Letter to Joseph Cottle, early April 1814, in *Letters* vol. 3, p. 468; cf. *Aids to reflection*, in *Works* vol. 9, p. 191. For Coleridge's use of the notion of awakening, and its Platonic overtones, see Cunliffe (1994), esp. pp. 212–14.

448. *The statesman's manual*, in *Works* vol. 6, p. 48, citing a passage from *The friend*. Holmes (1998, p. 361) notes the dynamic nature of Coleridge's understanding of beauty: as with religion here, he conceived of beauty as 'an explosion of energy perfectly contained' – and linked this with morality, where again dynamism and energy had to be balanced with duty and obligation.

449. *Works* vol. 10, pp. 119–20. The reference to an 'originating and perfective focal unity' points to

Coleridge's preoccupation with a 'total and undivided philosophy', an overriding transcendental synthesis of the kind he sought in German Romantic idealism (see introd. to ed. cit. of *Biographia literaria*, pp. lxxiii–lxxxi).

450. From *Songs of experience*, in CW p. 212; cf. the eponymous poem on p. 117. See Glen (1983), esp. pp. 96–8; and Thompson (1993) p. 185.

451. CW pp. 290–1; note that even 'obdurate Los' feels Pity (CW p. 328).

452. Ryan (1997) pp. 67–8.

453. See White (1964) p. 199.

454. As G. K. Chesterton (1910, p. 118) puts it, 'this irrational individual pity is the purely Christian element in the eighteenth century. This irrational individual pity is the purely Christian element in William Blake.'

455. 'The garden of love' from *Songs of experience*, in CW p. 215. Glen (1983, p. 160) comments on this: 'The picture is of a love that allowed "play" being subsumed by "instruction", freedom to actualize "joys and desires" by prescription. We can only guess at the particular crisis which may have prompted these lines; but even in 1788, it seems, Blake had been to "the garden of love" and found "thou shalt not" writ over the door."' See also 'The sick rose', from *Songs of experience*, CW p. 213; and the description of 'the Net of Religion' in *The first book of Urizen* (1794) (CW p. 235). He criticized the mainstream Christian Church because he felt it too, like the Deists, had restrained creative human energies through a grim rationalist tyranny (see White (1964) pp. 177–8). In poems like *The song of Los* (1795) Blake appears to reflect on the melancholy fact that attempts by organized religion 'to catch the joys of Eternity' have almost invariably ended in failure.

456. See the ed. cit. in the Bibliography to this chapter.

457. Supplementary passages to *The everlasting Gospel*, CW p. 757; cf. p. 758.

458. *Vala*, in CW p. 281. Cf. 'Between South Molton Street & Stratford Place, Calvary's foot' (*Milton*, in CW p. 484) or Eden and Felpham Vale (*Milton*, in CW p. 507), or 'Fibres of love from man to man thro' Albion's pleasant land./ In all the dark Atlantic vale down from the hills of Surrey' (*Jerusalem*, in CW p. 622).

459. 'The Divine Image', from *Songs of innocence* (1789), in CW p. 117.

460. Glen (1983, p. 150) notes the resonance between this poem and Pope's *The universal prayer*, though Blake's poem is not a prayer, but 'an exploration of the dynamics of prayer'. Blake does not assume the existence of God, or of Mercy, Pity, Peace and Love: he simply says that when in distress people instinctively pray to them: 'unobtrusively but exactly, Blake is showing how the conception of goodness grows out of the experience common to all human beings, even the most deprived, of dependence being acknowledged and answered' (p. 151). More important still, for Blake God *is* Mercy, Pity, Peace and Love – he is no unmoved mover, distant from the creation: God is our experience of these things (p. 152): or, more exactly, in these things (and, by implication, *only* in these things) we experience God – note the 'we' (pp. 154–5). Glen seems to go too far in arguing that the immanence of God in Mercy, Pity, Peace and Love, as put in the final stanza, is contingent upon its realization (p. 155).

461. *Literary remains* III.6; quoted in *Works* vol. 6, p. 55 n. 3, where Coleridge's observation that 'the act of praying was the very highest energy of which the human heart was capable, praying, that is, with the total concentration of the faculties' is also noted.

462. *The statesman's manual* in *Works* vol. 6, p. 71.

463. Letter to Joseph Cottle, 27 April 1814 in *Letters* vol. 3, p. 478): the immediate effect of praying is 'a penitent Resolution' (p. 479).

464. Letter to Joseph Cottle, 26 April 1814 in *Letters* vol. 3, p. 478.

465. His disinterested action in blessing the creatures at once seems to win him the ability to pray, just as his equally disinterested killing of the albatross earlier incurred his curse.

466. *The rime of the ancient Mariner* ll. 244, 288 and 614–18. For reflections on the ambiguities involved in this conclusion, see Prickett (1976) pp. 12–17.

467. *Jerusalem*, in CW p. 682. See also CW p. 420 and 'He can never be a Friend to the Human Race

who is the Preacher of Natural Morality or Natural Religion; he is a flatterer who means to betray'
(*Jerusalem*, in CW p. 681).

468. *Aids to reflection*, in *Works* vol. 9, p. 202.

469. *Hymns and spiritual songs*, in *Works* vol. 4, p. 350.

470. Rose (1965) p. 80.

471. For the hymns, see Watson (1997) pp. 133–70.

472. See David L. Wykes, 'From David's Psalms to Watts's Hymns: the development of hymnody among Dissenters following the Toleration Act', in R. N. Swanson (ed.), *Continuity and change in Christian worship* (Studies in Church history 35) (Woodbridge: Boydell, 1999) pp. 227–39.

473. Quoted in M. Spufford, *The importance of religion in the sixteenth and seventeenth centuries*, in Spufford (ed.), *The world of rural Dissenters, 1520–1725* (Cambridge UP, 1995) p. 95. For Watts' hymns, see Manning (1942), Escott (1962) (esp. pp. 225–6), Adey (1988) and Davie (1993) pp. 27–56.

474. His explicit sources include Tillotson (Sermon 21, vol. 1, p. 231; *Essays on the law and gospel, faith and works* 7, vol. 3, p. 692; *The sacrifice of Christ* 1, vol. 3, p. 746), Baxter et al. (Sermon 27, vol. 1, p. 290; Sermon 43, vol. 1, p. 470; *An exhortation to ministers* 4, in *An humble attempt*, vol. 3, p. 31), John Owen (Sermon 44, vol. 1, p. 482 footnote; Sermon 48, vol. 1, p. 533, 'the learned and pious Doctor Owen'; *Evangelical discourses* 11, vol. 1, p. 715; *A guide to prayer*, vol, 3, p. 110 and frequently elsewhere), Cotton Mather (*An exhortation to ministers* 4, in *An humble attempt*, vol. 3, p. 36), Bishop Gilbert Burnet (*A serious address to the people* 4, in *An humble attempt*, vol. 3, p. 77), Matthew Henry (*A guide to prayer* 2, vol. 3, p. 133). It is noteworthy that he also cites approvingly Thomas à Kempis and Fénelon (*A serious address to the people* 2, in *An humble attempt*, vol. 3, p. 49) for outdoing Protestants in the quality of their devotion. He also cites a wide variety of other sources: in one page of his *A guide to prayer* (2, vol. 3, p. 142) he cites an ancient Greek myth and an article in the *Spectator* for 14 June 1712. Rose (1965, pp. 98–112) also notes his (albeit not uncritical) indebtedness to Locke in respect of his educational work.

475. Sermon 1, in *Works* vol. 1, p. 1.

476. Sermon 1, in *Works* vol. 1, p. 1–2.

477. Sermon 31, in *Works* vol. 1, p. 327.

478. See Sermon 16 in *Works,* vol. 1, esp. pp. 176–80.

479. Sermon 16, in *Works* vol. 1, p. 176.

480. See, e.g., one of the *Hymns and spiritual songs*, vol. 4, p. 309, entitled 'Our comfort in the covenant made with Christ' – i.e. that between Father and Son). Adey, writing about Watts' *Divine and moral songs*, argues that Watts' God is both distant creator and tribal patriarch (1988, pp. 95–6), and that it is always God – not human beings – with whom Watts begins and on whom he centres all that he writes.

481. *Divine songs for children*, in *Works* vol. 4, p. 395.

482. Sermon 1, in *Works* vol. 1, p. 5.

483. Sermon 40, in *Works* vol. 1, p. 431.

484. *Evangelical discourses* 12, in *Works* vol. 1, p. 712.

485. Sermon 1, in *Works* vol. 1, p. 6.

486. *Essays on the law and gospel, faith and works* 7, in *Works* vol. 3, p. 687.

487. Sermon 1, in *Works* vol. 1, p. 6.

488. Sermon 1, in *Works* vol. 1, p. 8–9.

489. Sermon 3, in *Works* vol. 1, p. 25.

490. Sermon 15, in *Works* vol. 1, p. 170.

491. Sermon 43, in *Works* vol. 1, p. 471.

492. *Works* vol. 1, p. 35.

493. *Discourses of the love of God* 4, in *Works* vol. 2, p. 676.

494. The first edition (1707) has 'Where the young Prince of Glory dy'd' where the second (1709) has 'On which the Prince of Glory dy'd'.

495. The text from Galatians is 'But God forbid that I should glory, save in the cross of our Lord Jesus Christ, by whom the world is crucified unto me, and I unto the world' (KJV). For this hymn, see also Watson (1997) pp. 160–70.

496. *Hymns and spiritual songs*, in *Works* vol. 4, p. 349.

497. Rattenbury (1948, p. 22) stresses the strongly visual element in the hymn: it is, he suggests, a form of Protestant crucifix. But Davie (1993, p. 39) stresses the use of 'survey' rather than 'behold' or 'discern' or 'observe': Watts, like St Paul, 'surveys' the cross from a distance, omitting its immediate impact, its stink and disgrace – in this sense it is very unlike a crucifix (in fact in other hymns the physical aspects are paramount: e.g. 'Infinite grief! amazing woe!', in *Hymns and spiritual songs*, in *Works* vol. 4, pp. 325–6). Davie also points out (1993, pp. 41–2) the puzzle with the 'then' of verse 4 line 3 – meaningless unless it relates to the 'when' of verse 1 line 1 – i.e. it is only when I have indeed comprehensively *surveyed* the cross that I recognize its implications: my own death to all that is of the world.

498. Sermon 31, in *Works* vol. 1, p. 328. Cf. 'Survey the trees and the fields, how they bring forth food for you' (Sermon 37, in *Works* vol. 1, p. 398); cf. also *Horae lyricae*, in *Works* vol. 4, p. 457, and Samuel Johnson: 'my ardour to survey the works of nature . . . ' ('The vision of Theodore, the hermit of Teneriffe', from *The preceptor* (1748), repr. in D. Greene (ed.), *Samuel Johnson* (Oxford authors) (Oxford UP, 1994), p. 165).

499. Sermon 38, in *Works* vol. 1, p. 413. Cf. 'It is a peculiar delight of [St Paul] to survey the blessings we derive from Christ, and to run over the glories of the gospel in flowing language' (Sermon 37, in *Works* vol. 1, p. 395; cf. Sermon 38, in *Works* vol. 1, p. 412; *Death and heaven* 2, in *Works* vol. 2, pp. 33, 49, and 50; or the hymn 'My soul, survey thy happiness', linked with Sermon 38, in *Works* vol. 1, p. 416. Cf. also Sermon 44, in *Works* vol. 1, p. 480; *The holiness of times, places, and people* 1, in *Works* vol. 2, p. 516; and 3, in *Works* vol. 2, p. 535.

500. Sermon 3, in *Works* vol. 1, p. 34; cf. 'When I within myself retreat', from 'Happy solitude', *Horae lyricae*, in *Works* vol. 4, p. 480; cf. Thomas Ken's 'When of my heart I take survey', hymn for Trinity 12, in *The Christian year*, p. 273.

501. Sermon 12, in *Works* vol. 1, p. 141; cf. the hymn 'Great God, how infinite art thou':

> Nature and time quite naked lie
> To thine immense survey,
> From the formation of the sky
> To the great burning day

(*Hymns and spiritual songs*, in *Works* vol. 4, p. 317). Cf. Thomas Ken's famous 'Morning hymn', in *The Christian year* p. 1, with the lines 'Think how All-seeing God thy ways,/ And all thy secret thoughts surveys' and p. 114 'Thou, in all sin's recesses, doth survey/ Pollution with an unpolluted ray', hymn for Lent V.

502. *The doctrine of the passions* 4, in *Works* vol. 2, p. 585. See p. 52 above.

503. *The doctrine of the passions* 4, in *Works* vol. 2, p. 585.

504. *The doctrine of the passions* 16, in *Works* vol. 2, p. 607.

505. *Discourses of the love of God* 2, in *Works* vol. 2, p. 643.

506. *Discourses of the love of God* 2, in *Works* vol. 2, p. 644; cf. pp. 646–7 and 653; also *Reliquiae juveniles*, in *Works* vol. 4, p. 519.

507. See above, p. 52.

508. *Discourses of the love of God* 2, in *Works* vol. 2, p. 644; cf. p. 653.

509. *Discourses of the love of God* 7, in *Works* vol. 2, pp. 702–3.

510. p. 705.

511. *Death and heaven* 2, in *Works* vol. 2, p. 30.

512. It is worth noting that the five verses of the hymn proceed thus: reflection (v. 1)/ response (v. 2)/ reflection (v. 3)/ response (v. 4)/ concluding response (v. 5).

513. e.g. *Evangelical discourses* 5–6, in *Works* vol. 1, pp. 650–63; *The sacrifice of Christ* 2, in *Works* vol. 3, pp. 751–2.

514. *The sacrifice of Christ* 2, in *Works* vol. 3, p. 751–2.

515. Diane Tripp ('Daily prayer in the Reformed tradition: an initial survey', in *Studia Liturgica* 21 (1991) pp. 86–7) argues that Watts' imagery here is drawn from a traditional Reformed piety conceived as sacrifice, and that the notion of prayer as sacrifice (we offer ourselves as a thankful response to the grace of God) in Reformed spirituality is a vital one. This notion deeply

influenced the Reformed stress on a covenant sealed in baptism (p. 89).

516. Sermon 2, in *Works* vol. 1, p. 13.

517. Sermon 15, in *Works* vol. 1, p. 169; for moderation, see Sermon 28, in *Works* vol. 1, p. 294.

518. Sermon 23, in *Works* vol. 1, p. 246; cf. p. 251.

519. Sermon 19, in *Works* vol. 1, p. 207.

520. Sermon 31, in *Works* vol. 1, p. 330.

521. Sermon 48, in *Works* vol. 1, pp. 530–1 and 534.

522. *Evangelical discourses* 7, in *Works* vol. 1, p. 672; cf. *An exhortation to ministers* 1, in *An humble attempt*, in *Works* vol. 3, p. 8. This profoundly Christ-centred spirituality is worth comparing with the distinctive piety of the Moravians, with its emphasis on devotion to Christ's suffering and blood, for which see Podmore (1998) pp. 132–6. For Watts' relationship with the Moravians, see Podmore pp. 111–13.

523. Sermon 7, in *Works* vol. 1, p. 80.

524. *Evangelical discourses* 6, in *Works* vol. 1, p. 658.

525. See his fine sermon 'The right improvement of life', Sermon 39, in *Works* vol. 1, pp. 417–28.

526. Sermon 10, in *Works* vol. 1, p. 116.

527. *An exhortation to ministers* 2, in *An humble attempt*, in *Works* vol. 3, p. 24.

528. *An exhortation to ministers* 3, in *Works* vol. 3, p. 29.

529. Sermon 48, in *Works* vol. 1, pp. 533–4.

530. Sermon 1, in *Works* vol. 1, p. 4; cf. Sermon 18, p. 196.

531. Sermon 20, in *Works* vol. 1, p. 212.

532. *Evangelical discourses* 10, in *Works* vol. 1, p. 693; cf. *Essays on the law and gospel, faith and works* 6, in *Works* vol. 3, p. 676.

533. *Discourses of the love of God*, Preface, in *Works* vol. 2, p. 633. On the transforming nature of faith, see *Evangelical discourses* 10, in *Works* vol. 1, pp. 694–5.

534. Sermon 3, in *Works* vol. 1, p. 22.

535. p. 23.

536. p. 24. On the 'principle of holiness' or similar: in Sermon 48 Watts says that this 'principle of holiness' is the same as the Christian virtues which are given by the Spirit; see *Works* vol. 1, p. 537.

537. Sermon 3, in *Works* vol. 1, p. 30.

538. Sermon 9, in *Works* vol. 1, p. 100.

539. Sermon 9, in *Works* vol. 1, p. 103.

540. p. 107.

541. Sermon 10, in *Works* vol. 1, p. 113.

542. Sermon 38, in *Works* vol. 1, p. 406.

543. *A serious address to the people* 7, in *An humble attempt*, in *Works* vol. 3, pp. 97–8.

544. Sermon 6, in *Works* vol. 1, p. 69.

545. Sermon 36, in *Works* vol. 1, p. 389.

546. *A guide to prayer*, in *Works* vol. 3, pp. 118–19.

547. 'Complaint of desertion and temptations', *Hymns and spiritual songs*, in *Works* vol. 4, p. 343.

548. *A guide to prayer* 2, in *Works* vol. 3, p. 134.

549. For Watts' treatment of the Psalms, see Escott (1962) and Davie (1993). Watts' indebtedness to earlier psalmodists such as Tate and Brady is clear (see the detailed comparisons in Escott (1962) pp. 219–48). Davie (1993, p. 72) argues that Watts' and similar versions of the Psalms (e.g. those by Christopher Smart) were not intended to be sung congregationally but to be read. But at the end of his Preface Watts makes it clear that he hopes both congregations and private families will sing his psalms (*Works* vol. 4, p. 124). Watts himself acknowledges that he has consulted about twenty earlier versions of the Psalter (Preface to *The Psalms of David*, in *Works* vol. 4, p. 113). He sought to 'accommodate the book of Psalms to christian worship' (Preface to *The Psalms of David*, in *Works* vol. 4, p. 118; cf. Davie (1993) p. 71): Escott (1962, p. 125) argues that his key inspiration in this is Galatians and the Pauline notion of the freedom of the Spirit. 'They ought to be translated in such a manner as we have reason to believe David would have composed them if he had lived in our day' (*An essay for the improvement of psalmody*, in *Works* vol. 4, p. 378). Davie

(1993, pp. 83–4) stresses the fact that translators like Watts and Smart, notwithstanding their particular sectarian predispositions, were seeking *wisdom* above all in translating scripture – wisdom for their own generation. He also suggests that Watts might have been over-keen to domesticate scripture in seeking to appropriate it for his own folk – thus (e.g.) in Psalm 74 he makes no attempt to translate the reference to Leviathan in verse 14 whilst others like Smart valiantly do (1993, p. 85).

550. Escott (1962) p. 139 criticizes this.

551. *An essay for the improvement of psalmody*, in *Works* vol. 4, p. 119.

552. Preface to *The Psalms of David*, vol. 4, pp. 115–16.

553. Preface to *The Psalms of David*, in *Works* vol. 4, p. 117.

554. Sermon 5, in *Works* vol. 1, p. 59.

555. *A guide to prayer* 4, in *Works* vol. 3, pp. 174 and 178–9. We certainly must not suppose 'that noisy gesture, a distorted countenance, violence and vociferation are any signs of the presence of the divine Spirit' (p. 181). And we need to remember that the Spirit is not ours to command: it is 'a sovereign and free agent, and dispenses his favours in what measure he pleaseth, and at what seasons he will' (p. 183).

556. Sermon 6, in *Works* vol. 1, p. 66; cf. Sermon 11, in *Works* vol. 1, p. 124. This is in itself the consequence of Christ's incarnation and atonement (*A guide to prayer* 1, in *Works* 3, p. 113; cf. *Essays on the law and gospel, faith and works* 6, in *Works* vol. 3, pp. 671, 674).

557. Sermon 6, in *Works* vol. 1, p. 66.

558. In *Death and heaven* Watts argues that there must be degrees of life in heaven commensurate with differences here on earth: 'surely superior joys and glories must belong to superior powers and services' (2, in *Works* vol. 2, p. 40). It would hardly be fair for the thief reprieved on the cross to share the same degree of glory as St Paul. Watts neatly but unconvincingly argues that the parable of the labourers in the vineyard cannot apply to heaven (pp. 40–1)!

559. *Death and heaven* 2, in *Works* vol. 2, p. 43.

560. p. 43.

561. p. 63.

562. pp. 63–4.

563. p. 45.

564. p. 52.

565. Sermon 3, in *Works* vol. 1, p. 24.

566. Sermon 54, in *Works* vol. 1, p. 586. Watts goes on to celebrate the victories of Blenheim and Ramillies; cf. Sermon preached on the death of George I (1727), in *Works* vol. 1, p. 613. See also Sermon 12, p. 132; Sermon 45, p. 507; *Prayers composed for the use and imitation of children*, in *Works* vol. 3, pp. 519 and 537; *Hymns and spiritual songs*, in *Works* vol. 4, p. 297; *Horae lyricae*, in *Works* vol. 4, p. 428. Adey (1988 pp. 4–5) notes the striking link between monarchical patriotism and social concern in Watts' hymns, and the enduring influence of the former rather than of the latter. I am indebted to Dr Ken Rose for the important point that the patriotism of Dissenters in this period bore witness to their concern to be tolerated and respected at a time when many, weary of seventeenth-century 'enthusiasm', tarred all Dissent with that brush and saw it as vexatious and even subversive.

567. See the Preface to *Prayers composed for the use and imitation of children*, in *Works* vol. 3, p. 508.

568. Sermon 9, in *Works* vol. 1, p. 99.

569. Letter to Byrom, 25 April 1761, in Byrom, *Remains* vol. 2, p. 634. Lord Lyttleton (who died in 1773) was a poet and historian.

570. For a lucid exposition of this situation see Young (1998) chapters 3–4.

571. *The spirit of love* 2, in *Works* vol. 8, p. 45; cf. *An address to the clergy*, in *Works* vol. 9, pp. 11–12. Cf. *The spirit of prayer* 1, in *Works* vol. 7, p. 19. John Newton tells of his own relish for the beauties of classical composition, and his beginning to acquire 'what Mr. Law calls classical enthusiasm' (*An authentic narrative* 8, p. 24). Young (1998, p. 134) maintains that Law defended 'enthusiasm' so long as it was kindled by 'true Religion'.

572. For Law's life, see Walker (1973).

573. Walker (1973) pp. 13–21.

574. See Walker (1973) pp. 168–75.

575. Gibbon, *Memoirs,* pp. 15–17.

576. *The absolute unlawfulness,* vol. 2, pp. 143 and 145; cf. *Christian perfection* 10, vol. 3, pp. 150–70 and 11, vol. 3, pp. 170–95 – the evil of theatre-going is clearly an obsession of Law's: see *A serious call* 7, vol. 4, p. 60, &c.; and Brewer (1997) p. 333.

577. *The spirit of prayer* 2, in *Works* vol. 7, p. 53.

578. *Letters to a lady inclined to enter the Romish communion,* in *Works* vol. 9, p. 249.

579. Byrom, Journal entry for 19 April 1737, in *Remains* vol. 2, p. 112. See also Hobhouse (1927), and the letters of Law printed therein, and Rupp (1986) p. 239.

580. See Byrom's account of a conversation he had with Law in 1735: *Journal,* 7 June 1735, quoted in Talon (1950) pp. 156–8, and Talon's comments, p. 156 n. 35.

581. Hirst (1964, p. 189) notes that Law seems to have owned (and to have copied out himself) *An Hundred Queries upon the Mosaick Cabala* (dated 22 December 1781 and now in Dr Williams's Library) – this obviously suggests the influence of the Kabbalah (and the *Zohar* in particular) on Law.

582. See Gibbons (1996) p. 173. W. R. Inge argued (and Gibbons agrees) that Law was drawn to Boehme not by doctrines that were new to him, but by the forceful expression of ideas he already held (Gibbons (1996) p. 174). If (as seems likely) this is the case, Law's beliefs on (e.g.) chastity were entirely compatible with Boehme, though arrived at before he read Boehme (Gibbons (1996) p. 174). Hirst (1964, pp. 180–99) stresses the influence on Law of eighteenth-century English Behmenists like Andreas Freher (an immigrant from Germany) and Francis Lee.

583. *Letter* 5, in *Works* vol. 9, p. 153.

584. *Aids to reflection,* in Coleridge, *Works* vol. 9, p. 384; for the relationship between Coleridge and Law, and the possible influence of the former on the latter, see John Beer's note in ed. cit. of *Aids to reflection,* p. 567; cf. *Biographia literaria* 9, in *Works* vol. 7/1, p. 151, where Coleridge speaks of 'Behmen's commentator, the pious and fervid WILLIAM LAW'.

585. *Letter* 4, in *Works* vol. 9, p. 141.

586. *An earnest and serious answer to Dr Trapp,* in *Works* vol. 6, p. 45.

587. *The spirit of prayer* 1.1, in *Works* vol. 7, p. 3.

588. Letter to Mr Walker, January 1735, cited in Byrom, *Remains* vol. 2, p. 560.

589. *An address to the clergy,* 9.8. He takes a view similar to that of the *Theologia Germanica* in sharply distinguishing between the material and the spiritual worlds (though note that he says 'The truly spiritual man is he that sees God in all things, that sees all things in God, that receives all things as from Him, that ascribes all things to Him' (anti-Quaker text cited in Hobhouse (1927) p. 215).

590. *Christian perfection* 8, in *Works* vol. 3, p. 125.

591. *Christian perfection* 8, in *Works* vol. 3, p. 126; cf. *An earnest and serious answer to Dr Trapp,* in *Works* vol. 6, p. 45, directed to the clergy. Walker (1973, p. 54) describes *Christian perfection* as 'the harshest book that Law wrote'.

592. *An address to the clergy,* in *Works* vol. 9, pp. 32, 47.

593. *Letter* 6, in *Works* vol. 9, p. 159. Hoyles (1972, p. 124) argues that Law regards reason as a faculty completely opposite to the image of God in humanity; and, 'for Byrom and Law, the divine image constitutes the natural basis of illumination or enthusiasm'. See also Young (1998) pp. 127ff.

594. Law's distaste for marriage is already evident in *A serious call* and other early works (in *A serious call* Law explicitly agrees with the early Christian historian Eusebius in unequivocally setting the celibate life above the married (9, in *Works* vol. 4, p. 77–8)), but considerably amplified by his reading of Boehme (see Gibbons (1996) pp. 174–5).

595. *Remarks upon the fable of the bees,* in in *Works* vol. 2, p. 17. Law stresses further the primacy of reason in *The case of reason.*

596. *Christian perfection* 3, in *Works* vol. 3, p. 38. Later in the same work he indicates that the fallen human condition causes us to be both mad and foolish, i.e. fundamentally irrational (7, p. 100).

597. *An address to the clergy,* in *Works* vol. 9, pp. 29–30.

598. *Christian perfection* 7, in *Works* vol. 3, p. 107 – hence the spiritual value of fasting (pp. 108–18).

599. *The spirit of prayer* 1.1, in *Works* vol. 7, p. 4. An interest in landscape, or any Franciscan-like celebration of the creation, is entirely missing in Law's work.

600. *The spirit of prayer* 2, in *Works* vol. 7, p. 65.

601. *The spirit of love* 1, in *Works* vol. 8, p. 11.

602. *The spirit of love* 2, in *Works* vol. 8, p. 46. Cf. Boehme: 'If thou wilt enter again into the life-tree [i.e. of Eden], and be a twig on the only life of man, then thou must utterly forsake in thy mind and desire all whatsoever that is in this world; and become as a little child' (*Mysterium magnum* 24.20, vol. 1, p. 161). The key point here, well expressed by Hoyles (1972, pp. 127–8), is that for Law 'nature' does not mean conventional human nature in the way such a term is understood by deists, philosophers &c., but precisely the nature of the divine, through which we are regenerated. Hoyles even argues (p. 129) that Law's view of nature anticipates Freud in its stress on nature as essentially desire. In fact what happened was that Law was branded as an enthusiast for his views.

603. *The case of reason, or natural religion stated*, in *Works* vol. 2, p. 70.

604. p. 75. Cf. Boehme, *Mysterium magnum* 48.20–1, vol. 2, p. 450, where Boehme argues that we must offer our sins on the altar of Christ 'and with a full and free will die wholly to sin' – though note that Boehme warns against an excessive self-hatred here: 'a man ought not to be so foolish as to torment his whole life in his repentance and conversion, and to offer it up in the fire of death, without God's command; but he must sacrifice only the sin, and self-love of vanity' (48.31, vol. 2, p. 454).

605. *Christian perfection* 8, in *Works* vol. 3, p. 124.

606. p. 139.

607. p. 142.

608. *The spirit of prayer* 1.2, in *Works* vol. 7, p. 44.

609. Boehme, *Mysterium magnum* 41.55, vol. 1, pp. 381–2.

610. *Christian perfection* 6, in *Works* vol. 3, p. 83.

611. p. 86.

612. pp. 88–9.

613. *Christian perfection*, Introd., in *Works* vol. 3, p. 5; cf. 3, p. 45, and 5, p. 75.

614. *Christian perfection*, Introd., in *Works* vol. 3, p. 6.

615. p. 9.

616. p. 10.

617. 'We are Strangers to the Temper and Spirit of Piety' until we renounce the world (*Christian perfection* 5, in *Works* vol. 3, p. 72).

618. *The absolute unlawfulness of the stage-entertainment*, in *Works* vol. 2, p. 176.

619. *The absolute unlawfulness of the stage-entertainment*, in *Works* vol. 2, p. 180. Note that here Law's attitude to reason is positively emollient.

620. *Christian perfection* 2, in *Works* vol. 3, p. 23; see also p. 34; 9, p. 144; and *A serious call* 4, in *Works* vol. 4, pp. 30–42. Note the connection with Boehme: becoming is movement; perfect eternity is absolute repose.

621. *Christian perfection* 2, in *Works* vol. 3, p. 23.

622. See e.g. *Christian perfection* 2, in *Works* vol. 3, p. 26; and 3, p. 36.

623. e.g. *Christian perfection* 3, in *Works* vol. 3, pp. 39–40.

624. *Christian perfection* 4, in *Works* vol. 3, pp. 50 and 57.

625. *Christian perfection* 2, in *Works* vol. 3, p. 25.

626. pp. 29–30.

627. p. 30.

628. *An address to the clergy*, in *Works* vol. 9, p. 31.

629. *Christian perfection* 2, in *Works* vol. 3, p. 32. Hence Law's attack on the Quakers for their deprecation of the sacraments (see Hobhouse (1927) p. 213 and the text cited there).

630. *The spirit of prayer* 1.2, in *Works* vol. 7, p. 32; cf. 3, pp. 116–17). For this notion of a second, spiritual, birth, see Boehme, *Mysterium magnum* 50.16, vol. 2, p. 465; and Boehme, *The way to Christ discovered* 3.

631. *Of the nature and necessity*, in *Works* vol. 3, p. 168, cf. p. 181; and *The spirit of prayer* 1.2, in *Works* vol. 7, p. 30.

632. *An appeal to all who doubt*, in *Works* vol. 6, pp. 71–2.

633. p. 86; cf. *The spirit of prayer* 1.2, in *Works* vol. 7, p. 46: 'God is one, human Nature is one, Salvation is one, and the *Way* to it is one; and that is, the Desire of the Soul turned to God'.

634. *An appeal to all who doubt* 1, in *Works* vol. 6, p. 82.

635. As Hoyles (1972, p. 115) points out, this is his way of developing a spirituality at once interior and transforming, rather than latitudinarian or deist, rational and cold.

636. For a brief but rather laconic summary, see Walker (1973) chapter 6.

637. *A serious call* 1, in *Works* vol. 4, p. 7.

638. p. 8.

639. pp. 10–11.

640. p. 12.

641. *A serious call* 2, in *Works* vol. 4, pp. 16–21.

642. p. 21.

643. *A serious call* 3, in *Works* vol. 4, p. 22; *An appeal to all who doubt* 1, in *Works* vol. 6, p. 71.

644. *A serious call* 3, in *Works* vol. 4, pp. 26–7.

645. i.e. those good works expected of sheep; see *A serious call* 6, in *Works* vol. 4, p. 52.

646. p. 54. Law's remarks are clearly addressed to those who might be regarded as half-Christians, lukewarm and nominal in their religious allegiance and commitment.

647. *A serious call* 9, in *Works* vol. 4, p. 74; cf. 11, p. 100.

648. *A serious call* 4, in *Works* vol. 4, p. 36.

649. See e.g. *A serious call* 4, in *Works* vol. 4, p. 38.

650. *A serious call* 11, in *Works* vol. 4, p. 98.

651. *A serious call* 20, in *Works* vol. 4, p. 210.

652. *A serious call* 1, in *Works* vol. 4, p. 10; cf. 10, pp. 85 and 86: 'it is better to be holy, than to have holy prayers'; and cf. *The spirit of prayer* 3, in *Works* vol. 7, p. 115: 'People may be daily at the Service of the Church, and read long Prayers at home, in which are many Petitions for the Holy Spirit, and yet live and die, led and governed by the Spirit of the World' (3, pp. 120–1).

653. *Christian perfection* 12, in *Works* vol. 3, p. 197.

654. p. 197

655. p. 198.

656. p. 199–200.

657. *Works* vol. 1, p. 22.

658. *Works* vol. 1, p. 22.

659. *Christian perfection* 4, in *Works* vol. 3, p. 60.

660. Cf. *Christian perfection* 12, in *Works* vol. 3, p. 202: 'We must alter our Lives, in order to alter our Hearts, for it is impossible to *live* one way, and *pray* another.'

661. p. 205.

662. p. 210.

663. p. 211.

664. p. 211.

665. p. 210.

666. See e.g. *A serious call* 10, in *Works* vol. 4, p. 86: though note *A serious call* 14, *Works* vol. 4, pp. 128–9, where Law says that prayer is 'the nearest approach to God, and the highest enjoyment of him, that we are capable of in this life. It is the noblest exercise of the soul.'

667. *A serious call* 14, in *Works* vol. 4, p. 141.

668. *A serious call* 20, in *Works* vol. 4, p. 215.

669. p. 219.

670. p. 220; cf. *The spirit of prayer* 1.2, in *Works* vol. 7, p. 42.

671. *A serious call* 20 in *Works* vol. 4, p. 223.

672. p. 224.

673. *A serious call* 21, in *Works* vol. 4, p. 227.

674. p. 227.

675. p. 228.

676. p. 234.

677. p. 235.

678. p. 239.

679. *A serious call* 15, in *Works* vol. 4, p. 159.

680. *Christian perfection* 14, in *Works* vol. 3, pp. 236–7.

681. Flatus, in *A serious call* 12, in *Works* vol. 4, pp. 107–8.

682. *The spirit of prayer* 1.2, in *Works* vol. 7, pp. 27–8; cf. 3, p. 110.

683. *A serious call* 10, in *Works* vol. 4, p. 84. The word 'common' (common life, prayer, manner of living, &c.) recurs frequently in his work.

684. 'I am neither Protestant nor Papist . . . I cannot consider myself as belonging only to one Society of Christians, in separation and distinction from all others' (*Letter* 1, in *Works* vol. 9, p. 119).

685. *The spirit of prayer* 1.2, in *Works* vol. 7, p. 39.

686. There is little doubt that St Paul's life and journeys acted as a crucial catalyst for Wesley: see Rack (1992) pp. 111–12. Whitefield, similarly itinerant in his ministry, also echoes the ministry of St Paul (see, e.g., his own description of his leavetaking from Bristol in 1737, explicitly citing Acts; *Journals*, ed. Murray, p. 85).

687. *Journal* vol. 18, p. 382, for 4 May 1736.

688. The name 'Methodist', initially opprobrious, was originally applied to John Wesley as a gentle jibe at his fondness for spiritual discipline and assiduous devotion while an Oxford undergraduate. Wesley expected from his fellow-Christians the same high standards to which he aspired himself. In his *Journal* (vol. 23, p. 301, for 4 April 1784) he bewails the fact that so many Methodists have slipped from the intensely high levels of commitment with which they had started out. Later he writes 'Today I entered on my eighty-second year and found myself just as strong to labour, and as fit for any exercise of body or mind, as I was forty years ago . . . I am as strong at eighty-one, as I was at twenty-one, but abundantly more healthy' (*Journal* vol. 23, pp. 319–20, for 28 June 1784). A year later he is writing 'It is now eleven years since I have felt any such thing as weariness!' (*Journal* vol. 23, p. 369, for 28 June 1785).

689. Knox (1950, pp. 425 and 428) criticizes Wesley for having constantly to be in control, never delegating even when Methodism had acquired a substantial membership, endlessly busy. In his *Life*, Robert Southey suggests that 'it was scarcely possible that any man should not have been inflated upon discovering that he possessed a power over the minds of his fellow-creatures so strong, so strange, and at that time so little understood' (vol. 1, p. 209). Later he argues that Wesley sought nothing less than a second Reformation, 'whereby all that had been left undone in the former would be completed' (p. 261). On Wesley's love of controlling others, organizing things, and giving spiritual supervision or direction to others, see also Rack (1992) p. 95.

690. *Letters* vol. 6, p. 292, 1777. Not everyone agreed with this view. Samuel Johnson commented: 'John Wesley's conversation is good, but he is never at leisure. He is always obliged to go at a certain hour. This is very disagreeable to a man who loves to fold his legs and have out his talk, as I do' (Boswell, *Life of Johnson*, end of March 1778; quoted in Knox (1950) p. 431). In 1727 John wrote to his brother Samuel declaring 'Leisure and I have now taken leave of one another. I propose to be busy as long as I live' (quoted in Rack (1992) p. 82).

691. *Letters* vol. 3, p. 192, 1756.

692. *Letters* vol. 3, p. 203, 1756.

693. Thomas Church, accusing Wesley of enthusiasm, defines it as 'a false persuasion of an extraordinary divine assistance, which leads men on to such conduct as is only to be justified by the supposition of such assistance. An enthusiast is, then, sincere but mistaken' (*Letters* vol. 2, p. 204, 1745). Southey (*Life of Wesley* vol. 1, p. 42) notes that the term Methodists was still, in his day, indiscriminately applied to all enthusiasts; and elsewhere (vol. 1, p. 190) he describes Wesley as being at one point 'in the high fever of enthusiasm, and they among whom he conversed were continually administering cordials which kept the passion at its height'. Wesley himself defined 'enthusiasm' as 'a religious madness arising from some falsely imagined influence or inspiration of

God; at least from imputing something to God which ought not to be imputed to him, or expecting something from God which ought not to be expected from him' (*Sermons,* ed.Outler, 37, vol. 2, p. 50; cf. *Letters* vol. 4, p. 193, 1762). He was certainly often accused of it, and increasingly from 1739 onwards: e.g. by the anonymous *Amicus veritatis* who wrote to the *Bristol Weekly Intelligencer* in 1749, saying that 'Enthusiasm is the fountain from whence this evil [Methodism] flows' (quoted in *Letters* vol. 3, p. 26, 1750). Wesley defended himself against his anonymous critic, who also suggested that an enthusiast is one who adheres to principles uncontrollable by reason: 'I am still willing to be controlled by reason. Bring me stronger reasons for Infidelity than I have for receiving the Christian system, and I will come over to you to-morrow' (*Letters* vol. 3, p. 27, 1750). However, it is clear that accusations of enthusiasm persisted, and that Wesley eventually wearied of them ('the threadbare charge of enthusiasm', *Letters* vol. 4, p. 333, 1759).

694. *A letter to the author of 'The enthusiasm of Methodists and Papists compar'd'* (1750), in *Works* vol. 11, p. 364. Cf. Wesley's second letter (1751) to the same person (*Works* vol. 11, p. 417), where he asks the luckless bishop 'O sir, when will you deviate into truth?'

695. *Journal* vol. 19, pp. 121–2, 12 November 1739.

696. Thus he criticizes the 'enthusiasm' of a Mr John Brown, who believed that God had told him he was to be a king (*Journal* vol. 19, p. 304, 4 December 1742). Ronald Knox (1950, pp. 450–1) suggests that Whitefield was far more vulnerable to the charge of adopting an uncritical 'enthusiasm' than Wesley, with his more nuanced warnings against the excesses of the French writers.

697. Knox (1950, p. 449) suggests that Wesley uses the term 'enthusiasm' loosely (Wesley himself acknowledges the looseness of the term: *Sermons,* ed.Outler, 37, vol. 2, p. 48), though he defends him against the extreme subjectivism associated by contemporaries with the word: 'as a rule [Wesley] is the last man in the world to obey unaccountable impulses or make instinctive decisions' (p. 451). Rather he and his brother encouraged enthusiasm whilst not themselves being carried away by it (so Knox, p. 452), insisting instead on 'the Law and the Testimony' (i.e. scripture) as the ultimate source of authentication (p. 454; Wesley makes the same point in his defence against Thomas Church's accusation of his 'enthusiasm': *Letters* vol. 2, p. 205, 1745). Charles Wesley complains about 'that spirit of rebellion and enthusiasm which is so visible in our deluded brethren' in his *Journal* (vol. 1, p. 240, 13 June 1740).

698. *Letters* vol. 2, p. 65, 1745.

699. *Letters* vol. 2, p. 68, 1746; cf. the poem 'Zeal' in *Hymns and sacred poems,* pp. 13–15). He warns the Quakers of having 'a zeal, but not according to knowledge' (*Letters* vol. 2, p. 127, 1748).

700. *Letters* vol. 2, p. 95, 1747.

701. *Letters* vol. 2, p. 117, 1748. The lack of this criterion was, for him, the fatal weakness in Quakerism.

702. For the life of Wesley, see especially Rack (1992) and (more briefly) Wakefield (1992).

703. Rack (1992) p. 53; Wakefield (1992) pp. 166–7. For the influence of Susanna on John, see Rack (1992) pp. 55–6.

704. Southey, *Life* vol. 1, p. 25.

705. *Journal* vol. 19, pp. 39–45; Rupp (1986) p. 347; Rack (1992) p. 77.

706. The club was sometimes known as 'The Enthusiasts' or 'The Godly Club'; *Journal* vol. 18, p. 130, Preface. One of the late comers was George Whitefield.

707. In his *Journal* John gives as his motive for going 'singly this – to save our souls, to live wholly to the glory of God' (vol. 18, p. 137, 14 October 1735).

708. See Rupp (1986) p. 351 and Ward (1992) p. 310.

709. See Ward (1992) pp. 312–14 and Podmore (1998) pp. 29–71, the latter showing that Wesley's role in the foundation of the Fetter Lane Society was less significant than he and others have claimed.

710. *Journal* vol. 18, p. 244, 24 May 1738.

711. *Journal* vol. 18, p. 249.

712. *Journal* vol. 18, pp. 249–50; Southey, *Life* vol. 1, pp. 141–2.

713. *Journal* vol. 18. p. 250. See also Charles Wesley's *Journal* vol. 1, pp. 90–8 for his own intense spiritual experience at the same time.

714. In his notes on Southey's *Life*, Coleridge comments that 'this assurance amounted to little more than a strong *pulse* or throb of sensibility accompanying a vehement *volition* of acquiescence, – an ardent desire to *find* the position true, and a concurring determination to receive it as truth. That the change took place in a society of persons all highly excited, aids in confirming me in this explanation' (*Life* vol. 1, p. 142 note). But this is an inadequate explanation. For other interpretations of what happened on 24 May 1738, see Knox (1950, pp. 436–41), Rupp (1986, pp. 326–7), Wakefield (1992, p. 176), Ward (ed. cit. of Wesley's *Journal* vol. 18, p. 13), and Rack (1992, pp. 145–57).

715. Certainly Wesley himself constantly harked back to the 1738 experience as absolutely essential for all that followed. Emphasis on the sudden transforming nature of conversion in individuals' lives recurs regularly (e.g. *Journal* vol. 19, pp. 59–60, 15–20 May 1739); but he tells Bishop George Lavington of Exeter that 'conversion' is 'a term ... which I very rarely use, because it rarely occurs in the New Testament' (*A letter to the author of 'The enthusiasm of Methodists and Papists compar'd'*, in *Works* vol. 11, p. 368).

716. *Journal*, quoted in Rack (1992) pp. 187–8.

717. Rupp (1986) p. 358; Rack (1992) pp. 184–6. See also above, p. 21.

718. Podmore (1998, pp. 32–3) notes that Wesley applied to join the Moravians, though his request was refused.

719. Rupp (1986) p. 359.

720. *Letters* vol. 1, p. 616; quoted in Rupp (1986) p. 362. Whitefield frankly confessed in his diary that he 'had rather preach the Gospel to the unprejudiced, ignorant colliers, than to the bigoted, self-righteous, formal Christians. The colliers will enter into the Kingdom of God before them' (*Journals*, ed. Murray (1739), p. 243).

721. See Rupp (1986) pp. 368–72. However, there was a reconciliation towards the end of Whitefield's life (see Wesley, *Journal* vol. 22, p. 29, 31 January 1766: 'Mr Whitefield called upon me. He breathes nothing but peace and love.'

722. See Rack (1992) p. 212. The first Methodist conference met in June 1744, dealing with both doctrine and organization; and two years later the incipient circuit system began to emerge as well (p. 245).

723. Schmidt (1962–73) vol. 2/2, pp. 160–71; Rupp (1986) p. 401; *Journal* vol. 20, p. 378, Ward (1992) p. 378 n. 51, and Ward's n. 50 in *Journal* vol. 22, p. 152.

724. Some of the pain incurred by both of them in the process appears in Wesley's correspondence: see, e.g. *Letters* vol. 4, pp. 49–50, 52–4, 61–2, 75–8, 79–80 and 89. See also Wakefield (1992) p. 181. For John's relations with women, see Rack (1992) pp. 257–69 and, for a very particular view, Henry Abelove, *The evangelist of desire: John Wesley and the Methodists* (Stanford UP, 1990). His wife finally left him, and died in 1781.

725. Southey, *Life* vol. 2, p. 342.

726. Charles died three years earlier, in 1788.

727. For this subject, see Schmidt (1962–73) vol. 2/1, pp. 96–126; and Podmore (1998), esp. chapters 2–3 (which underline the crucial indebtedness of early Methodism to the Moravians).

728. *The nature, design, and general rules of the united societies.*

729. *The nature, design* 2, in *Works* vol. 8, p. 301.

730. Schmidt (1962–73 vol. 2/1, p. 107) notes the monastic overtones in some of the early Methodist documents.

731. *The nature, design* 3, in *Works* vol. 8, pp. 301–2.

732. p. 302.

733. *The nature, design* 4, in *Works* vol. 8, p. 302. This is no figure of speech: Wesley clearly believed (unlike, say, William Law) that God was as capable of wrath as of mercy: see Lindström (1946) pp. 69–70.

734. *The nature, design* 4–6, in *Works* vol. 8, pp. 302–3.

735. *Rules of the band-societies*, in Wesley, *Works* vol. 8, p. 305.

736. pp. 305–6.

737. p. 308.

738. Minutes of the First Annual Conference, quoted in Trickett (1990) p. 368.
739. Davies (1963, pp. 15–23) cites the early Montanists, medieval Waldensians and Franciscans, and post-Reformation Moravians and Pietists as key forebears of Wesley's movement.
740. *The character of a Methodist*, in *Works* vol. 8, p. 402.
741. See Young (1998) p. 151.
742. 'The main point is, with all and above all, study the Greek and Hebrew Bible, and the love of Christ' (*Letters* vol. 3, p. 163, 1756; cf. Trickett (1990) p. 364).
743. There is much debate about the extent of Wesley's indebtedness to eastern patristic writers like Ephrem the Syrian and St John Chrysostom, especially on his ideas of Christian perfection as essentially a dynamic, not a static, thing. But it should be noted that Wesley had also read deeply of Pseudo-Dionysius and other western 'mystical' writers; and here too it is crucial to remember that Wesley drew from whomsoever he found helpful for the task in hand, so that questions of sources are both unusually difficult and to some extent less relevant than with others. Rack (1992) is surely right to be cautious on the matter of eastern influence. For an example of Wesley's use of patristic theology, see *Letters* vol. 2, pp. 332–75 (1749), to Conyers Middleton.
744. *Letters* vol. 3, p. 12, 1749. This concern for the revival of primitive Christianity recurs (see, e.g., *Letters* vol. 4, p. 58, 1759; and his poem 'Primitive Christianity', *Works* vol. 8, p. 50. Cf. also hymns entitled 'Primitive Christianity', in *Hymns for children*, in vol. 6, pp. 439–41. In *Hymns and sacred poems* 1749 (vol. 4, p. 308), Charles Wesley begins a verse

> Workers with God, they now shall rear
> The church, that long in ruins lay,
> Her desolate estate repair,
> Her ancient piety's decay.

See also Whitefield's sermon 'The necessity and benefits of religious society' (1736) (1904 edn, Sermon 1, pp. 9–10); and Whitefield's reaction to a love-feast at Fetter Lane in 1739: 'Surely a primitive spirit is reviving amongst us' (*Journals*, ed. Murray, p. 194). William Cowper declared in 1781 that 'true Religion is working the same wonders now as in the first ages of the church' (Letter of 4 December 1781, *Letters and prose writings* vol. 1, p. 552).
745. Wesley explicitly, though not uncritically, acknowledges the former in *Journal* vol. 20, pp. 292–3, 27 July 1749, and the latter in *Journal* vol. 18, p. 121, Preface, and at the beginning of *Christian perfection*, in *Works* vol. 11, p. 428; for the latter, see Southey, *Life* vol. 1, pp. 30ff.). Wesley engaged in a fierce controversy with Law from 1760 onwards (see Southey, *Life* vol. 1, pp. 136–40; and Ward's note, *Journal* vol. 21, p. 278 n. 1): Wesley believed Law to be too much under the influence of the 'mystic' Boehme (for whom see Wesley's own *Thoughts upon Jacob Behmen*, which begins: 'What some seem most to admire in his writings, is what I most object to; I mean his philosophy and his phraseology. These are really his own; and these are quite new, therefore, they are quite wrong' (*Works* vol. 9, p. 588). In one letter in 1744 he wrote 'I love Calvin a little, Luther more; the Moravians, Mr Law, and Mr Whitefield far more than either' (*Letters* vol. 2, p. 25, 1744). But in 1756 he was writing to Law criticizing him for conflating true religion with philosophy and acutely commenting on Law's Boehme-inspired writing: 'Does not all this require a little more proof, and not a little illustration?' (*Letters* vol. 3, p. 337, 1756). Charles Wesley acknowledges his indebtedness to Law's *Serious call* in his *Journal* (vol. 1, p. 47, 1736) (but see also vol. 1, p. 191, 1739).
746. Wesley's devotion to them was far from uncritical: see, e.g., *Journal* vol. 19, p. 191, 21 April 1741; cf. vol. 19, p. 219, 3 September 1741. Yet he never lost a deep respect for the Moravians, and in a letter of 1745 to Thomas Church in which he sets out his view of them at length (*Letters* vol. 2, pp. 175–211) he said: 'I still think (1) that God has some thousands in our own Church who have the faith and love which is among them without those [the Moravians'] errors either of judgement or practice; (2) that, next to these, the body of the Moravian Church, however mistaken some of them are, are in the main, of all whom I have seen, the best Christians in the world' (*Letters* vol. 2, p. 179, 1745, to Thomas Church). See also *Letters* vol. 3, pp. 52–8 (to George James Stonehouse, 1750), wherein Wesley criticizes Moravian lack of concern with love of neighbour ('They no longer burn with love to all mankind, with desire to do good to all', *Letters* vol. 3, p. 56). Southey

(*Life* vol. 1, p. 300) stresses the formative influence of Peter Böhler on Wesley, as does Rack (1992, esp. pp 143ff.).

747. It concludes with an almost rhapsodic description of regeneration as 'an apprehension of beauty, an inner harmony achieved by the experiential discovery of the "divine sweetness" at a level unknown to the "reason" of the deist"' (see Edwards, *Treatise*, in *Works* vol. 1, pp. 252, 255, 324).

748. See esp. Orcibal (1965).

749. *Letters* vol. 1, pp. 207–10, 1736. In *An earnest appeal* he describes 'those who are styled "mystic divines"' as utterly decrying the use of reason (30, *Works* vol. 11, p. 55). He maintains that this credo includes rejection of public prayer (including the Eucharist) and of sensible devotion in any prayer, and rejection of the scriptures also (*Letters* vol. 1, pp. 208–9).

750. See, e.g., *Hymns and sacred poems* 1739, in *Poetical works* vol. 1, pp. 71–3 for a Tersteegen original translated by Wesley. For the spirituality of Tersteegen, see W. R. Ward, 'Mysticism and revival: the case of Gerhard Tersteegen', in J. Garnett and C. Matthew (eds), *Revival and religion since 1700: essays for John Walsh* (London: Hambledon, 1993) pp. 41–58.

751. *Journal* vol. 18, p. 213, 24–31 January 1738.

752. Cf. a late letter in which he refers to 'those poisonous writers the Mystics' (*Letters* vol. 8, p. 93, 1788). Wesley was for a while deeply influenced by the seventeenth-century mystical writers like Mme Guyon and the quietist Molinos (Guyon's works were not translated into English until late in Wesley's life, and in his *Journal* (vol. 19, pp. 272–3, 5 June 1742) he is very critical of her; but see vol. 22, pp. 245–6, where he calls her 'a woman of a very uncommon understanding and of excellent piety', 27 August 1770; and *Letters* vol. 6, p. 39 (1773), where he suggests that neither Guyon's nor Fénelon's writings 'are likely to do us any solid service'.

753. *Letters* vol. 6, p. 44, 1773. He is also suspicious of them because they derogate from the clear primacy of justification through faith (see *Letters* vol. 7, p. 128, 1782).

754. See the Preface to *Hymns and sacred poems* 1739, ed. cit. p. xxii: 'the religion these authors would edify us in is solitary religion'.

755. 'A thousand specious arts essay'd,/ Call'd the deep *Mystic* to my aid:/ His boasted skill the brute [= 'the beast and devil in my soul'] refined,/ But left the subtler fiend behind ('Galatians III.22' v. 8, in *Hymns and sacred poems* 1739, ed. cit. vol. 1, p. 84). This was the root also of Wesley's opposition to those advocating 'stillness' (i.e. attentive passivity before God) in 1740 – this notion seems to have been primarily Moravian in origin, but some manifestations of it may well have been influenced by Quietism (Podmore (1998) pp. 59–63; Rack (1992) p. 204). For illuminating discussions of Wesley's relationship with the 'mystics', see Knox (1950) p. 480; Whaling (introduction to *John and Charles Wesley*, p. 10); Rack (1992) p. 101. For his relationship with Roman Catholicism in general, see Butler (1995); for his indebtedness to Counter-Reformation piety in particular, see Duffy (1993).

756. *Letters* vol. 1, p. 152, 1734.

757. Cf. *Letters* vol. 7, p. 216 (written fifty years after the one just quoted): 'What, then, is religion? It is happiness in God, or in the knowledge and love of God . . . an heart and life devoted to God; or communion with God the Father and the Son; or the mind which was in Christ Jesus, enabling us to walk as He walked', 1784.

758. *Letters* vol. 2, p. 177, 1734.

759. *Letters* vol. 2, p. 268, 1746.

760. *A farther appeal* 1, 1:2, in *Works* vol. 11, p. 106. Lindström (1946, p. 34) notes that for Wesley 'awareness of original sin is not only awareness of it as inherent corruption: it embraces experience of the attendant guilt'.

761. *Sermons* ed. Sugden 1, vol. 1, p. 40.

762. See *Letters* vol. 1, pp. 22–3, 1725.

763. *Journal* vol. 21, p. 141, 9 April 1758. The Methodist Covenant Service which stems from this was originally created by others, but became what Ward calls 'neither a church nor an individual covenant, but the apostolic act of a society': it became standard for Methodists on New Year's Day or the first Sunday of the new year, as well as at other important occasions (see note by W. R. Ward, *Journal* vol. 21, p. 23 n. 82).

764. *Sermons* (ed. Sugden) 15, vol. 1, pp. 299–300; vol. 2, p. 227; cf. also Southey, *Life* vol. 1, p. 163 and vol. 2, pp. 76–8.

765. *Sermons* (ed. Sugden) 15, vol. 1, pp. 301–2; cf. *A farther appeal* 1, 1:5–6, in *Works* vol. 11, pp. 107–8.

766. *Sermons* (ed. Sugden) 15, vol. 1, p. 303; cf. 39, vol. 2, pp. 233–4.

767. *Sermons* (ed. Sugden) 39, vol. 2, p. 237; cf. Whitefield's Sermon on regeneration (1904 edn, Sermon 2, p. 38).

768. *Sermons* (ed. Sugden) 39, vol. 2, p. 240. Wesley's teaching on sanctification is not very precise. At one point he distinguishes it absolutely from justification: the latter is 'wholly distinct' from the latter, and 'necessarily antecedent' to it (*Journal* vol. 19, p. 96, 12–17 September 1739; cf. *Letters* vol. 2, p. 118, 1748). But elsewhere (*Letters* vol. 6, pp. 189–90) he speaks of justification and sanctification as virtually the same thing ('at the moment when we are justified, or when we are sanctified or saved from inbred sin'). He describes sanctification as 'both an instantaneous and a gradual work' (*Letters* vol. 5, p. 215, 1770) or 'the being made actually just and righteous' (*Sermons* (ed. Sugden) 5, vol. 1, p. 119), beginning the moment a man is justified (*Christian perfection* 17, in *Works* vol. 11, p. 452) (by contrast with which justification is defined as the forgiveness of our sins by God (*Sermons* (ed. Sugden) 5, vol. 1, pp. 120–1). An essential prerequisite for it is 'a will steadily and uniformly devoted to God'; but it is *not* essential to experience a continuing state of happy communion with God (*Letters* vol. 6, p. 68, 1774). Such a communion requires 'God's Spirit shining on His own work' (*Letters* vol. 6, p. 88, 1774). There are some useful observations in Lindström (1946, pp. 84–6) on the relationship between justification and sanctification.

769. *Journal* vol. 19, p. 17, 6 October 1738; cf. vol. 19, p. 97, 12–17 September 1739; cf. *Sermons* (ed. Sugden) 7, vol. 1, pp. 149–51.

770. *Journal* vol. 19, p. 18, 14–29 October 1738; *Letters* vol. 2, p. 138, 1748.

771. *Letters* vol. 2, p. 135, 1748.

772. *Letters* vol. 2, p. 136, 1748; cf. *Sermons* (ed. Sugden) 19, vol. 1, p. 391.

773. *Letters* vol. 3, p. 54, 1750. The Calvinist Whitefield makes the same point: 'to talk of my having the righteousness of Christ imputed to my soul, without my having the holiness of Christ imparted to it, and bringing forth the fruits of the Spirit as an evidence of it, is only deceiving ourselves' (Sermon on Jacob's ladder, 1904 edn p. 153).

774. *Letters* vol. 2, p. 137, 1748, written to his episcopalian opponent 'John Smith'.

775. Hence the significance of the text from 2 Peter (on participation in the divine nature) which precipitated Wesley's 1738 experience (see above).

776. It is noteworthy that Wesley was constantly having to define or defend his understanding of perfection in his correspondence; and in his *Life*, Southey notes Whitefield criticizing Wesley for appearing to argue that sinless perfection was attainable in this life, (vol. 1, p. 320). There was a major controversy within the Methodist movement on the matter in the 1760s (Rack (1992) pp. 334–42).

777. *Letters* vol. 4, pp. 298–9, 1765; cf. *Christian perfection*, in *Works* vol. 11, p. 428.

778. See *Sermons* (ed. Sugden) 35, vol. 2, pp. 152–6.

779. *Letters* vol. 3, p. 167, 1756; cf. *An answer to the Rev. Mr Dodd*, in *Works* vol. 11, p. 529, and *Letters* vol. 4, p. 10, 1758.

780. It is worth noting hymns that reflect on the reality of Christian backsliding (e.g. 'A prayer for restoring grace', *Hymns and sacred poems* 1742, in *Poetical works* vol. 2, pp. 120–2), where the nature of the Christian life as a slow and often contradictory progress towards heaven is sharply underlined.

781. *Christian perfection* 25, in *Works* vol. 11, p. 500.

782. *Christian perfection* 13, in *Works* vol. 11, p. 443. There is some lack of consistency here: Wesley did maintain that the state of perfection was wrought in the soul solely by faith, and 'consequently in an instant', even though accepting that 'a gradual work' might both precede and follow that 'instant' (*Letters* vol. 4, p. 187, 1761, to Charles Wesley; cf. *Letters* vol. 5, pp. 38–9, 1767 to the same; *Christian perfection* 18, in *Works* vol. 11, p. 460).

783. *Letters* vol. 7, p. 207, 1784. He is not always consistent here either: elsewhere (*Letters* vol. 3, p. 168) he says 'I still think that perfection is only another term for holiness, or the image of God in man.'

784. *Life*, vol. 2, p. 86.

785. *Hymns on scripture* in *The poetical works* vol. 10, p. 114. Cf. vol. 9, p. 130 and 291, 'And sinless at Thy feet to die'; p. 303 'And spotless in Thine arms expire'; vol. 10, p. 63 'Dwell within the sinless heart'; vol. 10, p. 77 'To walk before our God, and lead/ The sinless life of perfect grace'.

786. For this subject, see esp. *A farther appeal* 1 section 5, in *Works* vol. 11, pp. 138–76.

787. *Letters* vol. 2, p. 120, 1748.

788. *Sermons* (ed. Sugden) 10, vol. 1, p. 205; cf. 11, p. 222: 'God has made us thinking beings'. Wesley constantly returns to this compatibility of Christianity with human reason (see esp. *An earnest appeal* 20–2, in *Works* vol. 11, pp. 51–3, and 28, p. 55). Charles Wesley frequently writes about his opposition to 'stillness' (see e.g. *Journal* vol. 1, pp. 213–16 and 243: 'I read my Journal to the bands, as an antidote to stillness').

789. *Letters* vol. 3, p. 9 (to a Roman Catholic), 1749.

790. *Sermons* (ed. Sugden) 10, vol. 1, p. 207 – part of a wonderful passage.

791. *Sermons* (ed. Sugden) 10, vol. 1, p. 210.

792. p. 214. Lindström (1946, p. 156) notes that in Wesley's thought humility 'is given the primary significance of man's self-knowledge before God'.

793. *Letters* vol. 3, p. 222, 1757.

794. *Letters* vol. 3, p. 161, 1756; cf. pp. 163–4, 1756.

795. See *Sermons* (ed. Sugden) 29–31, vol. 2, pp. 38–83.

796. For Wesley on the boldness which is the fruit of assurance, see *Letters* vol. 1, p. 258, 1738, where he asks the Moravians: 'Have you that childlike openness, frankness, and plainness of speech so manifest to all in the Apostles and first Christians?' Cf. also *Letters* vol. 1, p. 188, 1735; *Letters* vol. 7, p. 304, 1785; *Hymns and sacred poems* 1739, in *The poetical works* vol. 1, p. 106 v. 6; pp. 177–9, translated from the German; *Hymns and sacred poems* 1740, vol. 1, p. 295 v. 7; *Hymns and sacred poems* 1742, vol. 2, p. 267. Southey (*Life* vol. 1, p. 11) describes Wesley's father as preaching 'boldly against the designs of the court', taking for his text the defiant response of Shadrach, Meshach, and Abed-Nego in Daniel 3. The stress on spiritual freedom is very important for Wesley: in *Christian perfection* Wesley notes the link between perfection and liberty, citing 2 Corinthians 3: we are set free by the Spirit from bondage to sin and death, and thus also freed from self-will, therefore 'desiring nothing but the holy and perfect will of God' (13, in *Works* vol. 11, p. 442).

797. *Letters* vol. 1, p. 16, 1725; see also Southey, *Life* vol. 1, p. 29.

798. *Letters* vol. 1, pp. 92–3, 1731; cf. *The character of a Methodist*, in *Works* vol. 8, p. 403). For the link between happiness and holiness, see *Letters* vol. 1, p. 114, 1731 and *Sermons* (ed. Sugden) 23, vol. 1, p. 476.

799. *A farther appeal* 2, 3:23, in *Works* vol. 11, p. 270. The use of the Song of Songs here ('Arise, and come away') is worth noting: it was by no means only Catholic writers who used it as an allegory of the spiritual life.

800. *Letters* vol. 1, p. 218, 1737.

801. *Sermons* (ed. Sugden) 11, vol. 1, pp. 234–5.

802. p. 235.

803. *Christian perfection* 10, in *Works* vol. 11, p. 434.

804. *The character of a Methodist* 8, in *Works* vol. 8, p. 404.

805. *Letters* vol. 6, p. 326, 1778; Southey, *Life of Wesley* vol. 2, p. 118. Whitefield is less positive: 'when the spirit of prayer began to be lost, then forms of prayer were invented', *Journal*, ed. Murray (1740), p. 483.

806. *Sermons* (ed. Sugden) 21, vol. 1, p. 428.

807. *Christian perfection* 25, in *Works* vol. 11, pp. 512–13.

808. *Letters* vol. 1, p. 112, 1731.

809. *Sermons* (ed. Sugden) 21, vol. 1, p. 431.

810. Whaling (*John and Charles Wesley*, introduction, p. 44) makes the important point that for the Wesleys feeling was not simply an emotional state, but analogous to the sense of touch: 'they were pointing to an inner, invisible realm that cannot be seen but whose internal reality, when activated by faith, is more certain than so-called rational or empirical evidences'. References to feeling and uses of the verb 'feel' appear very frequently in *Hymns and sacred poems*, and underline Whaling's point: see, e.g., 'The life of faith' (1740, in *The poetical works* vol. 1, pp. 209–21), esp. v. 4.

811. Cf. Southey, *Life* vol. 2, p. 10, on the Methodist John Pawson, who would 'pray, and weep, and roar aloud'.

812. *Journal* vol. 21, pp. 234–5, 25 November 1759. Cf. *Letters* vol. 8, p. 190, where he says to a Methodist lady: 'Never scream. Never speak above the natural pitch of your voice: it is disgustful to the hearers. It gives them pain, not pleasure. And it is destroying yourself.'

813. *Letters* vol. 8, p. 190, 1789.

814. Rupp (1986) pp. 409–10; Wakefield (1992) p. 169; Watson (1997) pp. 221–64.

815. See the memorable description, by Joseph Williams of Kidderminster, of a service at Bristol led by Charles Wesley: Southey, *Life of John Wesley* vol. 1, pp. 246–7. Rack argues (1992, p. 123) that hymn-singing was part of the enduring legacy of Moravian piety to Methodism.

816. *Directions for congregational singing*, in *Works* vol. 14, p. 466.

817. John Wesley, *Letters* vol. 4, p. 166, 1761.

818. Original in *Hymns and sacred poems* 1739, in *The poetical works* vol. 1, pp. 183–4. 'Welkin' = vault of heaven. The chorus was added by Wesley in 1743, but then consisted of the first two lines as above. In George Whitefield's hymn collection of 1753 it was altered to the version commonly sung today.

819. 'Charles Wesley will not contemplate any rest or bliss which cannot be shared' (Flew (1953) p. 72).

820. For 'the triumph of the skies', cf. *Funeral hymns* 42 v. 5 (in *The poetical works* vol. 6, p. 286): 'Thanks be to God who gave/ The victory and the prize!/ Join, all who own His power to save,/ The triumph of the skies!'

821. *Hymns on the Lord's Supper* 63, in Rattenbury (1948) p. 215: see also pp. 40–1.

822. See Allchin (1981, p. 27), who makes this point eloquently.

823. Heaven is a mountain-top where we shall 'salute our friends in light', *Hymns on the Lord's Supper* 52, in Rattenbury (1948) p. 211; cf. 98, p. 226. Allchin (1981, pp. 33–4) stresses that, because of his emphasis on union with Christ, Charles Wesley wants to proclaim our experience of heaven here and now. For hymns on the theme of glory, see, e.g., *Hymns on the Lord's Supper* 53, p. 211; *Hymns on scripture* in *The poetical works* vol. 11, p. 183 (on the Transfiguration); and vol. 12, p. 301 (on Acts 15.9).

824. See Hebrews 10.20 'through the veil, that is to say, his flesh'.

825. Matthew 1.23.

826. Isaiah 9.6: 'the everlasting Father, the Prince of Peace'. But Isaiah makes no reference to his being 'heaven-born'.

827. Malachi 4.2 (KJV) 'unto you that fear my name shall the Sun of righteousness arise with healing in his wings'; Matthew 13.43 (KJV) '... shall the righteous shine forth as the sun'. Cf. also 2 Samuel 23.3–4 'One who rules over people justly, ruling in the fear of God, is ... like the sun rising on a cloudless morning', where the image of the sun is applied to a ruler.

828. For this image in Wesley's hymns, see e.g. *Hymns and sacred poems* 1740, in *The poetical works* vol. 1, p. 316; also 1749, vol. 5, p. 231 (by Charles Wesley); 'rising Sun of righteousness', *Preparation for death* (vol. 7, p. 400); 'Till that Sun of righteousness/ All His heavenly rays display', *Hymns on scripture* (vol. 10, p. 165); and vol. 10, p. 173.

829. See esp. the hymns on Malachi 4.2 in *Hymns on scripture* vol. 10, pp. 133–4; cf. also this extract from 'Congratulation to a friend, upon believing in Christ' (*Hymns and sacred poems* 1739, vol. 1, pp. 180–3), v. 4 – this hymn immediately precedes 'Hark how all the welkin rings'):

> Blest be the Name that sets thee free,
> The Name that sure salvation brings;
> The Sun of Righteousness on thee
> Has rose with healing in His wings.

Cf. the penultimate verse of the hymn 'written in stress of temptation' ('Healing in his wings/ The Sun of Righteousness shall rise', *Hymns and sacred poems* 1740, vol. 1, p. 276). Cf. also 'Wrestling Jacob' v. 12, beginning 'The Sun of Righteousness on me/ Hath rose with healing in His wings', *Hymns and sacred poems* 1742, vol. 2, p. 175. Cf. also 'Risen, we know, Thou art,/ With healing in Thy wings', in *Hymns for New-Year's-Day* 1750 (vol. 6, p. 12). Cf. also 'O Sun of Righteousness, arise,/ With healing in Thy wing!' (from 'A prayer for the light of life', in *A collection of psalms and hymns* 1741, vol. 2, p. 12); and John Wesley's original poems in vol. 3, p. 171. Cf. 'As the great Sun of Righteousness/ Their healing wings display' (*Hymns on scripture* vol. 9, p. 134).

Other Evangelicals were fond of these texts too ('The Sun of Righteousness he eyes,/ With healing on his wings' (Newton, 'The happy change', *Olney hymns* 3:44, p. 288; 'It is the LORD who rises/ With healing in his wings' (Cowper, 'Joy and peace in believing', *Poems* 1, p. 188, *Olney hymns* 3:48, p. 291); 'The sun shone out upon us; and I trust, the Son of Righteousness arose on some with healing in His wings' (George Whitefield, *Journals* ed. Murray (1739), p. 263).

Wesley cites Malachi elsewhere (e.g. 'Suddenly return, and never . . .'; cf. Malachi 3:1; Flew (1953) p. 54). The theme of healing appears elsewhere in the Wesley hymns: cf. a 'Grace before meat' in *Hymns and sacred poems* (1739), in vol. 1, pp. 32–3, one verse of which begins

> Come, then, our Heavenly *Adam*, come!
> Thy healing influence give;
> Hallow our food, reverse our doom,
> And bid us eat and live (v. 5, p. 33).

Cf. also 'In temptation' (= 'Jesu, lover of my soul')(*Hymns and sacred poems* (1740), vol. 1, pp. 259–60) v. 4 'Heal the sick, and lead the blind'.

Davie (1993, pp. 87–8) criticizes Wesley here for not instead citing 2 Samuel 23.4, which refers to the sun rising but without the awkwardness of suggesting the sun having healing wings; but 2 Samuel 23.4 makes no reference to a sun 'of righteousness' which is Wesley's chosen scriptural image for the new-born Christ. Davie (1993, p. 88) goes on to express relief that Wesley didn't attempt to set the second part of Malachi 4.2 which speaks of calves leaping from their stalls! For a perceptive modern view of the significance of the 'healing wings' of Malachi, see Silvia Schroer, '"Under the shadow of your wings": the metaphor of God's wings in the Psalms, Exodus 19:4, Deuteronomy 32:11 and Malachi 3:20, as seen through the perspectives of feminism and the history of religion', in A. Brenner and C. Fontaine (eds.), *Wisdom and Psalms: a feminist companion to the Bible (second series)* (Sheffield: Sheffield Academic Press, 1998), pp. 264–82.

830. Thus in the hymn which follows this one ('Hymn for the Epiphany', *Hymns and sacred poems* (1739), vol. 1, pp. 184–5) verse 3 begins 'Mild He shines on all beneath,/ Piercing through the shades of death', which hardly suggests a mere inoffensiveness. See also the OED for early meanings of 'mild'.

831. See Boehme, *The way to Christ discovered* 3, p. 32; see also P. Deghaye, 'Jacob Boehme and his followers', in A. Faivre and J. Needleman (eds.), *Modern esoteric spirituality* (New York: Crossroads, 1993), pp. 234–5. The reference to the 'sons of earth' could also be from Boehme: the latter believed that each believer is first of all a human being born on earth: but each will be reborn spiritually while still on earth, born children of Wisdom 'after their bodies of light, which clothe them under their perishable covering even though they have not yet departed this earth'. Boehme also taught that Christ, although both human and divine, 'is a stranger in our earthly humanity' (*Mysterium magnum* 47.13, vol. 2, p. 439).

832. For the 'desire of nations', see Haggai 2.7; cf. Wesley's hymn 'The fifty-third chapter of Isaiah' (*Hymns and sacred poems* (1739), in vol. 1, p. 78), verse 2, which begins 'See the Desire of Nations comes,/ Nor outward pomp bespeaks Him near;/ A veil of flesh the God assumes'. Cf. also the last line of 'Though absent in body' (*Hymns and sacred poems* (1742), in vol. 2, p. 225): 'Come, Desire of nations, come!' Cf. also John Wesley's original poems, in vol. 3, p. 173 ('Dear Desire of nations, come,/ Come, and bring us all to God'); 'Come, thou Desire of nations, come,/ And take us all to God', in the ninth hymn 'for the Nativity of our Lord', vol. 4, p. 115; and 'Come, Thou Desire of nations, come' in the fifteenth hymn, vol. 4, p. 121. Cf. also 'Come, Thou Desire of nations now,/ And sprinkle all mankind!' (*Hymns on scripture* in vol. 9, p. 439).

833. 'My heart is fixed, O God', Psalm 57.7; cf. Psalms 108.1 and 112.7.

834. See the 'Hymn for a new-born child' (*Hymns for families*, in *The poetical works* vol. 7, pp. 68–9):

> Rise the woman's conquering Seed,
> In his ransom'd nature rise,
> Bruiser of the serpent's head,
> Give him back his paradise,
> Nature into grace convert,
> Grave Thine image on his heart.
>
> Cf.
>
> Rise, the woman's conquering Seed,
> Against our common foe,
> Bruiser of the serpent's head,
> Inflict the mortal blow . . . (*Hymns on scripture* 9:8)

Cf. also 'Galatians III.22' (*Hymns and sacred poems* 1739, 1:84) v. 5, lines 1–2:

> Awake, the woman's conquering Seed,
> Awake, and bruise the serpent's head!

Cf. also 'Romans IV.5' (*Hymns and sacred poems* (1739), vol. 1, p. 94) v. 1; 'To be sung in a tumult' v. 4, *Hymns and sacred poems* (1740), in vol. 1, p. 296: 'Christ, the woman's conquering Seed,/ Christ in us shall bruise thy head'; 'Avenge me of mine adversary', *Hymns and sacred poems* (1742), in vol. 2, p. 256; 'Awake, the woman's heavenly Seed,/ Thou Bruiser of the serpent's head', *Hymns on scripture* in vol. 9, p. 7 (on Genesis 3.15); 'Bruise his head, woman's Seed', in *A collection of psalms and hymns* (1741), in vol. 2, p. 29 – and, more generally, see 'Genesis III.15' in *Hymns and sacred poems* (1742), in vol. 2, pp. 66–8. Cf. also *Hymns and sacred poems* (1742), in vol. 2, p. 334.

835. *Select Psalms*, in *The poetical works*, vol. 8, p. 254. Cf. 'Who on Thy mystic body fall,/ Thy church, O Lord, they cannot shock' (*Hymns on scripture*, in vol. 11, p. 271, on Luke 22.18); and 'the mystic book' (= the Bible), *Hymns on scripture* vol. 12, p. 39; 'the mystical sign' (= baptism), vol. 12, p. 135.

836. *Hymns and sacred poems* (1740), in vol. 1, p. 225, v. 4.

837. *Hymns and sacred poems* (1740), in vol. 1, p. 356; cf. p. 360.

838. *Hymns and sacred poems* (1740), in vol. 1, p. 359; cf. p. 361 'who Thy mystic body are'.

839. *Hymns on scripture*, in vol. 9, p. 362, v. 2.

840. *Hymns on scripture*, in vol. 9, p. 98. Cf. 'And plunge in Thy immensity,/ And bathe for evermore!' Cf. also p. 313 'And quite absorb'd in love'; vol. 10, p. 49 'Absorb'd in the depths of His love!'; vol. 9, p. 335 'Lost in a boundless sea of love'; p. 357 and 'Implunged in that unknown abyss,/ That ocean of redeeming Love', vol. 13, p. 23; 'Resorb'd into the sea . . . In Thy immensity', vol. 13, p. 94; 'And wholly lost in Thee'; vol. 10, p. 174 'And give Thee up Thine own again,/ Absorb'd and lost in Thee.' 'While self is swallow'd up, and dies,/ For ever lost in Thee', vol. 13, p. 58. Cf. too 'Swallow up my soul in Thee' (in *Preparation for death*, in vol. 7, p. 404); 'plunged into the Deity' (*Select Psalms*, 8, in *The poetical works*, vol. 8, p. 60).

841. *Hymns on scripture*, in vol. 9, p. 309.

842. See, for example, *Hymns on scripture*, in vol. 10, p. 356, on Matthew 22.39.

843. *Hymns and sacred poems* (1749), in vol. 5, p. 27.

844. p. 321.

845. p. 350.

846. p. 418.

847. p. 408. See also 'Stamp me with the stamp Divine', p. 79; 'Stamp Thine image on our heart', p. 426; 'Stamp us with Thy Spirit's seal', *Funeral hymns*, in vol. 5, p. 315; cf. *Hymns on the Trinity*, in vol. 7, p. 327; 'Stamp'd with real holiness', *Hymns on scripture*, in vol. 9, p. 2; 'Jesus, Thou that image art,/ Seal Thy name upon my heart', *Hymns on scripture*, in vol. 9, p. 260. Note that Charles Wesley appears to use 'image' and 'likeness' to mean the same thing: 'After Thy likeness to wake up,/ Renew'd in sinless love', *Hymns and sacred poems* (1749), in vol. 5, p. 334. In heaven 'all our glorious foreheads [shall bear]/ The glorious stamp Divine', in vol. 5, p. 350. By 'image' he may

well mean 'character' ('And on my simple heart impress/ The character Divine', p. 417), the divine identity lost at the Fall; 'Stamp the image on our heart' (*Hymns on scripture*, in vol. 13, p. 23). Sometimes the image is spoken of as something we are to be clothed in (*Hymns and sacred poems* (1749), in vol. 5, p. 478). For his emphasis on fundamental change, see, e.g., *Hymns and sacred poems* (1749), in vol. 4, p. 320; *Hymns on scripture*, in vol. 13, p. 90 (on 1 Thessalonians 4.3); *Preparation for death*, in vol. 7, p. 390 'Change my nature into love'. In one place he uses 'portraiture' as synonym for 'image' (*Hymns on the Trinity*, in vol. 7, pp. 342–3). See also Allchin (1981) pp. 28–9.

848. My spirit all conform'd to Thine', *Hymns and sacred poems* (1749) (by Charles Wesley), in vol. 5, p. 66; 'To all Thine inward life restored,/ And outwardly conform'd to Thee', p. 149; 'Perfectly conform'd to Thee', *Hymns on scripture*, in vol. 9, p. 153. My heart 'pants for full conformity', p. 153. Cf. also Galatians 4.19: 'My little children, of whom I travail in birth again until Christ be formed in you'; and

> Israel, exult to prove
> How dear to God thou art,
> Object of His peculiar love
> Who made thee pure in heart;
> Feel all thy happiness,
> When Christ is form'd in thee,
> Consummate joy, and perfect peace,
> And spotless charity (*Hymns on scripture*, in vol. 9, p. 117).

849. The hymn 'Universal redemption' (*Hymns and sacred poems* (1740), in vol. 1, pp. 308–10) vigorously rejects Calvinist double predestination, taking the argument 'if *I* can be saved, anyone can'. See also Charles' *Journal* for Friday 22 September 1738: 'A dispute arising about absolute predestination, I entered my protest against that doctrine.'

850. See Rattenbury (1948) p. 59. In *Hymns on scripture* (in vol. 11, p. 389, on John 6.53), Charles explicitly criticizes a literal belief in the real presence unaccompanied by a recognition of 'the hidden mystery' at the heart of the Eucharist which he does not attempt to define further.

851. Cf. 'the heart of a crucified God' (*Hymns on scripture*, in vol. 13, p. 105).

852. 'Sinner, with awe draw near', *Hymns on the Lord's Supper* 39, in Rattenbury (1948), p. 207. *HLS* 30, pp. 204–5.

853. E.g. on Psalm 55 (*Select Psalms*, in *The poetical works* vol. 8, p. 12; 'agony of prayer', on Psalm 69 (p. 155); wrestling: 'And wrestle on in prayer' (*Hymns on scripture*, in vol. 9, p. 283); 'Which wrestles and receives in prayer/ Thy largest promises' (vol. 10, p. 310); 'To wrestle till the clouds remove,/ And Thou Thy name declare' (vol. 11, p. 46); 'Wrestling on in ceaseless prayer,/ We will not let Thee go' (vol. 11, p. 256; and the same line in vol. 12, p. 265 (on the apostolic church praying, on Acts 12.6); 'wrestle on in prayer unceasing' (vol. 13, p. 19); and

> On me that wrestling power bestow
> Which will not let th'Almighty go,
> Power to pray on, and never rest,
> Till, with Thy heavenly nature bless'd,
> I know Thee, Saviour, who Thou art,
> And bear Thine image on my heart.
> (*Hymns on scripture*, in vol.10, p. 79, on Hosea 12.3).

Cf. also vol. 9, p. 50; vol. 10, pp. 177 and 337; and *Select Psalms* in vol. 8, p. 88; and Charles' *Journal* (e.g. vol. 1, p. 363, 30 March 1744: 'at the time of intercession, we were enabled to wrestle for the nation with strong cries and tears').

854. *Hymns and sacred poems* (1749), in vol. 5, p. 255; by Charles Wesley. Note however that suffering, whilst for Wesley often sent by God, can never of itself be a good thing; only the blood of Jesus avails to save (see e.g. *Hymns for families*, in vol. 7, pp. 100–1, a prayer for one visited by sickness).

855. Charles Wesley, *Journal* vol. 1, pp. 381–2 (entry for 9 September 1744).

856. *Journal* vol. 20, p. 90.

857. *Letters* vol. 3, p. 13, 1749.

858. Quoted in *Johnsonian miscellanies*, ed. G. B. Hill (Oxford, 1897), vol. 2, p. 415.

859. From H. D. Best, *Personal and literary memorials*, cited in *Johnsonian miscellanies* 2, pp. 390–1.

860. Bate (1978) p. 275.

861. Richard Hurd, who was Samuel Johnson's own bishop at Lichfield and Coventry from 1775 to 1781, warned in a letter that the lives of the great 'were wretched in proportion to their greatness; that the hurry & tumult of their elevated state were inconsistent with their happiness, and that many a Cloud had obscur'd the lustre of their lives, which humbler mortals knew nothing of' (Letter 20 (1741), *The early letters* p. 53).

862. Letter to Hester Thrale 28 June 1783, in *Letters* vol. 4, p. 160.

863. Letter to William Adams, 30 March 1784, in *Letters* vol. 4, p. 305.

864. Boswell describes him as 'a steady Church of England man' (*Life of Johnson* chapter 82, p. 805; cf. Conclusion, p. 810).

865. See Suarez (1997) p. 200.

866. Hagstrum and Gray, Introduction to *Works* vol. 14, p. xl.

867. Boswell, *Life of Johnson*, chapter 79, p. 762.

868. See Bate (1978), esp. pp. 449–52. Johnson wrote a number of sermons, almost all of which were written for others to preach.

869. Sermon 16, in *Works* vol. 14, p. 174. For further strictures on the dangers of habit, see Johnson's 'Vision of Theodore, the Hermit of Teneriffe' (from *The preceptor*, 1748), repr. in *Samuel Johnson*, ed. D. Greene (Oxford authors) (Oxford UP, 1984), pp. 165–74.

870. *A journey to the western islands*, 'St Andrews', p. 6.

871. Suarez notes (1997, p. 197) that Johnson helped to popularize Joseph Trapp's sermons against 'enthusiasm', abridging them for the *Gentleman's Magazine* in 1739.

872. Sermon 13, in *Works* vol. 14, p. 143.

873. Sermon 27, in *Works* vol. 14, p. 290.

874. *A journey to the western islands of Scotland*, 'Raasay', p. 65.

875. Sermon 17, in *Works* vol. 14, p. 183.

876. Sermon 17, in *Works* vol. 14, p. 189.

877. Sermon 16, in *Works* vol. 14, p. 178.

878. Sermon 17, in *Works* vol. 14, p. 190.

879. Sermon 19, in *Works* vol. 14, p. 207.

880. Johnson argues that we should assume neither that those who suffer are deserving of it, nor that our own suffering is undeserved or worse than other people's (Sermon 15, in *Works* vol. 14, p. 168).

881. Sermon 19, in *Works* vol. 14, p. 213.

882. *A journey to the western islands*, 'Bamff', p. 22. Cf. 'Raasay', p. 65 (on the value of church buildings as helping to inculcate common values).

883. Sermon 4, in *Works* vol. 14, p. 41; cf. Sermon 13, p. 146.

884. Sermon 4, in *Works* vol. 14, p. 44; cf. Sermon 15, p. 161; Sermon 27, p. 294.

885. See *The Rambler* 150 (24 August 1751), in *Works* vol. 5, pp. 32–7; and Suarez (1997) p. 204.

886. *A journey to the western islands*, 'Mull', p. 139.

887. Sermon 10, in *Works* vol. 14, p. 112.

888. *Diary*, 1711–12, in *Works* vol. 1, p. 10.

889. Sermon 10, in *Works* vol. 14, pp. 110–11.

890. Sermon 2, in *Works* vol. 14, p. 26.

891. Sermon 5, in *Works* vol. 14, p. 56. Cf. Boswell, *Life of Johnson* chapter 43, p. 392: 'Dr Johnson showed how [evil] arose from our free agency, an extinction of which would be a still greater evil than any we experience.'

892. Sermon 2, in *Works* vol. 14, p. 21.

893. Boswell, *Life of Johnson* chapter 81, p. 791.

894. Sermon 2, in *Works* vol. 14, p. 25; cf. Sermon 15, pp. 163–4.

895. Sermon 2, in *Works* vol. 14, p. 22.

896. Sermon 3, in *Works* vol. 14, p. 33.

897. *A journey to the western islands*, 'Inch Kenneth', p. 148.

898. Sermon 3, in *Works* vol. 14, p. 34.

899. Sermon 3, in *Works* vol. 14, p. 35.

900. *Letters*, in *Works* vol. 1, p. 120.

901. See the excellent account by Bate (1978, pp. 455–6).

902. Letter to Hester Thrale 19 June 1783, in *Letters* vol. 4, p. 151; cf. *Johnsonian miscellanies* 2, p. 5; cf. also Boswell, *Life of Johnson* chapter 82, p. 806, on Johnson's refusal to take medicine when told he was dying, for fear it would cloud his mind.

903. *Works* vol. 1, pp. 45–6.

904. p. 46.

905. p. 46.

906. p. 50.

907. *Works* vol. 1, p. 319 (28 March 1782).

908. Letter to Bennet Langton, 21 September 1758, in *Letters* vol. 1, p. 167.

909. Boswell, *Life of Johnson*, chapter 65, p. 603.

910. Boswell, *Life of Johnson*, chapter 64, p. 595.

911. Boswell, *Life of Johnson*, chapter 65, p. 599.

912. Letter to Mrs.— (8 June 1762), in Boswell, *Life of Johnson*, p. 125. William Cowper (Letter of 27 August 1785, in *Letters and prose writings* vol. 2, p. 372) mentions Johnson's description of hope as 'the cordial of life, although it be the greatest flatterer in the world'.

913. See her essay *On the importance of religion to the female character*, in *Works* vol. 6, pp. 333–41, esp. p. 336.

914. See in particular the excellent accounts by Gibbons (1996, pp. 20–59), on attitudes to women; and by Vickery (1998, esp. the Introduction), on the social position of women.

915. E.g. the Tory Aphra Behn, the first professional woman writer to be buried at Westminster Abbey (Brewer (1997) p. 78).

916. 'Politeness was a tool which a well-born woman could use to extend her reach' (Vickery (1998) p. 9).

917. Vickery (1998) p. 9.

918. Gibbons points out (1996, p. 55) that the call for improved female education was not made primarily for the advancement of women but in order to help them serve their husbands better: see also pp. 56–7. For Wollstonecraft's relevance to spirituality, see Taylor (1997) (she argues that religion plays a much larger part in Wollstonecraft's thought that is usually supposed).

919. Wollstonecraft, *Maria*, chapter 1, p. 64.

920. For her life see Lowther Clarke (1944) pp. 118–25 (though he is unfairly disparaging of her work: see e.g. p. 118), and Gill (1994) pp. 49–51.

921. Rose (1991) p. 194.

922. See Hannah More's remarks in a letter to Horace Walpole, September 1791, in *Correspondence* vol. 31, pp. 357–8.

923. Published in 1804; Rose (1991) p. 190.

924. See, e.g., her poems for her dog (*Works* vol. 1, p. 111); Rose (1991) pp. 192–3; and Josephine McDonagh, 'Barbauld's domestic economy', in A. Janowitz (ed.), *Romanticism and gender* (English Association essays and studies, 1998) (Cambridge: D. S. Brewer, 1998), pp. 62–77.

925. For her life, see M. G. Jones, *Hannah More* (Cambridge UP, 1952).

926. See, among other works, her essay *Thoughts on the cultivation of the heart and temper in the education of daughters* (*Works* vol. 6, pp. 317–31).

927. For More's views on education, see Gill (1994) pp. 41–2.

928. See Rupp (1986) pp. 530–9; and Cowper's remarks on More as a writer (*Letters and prose writings* 3:103–4).

929. See M. G. Jones, *Hannah More* (Cambridge UP, 1952), pp. 87–91. For More's relationship with contemporary Evangelicalism, see pp. 97–102.

930. Letter to Horace Walpole, August 1792, in *Correspondence* vol. 31, p. 370.

931. A good example of More's conservative worldview can be seen in her Christmas hymn (*Works* vol.

6, pp. 22–4), in which she encourages servants and poor folk to be content with their lot since it was sanctified by Christ becoming human in just such circumstances. Yet in her hymn of praise for an abundant harvest (vol. 6, pp. 27–9) she exhorts people to use the surplus to 'feed the hungry poor'.

932. *Estimate*, in *Works* vol. 2, p. 289.

933. See vol. 1, p. 142: 'among those whom we now take the liberty to address, are to be found, especially in the higher class of females, the amiable and the interesting'.

934. Coleridge, Letter to Joseph Cottle, 27 May 1814, in *Letters* vol. 3, pp. 499–500.

935. Walpole, letter to Hannah More, 4 November 1789, in *Correspondence* vol. 31, p. 333.

936. Letter to Hannah More, 1 January 1792, in *Correspondence* vol. 31, p. 365.

937. *An estimate*, in *Works* vol. 2, p. 351.

938. *An estimate*, in *Works* vol. 2, pp. 299–300.

939. *Stories for persons of the middle ranks*, in *Works* vol. 1, p. 14.

940. *Hints towards forming the character of a young princess* 34, in *Works* vol. 4, p. 321.

941. p. 322. Cf. *Miscellaneous observations on genius, taste, good sense, &c* (*Works* vol. 6, pp. 353–4).

942. *Hints towards forming the character of a young princess*, in *Works* vol. 4, p. 323.

943. p. 324.

944. p. 324.

945. *Poems*, p. 301.

946. *Hints towards forming the character of a young princess*, p. 325.

947. p. 325.

948. pp. 325–6; cf. *Practical piety* vol. 2, p. 117.

949. *Hints towards forming the character of a young princess*, in *Works* vol. 4, p. 326.

950. p. 328.

951. p. 326.

952. *Practical piety* vol. 2, pp. 109, 112 and 119.

953. *Mary*, p. 33.

954. See the 'Advertisement' to *Mary*, ed. cit. p. 3.

955. *Mary*, p. 11.

956. p. 12. Taylor (1997, pp. 34–5) makes the important point that, in eighteenth-century England, only a freely-made ethical submission to God can free women from the dominion of men.

957. p. 15. Many contemporary women stress the beauty of nature and the presence of God within the created order: see, e.g., Anne Steele's hymn (*Hymns, Psalms and poems*, p. 25).

958. pp. 51–2.

959. *Maria*, p. 67.

960. *Thoughts on the devotional taste*, in *Works* vol. 2, p. 232. See also pp. 49–50.

961. p. 233.

962. p. 234.

963. p. 236.

964. p. 238. Cf. Hannah More: 'The Bible is not an exercise of ingenuity but of obedience' (*Practical piety* vol. 2, p. 121).

965. p. 239.

966. p. 239.

967. p. 241.

968. p. 245.

969. *Mary*, p. 5.

970. *Mary*, p. 25.

971. *Mary*, p. 46.

972. *Practical piety* vol. 1, pp. 5–6 and 23.

973. *Practical piety* vol. 1, p. 41.

974. *Stories for persons of the middle ranks*, in *Works* vol. 1, p. 168.

975. *Thoughts on the manners of the great*, in *Works* vol. 2, p. 280.

976. p. 281.

977. More, *On the importance of religion to the female character*, in *Works* vol. 6, pp. 337–8.

978. *The oeconomy of charity* vol. 2, pp. 50–1.

979. *Stories for persons of the middle ranks*, in *Works* vol. 1, p. 151.

980. *The oeconomy of charity* vol. 2, p. 19.

981. vol. 2, p. 33.

982. *Thoughts on the manners of the great*, in *Works* vol. 2, p. 258. She returns frequently to this subject: see, e.g., p. 262.

983. *The oeconomy of charity* vol. 2, p. 17. William Cowper gloomily notes (Letter of 31 May 1783, in *Letters and prose writings* vol. 2, p. 137) that 'the Sabbath is almost as obsolete in England as in France'.

984. *The oeconomy of charity* vol. 2, p. 25.

985. *Thoughts on the manners of the great*, in *Works* vol. 2, pp. 275–6.

986. *An estimate*, in *Works* vol. 2, p. 299.

987. *Practical piety* vol. 1, pp. 224–5.

988. *Practical piety* vol. 1, p. 102.

989. pp. 103–4.

990. p. 105.

991. p. 114.

992. p. 118.

993. pp. 128–9.

994. p. 224.

995. p. 135.

996. p. 136.

997. p. 137.

998. p. 138.

999. pp. 140–1.

1000. p. 147.

1001. p. 148.

1002. *An estimate*, in *Works* vol. 2, p. 289.

1003. *Hymns on scripture* in *The poetical works* vol. 12, p. 315, on Acts 16.13.

1004. Hannah More warns against a narrow disapproval of merriment, e.g. the author's preface to her Tragedies, in *Works* vol. 5, p. xiv.

1005. *Percy*, Act II, in *Works* vol. 5, p. 129.

1006. Defoe, *A tour through the whole island of Great Britain*, ed. P. Rogers (Harmondsworth: Penguin, 1986), pp. 227–8.

1007. See N. Pevsner, *Cornwall* (The buildings of England), 2nd edn rev. by E. Radcliffe (Harmondsworth: Penguin, 1970), pp. 205–6.

1008. See 'Spirituality and Dissent' earlier in this chapter.

1009. Letter to his son Isambard (1857), quoted in L. T. C. Rolt, *Isambard Kingdom Brunel* (Harmondsworth: Penguin, 1970), p. 419. For Brunel's life and work, see also D. Beckett, *Brunel's Britain* (Newton Abbot: David and Charles, 1980), esp. pp. 109–14.

1010. Rolt, pp. 243–4. Brunel died aged 53 on 15 September 1859, exhausted by a lifetime of astonishing achievement.

1011. On this essentially altruistic aspect of the English Industrial Revolution, see J. Bronowski, *The ascent of man* (London: BBC Publications, 1973), chapter 8, esp. pp. 262–5.

BIBLIOGRAPHY

Primary Works

Allestree, Richard, *The whole duty of man necessary for all families* (1657; London: John Beecroft, 1771)

Barbauld, Anna Laetitia, *Works*, 2 vols (London: Longman et al., 1825)

Berington, Joseph, *The state and behaviour of English Catholics from the Reformation to the year 1780* (London: Faulder, 1780)

Blake, William, *Complete writings*, ed. G. Keynes (London: Oxford UP, 1966)

Blake, William, *Water-colour designs for the poems of Thomas Gray*, with an introduction and commentary by G. Keynes (London: Trianon, 1971)

Boswell, James, *The life of Samuel Johnson* (1791; ed. J. W. Croker, London: John Murray, 1866)

Broughton, Thomas, *Serious advice and warning to servants, more especially those of the nobility and gentry* (1746; London: Rivington, 1763)

Burke, Edmund, *A vindication of natural society*, in *Works* (London: Rivington, 1815), vol. 1, pp. 1–80

Burke, Edmund, *A philosophical enquiry into the origin of our ideas of the sublime and beautiful*, in *Works* vol. 1, pp. 81–322

Burnet, Elizabeth, *A method of devotion*, 2nd edn (London: Downing, 1709)

Burnet, Gilbert, *A discourse of the pastoral care* (London: Rivingtons, 1821)

Butler, Alban, *The lives of the fathers, martyrs and other principal saints* (1756–9; Derby: Richardson, 1842), vol. 1

Butler, Alban, *Meditations and discourses*, ed. J. Lanigan (Dublin: James Duffy, 1840)

Butler, Joseph, *The analogy of religion, natural and revealed, to the constitution and course of nature*, ed. M.A. (London: Bell & Daldy, 1871), pp. 72–343

Butler, Joseph, *Fifteen Sermons*, ed. M.A. (London: Bell & Daldy, 1871), pp. 369–540

Byrom, John, *The private journal and literary remains*, ed. R. Parkinson, 4 vols (Manchester: Chetham Society, 1854–7)

Byrom, John, *Poems*, ed. A. W. Ward, 3 vols in 5 (Manchester: Chetham Society, 1894–1912)

Byrom, John, *Selections from the journals and papers of John Byrom, poet-diarist-shorthand writer 1691–1763*, ed. Henri Talon (London: Rockcliff, 1950)

Challoner, Richard, *The garden of the soul: or, a manual of spiritual exercises and instructions* (London: 1759)

Challoner, Richard, *Think well on't*, 5th edn (London: Meigham, 1749)

Challoner, Richard, *Meditations for every day in the year* (London: Burns & Oates, 1915)

Coleridge, Samuel Taylor, *Aids to reflection*, ed. John Beer (Collected Works 9) (London: Routledge & Princeton UP, 1993)

Coleridge, Samuel Taylor, *Biographia literaria*, ed. J. Engell and W. J. Bate (Collected Works 7/1 and 7/2) (London: Routledge & Princeton UP, 1983)

Coleridge, Samuel Taylor, *Lay sermons*, ed. R. J. White (Collected Works 6) (London: Routledge & Princeton UP, 1972)

Coleridge, Samuel Taylor, *On the constitution of the Church and State*, ed. J. Colmer (Collected Works 10) (London: Routledge & Princeton UP, 1976)

Coleridge, Samuel Taylor, *Letters*, ed. E. L. Griggs, 4 vols (Oxford: Clarendon, 1956–9)

Cowper, William, *Poems*, vol. 1 (1748–1782), ed. J. D. Baird and C. Ryskamp (Oxford: Clarendon, 1980)

Cowper, William, Hymns: see Newton, John

Cowper, William, *Letters and prose writings*, ed. J. King and C. Ryskamp, 5 vols (Oxford: Clarendon, 1979–86)

Defoe, Daniel, *The complete English tradesman*, in *Novels and miscellaneous works*, ed. W. Scott (Oxford: Talboys, 1841) vols 17–18

Defoe, Daniel, *The family instructor*, in *Novels and miscellaneous works*, ed. W. Scott (Oxford: Talboys, 1840) vols 15–16

Defoe, Daniel, *A journal of the plague year* (Shakespeare Head edn) (Oxford: Blackwell, 1928)

Defoe, Daniel, *Robinson Crusoe: an authoritative text, contexts, criticisms*, ed. M. Shinagel (Norton critical edition), 2nd edn (New York: Norton, 1994)

Defoe, Daniel, *Meditations*, ed. G. H. Healey (Cummington, MA, 1946)

Defoe, Daniel, *Religious courtship*, in *Novels and miscellaneous works*, ed. W. Scott (Oxford: Talboys, 1840) vol. 14

Defoe, Daniel, *Roxana, or, the fortunate mistress*, in *Novels and miscellaneous works*, ed. W. Scott (Oxford: Talboys, 1840) vol. 11

Defoe, Daniel, *Serious reflections during the life and surprising adventures of Robinson Crusoe* (1715), ed. G. A. Aitken (London: Dent, 1895)

Doddridge, Philip, *Works*, ed. E. Williams and E. Parsons, 10 vols (Leeds: Baines, 1802–5)

Doddridge, Philip, *The rise and progress of religion in the soul*, in *Works* vol. 1, pp. 211–466

Doddridge, Philip, *Sermons on public occasions*, in *Works* vol. 3, pp. 7–167

Doddridge, Philip, *Ordination sermons*, in *Works* vol. 3, pp. 171–279

Doddridge, Philip, *Hymns founded on various texts in the holy scriptures*, in *Works* vol. 3, pp. 433–643

Doddridge, Philip, *Letters*: see Nuttall, G. F., *Calendar of the correspondence of Philip Doddridge DD (1702–1751)* (Historical Manuscripts Commission, JP 26) (London: HMSO, 1979)

Edwards, Jonathan, *Treatise on the religious affections* (1746), in *Works*, ed. S. E. Dwight and E. Hickman (London, 1834; repr. Edinburgh, Banner of Truth, 1974), vol. 1, pp. 234–343

Gentleman's Magazine (1731–)

Gibbon, Edward, *The history of the decline and fall of the Roman Empire*, (1776–88; ed. in 3 vols by D. Womersley, London: Penguin, 1994)

Gibbon, Edward, *Memoirs of my life and writings* (Autobiography) (1796; ed. J. B. Bury, London: Oxford UP, 1907)

Gibbon, Edward, *A vindication, &c* (1779), ed. D. Womersley, in *History of the decline and fall* vol. 3, pp. 1106–84

Gibbon, Edward, *English essays*, ed. Patricia B. Craddock (Oxford: Clarendon, 1972)

Gibbon, Edward, *Miscellaneous works*, with introd. by D. Masson; (Globe edition) (London: Macmillan, 1895)

Goldsmith, Oliver, *The vicar of Wakefield* (World's classics) (London: Oxford UP, 1959)

Gother, John, *Spiritual works*, 16 vols (Newcastle: Coates et al., n.d. (1790))

Henry, Matthew, *Commentary on the whole Bible*, ed. L. F. Church (London: Marshall Morgan & Scott, 1960)

Hume, David, *Dialogues concerning natural religion*, in *Philosophical works*, ed. T. H. Green and T. H. Grose (London: Longmans, Green, 1882), vol. 2, pp. 375–408

Hume, David, *Of superstition and enthusiasm*, in *Essays moral, political, and literary*, ed. T. H. Green and T. H. Grose (London: Longmans, Green, 1875), vol. 1, pp. 144–50

Hume, David, *Of miracles* (*An enquiry concerning human understanding*, chapter 10), in *Essays moral, political, and literary*, ed. T. H. Green and T. H. Grose (London: Longmans, Green, 1875), vol. 2, pp. 88–108

Hume, David, *Of suicide* (*Unpublished essays* 2), in *Essays moral, political, and literary*, ed. T. H. Green and T. H. Grose (London: Longmans, Green, 1875), pp. 406–14

Hume, David, *The natural history of religion*, in *Essays moral, political, and literary*, ed. T. H. Green and T. H. Grose (London: Longmans, Green, 1875), vol. 2, pp. 309–63

Hurd, Richard, *Early letters, 1739–62,* ed. Sarah Brewer (Church of England Record Society) (Woodbridge: Boydell, 1995)

Johnson, Dale (ed.), *Women in English religion 1700–1925* (*Studies in Women and Religion*, 10) (New York: Edwin Mellen, 1983

Johnson, Samuel, *Diaries, Prayers, and Annals*, ed. E. L. McAdam Jr. with D. and M. Hyde (Yale edition vol. 1) (New Haven: Yale UP, 1958)

Johnson, Samuel, *A journey to the Western Islands of Scotland*, ed. M. Lascelles (Yale edition, vol. 9) (New Haven: Yale UP, 1971)

Johnson, Samuel, *Sermons*, ed. J. Hagstrum and J. Gray (Yale edition, vol. 14) (New Haven: Yale UP, 1978)

Johnson, Samuel, *Letters*, ed. B. Redford, 5 vols (Hyde edition) (Oxford: Clarendon, 1992–4)

Johnson, Samuel, *The Rambler*, ed. W. J. Bate and A. B. Strauss (Yale edition, vols 3–5) (New Haven: Yale UP, 1969)

Johnson, Samuel, *Johnsonian miscellanies*, ed. G. B. Hill, 2 vols (Oxford: Clarendon, 1897)

Jones, William, *Diary, 1777–1821*, ed. O. F. Christie (London: Brentano's, 1929)

Ken, Thomas, *The Christian year: Bishop Ken's Christian year, or hymns and poems for the holy days and festivals of the Church* (London: Montagu Pickering, 1868)

Ken, Thomas, *Prose works*, ed. W. Benham (London: Griffith et al., n.d.)

Ken, Thomas, *Works*, ed. W. Hawkins, 4 vols (London: John Wyatt, 1721) (poems)

Law, William, *Works*, 9 vols (London: Richardson, 1762; repr. Brockenhurst: 'G. B. Moreton' (= G. B. Morgan), 1892–3)

Law, William, *A serious call to a devout and holy life* (London: Griffith Farran Browne, n.d.)

Law, William, *A serious call to a devout and holy life* and *The spirit of love* in *Selected works*, ed. P. G. Stanwood (Classics of western spirituality) (New York: Paulist, 1979)

Leighton, Robert, *A practical commentary upon the First Epistle of St Peter*, ed. W. West, in *The whole works*, vols 3–4 (London: Longmans, Green, 1870)

More, Hannah, *Stories for persons of the middle ranks*, in *Works* (London: Fisher, Fisher & Jackson, 1834), vol. 1, pp. 1–246

More, Hannah, *An estimate of the religion of the fashionable world* (1791), in *Works* vol. 2, pp. 287–376

More, Hannah, *Thoughts on the importance of the manners of the great to general society*, in *Works* vol. 2, pp. 237–86

More, Hannah, *Hints towards forming the character of a young princess*, in *Works* vol. 4

More, Hannah, *Percy* (tragedy in 5 acts), in *Works* vol. 5, pp. 103–66

More, Hannah, *Poems*, with introd. by Caroline Franklin (The Romantics: Women Poets, 1770–1830 series) (London: Routledge/Thoemmes, 1996) (reprint of 1816 edn)

More, Hannah, *Practical piety; or, the influence of the religion of the heart on the conduct of the life*, 7th edn, 2 vols (London: Cadell and Davies, 1812)

More, Hannah, Miscellaneous essays, in *Works* vol. 6, pp. 257–358

Newton, John, *Works* (Edinburgh: Brown & Nelson, 1834)

Newton, John, *An authentic narrative*, in *Works*, pp. 1–33

Newton, John, *Letters on religious subjects*, in *Works*, pp. 35–126

Newton, John, *Cardiphonia; or, the utterance of the heart*, in *Works*, pp. 127–309

Newton, John, *Sermons preached in the parish-church of Olney* (*Olney sermons*), in *Works*, pp. 345–419

Newton, John, *Messiah; or 50 expository discourses on the series of scriptural passages which form the subject of Handel's celebrated oratorio of that name*, in *Works*, pp. 637–818

Newton, John (with William Cowper), *Olney hymns* (1779; London and Edinburgh: Nelson, 1853)

Smart, Christopher, *Hymns and spiritual songs*, in M. Walsh and K. Williamson (eds), *The poetical works of Christopher Smart, II: religious poetry, 1763–1771* (Oxford: Clarendon, 1983), pp. 1–97

Smart, Christopher, *Hymns for the amusement of children*, in M. Walsh and K. Williamson (eds), *The poetical works of Christopher Smart, II: religious poetry, 1763–1771* (Oxford: Clarendon, 1983), pp. 309–68

Southey, Robert, *The life of Wesley; and rise and progress of Methodism*, 3rd edn (with notes by Coleridge), 2 vols (London: Longman, 1846)

Steele, Anne, *Hymns, psalms and poems* (London: Daniel Sedgwick, 1863)

Sterne, Laurence, *The sermons of Mr Yorick*, ed. W. L. Cross, 2 vols (New York: J. F. Taylor, 1904)

Swedenborg, Emanuel, *Arcana coelestia*: Dole, G. F. (ed. and trans.) as *The universal human* (Classics of western spirituality) (London: SPCK/Paulist, 1984)

Swedenborg, Emanuel, *Soul–body interaction* (ed. and trans. G. F. Dole) (Classics of western spirituality) (London: SPCK/Paulist, 1984)

Trimmer, Sarah, *The oeconomy of charity; or, an address to ladies . . . with a particular view to the cultivation of religious principles, among the lower orders of people*, 2 vols (London: Johnson and Rivington, 1801)

Turner, Thomas, *The diary of Thomas Turner 1754–1765*, ed. D. Vaisey (Oxford UP, 1984)

Walpole, Horace, *Memoirs of King George II*, ed. J. Brooke, 3 vols (New Haven: Yale UP, 1985)

Walpole, Horace, *Correspondence with Hannah More* (Yale edition of Horace Walpole's correspondence, ed. W. S. Lewis, vol. 31) (New Haven: Yale UP, 1961)

Watts, Isaac, *Works*, ed. G. Burder, 6 vols (London: Barfield, 1810)

Wesley, Charles and John, *Hymns and sacred poems* (1739), in Osborn, G. (ed.), *The poetical works of John and Charles Wesley*, 13 vols (London: Wesleyan-Methodist Conference Office, 1868–72), vol. 1, pp. 1–194

Wesley, John. The following works are cited from the new edition of Wesley's works (earlier volumes published by OUP as 'The Oxford edition', later volumes published by Abingdon as 'The bicentennial edition'):

    vols 1–4 *Sermons*, ed. Albert C. Outler (Nashville: Abingdon, 1984–7)

    vol. 11 *The appeals*, ed. G. R. Cragg (Nashville: Abingdon, 1989)

    vol. 18 *Journal* and *Diaries* (1735–8), ed. W. R. Ward and R. P. Heitzenrater; (Nashville: Abingdon, 1988)

    vol. 19 *Journal* and *Diaries* (1738–43), ed. W. R. Ward and R. P. Heitzenrater (Nashville: Abingdon, 1990)

    vol. 20 *Journal* and *Diaries* (1743–54), ed. W. R. Ward and R. P. Heitzenrater (Nashville: Abingdon, 1991)

    vol. 21 *Journal* and *Diaries* (1755–65), ed. W. R. Ward and R. P. Heitzenrater (Nashville: Abingdon, 1992)

    vol. 22 *Journal* and *Diaries* (1765–75), ed. W. R. Ward and R. P. Heitzenrater (Nashville: Abingdon, 1993)

    vol. 23 *Journal* and *Diaries* (1776–86), ed. W. R. Ward and R. P. Heitzenrater (Nashville: Abingdon, 1995)

    The following works are cited from the editions given:

    Sermons: ed. E. H. Sugden, 2 vols (London: Epworth, 1921)

    A collection of forms of prayer for every day in the week in *Whole works* (1878 edn) vol. 11, pp. 232–77

    A collection of psalms and hymns (1741), in *The poetical works* (see under Wesley, Charles and John above) vol. 2, pp. 1–42

    A farther appeal to men of reason and religion in *Whole works* (1878 edn) vol. 8, pp. 55–277

    Hymns and sacred poems (1740), in *The poetical works* vol. 1, pp. 195–372

    Hymns and sacred poems (1742), in *The poetical works* vol. 2, pp. 43–366

    Hymns for children (1763), in *The poetical works* vol. 6, pp. 367–465

    Hymns for liturgical seasons (1746), in *The poetical works* vol. 4, pp. 105–204

    Hymns for the use of families, and on various occasions (1767), in *The poetical works* vol. 7, pp. 1–200

    Hymns for times of trouble and persecution (1745), in *The poetical works* vol. 4, pp. 1–90

    Hymns for those that seek and those that have redemption (1747), in *The poetical works* vol. 4, pp. 205–82

    Hymns on God's everlasting love (1741), in *The poetical works* vol. 3, pp. 1–106

    Hymns on the Lord's Supper: text in Rattenbury (1948) pp. 195–249

    Hymns on the Trinity (1767), in *The poetical works* vol. 7, pp. 201–348

    Letters, ed. J. Telford, 8 vols (London: Epworth, 1931)

    Miscellaneous hymns, in *The poetical works* vol. 6, pp. 1–366

    Original poems (1744), in *The poetical works* vol. 3, pp. 129–80

    A plain account of Christian perfection, in *Whole works* (1878 edn) vol. 11, pp. 428–524

    Preparation for death in several hymns (1772), in *The poetical works* vol. 7, pp. 349–421

    Short hymns on select passages of the holy scriptures (1762), in *The poetical works* vols 9–13

    Thoughts upon Jacob Behmen, in *Whole works* (1878 edn) vol. 9, pp. 588–93

    Versions and paraphrases of select Psalms, in *The poetical works* vol. 8, pp. 1–262

    See also: Whaling, F. (ed.), *John and Charles Wesley: selected writings and hymns* (Classics of western spirituality) (New York: Paulist, 1981)

Works, 3rd edn (with last corrections of the author), ed. T. Jackson (London: Mason 1829–31)

Whitefield, George, *Selected sermons*, ed. A. R. Buckland (London: Religious Tract Society, 1904)

Whitefield, George, *Journals*, ed. I. Murray (London: Banner of Truth Trust, 1960)

Wollstonecraft, Mary, *Mary* and *Maria*, and Mary Shelley, *Matilda*, ed. J. Todd (Harmondsworth: Penguin Classics, 1992)

Secondary Works

Ackroyd, Peter, *Blake* (London: Sinclair-Stevenson, 1995)

Adey, Lionel, *Class and idol in the English hymn* (Vancouver: British Columbia UP, 1988)

Allchin, A. M., *Participation in God: a forgotten strand in Anglican tradition* (London: DLT, 1988)

Barnard, L. W., 'The use of the patristic tradition in the late 17th and early 18th centuries', in R. Bauckham and B. Drewery (eds), *Scripture, tradition and reason: essays in honour of R. P. C.Hanson* (Edinburgh: T. & T. Clark, 1988), pp. 174–203

Bate, W. J., *Samuel Johnson* (London: Chatto & Windus, 1978)

Bebbington, D. W., *Evangelicalism in modern Britain: a history from the 1730s to the 1980s* (London: Routledge, 1989)

Beer, J. B., *Coleridge the visionary* (London: Chatto & Windus, 1959)

Besterman, Theodore, *Voltaire* (London: Longmans, 1970)

Bossy, J. *The English Catholic community 1570–1850* (London: DLT, 1975), esp. chapter 15

Bowersock, G. W. et al. (eds.), *Edward Gibbon and the decline and fall of the Roman empire* (Cambridge, MA: Harvard UP, 1977)

Brewer, John, *The pleasures of the imagination: English culture in the eighteenth century* (London: Harper-Collins, 1997)

Burrow, J. W., *Gibbon* (Past masters) (Oxford UP, 1985)

Butler, David, *Methodists and Papists: John Wesley and the Catholic Church in the eighteenth century* (London: DLT, 1995)

Chadwick, O., *The Popes and European revolution* (Oxford history of the Christian Church) (Oxford: Clarendon, 1981)

Chesterton, G. K., *William Blake* (Popular library of art) (London: Duckworth, 1910)

Clarke, W. K. Lowther, *Eighteenth century piety* (London: SPCK, 1944)

Cunliffe, Keith, 'Recollection and recovery: Coleridge's Platonism', in A. Baldwin and S. Hutton (eds), *Platonism and the English imagination* (Cambridge UP, 1994), pp. 207–16

Dallimore, Arnold A., *George Whitefield: the life and times of the great evangelist of the eighteenth-century revival* (London: Banner of Truth, 1970)

Davie, Donald, *A gathered church: the literature of the English dissenting interest, 1700–1930* (London: Routledge & Kegan Paul, 1978)

Davie, Donald, 'The language of the eighteenth-century hymn', in *Dissentient voice* (Notre Dame UP, 1982), pp. 67–82

Davie, Donald, *The eighteenth-century hymn in England* (Cambridge studies in eighteenth-century English literature and thought 19) (Cambridge UP, 1993)

Davies, Rupert, *Methodism* (Harmondsworth: Penguin, 1963)

Deacon, Malcolm, *Philip Doddridge of Northampton, 1702–51* (Northampton: Northamptonshire Libraries, 1980)

Duffy, E., 'Religious renewal in Augustan England', in D. Baker (ed.), *Renaissance and renewal in Christian history* (Studies in Church history 14); (Oxford: Blackwell for the Ecclesiastical History Society, 1977), pp. 287–300

Duffy, E., 'Richard Challoner 1691–1781: a memoir', in E. Duffy (ed.), *Challoner and his Church: a Catholic bishop in Georgian England* (London: DLT, 1981), pp. 1–26

Duffy, E., 'Wesley and the Counter-Reformation', in J. Garnett and C. Matthew (eds), *Revival and religion since 1700: essays for John Walsh* (London: Hambledon, 1993), pp. 1–20

Escott, Harry, *Isaac Watts, hymnographer* (London: Independent, 1962)

Everitt, Alan, 'Springs of sensibility: Philip Doddridge of Northampton and the Evangelical tradition', in

Landscape and community in England (London: Hambledon, 1985), pp. 209–45

Flew, R. N., *The hymns of Charles Wesley: a study of their structure* (London: Epworth, 1953)

Foley, B. C., *Some people of the penal times (chiefly 1688–1791)* (Lancaster Cathedral, 1991)

Gill, Sean, *Women and the Church of England from the eighteenth century to the present* (London: SPCK, 1994)

Glen, Heather, *Vision and disenchantment: Blake's Songs and Wordsworth's Lyrical Ballads* (Cambridge UP, 1983)

Hall, D. J., 'Plainness of speech, behaviour and apparel in eighteenth-century English Quakerism', in W. J. Sheils (ed.), *Monks, hermits and the ascetic tradition: papers read at the 1984 summer meeting and the 1985 winter meeting of the Ecclesiastical History Society* (Oxford: Blackwell, 1985), pp. 307–18

Heyd, Michael, *'Be sober and reasonable': the critique of enthusiasm in the seventeenth and early eighteenth centuries* (Leiden: E. J. Brill, 1995)

Hilton, J. A., '"The science of the saints": the spirituality of Butler's *Lives of the saints*', in *Recusant History* 15 (1980), pp. 189–93

Hindmarsh, D. B., *John Newton and the English Evangelical tradition* (Oxford: Clarendon, 1996)

Hirst, Désirée, *Hidden riches: traditional symbolism from the Renaissance to Blake* (London: Eyre & Spottiswoode, 1964)

Hobhouse, S., *William Law and eighteenth-century Quakerism* (London: Allen & Unwin, 1927)

Holmes, Richard, *Coleridge: early visions* (London: Hodder & Stoughton, 1989)

Holmes, Richard, *Coleridge: darker reflections* (London: HarperCollins, 1998)

Hoyles, John, *The edges of Augustanism: the aesthetics of spirituality in Thomas Ken, John Byrom and William Law* (Archives internationales d'histoire des idées 53) (The Hague: Martinus Nijhoff, 1972)

Jacob, W. M., *Lay people and religion in the early eighteenth century* (Cambridge UP, 1996)

Jones, Rufus M., *The later periods of Quakerism*, 2 vols (London: Macmillan, 1921)

Keynes, Geoffrey, *The library of Edward Gibbon*, 2nd edn (London: St Paul's Bibliographies, 1980)

Knox, Ronald, *Enthusiasm: a chapter in the history of religion* (Oxford: Clarendon, 1950)

Lindström, Harald, *Wesley and sanctification: a study in the doctrine of salvation* (Stockholm: Nya Bokförlags Aktiebolaget, 1946)

Luckett, Richard, 'Bishop Challoner: the devotionary writer' in E. Duffy (ed.), *Challoner and his Church* (London: DLT, 1981), pp. 71–89

Luria, K. P., 'The Counter-Reformation and popular spirituality', in L. Dupré and D. E. Saliers (eds), *Christian spirituality III: Post-Reformation and modern* (New York: Crossroad, 1989), pp. 93–120

Manning, Bernard, *The hymns of Wesley and Watts* (London: Epworth, 1942)

Mee, Jon, *Dangerous enthusiasm: William Blake and the culture of radicalism in the 1790s* (Oxford: Clarendon, 1992)

Nuttall, G. F. (ed.), *Philip Doddridge, 1702–51: his contribution to English religion* (London: Independent Press, 1951)

Nuttall, G. F. *The Puritan spirit: essays and addresses* (London: Epworth, 1967)

Orcibal, Jean, 'The theological originality of John Wesley and continental spirituality', in R. Davies and G. Rupp (eds.), *A history of the Methodist church in Great Britain*, vol. 1 (London: Epworth, 1965), pp. 81–112

Pibworth, N. R., *The gospel pedlar: the story of John Berridge and the eighteenth-century revival* (Welwyn: Evangelical Press, 1987)

Podmore, Colin, *The Moravian church in England, 1728–60* (Oxford: Clarendon, 1998)

Prickett, Stephen, *Romanticism and religion: the tradition of Coleridge and Wordsworth in the Victorian church* (Cambridge UP, 1976)

Rack, Henry D., *Reasonable enthusiast: John Wesley and the rise of Methodism*, 2nd edn (Nashville: Abingdon, 1992)

Rattenbury, J. E., *The eucharistic hymns of John and Charles Wesley* (London: Epworth, 1948)

Rivers, Isabel, *Reason, grace, and sentiment: a study of the language of religion and ethics in England, 1660–1780*, vol. 2 (Cambridge studies in eighteenth-century English literature and thought 37) (Cambridge UP, 2000)

Rogal, Samuel J., 'Swedenborg and the Wesleyans: opposition or outgrowth?', in Brock, E. J. et al., *Swe-*

denborg and his influence (Bryn Athyn, PA: The Academy of the New Church, 1988), pp. 295–307

Rose, J. K. H., *Dr Isaac Watts – his pedagogic writings and their place in 18th century education, together with introductory biographical material* (Leicester University MA thesis, 1965)

Rose, J. K. H., *Decline or rationalisation? The English grammar schools in the eighteenth century* (Keele University MA thesis, 1972)

Rose, J. K. H., *Ann and Jane Taylor as writers of improving verse for children in the early nineteenth century* Leicester University MPhil thesis, 1991

Rupp, E. G., *Religion in England 1688–1791* (Oxford history of the Christian Church) (Oxford: Clarendon, 1986) (review in *Journal of Ecclesiatical History* 39 (1988), pp. 151–2)

Schlenther, B. S., *Queen of the Methodists: the Countess of Huntingdon and the eighteenth-century crisis of faith and society* (Bishop Auckland: Durham Academic Press, 1997)

Schmidt, Martin, *John Wesley: a theological biography*, ET by N. P. Goldhawk, 2 vols in 3 (London: Epworth, 1962–73)

Shinagel, M. (1994): see under Defoe among Primary Works above

Starr, G. A., *Defoe and spiritual autobiography* (Princeton UP, 1965)

Suarez, Michael, SJ, 'Johnson's Christian thought', in Greg Clingham (ed.), *The Cambridge companion to Samuel Johnson* (Cambridge UP, 1997), pp. 192–208

Talon (1950): see under Byrom, among Primary Works above

Taylor, Barbara, 'For the love of God: religion and the erotic imagination in Wollstonecraft's feminism', in E. J. Yeo (ed.), *Mary Wollstonecraft and 200 years of feminisms* (London: Rivers Oram, 1997), pp. 15–35

Thompson, E. P., *Witness against the beast: William Blake and the moral law* (Cambridge UP, 1993)

Trickett, David, 'Spiritual vision and discipline in the early Wesleyan movement', in L. Dupré and D. E. Saliers (eds), *Christian spirituality III: Post-Reformation and modern* (World spirituality) (London: SCM, 1990), pp. 354–71

Vickery, Amanda, *The gentleman's daughter: women's lives in Georgian England* (New Haven: Yale UP, 1998)

Wain, John, *Samuel Johnson* (London: Macmillan, 1974)

Wakefield, G., 'John and Charles Wesley: a tale of two brothers', in G. Rowell (ed.), *The English religious tradition and the genius of Anglicanism* (Wantage: Ikon, 1992), pp. 165–94

Walker, A. K., *William Law: his life and thought* (London: SPCK, 1973)

Walsh, J. D., 'Origins of the Evangelical revival', in G. V. Bennett and J. D. Walsh (eds), *Essays in modern church history in memory of Norman Sykes* (London: A. & C. Black, 1966), pp. 132–62

Walsh, J. D., 'The Cambridge Methodists', in P. Brooks (ed.), *Christian spirituality: essays in honour of Gordon Rupp* (London: SCM Press, 1975), pp. 249–84

Walsh, J. et al. (eds), *The Church of England c.1689–c.1833: from toleration to Tractarianism* (Cambridge UP, 1993)

Ward, W. R., *The Protestant Evangelical awakening* (Cambridge UP, 1992)

Watson, J. R., *The English hymn: a critical and historical study* (Oxford: Clarendon, 1997)

Watts, Michael, *The Dissenters*, vol. 1 (Oxford: Clarendon, 1978)

Welch, Edwin, *Spiritual pilgrim: a reassessment of the life of the Countess of Huntingdon* (Cardiff: University of Wales Press, 1995)

West, Richard, *The life and strange surprising adventures of Daniel Defoe* (London: HarperCollins, 1997)

White, Helen C., *The mysticism of William Blake* (1927; repr. New York: Russell & Russell, 1964)

Young, B. W., *Religion and enlightenment in eighteenth-century England: theological debate from Locke to Burke* (Oxford: Clarendon, 1998)

2

Kinship and Sympathy

Spirituality and the Victorian age

All things are in motion around us, and the great heart of society is throb-
bing with manifold life. Science is startling the world with her brilliant
discoveries . . . Commerce is rousing the nations from their slumbers by
her invincible energy; is carrying her civilising influence into hitherto
untrodden regions and unnavigable seas; and is covering and enriching the
country of our birth with her glittering spoils. Despotism . . . is lifting her
dark and insulting brow, like a storm-cloud, before the face of peoples, and
with that mad ambition which is the sad but invariable inheritance of irresponsible power, is restless of guilty conquests. Regardless of the claims of
humanity and of the sacredness of life, it ministers with murderous hands
at the dreadful shrine of war, and heaps up its hapless victims, unmoved by
the remonstrances of earth or by the vengeance of heaven. Impiety, the
condensation of depravity, and often the foul progeny of superstition, has
collected its forces and furbished its arms. No longer a sullen and passive
thing, it has assumed the attitude of a proselyting power; it seeks to draw
into its vortex the great industrial classes of society . . . Wherever we turn
there is activity and progress, either for good or for evil. And shall the
Church of God be the only theatre of supineness and scene of retrogression and decay? Shall sloth, driven by the universal voice from the outer
court, find a refuge and a home in the holiest of all, and sit with flaccid
sinew and folded arms beneath the ark of the covenant . . . ? Such a disaster,
my brethren, would be the death-dirge of the nations, and might well fill
heaven with mourning, and the dark caverns of hell with grim and malig-
nant joy.[1]

These words, at once ponderous and urgent, were written by the great-great-grand-
father of the present writer, the Reverend James Phillippo Mursell, and form part of a
sermon he delivered at the Bloomsbury Chapel in London to mark the sixty-third
anniversary of the Baptist Missionary Society in 1855. Mursell was born at Lymington, and was for almost fifty years minister of Harvey Lane Baptist Church in
Leicester: he was active in local and national movements for social and political
reform, as well as in campaigning for the abolition both of the slave trade and of the
Established status of the Church of England.[2]

The rhetoric of Mursell's sermon for the missionary society is heavy-handed; but he was one of many prominent preachers who accurately gauged the challenge facing Christianity in the nineteenth century, and summoned the church to respond to it with a typically Victorian attack on sloth. But this was easier said than done. In a world of unprecedented change, in which science and commerce were burgeoning, and militarism and tyranny casting a shadow across the English Channel, how should the church respond? Was it to embrace the new utopias on offer, or engage with people of goodwill in building a better and juster world, or close the door on change and promote a defiant faith, a spirituality *contra mundum*, at the risk of becoming what Mursell called 'a theatre of retrogression'?

When James Phillippo Mursell died in 1885 at the end of a long and full life, he left a world unimaginably different from the one he entered in 1799. Samuel Butler, writing in his novel *The way of all flesh* of those living at the beginning of the century, said 'people were not so introspective then as we are now; they lived more according to a rule of thumb'.[3] The heightened introspection was not surprising: most rules and many truths had been subjected to searching and often sceptical enquiry by the time Victoria died in 1901; and few can have been unaffected by the experience, or by the other rapid and radical changes they saw around them. Mursell mentions four particular agents of change in his sermon – science, commerce, despotism, and what he terms 'impiety': each is worth a brief reflection.

In 1859, a scientist who had studied theology (among other subjects) at Cambridge published a book which began with the innocuous-sounding remark that cultivated plants appear to exhibit greater variety within any given family or genus than do those that grow in the wild.[4] Yet the book, Charles Darwin's *The origin of species*, was to usher in a revolution in scientific theory in a remarkably short time.[5] It is difficult, from the perspective of a century and a half later, to judge accurately how far the theory of evolution unsettled people's religious faith, though there can be little doubt that it did so to some degree.[6] Darwin showed how 'plants and animals, most remote in the scale of nature, are bound together in a web of complex relations'; and he argued that 'animals may partake from our common origin in one ancestor . . . we may be all netted together'.[7] Christians had to accept that human beings have kinship with animals as well as with God: the notion of 'sympathy' had to be given a new coinage. Indeed the word will become something of a *leitmotiv* in this chapter: it implies a likeness, some sense of common identity or kinship, between those sympathized with and those doing the sympathizing. After James Phillippo Mursell's death, the General Secretary of the Baptist Missionary Society praised his 'large and generous sympathy with the oppressed, with the despised negro in the days of his bondage and since, and with the poor and needy of every class'.[8]

But there were many for whom one question above all others will have recurred insistently: once we change this or that element of our beliefs, where shall we draw the line? Nor could Christians loftily dismiss the challenge of Darwin as a dull, earthbound affair that did not reach the higher levels of religious life: Darwin concluded his own book with a statement that reflected what could almost be called the spirituality of evolution, rooted not just in cold fact but in wonder and beauty:

There is grandeur in this view of life, with its several powers, having been originally breathed into a few forms or into one; and that, whilst this planet has gone cycling on according to the fixed law of gravity, from so simple a beginning endless forms most beautiful and most wonderful have been, and are being, evolved.[9]

The second agent of change identified by Mursell was commerce, 'rousing the nations from their slumber by her invincible energy'. The nineteenth century was the great age of English commerce. The quadrupling of the population during the course of the century, the ever-increasing migration from countryside to towns and cities, and major improvements in the technology of transport, all opened up hitherto undreamed-of opportunities.[10] The growth of cities was massively accelerated by the coming of the railways in the early part of the century, just as the growth of their suburbs was in turn made possible by the coming of the motor car in the later part.[11] The Industrial Revolution, begun in the eighteenth century, took wing in the nineteenth: grand or terrifying new factories sprang up across the land, and huge numbers came to them to find work. Nor were these changes confined to what was taking place within England. The growth of the British Empire, and with it of the shipping industry, also made possible vast increases in emigration (to overseas colonies) and immigration (above all from Ireland).[12]

These changes, of course, did not benefit everyone. The gap between rich and poor increased inexorably. Some acquired great wealth: others a bitter disillusionment. Civic pride and aspirations grew; but so did urban underclasses.[13] Above all, though, a new range of leisure opportunities began to become available to a slowly widening range of people: the public house, the music hall and the football pitch were to become formidable competitors with the churches for people's time and commitment on Sundays.[14]

No one explored the consequences of these changes more powerfully than Charles Dickens; and the very title of one of his finest novels, *Great expectations*, makes the main point eloquently: the Industrial Revolution and its concomitant changes enlarged expectations without necessarily enlarging opportunities. In the novel, the bleak constraints of life in the north Kentish marshes in the early years of the century are not intrinsically dehumanizing (and not at all so for the profoundly good character Joe Gargery); but as soon as young Pip's ambitions are aroused by coming into contact with wealth, the environment in which he has been brought up becomes stifling: he wants out. There was no way back to recover the myth of an older, gentler, more rural, more (as it seemed) *natural* life once the railways and factories had been built; but that did not stop many Victorians from writing or painting or building or speaking as though there were – not for nothing did the lure of a pseudo-medieval 'merry England' dominate the dreams of many, just as in the twentieth century many were content to allow so-called 'Victorian values' to dominate theirs.

James Phillippo Mursell's strictures about despotism, the third challenge he identifies, were no empty rhetoric. The continuing turmoil in France after the French Revolution and the reign and final defeat of Napoleon left an enduring mark on English minds: positively, it had been shown that tyranny could be overthrown;

negatively, it brought together freedom, atheism, and the overthrow of church and crown in a dangerous cocktail.[15] The brew was further spiced by the rise of nationalism and the ever-present fear of further war at home or abroad, a fear that became reality in the Crimea in 1854, in India in 1857, and in South Africa in 1899: democracy could not be taken for granted. Nor need despotism be seen as restricted to foreign tyrants: the Chartist riots of 1839 and the 'Peterloo' massacre of 1819, together with the rise of trades unions, reflects popular reaction against the growing power of industrialists; and, for some, what was seen as the state's unwarranted interference in the decisions of the Church of England (especially when issues of theological principle were at stake) was to prove the decisive factor in prompting conversion to Rome.

Finally, there was what James Phillippo Mursell calls 'impiety' and which might by a modern observer be called 'secularization', a process which, as Owen Chadwick points out, affected far more people than the intellectual tradition of 'enlightenment'.[16] In the same year that Darwin published *The origin of species*, John Stuart Mill produced his *On liberty*, arguing that each and every opinion had a right to be heard, and raising in acute form the question of how far moral and theological consensus was compatible with individual freedom.[17] Liberalism, rooted as it was in the dignity and status not of the state, or of the community, but of the individual, was to have a profound effect on the churches; and its rise was further fuelled by the rapid growth of journalism, allowing more and more people freedom to speak the hitherto unspeakable.[18] 'Liberal divinity', accelerated by the rise of biblical criticism in Germany, caused many to question for the first time the literal truth of scripture; and knowledge of the other great world faiths made it harder for some to affirm the unique claims of the Christian religion.[19]

These changes did not affect everyone, nor did they happen all at once; and none of them alters the fact that the nineteenth century was an era of expansion and renewal within all the main branches of English Christianity as well as in science and commerce. In part this was because religion often thrives when challenged, and did so then;[20] in part it reflects the fact that many people had a hard enough time of it surviving to worry about the latest insights of scientists or German theologians. The overwhelming majority of English people even at the end of the Victorian era believed in God. Admittedly some may have felt like the young Ernest Pontifex in Butler's *The way of all flesh*, who, 'like the farmers in his father's village, though he would not stand seeing the Christian religion made light of, . . . was not going to see it taken seriously';[21] but many others went further – the 1851 census showed that 39% of the population of England and Wales attended a place of worship on Sunday 30 March.

This bare statistic masks some important distinctions: it is certain that women went to church more frequently, and in larger numbers, than men;[22] it is fairly certain that country dwellers worshipped more often than those living in cities, and that immigrants or members of minority groups of any kind were more assiduous worshippers than others. And one recent scholar makes the important point that, where rural folk could, even in Victorian times, still conceive of their lives as being largely determined by unseen forces far more powerful than they were, city dwellers could often see for themselves both the symptoms and the causes of injustice and suffering, which must significantly have affected their world-view.[23] Nevertheless, Victorian England was profoundly religious; and even at the end of the nineteenth century most children were still being taught, by both parents and schoolteachers, to say their prayers.[24]

SPIRITUALITY AND THE ROMANTIC MOVEMENT

The nature of Romanticism

Among the plethora of '-isms' which were to affect the course of English spirituality during the Victorian era, one in particular demands further exploration, even though it resists easy definition. The nineteenth century was, as we have seen, a deeply religious age: it also a deeply spiritual one. The two were not necessarily the same thing; and the difference between them was, arguably, the result of Romanticism. In his 1965 Mellon Lectures, Isaiah Berlin argued that this elusive but crucial concept originated in German pietism, a branch of Lutheranism emphasizing an interior spirituality; and that this stress on the inward life was itself a reaction against the rhetoric and flamboyance of French culture following its effective victory over Germany in the Thirty Years War.[25] In a brilliant but polemical passage, Berlin goes on to say that this reaction

> was a very grand form of sour grapes. If you cannot obtain from the world that which you really desire, you must teach yourself not to want it. If you cannot get what you want, you must teach yourself to want what you *can* get. This is a very frequent form of spiritual retreat in depth, into a kind of inner citadel, in which you try to lock yourself up against all the fearful ills of the world. The king of my province . . . confiscates my land; I do not want to own land . . . The king has robbed me of my possessions: possessions are nothing. My children have died of malnutrition and disease: earthly attachments, even love of children, are as nothing before love of God. And so forth. This is the mood in which the German pietists operated. The result was an intense inner life, a great deal of very moving and very interesting but highly personal and violently emotional literature, hatred of the intellect, and above all, of course, violent hatred of France.[26]

Whether or not Berlin is right, there can be little doubt that Romanticism did indeed originate in Germany and was indeed characterized by a new introspection, a preoccupation with the self and the self's deepest aspirations and experience, a new emphasis on the (always unpredictable) wills and emotions and imaginations of human beings rather than merely on their rationality, a suspicion of grand external orders or forms, and a deep commitment to the integrity of the individual in his or her pursuit of beauty and meaning. The result was to help foster a profoundly spiritual view of life, if by 'spiritual' is meant a life rooted in enduring but invisible values such as love and beauty and justice, but without necessarily embracing the teachings of any given religion. Not the least of the effects Romanticism exerted on the Oxford Movement, as we shall see, was in driving its principal adherents to reclothe the spiritual in what they saw as its properly religious garments. But the appeal of Wordsworth and of George Eliot was surely in essence the result of their refusal to embody their deeply spiritual approaches to life in any particular religious tradition.[27]

Wordsworth and Shelley

There is space here only to indicate some of the areas in which two of the greatest figures of English Romanticism, William Wordsworth (1770–1850) and Percy Bysshe Shelley (1792–1822), affected the course of English spirituality. The first lies in their attitude to science. Wordsworth had no doubts about the important distinction, or complementarity, between the scientist and the poet:

> The Man of science seeks truth as a remote and unknown benefactor; he cherishes and loves it in his solitude: the Poet, singing a song in which all human beings join with him, rejoices in the presence of truth as our visible friend and hourly companion. Poetry is the breath and finer spirit of all knowledge; it is the impassioned expression which is in the countenance of all Science.[28]

The truth sought by the scientist is cold and uncompanionable; that sought by the poet is warm and alive. It is not difficult to see how appealing this approach could be to Christians seeking to affirm the integrity of a spiritual understanding of truth quite separate from, and untouched by, the inroads made by science.

Romanticism, spirituality, and social justice

An equally important area in which the Romantics influenced nineteenth-century English Christians is in their attitude to human nature. Wordsworth says that 'by our own spirits are we deified'.[29] He is clear that human beings have a vast self-transcending potential, all too rarely recognized:[30]

> Youth should be awed, religiously possessed
> With a conviction of the power that waits
> On knowledge, when sincerely sought and prized
> For its own sake, on glory and on praise
> If but by labour won, and fit to endure.[31]

And

> Neither vice nor guilt,
> Debasement undergone by body or mind,
> Nor all the misery forced upon my sight,
> Misery not lightly passed, but sometimes scanned
> Most feelingly, could overthrow my trust
> In what we *may* become.[32]

He is also clear that human beings are to think as well as to feel, even though he gives a very strong place to the affections.[33] The soul is the leading-star of the human person; yet Wordsworth's view of human nature is nuanced:

> Dust as we are, the immortal spirit grows
> Like harmony in music; there is a dark
> Inscrutable workmanship that reconciles
> Discordant elements, makes them cling together
> In one society.[34]

The soul's immortality is vital:

> the soul,
> Remembering how she felt, but what she felt
> Remembering not, retains an obscure sense
> Of possible sublimity, whereto
> With growing faculties she doth aspire,
> With faculties still growing, feeling still
> That whatsoever point they gain, they yet
> Have something to pursue.[35]

There is a good deal of Augustine here, and even more of Plato, but with the poet's careful avoidance (rather than explicit rejection) of any dogmatic precision.[36] But (and this is crucial) Wordsworth is not merely offering a vague spirituality cut off from the urgent concerns of this world. Near the end of *The prelude*, he excoriates the economist Adam Smith's *The wealth of nations* as making the pursuit of riches into a false idol, and asks with regard to the wealthy:

> Why is this glorious creature to be found
> One only in ten thousand? What one is,
> Why may not millions be?[37]

He passionately supports the provisions of the Poor Law Amendment Act (which established workhouses that, although in practice often grim and repressive, were designed in theory not simply to *accommodate* the poor but to *educate* and *advance* them):[38]

> Under how many various pressures of misery have men been driven thus, in a strain touching upon impiety, to expostulate with the Creator! and under few so afflictive as when the source and origin of earthly existence have been brought back to the mind by its impending close in the pangs of destitution. But as long as, in our legislation, due weight shall be given to this principle, no man will be forced to bewail the gift of life in hopeless want of the necessaries of life.

And he continues:

> Englishmen have, therefore, by the progress of civilisation among them, been placed in circumstances more favourable to piety and resignation to the divine will, than the inhabitants of other countries, where a like provision has not been established. And as Providence, in this care of our countrymen, acts through a human medium, the objects of that care must, in like manner, be more inclined towards a grateful love of their fellow-men.[39]

The connection Wordsworth makes between spirituality and poverty reflects his own relative prosperity: not all his fellow English were as privileged. Even so, it will be taken up by many others after him: what use is it to teach someone about prayer when they are hungry?

The importance of 'sympathy'

For Romantic poets like Wordsworth, then, the essence of the spiritual life is a love that actively embraces compassion and a recognition of human dignity. Their emphasis on compassion, or sympathy, again in the sense of shared suffering, is an important part of the Romantic legacy; and their understanding of it was drawn from Greek philosophy as much as from the Bible. In his influential *Analytical inquiry into the principles of taste*, published in 1805, Richard Payne Knight notes that, when the Stoic philosopher describes a great man struggling with adversity as 'a spectacle, upon which the gods might look down with pleasure', this is not because they enjoy watching people suffer, but because such suffering elicits their admiration, their *sympathy*.[40] 'All sympathies, excited by just and appropriate expression of energetic passion; whether they be of the tender or violent kind, are alike sublime; as they all tend to expand and elevate the mind.'[41] Sympathy, then, is no mere moralizing or intermittent burst of charity: Wordsworth speaks of

> the primal sympathy
> Which having been must ever be;
> In the soothing thoughts that spring
> Out of human suffering.[42]

For Wordsworth, this innate sympathy is rooted both in childhood and (and this is crucial) in our affinity with nature:

> No outcast he [the child], bewildered and depressed:
> Along his infant veins are interfused
> The gravitation and the filial bond
> Of nature that connect him with the world.
> Is there a flower, to which he points with hand
> Too weak to gather it, already love
> Drawn from love's purest earthly fount for him
> Hath beautified that flower; already shades
> Of pity cast from inward tenderness
> Do fall around him upon aught that bears
> Unsightly marks of violence or harm.[43]

The similarity with Darwin's stress on kinship is obvious. Shelley notes that sympathy makes us like what we contemplate; so Prometheus, staring at the Furies, says

> Methinks I grow like what I contemplate,
> And laugh and stare in loathsome sympathy.[44]

But, unlike Payne Knight, he uses compassion as an argument against design, and thus against a divine designer:

> A beautiful antelope panting under the fangs of a tiger, a defenceless ox, groaning beneath the butcher's axe, is a spectacle which instantly awakens compassion in a virtuous and unvitiated breast.[45]

And he wants to know how a universe created on such a basis can be made so by a loving God.[46]

Sympathy was not the only virtue to be given new impetus by the Romantics. Like Darwin, their response to the world around them was above all one of wonder, a wonder rooted in reverence rather than mere amazement.[47] Shelley maintains that life itself is astonishing:

> Life and the world, or whatever we call that which we are and feel, is an astonishing thing. The mist of familiarity obscures from us the wonder of our being. We are struck with admiration at some of its transient modifications, but it is itself the great miracle.[48]

The contemplation of nature

Now it is true that the Romantics saw the contemplation of the beauty of nature as possessing in itself a healing power. Thus, in *Tintern Abbey*, Wordsworth says that it bestows upon us

> that blessed mood,
> In which the burthen of the mystery,
> In which the heavy and the weary weight
> Of all this unintelligible world,
> Is lightened: – that serene and blessed mood,
> In which the affections gently lead us on, –
> Until, the breath of this corporeal frame
> And even the motion of our human blood
> Almost suspended, we are laid asleep
> In body, and become a living soul:
> While with an eye made quiet by the power
> Of harmony, and the deep power of joy,
> We see into the life of things.[49]

But he makes clear in the same poem that such contemplation is not enough. When he was young, and made his first visit to the ruined abbey, 'nature then . . . To me was all in all'.[50] But 'that time is past'; and this brings him to one of his most famous reflections:

> For I have learned
> To look on nature, not as in the hour
> Of thoughtless youth; but in hearing oftentimes
> The still, sad music of humanity,
> Nor harsh nor grating, though of ample power
> To chasten and subdue. And I have felt
> A presence that disturbs me with the joy
> Of elevated thoughts; a sense sublime
> Of something far more deeply interfused,
> Whose dwelling is the light of setting suns,
> And the round ocean and the living air,

And the blue sky, and in the mind of man:
A motion and a spirit, that impels
All thinking things, all objects of all thought,
And rolls through all things. Therefore am I still
A lover of the meadows and the woods,
And mountains; and of all that we behold
From this green earth; of all the mighty world
Of eye, and ear, – both what they half create,
And what perceive; well pleased to recognise
In nature and the language of the sense
The anchor of my purest thoughts, the nurse,
The guide, the guardian of my heart, and soul
Of all my moral being.[51]

It is vital to note the connections here between beauty and morality, between feelings and thought, heart and head.[52] In *The prelude*, Wordsworth sharply recalls how the experience of encountering a beggar abruptly prevents him lapsing into vaguely romantic mysticism ('His steadfast face and sightless eyes, I gazed,/ As if admonished from another world'[53]); and he significantly entitled Book 8 'Retrospect. Love of nature leading to love of man.'[54] The point is that nature teaches fundamental freedom and equality: in the world of nature (implicitly as opposed to cities) human beings can be free, working for themselves, attuned to the innate kinship of all things and the divine sympathy present in natural beauty.[55] In short, the universe may be beautiful; but the mind of a human being, in contemplating it, can become 'a thousand times more beautiful than the earth/ On which he dwells'.[56] And that beauty has sharply political implications: both Wordsworth and Shelley were passionate republicans, animated by a vision of a juster world rooted not in back-to-nature nostalgia, but in the indestructible freedom nature alone could teach us.[57]

Nonetheless, Wordsworth remains firmly convinced that living close to natural beauty is intrinsically ennobling;[58] and in this he was at one with Shelley, who shared much of Wordsworth's love of nature and his corresponding hatred of cities: 'Hell is a city much like London.'[59] Indeed Shelley believed that poets who celebrated the transforming and renewing power of nature were the key to the world's hope:

Through wood and stream and field and hill and Ocean
A quickening life from the Earth's heart has burst
As it has ever done, with change and motion,
From the great morning of the world when first
God dawned on Chaos; in its stream immersed,
The lamps of Heaven flash with a softer light;
All baser things pant with life's sacred thirst;
Diffuse themselves; and spend in love's delight,
The beauty and the joy of their renewèd might.[60]

It is perhaps Richard Payne Knight who most eloquently catches the relationship between beauty and morality:

The only moral good, that appears to result from either poetry, music, painting, or sculpture, arises from their influence in civilizing and softening mankind, by substituting intellectual, to sensual pleasures; and turning the mind from violent and sanguinary, to mild and peaceful pursuits . . . It is true, that excessive attention to any of these arts often withdraws the mind from the study or cultivation of others more important and beneficial: but it oftener withdraws it from indulgences, which are more criminal and destructive, both to the individual and society.[61]

Shelley: spirituality and atheism

It will become clear, in the course of this chapter, how greatly indebted many Christian theorists and practitioners of the spiritual life are to the Romantics: the recognition of science and spirituality as complementary, not inimical; the reverence given to human nature, a reverence rooted in sympathy and social justice; and the sense of nature as sacramental, bestowing upon the observer a moral as well as an aesthetic sense – all these were to exercise a crucial influence, especially on Tractarian and Roman Catholic writers, from Keble to Gerard Manley Hopkins and beyond. It would be easy to stop at this point, and conclude that the influence of the Romantics on Christianity was unequivocally positive, and that Wordsworth's own ambiguous religious faith was typical of his colleagues.[62] It seems more honest, however, to conclude this brief exploration with a look at the more overtly atheist spirituality of Shelley.[63] In one of his greatest poems, *Prometheus unbound*, the suffering hero delivers a ferocious attack on God:

> But thou, who art the God and Lord: O, thou,
>   Who fillest with thy soul this world of woe,
> To whom all things of Earth and Heaven do bow
>   In fear and worship: all-prevailing foe!
> I curse thee! let a sufferer's curse
> Clasp thee, his torturer, like remorse;
> Till thine Infinity shall be
> A robe of envenomed agony;
> And thine Omnipotence a crown of pain,
> To cling like burning gold round thy dissolving brain.[64]

For Shelley, the charge against Christianity was substantial. First, he maintained that both Protestants like Calvin and Catholics like St Dominic had taught that 'happiness is wrong';[65] secondly, their religion had been responsible for enormous suffering;[66] and thirdly, 'design must be proved before a designer can be inferred'.[67] He honoured the human Jesus as a noble person and outstanding spiritual teacher, but believed that identification with the Son of God had in effect obliterated the historical original.[68]

All this may leave the reader wondering why Shelley is included here at all, or indeed whether to speak of an 'atheist spirituality' is a contradiction in terms. The reason is clear: for Shelley, God must be, not ignored, but challenged: in *Prometheus unbound*, it is only the human soul which resists the omnipotence of Jupiter, chief of the gods:

Jupiter. Ye congregated powers of heaven, who share
The glory and the strength of him ye serve,
Rejoice! henceforth I am omnipotent.
All else had been subdued to me; alone
The soul of man, like unextinguished fire,
Yet burns towards heaven with fierce reproach, and doubt,
And lamentation, and reluctant prayer,
Hurling up insurrection.[69]

Prayer becomes precisely an assault on God, or more specifically on God's unbridled omnipotence. The moral of *Prometheus unbound*, and the essence of Shelley's own spiritual vision, are declared by Demogorgon in the poem's closing lines:

To suffer woes which Hope thinks infinite;
To forgive wrongs darker than death or night;
    To defy Power, which seems omnipotent;
To love, and bear; to hope till Hope creates
From its own wreck the thing it contemplates;
    Neither to change, nor falter, nor repent;
This, like thy glory, Titan [= Prometheus], is to be
Good, great and joyous, beautiful and free;
This is alone Life, Joy, Empire, and Victory.[70]

Why defy a God (or god) who does not exist? Because thereby we release within our-selves our innate longing (Shelley almost goes so far as to say our divinely-given longing) both for self-transcendence and for societies grounded in justice and freedom, something in which Shelley (like Wordsworth) passionately and persistently believed.[71] He could not accept a God who dispensed cruelly unfair fates to humans, because he wanted his fellow-humans to build a better world, and not passively or piously accept what fate dispenses:

That night the youth and lady mingled lay
In love and sleep – but when the morning came
The lady found her lover dead and cold,
Let none believe that God in mercy gave
That stroke.[72]

And Shelley never seems to have ceased hoping in values that were at once spiritual and social, romantic and political, and which in the end would triumph. In his poem to the west wind, written less than two years before his tragic and premature death off the Italian coast, Shelley bequeathed to the world not only his own best epitaph, but a form of prayer that in its defiant honesty and hope is extraordinarily moving. This is a secular *Benedicite*, protesting against the random finality of death and fate: if I die, the wind itself will give voice to the ideals by which I tried to live:

Make me thy lyre, even as the forest is:
What if my leaves are falling like its own!
The tumult of thy mighty harmonies

Will take from both a deep, autumnal tone,
Sweet though in sadness. Be thou, Spirit fierce,
My spirit! Be thou me, impetuous one!

Drive my dead thoughts over the universe
Like withered leaves to quicken a new birth!
And, by the incantation of this verse,

Scatter, as from an unextinguished hearth
Ashes and sparks, my words among mankind!
Be through my lips to unawakened earth

The trumpet of a prophecy! O Wind,
If Winter comes, can Spring be far behind?[73]

Spirituality and play

One other aspect of the Romantic legacy needs briefly exploring, both for its own intrinsic interest and for the influence it had: the significance of fantasy and play.[74] This is a complex subject: much nineteenth-century love of the medieval, the magical and the pseudo-mystical was not much more than a desire to escape the real world rather than to change it (though even when it was escapist it underlined another important dimension of Romantic influence on nineteenth-century religion: a love for, and desire to learn from, the past[75]). Thus (to take one example) the art of Edward Burne-Jones (1833–98) is suffused with dreamy and beautiful people, who are not (and are not intended to be) much earthly use. He wrote:

> I mean by a picture a beautiful, romantic dream of something that never was, never will be – in a light better than any light that ever shone – in a land no-one can define, or remember, only desire – and the forms divinely beautiful.[76]

There is no room in his art for the misshapen or the ugly: in his depiction of St George and the Dragon, the beast is a poor miserable thing unlikely to put up much of a fight. The reality of evil is sentimentalized away. But not all Romantic artists thought similarly. The composer Hubert Parry (1848–1918) wrote:

> Art is not solely for consolation – though that be one of its functions. It is not merely for refinement though that is one of its many benefits. It is not merely for interest though that may save many from folly and misspent lives. But to make men realize their fellowmen's conditions – and to know and feel the many sided aspects of their sufferings, and joys, and to enlarge their sympathies and their understandings.[77]

Parry was an agnostic, steeped in the philosophy of Schopenhauer and Nietzsche. But he wanted art to challenge the real world, not flee from it. And, from the point of view of Christian spirituality, the best purveyors of fantasy in Victorian England thought the same, interweaving the imaginary and the real rather than keeping them strictly separate. Hans Christian Andersen's fairy stories were very popular in

Victorian England: in *The snow queen*, Kay is rescued from his self-absorbed life and exile only when someone cares about him enough to come looking for him.[78] In Dickens' great novel *Little Dorrit*, the dreamy housekeeper Affery turns out, as even the villain recognizes, to have developed 'a fine susceptibility and spirituality', guessing the truth in her dreams.[79]

And, in sharply different ways, Charles Kingsley's *The water babies* and John Henry Newman's *The dream of Gerontius* are seeking ways to understand this world precisely by binding it in with another, just as Robert Louis Stevenson's *The strange case of Dr Jekyll and Mr Hyde* underlines what happens when that other world is cut adrift;[80] and Edmund Gosse, whose rigidly devout parents excluded any kind of fiction or fairy-stories from his childhood, found that all it did was to form him in scepticism.[81] The Victorian Nonconformist Robert Alfred Vaughan may have the last word: in his massive historical study of mysticism, he makes one of his characters say:

> Know that I was this morning reading Andersen's Märchen – all about Ole-Luk-Oie, his ways and works – the queer little elf. Upstairs he creeps, in houses where children are, softly, softly, in the dusk of the evening, with what do you think under his arm? – two umbrellas, one plain, the other covered with gay colours and quaint figures. He makes the eyes of the children heavy, and when they are put to bed, holds over the heads of the good children the painted umbrella, which causes them to dream the sweetest and most wonderful dreams imaginable; but over the naughty children he holds the other, and they do not dream at all . . . Is this to be treated as a simple child's tale? Far from it. There is a depth of philosophic meaning to it. Have not the mystics been mostly childlike natures? Have not their lives been full of dreams, manifold and strange – and they therefore, if any, especial favourites of Ole-Luk-Oie? They have accounted their dreams their pride and their reward. They have looked on the sobriety of dreamlessness as the appropriate deprivation of privilege consequent on carnality and ignorance; in other words, the non-dreamers have been with them the naughty children. To learn life's lessons well is, according to them, to enjoy as a recompence the faculty of seeing visions and of dreaming dreams. Here then is the *idea* of mysticism. You have its myth, its legend. Ole-Luk-Oie is its presiding genius.[82]

THE CHURCH OF ENGLAND
IN THE NINETEENTH CENTURY

Spirituality and the Oxford Movement[83]

Introduction

To move directly from Ole-Luk-Oie and fairy-tales to the sober realities of the Oxford Movement might appear bizarre or frivolous. But both drew much of their inspiration from the Romantic movement we have just been considering. Reverence for the visionary, the mystical, the *spiritual*; reverence for the past, and a longing to recover the pristine purity of earlier ages; above all, reverence for a form of truth which eluded scientific formulae, yet was crucial for human well-being – these things were to play a major role in the movement which took its name from the university city where it began, on 14 July 1833, with a sermon preached in the University Church by the then Professor of Poetry and Vicar of Hursley in Hampshire, John Keble (1792–1866). In the sermon he said:

> One of the most alarming [omens of increasing national apostasy], as a symptom, is the growing indifference, in which men indulge themselves, to other men's religious sentiments. Under the guise of charity and tolera-tion we are come almost to this pass; that no difference in matters of faith is to disqualify for our approbation and confidence, whether in public or domestic life.[84]

In short, anything goes, in both religion and morality. Keble did not have in mind anything remotely like the *laissez-faire* pluralism of the late twentieth century; but leg-islation which weakened the hold of the Church of England on Parliament, combined with the emancipation of the Roman Catholics in 1829, the Whig government's plans to reduce the number of Anglican bishops in Ireland, and the possibility of another bloody and anticlerical revolution in France, all helped to foster at Oxford a pervasive sense that, if the rot were not somehow stopped, all that orthodox Christianity stood for would be swept aside – and that the loss of the Church's voice at the centre of national life would lead, not to a generous ecumenical breadth, but to a dangerous moral and spiritual vacuum. It is easy to see this as a defence of privilege by a comfort-able élite; but, if we are to judge it on its own terms, it would be more accurate to see it as a defence of truth by those whose responsibility it was to teach it.

The names that the movement acquired (Oxford Movement, Tractarians, Anglo-Catholics) matter.[85] The University of Oxford was at the time an exclusively Anglican place, though moves were afoot (strongly resisted by Keble and his friends) to open it to Dissenters. Keble and his friends were, virtually to a man (*sic*), Tories, aca-demics, clergy: the movement never claimed to be representative, though it did seek to renew the whole church.[86] Nor did the movement lay claims to originality: it drew its inspiration partly from the eighteenth-century High Churchmen, partly from the poets and philosophers of Romanticism, partly from the great theologians of the Anglican settlement (Hooker, Andrewes, Laud, Jeremy Taylor and others), partly too from the scriptural scholarship and moral seriousness of the Evangelicals, but supremely from the universal Church's patristic inheritance (the study of which was itself, as we have seen, a feature of the seventeenth-century Church of England).[87]

The return to the past

This was not, of course, the first time the church had sought to renew itself by a 'return to sources' – indeed, given the historical nature of Christianity, every reform movement within it must have this character to some extent. But few if any previous movements had embarked upon the task with the precision and focused vision which was consequent upon the tightly knit nature of the group from which this one came. The scientific study of history has been seen as a nineteenth-century invention, although it could be argued that the Tractarians followed Gibbon in their historicism, exploring the past not for its own sake but in order to discover afresh enduring truths in danger of being lost.[88] In 1838 Keble and his friends (among whom the most influential were to be John Henry Newman (1801–90), Fellow of Oriel College and Vicar of the University Church, and Edward Bouverie Pusey (1800–82), Regius Professor of Hebrew and a Canon of Christ Church Oxford) began to publish a massive *Library of the Fathers*, which in the ensuing 47 years was to make available a vast quantity of patristic texts in English translation.[89]

Why this reverence for all things apostolic and patristic? Newman had no hesitation in saying later that he

> thought ... that the Apostolical form of doctrine was essential and imperative, and its grounds of evidence impregnable.[90]

In his immensely popular collection of poems *The Christian year*, Keble speaks of the 'earlier, purer days' of the Christian Church, and bids Christians learn from their scholars their 'own forgotten lore'.[91] It was what they saw as the purity and authenticity of early Christian doctrine which drew the Oxford Movement pioneers to it. Here at least was a truth you could rely on, rooted as it was in the centuries immediately following the life of the historical Jesus – a 'Catholic' truth, universal in scope and application.

This truth could lead Keble and his colleagues to an uncritical enthusiasm for all things patristic at the expense of all things Protestant (thus Pusey could speak of 'a horrible saying of the hard Calvin' about the damnation of unbaptized infants, whilst the same sentiment expressed by Tertullian is explained away: 'he probably uttered [it] to scare the heathen'[92]). But at its heart was the conviction that the Church of England had lost its way; that, as Keble put it, 'the Prayer Book is really the voice of the ancient Church';[93] so that to drink deeply of the wells of the earliest Christian centuries was to do what countless others would do after them: to discover how one's past could nourish one's future. And this was no archaeological excavation: as Richard Meux Benson, a later Tractarian, put it:

> It is not enough for us to know what was fixed [in patristic times] as the orthodox expression; we must have our minds trained affectionately in the orthodox consciousness, which is deeper and larger than the expression.[94]

What (to give a slightly later example) the composer Jean Sibelius was to do for Finland by drawing deep inspiration from the *Kalevala*, a nineteenth-century collection of Finnish national folklore, the early adherents of the Oxford Movement sought to do for the Church of England by their recovery of its patristic inheritance: to give it back its soul. This is, in a profound sense, an act of obedience, not to some external body of law, but to the Church's own innermost wellspring of life and truth.[95]

Tracts for the times

But patristic scholarship *tout court* was never going to be enough to fan the flames of a large movement. The second term used to describe Keble and his friends was 'Tractarian': it derived from the *Tracts for the times*, which began to be issued, by Newman, in

1833: a total of ninety were eventually produced, all anonymously. These too, it must be said, were clearly designed for a predominantly academic and clerical readership. Some were reprints of earlier texts, or catenas of quotations from patristic and seventeenth-century sources that confirmed Oxford Movement teaching; others were original pamphlets (or substantial treatises) on important theological subjects. Tract 72, reprinting Archbishop Ussher's views on prayer for the dead, concludes with a statement that well represents the aim of the whole series:

> to erect safe and substantial bulwarks for the Anglican believer against the Church of Rome, to draw clear and intelligible lines, which may allow him securely to expatiate in the rich pastures of Catholicism, without the reasonable dread, that he, as an individual, may fall into that great snare which has bewildered the whole Latin Church, the snare of Popery.[96]

This extract helps explain the third term used to describe adherents of the Oxford Movement: 'Anglo-Catholic'. Some of the Tracts had a particular relevance to spirituality. Thus Tract 84 (of 1838; written by Thomas Keble) is entitled *Whether a clergyman of the Church of England be now bound to have Morning and Evening Prayers daily in his parish church?* It consists of a collection of sixty-five quotations, first from the Prayer Book and then from various authorities ranging from Eusebius and Anglo-Saxon ecclesiastical canons to Jeremy Taylor, all answering the question in the affirmative. The writer argues that

> the duty itself is of such importance, one might perhaps say of so great necessity, for the maintenance of true religion, that it would be no more than right to make some venture, and, if need be, patiently to suffer discouragement and mortification for the sake of performing it.[97]

The Tract concludes with an impressive list of 'Daily and Occasional Services' held in London churches, taken from the (Anglo-Catholic) *British Magazine* of March 1838. The mix of erudition, practical information and (above all) instruction in the faith is characteristic of the whole series.

The Oxford Movement aroused both interest and opposition in large quantities. The publication of Newman's Tract 90 (entitled *Remarks on certain passages in the Thirty-Nine Articles*), attempting to show that, as Newman put it, 'the Articles are not written against the creed of the Roman Church, but against actual existing errors in it', caused a storm.[98] In the following year (1842) Newman left Oxford for Littlemore: in 1845 he was received into the Roman Catholic Church. Thereafter the effective leadership of the Oxford Movement lay with an unlikely group of Anglican academic priests: John Keble, who after ending his term as Professor of Poetry withdrew to parish life at Hursley until his death in 1866;[99] Edward Pusey, who after his wife's death in 1839 lived a simple but active life at Christ Church, Oxford, notwithstanding the furore that followed his sermon on the Eucharist there in 1843, leading to his suspension from preaching for two years;[100] John Mason Neale (1818–66), priest, scholar, novelist, and antiquarian, who was co-founder of what became the Ecclesiological Society, which sought to apply Tractarian principles to church architecture and liturgy;[101] and a number of disciples, among whom were Isaac Williams, poet and country priest, and Henry Parry Liddon, successively Vice-Principal of Cuddesdon Theological College and Chancellor of St Paul's Cathedral.[102] It will principally be these whose works form the basis of the exploration of Tractarian spirituality that follows.

In 1840 Pusey set down in a letter what he believed to be the central tenets of the Movement. In addition to the emphasis on patristic authority already mentioned, these included a 'high' doctrine of the episcopacy, the visible church, and the sacraments: the latter were to be seen not, as with Calvinists, as 'signs only of grace given independently of them', but as 'the very means by which we are incorporated into Christ, and subsequently have this life sustained in us'; 'regard for ordinances', such as daily public prayers, fasts, and the observance of feast days; 'regard for the visible part of devotion, such as the decoration of the house of God, which acts insensibly on the mind'; 'the necessity of continued repentance of past sins'; and belief in all the doctrines of the historic Creeds, especially that of the Trinity, as essential for salvation, rather than (as with some Protestants) an exclusive emphasis on justification by faith.[103] What kind of spirituality was elicited from these fundamental principles?

Spirituality and creation

In the first place, the Tractarians generally held a positive view of creation. In a sermon on Romans 7.22–3, Pusey stresses the Biblical teaching that all of creation, including its lowest parts, are to be taken up into glory.[104] Creation is stained through human misuse of it, a strikingly modern insight; but 'all nature, having suffered together, shall be restored together'.[105] For

> things animate and inanimate, as being the works of God . . . bear in themselves some likeness to their Maker, and traces of His Hands.[106]

But creation was there to be learnt from, and studied, not simply to be wondered at, though that did not prevent the Tractarians from delighting in its beauty:[107] on the contrary, its beauty was precisely a manifestation of its didactic and sacramental power. Hence the importance of 'the visible part of devotion' that Pusey refers to above, such as the decoration of the house of God. Pusey himself had in mind something relatively simple;[108] but Keble believed a beautiful building could draw the thoughts of worshippers 'away from the ordinary world, and lift them up to that world, where all is beautiful and glorious';[109] and J. M. Neale, horrified when a churchwarden in his first parish, at Crawley, suddenly clambered on the altar during the service in order to open the window, declared: 'the Protestantism of the people with respect to that is dreadful: it all arises from having a short Chancel'.[110]

The *non sequitur* here is more apparent than real: essential to the ideals of the Ecclesiological Society Neale helped to found was the recovery of that medieval Gothic style in which the size and height of the chancel emphasizes the overwhelming transcendence of God, as well as the holiness of his sacramental presence;[111] it also supremely articulates the spirit of a church standing over against the world, and scorning an easy conformity with it.[112]

The doctrine of reserve

This approach to creation has two major implications, which take us to the heart of Tractarian spirituality: first, the doctrine of reserve; secondly, the doctrine of the sacraments. In Tracts 80 and 87, another Tractarian, Isaac Williams, defined 'reserve' as 'a very remarkable holding back of sacred and important truths [in respect of God's dealing with humankind], as if the knowledge of them were injurious to persons unworthy of them'.[113] He says that

> there appears in God's manifestations of Himself to mankind, in conjunction with an exceeding desire to communicate that knowledge, a tendency to conceal, and throw a veil over it, as if it were injurious to us, unless we were of a certain disposition to receive it.[114]

Williams is not trying to argue for a hierarchy of truths, the higher of which are accessible only to a learned or priestly élite: rather he is seeking to guard the Church against two opposite hazards – on the one hand, an arid and speculative rationalism; on the other, 'enthusiasm', which he defines as 'a state of the mind when the feelings are strongly moved by religion, but the heart is not adequately purified or humbled'.[115] For Williams, the heart of Christianity is mystery, not in the sense of a riddle to be solved but in the sense of a living source of love and beauty that grasps and transforms you: like the apophatic theology of Pseudo-Dionysius and others, he wants to underline that, the closer you come to God, the less you have to say.[116] It is in worship, not in books, that true theology is expressed and lived.[117] Real Christian service is manifested in hidden acts of love and compassion; and it is rooted in the sacramental life of the church, in the continuing offering of prayer and praise at the altar. And it is by seeking to make that life our own, and thus to be changed, slowly and at great cost, into the Christlike people we were created to be, that we shall best proclaim the Gospel we believe.[118]

Sacramental spirituality

This brings us to the sacraments. In his controversial sermon 'The Holy Eucharist a comfort to the penitent' (1843), Pusey argues that baptism engrafts us onto the true vine; the Eucharist 'derives the richness and fulness of His life into the branches thus engraffed' [sic].[119] The main purpose of the Eucharist 'is the support and enlargement of life, and that in [Christ]' – and not just any life, but the life of Christ himself.[120] The perfection for which 'all the rational creation groans' is the perfection of union with Christ through the mystery of the Incarnation and the Eucharist.[121] (The insertion of the word 'rational' here is an intriguing qualification on St Paul's text in Romans 8.22, which says that 'the whole creation groaneth' (KJV), not just the rational part of it.) The 'immediate and proper end' of the Eucharist is

> union with Him Who hath taken our manhood into God, and the infusion into us of His Spirit and life and immortality, making us one with His glorified Humanity, as He is One in the Godhead with the Father.[122]

Pusey goes on to argue that frequent communion brings about a real change in the worshipper:

There is and ought to be a real consciousness that more frequent Communion should involve a change of life, more collectedness in God, more retirement, at times, from society, deeper consciousness of His Presence, more sacredness in our ordinary actions whom He so vouchsafeth to hallow, greater love for His Passion which we celebrate, and carrying it about, in strictness of self-rule and self-discipline, and self-denying love.[123]

The implications of this are important. In another of his sermons, Pusey says, traditionally enough, that

God made us for no other end than to be like Him; and, being like Him, to love Him and to enjoy Him, and to be filled with His love.

He made us after his own image; and

He willed to re-form each separate grace in us, line by line, Himself, but through ourselves; Himself evermore supplying His grace, and we, in each act, using it. He retraces that Image in us through the infusion of His grace, while we, using that grace, copy that Divine pattern. 'We all with open face, beholding, as in a glass, the glory of the Lord, are changed into the same Image from glory to glory, by the Spirit of the Lord' (2 Cor.3:18).[124]

Hence 'by beholding God, in His Glory, hereafter face to Face, we shall be made like Him in Glory. By beholding our Lord now on earth in His Holiness and His Love, we shall be transformed into some likeness of His Love and Holiness.'[125] We cannot see God here; but we can see him in Christ, whose life we seek to imitate, 'and through adoring love be conformed to Him'.[126] And it is supremely by imitating the self-emptying love of Christ that we achieve this.[127]

It is not surprising to find Pusey exploring a text like 2 Corinthians 3.18, with its visionary language of transformation into the likeness of Christ; but what *is* striking is the way he earths St Paul's text by stressing the need for us to incarnate in our lives the same unconditional love that Christ revealed in his. This process begins with faith, 'the root of the whole spiritual life of grace . . . the beginning of our spiritual existence'.[128] Through faith we are drawn to God:

The drawing of grace changes nature, and strengthens nature, reforms nature, subdues nature, but only if we be willing to be changed, reformed, subdued, strengthened. We are drawn with the cords of a man, not dragged as brutes.[129]

And Christ is constantly knocking on our doors:

by all things, good or evil, vanity or verity, nothingness or truth, remorse at evil or peace in good; the fading of this world, or glimpses of His own endless abiding Beauty; the dread of hell and of devils, or the brightness of the heavenly choirs and the echoes of the endless Halleluias; by the aweful death of the bad, or the frightfulness of a soul in deep sin, or by the calm beauty of souls in grace, which we half-see entering into the opened gates of Paradise; by the dryness of the ashes whereon we fed for bread, or the sweetness of His hidden Manna; the dreariness of His absence, or the light and life of His Presence, in something done for Him; by His Word, His preachers, His Sacraments, He stands at the door and knocks.[130]

Eucharistic spirituality: union with God

Pusey here makes very much his own the famous text from Revelation 3 ('Behold, I stand at the door and knock' (KJV)), beloved of Evangelicals. But he goes further. In a sermon for Ascension Day, Pusey explores the patristic theme of deification.[131] The humanity of Christ was not simply dissolved at the Ascension: it was deified.[132] And in the Eucharist we are united with his deified Body:[133] the indwelling of God the Holy Spirit in us 'ennobles, transforms, illumines, empowers, enlarges, transfigures, nay, they say boldly, "deifies" the soul'.[134] 'The Resurrection of Christ is the pattern of the resurrection of our poor bodies, but only, if we rise with Him in soul now.'[135]

This tremendous transcendental vision of the goal of human life begins at our baptism, when we are united with the Trinity, whose very life is intimate and loving union.[136] Yet at baptism this union is there only in potential, like a seed sown: it is increased whenever we pray to God, 'for we call Him into Himself' – a striking phrase – as well as when we receive Holy Communion.[137] And it is a union of love, so that 'every growth in love is growth of *His* Presence Who is Love':[138]

> We become like God, by His inward renewal of us . . . Love, which He creates, opens the heart for love which He is. Love, which He gives, enlarges the heart to receive larger love.[139]

The two principal sacraments of baptism and Eucharist, then, are at the epicentre of the spiritual life: what was begun in potential at baptism must be brought to fruition through our receiving the sacramental body of Christ at the Eucharist, in which the mystery of Christ's unique act of self-giving on the Cross is re-presented before us. Keble put this with eloquence and precision in a letter:

> The *suffering* Christ offered Himself *once for all* in satisfaction for the sins of the world; the *triumphant interceding* Christ offers Himself continually for the application of that great Atonement . . . And the Eucharist is this same Intercession transacted in Image and Mystery (not in mere shadow and figure) on earth, which in heaven takes place according to the glorious reality of that blessed place.[140]

This emphasis on the close link between the Eucharist and the sacrifice of Christ at Calvary is vital for the Tractarians:

> were it *only* a thankful commemoration of His redeeming love, or *only* a shewing forth of His Death, or a strengthening *only* and refreshing of the soul, it were indeed a reasonable service, but it would have no direct healing for the sinner. To him its special joy is that it is his Redeemer's very broken Body, it is His Blood, which was shed for the remission of his sins.[141]

Hence the intimate link between the Eucharist and the forgiveness of sins, a link that has already found expression in the Church's liturgy.[142] Keble stresses the physicality of the Eucharist: in it we receive, and reverence, Christ's risen body, which reminds us of the holiness of our own bodies also: 'When one Christian is kindly waiting on another, even in the way of bodily help . . . that Christian is really and truly waiting on Christ, honouring Him in his neighbour's body.'[143]

Two vital points follow from this. First, the presence of Christ in the Eucharist is precisely a spur, a reminder, a prophetic challenge to us to discern his presence also in our neighbour. 'Christ is in each Christian,' said Keble in a sermon, 'filling each more and more with Himself, in such measure as we try to keep Him with us', though differently in each.[144] But do we really contemplate his presence in one another?[145] Christ's presence is dynamic, and objective, not simply dependent upon whether or not we happen to notice him. We are already and always in his presence, inasmuch as he 'is present within and without, since nothing which He has created can displace Himself'.[146] 'The whole world is His Temple, for everywhere He is by Essence, Presence and Power.'[147] The exact *manner* of his presence remains mysterious: like Hooker, the Tractarians draw back from what they perceive as the over-definition of a profound mystery implied by the Roman dogma of transubstantiation.[148] But the *reality* of it for them is unquestionable.

Secondly, the Tractarian attitude to the Eucharist, and thus indirectly to the holiness of creation itself, led them to a profound commitment to social justice not immediately evident in most of the earliest works of Keble, Pusey and others, but directly consequent upon them. The Eucharist weaned people away from a perilous self-dependence: in his introduction to *Eucharistica*, a Tractarian devotional manual for Anglicans, Samuel Wilberforce (Bishop of Oxford and son of the slave-trade abolitionist William Wilberforce) warned against what he calls the low and degenerate mysticism which is everywhere abroad; which, setting out by seeking to promote the essence and inner life of piety, ends by destroying its very existence.[149] He means a narrowly individual piety concerned only with the self's own transformation. The Eucharist incorporates Christians into the whole life of the Church; and the spiritual life is to be seen in that firmly ecclesial context. Our bodies are holy, as well as our souls, because all of ourselves is destined for eternity.[150] The Church is 'our Mother';[151] but this is not simply a pious catchphrase. Rather, as Pusey put it,

> [The Church] herself ought to debate upon remedies, and should not leave to individual effort the work of the whole. We need Missions among the poor of our towns; organized bodies of Clergy living among them; licensed preachers in the streets and lanes of our cities; brotherhoods, or guilds, which should replace socialism; or sisterhoods of mercy, for any office of mercy, which our Lord wills to be exercised towards His members, or towards those His outcast ones whom love, for love of Him, might bring back to Him. We need Clergy to penetrate our mines, to migrate with our emigrants, to shift with our shifting population, to grapple with our manufacturing system as the Apostles did with the slave-system of the ancient world.[152]

Note here the stress on corporate pastoral care, rooted in the role of the church, and clearly distinct from political ideologies like socialism; note too the prominent role given to the clergy, and the imaginative vision of priesthood for contemporary society. This is Pusey writing about church councils. But it is also Pusey writing *for* the church of his own day, and doubtless not least for the priests and people of St Saviour's Leeds, the church he had himself quietly helped to pay for and to which he gave unstinting support.[153] Later Anglo-Catholics, as we shall see, will take this much further, arguing that Catholic truth and socialism are entirely compatible; but even then they will be drawing heavily on the thought of their Tractarian forebears.

Penance, sin and forgiveness

The spiritual vision of the early Tractarians, then, is a firmly corporate one: like St Paul in 2 Corinthians, Pusey and Keble almost invariably use the plural when writing about our transformation into the likeness of Christ. Holiness 'was made for all', not just for selected individuals.[154] But we cannot attain it on our own. Nor can we achieve it without prolonged and serious attention to the reality of sin in and around ourselves, another key dimension of Tractarian spirituality. Henry Liddon is interesting here: he acknowledges the power of Schopenhauer's typically sobering aphorism ('We do not perceive that certain days of our lives have been happy till they have given place to unhappy ones'[155]), and goes on to make clear that sin cannot be seen as an inherited flaw in human nature *ab initio*, nor as part of a Hegelian dialectical contradiction without which good would have no value.[156] Instead Liddon follows St James (1.15) in locating the roots of evil in human *desire*:

> [St James] says that desire when it hath conceived bringeth forth sin. He thus places the origin of moral evil in the created will, of which desire is the moral ingredient. Desire is, indeed, the raw material of moral life. It is neutral force which may become, under different circumstances, either sanctity or sin: and thus S. Augustine has defined virtue as 'love or desire ruled by true order.' Desire is part of the original outfit of every human being; a sympathetic impulse where by the various instincts and faculties of our nature are drawn towards something external to itself. What is that something?[157]

In human beings' original state, that 'something' was God, the only true object of our deepest desires.[158] The perverted misdirection of desire towards the things of time and sense is what causes sin.[159] Sin is not necessary to the existence of *goodness*; but it is necessary to the existence of *freedom*.[160] And God does not simply accept sin and evil. He fights against them, constantly seeking to bring good out of them.[161]

Much of this is patristic teaching, in this case drawn from the theology of St Augustine: its effect is to cause the Tractarians to see the spiritual life as a progressive thing, a process, in which as Pusey puts it 'we must either be stretching onward, or we shall be sinking back'.[162] As a consequence, the process of confessing our sins and receiving God's forgiveness plays a major role and requires further reflection here.

Pusey explores the theory of penance and absolution in a substantial preface he wrote to a translation of the French Abbé Gaume's *Advice on hearing confessions*.[163] He distinguishes between sacramental confession and spiritual direction;[164] and he justi-fies the frequent practice of the former by an unexpectedly homely analogy: just as frequent mowing gets rid of deep-rooted bindweeds which otherwise corrupt the entire lawn, so frequent confession is 'a help against some deep-rooted infirmity of our poor nature'.[165] Recourse to a priest is not, in Pusey's view, to derogate from the imme-diate and all-sufficient nature of Christ's personal relationship with the sinner;[166] nor is it to diminish the completeness of what Christ has achieved for us on Calvary. Rather, it is to co-operate with the work of grace first imparted to us at our baptism, thereby fostering what is inevitably a lifelong process of re-creation.[167] There is an admirable directness here: 'they are well nigh wasted hours,' he says, 'in which thou broodest sorrowfully over thyself, as though there were no hope, unless they issue in prayer to God'.[168] We must take action, seek the healing and wholeness we need and cannot attain alone.

Pusey and Keble explore the nature of what action is necessary in their letters of spir-itual counsel. This is the advice Keble gives to someone who is overwhelmed by a sense of sin:

> I think you had better begin immediately to prepare for what is called General Confession, by reviewing your whole history, and setting down your sins as well as you can; any book of preparation for the Holy Commu-nion will help you to do so. And, having this paper by you, you may add to it from time to time, as new faults occur, or old ones are remembered; and then when a good opportunity comes, you may pour it all out into your loving Lord's ear, through some one of His unworthy Priests.[169]

Later he tells the same person to do all of this 'as a religious exercise, as in God's presence, and a good deal on your knees'.[170] He is pastoral but firm with someone who appears to find it hard to avoid the presence of someone he is inappropriately fond of:

> do not think that this is beyond your power; you *know* that you can, if you will earnestly try, as in God's Presence, and with prayer to Him, you *can* resist and overcome temptations . . . By no means renew the intimacy which you speak of, under any specious fancy which may suggest itself to your mind of doing good to the other party. *Flight* is the approved remedy in such cases. Keep your distance and pray for her and for yourself.[171]

Tractarian spiritual direction
This kind of simple yet profound spiritual direction is characteristic of Tractarian spiri-tuality. In his Preface to Gaume's *Manual*, Pusey says that the office of spiritual director

> is, not to supersede, but to develop and deepen the sense of personal moral responsibility; to teach those who look to us for guidance, how to use the judgement which God has given them; to furnish them with clear princi-ples to discern right from wrong; to suggest to them how to discern, in the secret whispers of conscience, the voice of God the Holy Ghost . . . and to distinguish this from the human spirit, or Satan transformed into an angel of light; to train them to obey, not us, but Christ, the Master of both.[172]

He particularly warns against the dangers of directors encouraging an unhealthy dependence, or insisting on obedience to them rather than to God, citing F. W. Faber's *Growth in holiness*:

> The business of a director is not that of a pioneer. It is rather to go behind, and to watch God going before . . . He does not lead his penitents. The Holy Ghost leads them . . . He is not to have a way of his own applied to every one . . . It is a perilous thing to make a superstition of direction.[173]

This does not prevent the Tractarians from being firm when they feel it appropriate. 'Never compare thine own lot with that of another,' says Pusey in one of his sermons, many of which conclude with pithy spiritual guidance.[174] He rebukes one correspondent for being hypercritical, ending his letter: 'Our Lord bids us "Judge not." You do.'[175] And 'in telling a Sister's fault, think if it is from love of her'.[176] Keble warns of the risk of too interiorized a piety: 'I hold it to be a selfish and dangerous sort of thing for people to be always turning their eyes inward';[177] and he suggests that the therapeutic value of writing lies often simply in the act itself: 'I fancy the best way would be to write on till one was a little unburthened, and then put one's confessions in the fire.'[178] Here too it is important to note the vital interrelation between theology and practice, truth and Christian living:

> I should earnestly advise any person who wished to be well grounded in the truth, instead of reading controversial books . . . to go on taking for granted that the doctrine of the Church was true, *and acting upon it*. I believe this to be, I will not say the *best*, but the *only* way to come to a real grasp of holy truths.[179]

Above all, though, Tractarian spiritual direction is suffused with pastoral wisdom. Pusey tells a woman whose child has died to 'act day by day for the day', and not to look too far ahead at once.[180] And Keble tells an elderly priest suffering from depression that

> the more entirely we are made to feel the worthlessness of all that we have ourselves been or done, the more are we thrown, wholly and solely, upon the merits of Him, who is our only Hope; and this deep and bitter feeling may be our Lord's providential way of causing you to cast all your care upon Him . . . I am continually saying, in effect, to persons in such trouble as you sometimes feel, 'which do you really want of the Almighty? *Comfort* now, or pardon and acceptance hereafter?' The latter, of course: and it may be that the imperfection you complain of in the former, may greatly help towards that better thing.[181]

Pusey gently but shrewdly says to someone else burdened by suffering: 'I think that you are more likely to find comfort, when you cease to look for it and dwell more on the thought of God's great Love and pray for it. While we watch our feelings, we lose sight of God'[182] – this suspicion of the importance of feelings is characteristic of the Tractarians.[183] And he tells someone whose missionary work seems to have failed:

Not one thing which you have ever done for God, has been lost; not one is lost, or ever will be lost. While we each do the little we can do, we may leave the rest to Him.[184]

Spirituality and priesthood

It is vital to see that the attention given by the Tractarians to teaching about penance and spiritual direction was essential to their overall vision: if they could help individual Christians to deepen their spiritual lives, they could help bring about a renewal of the Church which in turn might precipitate a transformation of the nation. And here more than anywhere else their stress on the corporate is crucial: if one person's prayer, or participation in worship, develops, the whole body is enriched. So with the spirituality of the priesthood: texts like Newman's Tract 75, on the Roman breviary, might appear impossibly remote from most people's lives. But if priests were helped to become, not just stewards of the sacraments, but experienced spiritual guides (as Keble believed they should be), the life of the entire parish could be renewed. Here is Keble on St John the Baptist as a primary exemplar for contemporary priesthood:

> Let us try to enter into the spirit of that deep and affectionate loyalty . . . to our Lord, which is every where to be seen in the holy Baptist's character . . . 'Every day,' S.John seems to tell them, 'I have more and more of the same kind of satisfaction, which a true disinterested friend of any man has in his friend's happy marriage. Every day I rejoice more and more, in feeling that I am nothing, and that He is all; that He must increase, but I must decrease.'[185]

The theology and practice of prayer

This brings us finally to consider the Tractarians' understanding of prayer. Pusey describes prayer as an entering 'into the light of Eternal Brightness, to be kindled with the glow of everlasting Love, to enter, a bidden guest, into the unseen glory of the Divine Presence, and there, face to Face, to ask Him who is more ready to give than we to ask'.[186] What is noteworthy here is the interrelation of contemplative and petitionary prayer, fused in the central notion of the presence of God.[187] Hence, as Liddon says, prayer can never simply be petition: it is also praise and adoration, and a simple delighting in someone's presence:

> When we seek the company of our friends, we do not seek it simply with the view of getting something from them; it is a pleasure to be with them, to be talking to them at all, or about anything . . . So it is with the soul, when dealing with the Friend of friends – with God.[188]

Keble makes the same point with exquisite simplicity:

> with undivided heart,
> The shepherd talks with God apart,
> And, as he talks, adores.[189]

This notion of prayer as entering the presence of God is close to continental Catholic spirituality: Jean-Pierre de Caussade (1675–1751) speaks of the God who is everywhere present, and who may thus best be encountered in the midst of the routine and the everyday; and teachers like St François de Sales (1567–1622) and St Vincent de Paul (1581–1660) were supremely concerned with helping people to pray *in mundo*, to experience God's presence amongst them, and thus to reverence that presence both on the altar and in one's neighbour.[190] Yet this practising of the presence of God is not easy; and prayer requires perseverance: indeed Pusey suggests that earnest prayer is a condition of being heard by God;[191] and when we feel we are not being heard, we must do what the Canaanite woman and blind Bartimaeus did when faced with apparent rejection by Jesus or his disciples: cry out all the louder, for the longing to be heard is in itself holy: 'the longing of the soul is the Presence of Christ', as Pusey eloquently puts it.[192]

Hence the way to learn how to pray is precisely to begin praying, and constantly to seek to integrate the life of prayer with the whole life of the Christian: 'practise in life whatever thou prayest for, and God will give it thee more abundantly'.[193] Pusey elsewhere suggests that the promise of Jesus that God will answer our requests is said only to those willing to live as God's children.[194] Hence 'all prayer to God implies that we act as we pray';[195] and Keble entitled one of his sermons 'As we are, such are our prayers.'[196]

Prayer involves commitment, perseverance, keeping God company, as a child seeks out the company of its parent:

> it is coming before Him with your wants and petitions, as simply and as really as a child, being hungry, comes to his earthly father and asks for some bread. This is prayer: and we all know the need of it: but to practise it in earnest, *that* is the hard fight.[197]

And this capacity to 'stay in there' will in the end bear fruit. In his National Apostasy sermon, Keble said that the Church's work of intercession must continue no matter how badly she is treated by the secular authorities.[198] And intercession, sincerely practised, in turn gives the Church courage and strength to remonstrate at things that need attention or change.[199] It is again worth noting the stress on the corporate: prayer is anchored in the common worship of the whole Church, and supremely in the Eucharist.[200]

Hence we must bring our prayers, even our prayers of puzzlement and distress, into our worship: this, as Keble says, is the purpose of the Litany, 'how it reckons up almost all sorts of affliction and anxiety, and puts words in our mouth, asking for deliverance from them'.[201] Keble points out elsewhere that suffering can turn us in on ourselves; and sometimes it is good to offer God praise and thanksgiving in worship even when we are suffering, thereby deflecting our attention away from our own problems.[202] Hence the vital importance of providing, if possible, daily opportunities for common prayer in church. Pusey writes, in a short tract on fasting,

> I am the more convinced that the clergy are wrong in withholding daily prayers, that they underrate the willingness or the wish of their people to

go to Church, *if invited* . . . Surely we are neglecting to supply the cravings which either already exist, or might readily be awakened, when man has no earthly friend. And might not our poor, when destitute of employment, be led to the Church instead of to the ale-house?[203]

And, writing to someone after the death of their infant child, Keble says:

Since we are taught that there is a sympathy between Paradise and earth, at least between the saints in one, and the saints in the other, what if Christian parents by holy living, should be supposed to have this comfort among others, that their lost children still watch over them, or in some way or other know of their well doing?[204]

Conclusion

The achievement of the Oxford Movement was remarkable, though the extent of that achievement remains a matter of much debate.[205] Its influence took many forms, some of which will appear in the exploration of parish life that follows: the creation of (lay and clerical) guilds, giving devotional focus and identity to devout Anglicans;[206] the renewal of the religious life; the Anglo-Catholic missions in large cities, strongly influenced by French Catholic models of evangelism;[207] and above all the remarkable achievement of devoted Anglo-Catholic priests and people in some of the poorest urban areas in the land (which will be considered more fully in Chapter 3) – all these testify to the enduring power of the original Tractarian vision. In some respects, the most prosaic of testimonies remains the most powerful: the narrator says of the young priest Ernest Pontifex, in Samuel Butler's novel *The way of all flesh*, that 'it was surprising how many practices he now tolerated which in his youth he would have considered Popish'.[208] 'Tolerated' is too weak a word: the entire Church of England grew to value afresh a part of its Catholic inheritance which it might otherwise have allowed quietly to wither.

This is not to deny the limitations of the Oxford Movement. By no means all Anglo-Catholics came to be committed to social reform, or the care of the poor; many were, like Keble himself, deeply conservative, not only (or even primarily) in politics but in still holding to a vision of the church which modern secular realities no longer rendered tenable.[209] But here it is crucial to remember the profound threat they perceived, not just to the integrity of the Church of England, but to the spiritual health of the nation as a whole. In an intriguing footnote to one 1850 sermon, Pusey speaks of 'the teaching of the Church in her Catechism, and at the Baptism of every child' as 'one continuous ever repeated resistance' to control by the state.[210]

Arguably a more serious criticism of the early Tractarians is not that they were too conservative, but that they were too churchy: their view of the created world, though positive, had little of the visionary intensity of Wordsworth and Shelley, and images of an embattled church beleaguered in a hostile world frequently recur.[211] Nor is this only a matter of tone. The Oxford Movement reflected a desire to draw deeply from *within* the Church's spiritual tradition, and then to engage with the world – rather than to set about redefining or re-presenting the Gospel in the light of recent secular knowledge. Furthermore, despite the Tractarians' pastoral concern with the consequences of sin, the strongly corporate tone of much of their spirituality falters here: there is little questioning of the traditional assumption that everything is determined by God's overruling providence, an inclination patiently to accept suffering, rather than to challenge it, and little evidence of the kind of awareness of the dangers of deep-rooted injustices in society which will characterize the thinking of later Anglo-Catholics, or of a William Booth or a Cardinal Manning.[212]

Yet it would be not only uncharitable but unfair to end on such a note. Beneath the unemotional exterior, the tendency to extol 'that soothing tendency' (as Keble describes the quality in the Prayer Book he particularly wishes to commend[213]), and alongside the inevitably intellectual character of a movement nurtured in so atypical and distinctive a milieu, there is fire and vision in abundance. Take, for example, this remark of Pusey's: encouraging the faithful to receive Holy Communion frequently, he says that doing so gives us a direct foretaste of the life of heaven, and

> a union with God so close; that we cannot mostly, I suppose, imagine to ourselves, how we could daily thus be in Heaven, and in our daily business here below.[214]

One's first reaction in reading it might be to wonder whether the notion of heaven as a kind of eternity of Prayer Book Eucharists would be quite as universally appealing as Pusey appears to suppose (J. M. Neale's suggestion that heaven will be a little like the island of Madeira may seem more attractive[215]). But that is to miss the point entirely. Pusey was consumed by a longing to convey to all who would listen that we were created by a God of infinite love and glory, and that there is literally no limit to what that God can do, for us and for the world, if we consent to his gracious call. But that consent demands of us a willingness to remain faithful to a Church which is the sacrament of God's love: to commit ourselves to the daily round of worship and prayer, not seeking reward or instant gratification, until the slow inner process of consecration sets us (and, through us, creation itself) on fire, burning bushes ablaze with the divine presence:

> When I was in London there was a great ugly wall just in front of where I sat, but when the sun shone upon it it became all-glorious. That is like us: we are ugly, but when the grace of God shines on us we become very different. There now, look – see that wall! it is ugly enough in itself: now see! how resplendent![216]

Spirituality and the Liberal tradition

Introduction

It says a great deal for the breadth and vitality of the Church of England that, at nearly the same time as the great figures of the Oxford Movement were fashioning their theology, representatives of an entirely different tradition were actively at work. We have already noted the significance of John Stuart Mill's *On liberty*, and the rise of 'liberal divinity', above all in Protestant Germany. There is no sense in which either English Liberalism or German theology produced a school, or coherent body, of

English disciples: rather, one strand of English Anglican spirituality in the nineteenth century is characterized by some at least of the distinctive features that came to be associated with Liberalism in religion.

What were they? John Henry Newman had no doubts. In his *Apologia pro vita sua*, written in response to a charge made against him by Charles Kingsley, one of the figures to be explored here, Newman wrote:

> Liberalism is the mistake of subjecting to human judgment those revealed doctrines which are in their nature beyond and independent of it, and of claiming to determine on intrinsic grounds the truth and value of propositions which rest for their reception simply on the external authority of the Divine Word.[217]

That was a rallying-cry which Evangelicals as well as Tractarians might acknowledge. Broadly speaking, if Evangelicalism argued for the revelation of scripture as the sole repository of Christian truth, and Catholicism argued for that same revelation as interpreted by the Church, Liberalism argued for that revelation to be interpreted afresh in the light of other (usually contemporary) sources of truth and wisdom. By its very nature, therefore, it was less clear-cut in its doctrinal formulations than other traditions felt able to be, and in some respects scarcely merits the title of a movement at all. And the thinkers to be explored here differ considerably from one another on a range of issues. But insofar as the spirituality they sought to live by and promote reflected this underlying concern to engage with the world, not only in service but in the search for new ways of re-presenting Christian truth, they may be taken as representing a Liberal strain in the Anglican Christianity of their day.[218]

Frederick Denison Maurice (1805–72)

Something of the character of this kind of spirituality may be gleaned from the Dedication one of them wrote to his collection of sermons on the Prayer Book:

> To those who understand the Prayers of the Church best, the sufferers on sick beds; to those who often feel the need of them most, men toiling in the daily business of the world; to those who turn from them with the greatest aversion, persons harassed by doubts and confusions which seem to be mocked by their tone of calmness and trust; these Sermons are affectionately dedicated, by one who has learnt more of the inner meaning of the Prayer-Book from the first class than from all the instructions of divines; who never appreciated its practical, substantial character till he felt that the callings of the second class were as sacred as those of the recluse and devotee: and who by converse with the last, by experiencing their difficulties, by seeking to sympathize with them, by discovering his own incompetency to help them, has been led to know what guidance and comfort there is in it for such as never have found or expect to find a home in any religious party, rest in any religious theory.[219]

That was well said; and it was said by Frederick Denison Maurice. Born near Lowestoft, the son of a Unitarian minister, he went to Cambridge in 1823 in the hope of a legal career; but his refusal to subscribe to the Church's Thirty-Nine Articles excluded him from a degree and a fellowship, and he moved to London.[220] In due course he did become an Anglican, and in 1834 was ordained to a rural curacy before becoming Chaplain of Guy's Hospital in London in 1836, and in 1840 Professor of English Literature and History at King's College London. Six years later he was appointed Chaplain of Lincoln's Inn and Professor of Theology at the newly-created Theological School at King's. In the same year (1846) he founded Queen's College for women students. The political upheavals of 1848 had a profound effect on Maurice; and he became actively involved in social and political issues which in turn plunged him into theological controversy as well. After starting the Working Men's College in London in 1854, he became its Principal after being dismissed from King's for his religious views.[221] In 1860 he was given pastoral charge of a London church; and six years later he returned to Cambridge, this time as Knightsbridge Professor of Moral Philosophy. His last appointment was as incumbent of St Edward's, Cambridge, in 1870.

Maurice was a person of ideas, not an organizer; and his own ideas changed and developed in the course of his eventful life.[222] Among them were the notion of 'Christian Socialism', which he seems first to have defined in January 1850, though it would be wise not to read too much into that elusive term at this early stage in its development.[223] His thought reflects a rich mixture of sources: the Unitarianism of his childhood was certainly one of these;[224] and the influence of Plato, in varying ways, will be discernible in what follows, perhaps partly through the conduit of Coleridge.[225] His most famous work was *The Kingdom of Christ* (1838);[226] but he also published a number of biblical studies, the sermons on the Prayer Book already mentioned (1852), theological essays, and pamphlets.

Charles Kingsley (1819–75)

Certainly the most famous of Maurice's disciples was Charles Kingsley (1819–75), an even more colourful and complex character.[227] Born at Holne, in Devon, where his father was curate, Kingsley went to King's College London in 1836, and to Magdalene College Cambridge two years later. In 1842 he was ordained to the curacy of Eversley in Hampshire, where he spent much of the rest of his life: two years later he was made incumbent. His extraordinarily wide range of interests is reflected in his subsequent career: in 1863 he was elected a Fellow of the Geological Society, having three years earlier been appointed Regius Professor of Modern History at Cambridge, to the surprise of many people including himself. In 1869 he moved to Chester as a residentiary canon, and in 1873 to Westminster Abbey with the same role.

Kingsley described himself as 'an orthodox priest of the Church of England' who believed the theology of that church 'to be eminently rational as well as scriptural':[228] the desire to hold the two together is characteristic. But rationalism and scripture were not the only things he sought to hold on to. He was a keen amateur scientist of considerable ability, and deeply committed to scientific education, social justice, and women's suffrage.[229] His religious views reflect a broad ecumenism: thus his review of Vaughan's *Hours with the mystics* is generous both in his understanding of Catholic mysticism and in his appraisal of the Hindu Bhagavad-Gita (though he eventually concludes that 'Hindoo mysticism has failed of practical result . . . it has died down into brutal fakeerism', which reflects his occasional propensity for sweeping state-ments about things of which he knew relatively little[230]).

But the vital clue to understanding both Kingsley himself and his enduring impor-tance lies in his longing to make connections: he criticizes those who want to live in self-contained units of their own; and he has in mind not medieval mystics but Chris-tians of his own age, who by withdrawing into an inner citadel of impregnable truth 'leave the battle-field to rival demagogues'.[231] A charming tribute to Kingsley was paid to him by the Dean of Chester when he left there in 1873:

> All this enthusiasm for Natural Science . . . might at first sight seem out of harmony with the grave and formal traditions of cathedral life. Even if it were so, there could be no objection to this, but rather a great advantage in it. The clerical office ought to touch human interests on every side; an ancient institution ought to diffuse light into fresh places; the meeting of the old and the new never occurs more properly or more usefully, than in a cathedral . . . In our own cathedral, too, there seems a special invitation to associations of this kind. For not only do our Gurgoyes and Corbels betray the general mediaeval interest felt of old in animal and vegetable forms, but carvings in wood and stone, even in the interior of the church, show that here there was a lavish enjoyment of such observation and imitation. As an illustration of what I mean at this moment, I may say that in this building there are monkeys in the midst of the crockets of some canopies, and that Canon Kingsley, in the midst of Divine Service, was once observed to start, when his eye caught the sight of this strange creature in an unexpected place.[232]

Like Maurice, Kingsley was indebted to Platonism;[233] but he also drew deeply from classical and European folklore.[234] Maurice was an abiding influence on him; and he carried the banner of Christian Socialism himself for a while, though his political views were a unique mixture of co-operative action and educational reform.[235] His works include novels (many of a semi-historical kind, such as *Hypatia* and *Westward Ho!*), children's stories (supremely *The water babies* of 1862–3), *The hermits* (a study of the eremitical tradition in the early church), collections of sermons, and lectures on historical and ethical issues (notably *The Roman and the Teuton* and *Health and educa-tion*), which reflect his lifelong concern for social reform:

> Are you aware that more human beings are killed in England every year by unnecessary and preventable diseases than were killed at Waterloo or at Sadowa? Are you aware that the great majority of those victims are children?[236]

George John Romanes (1848–94)

One other person, lesser in his impact than Maurice or Kingsley, deserves mention here. George John Romanes was a distinguished biologist, and author *inter alia* of *Darwin and after Darwin*. In 1873 he wrote a study of prayer in which he sought to demonstrate the compatibility of Christian belief in a God who answers prayer with the insights of natural science.[237] By 1876, however, Romanes had written, anonymously, *A candid examination of theism* which was deeply sceptical;[238] but towards the end of his life he appears to have recovered the substance of his original belief in the God of Christianity.[239]

Spirituality and justice

In his novel *Alton Locke*, Kingsley describes a conversation between the narrator and a rural labourer he meets on the road. Having discussed the local clergyman, the narrator asks the labourer:

> 'But surely,' I said, 'all this religious knowledge ought to give you comfort, even if you are badly off.'
>
> 'Oh! religion's all very well for them as has time for it; and a very good thing – we ought all to mind our latter end. But I don't see how a man can hear sermons with an empty belly; and there's so much to fret a man, now, and he's so cruel tired coming home o' nights, he can't nowise go to pray a lot, as gentlefolks does.'[240]

The way, and the extent to which, a person approaches the spiritual life is crucially determined by his or her physical and social condition: this is a truth that Liberal Christians never forgot. It is not surprising, therefore, to find them holding together the personal and the spiritual, the corporate and the individual, in a manner not dissimilar from the Tractarians. Hence Maurice can say that 'the sense of Sin is essentially the sense of solitude, isolation, distinct individual responsibility'.[241] It is worth noting in this regard that Maurice takes the reality of evil with deadly seriousness: there is no easy tolerance of sin in his writing: 'the acknowledgment of an Evil Spirit is *characteristic* of Christianity'.[242]

This helps to give Maurice's spirituality an exceptionally alert, vivid sense. He believed that we are, at all times, surrounded by potential spiritual influences, both good and evil:[243] in fact he goes as far as to suggest that these influences take the form of messages to us. Thus memories can be understood as messages to us from those we once met, though he warns of inappropriate attempts to contact them: the only proper means of access to the spiritual world beyond is through the mediation of Christ.[244] This implies no passivity: the apostles, acting under the influence and leading of the Spirit, cast out demons.[245] But it does imply that we have to be good discerners of spirits.

This interrelation is fundamental to Maurice's spirituality; and it follows that there is for him a crucial sense in which our apprehension of the divine love and will, however fitful, must lead us to an active concern for others, and especially to struggle against injustice: reflecting on the text in the Revelation of John about the eating of the scroll, he says:

> But why should the book be sweet like honey in the mouth, if it is so full of woe? Why should it be bitter afterwards, if it is God's book? Ezekiel and St John had the same experience in this respect. Nor would our case, I conceive, be different if we did indeed eat the words, if they really entered

into us. There must be a sweetness unspeakable in the actual living taste of a Divine communication; in the assurance – felt in the blood, felt along the heart – that a portion of that law by which we are governed has been disclosed to us; that the love which lies beneath all law and is working at every moment for the welfare and renovation of the creatures which it has called into existence is showing itself forth in our very selves. Sweet as honey! But then the sense of this law defied in the world, defied in ourselves? of that love trampled upon and resisted in the kingdom of men and in the kingdom within us? Is there no revulsion in that?[246]

Any authentic experience of God, then, directly leads to love and service of others. And more: the creation as a whole is to be set free. Maurice is clear that

the whole of it must partake of the redemption; all creation must be continually ascending from under the law of death; there must be signs everywhere that the wings are expanding within the chrysalis; all must be aspiring to enter into the glorious liberty of the sons of God. Not only he who has kept weary watch o'er man's mortality, and has hoped against hope amidst the wrongs of nations and the sorrows of friends and the sins of his own heart; but also the student of nature, who discovers a wonderful order and beauty through the universe, and yet is tortured continually by the strangest visions of death and destruction; he also bears his part in the thanksgiving [commenting on Revelation 5.13–14].[247]

Spirituality and science

This implicitly acknowledges the value of what scientists and other seekers after knowledge contribute. Kingsley calls for a 'natural Theology . . . at once scriptural and scientific'.[248] It will be scientific in

approaching Nature at once with a cheerful and reverent spirit, as a noble, healthy, and trustworthy thing; and what is that, save the spirit of those who wrote the 104th, 147th, and 148th Psalms; the spirit, too, of him who wrote that Song of the Three Children, which . . . as long as it is sung in our churches, is the charter and title-deed of all Christian students of those works of the Lord, which it calls on to bless Him, praise Him, and magnify Him for ever?[249]

Kingsley realizes that a 'natural theology' will need to 'set forth a God whose character is consistent with all the facts of nature, and not only with those which are pleasant and beautiful'.[250] Hence any theology worthy of the name must wrestle with the difficulties of believing in God in a world where the innocent suffer, and with contemporary issues such as embryology and race.[251] Kingsley clearly accepts at least the fundamental principles of evolution and seeks to foster a piety compatible with them, rather than any retreat into a supernaturalism based on outright revelation. He says to scientists:

Your duty is to find out the How of things: ours, to find out the Why. If you rejoin that we shall never find out the Why, unless we first learn something of the How, we shall not deny that. It may be most useful, I had almost said necessary, that the clergy should have some scientific training . . . But our having learnt the How, will not make it needless, much less impossible, for us to study the Why.[252]

This is a vastly different perspective from that of the Tractarians, for reasons too obvious to need stating. The desire for a *rapprochement* between theologians and scientists is explicit:[253] indeed, far from idealizing the past, Kingsley argues that the present age is not as irreverent as was the age of the schoolmen, for then everyone was certain they knew all the answers.[254] He would have agreed with Thomas Love Peacock's Mr Flosky, a caricature of Coleridge, in *Nightmare Abbey*:

[The] word Old had great charms for him. The good old times were always on his lips; meaning the days when polemic theology was in its prime, and rival prelates beat the drum ecclesiastic with Herculean vigour, till the one wound up his series of syllogisms with the very orthodox conclusion of roasting the other.[255]

In Kingsley's view, the heavens and earth are being shaken by new questions, for example about the very possibility of the existence of hell.[256] The temptation for Christians is either to 'degenerate into a lazy scepticism, which believes that everything is a little true, and everything a little false', or 'degenerate into faithless fears, and unmanly wailings that the flood of infidelity is irresistible, and that Christ has left His Church'.[257] Neither are appropriate: Jesus Christ is the same yesterday, today and for ever;[258] and it may well be precisely Christ who is doing the shaking.[259] This is not to deny the importance of the supernatural: indeed Kingsley argues that once we ignore it we run the risk of thinking of nature 'only as something of which we can make use';[260] and to believe that (say) the cedars of Lebanon were made by God is to recognize their holiness.[261]

Spirituality and human transformation

Thus this approach insists on acknowledging that human beings have a spiritual nature as well as a physical one. George Romanes recognizes four elements in the human make-up; and he lists them in ascending order of importance: animality, intellectuality, morality, and spirituality. Of the latter two he writes:

Morality and spirituality are to be distinguished as two very different things. A man may be highly moral in his conduct without being in any degree spiritual in his nature, and, though to a lesser extent, vice versa. And, objectively, we see the same distinction between morals and religion. By spirituality I mean the religious temperament, whether or not associated with any particular creed or dogma.

There is no doubt that intellectual pleasures are more satisfying and enduring than sensual – or even sensuous. And, to those who have experienced them, so it is with spiritual over intellectual, artistic, &c. This is an objective fact, abundantly testified to by every one who has had experience: and it seems to indicate that the spiritual nature of man is the highest part of man – the [culminating] point of his being.[262]

The stress on experience here is worth noting: Charles Gore discusses it in his contribution to *Lux mundi*, a collection of essays which he edited in 1889 and which sought to reconcile Tractarianism with contemporary intellectual developments. He makes the point that, whatever the risks involved in appealing to experience,

> it is an essential part of the appeal which Christianity makes on its own behalf since the day Jesus Christ met the question 'Art thou He that should come, or do we look for another?' by pointing to the transforming effect of his work.[263]

If Christianity does not transform people, it is nothing. More: if it does not offer the potential to transform *all* people, it is nothing. This brings us to one of the central principles of Maurice's spirituality: his emphasis on God as universal father. In his study of the Prayer Book he writes: 'I claim it as the first and noblest distinction of our Prayers [= the BCP], that they set out with assuming God to be a Father, and those that worship him to be his children.'[264] We are not only children, but *forgiven* children;[265] and our spiritual nature depends first on our *childlikeness*.[266] Hence 'all Christian prayer is founded upon the actual manifestation of a father to his children'.[267] And this is supremely because God himself is revealed in the sending of his only son: 'the sense of filial dependence and trust' was the heart of Christ's life.[268]

Spirituality and inclusiveness

This stress on God's fatherhood is not only important for our understanding of prayer: it also reminds us of the universal vocation of Christianity. Everyone can claim God as father: 'the baptized Church is not set apart as a witness *for* exclusion, but against it'.[269] It is precisely because we are all spiritual beings that we need a *common* prayer book, 'not *special* prayers adapted to special temperaments and moods of character, but human; not refined and artificial, but practical; reaching to the throne of God, meeting the daily lowly duties of man'.[270] This is in itself a vital antidote against spiritual élitism:

> If our spiritual people will have their spirituality to themselves, if they do not like to acknowledge that all men have spirits, if they think that they bring a set of spiritual feelings with them, when they should come to be quickened and renewed by God's Spirit, they must go empty away. 'Blessed are the poor in spirit, for *theirs* is the kingdom of Heaven.'[271]

For Maurice, the great achievement of the Protestant Reformers lay in recognizing that 'the spiritual is also the practical'.[272] And the Prayer Book itself has two fundamental strengths: first, it integrates the spiritual with the everyday; secondly, it is for everyone. He is virulently critical of those he perceives as forever fretting about heresy, for to him this is to adopt an exclusiveness alien to the Gospel:

I am greatly afraid of heresy, but I believe it is most prevalent amongst those who are ever on the search for it: who are continually denying some portion of truth in the eagerness to convict their brethren of denying some other portion of it.[273]

Spirituality and Incarnation

One of Maurice's most penetrating insights is to point out that many Christians are themselves ambivalent about access to God:

I have spoken of a strange contradiction which there is in men's minds when they think of God. They feel as if it would be a dreadful thing to lose Him, and yet as if it would be a more dreadful thing to be brought near Him, to be in His open presence.[274]

This heightens the importance of the Incarnation, a central principle in Maurice's spirituality. The individual, he notes, is not crushed by the universal, but precisely fulfilled by it.[275] Spiritual life must be earthed in practice. This is Kingsley:

Grace, to be perfect, must shew itself by graciously forgiving penitents. Pity, to be perfect, must shew itself by helping the miserable. Beneficence, to be perfect, must shew itself by delivering the oppressed. The old prophets and psalmists saw as much as this; and preached that this too was part of the essence and character of God.[276]

This leads Liberal Christians to a fundamentally positive view of human life, which challenges the cold logic of natural selection. This is Kingsley again:

It is true – too true if you will – that all things live on each other. But is it not, therefore, equally true that all things live for each other? – that self-sacrifice, and not selfishness, is at the bottom the law of Nature, as it is the law of Grace?[277]

In becoming incarnate, God took upon himself the fullness of humanity, not merely the male part. Here too the emphasis is on inclusiveness, on a Gospel made available to all.[278] Emphasis on the Incarnation does not lead Maurice to neglect the other central dogmas of orthodox Christianity: the work of Christ and his self-giving love are firmly emphasised;[279] and the doctrine of the Trinity not only speaks of a God offering welcome to all:[280] it also leads us to another central plank of Maurice's thought, the Kingdom of Christ. Maurice argues that the propensity of human beings to live together in family units argues for the existence of a 'moral or spiritual constitution for mankind'.[281] Individual people *have* certain things, like habits or possessions; but they *are* brothers or uncles or children. We exist in and for relationships. And in all societies people 'have connected the ideas of fathers, children, husbands, brothers, sisters, with the beings whom they worshipped', God being in effect the husband of the nation in scripture.[282] The story of the Bible is that of a particular family or tribe being called to be God's chosen and covenanted people.[283]

There is thus something utterly natural about the Messiah, the heir of David's throne, being a human being as David was.[284] And this focuses a distinctive truth about the Israelite nation: that its king was only the visible representative of an invisible King, whereas other kings saw themselves as supreme authorities in their own right.[285] Hence the importance of Jesus' relationship with God as *Father*, stressing this essential relation between the visible Kingdom and its invisible King.[286] Hence too the importance of separating the priest from the lawgiver, the religious from the secular power, of seeing both as accountable to God.[287] This does not free us from our obligations to the secular state; but our obedience to it will be that of a human being and not that of a slave,[288] though sometimes we prefer slavery to servanthood and friendship.[289]

The Kingdom of Christ

What are the marks of this Kingdom? Maurice instances a number, of which we may single out three. The first and most obvious is baptism:[290] in it, a person 'is actually adopted into union with a Being above himself, and . . . the spirit of life, of power, of wisdom, is given to him'.[291] The very fact that it is granted to anyone irrespective of age or of spiritual wisdom or greatness is itself a prophetic sign, a sign of the spiritual *potential* of every human person.[292]

A second distinctive sign of the Kingdom is worship, and supremely the *continuity* of worship: the same forms and prayers have continued throughout time and across civilizations.[293] And it is in our acts of worship that the fellowship of all members of the Kingdom of Christ is most fully realized:[294] hence their importance.

Thirdly, a concern for the poor distinguishes the reality of the Kingdom of Christ. Maurice believes there is something distinctively English about the belief, which again the Prayer Book underlines, that Christianity is not primarily a system of control, but a society, and a way of life.[295] This vision has frequently been blurred or lost sight of: indeed Maurice believes that even the Methodists, whom he admires, were limited by their concern for people's souls more than for their bodies.[296] Such a response was

> not enough; men feel that they are not merely lost creatures; they look up to heaven above them, and ask whether it can be true that this is the whole account of their condition; that their sense of right and wrong, their cravings for fellowship, their consciousness of being creatures having powers which no other creatures possess, are all nothing. If religion, they say, will give us no explanation of these feelings, if it can only tell us about a fall for the whole race, and an escape for a few individuals of it, then our wants must be satisfied without religion. Then begin Chartism and Socialism, and whatever schemes make rich men tremble. Surely, what the modern assertors of a church system say about the duty of administering active charity to these sufferers, of showing that we do not merely regard them as pensioners on the national bounty, but as fellow-men for whom we are to make sacrifices – surely this language is far more to the purpose.[297]

Elsewhere Maurice goes further still:

> We have been sent into the world to do it good, and we have oftentimes been Jonahs in the vessel, the very causes of the storms which were shaking

it. This sin we are bound to confess, and to ask more humbly than any others for God's forgiveness.[298]

What made great saints like Francis of Assisi do what they did was not 'the craving for distant rewards in a future state', let alone 'the immediate reward of popular approbation', but 'an overpowering sense of the sympathy of the Saviour with every poor man, [and] an intense participation in that sympathy' – note the stress on sympathy here.[299]

Liberal spirituality and the religious life

It might be thought that so activist a view of the spiritual life would have little time or place for the contemplative element of Christian spirituality. It is true that in general Maurice has relatively little time for mysticism, warning of its 'morbid self-conscious tendencies',[300] and seeing it as a kind of Christian Buddhism.[301] But Kingsley's view is a nuanced one, worth careful examination: in *The hermits* he notes the formative influence of the early eremitical movement on the history both of Christianity and of human thought.[302] After telling the story of St Simeon Stylites, Kingsley concludes:

> Are we then to suppose that these old hermits had lost faith in God? On the contrary, they were the only men in that day who had faith in God. And, if they had faith in any other things or persons beside God, they merely shared in the general popular ignorance and mistakes of their own age; and we must not judge those who, born in an age of darkness, were struggling earnestly toward the light, as we judge those who, born in an age of scientific light, are retiring of their own will back into the darkness . . . They possessed what the world did not possess, faith in the utterly good and self-sacrificing God, and an ideal of virtue and purity such as had never been seen since the first Whitsuntide.[303]

Clearly Kingsley has little awareness of the deeper meaning of Christian asceticism; and he has little time for the exaltation of celibacy above marriage.[304] Some of his remarks are sweeping and unfair;[305] but, taken as a whole, he reveals a judicious evaluation of the role and importance of the monastic life:

> Monastic isolation from family and national duties especially fitted the fathers of that period for the task, by giving them leisure, if nothing else, to face questions with a lifelong earnestness impossible to the more social and practical Northern mind. Our duty is, instead of sneering at them as pedantic dreamers, to thank Heaven that men were found, just at the time when they were wanted, to do for us what we could never have done for ourselves; to leave to us, as a precious heirloom, bought most truly with the lifeblood of their race, a metaphysic at once Christian and scientific, every attempt to improve on which has hitherto been found a failure.[306]

The importance of sacrifice

This subject is of more than historical importance for an understanding of Liberal spirituality. For another crucial component was their emphasis on sacrifice, as the means by which we seek to live out what we believe. Maurice explored the subject in a series of sermons published as *The doctrine of sacrifice.* The notion was of course rooted in Jewish theology, for the Jews first recognized the crucial importance of sacrifice in bringing both God and humanity, and human beings themselves, together in unity.[307] For Maurice it was sacrifice which lay at the heart of the atonement: Christ's death was a sacrifice, 'the only complete sacrifice ever offered, the entire surrender of the whole spirit and body to God';[308] but it was propitiatory not in that humanity offered something to propitiate God but in that God wanted us to be free and proclaimed through the death of Christ 'the sure declaration of God's righteousness in the forgiveness of sins'.[309] And because Christ became sin for us (2 Corinthians 5.21), we can no longer (if we ever could) offer private or individual sacrifices to God for our sin: we can only offer the sacrifice of him who is offered for all the world.[310] Similarly our intercessions are his, are offered by his advocacy.[311] The sacrifice of Christ is a victory over the powers of evil; but it is also a pattern of self-giving that we are to make our own.[312]

Maurice argues that sacrifice is the most natural way of expressing our reverence for someone whom we worship, more natural (say) than simply speaking to him.[313] The story of Cain and Abel anticipates a crucial biblical truth: that 'sacrifice infers more than the giving up of a *thing*' – it involves the giving up of a person;[314] and it must be offered disinterestedly, without expectation of anything in response – failure to do this was Cain's sin.[315] Sacrifice is also a representative thing: we do it for others as well as for ourselves.[316] It is a commitment on our part to work with God for the building of a righteous world.[317] And, as is shown in the terrible story of Abraham and Isaac:

> [Abraham] had found sacrifice to be no one solitary act, no sudden expression of joy, no violent effort to make a return for blessings which we can only return by accepting; but that it lies at the very root of our being; that our lives stand upon it; that society is held together by it; that all power to be right, and to do right, begins with the offering up of ourselves, because it is thus that the righteous Lord makes us like Himself.[318]

And the notion of sacrifice lies at the heart of both our faith and our civic duty:

> Our fathers said that it was this God [the God of Abraham and of Jesus], and not any of the others, to which we were offered up. They said that when we were baptized He who breaks asunder the bonds of the captive, chose us as His redeemed children; that then and there we were sacrificed to Him and signed with the sign of sacrifice . . . That is our national consecration; that is our individual consecration. In the strength of that, we may go forth, we are pledged to go forth, against every false principle, and base, dishonourable practice, that enslaves ourselves and that enslaves the world . . . And never for a moment let us try to separate, or dream that we can separate, our individual life from our national. Our vocation is the same in the most private occupations, and when we are fulfilling what are called our duties as citizens. Every duty is a civic duty . . . When once we understand that, self-sacrifice can never be an ambitious thing – a fine way to get the reputation of saints or the rewards of another world. It will be regarded

as the true ground of all action . . . Think of this . . . as you eat that feast which is like the Jewish passover, because it is individual, because it is common, because it testifies of God as a Redeemer, because it testifies of Him as the avenger of all evil; but which is higher than the Jewish Passover, because it is human and universal, because in it we partake of a Sacrifice which has been offered to gather together in one the children of God that are scattered abroad – offered that they might be able to offer themselves as children to do their Father's work and will.[319]

The theology and practice of prayer

It remains to explore the theology and practice of prayer in the Liberal tradition. In a superb passage in one of his sermons, Charles Kingsley articulates its implications: to pray is to *become* a person:

> when [a person] prays, he is indeed a person. He is himself; and not ashamed, however sinful, to be himself; and to tell God about himself . . . You, each of you, have a right, as God's children, to speak to the God who made the universe. Therefore be sure, that when you dislike to say your prayers, it is because you do not like to be what you are, a person; and prefer – ah foolish soul – to be a thing, and an animal.[320]

If everything Kingsley wrote were on that level of inspiration, he would be one of the greatest figures in English spirituality. But it was Maurice who gave this approach to prayer its theological undergirding. In a magnificent exposition, he takes the prayer of Christ in John 17 as containing in itself the essence of all prayer, and expressing the longings of all people everywhere.[321] Christ's

> prayer was the acknowledgment of that which had been revealed to Him, His filial acceptance of that which had been prepared for Him. And surely . . . all prayer must be this. It is the acknowledging of that, be it sad or joyful, which has been given to us; it is the casting our experience upon Him who has brought us into it, and who understands it, because without Him we cannot go through it, or in the least understand it ourselves.[322]

The prayer gradually widens: it begins with just Christ and the Father, then includes the disciples, and finally extends to reach all who will believe through them. In Christ's prayer here, the disciples 'are taken out of the narrow exclusive sect-world by which they are surrounded, to be a family of witnesses for the Father and the Son'.[323] They were family members, not simply adherents; 'friends, not servants', awaiting the gift of the Spirit.[324] And 'what is prayer, but that intercourse of the Father with the Son, of the family with its Head, which this unity [of Father and Son] makes possible? And what is the object and result of all prayer but this, that what is true in the mind of God may be true in the actual condition of men?'[325]

Maurice's stress on our status as children of a heavenly Father recurs constantly, as has already been seen.[326] For him, prayer is the act of children acknowledging their need for a restored humanity, beginning with themselves.[327] In prayer, they fully realize themselves;[328] for in prayer the will gives itself up that it may be itself. It dies that it may enjoy life. In acknowledging another will as the only will, it attains its own freedom; even as in trying to have a being of its own, it becomes a slave. 'Father, not my will, but thine.'[329]

This is not to say that prayer is *purely* an act of human will and reason; rather the Spirit of God awakens them; 'the will and reason not called forth by him must remain for ever the torpid helpless victims of nature and sense', because without the leading of the Spirit a person's will and reason will forever be seeking their own autonomy.[330] And, once awakened, we must bring all of ourselves into our prayer: in a passage of visionary power, Maurice reflects on the human predicament in a grossly unjust world:

How do men rise out of the mire into which they are daily sinking more and more deeply? All would say, Not by acquiescence, but by protest. They affirm that mire is not the element in which human beings were meant to live. Though a hundred wish to abide in it, one or two continue to affirm for themselves, and for the rest, that that is not their state; if they can see no other, they can see there must be another. This protest and affirmation become prayer. They believe that somehow, or somewhere, they have a deliverer. If someone has consigned them to this misery, some other must be able to effect their salvation out of it . . . Whatever be the name of the Deliverer – in whatever region, near or distant, He may dwell – these inspirations have come from Him; He will second them. They ask him to save them from the oppressor . . . Whether the Author of the universe is the Oppressor or the Deliverer . . . this was what all the past ages were striving to know. What we say is, that the revelation of Jesus Christ was the solution of that question . . . Whatever makes the earth corrupt, whatever makes human beings corrupt, we believe to come not from His order, but from a breach of His order. We are bound, by our allegiance to Him, not to accept anomalies as laws, but to strive against them. We are bound to believe that He is stirring us to strive against them. We have a right to pray against them, whatever they may be, our prayers being merely the response to His inspirations – cries for the triumph of His will over that which opposes it.[331]

Hence:

We pray, because we feel that things are not as they ought to be; we pray, because we secretly confess or faintly hope that there may be some Power in the Universe which would set them right. We have very dim and confused notions what that Power can be, or why things should have gone into disorder in spite of it, or whether it is itself the author of our misery. Nevertheless, we pray.[332]

Conclusion

In his reflections on the Apocalypse, F. D. Maurice considers the liturgy of heaven, and addresses exactly the question raised by Pusey with which we concluded our exploration of the Tractarians:

> Oftentimes it has been said in Christian pulpits, that heaven is but the continuance of the worship upon earth. Those who have found that worship on earth very dreary and unsatisfactory, have said that they should prefer any Greek Elysium or Gothic Walhalla to such a heaven ... [But] all is worship there, because all are pursuing the highest good in contemplation and action; because all are referring their thoughts and acts to one centre, instead of scattering and dispersing them by turning to a thousand different centres; because each thinker and doer is forgetting himself in the object which he has before him, in the work which is committed to him ... The four living creatures, we shall find, are concerning themselves with all the movements and changes in the moral world; the very name of elders denotes that they are exercising the functions and faculties of judgment and direction over spiritual beings and over natural agents. Our worship must always be dreary, if it stands aloof from our daily life; if it does not interpret and transfigure that life.[333]

Both the worst and the best of Maurice are here: the prolix and rhetorical style; but also the constant interweaving of individual and corporate, of this world's needs and the next world's joys, of liturgy and life, which bring him to his sonorous conclusion. But Maurice is no unrealistic visionary: like Newman, he stresses the need to live in reality, not in illusion; like Newman, he knows that a key part of facing that reality is accepting our own status as sinners who are yet forgiven. To receive the absolution in the Eucharist 'is resigning a delusion, it is living in our true and simple state; still He only can make us reasonable beings'.[334] His continuing importance consists in his offering a wide-ranging theological analysis which both embraces the heart of orthodox Christianity and is open to the challenges of contemporary life and wisdom. His impatience with religious systems and some aspects of biblical literalism brought him furious opposition:[335] his legacy is a Christianity at once historical in its particularity and universal in its scope:

> A faith which boasts to be for humanity cannot test its strength unless it is content to deal with men in all possible conditions. If it limits itself to England, it will adapt itself to the habits and fashions and prejudices of England, of England too in a particular age. But doing this, it will never reach the hearts of Englishmen. You say, 'Try your Christianity upon the cotton-spinners of Manchester, upon the hardware men of Birmingham; if it fails with them, do you expect it will succeed in Persia and Thibet?' We know it will fail, it must fail in Birmingham and Manchester, if it addresses the people in those places mainly as spinners and workers in hardware. This has been the mistake we have continually made. We have looked upon these 'hands' as created to work for us; we have asked for a religion

which should keep the 'hands' in the state in which they will do most work and give the least trouble. But it is found that they are men who use these hands; and that which is a religion for hands, is not one for men.[336]

Charles Kingsley's writing lacks much of Maurice's depth and coherence; and some at least of his output is manifestly superficial. But he is one of only a few nineteenth-century spiritual writers to engage directly with the implications of contemporary scientific developments and insights. He has been associated with a 'muscular Christianity' which found little room for the feminine, and with a defensive disparagement of all things ascetic and Catholic. That is, as we have seen, unfair to him; and he did discern, in Christ's free act of self-sacrifice, the 'true manhood' to which all should aspire.[337] But notwithstanding the tiresome moralizing which surfaces in *The water babies*, or the intemperateness exemplified in his attack on Newman, Kingsley's achievement was to open to people the possibility of a profound Christian spirituality which was strong enough to embrace all that was best in the world instead of spurning it – and to do so with infectious enthusiasm.

Spirituality and parish life

Introduction

How churchgoing were the Victorians? We have already noted that the 1851 census showed that 39% of the total population attended a place of worship on 30 March of that year. Just over 20% – slightly more than half – were at Anglican churches, and a further 17% at Nonconformist ones.[338] One fifth of the adult population, then, went to an Anglican church on that particular Sunday. There are good grounds for thinking that the church was stronger in rural areas than in urban ones;[339] but even when that allowance is made the Church of England seems certainly to have remained a significant force, a real presence, in the spiritual and mental landscapes of a very large number of English people. But can we go any further? There is a question of identity here: scarcely any adherents of the Established Church in the nineteenth century would have described themselves as 'Anglicans' (although that term, for want of a better, will be used here): they would have thought of themselves as 'churchmen' or churchgoers, as distinct from 'Papists' or those associated with (Dissenting) chapels.[340] Much of what might be described as their spiritual lives will have been implicit, understated, unselfconscious, though of itself that makes it no less real.

Some things at least can be tentatively affirmed. It seems highly likely that prayers were said regularly in families, and that most homes contained a Bible, and many a Book of Common Prayer.[341] George Eliot's Adam Bede, whose spiritual life we shall consider later, opened the family Bible regularly for guidance, and read it every Sunday ('I've always lighted on some clear word to tell me where my work lay'[342]); and, in *The Mill on the Floss*, Mr Tulliver, no regular churchgoer, brings out the family Bible and insists on his son writing down in it the grim fate that had befallen the family, together with the boy's willingness to avenge it.[343] The family Bible, then, constituted a benchmark of the family's identity: a place to seek guidance, certainly, but also a place to record wrongs and a longing for justice.

Two adverse comments are worth quoting. George Eliot says of one of her fictional Midland villages:

> The inhabitants of Raveloe were not severely regular in their church-going, and perhaps there was hardly a person in the parish who would not have held that to go to church every Sunday in the calendar would have shown a greedy desire to stand well with Heaven, and get an undue advantage over their neighbours – a wish to be better than the 'common run'.[344]

Yet it is clear, from most of her novels, that the parish church played a major role in the lives of local people, and that failure to attend every Sunday morning did not necessarily imply a thin or non-existent spiritual life. In 1907, towards the end of the Edwardian era, George Bernard Shaw wrote:

> It is no use bothering because the parsons cant [sic] preach. What people really want them for is marriage, baptism &c. When the secular affirmations of these things are firmly established as popular superstitions, the parson will find himself superfluous to an extent that will astonish him. He may even have to preach religion; and then he will not be tolerated at all.[345]

Shaw's mordant wit conceals an important point; but even if it were true that large numbers of English people were ill at ease when parsons preached too much religion, it should not be taken as meaning that they lacked any significant spiritual life at all, or that the principal embodiment of Christianity available to them was nothing more than a lifeless dispenser of rites of passage. Beneath the surface, the mainstream Church of England in the Victorian and Edwardian eras may have had more vitality than it has often been given credit for.[346] Three more indicators of that vitality are worth briefly rehearsing.

Parish life in the Victorian era

First, a number of societies were formed during the nineteenth century, in response to specific needs. The (Church) Pastoral Aid Society (founded in 1836), the Additional Curates Society (1837), the Church of England Working Men's Society (1876), and the Church Army (1882) were concerned to help the church serve the poor, both by fostering vocations to the ordained ministry and by encouraging and equipping laypeople to work with them.[347]

Second, the Church of England played a major role in furthering education: the founding of the National Society (full title National Society for Promoting the Education of the Poor in the Principles of the Established Church) in 1811, and of a large number of diocesan educational bodies across the country during the century, was to be important in ensuring the propagation of good quality schools and educational programmes rooted in Christian principles;[348] and the foundation of teacher training colleges and theological colleges (beginning with Wells in 1838) significantly improved the education and spiritual formation of teachers and clergy alike. Third, very large numbers of new churches were built during the nineteenth century (most of them in the new urban areas) and even more were restored.[349] There is much debate about how effective this building programme proved to be;[350] but it certainly helped the Church to become a living presence in the midst of new and often wretchedly dis-advantaged communities.

It is worth looking in a little more detail at the state of Anglican parochial life during the nineteenth century; and one small window onto that life is offered by church mag-azines, which by the later part of the century were becoming increasingly popular.[351] Most were bound in with nationally-produced church inserts. Some had covers which are themselves instructive: thus the magazine of St Mark's Wolverhampton during the 1870s had on its front cover a railway engine and a paddle steamer as well as St Paul's Cathedral: this church (the cover seems to be saying) is here to proclaim no pseudo-medieval nostalgia, but a living faith for today.

Spirituality and urban life

We may begin with the cities and industrial areas. In Sheffield, a town where the Church of England was dominated by Evangelicals during the nineteenth century, there seems to have been a thriving parochial life, with a vast range of activities either run or actively supported by clergy and churchpeople;[352] though by the 1830s and 1840s there is evidence of widespread alienation of working-class people from the churches.[353]

Chesterton, in Staffordshire, was an industrial and mining area on the edge of the 'new' conurbation of Stoke-on-Trent. The parish church in the second half of the nineteenth century represented what might be called the 'moderate Catholic' tradi-tion: Holy Communion was celebrated every week, Morning and Evening Prayer were sung every Sunday and said on almost every weekday.[354] It was a difficult time: a massive explosion at a local colliery occurred in 1878, and poverty was widespread. In January 1880 the incumbent wrote of 'a time of unprecedented trial and distress . . . when mines stood idle, factories were closed, workshops empty, and men and women and children half starving by hundreds for want of the bare necessaries of life'.[355] The church was financially under great strain. And infant mortality (to judge by the deaths recorded month by month in the magazine) was distressingly high.

And yet the church exhibited striking signs of spiritual vitality. In 1879 the parish-ioners still raised £20 for home missions and £13 for foreign missions. A sick family club was set up in 1880;[356] there were already various church organizations (including a cricket guild), Sunday School, and district visitors.[357] The Guild of St Paul had monthly meetings with devotions and an address[358] (guilds grew up from the 1860s onwards, usually in parishes with a Tractarian tradition[359]). The special object of the Guild of the Holy Trinity was 'to deepen the spiritual life of its members'; the local branch was founded in 1873, and met monthly. A Young Men's Friendly Society branch was formed, the object of which was 'to knit together young men (chiefly of the working classes) in closer bonds of union, by forming a branch in *each* parish, where they may meet together for mutual instruction and amusement' with Associ-ates (e.g. the clergy) who would 'take an interest in [the members'] spiritual and temporal welfare, and be ready to meet them as friends'.[360] The parish was also very actively involved in education through both church school and Sunday school.[361]

St Mark's Wolverhampton was a parish church in the Evangelical tradition. Holy Communion was celebrated fortnightly on Sundays. Weekly prayer meetings took place on Saturday evenings, 'to see a blessing on the approaching Sabbath'.[362] There were men's and women's Bible classes, a Christian Union, temperance meetings and regular missionary society events and fund raising: instruction on private prayer was given on occasion through these organizations.[363] The church had its own lending library with over 1,000 volumes; and the incumbent wrote large numbers of small tracts. The Young Men's Society (with 70 members) had its own gymnasium and athletic class; and there was a Mutual Improvement Society, which met fortnightly. The Protestant tradition was reflected in the special meetings held to commemorate the 300th anniversary of the Spanish Armada in May 1888, at which fiercely anti-Roman principles were declared.

St Editha's church Tamworth represented a more central tradition of the Church of England. Towards the end of the nineteenth century Morning and Evening Prayer were said daily.[364] The Men's Bible Class met monthly: sixty of its members went on an outing on 18 July 1896; and one of a series of special services 'for Working Men in Working Clothes', held on 13 November 1896, was attended by forty people. In 1898 the diocesan bishop gave permission for the use of special services not included in the Prayer Book, such as a children's service and a service of intercession used after Evensong on Fridays. Special services were also held for particular concerns, such as the Boer War, or in aid of Indian famine relief.

Spirituality and rural life

In rural Staffordshire there is also evidence of extensive vitality in parish churches. The parish of Cheddleton, near Leek, had a moderate Tractarian tradition, with two eucharistic celebrations on most Sundays.[365] The Band of Hope, for children, had 20 members, each paying one penny on entry: they met every month. There were regular temperance meetings (reflecting the widespread problem of alcoholism), guild meetings, parochial social evenings, and days of intercession for overseas missions.[366] Inattention during worship was clearly a problem: an article entitled 'Irreverent conduct in church' complains of 'some young men (who are old enough to know better) [who] appear to have no better way of spending their time in Church than by scribbling in the Hymn Books'.[367]

The Staffordshire villages of Acton, Bednall, and Rickerscote, south of Stafford, had a combined population of about 500 in 1891. The parishes were central in churchmanship, with Holy Communion celebrated on three Sundays of the month at one of the churches. There were Bible Meetings every Thursday evening. At Christmas 1892 the Vicar awarded books and reward cards to 21 local children 'for accuracy and attention in learning their collects'.[368] Evangelism both local and international was clearly taken seriously: there was an active Missionary Association, all members of which were given prayer cards which they were asked to use 'regularly and earnestly';[369] and a Day of Intercession for the cause of Home Missions in our Land was held on 10 March 1897:

A special form of Prayer will be used at the Bednall Evening Service on that day, but all can send up their own supplication, when they use the familiar words '*Thy Kingdom come.*'[370]

The common life of the church

Material of this kind is inevitably anecdotal and impressionistic; but from it and similar sources a few tentative conclusions can be drawn. First, even the poorest parish churches exhibited a vigorous concern to support, in prayer and money, evangelistic and social work outside the parish itself: this included overseas missions and specific local concerns, such as the 'most successful Bazaar [held in the Borough Hall Stafford in November 1879, by local churches] in aid of the Stafford County Refuge for Discharged Female Prisoners'.[371] Second, the corporate life of the church was clearly seen as an instrument of spiritual growth: the incumbent of Milwich, a Staffordshire village, threw open the Rectory lawn for croquet and 'the very healthy and life-giving pursuit of bowls', and organized prayer meetings, with the explicit intention of fostering both spiritual and physical well-being.[372] Dora Greenwell quotes a clerical friend as saying that:

> There is something in Christianity, if we examine its history closely, which always for its full development requires an inner circle, a church within the church. It has found this in the Sect, the Order; it finds it too, in many an English parish, in a humble, healthful, almost unsuspected shape, in the work which, under good organization, grows up naturally about the Church. I once lived in a large manufacturing village, where a numerously attended Sunday-school became such a spiritual centre, and possessed all the attractive, binding energy I speak of; the more thoughtful persons of every class being drawn out as teachers, meeting the clergyman for prayer and reading of the Scriptures, with an especial reference to the common work; while *these* in their turn influenced the more seriously disposed young people, to whom the care of the very little ones was committed. I often recall these younger teachers, factory boys and girls, some of them even unable to read very fluently, yet most successful in the management of their infant classes . . . In all things we were as members, rejoicing and suffering *together*.[373]

The stress on the common life as fundamental to any healthy spirituality is crucial: 'how much Christian energy and love disappears, sinks below the surface . . . depressed by the low level of the surrounding atmosphere'.[374] And at the heart of Anglican common life remained the Book of Common Prayer, whose collects (as we have seen) children learned by heart and whose formularies and prayers must surely have permeated the hearts and minds of many like Dolly Winthrop, in George Eliot's *Silas Marner*, speaking of old Silas' former Dissenting friends:

> for what you talk o' your folks in your old country niver saying prayers by heart nor saying 'em out of a book, they must be wonderful cliver; for if I didn't know 'Our Father,' and little bits o' good words as I can carry out o'

church wi' me, I might down o' my knees every night, but nothing could I say.[375]

Dolly's 'little bits o' good words' were certainly drawn from the Prayer Book; and their very formality may have been as much help as hindrance. She only ever used the plural pronoun when referring to God, a habit 'which was no heresy of Dolly's, but only her way of avoiding a presumptuous familiarity'.[376] Another of George Eliot's characters, Adam Bede, is deeply aware of the value of the Prayer Book liturgy in forming spirituality (though, as we have seen, incumbents were increasingly supplementing its diet with new and more flexible material):

> To Adam the church service was the best channel he could have found for his mingled regret, yearning, and resignation; its interchange of beseeching cries for help, with outbursts of faith and praise – its recurrent responses and the familiar rhythm of its collects, seemed to speak for him as no other form of worship could have done.[377]

Spirituality and church buildings

Thirdly, the church building played a primary and perhaps increasing role as a centre for prayer. In the remote Peak District, the following appeared in the August 1900 issue of the church magazine referring to the tiny village of Calton:

> DAILY PRAYER AT THE CHURCH. Several considerations have led us to decide that we ought to have Daily Prayer in the Parish Church: (1) For one thing the church is near the Vicarage and therefore the state of the weather need not be taken into account; (2) For another: The Prayer Book speaks of 'The Order for Morning and Evening Prayer *daily to be said and used* throughout the year.' And further directs at the beginning of the book, in the part 'concerning the service of the Church': 'All Priests and Deacons *are to say daily* the Morning and Evening Prayer . . . that the people may come to hear God's Word and to pray with him' . . . (3) And most important of all, there is no doubt that to begin the day with prayer in the House of God brings a daily blessing to all who rightly take part in it.[378]

There is a price tag attached to this increased use of churches for daily prayer: the Tractarian tradition which encouraged this also discouraged the use of the building for other purposes, such as parish meetings, running the risk of making the church 'a resort for the devout rather than a resource for the community', as Frances Knight has put it.[379] Even so, the increasing popularity of choral music and public concerts, some of which took place in churches, helped to encourage people to use them. And, even when the concerts took place elsewhere, it is worth recalling the significance of all those Victorian oratorios, most of them long forgotten, in nurturing the spiritual life. The following announcement appeared in the Trent Valley Parochial Magazine (serving nine rural Staffordshire parishes) in June 1880:

> Two performances of the Oratorio 'Christ and His Soldiers' were given, under the patronage of the Lady Mary Sandon, in the Earl of Harrowby's

Schoolroom, Gayton, on Whit Tuesday May 18 [1880]. The oratorio is divided into two parts, 'The Life of Christ', and 'The Life of the Christian', and is composed of well-known hymns bearing on these subjects, set to music by Mr John Farmer, organist of Harrow School.[380]

Diocesan spirituality

Finally, it is worth stressing the efforts made by dioceses as a whole to foster the spiritual life of the clergy. Thus the Bishop of Lichfield appointed Wednesday 3 March 1880 as a 'Special Day of Devotion for the Clergy of the whole Diocese . . . that they should meet together on that day, at certain centres, for the purpose of united Prayer, Exhortation, and Meditation' – parishioners were notified in the hope that 'some of them may join, in heart and spirit, in the supplications which will be then offered up for a blessing upon the Ministry, and work of the Church.'[381]

EVANGELICAL SPIRITUALITY IN THE NINETEENTH CENTURY

Introduction: the 'Clapham Sect'

In the previous chapter, some of the principal features of English Evangelicalism became clear: the stress on a radical experience or process of conversion; the emphasis on a practical piety that (often, though not always) integrated prayer and Bible study with social action (Hannah More's 'practical Christianity'); the concern with family piety; and (as with the Tractarians) a desire to draw deeply from the pure wells of apostolic Christianity in order to renew the Church.

The nineteenth-century Evangelical movement built on these foundations, aided by Romantic stress on the value of emotions and the imagination in challenging the empirical realities of the observable world.[382] And the movement was further strengthened by continued fears of a resurgent papalist Catholicism.[383] It remained active in both the Church of England and the main branches of organized Nonconformity. The 'Clapham Sect' has already been briefly mentioned: the name arose from the work of a group of Evangelicals associated with John Venn (rector of Clapham from 1792 to 1813), and including Hannah More, Henry Thornton, and William Wilberforce.[384] Wilberforce's persistent and courageous leadership in championing the abolition of slavery was itself precipitated by his conversion to Evangelicalism as a result of reading Doddridge's *Rise and progress of religion in the soul*.[385] After his death in 1833, the effective leadership of the Evangelical movement fell to Anthony Ashley Cooper, Earl of Shaftesbury, whose mix of conservatism and social justice was to influence F. D. Maurice, despite the latter's different theological outlook.[386]

The effects of nineteenth-century Evangelicalism on the life of church and nation were extensive and enduring. Many major social reforms, together with the establishment of voluntary societies such as the RSPCA and NSPCC, were inspired by Evangelicals;[387] and, although it is impossible to calculate precisely, their influence on the spiritual lives of countless people was undoubtedly immense.[388] The movement as a whole encouraged a conservative attitude to the role of women; but many devout women (including hymn writers like Frances Havergal and Charlotte Elliott) will have found a new and deeper devotional life through their active involvement in it.[389]

As the century went on, however, latent fissures in the movement became more apparent. The spirituality associated with the regular Evangelical conventions held at Keswick from 1875 onwards tended to be more inward, more interested in inner holiness and spiritual growth, less concerned with social reform.[390] The arrival in England in 1873 of the American evangelists Dwight L. Moody (1837–99) and Ira D. Sankey (1840–1908) signified the beginnings of a major new period of Evangelical revivalism, of which the culmination was the ministry of Charles Spurgeon.[391] But not all Evangelicals were sympathetic to it: for older, more traditional Calvinist, Evangelicals, this American-style populist emotionalism was abhorrent. In what follows, the work of three major nineteenth-century Evangelicals, two Anglican and one Baptist, will be taken as representative.

Charles Simeon (1759–1836)

One of the most prominent Evangelicals within the Church of England in the earlier part of the century was the Cambridge priest Charles Simeon. He was born at Reading, of a wealthy family, and educated at Eton and King's College Cambridge, where he underwent a conversion experience in 1779. In 1782 he became a Fellow of King's, and in the following year was ordained priest and made Vicar of Holy Trinity Cambridge, a post he held until his death and which enabled him to exercise an influential preaching and pastoral ministry among undergraduates. He left behind a massive corpus of sermons and sermon outlines entitled *Horae homileticae*: a total of 2,536 of these fill 21 compendious volumes and form a commentary on every book of the Bible, as well as a resource for preachers.[392] Simeon is important because he sought to hold together both Calvinist and Arminian tendencies (present within English Protestantism since the sixteenth century) within Evangelicalism, and thus helped to preserve a dynamic Evangelical movement within the Established Church.

Charles Spurgeon (1834–92)

Arguably an even more important figure in English Evangelicalism is Charles Haddon Spurgeon (1834–92), for over 30 years minister of the Metropolitan Tabernacle in London. Spurgeon is an exemplary synthesis of Victorian enterprise and Evangelical individualism:[393] born at Kelvedon in Essex, of devout Puritan stock, he enjoyed a far less privileged upbringing than Simeon, because as a Dissenter he was barred from university education. He was baptized as an adult and in 1854 became minister of New Park Street (Baptist) Chapel in Southwark. His preaching soon made an impact: the congregation had to move to a music hall two years later in order to find adequate accommodation, and in 1861 the Metropolitan Tabernacle at the Elephant and Castle was built. Its swaggering classicism represents the peak of Evangelical confidence.

For over thirty years Spurgeon preached there, week by week, to a congregation of about 6,000. Where Simeon addressed the future leaders of society at Cambridge, Spurgeon spoke to a vast cross-section of London life. It was an astonishing achievement; and Spurgeon's ministry was clouded only by the 'Down Grade' controversy of 1887–8, when he left the Baptist Union because he believed the true and pure Calvinism so dear to him was being 'downgraded' by a new wave of more moderate leaders.[394]

In 1891 his health collapsed and he withdrew to France, still sending sermons by mail to be read in his absence. His death, on 31 January 1892, was a national event: a crowd of immense proportions attended his funeral.

Spurgeon's output of printed sermons was even more prodigious than Simeon's: 3,653 survive.[395] Not everyone was moved by them: one listener told a friend that

> my impressions fell below the lowest judgment I ever heard passed upon him. He has the gift of a fine voice . . . But I never heard any pulpit reading and speaking which in its level tone was more utterly common and empty of guiding intelligence or emotion . . . And the doctrine! It was a libel on Calvinism, that it should be presented in such a form. I never heard any attempt to exhibit the soul's experience that was more destitute of insight.[396]

The writer was George Eliot. But it would be foolish to dismiss Spurgeon as a ranting or ephemeral populist. He took his preaching seriously, spending hours in sermon preparation every week;[397] and he was very well aware of the perils of an easy popularity:

> Religion has become fashionable . . . It is reckoned to be reputable and honourable to attend a place of worship, and hence men are made religious in shoals . . . The whole nation appears to have been Christianized in an hour. But is this real? is this sincere? Ah! we fear not.[398]

What is fascinating and important about Spurgeon is that he was a Calvinist through and through, passionately concerned to present what he believed to be the only authentically scriptural Gospel in a manner that could change people's lives in the capital city in the late nineteenth century.[399] And, like Calvin (and notwithstanding George Eliot's strictures), he wanted to reach people's minds as well as their hearts: he refused to preach sermons 'with a view of driving you into religious fevers. Sturdy old Calvinism will not let us do that.'[400] His sermons show evidence of wide reading in Protestant piety; but his attitude to anything other than that is reflected in what he says of Butler's *Analogy of religion*:

> 'Butler's Analogy' is one of the most notable works in defence of revelation, and it is eminently calculated to impress the student with the truthfulness of our holy religion; but I should like to know whether there ever was a man, woman, or child truly converted to the Lord Jesus by 'Butler's Analogy.'[401]

J. C. Ryle (1816–1900)

Like his fellow Anglican Simeon, John Charles Ryle (1816–1900) came from a wealthy family and enjoyed a privileged education, at Eton and Christ Church, Oxford. But he was to be no stranger to suffering: in 1841 the family bank collapsed, and he experienced abruptly the effects of poverty; he lost his first wife after only three years of marriage, and his second ten years later after a protracted illness. He was ordained in 1841, and in 1880 became the first Anglican Bishop of Liverpool, a post he held until he died. Like Spurgeon, he was a convinced Calvinist: his work benefited from a more academic theological formation than Spurgeon enjoyed, though it lacks the latter's dynamic charge.[402] His series of essays, published in 1877 as *Holiness*, was intended to present a more restrained, thoughtful Evangelicalism as a counterblast to the increasingly popular revivalism already mentioned.

Conviction of sin: spirituality and Calvinism

The main foundations of nineteenth-century Evangelical spirituality are indeed traditionally Calvinist. Thus Simeon argues for the comprehensive nature of human fallenness, though it leads him to make a questionable distinction. The fact that human beings are, through the Fall, 'altogether polluted in every faculty of [their souls], and destitute of all true goodness' makes it hard to account for the evidence of moral goodness in non-Christians.[403] Ah, says Simeon: they may be *morally* good, in their relationships with one another; but they cannot be *spiritually* good, in the sense of being able to relate to God.[404] And this is because 'in the sight of God [we] are considered as guilty'.[405] The result is that

> a spirit of independence pervades every child of Adam, and is, perhaps beyond every thing else, the great effect and evidence of our apostasy from God.[406]

We have no longer (at least by nature) 'a creature-like spirit'.[407] And we are entirely unaware of our state of sinfulness. Piety, in short, can no longer be 'the natural product of [our] souls':[408] our souls are incapable of it.

It thus follows that a recognition of our inherent and profound sinfulness is a precondition of accepting God's free gift of justification. Unfortunately most people do not recognize it at all: 'our bereavement of heaven', says Simeon, 'is not felt as any evil; our bondage to sin is not at all lamented'.[409] But it is real all the same: sin is 'that vast moral disease which affects the whole human race', as Ryle puts it.[410] And, deep within all those whom God has called, is a longing for wholeness and freedom from bondage:[411] the very fact that this longing persists unsatisfied is itself evidence of its divine origin.[412] The work of conversion may be instantaneous (which Spurgeon prefers), or not; in either case, the process of transformation is lifelong. And Spurgeon's description of it is classically Puritan:

> Grace doth not reform us, but re-creates us: it doth not pare away here and there an evil excrescence, but it implants a holy and divine principle which goes to instant war with all indwelling sin, and continues to fight until corruption is subdued, and holiness is enthroned.[413]

Saving faith

The main ingredients of this kind of Calvinist piety have already been explored in detail in earlier chapters; and, given the explicit indebtedness of Spurgeon and others to earlier writers like John Owen and John Newton, there is no need to set out all the aspects of this theology again here.[414] Instead it might be worth pointing out a few of the distinctive aspects of nineteenth-century Evangelical spirituality, and in the process giving some flavour of its style and tone. This, for example, is Spurgeon on faith:

> While he had faith, Peter walked on the waves of the sea. That was a splendid walk; I almost envy him treading upon the billows. Why, if Peter's faith had continued, he might have walked across the Atlantic to America. But presently there came a billow behind him, and he said, 'That will sweep me away;' and then another before, and he cried out, 'That will overwhelm me;' and he thought – how could I be so presumptuous as to be walking on the top of these waves? Down goes Peter. Faith was Peter's life-buoy; faith was Peter's charm – it kept him up; but unbelief sent him down.[415]

There is a sense in which the Calvinist belief that all things are ordered by divine providence strengthens faith. Commending the fragile but courageous faith of Shadrach, Meshach and Abed-Nego, who are unsure as to whether God will save them from Nebuchadnezzar or not, Spurgeon says:

> We must not live and wait upon God with a kind of cupboard love, just as a stray dog might follow a man for bones; but we must speak well of our God even if he scourge us, for therein lies both the truth and the strength of faith.[416]

Sanctification

It follows from this that spiritual life, in the sense of a life lived under the guidance of the Holy Spirit, is a gift;[417] 'a vigorous and active principle', at once interior and personal, as Spurgeon puts it;[418] a quality of *perception*, in Simeon's words, 'which the natural man does not possess'.[419] And one of its most precious blessings is the ability constantly to discover new things as we grow in that life: 'what scenery surrounds the Christian, and what fresh discoveries he makes at every step! The Bible is always a new book.'[420] Even so, life after conversion is no picnic: 'Believe me, the life of grace is no dead level, it is not a fen country, a vast flat. There are mountains, and there are valleys.'[421] The Evangelicals are at one with the Tractarians in maintaining that, as Spurgeon puts it, 'the happiest condition of a Christian out of heaven is to live in the conscious enjoyment of the presence of the Lord Jesus'.[422] But they are equally aware that there are times when God feels absent, and both prayer and the sense of assurance are lost.[423]

The reason why the Christian's spiritual life can turn out to be so uneven is partly because, whilst justification is definitive and immediate, the process of sanctification, of becoming holy, is lifelong.[424] But it is partly also because the new nature that is God's gift to us at our new, spiritual birth, or regeneration, co-exists with the old one:[425] 'there is in every Christian two natures, as distinct as were the two natures of the God-Man Christ Jesus', each warring against the other.[426]

The victory has already been won for us, in the righteousness imputed to us when God, at Calvary, looks upon sinful humanity and 'sees' Christ taking its place;[427] but the lifelong process whereby our sanctification is accomplished demands all we have to give to it.[428] Even so, Christians have reason to celebrate: they are set free from bondage to sin. Ryle, typically cautious, suggests that the true signs of our election are not transient religious feelings, but habits of grace, and respect for Christ's law.[429] But Spurgeon goes further: we should celebrate our freedom:

> Atonement and jubilee ought to go together. Have you ever had a jubilee, my friends, in your hearts? If you have not, I can tell you it is because you have not had a day of atonement.[430]

And that freedom confers on each person an indestructible sense of self-worth:

> Liberty is the birthright of every man . . . There are some [in Great Britain] who are afraid to speak as men, who have to cringe and fawn, and bow, and stoop, to any one; who have no will of their own, no principles, no voice, no courage, and who cannot stand erect in conscious independence. But he is the free man, whom the truth makes free. He who has grace in his heart is free, he cares for no one; he has the right upon his side; he has God within him – the indwelling Spirit of the Holy Ghost; he is a prince of the blood royal of heaven.[431]

The new birth

An important point should be noted in passing here. For Simeon, the doctrine of regeneration, of a new birth, raises problems because it might be seen to clash with Anglican teaching on baptism. He defends the distinction between baptism and the new birth on the basis of John chapter 3;[432] and he is entirely loyal to Anglican teaching on the propriety of infant baptism. Baptism is a change of *state* 'for by it we become entitled to all the blessings of the new covenant. But it is not a change of *nature*.'[433] After all, Simon Magus was baptized but did not change. Simeon in effect sees baptism as the Christian equivalent of circumcision, an outward rite of admission rather than an inward rite effecting transformation.[434]

Our adoption as God's children has important pastoral implications. Indeed, one of Spurgeon's greatest strengths is his consistent ability to underline the pastoral implications of orthodox Calvinism. Here he is condemning adult paternalism:

> When the child is received into the church, it is with a kind of feeling that only the generous spirit of Christianity would enable us to be so wonderfully condescending, and so purely unselfish; for of course such young people cannot add much to the church, and it is by no means an occasion for killing the fatted calf, and beginning to eat and be merry. That spirit still lingers among us: I wish we could exterminate it![435]

But it has a more important implication. Our regeneration *unites* us with God, a fundamental principle of Calvinist spirituality.[436] Thus Spurgeon again:

> All the elect of God are in Christ Jesus by a federal union . . . [which] leads in due time, by the grace of God, to a manifest and vital union, a union of life, and for life, even unto eternal life, of which the visible bond is faith.[437]

This union is 'mystical and mysterious, but still most real, most true, and most effi-cient'.[438] And

> if we be one with Christ by a real and actual union, where Christ is we are, Christ's standing is our standing; and as Christ is nigh unto God, even so he hath raised us up together and made us sit together in heavenly places.[439]

In Christ is both male and female: 'The virtues, if I may so say, of both sexes were combined in our Lord . . . the feminine as well as the masculine of our common humanity. Human nature in its totality and completeness was fully possessed and thoroughly represented by him.'[440] And without a profound and enduring Christ-centredness, our religion will be rudderless and leaderless.[441]

Morality and duty

Something of the positive quality of this Evangelical spirituality is grasped by George Eliot in her early story 'Janet's repentance':

> Evangelicalism had brought into palpable existence and operation in Milby society that idea of duty, that recognition of something to be lived for beyond the mere satisfaction of self, which is to the moral life what the addition of a great central ganglion is to animal life. No man can begin to mould himself on a faith or an idea without rising to a higher order of experience: a principle of subordination, of self-mastery, has been intro-duced into his nature; he is no longer a mere bundle of impressions, desires, and impulses . . . The first condition of human goodness is some-thing to love; the second, something to reverence. And this latter precious gift was brought to Milby by Mr Tryan and Evangelicalism.[442]

This sense of consecrated duty is of course precisely what the Clapham Sect brought to burning issues of justice. There is less stress on social justice in the writings of Simeon, Spurgeon, or Ryle;[443] but there is a strong sense of compassion to the outsider. In a sermon on old age, Spurgeon argues that it is a time of particular memories, hopes, concerns, blessedness, and duties.[444] Above all, it is a time for childlike trust in God: the fact that God loves you in old age, when you can do so little for him, is a powerful encouragement.[445] And, in any case, as he says in a late sermon, all of us

> are pensioners upon the beneficence of our Lord Jesus Christ . . . We should long ago have broken any earthly bank, and drained the exchequer; but Christ has been to us like an ever-flowing fountain . . . communicating enough and to spare. What a purse![446]

The theology and practice of prayer

At the heart of Evangelical teaching on prayer is this conviction that we have been regenerated, born again, through the sacrifice of Christ on the cross: indeed it is pre-cisely in prayer that we can appropriate for ourselves doctrines which otherwise leave us cold: 'The way to get a doctrine is to pray till you get it,' wrote Spurgeon: 'pray yourselves into the truth', a sentiment which Tractarians would unquestionably have applauded, uniting as it does theology and the spiritual life.[447] And it is in the common prayer and worship of the church that the real power of the Gospel is manifested, a point Spurgeon makes with magisterial force:

> The aim of the church is not to provide out-door relief for the younger sons of the nobility; when they have not brains enough to win anyhow else their livelihood . . . Churches are not made that men of ready speech may stand up on Sundays and talk, and so win daily bread from their admirers. Nay, there is another end and aim from this . . . A church in London, which does not exist to do good in the slums . . . of the city, is a church that has no reason to justify its longer existing. A church that does not exist to reclaim heathenism, to fight with evil, to destroy error, to put down false-hood, a church that does not exist to take the side of the poor, to denounce injustice and to hold up righteousness, is a church that has no right to be. Not for thyself, O church, dost thou exist, any more than Christ existed for himself. His glory was that he laid aside his glory, and the glory of the church is when she lays aside her respectability and her dignity, and counts it to be her glory to gather together the outcasts, and her highest honour to seek amid the foulest mire the priceless jewels for which Jesus shed his blood.[448]

This is Spurgeon at his best; and it is worth noting, against those who assume that Calvinism led to a narrowly exclusive piety, that the church is there to pray for and care for the wicked, the poor, and the ignorant whether or not they are among the elect. It is also worth noting the stress on desire and longing that recurs in Spurgeon's work, and supremely in his teaching on prayer: 'the essence of all real prayer is desire. Words are but the habitation of prayer, the living tenant is desire.'[449] This is why 'there may be more prayer in the silent than in the fluent'.[450] 'Have you desires? – great, hungry, thirsty desires? Then bring them to the Lord.'[451] Eli could not read the desires of Hannah; but God could.[452] Simeon stressed this too: he says that one of the marks of true piety is that 'its desires are unbounded'.[453]

Spirituality and evangelism

Spurgeon's work abounds in pithy reflections which give some hint of his skill as a preacher; but they matter also because they help us to see how a thoroughly traditional Calvinism could be conveyed into a gospel of attractive warmth and power. His spiri-tuality is confident, full of joy; but it is marked by a recognition of the breaking process that inevitably precedes that. Thus he tells clergy that authentic ministry 'is sure to be heartbreaking' – beginning with your own.[454] He reproves apathetic Chris-tians:

> I have sometimes thought that certain unfriendly [Christians] must have been baptized in vinegar instead of water, from the sharp acid of the tem-perament. Surely the Spirit of God is a dove, full of peace, and love, and kindness, and not a bird of prey.[455]

Elsewhere he tells his congregation: 'some of you are not poor enough to be made rich by Christ'.[456] 'Come, brother, you did not reckon that such usefulness would ever fall to your lot, did you? Cheer up, and get to work. Wake up to holy energy.'[457] And, in a late sermon, 'In some of our churches everybody seems to be a little colder than everybody else. The members are holy icicles.'[458] He longed to see his people praying with enthusiasm and energy: 'You should see the man of God upon his knees. The posts of the doors of heaven move while he pleads with Jehovah.'[459] 'God loves earnest prayers. He loves impetuous prayers – vehement prayers.'[460] 'Secret prayer is one of the best tests of sincere religion.'[461]

Spirituality and scripture

Finally, it is worth noting the way these great preachers use the Bible to convey spiritual truth and comfort. It is not surprising to find them insisting on preaching and believing the whole Gospel, not some anodyne or emasculated substitute. 'It is not enough', said Simeon, 'to preach a scanty morality that we are called; but to publish the glad tidings of a full and free salvation.'[462] In a fine reflection on 2 Corinthians 3, Simeon tells his hearers that they must go to God as they are, unveiled, open:

> It is by putting off the veil from your own hearts, that you shall with 'open *unveiled* face behold his glory'; and, by beholding it, 'be changed into the same image from glory to glory, by the Spirit of the Lord.'[463]

Spurgeon's biblical expositions are also full of pastoral good sense. In a fine sermon on the parable of the lost sheep, he stresses the importance of what the shepherd does on finding the sheep: he lays it on his shoulders: 'it is an uplifting action', carrying the sheep without rebuke; 'it is an appropriating action', as though to say 'you are mine'; and it is a deed of service to the sheep: 'the sheep rides, the shepherd is the burden-bearer'.[464] The message is succinct, scriptural, and sustaining, the tone not flamboyant but direct.

Conclusion

It is easy for Simeon and Ryle to suffer by comparison with Spurgeon: they lack not only his populism, but his pastoral sense too. And the teaching of all three on the spiritual life is rooted in a theology more exclusivist than many will now, or did then, find acceptable. Ryle condemns 'that vague, dim, misty, hazy kind of theology which is so painfully current in the present age', and above all 'the extravagantly broad and liberal theology which is so much in vogue at the present time'.[465] But he also offers an important challenge to the Liberals: he invites them to ask themselves whether their religion provided any comfort at moments of crisis in life:[466] there could be little doubt that his had done so for him, and would continue to do so for many more. Yet it must be said that his spirituality is thin fare by comparison with Simeon's, his abhorrence of emotional revivalism a serious brake on any hint of open-hearted joy. Simeon's importance is considerable: he works hard, again and again, to show how full-blooded Evangelical Christianity is entirely compatible with human reason: 'the truth of God, though elevated above reason, is in perfect accordance with reason'.[467] And he bequeathed to the Church of England precisely that: an Evangelical inheritance at once exuberant and thoughtful, and certainly enduring (although the approaching tide of biblical criticism was to become, in the decades that followed, a new and unfamiliar challenge which English Evangelicalism was slow to address[468]).

But Spurgeon stands alone. He makes Ryle look like the loosest of Liberals in his vigorous castigating of all and sundry: Communists, Wesleyans, Mormons, Republicans, Tractarians, even (in the end) some of his fellow Baptists.[469] Yet even his polemical fire is in the end tempered by his pastoral warmth: 'we are too apt to ban and curse antagonists, instead of pitying and praying for them. It is not yours and mine to shut the door in any man's face, however depraved he may be; but still to stand and entreat him to come to the Saviour.'[470] And 'to walk the water is not an essential characteristic of faith, but to pray when you begin to sink is'.[471] There is a photograph of Spurgeon, reproduced at the beginning of Carlile's biography: it shows a short, bearded, grey-haired man with a stick, seated on a park bench. He sits stiffly, as if in pain or discomfort. But his eyes are full of fire; and there is a granitic strength about his expression. Here he is, late in his ministry but still at the height of his powers, conveying a Christianity at once heartwarming and adventurous, but above all *attractive*. No wonder they crowded to hear him:

> Amidst ten thousand allurements, faith is quite certain to choose that which appertains to boldness and to venturesomeness. John is full of love, he stops in the vessel; but Peter abounds in faith, and he must be doing some high action congruous to the nature of faith, and therefore he says, 'Lord, if it be thou, bid me come unto thee on the water.' That is the kind of thing for faith to do. Anybody can walk on the land, but faith is a water-walker. She can do, and act, and work where others fail . . . Faith loves to deal in great things; in marvellous adventure; in projects beyond human power. We are not to come to God and ask him to do for us what we can do for ourselves . . . Faith is a vessel expressly built for the deep seas. She is not a coaster, to keep close to the shore; she pushes out where she can neither see the shore nor fathom the depth . . . We must attempt some things which look like impossibilities, or we shall never keep up the esprit of the true soldiers of the cross.[472]

NONCONFORMIST SPIRITUALITY IN THE NINETEENTH CENTURY

It may appear strange to follow a section on Evangelical spirituality with another on that of Nonconformity, when the boundaries between the two were so blurred. Indeed, one could go further: nineteenth-century Nonconformity (and to some extent nineteenth-century Christianity) was dominated by Evangelicalism; and it was that kind of religion, heart-warming and socially activist, that touched the lives of millions of people, where the older rational Dissent, supremely exemplified in Unitarianism, remained largely a middle-class preserve.[473]

Even so, there were types and traditions within Nonconformity which were not adequately represented in the preceding section; and it is important, if the full richness and variety of Victorian Christianity is to be appreciated, for some account to be given of the kind of spirituality practised by those Dissenters who do not fit the mainstream Evangelical tradition. It is worth first noting a few more statistics from the religious census of 1851: just over 17% (2,878,543) of the total population on 30 March 1851 attended a Nonconformist service.[474] Of the Nonconformist denominations, the largest was the Wesleyan Methodists: 924,140 people (5.46% of the total population) attended one of their services on that day. After them came the Independents (or Congregationalists), with 655,935 (3.88%), and after them the Baptists with 499,604 (2.95%). Other Nonconformist groupings were smaller: the Primitive Methodists had 329,867 worshippers (1.95%), the Unitarians 34,110, and the Quakers 16,783. The Catholic Apostolic Church, founded by Edward Irving, had 4,908.

The sociology of Dissent has been well studied:[475] suffice it to say that, as a very broad generalization, English Victorian Nonconformity tended to appeal to artisan and lower-middle-class people whilst the Church of England drew more extensively from professionals and gentlefolk, though this is to ignore the fact that some very poor areas were better served by the Established Church as well as by Roman Catholicism.[476] As the century progressed, Dissent became more 'respectable', its chapels more consciously Gothic and less self-effacing, its ministers more educated. The result was a reduction in the prophetic or charismatic tone, but an increase in philanthropy. The Victorian emphasis on hard work, duty, enterprise, and making one's way in life must have favoured Dissent, and even made it more immediately capable of embracing at least some of the new insights of science. Thus one nineteenth-century Baptist could say that one of the cardinal principles of Nonconformity is 'the entire independence of the human mind'.[477] Margaret Oliphant catches something of its spirit at the opening of her novel *Salem Chapel*:

> Towards the end of Grove Street, in Carlingford, on the shabby side of the street, stood a red brick building, presenting a pinched gable terminated by a curious little belfry, not intended for any bell . . . This was Salem Chapel, the only Dissenting place of worship in Carlingford. It stood in a narrow strip of ground, just as the little houses which flanked it on either side stood in their gardens, except that the enclosure of the chapel was flowerless and sombre, and showed at the farther end a few sparsely-scattered tomb-stones . . . On either side of this little tabernacle were the humble houses – little detached boxes, each two storeys high, each fronted by a little flower-plot – clean, respectable, meagre, little habitations, which contributed most largely to the ranks of the congregation in the chapel. The big houses opposite, which turned their backs and staircase windows to the street, took little notice of the humble Dissenting community . . . Greengrocers, dealers in cheese and bacon, milkmen, with some dressmakers of inferior pretensions, and teachers of day-schools of similar humble character, formed the *élite* of the congregation. It is not to be supposed, however, on this account, that a prevailing aspect of shabbiness was upon this little community; on the contrary, the grim pews of Salem Chapel blushed with bright colours, and contained both dresses and faces

on the summer Sundays which the Church itself could scarcely have sur-
passed. Nor did those unadorned walls form a centre of asceticism and
gloomy religiousness in the cheerful little town. Tea-meetings were not
uncommon occurrences in Salem – tea-meetings which made the little
tabernacle festive . . . The Dissenters . . . aspired to no conquests in the
unattainable territory of high life, as it existed in Carlingford. They were
content to keep their privileges among themselves, and to enjoy their
superior preaching and purity with a compassionate complacence.[478]

And this is George Eliot's description:

Protestantism sat at ease, unmindful of schisms, careless of proselytism:
dissent was an inheritance along with a superior pew and a business connection, and Churchmanship only wondered contemptuously at Dissent
as a foolish habit that clung greatly to families in the grocery and chandler-
ing lines, though not incompatible with prosperous wholesale dealing.[479]

Primitive Methodism

One of the most interesting features of nineteenth-century Nonconformity was the
growth of Primitive Methodism, a popular religious movement originating in north
Staffordshire and consisting primarily of skilled artisans and the labouring poor. It was
founded by William Clowes (1780–1851), and Hugh Bourne (1772–1852);[480] but
much of the initial impetus came from the revivalist preaching of the American evangelist Lorenzo Dow, who began holding 'camp meetings' in the open air on the slopes
of Mow Cop, a 1,000-foot Pennine spur north of Stoke-on-Trent.[481] In 1807 the
Methodist Conference condemned these meetings;[482] and in the following year it
expelled Bourne, Clowes following in 1810. In 1811 their two small groups of followers combined, and in 1812 took the name of Primitive Methodists.[483] The name is
significant: it represented a desire to do for Methodism what the Oxford Movement
sought to do for the Church of England – to restore the purity of its original
teaching.[484] Though its appeal declined later in the century, it developed a strong following among the poor in rural and industrial (especially midland and northern)
areas. Many of their chapels were given biblical names like Bethel, Ebenezer, or Zion,
reflecting their sense of themselves as a chosen people like the Israel of the Old Testament.[485]

The role of women in Primitive Methodism is important: in a broadly democratic
organization, with no paid or professional ministry, women often exercised leadership
roles, if only indirectly. Dinah Maul of East Bridgford 'used to pray and sing as few
could', and was a class leader and 'a famous directress of penitents. When people were
in spiritual distress, still more when life was ebbing, the word would be, "Send for
Dinah."'[486] The emphasis on family or 'cottage' piety that pervaded its teaching
helped to produce a number of female preachers, from poorer social backgrounds
than more famous nineteenth-century religious women like Hannah More or Dora
Greenwell.[487]

Some of these women preceded Primitive Methodism: Ann Cutler, known as

'Praying Nanny', was a late-eighteenth-century female preacher from a poor Lancashire working family engaged in the cotton textile industry.[488] Even if the father
tended to preside at family prayers (and there is evidence to suggest that within Primitive Methodism mothers played a key role in this respect as well[489]), women would
spend time on Sundays teaching their children about the Bible and praying with
them, which underlines their vital spiritual role in the formation of their children: that
role might also include offering hospitality to ministers and at church meetings.[490]
The charismatic nature of Primitive Methodist piety seems also to have nurtured a
number of female visionaries.[491]

The kind of spirituality nurtured by the Primitive Methodist camp meetings is distinctive, and well worth brief further reflection. In the preface he wrote to his *A
collection of hymns for camp meetings*, Hugh Bourne pointed out that Christ 'and his
Apostles stamped a dignity on out-of-door worship, as they usually celebrated
worship in the open air'.[492] This is the spirituality of the Scottish Covenanters of two
centuries earlier, and there are interesting parallels between the two movements.[493]
Camp meetings could take place only on Sundays, when the labouring poor were free,
and could take various forms: preaching services, reading services, and what were
called 'Praying services'. This is what Bourne prescribed for the latter:

> Praying services should be carefully supported. They are the chief strength
> of the Camp Meetings, and give energy and dignity to the whole. They are
> held in four different ways:
>
> 1. The general praying service at the opening.
>
> 2. About a quarter past ten in the forenoon, a praying service should
> open in companies . . . if the congregation happen to be but small, they
> should nevertheless go out in companies, because the going out and
> coming in are a great relief both to body and mind; and are of great service
> to the people in other respects.
>
> 3. When a praying service, in companies, has gone on, with energy, for
> half an hour, they are usually summoned to the preaching stand. But if the
> pious praying labourers happen to be engaged with mourners, then the
> next service must be deferred or put off as the case may require.[494]

As with Wesleyan Methodists, the larger meetings were only one strand of the
common spiritual life of the Primitives. On Lovefeasts, Bourne writes:

> Lovefeasts usually open with singing and prayer. A piece is then sung by
> way of asking a blessing; after which the bread and water are served out,
> the Lovefeast collection is made, and a piece sung by way of returning
> thanks. The preacher makes a few remarks; the people rise in succession,
> and speak their own experience; and distant comers sometimes say a little
> about the works of God in other places. But none are allowed to run into
> useless exhortations, drag out to tedious lengths, or to speak unprofitably
> of others; and above all not to reflect upon or find fault, either with indi-
> viduals or societies.[495]

Note the sharing of testimonies and personal experiences, and the deliberate restraints on individuals dominating the proceedings. The emphasis on music is also significant: it played a vital role in Primitive Methodism (as Bourne's two substantial hymn collections suggest) and in Nonconformity in general – and not only in common worship. The radical journal *The Nonconformist* carried a review, in its issue of 4 October 1843, of *The people's music book* by James Turle (then organist at Westminster Abbey) and Edward Taylor.[496] The reviewer celebrated

> the rich source of pleasure which [music] opens up to families – the sweet bond of union into which it may be woven – how it enhances the attractions of home – how it may be made to elicit all the finer feelings, and to touch all the more delicate susceptibilities of the heart – what a graceful charm it gives to domestic relationships, and what a new interest it may throw around domestic devotion.

Jonathan Ireland, a nineteenth-century Primitive Methodist from Manchester, recalls the impact the movement made there in relation to music:

> Before the Primitive Methodists came to this city, and for some time after, it was very common to hear lewd or ribald songs sung in the streets, especially on the Lord's day. *But our movements drove them away by putting something better in their place.* We used to pick up the most effective tunes we heard, and then put them to our hymns; and at our camp-meetings people, chiefly young ones, used to run up to hear us, thinking we were singing a favourite song. But they were disappointed therein; nevertheless, they were arrested and often charmed by the hymn, which at times went with power to their hearts.[497]

Primitive Methodism also laid stress on smaller meetings specifically directed towards shared prayer. Bourne outlines their programme:

1. Open with singing for about 4, 5, or 6 minutes.
2. Spend 4, 5, or 6 minutes in prayer, ending with the Lord's prayer.
3. Sing about 2, 3, or 4 minutes.
4. Let the members of the society pray in quick succession, for about 2, 3, or 4 minutes each; with singing a verse or two occasionally, to vary the exercises.
5. In praying with mourners or in other particular cases, the exercises may be lengthened. But, in general, long exercises in public are injurious, and should be carefully avoided. And if any one trespass, by attempting to drag out to an improper length, then the leaders' meeting, or some other official authority, may determine what remedy shall be applied to such impropriety.
6. If exhortations be given, they may be from 2 or 3, to 6 or 8 minutes each.
7. Conclude in an hour, or an hour and a quarter.
8. On suitable occasions, prayer may again commence, and especially if there be souls in distress.

9. This outline may be judiciously varied in any point as circumstances may require.

10. In all kinds of meetings the general rules are as follow [sic]:– 1. Begin at the proper time. 2. Get into faith as much as possible, in order that the Holy Ghost may descend. 3. Kneel at prayer. 4. Stand in singing. 5. Sit in the time of preaching, exhortation, or discourse. Nevertheless in worship in the open air, if the ground be wet or unsuitable, the kneeling is sometimes dispensed with.[498]

These prayer meetings did not always follow Bourne's rules. The Primitive Methodist preacher Atkinson Smith was foreman on a farm at Messingham, which was owned by a Wesleyan local preacher

> who, like himself, was fully in the spirit of the revival. Master and man would often take the lead in services held in the large farm-kitchen, in the presence of the numerous children and servants who, in patriarchal style, lived under the same roof. Once, praise and prayer were still going on, with the blinds drawn and the candles burning, while the sun was already up and climbing the eastern sky. It was nothing to them that the struggling angel said, 'Let me go, the day breaketh.' It might break and dawn and shine; they said, 'We will not let thee go except thou bless us.'[499]

Bourne also emphasizes the value of personal prayer:

> In private prayer a person may, through the Mediator, enter into conversation with the Almighty, and lay open his whole soul unto him. He may press through temptation, grow into faith, and take hold of the strength of the Lord. At times, however, it is difficult to wrestle through the force of temptation, and get into the fulness of faith, till the Holy Ghost powerfully descends. But in this, as in other means, he that regardeth the clouds shall not reap.[500]

Finally, something needs to be said about Primitive Methodist ministers, almost all of whom were local part-time lay preachers, and some of whom (such as Joseph Capper of Tunstall, Stoke-on-Trent) were also involved in social and political activity on behalf of working-class people.[501] Charles Shaw, a nineteenth-century potter from Stoke-on-Trent who began as a child worker and later in life became a local preacher, recalls in his autobiography the impact of the early preachers:

> I saw the spell these men cast upon the multitudes to whom they spoke, by their simplicity, their rough energy, softened by their all-pervading compassion and their great theme. These men themselves, in a sense, were never anything but local preachers . . . There was nothing clerical about them. They were simply 'sinners saved by grace', telling in homely language how it had been done.[502]

Few if any of these ministers will have had any significant education; and there could be a conscious anti-intellectual bias in Primitive Methodism. Thus Bourne criticized people who wrote scriptural commentaries: 'they find no end in wand'ring mazes lost: O Lord, direct my soul into the plain Bible'.[503] And sometimes these lay ministers responded effectively when on the receiving end of lofty criticism about their lack of education. This is the reaction of the Primitive Methodist preacher John Benton (d.1856):

> Said a local preacher to him one day after hearing him try to preach at Cannock Common: 'You are bringing a scandal on the cause of Christ, you have had no learning, you do not understand grammar.' Benton's most effective answer was given some time after. He was preaching on a Good Friday afternoon . . . The room was crowded with colliers, and he had got but half-way through his discourse when a large part of the congregation became strangely affected: some groaned, others shrieked; some fell from their seats; and the whole assembly was thrown into consternation; he therefore closed the Bible, and went from his stand to pray for mourners; and when passing down among the people he saw his friend, the local preacher, standing and looking on with amazement. Said Benton to him: 'This is grammar!'[504]

More significantly, the spiritual education of children (both at home but even more in Sunday Schools) was a mainstay of this, as of all other nineteenth-century Nonconformist traditions. It is worth hearing once more from the Potteries labourer Charles Shaw, about the impact of Sunday School in the 1830s:

> To me, very soon, [Sunday School] was a life within my life. In the midst of a life of hardship and temptation, this inner life shed a brightness and a sweetness which always gave me an upward look and an upward aspiration. Sunday was verily an oasis in the desert to me . . . It gave me the only gladsome morning of the week. I got a washing that morning such as I had not time to get on other mornings. I had poor enough clothing to put on, but my eldest sister always helped me in my toilet on Sunday morning, and my hair got brushed and combed and oiled (with scented oil), so that I always carried a fragrance with me . . . Sundays brought sweetness into my life, and lifted me out of the demoralising influences of the working days.[505]

Spirituality and Liberal Nonconformity

If Primitive Methodism offers a case study of radical Nonconformist spirituality, we may return to the minister with whose words this chapter opened to explore a different species of Dissent. The ministry of James Phillippo Mursell (whom we first encountered at the beginning of this chapter) in a central Baptist church at Leicester gives us a glimpse of a spiritual life rooted in mainstream Nonconformity: Mursell, though like all Dissenters until 1854 barred from university education, was well-read and enjoyed the status of the full-time minister in a manner denied to the leaders of the Primitives.[506]

The Nonconformists were a formidable presence in Leicester, as in many other Victorian cities.[507] During Mursell's ministry there, the Unitarians at Great Meeting Chapel in East Bond Street commissioned Joseph Dare (1800–83) to lead their Domestic Mission among the urban poor of Leicester. Dare's annual reports of the Mission give a vivid picture both of widespread poverty and of the energetic activities of Nonconformists in seeking to combat this and other social ills.[508]

It was arguably the Baptists whose role in the social and spiritual life of Victorian Leicester was most significant, and Mursell's long ministry in the city centre was a major part of this.[509] His theology was broadly Calvinist, but the combination with a radical Liberalism in political terms makes for an interesting contrast with Spurgeon. Like Spurgeon, Mursell stresses the pervasive nature of human depravity: people err if they

> look upon the world as suffering under a sort of cutaneous affection, which will yield to the application of judiciously-selected molients, rather than as bowed down beneath a deep organic derangement which calls for the skilful and mighty hand of the Great and Divine Physician.[510]

Again like Spurgeon, but with a focus directed more towards social justice at home and evangelism overseas, Mursell wants to commend the attractiveness of God, which all Christians must seek to embody and communicate. 'Moral beauty is not a cold and a scenic thing, but a living and a plastic presence, touching into resemblance to itself whatever comes within its reach.'[511] And he continues:

> Superinduced on this capability of observing and of copying is the additional and semi-divine faculty of imparting . . . the life . . . which we imbibe and embody, so that in our turn we influence others, send forth our radiations, and . . . guide and solace the wandering and the lost . . . Christianity proposes to give to these capabilities an elevated direction, an appropriate end, and an all but infinite range. It calls us into blessed communion with the Father of our spirits, bids us copy and reflect the imitable perfections of our Redeemer, and impels us to spread the fragrance of His deeds and of His fame. Hence, my brethren, the rationale of Christian Missions.[512]

This is the beauty, the attractiveness, of Christianity; and its implications are not only evangelistic, but moral and spiritual as well. What we receive from God, and make our own by the practice of the Christian life, we are in turn called to convey to others; and the capacity of Christianity 'to unfold our nature' in this way, 'to draw forth its faculties, and to enlist its energies, is a proof of its innate power, an indubitable sign that it is not an artificially organised scheme, a grand and splendid theorem, but a substantial moral reality'.[513]

The extract from Mursell's sermon with which this chapter began illustrates his concern for overseas evangelism, a concern which was shared by large numbers of Christians from all the mainstream denominations.[514] Its relevance to the spiritual life consists in the enormous amount of prayer that missionary society members and others were encouraged to engage in on behalf of the work.[515] Moreover, for Mursell the Christian missions are 'the growth and the gauge of the spirituality of the Church';[516] and the key requirement is prayer:

> Let us be stirred to more earnest and believing prayer. This enterprise was born of prayer. It was the Monday evening prayer-meeting for the conversion of the world (first instituted, I think, in this county,) which awakened in the conscience of such men as Carey the sense of the inconsistency of prayer without practice.[517]

Mursell argues for a partnership between missionaries and indigenous Christians, with local people running local churches while the missionaries act like the apostles:

> Have we not, brethren, caught too little of the adventurous faith of the first planters of Christianity, and too little dared to leave our converts, as they left theirs to that Holy Ghost, who is the Author and Trainer of spiritual life . . . ?[518]

And he emphasizes that it is impossible to worry about spiritual or theological issues when you are starving.[519] He believed that all true knowledge is, by definition, germinant: 'to acquire knowledge with a view to insulate it is to offer violence to it, and to sin against its very nature':[520] hence his commitment to education at every level both at home and overseas. A wholesome spiritual life will recognize this, for it cannot be acceptable to say

> that the science of Christian morals is a theme for poets rather than for peasants, a tinted vision suffusing with colored rays the dreams of the enthusiast, instead of a plain reality fitted to guide the footsteps of the plodding traveller.[521]

Spirituality and social justice: the Salvation Army

An even more striking example of Nonconformist spirituality bearing fruit in concerted social action is that of the Salvation Army. William Booth (1829–1912) was born a member of the Church of England (at Sneinton, Nottingham). In 1844 he was converted during a Methodist revival campaign, and two years later became a street preacher and in 1855 a travelling evangelist. The Salvation Army regards its own beginning as being in a disused Quaker cemetery in Whitechapel, an area of massive poverty, where Booth was permitted to erect a preaching tent in 1865.[522] Booth became its first leader, or General, and, together with his devoted wife Catherine became a national figure.[523]

Booth has no doubt at all about the uselessness of trying to preach the Gospel or commend the spiritual values of Christianity to people who are starving:

> What is the use of preaching the Gospel to men whose whole attention is concentrated upon a mad, desperate struggle to keep themselves alive? You might as well give a tract to a shipwrecked sailor who is battling with the surf which has drowned his comrades and threatens to drown him. He will not listen to you. Nay, he cannot hear you.[524]

Booth's approach is direct, passionate, individualist: it is all very well, he says, for people to speak of the free play of natural laws leading to the survival of the fittest. 'But meanwhile what is to become of John Jones?'[525] It is important to note too (because it is often overlooked) Booth's concern to change the system that makes people poor or drunk or homeless, to tackle the causes as well as the symptoms.[526] His great work *In darkest England and the way out* (1890) not only contains a visionary blueprint for tackling England's massive problem of deprivation and inequality: it is also full of vivid anecdotes drawn from Booth's or fellow Salvationists' experience. Here is his description of an incident witnessed by a journalist in Whitechapel:

> I was stopped by a small crowd at a street corner. There were about thirty or forty men, women, and children standing loosely together . . . In the centre of the crowd was a plain-looking little woman in Salvation Army uniform, with her eyes closed, praying the 'dear Lord that he would bless these dear people, and save them, save them now!' Moved by curiosity, I pressed through the outer fringe of the crowd, and in doing so, I noticed a woman of another kind, also invoking Heaven, but in an altogether different fashion. Two dirty tramp-like men were listening to the prayer, standing the while smoking their short cutty pipes. For some reason or other they had offended the woman, and she was giving them a piece of her mind. They stood stolidly silent while she went at them like a fiend. She had been good-looking once, but was now horribly bloated with drink, and excited by passion. I heard both voices at the same time.
>
> What a contrast! . . . Clear and strong the voice [of the Salvationist], eloquent with the fervour of intense feeling, rang through the little crowd, past which streamed the ever-flowing tide of East End life. And at the same time that I heard this pure and passionate invocation to love God and be true to man I heard a voice on the outskirts, and it said this: 'You — swine! I'll knock the vitals out of yer!'[527]

More moving still is Booth's story of a 50-year-old chemist from Holloway in London who, driven to despair by poverty, tried to commit suicide together with his wife after both had tried to poison their only child (all three survived, and the chemist was put on trial for murder). In the moving letter he left for his brother and had intended as a farewell note, the chemist writes:

> May God Almighty forgive us for this heinous sin, and have mercy on our sinful souls, is the prayer of your miserable, broken-hearted, but loving brother, Arthur. We have now done everything that we can possibly think of to advert this wicked proceeding, but can discover no ray of hope. Fervent prayer has availed us nothing; our lot is cast, and we must abide by it. It must be God's will or He would have ordained it differently . . . Our clergyman has never called on us or given us the least consolation, though I called on him a month ago. He is paid to preach, and there he considers his responsibility ends, the rich excepted. We have only yourself and a very few others who care one pin what becomes of us, but you must try and

forgive us, is the last fervent prayer of your devotedly fond and affectionate but broken-hearted and persecuted brother.[528]

The anguish of a faith at once shattered and yet somehow still just alive is in itself eloquent witness to Booth's point: the life of prayer, and the spiritual values of the Gospel, cannot be separated from the physical and social conditions in which people live. It was a spirituality, not just of salvation but of survival, which William and Catherine Booth dedicated themselves to conveying. In the Victoria and Albert Museum there is a sampler of English embroidery with the following inscription, a moving witness to the terrible problem of high mortality rates among children and young adults in Victorian England:

On the Death of my Affectionate Mother

Lord thou wast pleased to bestow on me a Mother truly kind,
Whose constant care was to instil good precepts on my mind;
And plant the seeds of virtue in my young and tender breast,
Ere thou didst snatch her from my sight with thee to be at rest.
Grant me O Lord thy constant aid to do thy holy will,
that a tender Mother's pious wish may be in me fulfiled [sic].
Eliza Richardson aged 10 Years 1837.[529]

Unitarians and Irvingites

Finally, something needs briefly to be said about two small but significant strands of nineteenth-century Nonconformity. No part of this astonishingly diverse movement sought more single-mindedly to hold together the insights of Evangelicalism and of scientific rationalism than the Unitarians, though the result was a somewhat cerebral Christianity of little appeal to any but intellectuals.[530] Their outstanding representative in the nineteenth century was James Martineau, a distinguished theologian who became Principal of Manchester New College, a training centre for preachers. In his *The seat of authority in religion* (1890) he reflects Unitarian concern to combine the biblical with the scientific: he adumbrates a fundamental principle for a theology of the spiritual life in his exegesis of the first chapter of Genesis. He distinguishes the spirit that animates every human being (the *ruach*, or breath of life breathed by God into Adam), from the Holy Spirit of God. The effect of the breath of life

is in simply knowing it and becoming his own spectator. There is henceforth an 'inner man' that stands off from 'the outer,' to notice and apprehend its contents.[531]

The gift of the spirit or breath of life is a gift of self-consciousness, uniquely granted to human beings in the second account of creation in Genesis (chapters 2–3). The heavenly or Holy Spirit is different from this: 'in its proper home, it is as truly the essence of all living natures as "flesh" is here below'. There are the raw materials here for a distinctively Unitarian theology of the spiritual life, avoiding (as Unitarians must) any need to regard the Holy Spirit as divine in the manner of orthodox

Trinitarianism, and allowing an approach to Genesis 2–3 that might be compatible with science.[532]

Scarcely less gifted than James Martineau was Edward Irving, the Scottish Presbyterian minister who became the founder of the Irvingites, or Catholic Apostolic Church.[533] He moved from his first ministerial charge at Glasgow to be minister of the Caledonian Chapel at Hatton Garden in London in 1822 and swiftly established a reputation as a preacher. In 1825 he met Henry Drummond, a wealthy Scottish banker who had recently purchased Albury Park, near Guildford, which was to become a centre for the denomination. In 1831 Irving permitted speaking in tongues in his church, and in the following year was removed from the ministry of the Church of Scotland on grounds of heresy.[534] Irving and Drummond formed a new body which came to be called the Catholic Apostolic Church; Drummond became one of the first 'apostles' while Irving as pastor was given the title of 'angel'.

Irving died in 1834 aged only 42. He was a revivalist, but one deeply committed to what would later be called a Pentecostal theology: baptism in the Spirit, together with speaking in tongues, combined with a strong emphasis on eschatology and the imminent fulfilment of biblical prophecies.[535] His earlier works, which include a good deal of material on the spiritual life of Christians, are orthodox and full of wisdom. Here he is, in fine Nonconformist style, celebrating true Christian worship in the power and freedom of the Spirit:

> It is not the harmony of many voices in praise, nor the uniting of all voices into one in prayer; it is not the uncovered head, or the reverend bending of the knee, or the heartily uttered Amen. Still less is it the noble pile of Gothic or Grecian structure, the solemn voice or becoming dress of the priest . . . No, verily! It may be, it hath been, in a barn, in a cottage, under the open canopy . . . Oh no! my brethren; it is not the form and ceremony of the service, but it is the present Deity in every heart; it is the common inspiration of the Holy Spirit . . . this is it which possesseth the worshippers with the sacredness of the time and place, and makes them feel, This is none other than the house of God and the gate of heaven.[536]

Irving's book *On prayer* is a sustained attempt to explore the implications of biblical teaching and practice for contemporary prayer. He asks what constitutes a genuine prayer to which an answer might be expected, and suggests that the first and foremost criterion is whether it conforms to the knowledge of God's promises in scripture ('which are, as it were, the charter to go by'). Our prayer should be limited in scope and spirit to those promises: for 'without that knowledge [prayer] is an empty form, or rather a sinful liberty taken with the ear of God'.[537] Scriptural meditation is thus a vital adjunct to prayer;[538] and since these promises are a guide to our action as well as to our prayer, we must seek to achieve in action what we ask for in prayer:[539] prayer is 'the stepping-stone between holy conceptions and holy endeavours to bring these conceptions into being'.[540] This need not make prayer a dry affair: it is conducted in the language of affection and love.[541] Significantly, in view of his later beliefs, he emphasizes the importance of praying for the coming of Christ's kingdom, not only for ourselves but throughout the world;[542] and, in his treatise on the Psalms, he stresses the apocalyptic nature of psalmody, anticipating the final victory of the Messiah.[543]

ROMAN CATHOLIC SPIRITUALITY

Introduction

For English Roman Catholics, the nineteenth century witnessed some extraordinary developments. In 1829 the Catholic Emancipation Act marked a milestone in permitting Catholics to practise their religion, though a number of legal penalties remained in force.[544] In 1850 the episcopal hierarchy was restored, raising the Church's profile enormously. In 1884, Cardinal Manning opened the Brompton Oratory, whose triumphalist grandeur reflected the Church's increasing confidence. The wave of Irish immigration massively increased their numbers: there were about 80,000 in England in the 1760s, and about 1.3 million by 1903. And the numerical increase saw other developments: the rapid change of character from a largely rural to a largely urban denomination;[545] the development of episcopal and clerical control, replacing the power of the old recusant aristocrats;[546] and the growth of a (defensive or confident, depending on one's point of view) vigorous ultramontanism in Europe, ironically reflected in England by the neo-medieval Gothic splendour of A. W. N. Pugin's new churches.[547]

It is particularly important to recall the impact of the French Revolution here: the post-1815 conservative resurgence of Catholic militancy and papalist loyalty in France as a reaction to the 1789 Revolution powerfully heightened, even in England, the sense of a church establishing its identity over against the world. In 1854, the year Dissenters were admitted to Oxford and Cambridge, Pius IX declared the dogma of the Immaculate Conception, reflecting the surge of intense Marian devotion on the continent: this would increase still further after the Marian visions of St Bernadette Soubirous at Lourdes in 1858, which in turn stimulated a new fervour for pilgrimages there from England and across Europe.[548] And, in 1870, in the year that Rome fell to Vittorio Emmanuele I, thus reducing the temporal power of the popes to a tiny statelet around St Peter's Basilica, the papacy declared its own infallibility at the end of the First Vatican Council. Eight years later, Leo XIII's papal bull *Quod apostolici muneris* would condemn Socialism, Communism, and atheism as utterly incompatible with Roman Catholicism.[549]

The nature of nineteenth-century English Roman Catholicism

There were three distinct strands in nineteenth-century English Roman Catholicism. First, there were the old recusants, mostly landed gentry and aristocrats, who had in some areas kept the fire of the faith burning during the long years of persecution. It is easy to visualize these as tiny self-contained coteries of piety, having little impact on society around them. But their tenacious preservation of the old faith bore fruit: some recent scholarship has underlined the extent to which nineteenth-century Catholic piety was rooted in the old vernacular spirituality of the recusants, transmitted in particular through the teaching of popular books like Challoner's *Garden of the soul.*[550]

Second, there were the Irish immigrants whose numbers swelled English Catholicism during the century, and tilted its character significantly. They may well have been more regular churchgoers, as minority groups in foreign surroundings often are.[551] They brought with them to England their own piety; the use of the rosary as a home-based devotion may well owe a great deal to the practice of western Irish Gaelic-speaking Catholics.[552]

Third, there were the converts, mostly from Anglicanism: though relatively few in number, these were often prominent or articulate people (such as Newman and Manning), and helped to moderate the impact of huge numbers of Irish immigrants into the English Church.[553] It is not surprising that converts looked for a flamboyant, unapologetic Catholicism, especially when those who were ordained spent some years at Rome.[554] The converts were to become Rome's most effective apologists: all those whose thought is explored in this section were themselves converts.[555]

Two other important elements in Roman Catholic life need mentioning here, though the first (the rebirth of the religious life in England) will be considered later. The other was the influence of Catholic societies, which played a major role in fostering lay piety. By 1880 most English Catholic churches had some kind of society attached to them, and some had many.[556] Some were continental in origin, like the Franciscan tertiaries, or the Society of St Vincent de Paul (which was brought to England in 1844).[557] Some were specifically devotional, like the Apostleship of Prayer, or the Living Rosary;[558] not all were well supported. But all gave opportunities for laypeople to deepen their faith and devotional life.

Henry Edward Manning (1807–92)

Apart from John Henry Newman and Gerard Manley Hopkins, who will merit separate attention, four Roman Catholics may be taken as representative of nineteenth-century English spirituality. Henry Edward Manning was born in Hertfordshire, the son of a London merchant, and educated at Harrow and Oxford.[559] He had little to do with Newman or the other future Tractarian leaders while at university, and thereafter spent a year as a government clerk before being ordained in 1832. He spent nearly 18 years as first curate and then incumbent of the Sussex parish of Graffham and West Lavington, near Midhurst. Manning married the former rector's daughter Caroline Sergent: her death in 1837, aged only 25, was at once an irreparable blow and arguably the beginning of his serious interest in theology and the future of the Church.[560] In 1840 Manning, by now an enthusiast for Tractarian principles, was made Archdeacon of Chichester.[561] In 1850 the Gorham case, in which the Privy Council overruled the highest church court in England, helped to convince him that the Established Church was irretrievably tied to the state; and on 6 April 1851 he was received into the Roman Catholic Church. Thereafter his progress was rapid: in 1857 he was Provost of Westminster Cathedral chapter, and in 1865 he was made Archbishop of Westminster by Pius IX.[562]

Manning's leadership of the English Roman Catholic Church was outstanding. Here was this intelligent, austere, proud, and immensely able man, sprung from rural Anglicanism to Roman politics and national prominence. He had a profound commitment to issues of justice: in 1874 he delivered an address on 'The dignity and rights of labour' to the Mechanics' Institute at Leeds, and in 1889 intervened decisively in the crippling London dock strike, persuading employers and strikers to accept an honourable compromise, and thereby winning much respect not only for himself but for the Catholic Church too.[563] He stood with Salvationists against alcoholism, and with Josephine Butler against the Contagious Diseases Act.[564] He was passionately committed to the cause of education, especially of the poor, yet was unapologetically Ultramontane in theology. He wrote:

> The government of the Church is, in a strict and true sense, a monarchy; it is the kingdom of Jesus Christ. There is only one visible head; one only who has the twofold plenitude of jurisdiction and of doctrinal authority; one only who is independent of all authority on earth; one on whom all authorities in the Church depend; one supreme legislator, one supreme judge. He is sovereign and final.[565]

Yet there need be no contradiction here. Manning had witnessed the tensions within a church whose links with the state both allowed it access to the powerful, and constrained its freedom to run its own affairs. In the Rome of Pius IX he found a church sufficiently free from secular control (hence his reference to being 'independent of all authority on earth') to proclaim the Gospel without fear or favour; and that is precisely what he proceeded to do himself. It is significant that St Augustine is the writer he quotes most: there is something of Augustine in this shy but indomitable prelate.[566]

Frederick William Faber (1814–67)

Frederick William Faber was born in Yorkshire and educated at Shrewsbury, Harrow, and (like Manning) Balliol College Oxford, where (unlike Manning) he became active in the Oxford Movement. In 1839 he was ordained priest in the Church of England and in 1843 became Rector of Elton in Huntingdonshire. He made a number of continental tours which profoundly influenced him: indeed landscape and architecture as much as theology seem to have played a part in shaping his spiritual life;[567] and he became deeply attached to the rigorous but affective spirituality of St Philip Neri and St Alphonsus Liguori.[568] In 1845 he was received into the Roman Catholic Church, and spent some time in charge of a small religious community in Birmingham and Cheadle (Staffordshire) before joining the Oratory under Newman at Maryvale in Birmingham in 1848. A year later he was Superior of the new London Oratory, which in 1854 settled at Brompton.

Faber's Catholicism was more intense and emotional than Manning's: hence his difficult relations with Newman. But it would be wrong to dismiss him as an impulsive or extravagant figure. His books reflect wide reading among Catholic writers on the spiritual life, though there seems little doubt that he found in St Alphonsus Liguori a particularly congenial mix of papalism and exuberantly affective piety.[569] His hymns also reflect the influence of the Romantics (in 1830 he visited Wordsworth at Rydal Mount): both the hymns and much of his other writing are clearly concerned to help lay Catholics to grow in their faith. On 23 January 1862, a year before he died, he wrote a letter, in answer to a question on an abstruse point of mystical theology, which reveals the heart of his spirituality:

> I should hardly be a fair judge, for two reasons. First, my spiritual life has so changed during the past years that I can take little, if any, interest in

theological refinements, which once were the delight of my meditations. It seems as if God arrested me on the threshold, and so filled the *general* truth with surpassing sweetness, and at the same time with vague misty intelligence, that I cannot proceed to details, and I feel almost a dislike to having truths brought nearer or made clearer . . . Second, I am in my devotional instincts rather out of harmony with some of those you quote . . . There is something in that interior mincemeat of spirituality which I cannot digest. It seems never to forget itself, its postures, or the graceful arrangements of its toga, even in the presence of God. There is no St Francis-like childishness. No impulse, none of that intensely reverential familiarity, which belongs to Italian and Spanish saints.[570]

Alice Meynell (1847–1922)

Alice Meynell came from a literary background: her father was a close friend of Dickens, and her mother a nomadic, artistic character. Much of her childhood was spent in France and Italy. She became a Roman Catholic as a young adult, and in 1877 married Wilfrid Meynell. They settled in London, and had eight children, one of whom died in infancy. Both she and Wilfrid were writers; and, although Alice's output was relatively modest, it contains poetry of exceptional power and devotional intensity, among them the moving 'Letter from a girl to her own old age'.[571]

George Tyrrell (1861–1909)

George Tyrrell was born in Dublin, of a Protestant family; he became a Roman Catholic in 1879, and entered the Jesuit novitiate a year later.[572] Like Gerard Manley Hopkins, he underwent the full rigour of nineteenth-century Jesuit formation. It was not until 1893 that he was first sent to an ordinary parish;[573] and he survived there only a year before being sent to Stonyhurst to teach philosophy in 1894. It appears to be there that disagreements with his fellow Jesuits first surfaced; and in 1899 he was delated (reported) to Rome after the appearance of his 'A perverted devotion'.[574] The gathering storm-clouds did not stop Tyrrell continuing to write prolifically. In 1906 he was expelled from the Jesuits, and retired to Storrington in Sussex, where he died partially reconciled to the Church.[575]

Tyrrell was a complex person: far more humorous and outgoing than Newman or Manning, he nonetheless was prone to melancholy, worked excessively hard, and appears to have embodied a curious blend of pugnacity and placidity.[576] He produced a large amount of Catholic apologetics, most written in a vivid and effective prose style not unlike that of G. K. Chesterton. But his major importance for English spirituality consists in his interest in the relationship between theology and devotion.[577]

Spirituality and theology

'Catholicity', says the non-Catholic Dora Greenwell in her study of the French Dominican Lacordaire, 'is represented [by him] as ever working towards the whole of things.'[578] The search for an integrated faith, and above all for a close relationship between theology and prayer, is crucial for George Tyrrell. In the preface to his first published work (1897), he says that 'if the intellect needs the control of faith, faith is perfected and served by intellect. Therefore let not man sunder what God has joined together.'[579] In an 1899 essay ('The relation of theology to devotion'), Tyrrell insists on the vital connection between the two: devotion without [scholastic] theology becomes anthropomorphic and superstitious; theology without devotion becomes excessively abstract;[580] and abstract theology can rob faith of its power and devotion.[581] Hence:

> If [the purpose of the Creed] is the perfection and spiritual education of the individual believer, it attains this end only because it is the expression of the collective spiritual life of the Church at large – which life is normal and authoritative for the individual, and must be appropriated by him before any sort of healthy personality of belief can be developed. In no two souls could the words of the Creed stand for quite the same thing.[582]

Tyrrell even goes so far as to say that 'what I *feel* about life may be much truer than what I think or say about it – even to myself, i.e. it may be the product of a truer, though of an obscure and inexpressible intuition'.[583] This is not, however, to elevate feeling above thought or acts of the will:

> There is not a movement of the spirit in which knowledge, feeling, and will do not interpenetrate. When this is clearly recognized, it matters little from which of the three sides we approach the study of the spirit-life, since each entails the other two, and if we grasp one we grasp all . . . Religion does not consist in knowing; it does not consist in feeling; it does not consist in willing and doing, nor is it a sum or addition of all three; but it is a life, an operation in which the mind can view now under one, now under another of these aspects. It is not possible to feel with Christ, unless we think and will with Him, nor to think with Him, unless we feel with Him, for the spirit-life is one and indivisible.[584]

This concern to keep devotion and theology together in a period when they were constantly threatening to break apart (not least because of the highly schematic and scholastic nature of contemporary Roman theology) has important implications. It affects devotion to the eucharistic sacrament:

> The notion of the loneliness, the sorrows, the disappointments of the neglected Prisoner of Love in the tabernacle may be crude and simple; but it is assuredly nearer the truth than the notion of a now passionless and apathetic Christ, who suffered these things by foresight two thousand years ago, and whose irrevocable pains cannot possibly be increased or lessened by any conduct of ours.[585]

This may read strangely to some; but Tyrrell is trying to help his fellow-Catholics to value *both* popular (and sometimes sentimental) devotion to the Eucharist, *and* the insights of Catholic theology: indeed he is pastor enough to be aware that sometimes an unsophisticated lay piety is closer to the truth than a chilly intellectualism; and says so:[586] *lex orandi est lex credendi* – it is through true prayer that we apprehend true belief. Tyrrell makes this point well in his study of the Lord's prayer, the subject of his fine book *Lex credendi*. The first petition in it, 'Hallowed be thy name', reminds us that theology begins with the naming of God, as devotion begins with the experience of God. The two belong together: 'theology and devotion act and react upon each other'.[587] Failure to name God, or to name God correctly, is bound to lead to false devotion.

Tyrrell was not the only Roman Catholic to maintain the inseparability of dogma and devotion. Manning makes the same point, albeit in more precise and juridical terms, in his book on devotion to the Sacred Heart:

> There can be no Divine Truth which ought not to be an object of love and of veneration . . . If, when a divine truth is declared to us, our hearts do not turn to it, as the eye turns to the light; if there be not in us an instinctive yearning, which makes us promptly turn to the sound of the divine voice, the fault is in our hearts; for just in proportion as we know the truth we shall be drawn towards it.[588]

In short, we cannot love what we do not know.[589] But there are two kinds of theology: that taught by doctors of the Church, and that 'which comes not from books, but from God Himself; not from poring over learned pages, but by the infused light of the Holy Ghost'.[590] This is the theology of St Peter the fisherman, or of St Margaret Mary Alacocque, founder of devotion to the Sacred Heart.[591]

In the final analysis, Tyrrell and Manning parted company here: for Tyrrell, true religion must ultimately be mystery, never completely contained by neat dogmas.[592] This is not to commend obscurity for its own sake; but it is to beware of an excessive precision in theology:[593]

> Catholicism is characterised by a certain irrationality, incoherence, and irregularity – a certain irreducibleness to exact and systematic expression – which, far from being scandalous, is another presumption in its favour . . . Its very wildnesses and barbarisms point to the natural character of Catholicism, and distinguish it from all planned-out philosophical religions, whose over-trimness is an indication of their poverty and exhaustion; for nothing that lives and grows can keep its shape for long . . . Religions are growths, not manufactures . . . incoherencies and inconsistencies are a sign of natural life and growth; while artificial completeness means stagnation and death.[594]

Where G. K. Chesterton, in *Orthodoxy*, was brilliantly to hold together mysticism and dogmatic definition by his use of paradox, Tyrrell concluded that growth and mystery were too important to be so constrained, even though, as a good ascetic, he knew that growth happens best through restraint.[595] In the controversial article 'A perverted devotion', he attacked orthodox teaching on the certainty of eternal punishment in hell (as F. D. Maurice had done), precisely because it sacrificed mystery to easy certainty:

> The particular gratification that certain minds get out of the *materiality* of the fire [of hell] can only be accounted for by a nervous dread of in any way

making the doctrine mysterious, or removing it from the jurisdiction of common sense.[596]

And the reason mystery mattered so much to Tyrrell was because he wanted mystical religion to be accessible to everyone: hence his stress on love as its essential key.[597] He knew very well that mysticism was suspect in some quarters, either (for Protestants) because it was too Catholic or (for Catholics) because it was too esoteric.[598] But that only made it all the more important to hold together the mystical and the moral, a distinctive insight which Christianity alone maintains.[599]

In his last completed work (*Christianity at the cross-roads*) Tyrrell explores, in an essay entitled 'The truth-value of visions', the relationship between the subjective and the objective in the search for God. All of us, he argued, need to find harmony between ourselves and the transcendent, though none of us will ever achieve that completely in this life. Of course inward experience is not enough; yet God is revealed to us through our experiences insofar as we are affected by them.[600] It is immensely difficult for us to differentiate what we experience, separating the real from the illusory, the divine from the everyday. Yet he believed that

> by his inward experiences of felt harmony or discord with the transcendent, man can test the value of his religious notions and of the conduct they dictate. It is in these experiences that God guides him directly. There is no other language between the soul and God.[601]

In the final analysis, then,

> the only test of revelation [of this or any other kind] is the test of life – not merely of moral, but of spiritual, fruitfulness in the deepest sense. It must at once satisfy and intensify man's mystical and moral need. It must bring the transcendent nearer to his thoughts, feelings and desires. It must deepen his consciousness of union with God. This . . . was the 'evidence' to which Jesus appealed in proof of His 'possession' by God's spirit . . . Such, too, is the evidence of Christianity as a personal religion – its power over souls that are already Christian in sympathy and capacity . . . Any other 'sign,' be it miracle or argument, will appeal only to the faithless and perverse. It may puzzle them, but it will never convince them; it may convert them to the Church, but it cannot convert them to God; it may change their theology – it cannot change their hearts.[602]

As a 'Liberal Catholic' (a phrase he certainly preferred to the 'Modernist' label for which he was to be proscribed), Tyrrell sought to present a spirituality which would offer people a faith at once inward and firmly committed to the world around them: 'Catholicism', he wrote, 'is, more than other systems, a religion of the whole man, body, soul and spirit.'[603] He was acutely aware of the inherent risks of a liberalism so loose that it becomes no more than enslavement to passing fashions;[604] but in the final analysis he found that risk worth taking in order to avoid a petrifying and repressive orthodoxy.[605] The result, tragically, was to separate him from his Church; and that was tragic because so much of his thought abounds in insights and wisdom which later Catholics would have no difficulty in owning.

The mystery of the divine love

Others had less trouble in holding together the mystery of Christian faith and dogmatic certainty. Faber found the key in divine love, the centre of his understanding of the spiritual life: 'to love God is a bold and arduous undertaking'.[606] Two of his hymns articulate this well:

> There's a wideness in God's mercy,
>   Like the wideness of the sea:
> There's a kindness in His justice,
>   Which is more than liberty.
>
> There is no place where earth's sorrows
>   Are more felt than up in heaven;
> There is no place where earth's failings
>   Have such kindly judgment given.[607]
>
> How Thou canst think so well of us,
>   Yet be the God Thou art,
> Is darkness to my intellect,
>   But sunshine to my heart.[608]

For Tyrrell, God's love for us and ours for God are always essentially Trinitarian:

> All love seeks sympathy. If I see something beautiful I want another to enjoy it with me; and this points to a trinity of persons as satisfying the highest ideal of personal love; the Father loving the Son, in sympathy with the Spirit, the Father and Son loving the Spirit; and each giving Himself with the other, and each Person singly loving the other two as one, and rejoicing in their union and friendship.[609]

The work of grace

The notion of sympathy, implying a kinship of nature, is crucial here as in so much nineteenth-century spirituality.[610] But love is hard work;[611] and, more specifically, it involves co-operating with the work of grace within us. Faber here significantly moves away from the old Thomist teaching about grace co-operating with nature: he argues that ultimately the two are fundamentally opposed.[612] Renunciation and sacrifice thus become cardinal virtues for progress in the spiritual life: 'there is no pleasure to which we dare yield an unlimited assent'.[613] Furthermore 'the English habit of always standing up for our rights is fatal to perfection'.[614] The shadow of Roman obedience looms large here: indeed for Faber 'the papacy is itself only an incessant, continuous, unflinching martyrdom'.[615] And we must make that spirit our own: 'the only right spirit in which to serve Him is one of self-sacrifice and generosity'.[616]

It is easy to condemn this as negative or priest-dominated piety. But Faber has an important point to make here: he wants people to aspire after both a proper degree of self-knowledge and a willingness to forget oneself. He knows these are not easily reconciled, and says so on the first page of what is arguably his best book;[617] but getting it right is vital if we are to avoid both self-absorption and self-hatred; and 'the first effect of spirituality upon our minds is to sharpen our critical turn', especially (though not only) with regard to ourselves.[618] Furthermore, it demands that 'we should take great pains in our intercourse with others . . . Negligence on this point is the reason why many fail in their attempts after perfection.'[619] The trouble is our lack of will:

> A man will not get up at his proper time in the morning. He says he cannot; which is absurd, for there is no physical power holding him down in his bed. The fact is, he will not; he does not choose to do it; the virtue of it or the obedience of it is not worth the pain of it. He pleads that overnight he made a resolution to get up next morning, and asked the souls in Purgatory to get him up. The morning comes; the air is cold; meditation is uninteresting; sleep is pleasant. No souls have come from Purgatory to pull him out of bed, draw his curtains, light his fire, and the rest. It is not therefore his affair. He has done his part. He finished it all last night; but grace has not worked. What can he do? This is only a picture of a thousand other things. Multitudes who would have been nigh to saints remain nigh to sinners from this singular superstition about grace. What we want is not grace; it is will. We have already a thousand times more grace than we correspond to. God is never wanting on His side. It is the manly persistent will which is wanting on ours.[620]

Faber knows very well too that context matters: 'an hour's prayer amidst the blue skies and winelike air of the Mediterranean is an easier matter than an hour's prayer amidst the yellow drizzling fogs of London'.[621] But perseverance yields rewards, for real prayer has an effect which is obvious, and not at all the same as feigned piety: all of us know

> men who never miss their morning meditation, yet seem to be none the better for it . . . Not but that the habit of prayer is an excellent thing; only it is not the gift of prayer, and we are apt to exaggerate its importance from confounding it with the gift.[622]

The beauty of God

For all these writers, the beauty and attractiveness of God is the vital key to progress in the spiritual life. Manning stresses this in his treatise on devotion to the Sacred Heart, arguing that the beauty of God made flesh in the Incarnation draws us to him: 'if you live lives of prayer and piety and faith, [the vision of the divine beauty] is as visible before you as the beauty of the world which we see with our eyes of sense'.[623] And, unlike worldly beauty, this beauty has power to transform us into its own likeness, as St Paul says.[624] Thus:

> The Sacred Heart of Jesus, which is the love of God clothed in the sympathies of our humanity, has been not only glory and beauty, but an assimilating power, the principle of a new life, changing the inward hearts

of men and of nations into the likeness of itself . . . Wherever the hearts of men have been thus changed, first one by one, then by households, then by villages and towns and cities and peoples and nations, the world has changed its face.[625]

Note again the stress on 'sympathy', the oneness of God and humanity made possible through the Incarnation; but note also the characteristic way Manning sees our own spiritual growth as leading directly to the transformation of society as a whole. Like Faber, he has no doubt that this transformation will require a costly asceticism;[626] but our frailty and individuality are taken up into the life of the whole Church, which in his confident spirituality is 'rising perpetually towards its perfection'.[627] The crucial point is that it is in and through our participation in the life of the Church that we most fully discover the living presence of a God who loves us individually and yet is never ours alone. Manning celebrates that presence with a mixture of pastoral warmth and uninhibited theological confidence:

> They who love the Blessed Sacrament love it . . . because it is the most intimate way of conversing with Jesus. We converse with Him in our private chamber in our prayers; we converse with Him when we pray anywhere all the day long, by the roadside, or in the throng of men. But what is that to kneeling before the Blessed Sacrament? If every day you could speak for a quarter of an hour with your angel-guardian it would leave an impression on you all the day long . . . And yet, do you not see here the Lord of Angels and the King of Saints morning after morning in the Holy Mass? and may you not at any time come and kneel down here in His presence? and may you not converse with Him, not for a quarter of an hour only, but as long as you will? You may weary of His presence; He is never wearied of yours.[628]

In a quite different, more richly allusive way, Alice Meynell celebrates God's presence in creation in 'Christ in the universe':

> With this ambiguous earth
> His dealings have been told us. These abide:
> The signal to a maid, the human birth,
> The lesson, and the young Man crucified.
>
> But not a star of all
> The innumerable host of stars has heard
> How He administered this terrestrial ball.
> Our race have kept their Lord's entrusted Word.
>
> Of His earth-visiting feet
> None knows the secret, cherished, perilous,
> The terrible, shamefast, frightened, whispered, sweet,
> Heart-shattering secret of His way with us.

No planet knows that this
Our wayside planet, carrying land and wave,
Love and life multiplied, and pain and bliss,
Bears, as chief treasure, one forsaken grave.

Nor, in our little day,
May His devices with the heavens be guessed,
His pilgrimage to thread the Milky Way,
Or His bestowals there be manifest.

But, in the eternities,
Doubtless we shall compare together, hear
A million alien Gospels, in what guise
He trod the Pleiades, the Lyre, the Bear.

Oh, be prepared, my soul!
To read the inconceivable, to scan
The million forms of God those stars unroll
When, in our turn, we show to them a Man.[629]

Personal piety

The subtle interweaving here of the local and the cosmic, the incarnate and the universal, is powerful. It underlines another aspect of Catholic spirituality: the stress on the hiddenness of God, and the consequent need not only for an active participation in the public worship of the Church, but also for an interior piety. Faber is perceptively aware that, in busy Victorian society, this is no longer easy:

> There is no more privacy now . . . all society seems to be a collection of self-erected judgment-seats, before which anybody and everybody is being called daily, for every sort of action, even for the details and scandals of domestic life.[630]

So he recommends a pattern of spiritual life that is the mirror-opposite of a self-indulgent search for private fulfilment:

> Never keep a spiritual journal, a record of pious thoughts, or any vestige of a religious autobiography. I do not mean to say that the saints have not done so. But you must not do it. You will live in a land of dreams and conceits if you do, and though perhaps you do not believe it now, you will actually come at last to do and to say follies, in order to write them down afterwards. If you would know how the infatuation of keeping a journal is entangled with every root and fibre of self-love, throw your journal into the fire, and you will find out. Forget yourself, and what you have gone through. God remembers. Surely that is enough.[631]

It is this approach that can give asceticism its spring and pulse. Mortification for Faber is 'the love of Jesus, urged into that shape partly in imitation of Him, partly to express its own vehemence, and partly to secure, by an instinct of self-preservation, its own perseverance. There can be no true or enduring love without it.'[632] Mortification invigorates our prayer, and gives depth and strength to our sanctity.[633]

Devotion to Our Lady

Four other important aspects of Roman Catholic spirituality need brief exploration. The first is devotion to the Virgin Mary: for Tyrrell, she is the model of the Christian's inner, spiritual life, for in her alone he dwelt in all his fullness.[634] Some of Faber's celebrations of Mary are extravagant, but not all: 'what is the soul of the greatest saint, or even of the Prince of the Apostles, or still more, of the Immaculate Mother herself, compared with the Human Soul of Jesus, so peculiarly present in the Blessed Sacrament?'[635] Mary is our exemplar as one whose whole life and will were conformed to the will of God;[636] and we are to be God-bearers as she was. This is Tyrrell, reflecting on the centurion's words to Jesus ('Lord, I am not worthy . . . '):

> *Domine non sum dignus ut intres sub tectum meum.* My house is full of noise and tumult and worldly comforts and appliances, and the door is shut and barred, and the importunity of the midnight visitor is hateful to me. *Tantum dic verbo,* say but the word and my soul shall be healed. Change the inn to a cave; shatter the door and ruin the walls, 'that the King of Glory may come in.' Let Joseph go before to prepare the rude resting-place, and let Mary follow, and in the very midst of my soul bring forth her Firstborn. *Mater Divinae gratiae, ora pro nobis.*[637]

The Rosary was popular with every kind of Catholic, and may (as we have seen) have been especially beloved of the Irish communities.[638]

Eucharistic devotion

The second aspect of Catholic spirituality worth adverting to is devotion to the Blessed Sacrament, the subject of a long treatise by Faber. In an early work, Tyrrell says that sacraments are signs of the power of God to transform the physical: relics are a particular sign in this respect.[639] And, in more affective language, he quotes Jesus' words:

> 'I have greatly longed to eat this Pasch with you before I suffer.' Every single Mass is nothing more nor less than a renewal of that great paroxysm of our Saviour's passionate love for the soul.[640]

Faber celebrates the triumph of the glorified Christ in the sacrament:

> One moment, and the Body of our Lord as at the Right Hand of the Father, receiving in the splendour of its ravishing magnificence the worship of the prostrate hierarchies of heaven. Another moment, and what was bread is God.[641]

But at the end of his work he reminds us of the weakness of the eucharistic Christ; he is imprisoned, weak, in the Blessed Sacrament, suffering alone through his outraged, because rejected, love.[642] In a short but moving poem entitled 'In Portugal, 1912', Alice Meynell reflects on the God who is present even when the Eucharist can no longer be celebrated:

> In ambush at the merry board
> > The Victim lurks unsacrificed;
> The mill conceals the harvest's Lord,
> > The wine-press holds the unbidden Christ.[643]

Benediction of the Blessed Sacrament in churches was, together with Stations of the Cross and public recitation of the Rosary, the most prominent corporate devotional practice in nineteenth-century English Roman Catholic life.[644]

Penance

The third aspect of Roman Catholic spirituality worth noting is the practice of penance, which almost certainly increased significantly during the century, along with reparational devotions such as those to the Sacred Heart.[645] Tyrrell points the link between conviction of sin and intimacy with God: 'the more one grows in intimacy with Christ, the deeper is the sense of sin and our regret that, even to some extent unwittingly, we should have offended Him and must daily and hourly pain Him by our gross ways and ignorant inconsideration'.[646] Manning, emphasizing the costliness of the forgiveness won for us through Christ's sacrifice, goes on to say, in his book on penance, that

> there are two things which we shrink from seeing as they are, God and ourselves.[647]

In penance, we have to look directly at both. And 'we may never think that we know all we might of ourselves', nor need we fear when we see the worst of ourselves.[648] Acts of reparation are like St Mary Magdalene going to anoint Jesus' dead body in the tomb:[649] they are not essential to our receiving sacramental absolution; rather they are a free response of gratitude for the free gift of that forgiveness.[650]

The theology and practice of prayer

Finally, something needs to be said about Roman Catholic approaches to the theology and practice of prayer. In *All for Jesus*, Faber stresses exactly the point made by Tyrrell: the crucial interrelation of devotion, theology, and everyday life: prayer 'is an act in which vision, feeling, and will, the three factors of the spirit-life, designedly blend together and strive to attain their highest and deepest expression'.[651] For Manning, prayer is precisely the means by which we discover our status as children:

> The man that prays realises also the relation of God to himself as a father, and the personal relation of Jesus Christ to him as a kinsman and a brother and a friend. And, further, by the light of prayer and contemplation of God and of the Sacred Heart of Jesus, a man is 'changed into the same likeness from glory to glory, as by the Spirit of the Lord.'[652]

In prayer we become like God, just as through friendship a person can become like his or her friend:

> When Stephen stood before the council, his face shone like the face of an angel. The light of the presence of his Master in heaven fell upon it. And

they who live a life of prayer are being ever changed into the likeness of their Divine Lord. I do not mean that they are outwardly transformed; I do not mean that there come rays out of their hands or their side, or that there is any resplendent light upon their countenances; but I mean this, that there is a gentleness, a sweetness, a kindness, a lowliness, an attraction about their life which makes everybody at peace with them. Everybody draws near to them with a tranquil confidence and a rest of heart.[653]

Manning suggests the signs that accompany this: a denial of self, not in the sense of elaborate mortifications or long-winded prayers, but 'a true inward denial of self – a mortification of the intellect and heart and will';[654] charity towards others – again, not in the outward sense of almsgiving alone, but charity towards others' sins (often a more difficult achievement);[655] severity towards self: 'a sure token of a charitable heart will be that a man is gentle to everybody, but unsparing to himself';[656] mistrust of self, in the sense of avoiding a dangerous self-reliance;[657] and a spirit of praise:

the spirit of praise and the spirit of prayer ought to go together. But nothing is more certain than that we pray very often and that we praise but very seldom . . . And yet the whole of our eternity will be made up of praise, for then there will be no more prayer; and if we do not begin to learn the spirit of praise in this world, how shall we praise God in eternity?[658]

Tyrrell says that 'it is in praise that we feel our weakness and isolation most of all'. Hence praise is by definition inclusive: Christ 'whose own Heart is full of praise cannot rest till He has communicated the flame of His enthusiasm to all around him', including every single creature.[659] Hence the psalmist praying 'O magnify the Lord *with me*, and let us praise His Name *together*'. And the Christian has a pivotal, priestly role in this regard:

as in harmonized music the varying parts are bound together by their common relation to the melody through which they are related one to another; so in the *concentus* of creation it is through man and in reference to man that the voices of all other visible creatures are heard; and it is as harmonizing with the voice of the Son of Man, high above all, that our praises are acceptable.[660]

Thus to praise God is to lift eternity into the midst of the here and now. And that is exactly what happened in the Incarnation, the root of prayer and its theological foundation. This is Faber: in becoming human, God

mixes us up with Himself, makes our cause His, His interests ours, and we become one with Him. So by a mysterious communion the work of His prayers runs into our prayers, the wealth of His enriches the poverty of ours, the infinity of His touches, raises, and magnifies the wretchedness of ours. So that when we pray, it is not we who pray, but He who prays.[661]

This notion of prayer as something that God does in us recurs in Tyrrell's discussion of petitionary prayer in *Lex credendi*. He says that all such prayer is born of 'a divine discontent' which is

> God's own discontent; it is His knowledge of the contrast of the actual with the ideal; of things as they are with things as they ought to be . . . it is this knowledge as in some measure communicated to us and felt by us.[662]

Hence the desire within us that leads to prayer is not entirely *of* us, not simply there in virtue of our creation in God's image: it is born of God's longing to see a better world.[663] And God does not only pray in us: he works in us, too; 'the prayer is but the beginning of the work'.[664]

This is not to say that prayer will always be easy. Faber sensitively stresses the objective value of prayer even when nothing much seems to be happening:

> One word on what we call bad meditations. They are generally the most fruitful. The mere persevering at our prie-dieu the full time is an excellent and meritorious act of obedience. The mystery, which seems to lay no hold of us, is in reality soaking into our minds, and keeping us throughout the day more in the presence of God than we otherwise should have been . . . Whenever we have made a bad meditation, and cannot see that it is our own fault, we may be sure God means something by it, and it is our own business to find out what. It is no little thing to be able to endure ourselves and our own imperfections.[665]

SPIRITUALITY AND THE RELIGIOUS LIFE

The renewal of the religious life

The nineteenth century witnessed a renaissance of the religious life in England, and not only within the Roman Catholic Church. There are various theories as to why this happened. It could have been a reaction against the easy liberalism perceived by Roman and Anglo-Catholics to be such a serious threat to true religion.[666] It could, indirectly, have been a response to the need to serve the poor, and for corporate social reform and experiment, part of a wider pattern of diverse attempts to create new forms of community in a manner broadly analogous to the factory villages such as New Lanark in Scotland.[667] It could have been a part of the idealizing of the Middle Ages, the ideal of chivalry and the celebration of all things Gothic, part of Catholic Christianity's redefining of itself over against the world – a reaction against both an ever-increasing materialism and the new insights of science. It was certainly an integral part of the renaissance of Catholicism, both Anglican and Roman, in England during the century – integral not only to the Catholic tradition but to the Catholic vision of rebuilding society.[668]

Within the Roman Church, the religious communities grew steadily in number after Catholic Emancipation. The Benedictines came to Ramsgate in 1856, though their first school (at Ampleforth) was founded in 1814.[669] Herman Cohen, a convert

Jew who became a Discalced Carmelite, was sent to England to establish a community in Kensington, which he did, in 1861.[670] The Carthusians returned to England, at Parkminster in Sussex, in the 1870s.[671] Some religious orders were explicitly concerned to serve the poor, as with the Sisters of the Cross and Passion of Jesus Christ, whose English founder Elizabeth Prout (1820–64) sought to offer a consecrated religious life for women from poor backgrounds.[672]

Within the Church of England this vision of establishing communities who would live the Gospel among the poor and so witness to its truth certainly animated many, Pusey perhaps in particular:[673] in 1845 the first Anglican sisterhood was established at Park Village in London under his guidance.[674] Where he drew on the rule of St François de Sales for guidance in fostering a way of life for them, John Mason Neale proposed the Carthusian motto *Stat crux dum volvitur orbis* (The cross stands while the world revolves) for his new women's community at East Grinstead, which was founded in 1854.[675] (Neale was unusual among contemporary clergy in not only approving of women's communities but also believing that they did not need men to lead or guide them.[676])

Who joined these new communities? One recent suggestion, made by a member of the Community of St Mary the Virgin at Wantage (itself a product of the Oxford Movement), was that the demographic imbalance of the mid-nineteenth century made it inevitable that many women would never find marriage partners, thereby creating a reservoir of potential recruits;[677] but stronger motives were the deep commitment many made to the Catholic principles of holiness of life, reverence for scripture and tradition, and (perhaps above all) a willingness to devote oneself to the service of others: in an age which had no welfare state, and with widespread social need, many women seem to have become sisters more because they wanted to help the poor than because they wanted to live lives of exemplary holiness (though many were to end up achieving both).[678] Florence Nightingale argued that female religious communities achieved far more than the conventional family could ever do, and allowed a far greater degree of fulfilment among their members.[679]

In 1856 Charles Lowder, the Anglo-Catholic vicar of St Barnabas, Pimlico, set up a mission at St George's in the East consisting of unmarried priests living together inspired by a desire to evangelize and minister to the unchurched in London.[680] Clerical societies such as the Society of the Holy Cross were deeply influenced by the bold experiments of French Catholic pioneers, notably St Vincent de Paul.[681] On 25 July 1892 Charles Gore began the Community of the Resurrection with five other men, all celibate Anglican priests,

> who desired to combine together to reproduce the life of the first Christians, continuing steadfastly in the apostles' teaching and fellowship, in the breaking of bread and the prayers, and saying that none of the things which each possessed was his own, but having all things in common.[682]

Note the characteristic Tractarian stress on a desire to return to the wellsprings of apostolic Christianity. The community began at Oxford, moved with Gore to Radley, and in 1898 moved to Mirfield in Yorkshire.[683] Over twenty years earlier, Richard Meux Benson founded the Society of St John the Evangelist at Cowley in Oxford, where he was then incumbent. Benson, a committed Tractarian, became an important theologian of the renewed monastic life, thus bequeathing to the Church of England not only one of its most influential religious communities but a new theoretical blueprint for all it represented.[684]

The theology of the contemplative life

In his early work *Nova et vetera*, written for his fellow Jesuits, George Tyrrell offers a fine exposition of the theology of the contemplative life, citing the traditional monastic contrast between Martha and Mary:

> Martha flits here and there, comes and goes, but Mary sits, ever fixed in one unbroken gaze; and passes, unmoved, from life through death into fuller life; as it were, in a dream. Yet this highest life is also the most active and productive, and likest that of God, whose still gaze on the face of His Son is the cause of all movement and production . . . Great energy works tranquilly; the most divine and universal causes are likest God in their fruitful rest; furthest from solicitude and perturbation about many things . . . It is rather faith and philosophy, than sight and experiment, which assure us that the highest life must also be the most fruitful for others; that efficiency follows excellence. Those do most who seem to do nothing; those do nothing, who seem to do most. God and Nature work silently, secretly . . . The effect of the best and greatest work is felt only when its author is untraceable – or rather its authors, for it derives from a confluence of imperceptible streamlets. 'To be,' is more than 'to do', and does more.[685]

The image of God gazing in still contemplation on the face of his Son as the origin of all that is fruitful; the notion of energy working in tranquillity (a notion which, however, some factory workers might have taken issue with); and the stress on what is greatest being what is most anonymous – all these are traditional insights drawn from monastic and patristic sources, albeit expressed with warmth and eloquence. But Dora Greenwell, an Anglican, offers a quite different and more contemporary theology of the religious life in her biography of Lacordaire:

> The ideal of Christianity which we now most love to contemplate is that which is attained by the full and pure development of natural life, with all its rich capabilities of beauty and excellence. Yet in nature itself there still remains waste and barren ground that offer no hope of harvest; there are jungles never to be cleared; wells of Marah unsweetened by any healing leaf; places given over to perpetual desolation . . . In Nature itself, according to one of Lacordaire's deepest sayings, there is something which can only be justified from the point of view which grace assumes – a manifest loss and failure – many unfulfilled prophecies, many broken promises. In nature there is decay and death, a deep confession of inadequacy, a solemn appealing litany of anguish, a great continual cry to which there is no answer found, save in the cry which went up from God himself upon the

cross. Like cures like. The hurts of the soul are only to be healed through a deepened wound; its truest life is to be won through voluntary death . . . In the monastic life the principle of self-abnegation, essential to the very nature of Christianity, is raised to the degree of self-immolation.[686]

This is a remarkable passage. The frank recognition of the gross randomness and pain that are built into the very fabric of nature, dispelling too easy a Romantic reverence; and the conviction that only a self-sacrifice freely entered upon can offer healing and meaning for such a nature and such a world, lead Greenwell to a profound analysis of what drove (or perhaps called) Lacordaire to the ascetic life he made his own. Greenwell goes on to say that the religious life embodies this principle of self-denial in two ways: from outside, it is a common life of simplicity, order, fraternity, and freedom from worldly desires; from within, and considered supernaturally, there is 'an awful yet tender sense of familiarity with God', a passionate longing for intimacy with God, which is precisely the fruit of a willing break with what most would regard as the natural means of human fulfilment.[687]

And that break is itself a 'heroic imitation of the Saviour's Passion'.[688] The heroism consists in Lacordaire's adoption of uncompromisingly harsh ascetic practices, such as flagellation, which Greenwell defends thus:

> Strange, fantastic, and mistaken as seem to us many of the forms his deep convictions prompted, we must not attribute them to a Manichean contempt of the body; but rather refer them to his desire to be a sharer in that death which his Saviour and God tasted once for every man, and to his longing to fill up for the Church's sake that which in His Lord's unexampled suffering was left behind.[689]

And she considers this to have implications for all, not just for Catholics:

> There is many a loving, believing heart who never heard or read of solidarity, reversibility or expiation, who yet lives and works and prays in the strength of thoughts to which it would not be able to give clear dogmatic expression. The gospel tells us that we are 'every one members one of another, and that no man, either in Christ or Adam, liveth or dieth to himself' – truths which bring into every action the sense of possibly infinite loss and gain we know not to how many. Catholicity gives this sense of mutual accountability a firm theological basis in that unalterable sense of the presence of Christ within His Church and the union of all its members in Him, which makes all within it linked and interdependent, even to the other after world and the souls it has received from this. But Protestantism also holds to these truths by their heart; and when our National Church had fallen on evil and degenerate days, it was not a Romanist who said, 'It is because we have so few high saints among us that we have so many low sinners.'[690]

The clue, then, to the source of meaning and purpose in the face of nature's terrible randomness lies in Christians' fundamental sense of mutual indwelling and co-responsibility mediated through the presence of Christ among us. Greenwell notes that Lacordaire's spirituality did not end in ferocious asceticism: it manifested itself also in a commitment to justice and public affairs.[691] But even if it had not, it would still have played its part in the redemption of the world.

Spirituality and vocation

How are people to know whether they are called to the religious life? R. M. Benson acknowledges that

> the natural ear is deaf to the meaning of the Voice [of God] because the heart is not kindled with the life of love. The Voice of the Heavenly Speaker is, to the natural mind, only like the notes upon a printed stave. The intellect may accept them as true to the laws of harmony, but there is no vibration, no responsive sympathy, no unity of love. The loving heart, quickened by the Holy Ghost to the Divine Word, is responsive to that which it hears.[692]

So it can only be a person who is animated by love who will recognize the divine call. Even then, responding to this call is hard work:

> when God draws us to Himself we are very apt to feel the long-continuing strain whereby God would draw us out of ourselves. The progress may often be wearisome. We seem to get no nearer; but what we feel is the gradual loss of self.[693]

'The progress is not only onward. *That gives pleasure. But* upward. *That makes us feel the burden of our nature.*'[694] The stress here on a divine call to leave all behind and rise up, away from all fleshly entanglements, towards God alone is strongly Platonic in both positive and negative senses: positively, in Benson's implicit stress on the divine attractiveness, drawing us towards himself; negatively, in the implied abandonment of all that is material. This negative assessment of the world is strengthened by Benson's emphasis on the reality of evil in the world, an emphasis which recalls that of the desert fathers. Evil

> was not an abstraction which [Christ] could deplore. It was a personal organization of rebellion against God.[695]

Satan has personality: *evil is not abstract but real.*[696] And Benson follows the wisdom of the desert by maintaining that the primary response of those called to the religious life is to fight evil primarily by withdrawing from the world, by mortification, the freely offered sacrifice of one's life described by Dora Greenwell above.[697] Yet this mortification has a positive content: it is an imitation of Christ, and specifically an imitation of St John the Baptist's declaration that Christ must increase while he decreases. Benson points here to how ascetic spirituality gives meaning and purpose to life, grace redeeming nature; whereas ageing and physical decline is natural, the free giving up of this world's pleasures in following Christ is the work of grace:

S.John [Baptist] was not only to decrease by a law of physical necessity. His decrease was the appointed pathway by which he should attain to the fulness of personal glory, whereby his ministerial glory should be consummated. If he had not seen the things of earth die from before his eyes, he could not have opened his eyes to the coming glory of the Kingdom whereof he taught . . . He was not to hold earthly fellowship with Christ, although they were so closely bound together, both by the ties of nature, and in the relationship of their ministerial offices. He rejoiced in the Bridegroom with the simplicity of love, looking forward to have fellowship with Him in the glory of the Kingdom to be revealed hereafter. He must show himself worthy to be with Christ there, by accepting the difficulties of nature which were appointed for him here. So it is with us now.[698]

The mystery of the Eucharist in the religious life

The problem for us is that this acceptance must be not just an external but an internal one. The religious life in this respect is rooted in the Eucharist, where the triumphant victory of Christ over the powers of evil is re-presented at the altar and we offer ourselves, along with Christ, to the Father. This external, liturgical process must be internalized, appropriated by each individual participant in the eucharistic mystery:

> we cannot ask God to accept Christ in ourselves, save as we are cultivating that indwelling Presence which we present. Our law of life can no longer be the law of a merely external command. It must be the law of 'the engrafted Word,' the Word made Flesh, Who has united us to Himself in His holy Self-oblation to the Father: the law of liberty, of Divine sonship, of eternal communion with God.[699]

This brings us to a vital point. Like Dora Greenwell, Benson consistently locates any response to God's call within the corporate life of the body of Christ:

> the act of communion with Christ is not an act producing merely an individual result. If our hearts rise up to God in Christ, as they ought to do, in Holy Communion, they must also expand so as to include all the sympathies of Christ's mystical Body. We can no more live by a separated individuality of spiritual fellowship with Christ, than a finger can live if separated from the life of the hand to which it belongs.[700]

This is not Platonic, but Pauline, the Hebrew tradition balancing the Greek in a manner characteristic of the best in early Christian theology. And note at its heart a striking phrase: 'all the sympathies of Christ's mystical body'. This is crucial for Benson: insisting again that dying to self is not something negative, he goes on to say that 'by a real living sympathy with [Christ] in the joy of His Holy Kingdom we acquire the holiness which belongs to His people'.[701] And it is this freely embraced sympathy, this shared suffering with Christ, that animates the prayer of those called to the religious life. The daily round of monastic offices, the time given to meditation and personal prayer and seeming renunciation of the world are not merely an appointment of arbitrary devotion by authority, but in making such appointment, the Church is accepting, hallowing, developing, utilising, a law of our human nature. The law of sympathy in contemplation was given to us by God for this very purpose. Mankind was formed to find delight in Truth; not merely after the manner of individual intelligences, but with the consciousness of common joy in one Life-giving object. And thus we were not only to find our Life in the knowledge and Love of God, but in the Love of one another, which that knowledge sustains and purifies.[702]

The nature and purpose of the religious life

Thus the central wellspring of the religious life is not an act of self-sacrifice for its own sake, but a rediscovery, precisely through the free offering of ourselves, of our hidden but obscured kinship with Christ, a sympathy with him that is at once ontological and moral: ontological, because it frees us to rediscover our true nature as images of Christ; moral, because it leads us to an active participation in (a sympathy with) the sufferings of the world. And from this flow important consequences. First, in the religious life the common precedes the individual (itself a prophetic witness in an increasingly individualized society like Victorian England). Thus for Benson holiness begins with the corporate holiness of the Church, the Holy Spirit dwelling in the common life of all the baptized. And even though he acknowledged that 'we cannot share this life except in proportion as we call it into individual exercise personally for ourselves', individual holiness is derived from the corporate holiness of the Church, rather than the other way round.[703]

Secondly, the religious life is rooted in constant intercession for the whole body of Christ, a deep and strong sympathy giving birth to 'large-hearted energy'.[704] For Benson, meditation is 'an energy of the soul in Communion with God'.[705] The purpose is to hand ourselves over to

> that blessed control of the Holy Spirit which, while it does render us intensely quiescent beneath the power of His all-comprehending operation, does nevertheless raise us to an intensity of spiritual energy far surpassing anything which can be derived from any human guide.[706]

And, because here too our own progress in the spiritual life is derived from that of the whole Body of Christ,

> we are not to measure the value of our mental prayer by any pleasure experienced in attempting it. Probably it is quite the reverse. Prayer on our part is not merely an approach to God, but a conflict with Satan. Body and mind naturally droop. Moses needed to have his hands upheld.[707]

Thirdly, the religious life is a process of total transformation. Benson bewails our reluctance to be changed:

> We cannot expect to move the hearts of others save by the power of the Holy Ghost. But that power needs to be sought. Our Lord is ever waiting

to be gracious, ready to give. We, alas! are content with a scanty supply when we have abundance of grace within our reach, if we would only ask for it. We have so little anxiety to be transformed![708]

'We are not following Jesus truly unless we . . . acquire an experimental consciousness of His supernatural characteristics. As we follow Him, we learn what following Him means.'[709]

We learn to act by first learning simply how to be. We learn to be happy by freely renouncing all that makes for worldly happiness. We learn to discover our own deepest fulfilment by setting the life and well-being of the community before those of individuals within it. These central paradoxes of the religious life find their meaning in the mystery of Christ: our sympathy, our shared suffering with Christ's is in turn the means by which we enter into, and help to transform, the involuntary suffering of Christ's creatures, both animal and human.[710] Yet none of this would be possible had God not in Christ first had sympathy with us, by coming to share our lives. Incarnation is central to nineteenth-century monastic theology, as it was to Tractarian thought. 'We cannot be satisfied', wrote Benson in a letter, 'unless we become like Him . . . God is not *degraded, but* man is elevated *by the Incarnation of our Lord Jesus Christ.*'[711]

CASE STUDIES

A severe and beautiful religion: John Henry Newman (1801–90)

Newman's life

Newman's long life virtually straddled the nineteenth century: he was at once a man *of* his time and a man *against* it; and the two need to be held together, for he was certainly no crude reactionary any more than someone who welcomed uncritically the wisdom of his age. He was nurtured in Anglican Evangelicalism; but his faith was proved and hammered out through the crucible of the Oxford Movement's birth and early growth. He spent his life in colleges and other religious institutions peopled largely by celibate men. That narrowed his perspective; but it also sharpened it. Perhaps more than anything else, Newman was a courageous person: he is the mirror-opposite of, for example, Thomas Love Peacock's Reverend Mr Larynx, the 'good-natured, accommodating divine' who would agree with whoever it was he happened to be speaking to at the time.[712] In page after page of Newman's enormous written legacy, in pastoral letter and theological treatise, one feels the enormous hidden strength of someone who scorns compromise and seeks only to share the truth by which he tries to live.

That life began in London, in 1801. Newman went to boarding school aged seven, and spent virtually the rest of his life in communal institutions. This could not have come naturally: he was shy, not gregarious. 'I am very quiet here and to myself,' he wrote from Trinity College Oxford, which he entered in 1817.[713] His election as a Fellow of Oriel College in 1822, a year after his father's bankruptcy shamed and impoverished the family, was an event he always looked upon as the turning point of his life.[714] In 1824, by now ordained in the Church of England, he was made curate of

St Clement's, Oxford, and rapidly began a visitation of the entire parish. This too did not come naturally;[715] but we get hints of his persevering pastoral concern from his diary: 'MONDAY 13 SEPTEMBER [1824] visited Swell (who was very rude).'[716] A few pages later we read: 'gave port wine to Swell'.[717] Within two months Swell's death is recorded.[718] We know, and need to know, no more. And the entry for Michaelmas Day 1824 is similarly laconic, and the more moving for its lack of emotional expression:

WEDNESDAY 29 SEPTEMBER Aunt came to town Dr Clutterbuck came for the last time – at 3 to ten at night my dear Father ceased to breath [sic] – Charles, Francis and myself slept in the parlour in our clothes. *my Father died.*[719]

Newman was shy, neither given to overt emotional display nor lacking in deep feelings: it was simply that 'I have an enormous dislike to puffing'.[720] Like many shy people, he could express himself far better by the written word than in person.[721]

Newman's ministry in a conventional parish was short-lived: in 1826 he resigned his curacy on becoming a tutor at Oriel, and in 1828 became Vicar of the University Church. His involvement with Keble and Pusey at the heart of what came to be called the Oxford Movement has been chronicled many times;[722] but it is still worth remembering that he 'ever considered and kept the day [of Keble's National Apostasy sermon] as the start of the religious movement of 1833'.[723] Another 'cardinal point of time' came in March 1836: his dear friend Hurrell Froude died, soon to be followed by his mother, whilst Newman became a user of the Roman breviary and presided over the birth of the new *Library of the Fathers.*[724] Another such point came in 1842: Newman withdrew from Oxford to live with a small community at Littlemore, just outside the city; in 1843 he resigned as vicar and two years later, on 9 October 1845, was received into the Roman Catholic Church. The move took place almost exactly half way through his life.

The difference in lifestyle must have been at once radical and inconsequential: radical because he was no longer his own master, inconsequential because he continued living in communities of one kind or another, and in 1848 established the first English Oratory (that is, house of the Oratorian Order founded by St Philip Neri) at Maryvale in Birmingham – he may well have seen this as in some respects a kind of replica of the fellows' common room at Oriel.[725] His choice of the Oratorians is of course significant: in 1846 he wrote from Littlemore to F. W. Faber, soon to become a fellow Oratorian:

I have long felt special reverence and admiration for the character of St [Philip] Neri, as far as I knew it . . . I wish we could all become good Oratorians, but that, I suppose, is impossible.[726]

Superficially, much of the rest of Newman's long life is a history of controversies. There was the long and exhausting process of trying to work with the Irish Roman Catholic bishops, who wanted him to found and develop a Catholic University at Dublin, but on their own terms, which occupied most of the 1850s. In the 1860s he faced serious criticism from Rome because of an article he had written entitled 'On

consulting the faithful in matters of doctrine'. He engaged in a fierce dispute with
Charles Kingsley, who had impugned his integrity, and became embroiled in an
intra-Catholic argument about whether or not to found a Catholic mission to the
University of Oxford. In the 1870s he was involved in debates about papal infallibility.
In 1879, however, he was made Cardinal, a rare and remarkable honour for someone
who was not even a bishop. All these events touched Newman deeply: he was intensely
sensitive, yet not at all averse to controversy – in this sense he was quintessentially
Victorian. The debate with Kingsley elicited one of his greatest works, his semi-
autobiographical *Apologia pro vita sua*: in it he said he was

> not unwilling to draw an opponent on step by step, by virtue of his own
> opinions, to the brink of some intellectual absurdity, and to leave him to
> get back as he could . . . Also I used irony in conversation, when
> matter-of-fact men would not see what I meant.[727]

The scorn, subtlety, and lofty disdain of non-intellectuals may surprise. But we
should attend to what he wrote in 1849: 'persons form *lasting* attachments far more by
their *views* of things than their *feelings*'.[728] This is a highly contentious statement; but
Newman had no doubt about it. If he was vituperative, it was not from lack of charity
but from precisely that charity which came from setting truth first. The point becomes
clear in his correspondence. Thus, in a moving letter to Fr Bernard Dalgairns, a fellow
Oratorian, on a sensitive issue, he writes: 'I think it best to state the case as it really
stands.'[729] And the truth matters most, because it alone gives life meaning and hope:
for Newman, as Owen Chadwick has put it, 'the only argument for Christianity that
proves anything is that it works'.[730] In such a context, controversy over an issue of
truth may even be a good thing; and Newman told the Catholic Bishop of Brechin
that 'controversy though unpleasant as a dose of medicine, like medicine does great
good'.[731]

This could make Newman cruelly dismissive: he told a correspondent that he had
no time for the young Catholic architect A. W. N. Pugin: 'What Mr Pugin writes I do
not know, and do not much interest myself about – because he does not talk or write
like a sensible man.'[732] But he reserved his fiercest polemic for ideas or movements,
rather than people, which he believed to be dangerous and wrong.[733] Evangelicals were
fortunate to get away with being described as 'the peculiars';[734] but Liberalism was less
fortunate.[735]

So clear and unambiguous an approach to truth caused Newman to oppose all 'latitudinarianism, indifferentism, republicanism, and schism, a spirit which tends to
overthrow doctrine', as he put it in an letter to his mother written long before the
Oxford Movement was under way.[736] Note the 'republicanism': although he described
himself as 'neither Whig nor Tory',[737] he was by temperament profoundly conservative: 'progress' for him too easily meant the overthrow of truth. He recalls in the
Apologia holding 'that it was unchristian for nations to cast off their governors, and,
much more, sovereigns who had the divine right of inheritance'.[738] But his real
concern was not so much to defend the monarchy as to defend the Church, and as an
Anglican he opposed any political change which might lead to interference in its life.
This led him to call for Nonconformists to remain excluded from Oxford, to support

the conservative bishops who opposed the Reform Act – and later to question the whole nature of establishment. Rationalism (in the sense of a truth attained by reason alone) and Romanticism (in the sense of a truth discovered, or invented[739]) were enemies too; and he had no time for anything which might lead to a vague spirituality:

> I am up in arms against the Shelleyism of the day, which resolves religion into feeling, and makes it possible for bad men to have holy thoughts. Doubtless no religious emotion is worth a straw, or rather it is pernicious, if it does not lead to practice.[740]

The nature of Catholic truth

In a sermon he wrote entitled 'Feasting in captivity', Newman describes Catholic faith as both severe and beautiful. The key is to keep the two together:

> One danger there is: that of our attempting one of these aspects of con- stituent portions of the Christian character while we neglect the other. To attempt Apostolical Christianity at all, we must attempt it all. It is a whole, and cannot be divided; and to attempt one aspect of it only, is to attempt something else which looks like it, instead of it. 'All is not gold that glitters,' as the proverb goes; and all is not Catholic and Apostolic which affects what is high and beautiful, and speaks to the imagination. Religion has two sides, a severe side, and a beautiful; and we shall be sure to swerve from the narrow way which leads to life, if we indulge ourselves in what is beautiful, while we put aside what is severe.[741]

There seems little doubt that Newman found the severe more congenial than the 'high and beautiful' (and he certainly had little time for ritualism[742]); but that is not the point. This notion of truth as an indivisible whole is important for a number of reasons. First, it was essential to patristic Christianity: we have already seen the importance of this for the Tractarians, and for Newman (whose patristic scholarship was immense) it was vital. He had a profound reverence for the past: 'the Apostles lived eighteen hundred years since; and as far as the Christian looks back, so far can he afford to look forward'.[743] And he took from patristic theology a central paradox: that God was unchanging and unchangeable, whilst human beings must be transformed into the divine likeness they had lost. Hence the mix of conservatism and radicalism in his spirituality: hence too his commitment to a faith that is invariably demanding, even severe:

> Men admire religion, while they can gaze on it as a picture. They think it lovely in books: and as long as they can look upon Christians at a distance, they speak well of them.[744]

> That religion is true which has power, and so far as it has power; nothing but what is divine can renew the heart.[745]

Hence also his emphasis on the work of the Holy Spirit, another vital aspect of patris- tic theology: the Spirit works on the chaos of our lives, 'bringing . . . the voice of Truth in the hearts of all rational beings, tuning them into harmony with the intimations of God's Law, which were externally made to them'.[746]

But there is another reason why it is vital to assent to the truth as an indivisible whole, for only then does it come alive. And the place where it supremely comes alive is in worship and prayer. In a letter of 1835 Newman wrote:

> No mode of teaching can be imagined so public, constant, impressive, permanent, and at the same time reverential than that which makes the forms of devotion the memorial and declaration of doctrine – reverential because the very posture of the mind in worship is necessarily such. In this way Christians receive the Gospel literally on their knees, and in a temper altogether different from that critical and argumentative spirit which sitting and listening engender.[747]

As a Roman Catholic, he developed this point further:

> There is a marked contrast in Catholicity between the views presented to us by doctrine and devotion respectively. Doctrines never change, devotions vary with each individual. Catholics allow each other, accordingly, the greatest licence, and are, if I may so speak, utter *liberals*, as regards devotions, whereas they are most sensitive about doctrine. That Mary is the Mother of God is a point of faith – that Mary is to be honored and exalted in this or that way is a point of devotion.[748]

Here Newman is at his furthest distance from Liberalism, as he says himself: the truth cannot and does not alter; it is supremely learned from the past, and most firmly apprehended on our knees. He says in a sermon:

> we all see the Creed, but who comprehends it fully? All we can hope is, that we are in the way to understand it; that we partly understand it; that we desire, pray, and strive to understand it more and more. Our Creed becomes a sort of prayer.[749]

The nature of assent

The Creed is thus a given: it is (to use one of Newman's favourite words) *real*; and that reality is authenticated in the effect it has on human lives. But how can a bare doctrinal statement have any effect on lives, especially if we do not understand it anyway? Newman explored this question in his most dauntingly severe book, *A grammar of assent* (1869). He begins by distinguishing between 'notional propositions' (of a general kind, like 'man is an animal'[750]) and 'real propositions' (such as 'Philip was the father of Alexander'). In fact we need both: we need 'notional' propositions to enable us to relate to things of which we have no direct experience ourselves; and we need 'real' propositions because they alone are rooted in concrete instances. Thus

> to apprehend notionally is to have breadth of mind, but to be shallow; to apprehend really is to be deep, but to be narrow-minded . . . Without the apprehension of notions, we should for ever pace round one small circle of knowledge; without a firm hold upon things, we shall waste ourselves in vague speculations. However, real apprehension has the precedence, as being the scope and end and the test of notional . . . Experiences and their

images strike and occupy the mind, as abstractions and their combinations do not.[751]

So far so good, though Newman cannot resist introducing a polemical element by declaring that Protestant assent tends to be notional, that is, primarily directed towards abstract propositions and principles, whereas Catholic assent tends to be real, that is, directed to the concrete presence and reality of Christ in the sacrament, or Our Lady, or angels.[752] But the really important point is that having a notional assent in the reality of God may not actually lead you to change your life in any way; making a real assent to the reality of God *must* do so.[753]

What we have to do, then, is to make a 'real assent' to the truth presented to us in (say) the historic creeds. And to do that need not mean fully understanding what we are assenting to: we can apprehend something that is essentially mysterious, like the truth revealed in poetry or music.[754] We must be careful to distinguish *inference* from *assent* here: we may *infer* that Christ died on the cross, by examining the evidence, without *assenting* to it.[755] Inference, then, has no effect on our lives; notional assent has only a limited amount. But real assent is transforming; and that is what Christians mean by belief in God:[756]

> 'There is a God,' when really apprehended, is the object of a strong ener-
> getic adhesion, which works a revolution in the mind; but when held
> merely as a notion, it requires but a cold and ineffective acceptance,
> though it be held ever so unconditionally.[757]

And the reason why assent affects us where inference does not is a crucial one: it is because an act of inference is conditional: you do not have to commit yourself, and even if you do you can change your mind whenever you want. But for Newman an act of assent is unconditional;[758] once you start making it conditional, or introducing degrees of assent, you destroy its unique character.[759] The analogy with human love again may help to clarify what Newman is saying: a commitment which can at any time be reversed is in reality (and this is what he is talking about) not a commitment, not an *assent*, at all. Real assent involves more than the emotions: it involves the mind and the will as well.[760] The question, of course, is whether something like the doctrine of the Trinity can be apprehended, and assented to, in the way that a beautiful person can.[761] Newman argues not only that it can, but that *anything* to which we really assent will affect us. He is well aware that we can give 'real assent' (which he also calls 'belief') to something that is not true, but beautiful:

> Belief . . . being concerned with things concrete, not abstract, which vari-
> ously excite the mind from their moral and imaginative properties, has for
> its objects, not only directly what is true, but inclusively what is beautiful,
> useful, admirable, heroic; objects which kindle devotion, rouse the
> passions, and attach the affections; and thus it leads the way to actions of
> every kind, to the establishment of principles, and the formation of
> character, and is thus . . . intimately connected with what is individual and
> personal.[762]

All these things have the power to change us if we give our assent to them. Only when we do that is the heart reached by them. And

> the heart is commonly reached, not through the reason, but through the imagination, by means of direct impressions, by the testimony of facts and events, by history, by description. Persons influence us, voices melt us, looks subdue us, deeds inflame us. Many a man will live and die upon a dogma: no man will be a martyr for a conclusion . . . No one, I say, will die for his own calculations: he dies for realities. This is why a literary religion is so little to be depended upon; it looks well in fair weather; but its doctrines are opinions, and, when called to suffer for them, it slips them between its folios, or burns them at its hearth.[763]

'Life is for action. If we insist on proofs for every thing, we shall never come to action: to act you must assume, and that assumption is faith.'[764] Hence:

> It is assent, pure and simple, which is the motive cause of great achievements; it is a confidence, growing out of instincts rather than arguments, stayed upon a vital apprehension, and animated by a transcendent logic, more concentrated in will and in deed for the very reason that it has not been subjected to any intellectual development.[765]

The dogmas themselves, then, do not change, even though our modes of assenting to them do. Believing in them, in the sense of giving our real assent to them, is the first and essential step to appropriating their transforming power in our lives:

> Knowledge must ever precede the exercise of the affections . . . We love our parents, as our parents, when we know them to be our parents; we must know concerning God, before we can feel love, fear, hope, or trust towards Him. Devotion must have its objects . . . in religion the imagination and affections should always be under the control of reason . . . Sentiment, whether imaginative or emotional, falls back upon the intellect for its stay, when sense cannot be called into exercise; and it is in this way that devotion falls back upon dogma.[766]

This emphasis on knowledge is not always appealing, because not everyone wants to know why things are the way they are. Newman says in a sermon:

> A great number of men live and die without reflecting at all upon the state of things in which they find themselves. They take things as they come, and follow their inclinations as far as they have the opportunity. They are guided mainly by pleasure and pain, not by reason, principle, or conscience; and they do not attempt to *interpret* this world, to determine what it means, or to reduce what they see and feel to system.[767]

The emphasis on 'system', on clarity and structure and order, is characteristic. So is the implied stress on true religion as demanding, severe even. People do not like the tie of religion, they do not like dependence. To trust another, much more to trust him implicitly, is to acknowledge oneself to be his inferior; and this man's proud nature cannot bear to do. He is apt to think it unmanly, and to be ashamed of it.[768]

Newman returns to this point constantly: the world prefers 'the brighter side of the Gospel, its tidings of comfort, its precepts of love; all darker, deeper views of man's condition and prospects [are] conveniently forgotten'.[769] But 'this is the religion *natural* to a civilized age, and well has Satan dressed and completed it into an idol of the Truth'.[770] 'Everything is bright and cheerful. Religion is pleasant and easy; benevolence is the chief virtue; intolerance, bigotry, excess of zeal, are the first of sins.'[771] Novelty is all. He even goes on to say that

> it would be a gain to this country, were it vastly more superstitious, more bigoted, more gloomy, more fierce in its religion, than at present it shows itself to be.[772]

This is not because such a state is good in itself, but because it is infinitely better than 'a heathen obduracy, and a cold, self-sufficient, self-wise tranquillity'.[773] Hence:

> In truth, we have had enough, if we would be wise, of mere political religion; which, like a broken reed, has pierced through the hand that leaned upon it.[774]

Hence too Newman's own ultimate rejection of a church too closely linked with the state, and his decision to submit himself to a church which unambiguously determines what is truth: for without that, Christians are left merely to depend upon their own judgements (or, worse, told what to believe by politicians). Newman is a fierce opponent of private (that is, individual preference and judgement), reacting against its contemporary popularity.[775] He would have had no time for Charles Kingsley's enthusiastically eclectic faith; and he certainly had none for a Protestant understanding of truth:

> I conclude . . . that there is neither natural probability, nor supernatural promise, that individuals reading Scripture for themselves, to the neglect of other means when they can have them, will, because they pray for a blessing, be necessarily led into a knowledge of the true and complete faith of a Christian.[776]

And the way to apprehend, and live by, 'the true and complete faith of a Christian' is first to understand ourselves:

> To understand that we have souls, is to feel our separation from things visible, our independence of them, our distinct existence in ourselves, our individuality, our power of acting for ourselves this way or that way, our accountableness for what we do.[777]

As we come to recognize the enduring worth of our souls, so 'we begin, by degrees, to perceive that there are but two beings in the whole universe, our own soul, and the God who made it'.[778] Even our neighbours are, in this world, strictly speaking, irrelevant – 'nothing to us here', though they will be in the next.[779] (This is not as narrow as it sounds: elsewhere Newman makes clear that 'if we have but once seen any child of Adam, we have seen an immortal soul'.[780]) In any case, this preoccupation with our own standing before God brings us to see ourselves as *creatures*, not independent autonomous units.[781] And, unlike other creatures, man

> is a being of progress with relation to his perfection and characteristic good. Other beings are complete from their first existence . . . but man begins with nothing realized . . . and he has to make capital for himself by the exercise of those faculties which are his natural inheritance.[782]

Justification and the new birth of baptism

How do we do that? Partly by obedience, a crucial virtue for Newman: 'our only safety lies in obedience; our only comfort in keeping it in view'.[783] But such obedience is in itself a response to the working of grace: for Newman, justification is not something conferred upon us extrinsically, and to which we respond by seeking to grow in holiness; rather it is given to those 'who by [God's] grace are moved to do their duty'.[784] Thus:

> God's declaring us righteous renews us, as in the beginning He spake the Word, and the world was created.[785]

And it renews us by making Christ's presence a reality for us:

> Christ's sacred Presence, which shines forth in the heart straight upon the word of justification, creates a renewal there as certainly as a light involves illumination, or fire heat.[786]

This is a vital point for Newman. Justification does not simply confer on us a new *status* before God, nor even only make possible for us a *relationship* with God: it actually makes God *present* to us. To be justified is not simply to be extrinsically set at rights with God, but to be granted 'the glorious Shekinah of the Word Incarnate, as the true wedding garment in which the soul must be dressed'.[787] And:

> The long practised Christian, who, through God's mercy, has brought God's presence near to him, the elect of God, in whom the Blessed Spirit dwells, he does not look out of doors for the traces of God; he is moved by God dwelling in him . . . this is the state of mind to which vigorous prayer and watching tend.[788]

So to be justified is to be reborn; and this rebirth is supremely manifested at baptism. The coming of the Holy Spirit in baptism is a 'wonderful change from darkness to light';[789] by it, the Spirit 'impresses on us our Heavenly Father's image, which we lost when Adam fell, and disposes us to seek His presence by the very instinct of our new nature'. This is vital: baptism 'gives us grace to change our natures'.[790] In fact:

If we have been made God's children, we cannot unmake ourselves; we can never be mere natural men again. There is but the alternative of our being His children still, though erring ones, and under rebuke.[791]

In baptism, the Spirit 'unites us to all holy beings', thereby drawing us out of the prison of our own self-absorption, and conferring on us the privilege of sonship;[792] it also dwells in us habitually, giving us a form of words (the Our Father) by which we can pray. And our new birth in baptism is made possible through God's own birth at Christmas: 'the greater Mystery of the Incarnation is made to envelope and pledge to us the mystery of the new birth'.[793] 'Our Saviour's birth in the flesh is an earnest, and, as it were, beginning of our birth in the Spirit. It is a figure, promise, or pledge of our new birth, and it effects what it promises. As He was born, so are we born also; and since He was born, therefore we too are born.'[794] And in Baptism we come to share the glory of the transfigured Christ:

> By this new birth the Divine Shechinah is set up within [the Christian], pervading soul and body, separating him really, not only in name, from those who are not Christians, raising him in the scale of being, drawing and fostering into life whatever remains in him of a higher nature, and imparting to him, in due season and measure, its own surpassing and heavenly virtue. Thus, while he carefully cherishes the Gift, he is, in the words of the text, 'changed from glory to glory, even as by the Spirit of the Lord.'[795]

The nature and importance of conscience

Newman distinguishes between the objective presence of Christ in the Eucharist and the particular (and generally very unexpected) visitations of God in daily life.[796] God sees us, exactly as we are, all the time, and calls us by name, loving us from all eternity. 'What a thought is this, a thought almost too great for our faith! Scarce can we refrain from acting Sarah's part, when we bring it before us, so as to "laugh" from amazement and perplexity. What is man, what are we, what am I, that the Son of God should be so mindful of me?'[797] We can contemplate God in everything that we do,[798] with a

> feeling of simple and absolute confidence and communion, which soothes and satisfies those to whom it is vouchsafed. We know that even our nearest friends enter into us but partially, and hold intercourse with us only at times; whereas the consciousness of a perfect and enduring Presence, and it alone, keeps the heart open . . . This is what is meant by the peace of a good conscience; it is the habitual consciousness that our hearts are open to God, with a desire that they should be open.[799]

In fact it is precisely by means of 'the peace of a good conscience' that we do become aware of the divine presence within and around us.[800] For Newman, the existence of our conscience is effectively the starting-point for belief in God.[801] Conscience involves recognizing the presence of Christ within us: Christ

> is present with him – present not externally, not in nature merely, or in providence, but in his innermost heart, or in his *conscience*.[802]

So, by becoming aware of Christ's presence in us – a presence demanding both our reverence and our obedience – we begin to make progress in the spiritual life. And this is hard work, which is why so few bother: 'the absence of a vigilant walk, of exact conscientiousness in all things, of an earnest and vigorous warfare against our spiritual enemies, in a word, of strictness, this is what obscures our peace and joy. Strictness is the condition of rejoicing.'[803] Here too, one feels, severity has the edge on beauty in Newman's spirituality; but that is because he bewails our failure to go deep enough into the Christian life, and as a result to get so little out of it, preferring either a lather of emotion or 'a system of duties with little of privilege or comfort'.[804]

The theology and practice of prayer

Much of what has been said so far needs to be borne in mind in considering Newman's understanding of prayer, which 'is to spiritual life what the beating of the pulse and the drawing of the breath are to the life of the body'.[805] Prayer is '(if it may be said reverently) *conversing* with God':[806] the qualification in parentheses is instructive. Newman speaks of prayer as a teacher might, and in the best possible sense:

> A man is no longer what he was before; gradually, imperceptibly to himself, he has imbibed a new set of ideas, and become imbued with fresh principles. He is as one coming from kings' courts, with a grace, a delicacy, a dignity, a propriety, a justness of thought and taste, a clearness and firmness of principle, all his own. Such is the power of God's secret grace acting through those ordinances which He has enjoined us; such the evident fitness of these ordinances to produce the results which they set before us. As speech is the organ of human society, and the means of human civilization, so is prayer the instrument of divine fellowship and divine training.[807]

Furthermore, prayer introduces us into God's presence, and (here we touch on an eschatological dimension in Newman's work) prepares us for Christ's coming: 'he who cannot pray for Christ's coming, ought not in consistency to pray at all'.[808] Above all, prayer presupposes an act of 'real assent' of the kind explored earlier. Indeed Newman goes so far as to say that it depends on a quality of *certitude* which persists and underpins all our devotions:

> without certitude in religious faith there may be much decency of profession and of observance, but there can be no habit of prayer, no directness of devotion, no intercourse with the unseen, no generosity of self-sacrifice.[809]

Why? Because prayer *is* communion, is the means by which we become conscious of the actual presence of the God to whose existence and authority we have unconditionally assented.[810] And it requires structure, discipline, pattern, as does any relationship, though that is not really the reason for Newman's preference for formal over informal prayer. Rather it is because he is unimpressed with affective prayer, as he generally is with the use of the emotions in the spiritual life: it can lead to a dangerous subjectivity.[811] Furthermore forms have a vital role in guarding against chaos:

We *must begin* religion with what looks like a form. Our fault will be, not
in beginning it as a form, but in continuing it as a form. For it is our duty
to be ever striving and praying to *enter* into the real spirit of our services,
and in proportion as we understand them and love them, they will cease to
be a form and a task, and will be the real expressions of our minds. Thus
shall we gradually be changed in heart from servants into sons of Almighty
God.[812]

It is crucial to see that formality, in the sense defined here, and reverence are indispensable in Newman's understanding of prayer: he condemns 'the familiarity with
which many persons address our Lord in prayer, applying epithets to Him and
adopting a strain of language which does not beseem creatures, not to say sinners', and
a corresponding 'irreverence in church, sitting instead of kneeling in prayer . . . and,
much more, looking about when prayers are going on, and observing what others are
doing'.[813] What may appear dead forms to those who are spiritually dead are living
ones to those who are alive.[814] 'To be present at extempore prayer, is to *hear prayers*';[815]
and prayers formed at the present moment are likely to be irreverent, unworthy of the
majesty of the God to whom they are offered.[816] But the real danger is again that of our
making private judgements and forming private habits which happen to suit us, and
which can then be dropped when we feel like it, thereby insidiously weakening our
resolve to continue praying, until like Samson we suddenly wake up and discover we
have lost God altogether.[817]

How then should we pray? In a letter of 1837 to Henry Wilberforce Newman
commends the use of the (Latin) breviary devotions: they are 'very unexciting, grave,
and simple', and provide a balanced diet of prayer for every day of the year.[818] He
commends the way the breviary sets the bulk of our prayer in the morning – 'when our
time is more our own and our mind most fresh. To leave the body of our prayers for
night, is like putting off religion to a deathbed . . . Morning services *secure* the day's
devotion.'[819] He has much to say about the Psalms, which 'should be the basis of all
devotion – the more one knows of them, the more surprising they are – of course,
being inspired'.[820] And their ruling idea is

> that the weak, the oppressed, the defenceless shall be raised to rule the
> world in spite of its array of might, its threats, and its terrors; that 'the first
> shall be last, and the last first.'[821]

It is interesting, but perhaps not surprising, to find Newman describing the monumental Psalm 119 (easily the most formally structured in the Psalter) as 'the standing
prayer of the Church Militant in every age, as of old time for things longed for, so now
for things pledged to it'.[822]

But prayer is not just words, however indispensable these are because they insert us
into the continual rhythm of the Church's prayer. Newman also speaks about contemplative prayer, and especially the contemplation of Christ: thus, when we are
suffering, we must try to tear ourselves away from a profound self-absorption by contemplating the suffering Christ (which in itself is possible only through grace).[823] It
may in fact be precisely in times of suffering (though it need not be so) that we begin,

by a process of meditation on the truths of scripture, to appropriate those truths as living realities:

> To the devout and spiritual, the Divine Word speaks of things, not merely of notions. And, again, to the disconsolate, the tempted, the perplexed, the suffering, there comes, by means of their very trials, an enlargement of thought, which enables them to see in it what they never saw before. Henceforth there is to them a reality in its teachings, which they recognize as an argument, and the best of arguments, for its divine origin. Hence the practice of meditation on the Sacred Text; so highly thought of by Catholics. Reading, as we do, the Gospel from our youth up, we are in danger of becoming so familiar with them as to be dead to their force, and to view them as a mere history. The purpose, then, of meditation is to realize them; to make the facts which they relate stand out before our minds as objects, such as may be appropriated by a faith as living as the imagination which apprehends them.[824]

He commends traditional meditation on the life of Christ:[825] 'we must try to live as if the Apostles were living, and we must try to muse upon our Lord's life in the Gospels, not as a history, but as if a recollection'.[826] Note here Newman's preference for returning to sources, as well as his emphasis on practising the presence of Christ.

None of this will be easy: prayer is hard work,[827] which is why we need love, 'the one thing needful', to embark upon it.[828] Christ commands us to 'watch and pray': watching means avoiding evil and being aware of our susceptibility to submit to temptation:[829]

> Is it an easy thing to pray? It *is* easy to wait for a rush of feelings, and then to let our petitions be borne upon them . . . but it is not at all easy to be in the habit day after day and hour after hour, in all frames of mind, and under all outward circumstances, to bring before God a calm, collected, awakened soul.[830]

Praying attentively is difficult; but it is also a *habit*, and making it so is what helps to make it effectual.[831] Hence the great benefit of public worship is that 'it statedly interferes with the urgency of worldly excitements', thereby calming and steadying the mind.[832] And all this takes time:

> No one, then, when he first turns his thoughts to religion, finds it easy to pray; he is irregular in his religious feelings; he prays more earnestly at some times than at others; his devotional seasons come by fits and starts; he cannot account for his state of mind, or reckon upon himself; he frequently finds that he is more disposed for prayer at any time and place than those set apart for the purpose. All this is to be expected; for no habit is formed at once.[833]

We must therefore begin to pray by composing ourselves and kneeling down quietly 'as to a work far above us . . . meekly repeating the wonderful words of the Church our Teacher'.[834] Once we are formed in the habit of prayer, our entire lives will become prayer: we shall see God in all things, and can be said almost literally to pray without ceasing.[835]

The great strength of this approach is in its capacity to transform us, slowly and painfully, into the holy people we are created to be: and transformation, as the word implies, requires form, structure, order, rhythm, if the chaos that exists as much within us as it did at the dawn of creation is not to erupt and overwhelm us again. Only thus can we put down roots deep into the life of God, roots that will sustain us in times of darkness. Seen in this light, prayer becomes part of the very essence of the Church's life, to be engaged in not in search of immediate benefits or emotional gratification but precisely in order to be conformed into the likeness of Christ. And the prayers of those most hidden from worldly view may be the most precious of all, a thought which elicits from Newman a moment of inspired eloquence:

> Alas! there must be something wrong among us; when our defenders recommend the Church on the mere plea of its activity, its popularity, and its visible usefulness, and would scarcely scruple to give us up, had we *not* the many on our side! If our ground of boasting be, that rich men, and mighty men, and many men love us, it never can be a religious boast, and may be our condemnation. Christ made His feast for 'the poor, the maimed, the lame, and the blind.' It is the widow and the fatherless, the infirm, the helpless, the devoted, bound together in prayer, who are the strength of the Church. It is their prayers, be they many or few, the prayers of Mary [as in Mary and Martha] and such as Mary, who are the safety, under Christ, of those who with Paul and Barnabas fight the Lord's battles. 'It is but lost labour to rise up early, to sit up late, to eat the bread of sorrows,' if prayers are discontinued. It is mere infatuation, if we think to resist the enemies who at this moment are at our doors, if our Churches remain shut, and we give up to prayer but a few minutes in the day.[836]

Finally, prayer is a sharing in the continuing intercession of Christ, and keeping that in mind enlarges our perspective when we pray:

> Viewed in his place in 'the Church of the First-born enrolled in heaven,' with his original debt cancelled in Baptism, and all subsequent penalties put aside by Absolution, standing in God's presence upright and irreprovable, accepted in the Beloved, clad in the garments of righteousness, anointed with oil, and with a crown upon his head, in royal and priestly garb, as an heir of eternity, full of grace and good works, as walking in all the commandments of the Lord blameless, such an one, I repeat it, is plainly in his fitting place when he intercedes. He is made after the pattern and in the fulness of Christ – he is what Christ is. Christ intercedes above, and he intercedes below. Why should he linger in the doorway, praying for pardon, who has been allowed to share in the grace of the Lord's passion, to die with Him and rise again? He is already in a capacity for higher things. His prayer thenceforth takes a higher range, and contemplates not himself merely, but others also. He is taken in the confidence and counsels of his Lord and Saviour.[837]

Conclusion

There is an intriguing moment at the beginning of *A grammar of assent*: Newman tells us that there are three ways we can hold a proposition – inference, doubt, and assent. Of these, he will not discuss doubt at all; indeed he dismisses it with a single observation.[838] Assent is an absolute, unconditional thing ('the absolute acceptance of a proposition without any condition'[839]): there is simply no room for doubt in it. Why? Because 'we cannot without absurdity call ourselves at once believers and inquirers also'.[840] Doubt is for Liberals:

> And ye [Liberals] have caught some echoes of its lore,
>   As heralded amid the joyous choirs;
>   Ye mark'd it spoke of peace, chastised desires,
> Good-will and mercy, – and ye heard no more;
> But, as for zeal and quick-eyed sanctity,
> And the dread depths of grace, ye pass'd them by.
> And so ye halve the Truth; for ye in heart,
>   At best, are doubters whether it be true.[841]

This massive certainty, this rigorous exclusion of question-marks, is both impressive and daunting, like mountains in winter. And it brings us finally to the dilemma with which Newman confronts us. There is a sense in which, of all the great spiritual writers considered in this book, he is the most difficult to assess, for the very reasons that led him on the journey to Rome: because he, like the truth which animated him, is indivisible, not susceptible of being taken piecemeal. Its strength is his: an intellectual integrity and coherence of extraordinary power, a vision of the spiritual life capable of anchoring those who make it their own in a tradition that reaches back to the wellsprings of Christianity, and in which Catholic truth becomes a living source of inexhaustible riches for those who submit themselves to its overriding demands. And that strength is all the more impressive for being so contrary to so much that was ephemeral and superficial at the time.

Yet it is also daunting, severe rather than beautiful, forbidding rather than attractive, and not only for the reasons already given. In an early sermon Newman wrote: 'Heaven . . . is not like this world; I will say what it is much more like – *a church.*'[842] And when, much later in his long life, Cardinal Manning, with whom Newman always had a tense relationship, invited him to join the Senate of a proposed (Catholic) Kensington College, Newman refused, on the grounds that it would be a part of the University of London; and that was

> a body which has been the beginning, and source, and symbol of all the Liberalism existing in the educated classes for the last forty years.[843]

At the age of 72, and with the painful experiences in Dublin behind him, one could scarcely blame Newman for declining. But the reason is instructive. Newman's is a wholly uncompromising, radically supernatural spirituality, intensely compassionate to people's spiritual needs and the salvation of their souls, entirely uninterested in their physical needs. 'It is not', he wrote in his *Lectures on certain difficulties felt by Anglicans*, 'by frames of mind, it is not by emotions, that we must judge of real religion; it is the having a will and a heart set towards those things unseen.'[844] In a famous, or notorious passage in the same work (which he repeated in his *Apologia*), he went further still: the Church

> holds that it were better for sun and moon to drop from heaven, for the earth to fail, and for all the many millions who are upon it to die of starvation in extremest agony, so far as temporal affliction goes, than that one soul, I will not say, should be lost, but should commit one single venial sin, should tell one wilful untruth, though it harmed no one, or steal one poor farthing without excuse. She considers the action of this world and the action of the soul simply incommensurate, viewed in their respective spheres.[845]

It is important not to lose a sense of perspective here: Newman is, albeit in his most polemical manner, wanting to hammer home the terrible damage done by sin, not only to our bodies but even more to our souls.[846] Even so, one can be forgiven for hesitating in the face of so uncompromising a statement. There is little interest in the world of nature in Newman, little concern for social justice or the affairs of the world. This may be the fault of his context rather than of his personality; but it unquestionably limits his appeal. More seriously, perhaps, one may be entitled to wonder whether the theology of apostolic and patristic Christianity was anything like as homogeneous and coherent as he certainly believed it to be.[847] In the final analysis, some will draw back before a faith so certain as this, even though its pervasive severity is always shot through with an even more pervasive sense of hope, and a hope all the more powerful for the unsparing honesty and rigour with which it is set forward. At the very end of his *Lectures on the prophetical office of the Church*, Newman reminds his hearers that the Church's history has always been one of trouble and disorder:

> every century is like every other, and to those who live in it seems worse than all times before it. The Church is ever ailing, and lingers on in weakness . . . The Saints are ever all but failing from the earth, and Christ all but coming; and thus the Day of judgment is literally ever at hand, and it is our duty ever to be looking out for it, not disappointed that we have so often said, 'now is the moment,' and that at the last, contrary to our expectation, Truth has somewhat rallied. Such is God's will, gathering in His elect, first one and then another, by little and little, in the intervals of sunshine between storm and storm, or snatching them from the surge of evil, even when the waters rage most furiously . . . 'The waves of the sea are mighty, and rage horribly; but yet the Lord, who dwelleth on high, is mightier.'[848]

'Pied beauty': Gerard Manley Hopkins (1844–89)

Introduction

If Newman's spirituality appeared more severe than beautiful, that of the Jesuit priest and poet Gerard Manley Hopkins might seem to be the opposite. This is an extract from a sermon he preached in the Lancashire parish of Bedford Leigh:

There met in Jesus Christ all things that can make man lovely and loveable. In his body he was most beautiful . . . we have . . . accounts of him written in early times. Another proof of his beauty may be drawn from the words *proficiebat sapientia et aetate et gratia apud Deum et homines* (['he increased in wisdom and stature, and in favour with God and man'] Luc.ii 52) . . . But he could not have pleased by growth of body unless the body was strong, healthy, and beautiful that grew. But the best proof of all is this, that his body was the special work of the Holy Ghost. He was not born in nature's course, no man was his father; had he been born as others are he must have inherited some defect of figure or of constitution, from which no man born as fallen men are born is wholly free unless God interfere to keep him so. But his body was framed directly from heaven by the power of the Holy Ghost, of whom it would be unworthy to leave any the least botch or failing in his work . . . I leave it to you, brethren, then to picture him, in whom the fulness of the godhead dwelt bodily, in his bearing how majestic, how strong and yet how lovely and lissome in his limbs, in his look how earnest, grave but kind. In his Passion all this strength was spent, this lissomness crippled, this beauty wrecked, this majesty beaten down. But now it is more than all restored, and for myself I make no secret I look forward with eager desire to seeing the matchless beauty of Christ's body in the heavenly light.[849]

There is something Grecian, homoerotic almost, in this contemplation of Christ's physically beautiful body; and the rejection of 'the least botch or failing' in it is a strange remark from the poet whose 'Pied Beauty' celebrates 'all things counter, original, spare, strange; /Whatever is fickle, freckled'.[850] One wonders what the parishioners made of it (they had little time to make anything of it, since Hopkins' curacy there lasted only three months). The paradox is heightened by the fact that Hopkins rarely if ever appears to have used even a single word without careful thought. Yet the paradox is more apparent than real. The priest-poet who can celebrate the beauty and attractiveness of God in the most direct and physical manner can also, with no less directness and honesty, help us to see the world exactly as it is.[851]

The life of Hopkins

If Newman's life appears to many to have been withdrawn and secluded, Hopkins' is likely to appear stranger still.[852] He was born in east London, the eldest of a large family: his father Manley Hopkins was an insurance adjuster.[853] In 1852 the family moved to Hampstead, and in 1854 Hopkins went to Highgate School, proceeding to Balliol College Oxford nine years later. Hopkins acquired a great love of the Latin and Greek classics here, as well as becoming intensely religious, deeply influenced by the Tractarian H. P. Liddon.[854] On 21 October 1866 he was received into the Roman Catholic Church by Newman, and two years later entered the Jesuit novitiate at Roehampton. His journal is laconic on the subject: 'May 5 [1868]. Cold. Resolved to be a religious.'[855]

Jesuit formation at the time was minutely organized, utterly separated from the secular world: a life of precisely calibrated routine and order; as Norman White puts it, 'Nothing happened, constantly.'[856] After spending two years at Roehampton, Hopkins continued his formation first at Stonyhurst and later (in 1874) at St Beuno's in Wales. It was there, in 1877, that he was ordained priest. Disappointed at his superiors' decision not to allow him to complete his final year of studies, he served as a curate successively in London (Farm Street), Oxford (St Aloysius), Bedford Leigh, Liverpool, and Glasgow. In 1881 he made a long retreat, from which most of his extant spiritual writings emerged. In the following year he was sent back to Stonyhurst to teach novices, and two years later was appointed Professor of Greek at University College Dublin, where he died of typhoid five years later, on 8 June 1889.

Hopkins' classical education was a major influence on him, as was his interest in architecture, the close observation of which will have helped to shape his acute ability to observe the detail and texture of landscape. He seems also to have been deeply attracted by both the countryside and the Catholic associations of the area of North Wales around St Beuno's.[857] He was very interested in philology both classical and contemporary, in the sound of words as well as their associations. He learnt Welsh while at St Beuno's.[858]

As a child, Hopkins was precocious and sensitive; and the effects on him of his sternly male education culminating in the ferocious regimentation of his Jesuit training must have been immense. It is instructive to note that in an early sermon he referred to God not only as the king but as 'the general we are to obey', presumably just one level above the general of his Order.[859] Yet it would be unwise to settle for a picture of Hopkins as a lonely and repressed solitary: the recent discovery of a witty poem 'Consule Jones', written for his fellow-Jesuits at St Beuno's, suggests a gentler, more humorous Hopkins.[860] Like Newman, he seems not to have been at ease in the company of parishioners. He records an incident that took place while he was working in Liverpool:

> After this sermon one of my penitents told me, with great simplicity, that I was not to be named in the same week with Fr Clare [the Rector, and a fine preacher]. 'Well,' I said, 'and I will not be named in the same week. But did you hear it all?' He said he did, only that he was sleeping for parts of it.[861]

It is hard to blame the parishioner for sleeping, or Hopkins for leaving him cold: the nature of his Jesuit formation is unlikely to have made preaching to Liverpool parishioners easy. Again, though, we should avoid jumping to conclusions: Hopkins was no narrow aesthete despite his formation. In 1875 he read in *The Times* about the wreck of the Scottish-built transatlantic steamer *Deutschland*, at the mouth of the Thames, and the loss of large numbers of crew and passengers – including a small group of nuns who had already been expelled from Protestant Prussia because of their faith. It led to one of his greatest poems, and one which, while influenced by classical form and Catholic faith, is acutely sensitive to the tragic suffering of those who were shipwrecked.[862] And even the stern Jesuit training had its pastoral advantages: in one of his sermons preached at Bedford Leigh, he uses Ignatian-style meditation in a sermon on Jesus' healing of the paralytic, encouraging the congregation to

imagine . . . the surprise of those assembled there, the sound of feet scram-
bling on the tiles, the light of heaven breaking in, a mattress coming
through swung by four ends of rope.[863]

Hopkins and medieval theology

Of the many literary influences which helped to shape Hopkins' spirituality, one in
particular is worth stressing: the medieval philosopher Duns Scotus.[864] It is possible to
see this simply as Hopkins' love of all things medieval, along with his passion for
Gothic architecture and the kind of medieval mysticism reflected in a poem like *Rosa
mystica*.[865] But the influence went far deeper: Hopkins also accepted Scotus' view that
the Incarnation was the culmination of God's eternal plan for creation, not the sad
consequence of the Fall.[866] The great Swiss theologian Hans Urs von Balthasar has also
shown how Scotus' concept of *haecceitas* (literally the 'thisness' of things, and hence an
emphasis on individual form and identity) profoundly influenced Hopkins:

> Any consideration of 'form in general' . . . becomes preparation for what
> Hopkins intended by the always unique oneness of the individual form
> that only emerges in the Christian encounter between the absolutely
> personal and free God and the fully personal creature . . . and just this
> fundamental experience had to lead Hopkins back to Ignatius and his
> *Spiritual exercises*, where for the first time in the history of Christian spiri-
> tuality everything is placed on the knife edge of the mutual election that
> takes place between God and man, behind which retreats any considera-
> tion of 'perfection in general.'[867]

Hence, Balthasar argues, Hopkins has to be seen as priest, poet, and theologian all
at once: the various vocations cannot be separated.[868] Scotus 'had been the first to
maintain philosophically the uniqueness of things, withstanding the temptation
to dissolve them into general ideas, forms or laws. This too was Hopkins' object: to
express the irreducibly unique, or at least to evoke it, which clearly brought with it the
danger of "oddness."'[869] Both Scotus and Hopkins had an eye for the uniquely individual, the 'dappled' things and people: both were also preoccupied with the relation
between the particular and the universal.[870] Hopkins was not alone in this: his
near-contemporary and fellow-Jesuit George Tyrrell says:

> it is greater skill which deals with more difficult and stubborn matter, and
> detects a possible beauty latent in that which is crabbed and deformed.[871]

'Inscape' and 'instress'

But Hopkins *was* alone in the terms and approach he used. He explores the relationship between the universal and the particular in his use of two distinctive concepts
which are crucial for understanding his spirituality. 'Inscape' is God's design, present
in the created world – the form or identity of a thing as it is, and that which prevents it
from being something else: it is what you see or perceive to be present in something.
'Stress' and 'instress' are the way that design works out in practice in human minds and
wills, and how you appropriate and respond to what you see: it is thus crucial for spiri-

tuality.[872] The influence of Scotus' *haecceitas* is important here too; but that of other Christian philosophers, such as Augustine, may be significant as well.[873]

Hopkins' sensitivity to what he sees is not restricted to his poetry. In his *Journal* for 1867 there is a moving passage about his observation of two ash trees in Finchley: he notes the beauty that is the result of looking at them in such a way that the two trunks nearly merge, and the beauty that is manifest in the rich and complex detail of their leaves and branches. His attention to detail is striking.[874] But more important still is what he says in one of his sermons, which is worth quoting at length:

> Search the whole world and you will find it a million-million fold con-trivance of providence planned for our use and patterned for our admiration. But yet this providence is imperfect, plainly imperfect. The sun shines too long and withers the harvest, the rain is too heavy and rots it or in floods spreading washes it away . . . we contend with cold, want, weakness, hunger, disease, death, and often we fight a losing battle, never a triumphant one; everything is full of fault, flaw, imperfection, shortcom-ing; as many marks as there are of God's wisdom in providing for us so many marks there may be set against them of more being needed still, of something having made of this very providence a shattered frame and a broken web. Let us not now enquire, brethren, why this should be; we most sadly feel and know that so it is. But there is good in it; for if we were not forced from time to time to feel our need of God and our dependance on him, we should most of us cease to pray to him and to thank him. If he did everything we should treat him as though he did nothing, whereas now that he does not do all we are brought to remember how much he does and to ask for more. And God desires nothing so much as that his creatures should have recourse to him.[875]

This may be classical Ignatian spirituality; but it is expressed in Hopkins' own way, and underlines the rigour and directness of his approach to nature and life. Sometimes nature is terrifying, as in 'The wreck of the Deutschland':

> Wiry and white-fiery and whirlwind-swivelled snow
> Spins to the widow-making unchilding unfathering deeps.[876]

The 'widow-making unchilding unfathering deeps' vividly embody all that God is not: destructive, inanimate. This is the dark watery primordial chaos of Genesis 1 or the nightmarish opening verses of Psalm 69, a chaos at once tamed by the Creator and yet constantly threatening to break out and overwhelm all that has been created. For Hopkins, disorder is a negative reality, a state of non-being, yet with evil potential in precisely the way that chaos has in scripture:

> We are to hate disorder because it is the soil of sin, being by itself a negative thing without natural ugliness. You must consider its known conse-quences. It is like sleep in a pointsman, steersman, or sentinel.[877]

There is a moral element implied here: disorder is an absence of something, of subor-dination or obedience to God: sin, by contrast, is positive disobedience.[878] Elsewhere

Hopkins stresses the creative power of God's presence in creation, as in 'God's Grandeur', where God is present both in the storm and the sunrise.[879]

Spirituality and suffering

These perceptions bring us back to 'The wreck of the Deutschland'. Having described the violent and destructive power of the sea, Hopkins speaks of how God looks upon the exiled and drowning nuns, and sees beauty in tragedy:

> Loathed for a love men knew in them,
> Banned by land of their birth,
> Rhine refused them, Thames would ruin them;
> Surf, snow, river and earth
> Gnashed: but thou art above, thou Orion of light;
> Thy unchancelling poising palms were weighing the worth,
> Thou martyr-master: in thy sight
> Storm flakes were scroll-leaved flowers, lily showers – sweet
> heaven was astrew in them.[880]

This is a remarkable passage: one distinguished scholar has read into it a virtual illustration of the Lutheran notion of God's righteousness.[881] God looks upon human sorrow and innocent suffering and sees enduring goodness and beauty; and the 'tall nun' looks at the grim chaos around her and sees the hand of God:

> Ah! there was a heart right!
> There was single eye!
> Read the unshapeable shock night
> And knew the who and the why.[882]

Her suffering and her faith become in some sense redemptive for her fellow victims.[883] And behind the terrible scene Hopkins sees God, present even in the wreck,

> Stanching, quenching ocean of a motionable mind;
> Ground of being and granite of it: past all
> Grasp God, throned behind
> Death, with a sovereignty that heeds but hides, bodes but abides.[884]

In the last sonnets, sometimes called the 'Sonnets of desolation', probably written near the end of his life in Dublin, Hopkins struggles with despair and death in powerful though ambiguous verse, culminating in his own experience of wrestling Jacob:

> Nay in all that toil, that coil, since (seems) I kissed the rod,
> Hand rather, my heart lo! lapped strength, stole joy, would laugh, cheer.
> Cheer whom though? The hero whose heaven-handling flung me, foot trod
> Me? or me that fought him? O which one? is it each one? That night, that year
> Of now done darkness I wretch lay wrestling with (my God!) my God.[885]

In the fine 'Nondum' (1866), Hopkins speaks to a God who does not answer and remains constantly silent. It ends:

> Oh! till Thou givest that sense beyond,
> To shew Thee that Thou art, and near,
> Let patience with her chastening wand
> Dispel the doubt and dry the tear;
> And lead me child-like by the hand
> If still in darkness not in fear.
>
> Speak! whisper to my watching heart
> One word – as when a mother speaks
> Soft, when she sees her infant start,
> Till dimpled joy steals o'er its cheeks.
> Then, to behold Thee as Thou art,
> I'll wait till morn eternal breaks.[886]

And the catastrophe of the wrecked *Deutschland* causes Hopkins to ponder both the mystery of God's existence and the arbitrariness of tragedy.[887] For Hopkins, as for George Herbert, God is both lover and tyrant, both intimately present and fearsomely distant:

> Thou art lightning and love, I found it, a winter and warm;
> Father and fondler of heart thou hast wrung.[888]

Hopkins goes on to ask why God could not protect those passengers who drowned in the wreck;[889] and he describes the 'tall nun' who, according to reports, at midnight stood on a table in the saloon of the grounded ship, thrust her body through the skylight, and kept exclaiming, in a voice heard by those in the rigging above the roar of the storm, 'My God, my God, make haste, make haste!'[890]

Exile and death

Two themes recur both in this and other poems. The first is exile, a familiar idea in both poetry and spirituality, and an experience which Hopkins himself underwent during the lonely final years of his life in Dublin. 'The wreck of the Deutschland' is informed by sensitivity for the exiled nuns; and in 'Pilate' he writes: 'This outer cold, my exile from of old / From God and man, is hell no doubt.'[891] The second is death, a subject which seems to have preoccupied Hopkins as it did many Victorians.[892] In an early poem he reflects on the unpredictable omnipresence of death, articulating the transient nature of created things:

> I had a dream. A wondrous thing:
> It seem'd an evening in the Spring;
> – A little sickness in the air
> From too much fragrance everywhere:–
> As I walk'd a stilly wood,
> Sudden, Death before me stood:
> In a hollow lush and damp,

He seem'd a dismal mirky stamp
On the flowers that were seen
His charnelhouse-grate ribs between,
And with coffin-black he barr'd the green.
'Death,' said I, 'what do you here
At this Spring season of the year?'
'I mark the flowers ere the prime
Which I may tell at Autumn-time.'
Ere I had further question made
Death was vanish'd from the glade.
Then I saw that he had bound
Many trees and flowers round
With a subtle web of black,
And that such a sable track
Lay along the grasses green
From the spot where he had been.
    But the Spring-tide pass'd the same;
Summer was as full of flame;
Autumn-time no earlier came.
And the flowers that he had tied,
As I mark'd, not always died
Sooner than their mates; and yet
Their fall was fuller of regret:
It seem'd so hard and dismal thing,
Death, to mark them in the Spring.[893]

The theology and practice of prayer

The sense of two worlds interpenetrating one another, so palpable in this poem, brings us to Hopkins' understanding of prayer. Balthasar rightly draws attention to an important passage in Hopkins' spiritual writings about the relationship of prayer and grace. For Hopkins, the 'prevenient grace' of classical theology '*rehearses* in us our consent beforehand', that is, before we have consented to co-operate with it: as Balthasar puts it, this prevenient grace is for Hopkins 'the Augustinian being drawn (*delectatio*) to God, expressed here in more personal terms'.[894] As God's grace penetrates us, a new horizon is opened to us; and Hopkins says:

> It is into that possible world that God for the moment moves his creature out of this one . . . This shift is grace.[895]

In Hopkins' view, it is only at this point that the creature has to decide whether or not to co-operate with the divine grace, and say Yes to God:

> and this least sigh of desire, this one aspiration, is the life and spirit of man . . . And remark that prayer understood in this sense, this sigh or aspiration or stirring of the spirit towards God, is a *forestall* of the thing to be done, as on the other side grace prevenient is God's forestall of the same, and it is

here that one creature, one man, differs so much from another: in one God finds only the constrained correspondence with his forestall . . . in another he finds after this an act of choice properly so called. And by this infinitesimal act the creature does what in it lies to bridge the gulf fixed between its present actual and worser pitch of will and its future better one. For the forestall on God's part, in which the creature's correspondence is bound up, is a piece bodily taken out of the possible world, the 'burl of being', of that creature and brought into this actual one.[896]

The language is characteristically original, but infinitely worth paying attention to, for the point matters. Prayer for Hopkins is this 'sigh or aspiration', which is itself a kind of response or answer to God's gift of grace: God's 'forestalling' opens up new possibilities to us, gives us glimpses of new horizons or ways of seeing, and is a kind of invitation,

> a prophecy, a forecast, not of the certain future, for it leaves us free still to discard and unmake that future: therefore of a possible future.[897]

God's initiative here is only one manifestation of the infinitely greater initiative taken in Incarnation, when the Son of God came forth from the Father

> to give God glory and that by sacrifice, sacrifice offered in the barren wilderness outside of God, as the children of Israel were led into the wilderness to offer sacrifice. This sacrifice and this outward procession is a consequence and shadow of the procession of the Trinity, from which mystery sacrifice takes its rise.[898]

The point is important for understanding Hopkins' view of prayer. God is constantly revealing, communicating himself, supremely through Christ in Incarnation and in the sacraments, but also through his divine energy or prevenient grace, which we experience in the form of an invitation to look outside and beyond ourselves, to glimpse hitherto undreamed-of possibilities in the 'this-ness', the reality as it is, of the world around.

In a profound sense, then, God himself is the true 'inscape' of all things; but, as Hopkins says in 'The wreck of the Deutschland', 'his mystery must be instressed, stressed', must be *received* by us. We need to be spiritual radio aerials, constantly attentive and sensitive to the hidden but active divine presence around us. 'Elected Silence, sing to me' is the haunting opening of his poem 'The habit of perfection'.[899] In prayer, we respond to God's longing to draw us out of the grim realities of the world as it is and reveal to us the best of all possible worlds. Like the Song of Songs (whose influence is perceptible in Hopkins' poem 'The elopement'), the divine call is an invitation of love.

This is not, however, to say that the spiritual life is all beauty and adventure. In a sermon, Hopkins speaks of love as *obedience*, a crucial virtue in his Jesuit formation:

> Love of God means the preferring his will to ours: it is the love of a subject for his ruler. Love for Christ is enthusiasm for a leader, a hero, a love for a bosom friend, love for a lover.[900]

And towards the end of his life, during a retreat in Dublin, Hopkins writes:

> our lives and in particular those of religious, as mine, are in their whole
> direction, not only inwardly but most visibly and outwardly, shaped by
> Christ's. Without that even outwardly the world could be so different that
> we cannot even guess it. And my life is determined by the Incarnation
> down to most of the details of the day. Now this being so that I cannot
> even stop it, why should I not make the cause that determines my life, both
> as a whole and in much detail, determine it in greater detail still and to the
> greater efficiency of what I in any case should do, and to my greater happi-
> ness in doing it? . . . The Incarnation was for my salvation and that of the
> world: the work goes on in a great system and machinery which even drags
> me on with the collar round my neck though I could and do neglect my
> duty in it.[901]

Conclusion

The radical obedience demanded of the Jesuit, the unequivocal submission of one's
own will and preferences in favour of Christ's will for us, may not appeal to many. But
it is important to remember the point made above: for Hopkins, the Incarnation is
not only, or even primarily, a corrective made necessary by human sin, but the
crowning moment of the divine plan for the universe, the revelation in human form of
a God whose energy and love never ceases to call us. In that perspective, the strangeness of Hopkins' admiration of the beautiful Christ with which we began melts away:
Christ incarnates the fullness of humanity, and what he is, we can become in him:

> For Christ plays in ten thousand places,
> Lovely in limbs, and lovely in eyes not his
> To the Father through the features of men's faces.[902]

Once we see that, our own ordinariness and failures are irradiated by grace: as
Hopkins says:

> I am all at once what Christ is, since he was what I am, and
> This Jack, joke, poor potsherd, patch, matchwood, immortal diamond,
> Is immortal diamond.[903]

And, in one of the late 'Sonnets of desolation', Hopkins, in densely allusive language,
seems to be saying: we cannot wring joy from God, cannot claim or control God – but
when we least expect it, he will smile on us:

> come, poor Jackself, I do advise
> You, jaded let be; call of thoughts awhile
> Elsewhere; leave comfort root-room; let joy size
> At God knows when to God knows what; whose smile
> 'S not wrung, see you; unforeseentimes rather – as skies
> Betweenpie mountains – lights a lovely smile.[904]

The sympathetic sacrifice: Dora Greenwell (1821–82)

Introduction

Of those explored in these case studies, Dora Greenwell is easily the least known. The very difficulty of categorizing her is likely to be one of the reasons for this. An Anglican, and broadly an Evangelical, she wrote one biography of a French Dominican and another of an American Quaker – and she dedicated a third book to the American evangelists Moody and Sankey.[905] Her love of fantasy and myth, and her vast reading, may have further helped to loosen her sense of belonging within any one of the specific spiritual traditions of English Christianity considered in this chapter.[906] She was a layperson, and a single woman, and wrote about that too. And some of her poetry is frankly of indifferent quality.

Nor is her life overtly interesting.[907] Born at Greenwell Ford, in County Durham, her father was a country gentleman. Her favourite brother, Alan, was to be an Anglo-Catholic priest.[908] Dora and her parents went to live with Alan at his rectory in Lancashire after Dora's father experienced severe financial difficulties. In 1854, she and her mother settled in Durham, where Dora's best work was produced.[909] After her mother's death Dora lived variously in London, Torquay, and Bristol. Ill-health dogged her for much of her life.

Greenwell left behind her a small body of written work, of uneven quality. Two of the prose works, *Two friends* (1862) and *Colloquia crucis* (1871), are written as extended spiritual dialogues with a clerical friend. Her book of essays (1866) includes an important piece on prayer and another on the role of single women.[910] Her biography of the Dominican Jean-Henri-Baptiste Lacordaire (1802–61), a key liberal influence during the second Catholic revival in post-Revolution France, is an absorbing study: she celebrates his erudition and compassion, his combination of 'high thinking and plain living',[911] his commitment to the vital principle of sacrifice, and his passionate liberalism in upholding Christian truth and values.

Greenwell's study of the American Quaker John Woolman (1871) celebrates the life of someone who combined a tendency to quietism with a strong commitment to social justice.[912] The poems in *Carmina crucis* (1869), and the essays in *Liber humanitatis* (1874), contain much of her best work. In 1868, after wide reading and some pioneering work on the subject, she wrote an article 'On the education of the imbecile' (published in the *North British Review* that year), for the Royal Albert Idiot Asylum in Lancaster: her advocacy of the rights of the mentally ill is impressive.[913]

Greenwell drew from a remarkably wide range of sources, from Dante and T. H. Huxley to the *Rubaiyat* of Omar Khayyám (which she describes as 'that splendid, darkly-atheistic poem'[914]). Among the theological writers she cites in the collection of extracts she published as *A basket of summer fruit* were St Bernard, Cowper, Coleridge, Luther, Baxter, Madame Guyon, Faber, Wesley, St John of the Cross, and the Scottish Covenanter Samuel Rutherford.[915] She was widely read in French, German and Italian literature, poetry and theology.[916] She had a wide range of friends, among them Josephine Butler, Christina Rossetti, Elizabeth Barrett Browning and the woman poet Jean Ingelow.[917] But she was no ivory tower intellectual: in addition to her work with the mentally ill, she regularly visited Durham pitmen and prisoners, and was actively involved in a number of social causes: the treatment of children at work, the victims of the Irish famine of 1847 and the collapse of the Lancashire cotton industry in 1863. She opposed vivisection, was an early advocate of women's franchise, and was passionately engaged in the campaign for the abolition of slavery. One of her friends recalled that 'in her whole nature there was a love of what was free and lavish', like tropical flowers and richly evocative scents.[918]

The mystery of sacrifice

Something of what lies behind this intriguing eclecticism may be suggested by what she quotes Lacordaire as saying: 'Above all things, *have a life* – your own life; live to a centre of lofty and consistent aims.'[919] This could be taken as implying a comfortable dilettantism; but the existence of another overriding influence appears in what she says of Mme Guyon's work:

> It seemed to her that the Gospel exhibited itself not merely as a plan for escaping punishment, but as *containing also the element of spiritual restoration and of inward life.* She regarded the new life in Christ, when perfected, as being the same as Christ's life, or God's life, and those persons who have experienced the inward spiritual renovation to the extent of pure or perfect love as being truly one with God. At this great object she advised all to aim.[920]

Guyon is talking about a *fixed* state, based on principle rather than feeling, which enables people to draw fruit from whatever life throws at them.[921] But it presupposes a complete submission of the soul's will before the will of God.[922] It is clear that Greenwell approves of this, which is remarkable given her equally strong advocacy of compassion and social justice. Thus she commends the fact that there is 'something sublime in the passivity of the early Quakers; unresisting and yet persisting, they are at the same time "reeds shaken by the wind", and "prophets, yea, and more than prophets."'[923]

The clue to this paradox, a combination of persistent individual searching for truth with a deep resignation to the will of God, lies in the mystery of sacrifice:

> it is our personal initiation into this mystery of sacrifice which is as regards the life which is in Christ Jesus its true sacrament, enabling the soul to pass into real and intimate communion with him.[924]

Greenwell's whole point is that we must let God work within us, inwardly transforming us, before we are able to work for God in the world.[925] She quotes another French priest, Lammenais, who said that 'sacrifice is the base and essence of all true society': 'there is nothing fruitful except sacrifice';[926] and she notes that 'Lacordaire's conception of the priestly office was that of an absolute and perpetual sacrifice'.[927]

Greenwell argues that behind this view of sacrifice lies the fundamental Catholic emphasis on solidarity, of our mutual accountability one to the other, which must also be at the heart of our prayer.[928] Understood in this context, the expiatory aspect of sacrifice becomes important:

In writing to console a father for the death of a son in early life, Lacordaire says: 'In losing one whose future appeared uncertain, we might believe that God was willing to save him, comparatively untried; but if, on the contrary, his life has been pure and holy, we are justified in believing that he has been a victim for the salvation of others, and that his blood will weigh in the balance wherein God will judge the world.'

Greenwell is not uncritical of some aspects of this doctrine. But it does at least take with the utmost seriousness the suffering and pain and 'all the unutterable blank and waste of natural life', and give them real value.[929] Hence our own sacrifices will never be in vain if they represent a free uniting of one's own meagre life and will with those of Christ: 'a Christian need never grieve over his deficient gifts, his scanty resources; let him unite himself to his Saviour's great continual work, and his own is already done.'[930]

This pervasive emphasis on sacrifice as a crucial dimension of any authentic spiritual life also has implications for Christian prayer. Greenwell notes that since the Fall there has been no prayer without sacrifice; and in the teaching of Christ prayer and sacrifice are never disunited:[931] 'sacrifice makes prayer possible; it opens the way to God'.[932] This is because it is supremely the cross that

> *binds* the soul to prayer. It is this sight that makes of every awakened soul a priest, an intercessor, no longer bringing, as does the mere nominal believer, his 'fruit of the lips' . . . but offering up to God *sacrifice through sacrifice*; no longer trusting in its own repentance, its own faith, its own prayer, but joining its every petition to the might of that prevailing blood, which is '*itself the* most powerful of all intercessions' (F. W. Faber).[933]

Hence by offering up our own will with our prayer, along with the one sacrifice of Christ, we pray truly.[934] Prayer 'is at once self-assertion and self-surrender':[935] it is free precisely 'because it is depending'.[936] Hence the power of the Psalms, which make sense only when we see them as 'covenant prayers', the fruit of a love that 'cannot exist but in reciprocity, [that] claims much, and yet continually brings something of its own'.[937] In prayer we are fellow-labourers with God, which is why prayer is work.[938]

Suffering and the divine love

Yet all this raises a major question: what about those who, unlike Lacordaire, suffer involuntarily? Greenwell ponders this in one of many lengthy footnotes to be found in her books. She suggests that

> a life filled with pain is perhaps meant by God to be a life filled with prayer. However blank and unintelligible it may be to men, its Godward aspect may be full of meaning. Stript of leaf and blossom, it may stand bare like a cross, appealing and interceding.

This is not at all to say that suffering is *medicinal*, let alone that it is good; but it is to say that it may be *expiatory*, in the manner of St Paul as well as of Lacordaire:

The Church of Rome, in its profound appreciation of that saying of St Paul's, 'I fill up that which is behind of the afflictions of Christ,' discovers in pain, even in that which is simply physical and inarticulate, a power which in the extent of its working can be but dimly guessed at, – a mighty power of *expiation*, ever joining itself to the one atonement, inseparable from that work, which has given a value to all suffering . . . Lacordaire, in words that do not at once disclose their awful depth of meaning, speaks of earth's mute and many sufferers as being 'the obscure victims of the cross which has saved them.'[939]

It may even be, she suggests, that our prayers in moments of agony are in some special manner granted immediate access to God: 'when the heart is driven into its deepest recess, it finds itself nearest to its God; but let its distress stop short of despair, which makes prayer impossible'.[940] In her study of the Quaker John Woolman she again reflects on the notion of expiation; but this time it is the sympathy, the shared suffering, of the wounded prophet which becomes redemptive. She movingly depicts Woolman making his own the desperate prayers of black slaves:

'It hath been computed that near one hundred thousand negroes have of late years been annually taken from the African coast by ships employed in the English trade. In procuring these slaves many children are stolen privately; wars are also encouraged among the negroes; *but all is at a great distance*. Many groans arise from dying men which we hear not. Many cries are uttered by widows and fatherless children which reach not our ears. Many cheeks are wet with tears, and faces sad with unutterable grief, which we see not. Cruel tyranny is encouraged! The hands of robbers are strengthened, and thousands reduced to abject misery who never injured us. In a feeling of the misery of these people, and of that great offence which is ministered to them, my tears have often been poured out before the Lord. And often under the sense of a deep revolt, and an overflowing stream of unrighteousness, my life has been a life of mourning, and tender desires are raised in me, that the nature of these practices may be laid to heart.'[941]

'These pages', Greenwell argues, 'show [Woolman] to us as a weeping prophet, as one of those men upon whose foreheads, because they sigh and cry for the abominations that be done upon the earth, God's mark of acceptance is set.'[942] This is spiritual compassion of the profoundest kind; and it brings us to the heart of the matter. For Greenwell it is

that deepened spirituality, which, like an extended natural science, is so continually widening the field of remote, unsuspected affinities, that at last few things stand before it alone or unallied; the grandeur of the whole connects them all, and the sense of great or little almost disappears. The things which bear upon man's spiritual and immortal destinies are not to be appreciated by number of weight or measure; and human life, when viewed under its moral significance, assumes the aspect of one of those grand prophetic visions, where 'the meanest things of every day,' the caldron and the hooks, the measuring-rod and the plumb-line, stand in the closest relation to the opened heaven and the glory of the terrible crystal – the throne, and Him that is seated upon it.[943]

This is a remarkable passage. Twelve years before Greenwell wrote *John Woolman*, Charles Darwin published, in *The origin of species*, his exploration of 'the nature of the relationship, by which all living and extinct beings are united by complex, radiating, and circuitous lines of affinities into one grand system'.[944] Here is Greenwell articulating a spiritual vision in which all things belong together; and its central pivot is the Cross, by and through which God's unconditional sympathy with a suffering world is manifested. The Cross thus stands at the centre of any spirituality worthy of the name, not because it 'explains the enigma of a blighted creation, or to infer that life and nature are not equally a problem whether we contemplate them from a Christian or a Pagan point of view', but because 'it consoles, as Love itself consoles, by the very presence of its sympathy. It is man's desolation met by the desolation of God.'[945]

Prayer

It is vital to see, first that this pivotal doctrine of sacrifice and sympathy is absolutely central for Greenwell, because it articulates the way of God with humanity; and, secondly, that for her the divine compassion is no mere paternalism from on high, but the manifestation of a profound kinship between humanity and its Creator. The first point is clear: for Greenwell 'the very idea of prayer is founded upon the belief in God's sympathy with man'[946] – a sympathy which culminates in the Incarnation: God's sympathy causes him to act, supremely (though not only) in becoming flesh: 'the facts of Christianity are *a mighty interference*'.[947] It follows that God can answer prayer, interfering in the natural processes of the universe as he has already done in becoming incarnate – but also that God can only do this when our prayer is a free surrendering of our own wills, so that God can use our freedom to accomplish his purposes. Greenwell has no time for a naive or simplistic approach to petitionary prayer:

> Only yesterday I heard a most charming lady telling a little girl who sat upon her knee, how her pony-carriage had lately run over a little boy, and how her horse rearing suddenly, had actually cleared the child without hurting him. The little girl listened with riveted attention. Then said the lady, '*Who* was it *made* the horse rear up just at that moment?' 'Who is it that always takes care of children, of *good* children?' 'Who puts them under the care of His pretty bright angels?' etc. I do not doubt but this, joined with the affectionate, reverent looks and tones of the speaker, made a good impression on a childish mind; but what could be more *false*? What if the horse had *not* reared? Was the child a wicked child, or God an unmindful God? . . . Surely there is a sense of God's overruling Providence far deeper than this, which looks behind events to principles; which trains the mind not to abject submission to a power which cannot be resisted, but to the free, loving resignation which a spiritual being renders to a Spirit, with whom love and obedience, *and an imparted affinity* have surely, though not yet perfectly, united him.[948]

Note the 'imparted affinity', underlining the points made above: it leads to the second point, the kinship between humanity and God, a kinship imparted in the Incarnation. And this introduces us to a central paradox: prayer is at once 'free, loving resignation', and yet it is no grovelling self-abasement:

> When I turned to the Psalms and Prophets, I was greeted by a voice which seemed silent in the continually reiterated *culpa mea, maxima culpa* of ordinary Christian prayer. I was met by a strain of bold and tender expostulation to which God himself seems to invite man, when He says, 'Come now, let us *reason* together.' I heard man address his Maker in language far indeed, far removed from the abjection of the books of devotion I had always used. I listened to words now of tender complaining, now of sorrowful and indignant pleading, to words such as on earth may pass between friends who deeply love, but do not as yet wholly understand each other.[949]

Greenwell introduces the Tractarian doctrine of reserve to assist in exploring this paradox. Prayer is the 'will of man brought to bear upon the will of God';[950] and although God's *nature* cannot change, God's *will* surely can.[951] She argues that 'all that we see around and within us testifies to the presence of a mighty opposing agency, and bears witness, also, to a reserve or economy of grace, a hiding of God's power, in which we can, even in this hiding, as through a glass darkly, even now discern a merciful purpose'.[952] Again, then, prayer is *work*, and we shouldn't expect it to be any easier than is the continuing work of redemption.[953]

This reserve enters into our prayer too:

> It is not every faithful Christian who can say unto his Lord, 'Thou hast given me my heart's desire, Thou hast not denied me the request of my lips'; neither can all of God's children join in that fervent ascription of the Psalmist's, 'I love the Lord *because* He has heard the voice of my petitions.' We hear another, a deeper voice exclaim, 'O my God, I cry in the day-time and Thou hearest not, and in the night season also I take no rest.'[954]

And yet this does not stop us praying; and what keeps us at it is *faith in prayer itself*. For '*Prayer is the instinct of the redeemed soul*.'[955] And it is always a corporate activity, a participation-in, or sympathy-with, the entire Body of Christ: 'intercession is the mother tongue of the whole family of Christ'.[956]

Spiritual anthropology

It is with this in mind that we may conclude by considering the other principal aspects of Greenwell's spirituality. She has a typically rich and subtle view of human nature, set out in an essay in *Liber humanitatis*.[957] She first notes that animals, though possessing consciousness as humans do, do not possess *choice*: an animal has no will.[958] She continues by stressing the inseparability of body and soul, mind and matter: scripture does not allow us to posit a soul that is utterly separable from the body:

the relation between mind and matter in the organized being of man is so intimate, their dependence and interdependence so close and radical, that though they are no doubt separable forces, we know not, nor probably shall ever know, where the action of one ceases and that of the other begins.[959]

Furthermore 'it is to the agency of the senses, that man owes many of his sweetest feelings of affection, his loftiest aspirations after excellence';[960] and 'those whom we really love are as dear to us in their bodies as they are in their souls'.[961] Hence too the importance of music, which, in its subtle appeal to both mind and senses, soul and body,

> opens a door, even into heaven – one that no man can shut. Our senses, and the nerves connected with them, are minute threads, conductors into a mighty, compactly-welded system which leads us into the very core of nature, and up to the very heart of God.[962]

Hence for Greenwell 'there is a real, close and subtle link between the sensual and the spiritual regions in man's nature'.[963] The spiritual takes priority, for it is, in her view, the source and principle of human freedom.[964] But the spiritual can also be demonic: 'if we consider this we shall see how it is that some (so-called) religious persons are not moral'.[965] Hence the vital importance of holding the sensual and the spiritual together; for

> when these two apparently opposing poles in our nature are touched, and touched *together* to their finest issues, a glow seems to spread over the whole outward world, of which the merely rational, intelligent man, though he were to stand and gaze before it for a millennium, would know nothing. All that is jarring and dissonant is hushed; creation itself is self-reconciled, touched outwardly with tender light, suffused with inner warmth and intimate joy. All things seem to burst forth in sudden beauty.[966]

This is dangerous, and could easily become a narcissistic escapism: 'the mind loses its critical, distinguishing property, yields to passive enjoyment, and asks for nothing beyond what the moment gives'.[967] Yet the rich interrelation of the sensual and the spiritual is capable of experiences of which reason will never be capable, such as the mother's tender love for her child.[968] Hence 'it can never be well with man until his whole nature is restored'.[969] Our spiritual and physical natures cannot do without each other.

And this, as we might expect, has important consequences. In her early *On the education of the imbecile*, Greenwell argues that the very dependence of the soul on the body is itself an argument for taking the body seriously:

> the more we learn of the soul's dependence upon the body, the more we recognise its actual, if not entire subjugation to the organism it has to work through, the more thoroughly we shall believe in the soul's distinct existence, and separate power and freedom. When we have learnt all that is at

present known about brain and cell, and nerve and tissue, we shall find
that we have extended, and not in any degree exhausted, the study of the
rational, affectionate man.[970]

Both body and soul are 'originally beautiful, originally noble; each is "created free,
although born in chains."'[971] Yet physiology needs something greater than itself to
complement it: 'physiology stands in need of Christianity as its complement'.[972]
Christ is 'the restored perfection of *our whole nature*, the marriage of the purified soul
with the glorified body – a union without which neither can exert its full powers or
know its true blessedness'.[973]

It is important to stress that for Greenwell this concern to hold together sense and
spirit, soul and body, involves precisely the fulfilment of both, and in particular opens
up to us a spiritual world of otherwise unimaginable richness. Greenwell articulates
this powerfully in *Colloquia crucis*:

> There is a spiritual world within man as well as one without and beyond
> him; a world upon which . . . many of the abnormal conditions of our own
> nature, such as dreams, delirium, and insanity, give us strange out-looks;
> indeed, our own nature, without passing into these extreme transforma-
> tions, can sometimes, when wound up to its highest pitch, through
> religious enthusiasm or other vehement emotion, touch upon the borders
> of a super-sensual world; a world of which our present life is but the pale
> shadow; a world of fuller bloom, of freer life, and of richer energy. A
> super-sensual world I have called it, yet is it one fearfully allied with sense,
> and one to which the senses open the door, while through them man is as it
> were *wooed* to enter upon the strange and ruined splendour of a palace that
> was once his home.[974]

The importance of dreams and fantasy

How do we gain access to this spiritual world? First, in our dreams, and in all that we
so easily dismiss as illusion in human life. In *On the education of the imbecile* Greenwell
says that we can learn much from what is disordered in human nature: 'in dreaming
. . . the soul is often stirred to depths of anguish, and raised to heights of ecstasy, such
as actual life under its present limited conditions can never admit it to.'[975]

Secondly, we gain access through fairy-tale and folk-lore, where again the creative
value of illusion and imagination is essential. In an essay entitled 'Folk-lore', Dora
Greenwell says that true folk-lore 'demands, on the part of the [hearer], that sort of
uncritical self-surrender which is not possible to a cultivated, introvertive, reflective
era'.[976] It is something associated above all with childhood; 'and hence all minds that
are most deeply imbued with the essential spirit of poetry have been most quick to
recognise that unity between the poetic and the childlike nature'.[977] The poet can
enter the 'vast, illimitable, and still *beyond*' region which the child knows well, and in
which it plays:[978]

> I can remember, when a very little girl, playing along with one of my
> brothers in a half-darkened hayloft with two kittens and an old stable

lantern, which we had agreed should stand good for 'two Chinese princesses in a pagoda.' So far as I can now recall my own private sentiments, I do not believe I really thought they were *quite* princesses, but I am sure that I did not imagine them to be at all kittens! The glory about them was a real thing. I believe it is this power of creating and absolutely yielding to an illusion which is in the first instance voluntary and conscious, which makes play so entrancing to children, and the utter want of ability to do so which in after life makes play to grown-up people such very hard work – mere playing at playing.[979]

This rich semi-illusory world may be what animals experience when they dream: 'It is not impossible that animals owe much of the happiness which . . . we may be certain they possess, to a continual half-conscious dream in which they are at one with all their surroundings.'[980] And she continues:

All persons whose nature is at all idealistic will be at times conscious of a strange feeling, experienced sometimes at very long widely-separated intervals, when the sensitive individual and the sensuous world seem to meet and fully mingle. At such times the world seems beautiful, and individual life wide, warm, and young. All is quiet and dreamlike, yet full of expectancy and wonder; the most ordinary prosaic scenes become magical, without ceasing to be homely and familiar. The market-place, for instance, of some old provincial city will appear to be filled with clear golden sunlight, where the shops, the ancient houses, the strange uncouth signboards, the militiamen gossiping and lounging about the doors of the public-houses, will remind one of some story by Tieck or Hoffman, where an alluring *diablerie* lies hidden under life's apparent matter-of-fact routine; where people stand about the streets chatting, smoking, idling; yet the student who is passing along is, for aught we know, an adept or a Rosicrucian; and the wandering wizened pedlar, who is crying his goods so cheerily, may possibly be ready to sell you the *peau de chagrin*, or to traffic with you for your own soul, just as it may happen to suit him and you. There is a spell abroad.[981]

But if folk-lore and the world of play refuse to separate the supernatural from the natural, they do insist on separating good from evil, a distinction central to all fairy-tales. 'It may be observed that folk-lore generally bears a strong witness to that instinctive belief which seems part of man's reasonable nature, in two great opposed central forces of good and evil, to the *living* heart of which whatever of right belongs to either naturally converges, and draws along with it whatever flotsam and jetsam it finds in its way. Good coheres together, so does evil.'[982]

Greenwell goes on to stress the fact that in much folk-lore evil derives its power from nature, which is not as friendly to human beings as is often supposed:

Who can wonder that the agricultural labourer, the miner, or the fisher on the lonely seas, should be in general so utterly insensible to the charm more cultured spirits feel so deeply, in her more stern and savage moods, which to him are simply suggestive of added toil, difficulty, danger, and possibly death. To say the least they are but to him, in the words of a Southern servant, who, riding with his master through some of the most wild and beautiful scenery in Westmoreland, answered to his admiring appealing 'Well, Anthony, what do you think of all this?' by simply, '*Very bare pasture, sir.*'[983]

Greenwell's point here is not so much the unimaginativeness of working people but precisely their ability to see what aesthetes may not: the enduring capacity for evil that exists in the natural world; and she fascinatingly links this with St Paul's idea that even the outward creation 'groans, being burdened'.[984]

Greenwell's stress on the value of fantasy must, however, always be held together with her overriding emphasis on the integrity of the sensual and the spiritual – and, beyond both, the principle of sacrifice. In the final analysis 'there is a sadness in all Idealism; it lifts the soul into a region where it cannot now dwell; it must return to earth, and it is hard for it not to do so at the shock of a keen revulsion'.[985] It is like the apostles descending from the mount of Transfiguration.[986] It is even more like what Christians believe God did at Christmas.

Women and the spiritual life

A final point needs to be made. Greenwell has a typically original approach to the role of women in the spiritual life. She accepts the teaching of Genesis in envisaging female nature as less complete within itself; but she deprecates the notion that this renders women somehow inferior. 'A woman's best praise can no longer consist, as it has done hitherto, in being told that she has written *like a man*.'[987] She wants to see the Church doing more to make use of the distinctive contributions women can offer:

> To a society, unrenewed in the mass, the hidden life of a Christian remains a mystery, requiring to be translated into the intelligible language of a life of holy love, so that those who run may read . . . the Christian faith needs at first to be presented, not as a doctrine, but as a life.[988]

This is where women, especially single women, who have offered their lives as a sacrifice for the good of the community, have a crucial part to play. It is precisely women who embody the divine sympathy:

> to her, *sympathy is power*, because to her it is knowledge; and it is this ability to feel with others, as well as for them, that takes all hardness or ostentation from instruction and counsel – all implied superiority from pity and consolation. The woman, or man, of true feeling does not *come down* upon the sinner or sufferer, from another region, but is always, for the time being, on a level with those that are addressed – even able to see things as they see them.[989]

Conclusion

Dora Greenwell's achievement is a unique drawing-together of a vast range of insights and truths into a coherent whole. Some of her writing is obscure, and some sentimental. But she works hard to produce a way of seeing the world, and of living in it, which both accepts some of the insights of science and yet is firmly anchored in a distinctively Christian framework and dynamism. She anticipates Chesterton in her vigorous use of paradox, and Evelyn Underhill in her thoroughgoing exploration of the mystery of sacrifice. And she comes across, not as some stereotypical Victorian spinster, but as a romantic with a tough and rigorous intellect, a prophet with time to play, a fighter for social justice with a glint of mischief in the eye. 'That is a miserable idea', she exclaimed once to a friend, 'of perfection – to make the two ends *meet*. I should like them to *tie in a handsome bow*.'[990]

Spirituality and the Victorian novel: George Eliot and Charles Dickens

The inclusion of some reflections on two of the greatest Victorian novelists can be justified on several grounds, in ascending order of importance: first, because their novels were far more widely read than (say) the poems of Shelley or the sermons of Newman – nearly all of them were serialized in monthly instalments; secondly, because their authors' awareness of the experiences and aspirations of 'ordinary' people was as great as, if not greater than, that of many clergy, let alone 'spiritual' writers; thirdly, because the insights the novels have to offer in relation to the spiritual life justify their inclusion anyway, even though neither of the authors to be considered here was conventionally religious. What follows makes no claim to be a comprehensive survey of a subject already copiously explored by others: rather it is a reflection on some aspects of the novels that are relevant to English spirituality.

The lives of Charles Dickens (1812–70) and George Eliot (1819–80) are too well known for anything but the briefest summary to be required. Dickens was born in Portsmouth, of a family that was soon to be constantly threatened by debt and did in fact spend some months in the Marshalsea debtors' prison while Dickens was a boy. He had, therefore, little formal education, and earned his living principally as a journalist. His major novels, from *Pickwick papers* (1836–7) onwards, first appeared in cheap and accessible serial form, and were almost all hugely popular, reflecting his social concern and passionate advocacy on behalf of the urban poor. George Eliot (whose real name was Mary Ann (Marian) Evans) was born in the Midlands countryside, the youngest surviving child of an estate agent. As a young adult she was deeply influenced by progressive intellectual thought, and was for a while assistant editor of the radical *Westminster Review*. In 1851 she met George Henry Lewes, a literary figure in London, who was separated from his wife: in 1854 the two began to live together, and remained together until his death in 1878. The first of her major fictional works, *Scenes from clerical life*, was published in 1858, and the last, *Daniel Deronda*, in 1876.

Neither Dickens nor Eliot was conventionally religious. Dickens did for a time attend a school at Chatham run by a young Baptist minister; but he had little time for formal religion, and frequently excoriated it in his novels. This is how he describes the deeply unappealing Mrs Joe in *Great expectations*:

> Mrs Joe was a very clean housekeeper, but had an exquisite art of making her cleanliness more uncomfortable and unacceptable than dirt itself.

Cleanliness is next to Godliness, and some people do the same by their religion.[991]

There is no shortage of other examples.[992] What his novels communicate vividly is a profound sense of the *unattractiveness* of so much conventional piety. He is aware that this sense could arise from simple misunderstanding: thus Pip, in *Great expectations*, remembers thinking as a child that the fact that he was to 'walk in the same all the days of my life', as the Prayer Book Catechism stipulates,

> laid me under an obligation always to go through the village from our house in one particular direction, and never to vary it by turning down by the wheelwright's or up by the mill.[993]

But he is also aware that some professedly religious people are at best otherworldly, and at worst downright nasty. Arguably the nastiest of all is the unspeakable Mrs Clennam in *Little Dorrit*, whose son (as he supposes) recalls

> the sleepy Sunday of his boyhood, when, like a military deserter, he was marched to chapel by a picquet of teachers three times a day, morally handcuffed to another boy; and when he would willingly have bartered two meals of indigestible sermon for another ounce or two of inferior mutton at his scanty dinner in the flesh. There was the interminable Sunday of his nonage; when his mother, stern of face and unrelenting of heart, would sit all day behind a bible – bound like her own construction of it in the hardest, barest, and straitest boards.[994]

He recalls the family household: 'at the heart of it his mother presided, inflexible of face, indomitable of will, firmly holding all the secrets of her own and his father's life, and austerely opposing herself, front to front, to the great final secret of all life'.[995] A hint of what that 'final secret' is for Dickens appears at the end of the novel, when the grim unforgiving nature of Mrs Clennam's piety is met and overcome by the gentle redemptive forgiveness of Little Dorrit's.[996] Sympathy, not religious observance, is what counts. The point is beautifully illustrated in *Great expectations*: young Pip tells good Joe Gargery that he has lied, that he thinks he has lied because he is common, and that (for the first time in his life) he wishes he were not common:

> This was a case of metaphysics, at least as difficult for Joe to deal with, as for me. But Joe took the case altogether out of the region of metaphysics, and by that means vanquished it.
>
> 'There's one thing you may be sure of, Pip,' said Joe, after some rumination, 'namely, that lies is lies. Howsever they come, they didn't ought to come, and they come from the father of lies, and work round to the same. Don't you tell no more of 'em, Pip. *That* ain't the way to get out of being common, old chap . . . If you can't get to be oncommon through going straight, you'll never get to do it through going crooked.'[997]

'That was a memorable day for me,' says Pip afterwards, 'for it made great changes in me.'[998] Like the Calvinist, he undergoes a profound conviction of sin; but there is little that is specifically religious either about the experience or about what follows.

George Eliot's relationship to conventional religion was altogether more complex. At school she became a convert to Evangelicalism (though she was never a Dissenter);[999] her encounter with a freethinking Coventry manufacturer alienated her from Christianity, though she remained strongly influenced by Christian concepts of love and duty. In 1859 she wrote in a letter:

> I think I hardly ever spoke to you of the strong hold Evangelical Christianity had on me from the age of fifteen to two and twenty and of the abundant intercourse I had had with earnest people of various religious sects. When I was at Geneva, I had not yet lost the attitude of antagonism which belongs to the renunciation of *any* belief – also, I was very unhappy, and in a state of discord and rebellion towards my own lot. Ten years of experience have wrought great changes in that inward self: I have no longer any antagonism towards any faith in which human sorrow and human longing for purity have expressed themselves; on the contrary, I have a sympathy with it that predominates over all argumentative tendencies. I have not returned to dogmatic Christianity – to the acceptance of any set of doctrines as a creed, and a superhuman revelation of the Unseen – but I see in it the highest expression of the religious sentiment that has yet found its place in the history of mankind, and I have the profoundest interest in the inward life of sincere Christians in all ages.[1000]

The letter reflects the nuanced and sensitive attitude she was to adopt to the religion she had rejected, and introduces us to the vital concept of sympathy to which we shall return. That rejection was certainly not uninformed: Eliot translated one of the pillars of nineteenth-century German Liberal divinity: David Strauss' *Life of Jesus* (1846), as well as the even more radical *The essence of Christianity* by Ludwig Feuerbach (1854). What she lost was not her spirituality but the doctrinal beliefs which had hitherto underpinned it; and that left her with an abiding suspicion, not of those who could still in good conscience accept such beliefs, but of those whose lives failed to reflect their beliefs. In *The mill on the floss* she reproves people who reject others on the grounds that 'society' demands it, whilst claiming assent to the higher authority of God:

> That authority had furnished a very explicit answer to persons who might inquire where their social duties began, and might be inclined to take wide views as to the starting-point. The answer had not turned on the ultimate good of society, but on 'a certain man' who was found in trouble by the wayside.[1001]

Eliot had less time for Evangelicals than for mainstream Anglicans and Nonconformists. An article she wrote in 1855 lambasts (Evangelical) preachers: 'the clergy are, practically, the most irresponsible of all talkers';[1002] and she finds little trace of 'really spiritual joys and sorrows' in the discourses of the luckless Dr Cumming she is reviewing. But she retains a deep respect for many other aspects of religious practice, perhaps especially for worship. In *Adam Bede*, Lisbeth is helped by the funeral service for her husband:

Lisbeth had a vague belief that the psalm was doing her husband good; it was part of that decent burial which she would have thought it a greater wrong to withhold from him than to have caused him many unhappy days while he was living. The more there was said about her husband, the more there was done for him, surely the safer he would be. It was poor Lisbeth's blind way of feeling that human love and pity are a ground of faith in some other love.[1003]

This can be read simply as a celebration of 'implicit' religion. But the reference to 'pity' is significant, as we shall see. Contrast Lisbeth's response to liturgy with that of another character in *Adam Bede*, the tragic Hetty:

Religious doctrines had taken no hold on Hetty's mind: she was one of those numerous people who have had godfathers and godmothers, learned their catechism, been confirmed, and gone to church every Sunday; and yet, for any practical result of strength in life, or trust in life, have never appropriated a single Christian idea or Christian feeling.[1004]

In general terms, then, Eliot is inclined to judge religious beliefs not simply by the *general* effect they have on those holding them, but by the *specific* criterion of whether those who hold them manifest the virtue of sympathy, or compassion, or pity. Before exploring this in more detail it is worth briefly looking at a few more examples of how she describes religious beliefs and people. In her first major fictional work, *Scenes from clerical life*, she writes:

Religious ideas have the fate of melodies, which, once set afloat in the world, are taken up by all sorts of instruments, some of them woefully coarse, feeble, or out of tune, until people are in danger of crying out the melody itself is detestable.[1005]

She leaves open the question of whether the melody really *is* detestable, or has simply been unlucky in its choice of performers. In *Middlemarch* Mr Bulstrode is described, not as a hypocrite, but as 'simply a man whose desires had been stronger than his theoretic beliefs, and who had gradually explained the gratification of his desires into satisfactory agreement with those beliefs'.[1006] And in *The mill on the floss* (in a chapter exquisitely entitled 'A variation of Protestantism unknown to Bossuet'[1007]), she describes the piety of the townsfolk in her fictional East Anglian river port with subtlety and humour:

Their theory of life had its core of soundness, as all theories must have on which decent and prosperous families have been reared and have flourished; but it had the very slightest tincture of theology. If, in the maiden days of the Dodson sisters, their bibles opened more easily at some parts than others, it was because of dried tulip petals, which had been distributed quite impartially, without preference for the historical, devotional, or doctrinal. Their religion was of a simple, semi-pagan kind, but there was no heresy in it, if heresy properly means choice, for they didn't know there was any other religion, except that of chapel-goers, which appeared to run in families, like asthma . . . The religion of the Dodsons consisted in revering whatever was customary and respectable: it was necessary to be baptised, else one could not be buried in the churchyard, and to take the sacrament before death as a security against more dimly understood perils; but it was of equal necessity to have the proper pall-bearers and well-cured hams at one's funeral, and to leave an unimpeachable will. A Dodson would not be taxed with the omission of anything that was becoming.[1008]

In *Romola*, a historical novel set in Renaissance Florence, she explores the matter altogether more seriously. She says of the ascetic reforming Dominican Savonarola that his

need of personal predominance . . . his enigmatic visions, and his false certitude about the divine intentions, never ceased, in his own large soul, to be ennobled by that fervid piety, that passionate sense of the infinite, that active sympathy, that clear-sighted demand for the subjection of selfish interests to the general good, which he had in common with the greatest of mankind.[1009]

What is really interesting is what follows. Romola is drawn to Savonarola after the collapse of her marriage to Tito, not because of his dogmatic certainty, or even because he had wisely warned her not to run away, but because by submitting herself to his teaching

she had found an immediate satisfaction for moral needs which all the previous culture and experience of her life had left hungering. Fra Girolamo's voice had waked in her mind a reason for living, apart from personal enjoyment and personal affection; but it was a reason that seemed to need feeding with greater forces than she possessed within herself, and her submissive use of all offices of the Church was simply a watching and waiting if by any means fresh strength might come. The pressing problem for Romola just then was not to settle questions of controversy, but to keep alive that flame of unselfish emotion by which a life of sadness might still be a life of active love.[1010]

This is crucial: Christian faith and practice gave Romola a degree of objectivity, an awareness of what would now be called a 'significant other', which her life otherwise now lacked. It proved, however, only a transient support. At the novel's terrible climax, Romola uncovers and undermines the essentially self-regarding basis of Savonarola's piety:

'Do you, then, know so well what will further the coming of God's kingdom, Father, that you will dare to despise the plea of mercy – of justice – of faithfulness to your own teaching? Has the French king, then, brought renovation to Italy? Take care, Father, lest your enemies have some reason when they say, that in your visions of what will further God's kingdom you see only what will strengthen your own party.'

'And that is true!' said Savonarola, with flashing eyes. Romola's voice had seemed to him in that moment the voice of his enemies. 'The cause of my party *is* the cause of God's kingdom.'

'I do not believe it!' said Romola, her whole frame shaken with passionate repugnance. 'God's kingdom is something wider – else, let me stand outside it with the beings that I love.'

The two faces were lit up, each with an opposite emotion, each with an opposite certitude. Further words were impossible.[1011]

This tremendous passage reveals more of Eliot's own piety. Slightly later in *Romola* she suggests that all 'energetic belief' has as its implicit formula a ring of egoism (which might be one of the reasons she disliked Spurgeon's preaching); but she nonetheless acknowledges that, if the danger of such belief is that it risks turning demonic, the comparable danger of resorting solely to 'tender fellow-feeling' is that it 'is apt to be timid and sceptical towards the larger aims without which life cannot rise into religion'.[1012] It is a hard dilemma: Romola herself finally finds a way of resolving it; but Savonarola does not, and pays the terrible penalty. But even then Eliot does not altogether dismiss him: as he dies in the flames, he experiences

> the agony of sinking from the vision of glorious achievement into that deep shadow where he could only say, 'I count as nothing: darkness encompasses me: yet the light I saw was the true light.'[1013]

There is a similarly climactic moment at the end of Eliot's last novel, *Daniel Deronda*, in which Gwendolen has to face the extraordinary fact (extraordinary not only to her but to many of Eliot's readers) that Deronda is Jewish, will marry a Jewish woman and will devote the rest of his life to the Zionist cause. Eliot comments:

> There comes a terrible moment to many souls when the great movements of the world, the larger destinies of mankind, which have lain aloof in newspapers and other neglected reading, enter like an earthquake into their own lives . . . Then it is that the submission of the soul to the Highest is tested, and even in the eyes of frivolity life looks out from the scene of human struggle with the awful face of duty, and a religion shows itself which is something else than a private consolation.[1014]

Behind Eliot's own writing lies the thought of those she had read and studied, and perhaps especially of Feuerbach and Darwin. Feuerbach taught her that religious belief is, in his view, an imaginative necessity for human beings, and a projection of our interest in our own species:

> religion is the childlike condition of humanity . . . Hence the historical progress of religion consists in this: that what by an earlier religion was regarded as objective, is now recognised as subjective; that is, what was formerly contemplated and worshipped as God is now perceived to be something *human*.[1015]

It is worth noting that Feuerbach did acknowledge the need for some kind of objective reference point in human lives: 'we know the man by the object, by his conception of what is external to himself; in it his nature becomes evident; this object is his manifested nature, his true objective *ego*'.[1016] But this still reads as though the external object or aim is somehow reducible to a projection of the subject.[1017]

Eliot read Darwin's *The origin of species* when it appeared;[1018] and she herself wrote about the 'Development theory', meaning not only the idea that organisms evolve from earlier ones, but also that, as her partner G. H. Lewes put it in 1855:

> A change has come over the spirit of enquiry . . . In Geology, in Physiology,
> in History and in Art, we are all now bent on tracing the phases of develop-
> ment. To understand the *grown* we try to follow the *growth*.[1019]

Quite apart from its implicit questioning of the need for a creator at all, the influence of Darwinism on English spirituality could broadly be said to have been both destructive and constructive: destructive, in arguing for the survival of the fittest at the expense of the others, and thus for the primacy of competition as a motivating force in life; constructive, in pointing to the primal kinship that exists between human beings and other species (and indeed with primitive human beings), a kinship that aroused in Victorian England a deepened and more enlightened sympathy. And it is this concept of sympathy, which has already appeared frequently in the course of this chapter, to which Eliot and Dickens make a significant contribution.

The idea recurs frequently in Dickens' work. In *Great expectations*, he presents the narrator, Pip, as someone whose youthful act of generosity (prompted by fear) is replaced by snobbery and self-centredness once he inherits money, but whose character is transformed at the end of the novel as he becomes compassionate towards his threatened benefactor Magwitch. As Magwitch dies, Pip

> thought of the two men who went up into the Temple to pray, and I knew
> there were no better words that I could say beside his bed, than 'O Lord, be
> merciful to him, a sinner!'[1020]

Yet that sympathy costs Pip little. In the later novel *Little Dorrit*, we have already noted that the eponymous central character exhibits a capacity for compassion that becomes redemptive, not only with regard to the fearsome Mrs Clennam, but also with regard to the much more significant character Arthur Clennam, whose sudden catastrophic business failure and imprisonment is redeemed by her enduring love. This could be seen simply as one person showing to another the very compassion she had already received from him. But it is not that simple. Both Little Dorrit and Arthur Clennam experience what would now be described as 'deprived' childhoods, the latter (as we have seen) emotionally deprived, the former physically so. Both, however, succeed in enduring this deprivation without recourse to festering resentment or brutalization, a point all the more notable in the work of a writer acutely conscious of just how destructive any kind of deprivation can be. Thus Dickens describes Arthur Clennam as a man who had deep-rooted in his nature, a belief in all the gentle and good things his life had been without. Bred in meanness and hard dealing, this had rescued him to be a man of honorable mind and open hand. Bred in coldness and severity, this had rescued him to have a warm and sympathetic heart. Bred in a creed too darkly audacious to pursue, through its process of reversing the making of man in the image of his Creator to the making of his Creator in the image of an erring man, this had rescued him to judge not, and in humility to be merciful, and have hope and charity.[1021]

Dickens does not explain *why* or *how* Clennam is like this: he simply tells us that he is. Had he been like his mother, damaged beyond redemption by a deformed religiosity, Little Dorrit's compassion would doubtless have done him little good. It is, then, in part a question of how we ourselves handle what is done to us which determines our capacity to receive the free gift of others' compassion when we most stand in need of it.

But only in part. In the famous adventure story *A tale of two cities*, Dickens goes further. The ultimate triumph of goodness is possible only because a hitherto worthless character performs an act of compassion that costs him his own life, but through which he discovers at the very end an inner peacefulness that had otherwise eluded him.[1022] Romola, in George Eliot's novel, points the moral:

> 'If you mean to act nobly and seek to know the best things God has put within reach of men, you must learn to fix your mind on that end, and not on what will happen to you because of it. And remember, if you were to choose something lower, and make it the rule of your life to seek your own pleasure and escape from what is disagreeable, calamity might come just the same.'[1023]

Sympathy – or indeed the discovery of any enduring meaning in life – involves sacrifice, or at the very least the risk of it. Eliot's own novels are full of this subject. Sympathy is 'the one poor word which includes all our best insight and our best love';[1024] In 1869 she wrote, in a letter to Harriet Beecher Stowe that reflects the influence of the 'Development theory':

> I believe religion . . . has to be modified – 'developed,' according to the dominant phrase – and that a religion more perfect than any yet prevalent, must express less care for personal consolation, and a more deeply-awing sense of responsibility to man, springing from sympathy with that which of all things is most certainly known to us, the difficulty of the human lot.[1025]

And, in perhaps her greatest novel, *Middlemarch*:

> There is no general doctrine which is not capable of eating out our morality if unchecked by the deep-seated habit of direct fellow-feeling with individual fellow-men.[1026]

It is exactly the lack of this sympathy that she finds so disagreeable in some religious people. And in her critique of the Evangelical Dr Cumming she articulates her criticisms in detail:

Dr Cumming's theory ... is that actions are good or evil according as they are prompted or not prompted by an exclusive reference to the 'glory of God.' God, then, in Dr Cumming's conception, is a being who has no pleasure in the exercise of love and truthfulness and justice, considered as effecting the well-being of his creatures; He has satisfaction in us only in so far as we exhaust our motives and dispositions of all relation to our fellow-beings, and replace sympathy with men by anxiety for the 'glory of God.' The deed of Grace Darling, when she took a boat in the storm to rescue drowning men and women, was not good if it was only compassion that nerved her arm and impelled her to brave death for the chance of saving others; it was only good if she asked herself – Will this redound to the glory of God? ... A man is not to be just from a feeling of justice; he is not to help his fellow-men out of goodwill to his fellow-men; he is not to be a tender husband and father out of affection; all these natural muscles and fibres are to be torn away and replaced by a patent steel-spring – anxiety for the 'glory of God.' Happily, the constitution of human nature forbids the complete prevalence of such a theory. Fatally powerful as religious systems have been, human nature is stronger and wider than religious systems, and though dogmas may hamper, they cannot absolutely repress its growth ... But next to that hatred of the enemies of God which is the principle of persecution, there perhaps has been no perversion more obstructive of true moral development than this substitution of a reference to the glory of God for the direct promptings of the sympathetic feelings.[1027]

It is fascinating to speculate on how John Henry Newman might have responded to this argument. Eliot herself later concedes that orthodox Christianity is not fairly represented here: and that belief in a God whose love and sympathy reaches its culmination in Jesus as 'God manifest in the flesh' has fostered and enlarged the love and sympathy of millions of adherents. Her criticism is both with *perversions* of Christian doctrine, notably as represented by Dr Cumming, and with the *exclusiveness* of Christian faith insofar as it may suggest that there is no genuine compassion outside it.[1028]

Eliot is in no doubt that suffering itself is intrinsically destructive.[1029] Nor does she perceive nature as somehow possessing a capacity to elicit our highest feelings, in the way that Wordsworth did.[1030] What she is arguing is that

surely, surely the only true knowledge of our fellow-man is that which enables us to feel with him – which gives us a fine ear for the heart-pulses that are beating under the mere clothes of circumstance and opinion. Our subtlest analysis of schools and sects must miss the essential truth, unless it be lit up by the love that sees in all forms of human thought and work, the life and death struggles of separate human beings.[1031]

This capacity to sympathize comprises a number of ingredients. First, it has to do with feelings. Eliot shows us what she means by this in *Adam Bede*, where Adam says to his brother:

'Nay, Seth, lad; I'm not for laughing at no man's religion. Let 'em follow their consciences, that's all. Only I think it 'ud be better if their consciences 'ud let 'em stay quiet i' the church – there's a deal to be learnt there. And there's such a thing as being over-speritial; we must have something beside Gospel i' this world. Look at the canals, an' th' aqueducs, an' th' coal-pit engines, and Arkwright's mills there at Cromford; a man must learn summat beside Gospel to make them things, I reckon. But t'hear some o' them preachers, you'd think as a man must be doing nothing all's life but shutting's eyes and looking what's a-going on inside him. I know a man must have the love o' God in his soul, and the Bible's God's word. But what does the Bible say? Why, it says as God put his sperrit into the workman as built the tabernacle, to make him do all the carved work and things as wanted a nice hand. And this is my way o' looking at it: there's the sperrit o' God in all things and all times – weekday as well as Sunday – and i' the great works and inventions, and i' the figuring and the mechanics. And God helps us with our headpieces and our hands as well as with our souls; and if a man does bits o' jobs out o' working hours . . . he's doing more good, and he's just as near to God, as if he was running after some preacher and a-praying and a-groaning.'[1032]

'Feelings' here are not simply a spontaneous rush of emotion: they have to do with what is essentially spiritual in our make-up – and, as Christians would want to say, with the work of the Holy Spirit within and around us. Adam, an uneducated labouring man, is intensely aware of these spiritual realities:

'There's things go on in the soul, and times when feelings come into you like a rushing mighty wind, as the Scripture says, and part your life in two a'most, so as you look back on yourself as if you was somebody else. Those are things as you can't bottle up in a 'do this' and 'do that;' and I'll go so far with the strongest Methodist ever you'll find. That shows me there's deep, speritial things in religion. You can't make much out wi' talking about it, but you feel it.'[1033]

Secondly, sympathy involves a contemplative ability to see what is really happening to people, a point sharply made by Dickens in *Oliver Twist*: noting how we all too easily read into situations what we want to see there, rather than what *is* there, he says:

Men who look on nature, and their fellow-men, and cry that all is dark and gloomy, are in the right; but the sombre colours are reflections from their own jaundiced eyes and hearts. The real hues are delicate, and need a clearer vision.[1034]

George Eliot constantly stresses the importance of realism, in the sense of seeing accurately what is really happening, what is *true*. She wrote in an early essay:

The notion that peasants are joyous, that the typical moment to represent a man in a smock-frock is when he is cracking a joke and showing a row of sound teeth, that cottage matrons are usually buxom, and village children necessarily rosy and merry, are prejudices difficult to dislodge from the artistic mind, which looks for its subjects into literature instead of life . . . But no one who has seen much of actual ploughmen thinks them jocund; no one who is well acquainted with the English peasantry can pronounce them merry.[1035]

Thirdly, as we have seen, true sympathy involves the willingness to cope with adversity creatively, in the manner of Little Dorrit, who is a supremely convincing example of the *attractiveness* of the good. By contrast another character in the same novel, the enigmatic and reclusive Miss Wade, has been brutalized by her own repressive upbringing. In Eliot's *Silas Marner*, the eponymous hero is, as it were, always on the receiving end, first of adversity and later of blessing; but he is not simply a passive recipient of both – the way he handles the one determines his capacity in time to receive and respond to the other.

Finally, true sympathy involves a costly willingness to act for and with others; and it is this in the end which authenticates it:[1036] 'the tale of the Divine Pity was never yet believed from lips that were not felt to be moved by human pity'.[1037] And Eliot represents the fervent Primitive Methodist preacher Dinah as seeking in prayer exactly the sympathy Eliot writes about:

> She closed her eyes, that she might feel more intensely the presence of a Love and Sympathy deeper and more tender than was breathed from the earth and sky. That was often Dinah's mode of praying in solitude. Simple to close her eyes, and to feel herself enclosed by the Divine Presence; then gradually her fears, yearning anxieties for others, melted away like ice-crystals in a warm ocean.[1038]

In this connection it is perhaps Daniel Deronda, in Eliot's eponymous novel, who is her most fully developed exemplar of sympathy. He 'had the stamp of rarity in a subdued fervour of sympathy, an activity of imagination on behalf of others, which did not show itself effusively, but was continually seen in acts of considerateness that struck his companions as moral eccentricity'.[1039] It involved an inclination to 'take care of the fellow least able to take care of himself';[1040] 'persons attracted him . . . in proportion to the possibility of his defending them, rescuing them, telling upon their lives with some sort of redeeming influence; and he had to resist an inclination, easily accounted for, to withdraw coldly from the fortunate'.[1041]

At the same time, Deronda is a thinker – not someone simply drawn by the pull of sentiment or pity. 'He wanted some way of keeping emotion and its progeny of sentiments – which make the savours of life – substantial and strong in the face of a reflectiveness that threatened to nullify all differences.'[1042] Later, Eliot shows that what she has in mind is an emotional intelligence:

> since the unemotional intellect may carry us into a mathematical dreamland where nothing is but what is not, perhaps an emotional intellect may have absorbed into its passionate vision of possibilities some truth of what will be – the more comprehensive massive life feeding theory with new material, as the sensibility of the artist seizes combinations which science

explains and justifies . . . We must be patient with the inevitable makeshift of our human thinking, whether in its sum total or in the separate minds that have made the sum. Columbus had some impressions about himself which we call superstitions, and used some arguments which we disapprove; but he had also some true physical conceptions, and he had the passionate patience of genius to make them tell on mankind. The world has made up its mind rather contemptuously about those who were deaf to Columbus.[1043]

This brings us finally to the notion of prayer as it is explored in these novels. Eliot confesses to finding prayer intellectually impossible;[1044] and Romola also finds the notion of prayer impossible at a critical moment for her, despite her religious submission to Savonarola: 'the activity of her thought excluded a mental state of which the essence is expectant passivity'.[1045] Dickens, however, is more positive, albeit ironically. One of his innumerable and unforgettable characters is Jerry Cruncher, in *A tale of two cities*: a bank clerk by day and a body-snatcher by night, with stand-up hair and a devout Christian wife. He cannot bear to allow his wife to pray because of the fear that this might affect his lifestyle. She says pleadingly to him: 'I was not praying against you; I was praying for you.' And he retorts, to her and their son:

> 'You weren't. And if you were, I won't be took the liberty with. Here! your mother's a nice woman, young Jerry, going a praying agin your father's prosperity. You've got a dutiful mother, you have, my son. You've got a religious mother, you have, my boy: going and flopping herself down, and praying that the bread-and-butter may be snatched out of the mouth of her only child.'
>
> Master Cruncher (who was in his shirt) took this very ill, and, turning to his mother, strongly deprecated any praying away of his personal board . . .
>
> Mr Cruncher's temper was not at all improved when he came to his breakfast. He resented Mrs Cruncher's saying grace with particular animosity.
>
> 'Now, Aggerawayter! What are you up to? At it agin?'
>
> His wife explained that she had merely 'asked a blessing.'
>
> 'Don't do it!' said Mr Cruncher, looking about, as if he rather expected to see the loaf disappear under the efficacy of his wife's petitions. 'I ain't a going to be blest out of house and home. I won't have my wittles blest off my table. Keep still!'[1046]

CONCLUSION: THE SPIRIT OF DIVINE DISCONTENT

In 1908 the Secretary of the Bank of England resigned. His departure was not greatly lamented, though no scandal had precipitated it. He had simply lost interest in his job. Within a few months his latest book was published: it too attracted little interest at the time, being generally thought to be inferior to his previous work, which had appeared to general acclaim.[1047] This is its opening paragraph:

The Mole had been working very hard all the morning, spring-cleaning his little home. First with brooms, then with dusters; then on ladders and steps and chairs, with a brush and a pail of whitewash; till he had dust in his throat and eyes, and splashes of whitewash all over his black fur, and an aching back and weary arms. Spring was moving in the air above and in the earth below and around him, penetrating even his dark and lowly little house with its spirit of divine discontent and longing. It was small wonder, then, that he suddenly flung down his brush on the floor, said 'Bother!' and 'O blow!' and also 'Hang spring-cleaning!' and bolted out of the house without even waiting to put on his coat. Something up above was calling him imperiously, and he made for the steep little tunnel which answered in his case to the gravelled carriage-drive owned by animals whose residences are nearer to the sun and air. So he scraped and scratched and scrabbled and scrooged, and then he scrooged again and scrabbled and scratched and scraped, working busily with his little paws and muttering to himself, 'Up we go! Up we go!' till at last, pop! his snout came out into the sunlight, and he found himself rolling in the warm grass of a great meadow. 'This is fine!' said the Mole. 'This is better than whitewashing!'[1048]

The wind in the willows soon established itself as one of the great classics of children's literature. Its author, Kenneth Grahame (1859–1932), was a strange man: part-recluse, part-country gentleman, part-banker, he idealized his own childhood (though it was only intermittently happy) and in some respects was never really at ease in the world of adults.[1049] Even more than his earlier books, *The wind in the willows* celebrates a childlike world of friendship and fantasy, in the process evoking a rural way of life that had long vanished if it had ever even existed.

The book is easy to criticize: all the principal characters are male; it can be read as a cryptic attack on everything (from railways to incomers) that threatens the settled tranquillity of the country gentleman; and the famous religious experience ('The piper at the gates of dawn') is, for many at least, curiously unconvincing. Yet Grahame's achievement was still remarkable. He poured his heart into the book: when E. H. Shepard was asked to produce illustrations for it, he recalled Grahame saying to him: '"I love these little people, be kind to them." Just that.'[1050]

In its indebtedness to Romanticism, its enterprising characters (gently hinting at a Darwinian kinship between humans and animals), its sensitivity to both the beauty and the cruelty of nature, its subtle dialectics first of exile and home, and then of sympathy and selfishness, but perhaps above all in its evocation of the 'spirit of divine discontent and longing' that drew the Mole out of his home in search of a new and exciting world, *The wind in the willows* catches some of the central themes of English spirituality in the Victorian era. Yet its own context is tragically at odds with the timeless world it evokes. Grahame wrote it for his and his wife Elspeth's only child, Alastair: Grahame idealized his son just as he had his own childhood. But Alastair was born half-blind, grew up precocious and sensitive, was cruelly bullied at school; and, on 7 May 1920, he was found dead on a railway track at Oxford. He was buried on what would have been his twentieth birthday. Kenneth and Elspeth, devastated at their son's suicide, withdrew into themselves, and spent most of the rest of their lives travelling abroad. Their own personal idyll, such as it was, had been shattered even more definitively than the weasels and stoats destroyed the pipedreams of Mr Toad.

So *The wind in the willows*, and the tragic life of its author, turned out to be not only reminiscent of a bygone age but prophetic of a new one. The 'spirit of divine discontent and longing' that drew Mole from his whitewashing was to draw countless young women and men, from across Europe and beyond, to the mud and madness of the Great War. Kenneth and Elspeth Grahame's terrible bereavement would be repeated millions of times over in the lives of families who lost loved ones in the almost unimaginable horrors the twentieth century was to bring. In an earlier book, *The golden age* (which by a curious twist of fate was beloved of the German Kaiser, Wilhelm II), Grahame describes (again autobiographically) the moment at which a young boy has to bid farewell to his brother, who is going away to school.[1051] His words can speak for all who sensed, when Victoria died in 1901, that a whole way of life was dying with her, and that no one quite knew what would take its place:

> As I looked at Edward, in new clothes of a manly cut, with a hard hat upon his head, a railway ticket in one pocket and money of his own in the other ... I began to feel dimly how great was the gulf already yawning betwixt us. Fortunately I was not old enough to realise, further, that here on this little platform the old order lay at its last gasp, and that Edward might come back to us, but it would not be the same Edward of yore, nor could things ever be the same again.[1052]

NOTES

1. J. P. Mursell (1855) pp. 246–7.
2. For Mursell's life, see Arthur Mursell (1886). For his ministry in Leicester, see further below. For the Mursell family's significance within the Baptist Union locally, see T. S. H. Elwyn, *The Northamptonshire Baptist Association: a short history, 1764–1964* (London: Carey Kingsgate, 1964) p. 93.
3. *The way of all flesh* chapter 6, p. 20.
4. Darwin, *The origin of species* chapter 1, p. 71.
5. Chadwick argues (1970, p. 5) that between the publication of *The origin of species* (1859) and *The descent of man* (1871) the doctrine of evolution achieved wide acceptance. See also R. M. Young, 'The impact of Darwin on conventional thought', in A. Symondson (ed.), *The Victorian crisis of faith* (London: SPCK, 1970).
6. See e.g. Chadwick (1975), esp. chapter 7; Bebbington (1989) p. 142.
7. Darwin, *The origin of species* chapter 3, pp. 124–5. The second quotation is from his notebook, quoted by J. W. Burrow, introd. to *The origin of species*, p. 41.
8. Minutes of the Baptist Missionary Society 17 November 1885, quoted in Mursell (1886) p. 176.
9. Darwin, *The origin of species* chapter 14, pp. 459–60. More recent atheist scientists have sought to develop the spirit of wonder as an integral dimension of scientific enquiry: see e.g. Richard Dawkins, *Unweaving the rainbow: science, delusion and the appetite for wonder* (Harmondsworth: Penguin, 1998).
10. The population of England increased from 8.9 million in 1801 to 35.5 million in 1901. And whereas 76.2% of the population lived in rural areas in 1801, only 22% of them did in 1901.

Between 1780 and 1860 huge numbers of people, whose families had worked on the land since families existed, moved into towns and cities (by 1901 more than 75% of the population of England and Wales lived in towns). The population growth rate was far faster than that of Germany, Italy, Russia, or France.

11. See Briggs (1968) pp. 12–15. The railway was one of the great features of the century. By the end of 1838 there were 500 miles of track in use; by 1843, 2,036 miles. A further 8,731 miles were sanctioned during the feverish 'railway mania' of 1845–7. Crewe (which had not even figured as a place name in the 1841 census) grew during this period, entirely as a railway town (Briggs (1983) p. 210). By that time the railways were no longer a novelty: they altered established patterns of life, encouraged equality (not always popular with the upper classes), transformed townscapes (Briggs (1983) p. 212), and vastly accelerated the move to the cities (Digby (1982) pp. 29–30). They effectively began the seaside town holiday phenomenon (Briggs (1983) p. 214): from London alone people could choose between Eastbourne, Brighton, Worthing or Southend, each having its own tone. The architecture of Victoria station (1860) was neither Doric, like Euston, nor Gothic, like St Pancras: rather 'it pointed resolutely to the commuter age' (Briggs (1983) p. 214). The railway encouraged community: you never knew whom you might meet. The private car encouraged the opposite (p. 216): the first English four-wheel car appeared in 1895.

12. Briggs (1983) p. 222. He points out (p. 224) that between the 1880s and 1914 over 4,500,000 square miles were added to the 'red' areas of world maps.

13. In 1801 (the first census, itself a landmark) there were only 15 towns of over 20,000 people: by 1891 there were 63. Leeds, Manchester, Sheffield and Birmingham increased by over 40% between 1820 and 1830 (the decade of most rapid growth); that of Manchester almost doubled between 1851 and 1901 and that of Salford almost trebled – see Briggs (1983) p. 194.

14. See Bebbington (1989), esp. pp. 113 and 142.

15. See Chadwick (1975) p. 88.

16. Chadwick (1975) p. 9: 'Enlightenment was of the few. Secularization is of the many.' G. K. Chesterton would later describe the Victorian era as being that of 'the first generation that ever asked its children to worship the hearth without the altar' (*Autobiography* (London: Hutchinson, 1937) p. 27).

17. For this subject, see the excellent discussion in Chadwick (1975).

18. For nationalism see Chadwick (1975) pp. 128–30; for journalism, see p. 38.

19. David Friedrich Strauss' *Life of Jesus* (1835) marked the beginning of a new interest in a historical reconstruction of the events described in the Gospels: it was translated into English by George Eliot in 1846. See also Chadwick (1966) p. 530 and Wheeler (1990) pp. 8–11. The Frenchman Stanislas Julien's *Voyages des pèlerins bouddhistes* (1853–7) was published in England in 1857; see also Max Müller, 'Buddhism and Buddhist pilgrims: a review' (London: Williams and Norgate, 1857). Mrs Speir published her *Life in ancient India* shortly before that. Müller's article was attacked in a letter to *The Times* (24 April 1857) by Francis Barham, who argued that the Buddhist notion of *nirvana* meant, not utter annihilation, but union and communion with God. The number of English Jews increased sharply during the years 1881–1905 as a result of immigration from eastern Europe and Russia: see McLeod (1996) pp. 45–7. The Nonconformist Robert Alfred Vaughan published his *Hours with the mystics*, an exploration of mysticism from the Bhagavad-Gita to Swedenborg, in 1856.

20. Chadwick (1975) pp. 92–3 and 117–18.

21. *The way of all flesh* chapter 47, p. 182.

22. Bebbington (1989) p. 129.

23. See Watts (1995) pp. 129–30.

24. See McLeod (1996) pp. 75–80.

25. See Berlin (1999). For Pietism, and its relationship with Romanticism, see also Peter C. Erb's introduction to *Pietists: selected writings* (Classics of western spirituality) (New York: Paulist, 1983), p. 5.

26. Berlin (1999) p. 37.

27. For the relationship of Wordsworth and his contemporaries to religion, see esp. Prickett (1976)

and Ryan (1997). For George Eliot, see further below.

28. Wordsworth, Preface to the second edition of the Poems, in *Complete poetical works*, p. 738.

29. 'Resolution and independence' (1802), from *Poems of the imagination*, in *Complete poetical works*, p. 156.

30. See, e.g., 'The primrose of the rock' (1831), in *Poems of the imagination* 43, in *Complete poetical works*, p. 179.

31. *The prelude* 3, in *Complete poetical works*, p. 512.

32. *The prelude* 8, in *Complete poetical works*, p. 555.

33. See 'Devotional incitements' (1832), *Poems of the imagination* 46, in *Complete poetical works*, p. 182.

34. *The prelude* 1, in *Complete poetical works*, p. 499.

35. *The prelude* 2, in *Complete poetical works*, p. 506.

36. For Wordsworth's Platonism, see Prickett (1976), esp. p. 81. Shelley was also a passionate Platonist and Hellenophile ('I had rather be damned with Plato and Lord Bacon, than go to Heaven with Paley and Malthus', Shelley, Preface to *Prometheus unbound*, in *Complete poetical works*, p. 207; cf. *Hellas*, Prologue, ll. 94–5, where Christ describes himself as 'a burning morrow' to Plato; *Complete poetical works*, p. 450).

37. *The prelude* 13, in *Complete poetical works*, p. 580.

38. For the Poor Laws, see the succinct summary in Digby (1982).

39. 'Postscript' (1835), in *Complete poetical works*, pp. 757–9. The reference to expostulating with the Creator is to the complaint of Adam against God in Milton's *Paradise lost*.

40. Payne Knight, *Analytical inquiry* 3.1, p. 323.

41. p. 331.

42. *Intimations of immortality* 10, in *Complete poetical works*, p. 462.

43. *The prelude* 2, in *Complete poetical works*, p. 505. Cf. 8, p. 553:

> Of sympathy, inspiring and inspired,
> When everywhere a vital pulse was felt,
> And all the several frames of things, like stars,
> Through every magnitude distinguishable,
> Shone mutually indebted, or half lost
> Each in the other's blaze, a galaxy
> Of life and glory. In the midst stood Man,
> Outwardly, inwardly contemplated,
> As, of all visible natures, crown, though born
> Of dust, and kindred to the worm; a Being,
> Both in perception and discernment, first
> In every capability of rapture,
> Through the divine effect of power and love;
> As, more than anything we know, instinct
> With godhead, and, by reason and by will,
> Acknowledging dependency sublime.

In the Preface to the 2nd edn of his Poems, Wordsworth argued that 'we have no sympathy but what is propagated by pleasure; I would not be misunderstood; but wherever we sympathise with pain, it will be found that the sympathy is produced and carried on by subtle combinations with pleasure' (*Complete poetical works*, p. 738). Again, this is surely not to argue that we gain any pleasure from others' sufferings, but that their sufferings elicit both our admiration, and our active readiness to alleviate them.

44. *Prometheus unbound* 1, ll. 450–1, in *Complete poetical works*, p. 218; cf. *On love* p. 201: 'there is something within us which, from the instant that we live, more and more thirsts after its likeness'.

45. *A refutation of deism*, p. 52.

46. See esp. his *Refutation of deism* and *Essay on Christianity*.

47. Wordsworth distinguishes between wonder and 'legitimate admiration': the former is 'the natural product of Ignorance', the latter a wholly good thing (Essay, supplementary to the Preface to the

second edition of his poems, in *Complete poetical works*, p. 747). Richard Payne Knight puts astonishment above awe and respect (*An analytical inquiry* 3.1, p. 373), though of itself astonishment is not necessarily noteworthy:

> If [the author of this book] . . . had walked up St James's Street without his breeches, it would have occasioned great and universal *astonishment*; and if he had, at the same time, carried a loaded blunderbuss in his hands, the astonishment would have been mixed with no small portion of *terror*: but I do not believe that the united effects of these two powerful passions would have produced any sentiment or sensation approaching to sublime.

Note the influence of Descartes's view here: see p. 52 above. George Eliot describes her reaction to a painting in Dresden in 1858 as 'a sort of awe, as if I were suddenly in the living presence of some glorious being' (*Journals*, p. 325).

48. *On life*, p. 193.
49. *Tintern Abbey*, in *Complete poetical works*, p. 164. Note the potential of the affections here. Cf. *The prelude* 2 (*Complete poetical works*, pp. 506–7), where Wordsworth says

> 'Twere long to tell
> What spring and autumn, what the winter snows,
> And what the summer shade, what day and night,
> Evening and morning, sleep and waking thought,
> From sources inexhaustible, poured forth
> To feed the spirit of religious love
> In which I walked with Nature . . .
> Ye mountains! thine, O Nature! Thou hast fed
> My lofty speculations; and in thee,
> For this uneasy heart of ours, I find
> A never-failing principle of joy
> And purest passion.

50. *Tintern Abbey*, in *Complete poetical works*, p. 164.
51. pp. 164–5.
52. Gill (1998, p. 44) makes the point that nothing Wordsworth says here *requires* a theological interpretation, just as nothing *contradicts* one.
53. *The prelude* 7, in *Complete poetical works*, p. 545.
54. *Complete poetical works*, p. 547.
55. See *The prelude* 8, in *Complete poetical works*, pp. 548–50. Wordsworth's hostility to cities is explicit in *The excursion* 8, ll. 117ff., in *Complete poetical works*, p. 683. Cf. also *The prelude* 6, in *Complete poetical works*, p. 530, and the very end of the same poem (14, p. 585), where the link between natural beauty and morality is strongly made.
56. *The prelude* 14, in *Complete poetical works*, p. 588.
57. For Wordsworth's anguish because the Church of England's prayers for the King's victory clashed with his own enthusiasm for the French Revolution, see *The prelude* 10, in *Complete poetical works*, p. 565, and Ryan (1997) p. 86. For Shelley's republicanism, see the remarks of Mary Shelley on *The mask of anarchy* in Shelley, *Complete poetical works*, p. 345.
58. At the very end of his Postscript of 1835 (*Complete poetical works*, p. 763) he quotes an earlier poem of his own:

> my theme
> No other than the very heart of man,
> As found among the best of those who live,
> Not unexalted by religious faith,
> Nor uninformed by books, good books, though few.
> In Nature's presence.

59. Shelley, *Peter Bell the Third* 3, in *Complete poetical works*, p. 350.
60. *Adonais* 19, on the death of Keats, in *Complete poetical works*, p. 436.
61. *An analytical inquiry* 3.3, pp. 454–5.
62. See Ryan (1997) for an exploration of this.

63. For a sensitive discussion of Shelley and religion, see Ryan (1997), pp. 193–223.

64. *Prometheus unbound* 1, ll. 282–91, in *Complete poetical works*, p. 214.

65. Shelley, *Peter Bell the Third* 6, in *Complete poetical works*, p. 358.

66. *A refutation of deism*, in *Works* vol. 6, p. 37.

67. p. 46. Cf. 'Nothing exists but as it is perceived' (*On life*, p. 196; though note that in Shelley's view poetry broadens the limitations of our surroundings: 'poetry defeats the curse which binds us to be subjected to the accident of surrounding impressions': *A defence of poetry*, in *Complete works* vol. 7, p. 137). 'Poets are the unacknowledged legislators of the world' (p. 140).

68. In *Prometheus unbound*, Prometheus, looking on the crucified Jesus, says

    O, horrible! Thy name I will not speak,
    It hath become a curse.

    (*Prometheus unbound* 1, ll. 603–4, in *Complete poetical works*, p. 221). Cf. 'Hellas', p. 480; and *Essay on Christianity*, p. 239, where he says that 'the interpreters of [Jesus'] doctrine have confounded the good and the evil principle'.

69. *Prometheus unbound* 3, ll. 1–7, in *Complete poetical works*, p. 242.

70. *Prometheus unbound* 4, ll. 570–8, in *Complete poetical works*, p. 268. Note here the Greek influence, the celebration of beauty, of immortality and immutability.

71. See especially the blazing vision of a restored republican Greece in his poem 'Hellas', esp. ll. 1084–1100, in *Complete poetical works*, pp. 477–8, and Shelley's own eloquent comments on it, pp. 478–9.

72. 'The sunset' (1816), in *Complete poetical works*, p. 529.

73. 'Ode to the west wind', in *Complete poetical works*, p. 579. For Mary Shelley's account of her husband's death, see pp. 675–80. Paul Foot argues that the wind here represents both a source of chaos and the free wind of revolution bringing a brighter day: the last verses express, not self-pity, but Shelley's own longing, at a time when he was censored, abroad and politically powerless, to have a share in bringing about the new world he dreamed of (*Red Shelley* (London: Sidgwick and Jackson, 1980) pp. 224–6).

74. See Berlin (1999, pp. 85–6) for Schiller's concept of *Spieltrieb*, 'play-drive', which frees us from imprisonment to passions and other drives we cannot master by allowing us to play, which is supremely what happens when we engage in art of any kind.

75. For this, see esp. Prickett (1992) pp. 200–1.

76. Quoted in guide to Burne-Jones exhibition (Birmingham, 1998). The Aesthetic movement with which he was associated sought to undo the link between art and morality which was prized by Victorian culture in general, celebrating instead 'art for art's sake' (Alan Crawford, 'Burne-Jones as a decorative artist', in S. Wildman and J. Christian (eds), *Edward Burne-Jones: Victorian artist-dreamer* (New York: Metropolitan Museum of Art, 1998) p. 11; and Wildman and Christian, p. 112).

77. Parry, quoted in Dibble (1992), pp. 359–60. Cf. Isaiah Berlin: 'The business of a work of art is to liberate us, and it liberates us by ignoring the superficial symmetries of nature, the superficial rules, and by sharp transitions from one mode into another – from poetry to prose, from theology to botany or whatever – knocks down a great many of the conventional divisions by which we are hemmed in and cribbed and imprisoned' (1999, p. 111).

78. Andersen's fairy stories were immensely popular in Victorian England.

79. *Little Dorrit* Book 2 chapter 30, p. 737.

80. For a valuable exploration of this theme, see Prickett (1979).

81. Gosse, *Father and son*, p. 22.

82. *Hours with the mystics*, vol. 1, pp. 34–5.

83. This section will concentrate on the principal figures of the Oxford Movement itself (especially Pusey and Keble): the spirituality of later Anglo-Catholicism, together with that of the Christian Socialists, is explored in Chapter 3.

84. Keble, *Assize sermon on national apostasy*, p. 18.

85. The name 'Oxford Movement' seems to have been established early; Newman refers to it as this in a letter of 1872 (*Letters and diaries* vol. 26, p. 201). It seems frequently to have been described by

opponents as 'Puseyism'. In 1844 J. M. Neale was referring to 'us Anglo-Catholicks' (*Letters*, p. 77). The term 'High churchman' originated soon after 1688, and implied a doughty defender of the church (and usually a Tory too).

86. Some early adherents, like William Palmer, did want a broad-based popular movement in defence of the Church, while Newman wanted a narrower and more élitist movement restoring ecclesial authority (Chadwick (1966) p. 73).

87. For the influence of the earlier High Church movement on the Tractarians, see esp. Nockles (1994) and Chadwick (1990) p. 9. The Tractarian view of scripture is captured in Keble's remark that 'A Bible is . . . an outward visible sign, a kind of sacrament, seen by the eye, of the Presence of our Lord Jesus Christ', *Sermons for the Christian year* 1.31 (on Psalm 119), p. 313; cf. also Keble's sermon on the Prayer Book Collect for the Second Sunday in Advent, 1.25, pp. 257–64.

88. See Ward (1986) for the Oxford Movement and history.

89. The publication extended over 47 years, from the publication of St Augustine's *Confessions* in 1838 to the latter part of St Cyril on St John in 1885 (Liddon, *Life of Pusey* vol. 1, p. 435): a total of 48 volumes were published, including 13 patristic and ancient writers (the small number of authors included seems to have been Pusey's deliberate intention to focus on the pre-eminent patristic authors (Liddon, pp. 435–6)). Two years later, in 1840, a committee was established to produce the parallel Library of Anglo-Catholic Theology (making available the quintessence of seventeenth-century English divinity): the first of 83 volumes was published in 1841.

90. Newman, *Apologia*, p. 44.

91. 'The Epiphany', in *The Christian year*, p. 28, and 'Tuesday in Easter Week', in *The Christian year*, p. 77.

92. Pusey, *What is of faith*, p. 11.

93. *Sermons for the Christian year* 1.34, p. 346.

94. Benson, *The followers of the Lamb*, p. 12.

95. Obedience plays a key role in Tractarian spirituality: not servile obedience to an increasingly secular state, but the freely given obedience of a child to its parents: see Isaac Williams' Tract 86 (*Indications of a superintending providence in the preservation of the Prayer Book and in the changes which it has undergone*), in which he gives a detailed résumé of how the compilers of the Prayer Book subtly heightened the sense of Christians as servants of God, rather than children, so as in turn to foster in us a spirit of unconditional obedience: see esp. pp. 9–10. It leads him (pp. 63–4) to a forceful though unsatisfactory critique of Wesley, accusing him of offering people too easy an assumption that our adoption as children of God removes the need for us also to be obedient servants: we must first (says Williams) be humiliated, seek repentance, and through the providential formularies of the Prayer Book will discover in our suffering our true status as sons and daughters of God (Tract 86, pp. 72–3). This extraordinary argument is not only unfair to Wesley: it entirely misses the central thrust of the parable of the Prodigal Son. Williams' tract is, however, of interest from the point of view of the theology of the Prayer Book itself: for this, see chap. 5 of vol. 1 of the present work.

96. Tract 72, *Tracts for the times* vol. 3, p. 54.

97. Tract 84, *Tracts for the times* vol. 5, p. 36.

98. Tract 90, *Tracts for the times* vol. 6, p. 59.

99. For Keble see Rowell (1983) pp. 21–42.

100. For Pusey, see Liddon's *Life*; Rowell (1983) pp. 71–97, and Butler (1983).

101. For Neale, see his *Letters*, edited by his daughter, Litvack and Rowell (1983) pp. 98–115.

102. Liddon's works include a classic biography of Pusey; the Bampton Lectures of 1866, published as *The Divinity of Our Lord and Saviour Jesus Christ*; and *Some elements of religion*, Lent lectures delivered at St James Piccadilly in 1870. For Liddon see Rowell (1983).

103. Text quoted in Liddon, *Life of Pusey*, vol. 2, pp. 140–1.

104. 'Groans of unrenewed and renewed nature' (*Parochial sermons* 2.17, pp. 304–5).

105. pp. 309–10.

106. p. 310. It should be noted that this doesn't lead Pusey to a very positive evaluation of our response to creation: we must look beyond it to its Creator (p. 322).

107. See the marvellous description Pusey gives in his journal of his view of Mont Blanc in 1822; Liddon, *Life of Pusey*, vol. 1, pp. 34–5.

108. See Liddon, *Life of Pusey*, vol. 2, pp.476–7.

109. *Sermons for the Christian year* 11.19, pp. 230–1; cf. 11.5, p. 65; 11.20, pp. 242–4.

110. *Letters*, p. 37.

111. Chadwick (1966) pp. 212–21; Rowell (1983) pp. 101–4; Fisher (1995) pp. 20–1.

112. For this strand in the recovery of Gothic architecture, see Dixon and Muthesius (1978) p. 187.

113. *On reserve in communicating religious knowledge* (Tract 80), *Tracts for the times* vol. 4, p. 3.

114. p. 3. He cites examples from scripture (such as Christ's use of parables, pp. 8–11), though some of these are very curious (such as St Peter expelling all the onlookers when raising Tabitha, p. 26).

115. p. 55.

116. pp. 124–5.

117. For Pusey's strictures on excessive study, see his Letter to — (1838), cited in Liddon, *Life* vol. 2, pp. 47–51.

118. For Jesus as exemplar of the doctrine of reserve, see also Keble, *Sermons for the Christian year* 11.5, pp. 64–5; for the implications of this doctrine for evangelism, see R. M. Benson, *Letters*, p. 37. For Newman's understanding of reserve, see further below.

119. Pusey, *The Holy Eucharist*, p. 4.

120. pp. 4 and 10.

121. p. 14.

122. p. 27.

123. pp. 30–1.

124. Pusey, *Parochial and cathedral sermons* 15, pp. 200–1.

125. p. 201.

126. pp. 202–3.

127. pp. 203–4.

128. Pusey, *Parochial sermons* 2.1, p. 1.

129. p. 16.

130. Pusey, *Parochial and cathedral sermons* 21, pp. 304–5.

131. Pusey, *Parochial sermons* 2.13, pp. 225–8 with lengthy footnote. See also A. M. Allchin, *Participation in God* (London: DLT, 1988) pp. 48–62.

132. Pusey, *Parochial sermons* 2.13, p. 229.

133. p. 235.

134. Pusey, *Parochial and cathedral sermons* 36, p. 474, citing St Gregory Nazianzen.

135. Pusey, *Parochial and cathedral sermons* 30, p. 414; cf. Liddon, *Some elements of religion*, p. 114.

136. Pusey, *Parochial and cathedral sermons* 38, p. 497.

137. Pusey, *Parochial sermons* 2.15, pp. 280–1.

138. p. 281.

139. Pusey, *Parochial sermons* 2.20, p. 360.

140. *Letters of spiritual counsel*, p. 219. For Keble's views on the real presence of Christ at the Eucharist, see pp. 209–11.

141. Pusey, *The Holy Eucharist*, p. 18.

142. p. 24.

143. *Sermons for the Christian year* 6.6, p. 62. Note, though, that Keble sees the soul as infinitely more precious than the body: 'Your soul is yourself, not your body: and when death comes, and the soul and body are parted, it is not *you* that will lie dead, and be buried' (*Sermons for the Christian year* 3.11, p. 113).

144. Keble, *Sermons for the Christian year* 7.13, p. 118; cf. 1.37, pp. 372–81.

145. Keble, *Sermons for the Christian year* 5.20, p. 203.

146. Pusey, *Parochial and cathedral sermons* 39, p. 504.

147. p. 511.

148. See Newman, Tract 90, *Tracts for the times*, pp. 54–5.

149. Wilberforce, introd. to *Eucharistica*, p. xi.

150. Keble, *Sermons for the Christian year* 3.11, p. 113; cf. Liddon, *Some elements of religion*, pp. 114–17.
151. Keble, *Sermons for the Christian year* 1.3, p. 31.
152. *The Councils of the Church*, pp. 4–5.
153. See Liddon, *Life* vol. 2, p. 466. The church was consecrated in 1845.
154. Pusey, *Parochial and cathedral sermons* 12, p. 167.
155. From Schopenhauer's *Die Welt als Wille und Vorstellung* 67.59, quoted in Liddon, *Some elements of religion*, p. 131.
156. Liddon, *Some elements of religion*, pp. 138–9.
157. Liddon, ibid., pp. 148–9.
158. p. 149.
159. p. 150.
160. Liddon, *Christmas sermons* 12, p. 197.
161. *Christmas sermons* 12, p. 198.
162. *Parochial and cathedral sermons* 13, p. 180.
163. (or *Manual for confessors*). The Manual itself is a substantial compilation of extracts from the works of St François de Sales, St Charles Borromeo, St Philip Neri, St Francis Xavier, and other spiritual writers, abridged and translated, presumably by Pusey himself, and reflects the pervasive influence of French Catholic spirituality on the Tractarians. For Pusey as confessor and spiritual director, see the article by K. Denison, in Butler (1983), pp. 210–30. For another central exposition of Tractarian theology of penance, see Keble, *Sermons for the Christian year* 1.45, pp. 458–68.
164. Pusey, Preface to Gaume, p. cxliii.
165. Preface to Gaume, p. clv.
166. Preface to Gaume, p. clxix.
167. Pusey, *Parochial sermons* 2.11, p. 192.
168. p. 193.
169. *Letters of spiritual counsel*, p. 98.
170. *Letters of spiritual counsel*, p. 100.
171. *Letters of spiritual counsel*, p. 114.
172. Pusey, Preface to Gaume, p. clxi.
173. Faber, *Growth in holiness*, quoted in Pusey, Preface to Gaume, pp. clxvi–clxvii. Cf. also Pusey's quotation from Fr Thomas (T. T.) Carter, Preface to Gaume, p. clxii. On the same page Pusey summarizes the point: 'Direction, rightly understood, is only "ghostly counsel and advice" become habitual.' Cf. Keble, *Letters of spiritual counsel*, p. 159: 'Beware of hero worship.'
174. *Parochial sermons* 2.9, p. 158.
175. *Spiritual letters*, p. 78.
176. *Spiritual letters*, p. 333.
177. Keble, *Letters of spiritual counsel*, p. 3; cf. Pusey, *Spiritual letters*, pp. 69–71.
178. Keble, *Letters of spiritual counsel*, p. 7.
179. *Letters of spiritual counsel*, p. 77.
180. Pusey, *Spiritual letters*, p. 13.
181. Keble, *Letters of spiritual counsel*, pp. 177–8. Cf. Pusey's advice to a correspondent: 'Do not dwell on past failures in themselves; but tell God, "Would, O my God, I had not, in this or this or this, offended Thee." And He will make it as if it had not been. Fear not. Jesus intercedes for you ever, and He is Almighty' (*Spiritual letters*, p. 21; cf. p. 93 'Do not look back at former years with regret.').
182. Pusey, *Spiritual letters*, p. 109.
183. Cf. Pusey: 'to speak of feelings is a great ill', *Spiritual letters*, p. 309. Keble: 'we must live by rule: it is quite a mistake . . . to trust to our own feelings only, if we are not going on regularly by rules of goodness' (Keble, *Sermons for the Christian year* 9.5, p. 46). 'As our day begins with prayer, so it must go on by rule. We dare not surely live by random' (9.41, p. 448). Keble warns of the dangers of 'trusting to religious emotions' (5.4, pp. 36–45). He warns a penitent not to 'go upon *feeling*, one way or the other, but upon calm consideration, with prayer', and not to lessen their sense of

their own responsibility (Keble, *Letters of spiritual counsel*, p. 172).

184. *Spiritual letters*, p. 114.

185. *Sermons for the Christian year* 10.29, on John 3.30, pp. 270–1.

186. Pusey, *Parochial and cathedral sermons* 19, p. 278.

187. Cf. Keble: 'What an aweful thing is prayer, when you regard it in this light, that it is coming into the immediate Presence of the great God of heaven and earth' (*Sermons for the Christian year* 8.16, p. 169).

188. Liddon, *Some elements of religion*, p. 178.

189. *The Christian year*, p. 57.

190. *Self-abandonment to the Divine Providence* trans. Algar Thorold (London: Burns & Oates, 1933; rev. 1959; repr. Collins, 1971), p. 73. This text was compiled by Fr Henri Ramière SJ from de Caussade's writings in 1861, but the underlying spirituality is the same. Pusey translated a number of continental spiritual texts; and the influence of French Catholic spiritual and pastoral theology on the Tractarians was extensive. See Rowell (1983) and, for François de Sales and Vincent de Paul, the articles by Michael J. Buckley and Keith P. Luria in *Christian spirituality III: post-Reformation and modern* (World spirituality) (New York: Crossroad, 1989).

191. *Parochial sermons* 2.10, p. 169. Cf. Keble: 'when God has a great work in hand . . . and calls upon us, as He always does, to pray for it, He means that we must not be content with one, two, or three prayers: we must lead a whole life of prayer' (*Sermons for the Christian year* 11.14, p. 169). Elijah prayed for three years and a half, 'and his prayer is at last answered' (p. 171).

192. *Parochial sermons* 2.16, pp. 299–300 and *Parochial and cathedral sermons* 14, p. 194. Liddon (*Some elements of religion*, pp. 5–7) says that the fact that we desire God, and a deeper sense of meaning in life than materialism can offer, is in itself evidence of the existence of God.

193. Pusey, *Parochial sermons* 2.10, p. 179; cf. Pusey, *Spiritual letters*, p. 20: 'The power to pray comes with praying.'

194. *Parochial and cathedral sermons* 19, p. 275.

195. Pusey, *Parochial and cathedral sermons* 22, p. 321.

196. Keble, *Sermons for the Christian year* 8.39, pp. 406–16.

197. Keble, *Sermons for the Christian year* 8.10, p. 99.

198. *Sermon on national apostasy*, p. 22.

199. *Sermon on national apostasy*, p. 23.

200. Keble, *Sermons for the Christian year* 7.6, p. 50.

201. Keble, *Sermons for the Christian year* 9.7, p. 68. Cf. Pusey: 'If we would but pour out into the ears of God the complaints, with which we in our hearts bemoan ourselves, or which we vent to one another! Would, my brethren, that instead of restlessly tossing to and fro, we would go straight to the Throne of God' (*Parochial and cathedral sermons* 19, p. 282; cf. *Spiritual letters* p. 22: 'There is no use in complaining, except to God.')

202. *Sermons for the Christian year* 9.22, pp. 234–5. Cf. also 7.6, p. 50, on the Eucharist as the natural focus for all our prayer.

203. Tract 66, *Tracts for the times* vol. 2/1, p. 13. In his lectures on Daniel, Pusey notes that Daniel's practice of praying thrice daily is rooted in Psalm 55.17 (ed. cit., pp. 556–7).

204. *Letters of spiritual counsel*, p. 9.

205. See Yates (1983) p. 144: in c.1900 vestments were worn in only about 12% of churches in southern England. Yet by the same date the eastward position in the Eucharist, lighted candles and the mixed chalice had become the norm in several dioceses. See also Yates (1991).

206. See Bodington (1905) pp. 164–72 and, more generally, his study of devotional books (1908).

207. For these see esp. Kent (1978) pp. 236ff.

208. Butler, *The way of all flesh* chapter 50, p. 200.

209. See Rowell (1983) p. 39. Keble's conservatism appears frequently: see, e.g., his reverence for Charles I, who 'didst love to trace [the Church's] daily lore' (*The Christian year*, p. 203); his insistence that 'each one [in the Christian household] will know his place, and will keep to it' (*Sermons for the Christian year* 9.28, p. 306). In his *Sermons for the Christian year* 3.40 (on the Litany), Keble encourages people to pray for the queen, that she may vanquish all her enemies, who 'are also the

enemies of God and His Church' (see esp. p. 406), whilst rejecting any state control of the church, which is almost contradictory.

210. *Parochial and cathedral sermons* 21, p. 318.

211. See, e.g., in Keble's *The Christian year*, references such as 'faith grows rare' (Fifth Sunday after Easter, in *The Christian year*, p. 86): 'the sinful world around' (Whitsunday, p. 93); 'The holy house is still beset/ With leaguer of stern foes' (Second Sunday after Trinity, p. 103); 'the thankless deep' (Fifth Sunday after Trinity, p. 109).

212. E.g.: 'Patience makes the soul to be of one mind with God, and sweetens all the ills of life. It casts the light of Heaven upon them, and transforms them into goods' (Pusey, *Parochial sermons* 2.5, p. 84). Pusey assumes that 'everything . . . is ordained or overruled by God' (p. 88); so we must simply endure with patience what is evil or painful. He can go so far as to say that 'every evil is, in God's purpose, a medicine to our soul, bitter, painful, but full of everlasting health' (p. 95). He does acknowledge that we may well need to complain in the face of evil; but we should complain *to* God, not *of* God (p. 96). Elsewhere Pusey says 'Allow thyself to complain of nothing (not even of the weather), knowing that everything is ordained or overruled by God' (*Parochial sermons* 2.9, p. 158).

213. *The Christian year*, p. 1.

214. *The Christian year*, p. 28; cf. Keble, *Sermons for the Christian year* 10.39, p. 365.

215. 'It is only wonderful to think, if earth is so transcendently and ravishingly lovely, what Heaven must be!' (from Madeira, 1843) J. M. Neale, *Letters*, p. 66.

216. Pusey, *Spiritual letters*, pp. 330–1.

217. Newman, *Apologia*, p. 288.

218. Reflecting on the theological debate of his day, John Stuart Mill wrote in about 1861: 'When the philosophic minds of the world can no longer believe its religion, or can only believe it with modifications amounting to an eventual change of its character, a transitional period commences, of weak convictions, paralysed intellects, and growing laxity of principle, which cannot terminate until a renovation has been effected in the basis of their belief, leading to the evolution of some faith, whether religious or merely human, which they can really believe: and when things are in this state, all thinking or writing which does not tend to promote such a renovation, is of very little value beyond the moment' (*Autobiography*, quoted in David L. Edwards (1971) p. 141).

219. Maurice, *The Prayer-Book*, pp. iii–iv. For Maurice's attitude to the Prayer Book and his contribution to Anglican liturgy, see J. N. Morris, '"A fluffy-minded Prayer Book fundamentalist"? F. D. Maurice and the Anglican liturgy', in R. N. Swanson (ed.), *Continuity and change in Christian worship* (Studies in Church history 35) (Woodbridge: Boydell, 1999) pp. 345–60.

220. Both Cambridge and Oxford Universities were at that time still exclusively Anglican.

221. Specifically for his refusal to accept the existence of hell.

222. See Reardon (1971) pp. 203–4.

223. See Carpenter, Introduction to Maurice's *Theological essays*, p. 8; Reardon (1971) p. 208; Norman (1987) pp. 19–21.

224. See esp. his *Theological essays* as well as *The Kingdom of Christ*.

225. See Vidler (1948) p. 32.

226. Its full title was *The Kingdom of Christ, or hints to a Quaker respecting the principles, constitution and ordinances of the Catholic Church*. It originally appeared as a series of letters, then (still in 1838) published as a book in 3 volumes. For the second edition (1842) in 2 volumes, Maurice completely rewrote and reconstructed the work (see A. R. Vidler's Introduction to the 2nd edn, pp. 8–9). The structure of the book, based upon the advancement of a particular Christian truth followed by the objections to it which are held by Quakers, 'Pure Protestants', rationalists, and Roman Catholics (to whose beliefs and practices Maurice appears to have a particularly strong objection), makes it feel ponderous.

227. For Kingsley's life, see the *Life* and letters written by his wife, and Chitty (1974). Chitty has had access to hitherto unpublished love letters and drawings (some of which she prints) which reveal the intensely sensual aspect of Kingsley's nature.

228. *Westminster sermons*, Preface, p. vii.

229. For his commitment to science, see his *Health and education*, pp. 156–7. For his commitment to women's suffrage, see his letter to John Stuart Mill of 1869, quoted in *Life* vol. 2, p. 295.

230. Kingsley, *Miscellanies* vol. 1, p. 349. Maurice was a pioneer in the study of other great world faiths and their relationship to Christianity: see his *Religions of the world* (1846).

231. *Miscellanies* vol. 1, p. 353.

232. Quoted in Kingsley, *Life* vol. 2, p. 412.

233. See *The water babies* chapter 4, p. 105.

234. Chadwick (1990) p. 109.

235. Stewart Headlam (*The Socialist's church*, p. 1) acknowledges Maurice and Kingsley as the principal founders of Christian Socialism. For Kingsley's socialism, see Norman's stern but just criticism (1987, p. 35).

236. *Health and education*, p. 135.

237. Its full title was *Christian prayer considered in relation to the belief that the Almighty governs the world by general laws* (published in 1874 with an appendix on *The physical efficacy of prayer*).

238. See Charles Gore's preface to Romanes' *Thoughts on religion*.

239. See *The life and letters of George John Romanes*, written by his wife; and Gore's preface to *Thoughts on religion*.

240. *Alton Locke*, p. 133.

241. *Theological essays*, p. 37; cf. *The Gospel of St John* 21, p. 338.

242. *Theological essays*, pp. 45 and 46; cf. *The doctrine of sacrifice*, p. 179, where sin is seen as 'conscious separation from a pure and holy will'.

243. *The Epistles of St John* 14, p. 220.

244. pp. 222–6.

245. p. 225.

246. *Lectures on the Apocalypse* 10, p. 149.

247. *Lectures on the Apocalypse* 5, pp. 78–9.

248. See Preface to *Westminster sermons*, esp. p. xii.

249. p. xii.

250. p. xiii.

251. pp. xiv–xviii.

252. pp. xxi-xxii.

253. See also Kingsley, *Westminster sermons* 5, p. 58.

254. *Westminster sermons* 8, p. 86.

255. Peacock, *Nightmare Abbey*, p. 360.

256. Kingsley, *Westminster sermons* 8, p. 86. See Maurice's *Theological essays*, esp. p. 319.

257. Kingsley, *Westminster sermons* 8, p. 93.

258. p. 94.

259. p. 95.

260. *Westminster sermons* 16, p. 181.

261. pp. 184–5.

262. *Thoughts on religion*, pp. 143–4.

263. 'The Holy Spirit and inspiration', p. 230.

264. *The Prayer-Book* 1, p. 7. Hence 'Almighty and most merciful *Father*' (p. 8).

265. *The Prayer-Book* 3, p. 40.

266. 'Then only could men fully believe themselves to be spirits when they fully believed God to be their Father', (*The Prayer-Book* 4, p. 54).

267. *The Prayer-Book* 11, p. 164.

268. *The Gospel of St John* 20, p. 314.

269. Maurice, *The Prayer-Book* 1, p. 11; cf. 4, p. 60; cf. Vidler (1948) p. 73.

270. Maurice, *The Prayer-Book* 1, p. 13.

271. p. 13.

272. p. 13.

273. p. 15.

274. *The Epistles of St John* 15, p. 240.

275. *The Gospel of St John* 20, p. 305, reflecting on Jesus' love for Martha and Mary.

276. *Westminster sermons* 1, p. 7.

277. *Health and education*, p. 197. Kingsley is reflecting here another strand in nineteenth-century thought about origins. Richard Holmes (*Coleridge: darker reflections* (London: HarperCollins, 1998) p. 540 n*) argues that Coleridge belonged to an alternative intellectual tradition to that of Darwin, a tradition rooted in German Naturphilosophien that observed the same phenomena of evolutionary ascent in terms of an emerging 'altruism'.

278. The Tractarian Henry Parry Liddon noted that 'one object of the Divine Incarnation was to put woman's life on a totally new footing within the precincts of the Church of the redeemed (*Christmas sermons* 5, p. 83; cf. 6, pp. 99–100). See also the writings of F. W. Robertson, a Liberal Anglican priest who stressed the gender inclusiveness of the incarnate Christ in a striking manner: esp. *Life and letters* vol. 2, p. 51; cf. letter of 18 Nov 1849, vol. 1, p. 287; and vol. 1, p. 49.

279. *Theological essays*, p. 109; cf. *The Gospel of St John* 19, p. 292, on the paradox of Christ's freedom and obedience to the Father.

280. *The Gospel of St John* 26, p. 412.

281. *The Kingdom of Christ* 2.2, vol. 1, p. 228.

282. pp. 229 and 242.

283. *The Kingdom of Christ* 2.3, vol. 1, pp 237ff.

284. p. 245.

285. p. 248.

286. p. 249.

287. See *The Kingdom of Christ* 2.5, vol. 2, p. 197.

288. *The Prayer-Book* 13, pp. 206–8; cf. 14, p. 222.

289. *The Prayer-Book* 16, p. 251.

290. *The Kingdom of Christ* 2.4, vol. 1, p. 258.

291. p. 276; and see Vidler (1948) pp. 94–120.

292. *The Kingdom of Christ* p. 276; cf. *The Prayer-Book* 1, p. 7. The other key signs Maurice takes to be the creeds, the Eucharist, the existence of an ordained ministry, and the Bible; for his treatment of these, see Vidler (1948) pp. 122–54.

293. *The Kingdom of Christ* 2.4, vol. 2, pp. 35–6.

294. p. 36.

295. *The Kingdom of Christ* 3.1, vol. 2, pp. 315–16; cf. *The Prayer-Book* 8, pp. 124–5: 'when men are leagued in support of a system they will resort to craft and dishonesty in defence of it'.

296. *The Kingdom of Christ* 3.2, vol.2, p. 335. For his historical sketch see vol. 2, pp. 316–19.

297. pp. 335–6.

298. *The Prayer-Book* 3, p. 49.

299. *The Prayer-Book* 15, p. 239.

300. *The Prayer-Book* 1, p. 12.

301. *The religions of the world* 2.3, p. 212.

302. p. 17; cf. *The Roman and the Teuton*, p. 178.

303. *The hermits*, pp. 198, 214–15 and 218.

304. *The Roman and the Teuton*, p. 29. See also Chitty (1974) for a revealing description of Kingsley's personality and its strongly sensual side; hence, at least in part, his dislike of Newman – though, as Chitty points out (p. 236) 'Newman stood for the things that Kingsley most disliked and feared in himself'.

305. e.g. his view of the eastern hermits as 'mere self-torturing fakeers' (*The hermits*, p. 169); or the reference in *The water babies* to 'nasty . . . smelly old monks' (chapter 5, p. 143).

306. *Hypatia*, Preface, p. xv. Chadwick (1990, p. 126 and p. 127 n. 35) suggests that the ambivalence evident in Kingsley's evaluation of asceticism may derive from the clash between his own sexual obsessions, and his love of the classical and medieval past. But there must have been no shortage of contemporary Christians who would have viewed monastic asceticism with even more disapproval than he did.

307. *The Gospel of St John* 21, pp. 332–3.
308. *Theological essays*, p. 113.
309. *The doctrine of sacrifice*, p. 159.
310. *The doctrine of sacrifice*, pp. 196–7.
311. pp. 261–3.
312. pp. 217–47.
313. p. 6.
314. p. 15.
315. p. 16.
316. p. 24.
317. p. 35.
318. pp. 43–4.
319. pp. 63–6; cf. *The Kingdom of Christ* 2.4, vol. 2, pp. 71–2.
320. *Westminster sermons* 15, pp. 177–8.
321. *The Gospel of St John* 26, p. 413.
322. pp. 413–4.
323. p. 417.
324. p. 418.
325. p. 419.
326. See also *The Epistles of St John* 7, p. 115.
327. *The Kingdom of Christ* 2.4, vol. 2, pp. 51–2.
328. p. 37.
329. p. 37.
330. p. 38. For this stress on the vital role played by the Holy Spirit see also Gore's fine essay 'The Holy Spirit and inspiration', in *Lux mundi*, pp. 230–66.
331. *Lectures on the Apocalypse* 19, pp. 288–9. Cf. Maurice's discussion of the prayer of the Psalms, in *The Prayer-Book* 6, pp. 95–6. Cf. also F. W. Robertson, *Life and letters* vol. 2, p. 279, for a similar approach, albeit less eloquently expressed.
332. *The Epistles of St John* 18, p. 288.
333. *Lectures on the Apocalypse* 4, pp. 63–4.
334. *The Prayer-Book* 17, pp. 273–4.
335. Maurice's Liberalism did not exclude a good deal of biblical literalism, though: see, for example, how he conceives of the role of the four living creatures in the reflections on Revelation just cited.
336. *Religions of the world* 2.4, p. 248.
337. For this, see Sean Gill, 'How muscular was Victorian Christianity: Thomas Hughes and the cult of Christian manliness reconsidered', in R. N. Swanson (ed.), *Gender and Christian religion* (Studies in Church history 34) (Woodbridge: Boydell, 1998) pp. 421–30).
338. Figures quoted in Watts (1995) p. 28.
339. See Norman (1976) pp. 126–7; Watts (1995) p. 114. In some rural areas the parish church was the only available place of worship anyway: see Knight (1995) chapter 2, esp. p. 31 n. 34.
340. See Knight (1995) p. 2 n. 1.
341. Knight (1995) p. 37.
342. *Adam Bede* chapter 3, p. 37.
343. *The mill on the floss*, Book 3 chapter 9, pp. 354–7.
344. *Silas Marner* chapter 10, p. 80.
345. *Bernard Shaw: collected letters*, ed. Dan H. Laurence, vol. 2 (1898–1910) (London: Max Reinhardt, 1972), p. 702.
346. See the recent study by Frances Knight (1995), and the valuable article by R. Arthur Burns ('A Hanoverian legacy? Diocesan reform in the Church of England c.1800–1833', in Walsh (1993), pp. 265–82).
347. Norman (1976) pp. 161–2. He points out that within a decade, the Working Men's Society had 10,000 members.
348. See Chadwick (1966) pp. 337–8; Knight (1995) pp. 191–5.

349. Chadwick (1966) p. 84.

350. See Wickham (1957) pp. 77–8, on Sheffield; Norman (1976) pp. 126–9. There is some evidence (e.g. rise in baptisms) to show that in the later nineteenth century the Church of England had made much progress in poorer urban areas; see McLeod (1996) p. 74.

351. The material for what follows is largely drawn from parish and diocesan magazines from the diocese of Lichfield, from a variety of ecclesiastical traditions and geographical communities. The anecdotal nature of much of the material may, it is hoped, be compensated for by the immediacy it conveys. I am indebted to the staff of Staffordshire County Records Office for making this material available.

352. Wickham (1957) pp. 82–3.

353. p. 85. J. C. Symons (*Report on the trades of Sheffield and the moral and physical conditions of the young persons employed in them*, 1843) wrote of 'the melancholy amount of immorality among children of the working-class . . . attendance at places of worship is by no means a practice with the youth of Sheffield . . . churches and chapels are unfilled and the schools scantily attended, and this remark applies also to the greater part of the Wesleyan and other denominations' (quoted in Wickham (1957) pp. 89–90); and see the report of Dr G. Calvert Holland, a Sheffield physician, who in 1843 published *Vital statistics of Sheffield*, commissioned by the Town Trustees, and came to similar conclusions (quoted in Wickham (1957) p. 92) – though as Wickham points out (p. 93) this tells us little about people's personal spirituality.

354. Evening Prayer was said only on Mondays, Wednesdays and Fridays, at 7 p.m. On Wednesdays a sermon was preached at it. Morning Prayer was said daily at 9.45 a.m.

355. *Chesterton Parish Magazine* 25, January 1880.

356. *Chesterton Parish Magazine* 25, January 1880.

357. *Chesterton Parish Magazine* 15, March 1879.

358. E.g., in January 1880, on Temperance; by the vicar; *Chesterton Parish Magazine* 17, November 1879.

359. See Knight (1995) p. 42.

360. *Chesterton Parish Magazine* 23, November 1879.

361. See 23, November 1879.

362. Information taken from monthly parish magazines, 1885–8. A determination to try to keep Sunday as a holy day amidst ever-increasing business appears frequently in Victorian religious writings: see, e.g., the article 'In what ways can wives and mothers best promote the revival of piety in the Church?' in *The British Mothers' Magazine* IV (1848), text in Johnson (1983) pp. 127–8.

363. E.g. to the Christian Union on 22 June 1885.

364. All information is taken from the church registers; in Staffordshire CRO.

365. *Cheddleton Parish Magazine* 40, April 1889, Staffordshire CRO.

366. From 1874 this took place annually on 29 November: see *Cheddleton Parish Magazine* 47, November 1889.

367. *Cheddleton Parish Magazine* 58, October 1890.

368. *Cheddleton Parish Magazine* 5.2, February 1893.

369. *Cheddleton Parish Magazine* 3.3, March 1891.

370. *Cheddleton Parish Magazine* 10.3, March 1897.

371. *Trent Valley Parochial Magazine* 11.11, November 1879.

372. *All Saints' Church Milwich Monthly Magazine*, issues of December 1904, April 1905, and July 1905; Staffs CRO.

373. Greenwell, *Two friends*, pp. 101–3.

374. p. 108.

375. *Silas Marner* chapter 16, p. 144.

376. *Silas Marner* chapter 10, p. 84. For the significance of the Prayer Book in nineteenth-century lay piety, see Knight (1995) pp. 37–44.

377. *Adam Bede* chapter 18, p. 199. Cf. the remarks of Dolly Winthrop in *Silas Marner* chapter 16, p. 144.

378. *Our Parish Magazine* (Alstonefield Rural Deanery), August 1900.

379. Knight (1995) p. 71.

380. *Trent Valley Parochial Magazine* 12.6, June 1880; Staffordshire CRO.

381. Quoted in *Trent Valley Parochial Magazine* 12.3, March 1880. Quiet days for clergy took place: see e.g. 12.10, October 1880.

382. See Bebbington (1989) pp. 75–81.

383. Chadwick (1966) p. 440.

384. See Hennell (1958) pp. 169–214.

385. See Hugh Thomas, *The slave trade* (London: Macmillan, 1997), esp. pp. 511–35.

386. See Bradley (1976) p. 17; Edwards (1971) pp. 125–56.

387. See Bradley (1976), esp. pp. 136–7; Hennell (1979) p. 4.

388. See Watts (1995) pp. 1ff.

389. See Bebbington (1989) p. 175.

390. See Bebbington (1989) pp. 151–2.

391. For this movement, see esp. Kent (1978) chapter 4 and Bebbington (1989) pp. 162–4.

392. For the sermons, see C. Smyth, *The art of preaching: a practical survey of preaching in the Church of England, 1747–1939* (London: SPCK, 1940) pp. 174–5. For Simeon in general, see Smyth's *Simeon and church order* (1940).

393. This point is well made by Gordon (1991, p. 167). For Spurgeon, see Carlile (1933) and Bacon (1967), as well as Gordon.

394. For this controversy, see Spurgeon's own articles in his own magazine, *The Sword and the Trowel* (esp. 'Another word concerning the Down-Grade', August 1887). For its context, see Bebbington (1989) p. 145.

395. Now available on a single CD-ROM: see Bibliography.

396. George Eliot, letter of 18 November 1870 to Sara Sophia Hennell, in *Letters* vol. 5, p. 121.

397. See e.g. *Sermons* 36, vol. 1, p. 491, for his view of the value of serious study.

398. *Sermons* 68, vol. 2, p. 186.

399. 'It is our firm belief, that what is commonly called Calvinism, is neither more nor less than the good old gospel of the Puritans, the Martyrs, the Apostles, and of our Lord Jesus Christ' (Preface to vol. 1 of *Sermons* (1855), p. 3; cf. *Sermons* 7, vol. 1, p. 100; 11, vol. 1, p. 172; 27, vol. 1, p. 380; 42, vol. 1, p. 551). For Spurgeon, 'the Arminian gospel is the shell without the kernel' (*Sermons* 26, vol. 1, p. 365). He adheres to Calvinist orthodoxy about the two covenants (*Sermons* 93, 'God in the covenant', vol. 2, pp. 507–19).

400. *Sermons* 58, vol. 2, p. 73.

401. *Sermons* 1774, vol. 30, p. 255.

402. Gordon (1991, p. 219) notes that one of his favourite words was 'solid'. For Ryle, see Hennell (1979) and Gordon (1991) pp. 203–28.

403. *Appeal to men of wisdom and candour*, in *Let wisdom judge*, pp. 40–9 (preached in 1815).

404. p. 41.

405. Simeon, *Horae homileticae* vol. 1, p. 15.

406. *Appeal to men of wisdom and candour*, in *Let wisdom judge*, p. 41.

407. p. 42.

408. p. 46.

409. *Horae homileticae* vol. 1, p. 670.

410. *Holiness*, p. 2.

411. Spurgeon, *Sermons* 42, vol. 1, p. 556.

412. Spurgeon, *Sermons* 31, vol. 1, pp. 426–9. See also Simeon, *Evangelic and Pharisaic righteousness compared*, in *Let wisdom judge*, p. 82.

413. *Sermons* 881, vol. 15, p. 491; cf. 1781, vol. 30, p. 370: 'The gospel does not renew a sinner for a season, and then leave him to relapse; but it gives an endless life, implants a deathless principle, and secures ultimate perfection.'

414. Spurgeon frequently cites Bunyan, Owen, Luther and Calvin; he also cites George Herbert, Cowper, Newton, and Doddridge, albeit not always uncritically – see, e.g., *Sermons* 45, vol. 1, p. 602.

415. *Sermons* 3, vol. 1, p. 50.
416. *Sermons* 1767, vol. 30, p. 149.
417. *Sermons* 864, vol. 15, p. 238.
418. *Sermons* 864, vol. 15, p. 244.
419. Simeon, *The offices of the Holy Spirit*, in *Let wisdom judge*, p. 140.
420. Spurgeon, *Sermons* 876, vol. 15, p. 426.
421. Spurgeon, *Sermons* 880, vol. 15, p. 478.
422. *Sermons* 3552, vol. 63, p. 87; cf. Ryle, *Holiness*, p. 249.
423. Spurgeon, *Sermons* 3552, vol. 63, pp. 91–2.
424. Spurgeon, *Sermons* 10, vol. 1, p. 132; cf. 30, vol. 1, p. 416; Ryle, *Holiness*, pp. 15–33.
425. Spurgeon, *Sermons* 20, vol. 1, p. 283.
426. Spurgeon, *Sermons* 83, vol. 2, p. 378; cf. *Sermons* 882, vol. 15, p. 498.
427. Spurgeon, *Sermons* 1796, vol. 30, p. 593; and cf. 1771, vol. 30, p. 213: 'the general religion of mankind is *"do"*, but the religion of a true Christian is *"done"*'.
428. Spurgeon, *Sermons* 83, vol. 2, p. 388.
429. *Holiness*, pp. 24–9.
430. *Sermons* 95, vol. 2, p. 545.
431. Spurgeon, *Sermons* 9, vol. 1, pp. 116–17. This is a point to which he constantly returns: 'the salvation of great saints often depends upon the salvation of little ones' (*Sermons* 6, vol. 1, p. 95); we are all kings and priests of God (10, vol. 1, p. 135); 'a Christian is a king. He is not simply *like* a king, but he *is* a king, actually and truly' (10, vol. 1, p. 135); 'to be a saint is a far more honourable thing than to be a Duke' (1796, vol. 30, p. 591).
432. *Appeal to men of wisdom and candour*, in *Let wisdom judge*, pp. 53–4.
433. p. 58.
434. See p. 61. Anglo-Catholics of course believed in 'the unconditional Regeneration of all Infants . . . by the Sacrament of Holy Baptism', as J. M. Neale put it in 1850 (*Letters*, p. 133).
435. *Sermons* 1785, vol. 30, p. 420.
436. *Sermons* 1757, vol. 30, p. 8; cf. 1759, vol. 30, p. 26.
437. *Sermons* 851, vol. 15, p. 48. Gordon (1991, pp. 162–3) stresses the importance of the theme of union with God for Spurgeon.
438. *Sermons* 851, vol. 15, p. 49.
439. p. 49; cf. 851, vol. 15, p. 60, for Moses as a type of this union with God.
440. *Sermons* 3553, vol. 63, p. 101.
441. *Sermons* 3555, vol. 63, p. 126.
442. 'Janet's Repentance', in *Scenes of clerical life*, pp. 320–1.
443. Thus Spurgeon simply assumes that God divinely ordains some to be rich and others poor (*Sermons* 77, vol. 2, p. 308), though he does maintain that 'very frequently good men are poor men' (*Sermons* 99, vol. 2, p. 585). The people of God are poor partly because then God can display his sovereignty in them (p. 588); but partly too because 'a poor man is the image of Jesus Christ, if he be a Christian' (p. 590 – note the qualification). Cf. also pp. 592–5; *but* see further below, on the role of the church.
444. *Sermons* 81, vol. 2, pp. 357–73, preached in 1856.
445. p. 366.
446. *Sermons* 3555, vol. 63, p. 131.
447. *Sermons* 79, vol. 2, p. 340.
448. *Sermons* 897, vol. 15, p. 720.
449. *Sermons* 1802, vol. 30, p. 681.
450. p. 682.
451. p. 683.
452. p. 686.
453. Simeon, *Horae homileticae* vol. 4, p. 67.
454. *Sermons* 862, vol. 15, p. 212; cf. 1774, vol. 30, p. 252: 'An experience of breaking down and of

soul-horror is necessary to prepare a man for after-usefulness among the convicted, the desponding, and the despairing.'

455. *Sermons* 1790, vol. 30, p. 505.

456. *Sermons* 1798, vol. 30, p. 629.

457. *Sermons* 1814, vol. 30, p. 875.

458. *Sermons* 2182, vol. 37, p. 10, read aloud in his church in 1891 during Spurgeon's last illness.

459. *Sermons* 1805, vol. 30, p. 728.

460. Spurgeon, *Sermons* 59, vol. 2, p. 83.

461. *Sermons* 16, vol. 1, p. 225.

462. Simeon, *Horae homileticae* vol. 1, p. 673.

463. Simeon, *Horae homileticae* vol. 1, p. 552, preaching on Exodus 34 and citing 2 Corinthians 3:18.

464. *Sermons* 1801, vol. 30, pp. 673–5.

465. *Holiness*, pp. 10–11.

466. *Holiness*, p. 11.

467. *The offices of the Holy Spirit*, in *Let wisdom judge*, p. 142.

468. See Bebbington (1989) pp. 86–91 on nineteenth-century Evangelical attitudes to biblical inerrancy, stressing that those attitudes were far more nuanced than is often supposed. For twentieth-century attitudes, see pp. 184–91. For nineteenth-century approaches to biblical interpretation, a good starting-point is Benjamin Jowett's essay 'On the interpretation of Scripture' in *Essays and reviews* (1860).

469. For examples of Spurgeon's polemic, see *Sermons* 27, vol. 1, p. 374 (against Communists and Republicans); 49, vol 1, p. 660 (against Wesleyans); 850, vol. 15, p. 39 (against Tractarians); and 2085, vol. 35, pp. 339–53, for a classic delineation of his uncompromising faith.

470. *Sermons* 1781, vol. 30, p. 359.

471. *Sermons* 3562, vol. 63, p. 209.

472. *Sermons* 3562, vol. 63, pp. 203–7.

473. See Watts (1995) pp. 1ff. for a good discussion of this.

474. Figures from Watts (1995) p. 28.

475. See esp. Watts (1995) for a comprehensive exploration.

476. George Eliot has the Rector say of the appeal of Dissent: 'the promise is sweeter when this life is so dark and dreary, and the soul gets more hungry when the body is ill at ease' (*Adam Bede* chapter 8, p. 93).

477. James Phillippo Mursell (1840) p. 5.

478. Oliphant, *Salem Chapel*, pp. 1–2. She drew much of the detail for this description from her own Free Church of Scotland church in Liverpool. For Oliphant, see Cunningham (1975) pp. 231–48.

479. *The mill on the floss*, Book 1 chapter 12, pp. 184–5.

480. For Clowes and Bourne see first Kendall (1905): for Bourne, the more significant of the two, see also the biographies by Ashworth (1888) and Wilkinson (1952). Like George Fox and John Wesley (both of whom strongly influenced him), Bourne became a travelling evangelist, covering immense distances.

481. For Dow see Kendall (1905) vol. 1, esp. p. 59; Kent (1978) pp. 38–70; Watts (1995) pp. 139–40; for Mow Cop see Kendall (1905) vol. 1, p. 17.

482. Kendall (1905) vol. 1, p. 77.

483. Watts (1995) pp. 32–3.

484. See Kendall (1905) vol. 1, pp. 132–5.

485. For the sociology and spread of the movement, see Chadwick (1966), Watts (1995), and (exhaustively) Kendall (1905) (an invaluable but ill-organized book). Kent (1978, p. 39) suggests that in the first half of the nineteenth century the movement thrived as the religious expression of a demand for change, but flagged in the second half as it lost contact with the wave of social protest that led to trade unionism. Nevertheless it was unquestionably a working-class religious movement, even though it also encompassed a wide variety of backgrounds in its adherents: for a detailed study, see Ambler (1989).

486. Quoted in Kendall (1905) vol. 1, p. 246. Ambler (1989, p. 47) suggests that Primitive Methodist women preachers in Lincolnshire helped to sustain rural workers during a time of social change by emphasizing the centrality of religious experience that was rooted in the home.

487. See Valenze (1986) for an important exploration of this area. She suggests (p. 48) that Victorian Britain tended to narrow religion to church-going, Sunday Schools and private piety of a middle-class kind. But 'in places inaccessible to chroniclers of culture, in ways not in accordance with polite society, common women developed a unique form of female ministry, derived from specific circumstances of laboring life' (p. 50).

488. Valenze (1986) pp. 52–3. See also W. Bramwell, *A short account of the life and death of Ann Cutler* (Sheffield, 1796).

489. See Wilson (1998) p. 354.

490. See Wilson (1998).

491. Kendall (1905) vol. 1, p. 153. The authenticity of their visions was determined by the nature of the revelations to which they gave rise once the individual emerged from the experience.

492. Bourne, *A collection*, Preface (no page no.).

493. See James Barr, *The Scottish Covenanters* (Glasgow: John Smith, 1946), for a comprehensive if over-committed account, and also W. Makey, *The church of the Covenant, 1637–1651* (Edinburgh: John Donald, 1979), for its origins. The working-class membership, open-air worship, love of cheerful singing and harmless recreations, democratic structures and fierce courage in the face of intolerance are all similarities.

494. Bourne, Preface to *The large hymn book*, section entitled 'On worship'.

495. Bourne, Preface.

496. *The Nonconformist* 3, pp. 685–6, issue of Wednesday 4 October 1843.

497. Quoted in Kendall (1905) vol. 2, p. 33.

498. Bourne, Preface to *The large hymn book*.

499. Quoted in Kendall (1905) vol. 1, p. 424.

500. Bourne, Preface to *The large hymn book*.

501. For Capper, see Kendall (1905) vol. 1, pp. 339–41, and (for other examples) vol. 2, pp. 186–8.

502. Charles Shaw, *When I was a child*, p. 232.

503. Bourne, *Journal*, quoted in Kendall (1905) vol. 1, p. 140. Even so, he proved to be an able publisher and correspondent, unlike his colleague Clowes (Kendall (1905) vol. 2, p. 1).

504. Quoted in Kendall (1905) vol. 1, pp. 96–7.

505. *When I was a child*, pp. 7–9.

506. Though he too warned of the dangers of excessive study: 'learning, however important, is neither the first nor the second requisite in the service of Jesus Christ' (quoted in Mursell (1886) p. 149, referring to his father's labours among the poor round Lymington).

507. See K. D. M. Snell, *Church and chapel in the North Midlands: religious observance in the nineteenth century* (Leicester University Department of English Local History, Occasional Papers, 4th Series no. 3) (Leicester UP, 1991), p. 23; in fact Briggs (*Victorian cities*, pp. 370–1) argues that the city was 'virtually taken over by the Nonconformists in 1836'). In the 1851 census the Baptists represented 14.6% of the worshipping population in Leicester, Anglicans representing 35.9%, Methodists (Wesleyan and Primitive) 5.7% and Independents 4.8% (Snell (1991) p. 60). Yet in 1862 nearly half the town's population did not worship regularly at all (Haynes (1991) p. 83). Briggs (1968, p. 68) notes that Nonconformist attendance made up more than 50% of total church attendances in the 1851 census in Bradford, Leeds, Oldham, Wolverhampton and Sheffield, and between 40 and 50% in Birmingham, Manchester, Salford and Newcastle. Furthermore Nonconformists often played a disproportionately prominent part in civic life: thus they were very active in Manchester in promoting the Anti-Corn Law League (Briggs (1968) pp. 123–5). In Birmingham Nonconformist ministers were 'the first people boldly to proclaim a "civic gospel"' (p. 195): the great Baptist preacher George Dawson (1821–76) opened his own church (the Church of the Saviour) in the city centre (in 1847), where he preached regularly to the citizenry on a vast range of public issues until his death (Briggs (1968) pp. 195–6); and his successor Charles Vince was even more involved in Liberal politics and educational issues. Many of

Birmingham's most prominent families were Unitarians (including Joseph Chamberlain) (p. 198), though they remained a small minority (p. 202).

508. See Haynes (1991) for extensive and vivid extracts from Dare's reports.

509. Temple Patterson (1954, p. 231) describes the Baptists in Leicester in the 1830s as 'the shock-troops of local Radicalism'. Not all Baptists were as politically active, however: Mursell's own distinguished predecessor Robert Hall largely abjured political involvement (Watts (1995) pp. 355–6). For Mursell's campaigning activities in Leicester, see Temple Patterson (1954), Mitchell (1983), and Watts (1995) p. 427. For his involvement in the campaign to end the payment of church rates and end the establishment of the Church of England, see the early issues of *The Nonconformist* (which he helped to establish), esp. the first issue (1841), p. 2; vol. 1 no. 16 (28 July 1841), p. 274; vol. 3 no. 136 (25 October 1843), pp. 723–4; vol. 3 no. 145 (27 December 1843), p. 865. Mursell's collected *Letters on education* were reprinted in 1871. In 1830 he with 11 others (mostly Unitarians and Baptists) formed the Leicester and Leicestershire Political Union (Mitchell (1983) p. 68; Temple Patterson (1954) p. 188), membership of which eventually grew to over 4000: they sought municipal reform, the ending of tithes and church rates, repeal of the Corn Laws and of tax on newspapers, abolition of slavery, the adoption of household suffrage, the ballot and the removal of disabilities affecting Dissenters (Mitchell (1983) p. 69). Mursell sought successfully to establish a Mechanics' Institute in the town (p. 40), and celebrated the final passing of the Reform Bill in 1832. He attacked corruption in the government of Leicester (p. 41) and took a keen interest in issues like the amendment of the Poor Law, national education for all, the removal of religious disabilities, the abolition of church rates &c. (p. 42; Watts (1995) p. 427). He furiously opposed the Tory supporters in Leicester of the Duke of Wellington, and in 1835 Tory control of Leicester collapsed. In 1838 Mursell proposed a plan to support the impoverished framework-knitters (suffering from a depression in the hosiery industry): his appeal to employers and employed to work more closely together, together with the suggestion of a union, influenced both sides towards reconciliation (Temple Patterson (1954) p. 299). During the time of the Chartist riots Mursell sided with the poor, though refused to countenance violence (Mursell (1886) p. 60; Temple Patterson (1954) p. 302). In 1844 he spoke out prominently against the church rate and also in favour of Daniel O'Connell, who had been imprisoned for sedition (p. 62).

510. Mursell (1855) p. 218. He follows patristic theology in arguing that the Gospel 'seeks to revive His image' in the breasts of human creatures (p. 222).

511. Mursell (1855) p. 211.

512. Mursell (1855) p. 212.

513. p. 212. Mursell stresses that, if Christianity is to have the power to transform us, we must not pick and choose our personal opinions of it (p. 224; cf. p. 227: 'a correct, a jealous and an unreserved regard to Christian truth is the fairest and only effective method of drawing forth its resources and of putting it to an experimental test'). 'The spiritual phenomena which are at once the fruits and symbols of its power will be but faintly revealed and but feebly sustained . . . in that heart or in that community which contemplates it in parts, and which fails to recognise it in its beautiful and its stupendous proportions' (p. 228). Hence the dangers of diluting the Gospel by being *too* accommodating in presenting it (p. 242).

514. The theme appears regularly in Tractarian preaching (e.g. Keble, Sermon 'Missionary work the duty of all', in *Sermons for the Christian year* 11.18, pp. 209–22). 'The Spirit of Christ . . . and His spouse the Church, are for ever doing missionary work' (p. 213). We must do what we can to support the work of the SPG and others, not expecting immediate results, but giving like the widow with her mite (p. 221). Richard Meux Benson, founder of the Anglican Society of St John the Evangelist, saw a crucial part of its role in England as upholding the society's missionary work overseas in continual intercession (Benson, *The followers of the Lamb*, p. 17).

515. Watts (1995) p. 20.

516. Mursell (1855) p. 229.

517. Mursell (1867) p. 17. William Carey was a predecessor of Mursell's as minister of Harvey Lane Baptist Church, whose 1792 pamphlet *An enquiry into the obligation of Christians to use means for*

the conversion of the heathen was to have a major effect on the development of nineteenth-century overseas missionary work (Neill (1964) p. 261; Watts (1995) pp. 6ff.). For a general survey of this subject see Neill (1964) pp. 261–321 as well as Watts, who argues (1995, pp. 19–20) that the missionary societies were far less narrowly imperialist than has often been thought. The Primitive Methodists sent missionaries to Fernando Po and various parts of Africa (Kendall (1905) vol. 2, pp. 481–506).

518. Mursell (1867) p. 37.

519. Mursell (1855) p. 210.

520. Mursell (1871) p. 15.

521. Mursell (1856) p. 30.

522. Sandall (1947) vol. 1, p. 37; Chadwick (1970) p. 288. Sandall (1947, vol. 1, p. 41) suggests that year as the effective birth of the movement, though it was originally the East London Christian Mission (formally set up under that name in 1867) (Sandall (1947) vol. 1, p. 72).

523. The name 'Salvation Army' began to be used of his followers in 1878: the military imagery was popular among revivalists at the time (e.g. Sabine Baring-Gould's 1864 hymn 'Onward Christian soldiers') (Sandall (1947) vol. 1, pp. 226–7; Chadwick (1970) pp. 290–1; it is interesting that Manning disapproved of it – 'S.Paul did not go [on his journeys] in array, nor with the pomp and circumstance of war' ('The Salvation Army', in *Miscellanies* 3 (London: Burns and Oates, 1888), p. 197). The new name was not legally established until 1880 (Sandall (1947) vol. 1, pp. 233–4). In 1878 the Army had 50 corps and 88 officers; by 1883 it had 528 corps and 1,340 officers in Britain; by 1886, 1,006 corps and 2,260 officers in Britain (p. 293). In the last years of his life Booth won national esteem, was received by Edward VII and received an honorary doctor of laws degree at Oxford.

524. Booth (1890) p. 45.

525. Booth (1890) pp. 79–80.

526. See pp. 82–9.

527. Quoted in Booth (1890) pp. 164–5.

528. Quoted in Booth (1890) pp. 41–2.

529. Victoria and Albert Museum, textiles department, T.3–1930. Note, in this regard, the inclusion of 'a child's lamentation for the death of a dear mother' in *Hymns for infant minds*, produced by two East Anglian Congregationalist sisters, Ann (1782–1866) and Jane (1783–1824) Taylor, pp. 72–3.

530. For the Unitarians in the nineteenth century see Chadwick (1966) pp. 391ff.; Watts (1995), esp. pp. 90–1.

531. Martineau, *The seat of authority* Book 4 chapter 2, pp. 383–4.

532. Martineau also wrote *Types of ethical theory* (1885) and *A study of religion* (1888).

533. See his *Collected writings* in 5 volumes (London, 1864), Strachan (1973), Hennell (1979), and Bebbington (1989) pp. 78–81.

534. Chadwick (1966) p. 36; Hennell (1979) p. 9.

535. Hennell (1979) pp. 10–11. His condemnation by the Church of Scotland was, however, primarily because of his views on Christ's human nature: he argued that it was holy not because it came from God, i.e. inherently, but because of the inworking or energizing of the Holy Spirit upon it (Strachan (1973) p. 48).

536. *On praise*, in *Works* vol. 3, pp. 212–13.

537. *On prayer*, in *Works* vol. 3, pp. 8–10.

538. pp. 11–12.

539. pp. 20–1 and 87–95.

540. p. 22.

541. See pp. 69 and 82–3.

542. pp. 150–62.

543. Irving, *The book of Psalms*, in *Works* vol. 1, pp. 402–8. Irving says that the reason the Psalms 'have found such constant favour in the sight of the Christian Church . . . is to be found in this – that they address themselves to the simple instinctive feelings of the renewed soul, which are its most

constant and permanent part' (p. 389). The cursing psalms and texts remind us that 'rebuke is a form of charity; and censure, and excommunication, yea, and total abandonment for a while. Truth is always a form of charity; or, to speak more properly, truth is the soul of which charity is but the beautiful, graceful, and lovely member' (p. 398).

544. Including a prohibition on Roman Catholics from using ecclesiastical titles and names of sees already used by the Church of England (and hence of course from implicitly claiming to be *the* pre-Reformation English church), and prohibition from performing their rites in public, or becoming members of a religious order; see Chadwick (1966) pp. 18–19.

545. Chadwick (1970) p. 402.

546. Bossy (1975), Newsome (1993) p. 189.

547. 'Ironically' because Pugin, as a lover of Gothic, hated Roman Baroque. For Pugin see Dixon and Muthesius (1978), esp. p. 182; Prickett (1979) p. 17; Rosemary Hill, 'To stones a moral life: how Pugin transformed the Gothic Revival', in *The Times Literary Supplement* (18 September 1998), pp. 21–2; and Judith Champ, 'Goths and Romans: Daniel Rock, Augustus Welby Pugin, and nineteenth-century English worship' in R. N. Swanson (ed.), *Continuity and change in Christian worship* (Studies in Church history 35) (Woodbridge: Boydell, 1999), pp. 289–319.

548. Chadwick (1975) p. 124.

549. *Quod apostolici muneris* was to some extent anticipated by Pius IX's *Quanta cura* of 1864, to which was appended the *Syllabus errorum* that condemned a wide range of contemporary intellectual movements regarded as heretical. In 1896 Leo's bull *Apostolicae curae* famously described Anglican ordinations as 'absolutely null and utterly void'.

550. See Heimann (1995). *The garden of the soul* was easily the most frequently-reprinted manual of devotion in RC English circles between 1850 and 1914 though in nineteenth-century editions it was progressively expanded (Heimann (1995) pp. 71–82). Heimann's argument is that the devotional tone of Challoner and his predecessors was adjusted, rather than replaced, so as to allow for the desire for a more affective and warm piety suited to the new circumstances of the nineteenth century (p. 89). 'It was an invigorated English recusant tradition, not a Roman one, which was most successful in capturing the imagination of Catholics living in England from the middle of the nineteenth century to the early years of the twentieth' (p. 137). It is worth reading Crichton's article (1996), which comments on Heimann's thesis.

551. See Chadwick (1975) p. 102.

552. Crichton (1996) p. 327.

553. Henry Chadwick (1990) p. 60.

554. Chadwick (1966) pp. 279–81.

555. Doubtless this was in part the result of a felt need to justify to former colleagues, and to themselves, their decisions to convert.

556. Heimann (1995) p. 125.

557. Heimann (1995) p. 127.

558. p. 135.

559. For Manning see esp. Newsome (1993), a deeply impressive study, and Pereiro (1998). Manning's earliest biographer, E. S. Purcell, was wretchedly biassed; and this, together with Lytton Strachey's famous portrayal ('the face of smiling asceticism . . . as [he] passed in triumph from High Mass at the Oratory to philanthropic gatherings at Exeter Hall', (*Eminent Victorians* (Harmondsworth: Penguin, 1948), p. 13), badly tarnished Manning's subsequent reputation. For Manning's relationship with the early Tractarians at Oxford, see Norman (1984) pp. 246–7.

560. See Newsome (1993) pp. 82–3; Norman (1984) p. 248.

561. Newsome (1975) p. 296.

562. See Norman (1984) p. 251; Newsome (1993) p. 249.

563. Newsome (1993) pp. 333–7.

564. Though, as Norman (1984, p. 281) points out, he was conservative about the role of women in general.

565. *The pastoral office*, p. 31. He does go on to acknowledge that bishops frequently fail to live up to their lofty calling (p. 177); but it is hard to imagine a more grandiose theology of episcopacy.

566. Newsome (1993) p. 290; Pereiro (1998) p. 78.

567. See, e.g., the impact made on him by the charterhouse (Carthusian monastery) at Pavia; Bowden (1869) pp. 84–6. Bowden (1869, p. 3) notes his early love of natural beauty.

568. Bowden (1869) p. 179.

569. Sharp (1983).

570. Letter to M. Watts Russell, quoted in Bowden (1869) pp. 427–8.

571. For Alice Meynell, see the eloquent and moving tribute by G. K. Chesterton in his *Autobiography* (London: Hutchinson, 1937), pp. 286–7.

572. Sagovsky (1990) pp. 12–17. Sagovsky's biography is an outstandingly balanced and perceptive account: much writing about Tyrrell appears to be influenced by whether or not the author approves of Tyrrell's later break with Rome.

573. At St Helen's: see Petre (1912) vol. 2, pp. 36–7. Petre's two-volume study is an indispensable source of information about Tyrrell, but needs to be balanced by Sagovsky.

574. Petre (1912, vol. 2, p. 80), says that Tyrrell, infuriated at being delated, destroyed an almost-complete book on St Ignatius' *Spiritual exercises*, which if true may have been a serious loss to English spirituality.

575. In 1899 Tyrrell was already writing to a friend expressing his disapproval of nearly all his Jesuit colleagues ('That I am totally out of sympathy with all but a mere handful of the body is indeed a pain to me; but whose fault is it? . . . Certainly I should never recommend anyone to enter the English Province as I know it': letter quoted in Petre (1912) vol. 2, p. 74). He reverenced St Ignatius Loyola, but intensely disliked what he saw as the later systematic accretions built upon his teaching (pp. 77–84). In 1900 the English Catholic bishops produced a pastoral letter 'The Church and Liberal Catholicism' which infuriated Tyrrell (Petre (1912) vol. 2, pp. 146–61). In 1903–4 Tyrrell wrote his 'Letter to a Professor', which was eventually to precipitate his dismissal from the Society (Petre (1912) vol. 2, pp. 193–6). In 1904 he wrote to the Jesuit General telling him that he now had 'no affection for and no belief in the existing Society, which seems to me essentially false to its original spirit and aims' (letter in Petre (1912) vol. 2, p. 229). It became difficult for Tyrrell to find any means by which he could leave the Society and remain a priest. In 1906 extracts from Tyrrell's 'Letter to a Professor' were published in the *Corriere della Sera*: when Tyrrell refused to repudiate these, he was expelled from the Jesuits. On 14 February 1906 he said his last Mass, at Eastbourne (Petre (1912) vol. 2, p. 262). In 1907 Pius X's encyclical *Pascendi* condemned Modernism and led to Tyrrell's virtual excommunication after he attacked the encyclical in a letter to *The Times*. In 1908 the Prior of the Premonstratensians at Storrington refused Tyrrell permission to attend the Sunday Mass in what appears to have been a peculiarly hurtful episode (Petre (1912) vol. 2, pp. 363–5). For the very moving story of his death and burial, see Petre (1912) vol. 2, pp. 420–46.

576. See the remark of Sagovsky (1990, p. 41): 'As an incorrigible idealist, he believed in the Roman Church with a kind of visionary fervour . . . Bit by bit, he lost his confidence in the system, but the more this happened, the more he clung to his hope for a renewal of the Church by a return to the sources.'

577. He regarded his 1899 article 'The relation of theology to devotion' (later printed as 'Lex orandi - lex credendi' in *Through Scylla and Charybdis*) as the keynote of his thought (Petre (1912) 2nd series, p. 98). Much of his output is designed to popularize Catholic teaching, and was produced as sermons or articles in the Jesuit periodical *The Month* (from 1886 to 1904). Some of his early work (notably *Nova et vetera* (1897), which originated in domestic conferences given to Jesuit lay-brothers) is outstanding.

578. *Lacordaire*, p. 242.

579. *Nova et vetera*, Preface, p. vi.

580. *The faith of the millions*, 1st series, p. 240: this essay first appeared in *The Month* (November 1899) and later as 'Lex orandi, lex credendi' in *Through Scylla and Charybdis*, pp. 85–105: clearly it was very important for Tyrrell.

581. *The faith of the millions*, 1st series, p. 243.

582. *Lex credendi*, Preface, p. x.

583. *Lex credendi*, p. 14.

584. *Lex credendi*, p. 16; cf. pp. 138–9.

585. *Lex credendi*, p. 245.

586. Displaying esoteric knowledge for the sake of it is useless (p. 246).

587. *Lex credendi*, p. 141.

588. *The glories of the Sacred Heart*, pp. 82–3.

589. *The glories of the Sacred Heart*, p. 83. See Pereiro (1998) p. 120.

590. Manning, *The glories of the Sacred Heart*, p. 114.

591. pp. 115–16. Cf. also Faber (*Growth in holiness* 5, p. 50): 'a mistake in doctrine is doubly dangerous when it is worked up into the spiritual life. It poisons everything.'

592. 'There is a most unpardonable narrowness as well as impertinence in the desire to represent the intercourse between the created spirit and its indwelling Creator in terms as sharp and exact as those which describe the dealings of father and son' (*Hard sayings*, p. viii).

593. pp. x–xi.

594. *Through Scylla and Charybdis*, pp. 24–5 and 47.

595. It is through mortification and the cross that we grow most truly and fruitfully (*Nova et vetera*, pp. 120–1).

596. *Essays on faith and immortality*, p. 166. 'A perverted devotion' first appeared in *The Weekly Register*, 16 December 1899, and was subsequently reprinted in *Essays on faith and immortality*, ed. M. D. Petre, pp. 158–71; see also Petre (1912) vol. 2, pp. 112–30. It was precisely this article that precipitated his eventual condemnation.

597. 'If love be mysticism, then we have the key to all mysticism within ourselves' (essay 'What is mysticism?' (1897), *The faith of the millions*, 1st series, p. 271). 'Love itself is a contemplative act – *complacentia boni* – a gazing with delight upon the Fair and True: the mind's embrace of that which is its food and eternal life' ('The true and the false mysticism' (1899), *The faith of the millions*, 1st series, p. 275). 'All love is mystical in that it refuses the exact analysis of reason which, without contradicting, it ineffably transcends; still more must the union between the Creator and the created soul be of a nature dimly apprehensible; something to be felt rather than said' (p. 283). And this is not the privilege of an elect few, 'but an obligation binding upon all'. 'Catholicism . . . is a language in which the simplest and the subtlest can hold converse with Heaven on the shallowest themes and the deepest' (*Through Scylla and Charybdis*, p. 56).

598. *The faith of the millions*, 1st series, p. 279.

599. See *Lex credendi*, p. 32. The unity between the two which Tyrrell stresses here is important because it alone brings us true peace, 'the peace of the heart whose many loves are gathered up and converge into one' (*Nova et vetera*, p. 56; cf. pp. 387–8).

600. *Christianity at the cross-roads*, p. 109.

601. *Christianity at the cross-roads*, p. 111.

602. pp. 112–13.

603. *Through Scylla and Charybdis*, p. 28; cf. Tyrrell's early (1898) essay '"Liberal" Catholicism', in *The faith of the millions*, 1st series, p. 74.

604. *The faith of the millions*, pp. 82–3.

605. 'Reflections on Catholicism', in *Through Scylla and Charybdis*, pp. 20–84, esp. p. 79: 'liberal Catholicism has no necessary connection with a minimising tendency as to doctrine or discipline. What it excludes is the negative, militant, intolerant spirit, whether of orthodoxy or heterodoxy, whether conservative or progressive.'

606. *Growth in holiness* 8, p. 94.

607. Faber, Hymn no.102, 'Come to Jesus', in *Hymns*, p. 343.

608. Hymn no.119, in *Hymns*, p. 391.

609. *Nova et vetera*, p. 82.

610. It is interesting to note that Manning, in describing the Incarnation, describes God as coming 'in our humanity as our kinsman' so that he might draw all his kinsfolk to live with him in heaven (Manning (1876) pp. 62–3).

611. Tyrrell, *Nova et vetera*, p. 18: love requires 'laborious exercise'.

612. *Growth in holiness* 8, pp. 95–6.

613. p. 96.

614. *Growth in holiness* 9, p. 114.

615. *The Blessed Sacrament* 2.1, pp. 146–7.

616. *Growth in holiness* 4, p. 34. Self-denial, though unpalatable to nature, is essential to the workings of grace (pp. 39–40). This alone conduces to setting us free in the way Jesus was free (pp. 44–5).

617. *Growth in holiness* 1, p. 1.

618. *Growth in holiness* 6, p. 69.

619. p. 63.

620. *Growth in holiness* 2, p. 14.

621. p. 18.

622. p. 19. Cf. Tyrrell, *Nova et vetera*, p. 123: 'every good desire or prayer or effort elicited from our heart by that love which is the one secret cause of all good . . . is an energy set free that can never be ultimately lost or destroyed'.

623. *The glories of the Sacred Heart*, p. 173.

624. In 2 Corinthians 3; see p. 174.

625. pp. 175–6.

626. p. 203.

627. Manning, *Sermons on ecclesiastical subjects* (1872) vol. 3, p. 251.

628. Manning, *The glories of the Sacred Heart*, pp. 157–8.

629. Meynell, *Poems*, p. 92.

630. *The Blessed Sacrament* 2.7, p. 249.

631. *The Blessed Sacrament* 2.7, p. 253.

632. *Growth in holiness* 11, p. 138.

633. *Growth in holiness* 11, pp. 149–51.

634. *Hard sayings*, p. 27.

635. *The Blessed Sacrament* 1.7, pp. 128–9. See his Hymn no. 49 ('The grandeurs of Mary'), in *Hymns* p. 184, for a different Mariology.

636. Faber, *Growth in holiness* 5, p. 49.

637. Tyrrell, *Nova et vetera*, pp. 77–8.

638. See also Heimann (1995) pp. 60–1. Faber says 'I cannot conceive a man being spiritual who does not habitually say the Rosary' (*Growth in holiness* 15, p. 247).

639. *Nova et vetera*, p. 29.

640. *Nova et vetera*, p. 406.

641. *The Blessed Sacrament* 2.3, p. 168.

642. Faber, *The Blessed Sacrament*, pp. 576–83.

643. Meynell, *Poems*, p. 81.

644. Heimann argues (1995, pp. 46–9) that the origins of Benediction, at least in its English manifestation, were from Challoner: 'it would be difficult to find a more quintessentially old-Catholic devotion' (1995, p. 51). In the nineteenth century it seems to have been popular with all strata of Roman Catholic society. Crichton (1996), modifying Heimann's arguments, warns that the term 'Benediction' could mean a variety of things from 'Evening Service' to the full eucharistic exposition rite. For Stations of the Cross, see Heimann (1995) p. 42.

645. See Heimann (1995) pp. 150–2.

646. *Nova et vetera*, p. 42.

647. *The love of Jesus to penitents*, pp. 34–5 and 22–3.

648. pp. 48–9.

649. pp. 75–6.

650. pp. 75–7 and 89. Not everyone agreed that reparation was a virtue at all: in Dickens' *Little Dorrit*, one of the central characters asks his lawyer how he can make reparation after he and his partner are ruined in a financial collapse. The lawyer answers 'I *don't* like the term "reparation," sir, except as a lever in the hands of counsel' (*Little Dorrit* Book 2 chapter 26, p. 684).

651. *All for Jesus*, p. 118; cf. Tyrrell, *Lex credendi*, p. 83.

652. Manning, *The glories of the Sacred Heart*, p. 239.
653. p. 240.
654. pp. 251–2.
655. pp. 254–6.
656. p. 256.
657. pp. 260–1.
658. p. 262.
659. *Nova et vetera*, p. 91.
660. pp. 92–3; cf. pp. 117 and 243.
661. *All for Jesus*, p. 117.
662. *Lex credendi*, p. 134.
663. p. 135.
664. p. 151; cf. p. 211: 'with the right and duty of praying for [the ends of the Kingdom] comes the right and duty of working for them'. Cf. p. 218.
665. *Growth in holiness* 15, p. 229.
666. See Ward (1986), esp. p. 219.
667. See Aspinwall (1985).
668. Anson (1964, pp. 193–8) details various pre-nineteenth-century attempts at renewing the eremitical life in England; Allchin (1958, chapter 1) explores the extent to which an implicit, and sometimes explicit, approval of monasticism remained present within Anglican thought from the sixteenth century until the nineteenth century, finding occasional reflection in communities like Little Gidding. But none of this alters the sense in which the recovery of the religious life in the nineteenth century was a genuinely new development, a renaissance.
669. See Philip Jebb and David M. Rogers, 'Rebirth', in *The Benedictines in Britain* (London: British Library, 1980), pp. 92–102.
670. Anson (1964) pp. 205–6.
671. The Jesuit journal *The Month* records the historic visit of Queen Victoria to the Grande Chartreuse in 1887. Visiting an English monk, she gave him a silver cross which he could not keep; so he gave it to the Prior having written on the back of it 'Regina dedit; regula abstulit; sit Nomen Domini benedictum' (The queen gave; the Rule hath taken away; blessed be the name of the Lord). *The Month* 17 (1887), p. 474 n. 4. For a woman to be allowed to enter the Grande Chartreuse was extraordinary.
672. See Hamer (1994).
673. See Liddon, *Life of Pusey* vol. 3, pp. 1–2 and 19.
674. Liddon; Allchin (1958) pp. 127–36; Mumm (1999) pp. 6 and 68–9. Mumm suggests (pp. 157–8) that Pusey's guidance, here as elsewhere in regard to religious communities, was consistently detrimental to community survival.
675. In 1895 this motto was altered to *Per angusta ad augusta* (Neale, *Letters*, p. 118). Neale in fact based its original rule on that of Clewer (p. 234). See Allchin (1958) pp. 96–113.
676. Mumm (1999) p. 157.
677. Ann Frances CSMV (1985) p. 372. For the Wantage community, see Mumm (1999) pp. 8–9: Mumm notes that this was one of the very few communities which did not discriminate between sisters on the basis of their social status.
678. See Mumm (1999) chapter 2, esp. pp. 15 and 46. She points out that most Anglican sisterhoods were founded in poor areas (p. 95).
679. See the extract from her *Suggestions for thought for seekers after religious truth among the artisans of England* (1860) cited in Mumm (1999) p. 167.
680. Kent (1978) p. 255.
681. See Kent (1978) pp. 236–94 and Allchin (1958) p. 38.
682. Prestige (1935) p. 138.
683. In 1902, when Gore was made a bishop, he was succeeded by Walter Frere as Superior; see Prestige (1935) p. 217, and Alan Wilkinson, *The Community of the Resurrection: a centenary history* (London: SCM, 1992).

684. For Benson, see Allchin (1958); the memoir by Arthur Hall in Benson's *Letters*. He left a number of significant works, including some fine spiritual letters, numerous meditations for the use of religious and others, and a study of the Psalms (*The war song of the Prince of Peace*).

685. *Nova et vetera*, pp. 100–1.

686. *Lacordaire*, pp. 132–3.

687. pp. 134–5.

688. p. 136.

689. p. 146.

690. pp. 150–1.

691. pp. 155–7.

692. *The followers of the Lamb*, pp. 129–30.

693. p. 131.

694. p. 131.

695. p. 136.

696. p. 146.

697. pp. 37–40.

698. pp. 203–4.

699. p. 98.

700. p. 118.

701. Benson, *Letters*, p. 49.

702. Benson, *Benedictus Dominus*, vol. 1 Preface, pp. v–vi.

703. Benson, *Letters*, p. 321.

704. *The followers of the Lamb*, p. 119.

705. *Benedictus Dominus* vol. 1, Preface p. vii.

706. p. vii.

707. *The followers of the Lamb*, p. 6.

708. *Letters*, p. 199.

709. Benson, *The final Passover* vol. 1, p. 20.

710. See Benson, *The followers of the Lamb*, pp. 76–8.

711. Benson, *Letters*, pp. 195–6; cf. pp. 314–16.

712. Peacock, *Nightmare Abbey*, p. 361.

713. *Letters and diaries* vol. 1, p. 47. He speaks of being 'stared at', (vol. 1, pp. 36, 40).

714. Quoted in Ker (1988) p. 18.

715. 'I rather dread the two thirds of the parish which are to come,' he wrote to his mother, after visiting one third (*Letters and diaries* vol. 1, p. 180, 28 July 1824).

716. *Letters and diaries* vol. 1, p. 191.

717. p. 196.

718. 16 November 1824; vol. 1, p. 198.

719. *Letters and diaries* vol. 1, p. 193.

720. Letter to Henry Wilberforce, 28 March 1855, in *Letters and diaries* vol. 16, p. 429.

721. See the acute remarks of Newsome (1993) p. 124.

722. See especially Rowell (1983), Ker (1988), and Newsome (1993).

723. *Letters and diaries* vol. 4, p. 5, n. 2.

724. *Letters and diaries* vol. 5, pp. 246–7. For Newman and the breviary, see Withey (1992).

725. See *Letters and diaries* (17 February 1849), vol. 13, p. 56.

726. 1 February 1846, *Letters and diaries* vol. 11, p. 105. Later he refers to Neri as 'the most angelic of saints' (11 June 1854, in *Letters and diaries* vol. 16, p. 153).

727. *Apologia*, p. 45.

728. *Letters and diaries* vol. 13, p. 64.

729. *Letters and diaries* vol. 16, p. 235.

730. Chadwick (1983) p. 3.

731. Letter to Alexander Forbes, Bishop of Brechin, 6 April 1686, in *Letters and diaries* vol. 24, p. 58. Cf. vol. 21, p. 62, where he says in a letter of 27 February 1864: 'controversy, which was never

pleasant to me, is quite a trouble to me at my age'. Wilfred Ward has pointed out that each of Newman's major failures in life led to immensely productive consequences: the *Apologia* after Kingsley's attack, the *Essay on development* after the opposition to Tract 90, the *Grammar of assent* after the failure of his Oxford plans (see Newsome (1975) pp. 295–6).

732. Letter of 7 April 1850, in *Letters and diaries* vol. 13, p. 460.

733. Note here that for Newman 'idea' connoted not some speculative abstraction, but (as with Plato) the deepest reality itself. See David Tracy, 'Recent Catholic spirituality: unity amid diversity' (*Christian spirituality III: post-Reformation and modern*, ed. Dupré and Saliers (London: SCM Press, 1990), p. 146.

734. Letter to Hurrell Froude, 1 February 1836, in *Letters and diaries* vol. 5, p. 222.

735. For Newman's definition of it, see p. 202 above. See also *Apologia*, p. 48.

736. 13 March 1829, *Letters and diaries* vol. 2, pp. 129–30.

737. *Letters and diaries* (1833), vol. 3, pp. 293.

738. *Apologia*, p. 30; he was speaking of the deposition of the Bourbons in France.

739. See Berlin (1999) p. 87: for the Romantics, 'ideals are not to be discovered at all, they are to be invented' – as art is. For Newman's relationship with Romanticism, see D. Nicholls and F. Kerr (eds), *Newman: reason, rhetoric and Romanticism* (Bristol, 1991).

740. Letter of 16 April 1833, in *Letters and diaries* vol. 3, p. 292.

741. *Sermons bearing on subjects of the day*, p. 391.

742. 'I have myself a very great repugnance to reviving obsolete usages on private authority without very strong reason for doing so' (letter of 1842, quoted in Ker (1988) p. 252). Cf. also *Parochial and plain sermons* (hereafter PPS) 2.23: 'I wish I saw any prospect of this element of zeal and holy sternness springing up among us, to temper and give character to the languid, unmeaning benevolence which we misname Christian love. I have no hope of my country till I see it' (p. 409). Only when hope and fear go together will there be hope for humankind (p. 410).

743. PPS 3.17, p. 641. For Newman, memory of the past, and the virtue of long silent patient attention to things of the spirit, has a particularly creative effect (see PPS 4:17, p. 900).

744. PPS 1.12, p. 106.

745. *Sermons bearing on subjects of the day*, p. 346.

746. PPS 2.19, p. 365. Cf. PPS 3.18, p. 365. See also Ker (1988) p. 91.

747. Letter to James Stephen, 16 March 1835, in *Letters and diaries* vol. 5, p. 46.

748. Letter to Mrs William Froude, 2 January 1855, *Letters and diaries* vol. 16, pp. 341–2.

749. PPS 5.3, p. 986.

750. Though normally notional terms will be plural ('rabbits eat voraciously') and real ones singular ('my pet rabbit eats lettuce').

751. *A grammar of assent* 3, p. 34, and 4, p. 37.

752. *A grammar of assent* 4.1, pp. 55–8.

753. *A grammar of assent* 4.2, pp. 86–7.

754. *A grammar of assent* 4.1, p. 46. Newman explores this in his understanding of 'reserve'. Basically this means either a deliberate holding-back in communicating what people might not be ready to understand, or conveying a truth in a manner that makes it more palatable or assimilable to the recipient, like a doctor telling bad news to a patient (Newman also calls this second sense 'economy'). It is in this respect that poetry can be so valuable as a means of conveying truth (see the helpful analysis in Newsome (1993), p. 76). In a letter (to Richard Holt Hutton) of 1 March 1872, Newman writes:

> I have . . . looked at St Francis [Xavier]'s exposition of the Creed. That it is fresh, impressive, beautiful, suited to its hearers, I suppose will be generally allowed; but, as to the truth of every word of it, well, it seems to me a *Meditation* on the Creed, a quickening of it into substance and reality. Catholics are apt to gabble it over; St Francis impressed it as a living fact upon the hearts of his audience. It is in his hands reason elevated by imagination. The only way to make heavenly truths alive within us is thus to submit them to an economy. Educated men may do this for themselves in meditation, knowing what they are doing; they don't confuse such clothing with the outline of faith. Nor indeed do the common people; nay does not St Francis

virtually even tell them that he has added to the Creed his own thoughts . . . ?

This is how we talk to children. I recollect how as a child I used to say of a story 'tell it again,' 'tell it again,' – children thus feed their imagination – they realize facts in their own colouring and shape. It is all they can do . . . And so, as to speeches put in Scripture into the mouths of sacred persons – 'Let there be light' – 'lest he put forth his hand etc' 'They will reverence my son' 'I go to *prepare* a place for you', etc. These surely are modes of bringing home to the mind ideas which primitive language cannot express otherwise, or primitive races and uneducated minds receive; – nay no language and no human mind; – but there is no necessary confusing of them, I think, in the mind of the Catechumen, with the credenda which are definite articles, direct and terse. (*Letters and diaries* vol. 26, pp. 39–40)

Cf. Faber's

> The awful spirit of reserve, that dwells
> In nature's forms and shadows . . .
> ('Admiration of nature', in *Poems*, pp. 212–13)

755. We most frequently infer notional propositions, which are by definition abstract; whereas we most frequently assent to real propositions (*A grammar of assent* 4, pp. 40–1).

756. *A grammar of assent* 4.3, pp. 89–90.

757. *A grammar of assent* 5.2, p. 126.

758. *A grammar of assent* 6, p. 158.

759. *A grammar of assent* 6.1, pp. 174–6.

760. Newman distinguishes between theology and religion: the former deals with notional assent, the latter with real assent. He uses the term religion to mean something very close to 'spirituality'. In *A grammar of assent* he defines 'religion' as 'the knowledge of God, of His Will, and of our duties towards Him' (10.1, p. 389).

761. *A grammar of assent* 5.2, pp. 126–7.

762. *A grammar of assent* 4.3, pp. 90–1.

763. pp. 92–3.

764. p. 95. Newman says that great people come upon or apprehend the truth without always being able to explain why it is true, or even how it is they have come to apprehend it. It belongs to second-rate, though still important, people to come along after them and prove what the great apprehended without the need of proof (*Lectures on the prophetical office of the Church*, quoted in *A grammar of assent* 9.3, p. 380). This is what he means by the 'illative sense' in operation, right judgement: see *A grammar of assent* 9.2, p. 353.

765. *A grammar of assent* 7.1, p. 216.

766. *A grammar of assent* 5.1, pp. 120–1.

767. PPS 6.7, p. 1239.

768. PPS 1.15, p. 128.

769. PPS 1.24, p. 199.

770. p. 199.

771. p. 200.

772. p. 205.

773. p. 205. This element of uncompromising fierceness and sobriety in Newman's Anglican spirituality is noted by Newsome (1993, pp. 111–13), who compares Newman at this time with Manning, whose sermons reflected more the primacy of love than of fear. See also note 742 above.

774. *Lectures on the prophetical office of the church*, Introd., p. 13.

775. 'This is a day [= an age] in which there is (rightly or wrongly) so much of private judgment . . . that it involves individual profession, responsibility, and recompense in a way peculiarly its own' (PPS 5.3, p. 980); and see esp. his 1841 essay 'Private judgment', repr. in *Essays critical and historical* vol. 2, pp. 336–74.

776. *Lectures on the prophetical office of the church*, 6, p. 203. The issue of *sola scriptura* was the key one for Newman in the controversy over the appointment of R. D. Hampden as Regius Professor of Divinity at Oxford: Hampden argued strongly for it (Newsome (1993) pp. 98–9).

777. PPS 1.2, p. 16.

778. PPS 1.2, p. 17.
779. PPS 1.2, p. 17.
780. PPS 4.6, p. 787.
781. As time passes, people 'will find that independence was not made for man – that it is an unnatural state . . . No, we are creatures; and, as being such, we have two duties, to be resigned and to be thankful' (PPS 5.6, p. 1012).
782. *A grammar of assent* 9.1, p. 349.
783. 'Private judgment' (1841), in *Essays critical and historical* vol. 2, p. 343. See also PPS 8.14, pp. 1682–90, a sermon entitled 'Obedience to God the way to faith in Christ'; and *A grammar of assent* 6.1, p. 169. In PPS 3.4, he commends King David as an exemplar of obedience (p. 518), and notes how Joseph was able to cope with imprisonment in Egypt because of the 'settled habits of virtue which he could call to his aid at a moment's notice' (p. 519) – an appealing thought.
784. *Lectures on justification* 1, pp. 1–2.
785. *Lectures on justification* 6, p. 171.
786. p. 172.
787. *Lectures on justification* 8, p. 218.
788. PPS 1.6, p. 52; cf. PPS 5.16: 'A true Christian . . . may almost be defined as one who has a ruling sense of God's presence within him', p. 1102.
789. PPS 2.19, p. 368.
790. PPS 7.16, p. 1545.
791. *Lectures on the prophetical office of the church* 14, p. 407.
792. PPS 2.19, p. 370.
793. PPS 3.18, p. 651.
794. PPS 5.7, p. 1015.
795. PPS 3.18, p. 652.
796. For these particular visitations, see PPS 2.10, pp. 297–8.
797. PPS 3.9, p. 563.
798. PPS 3.18, p. 653.
799. PPS 5.22, p. 1160.
800. See PPS 2.2, p. 239.
801. *A grammar of assent* 5.1, p. 105.
802. PPS 5.16, p. 1102.
803. PPS 4.9, p. 820.
804. PPS 4.9, p. 822.
805. PPS 7.15, p. 1539; cf. *A grammar of assent* 10.1, p. 403.
806. PPS 4.15, p. 878.
807. PPS 4.15, p. 880.
808. PPS 5.4, pp. 993–4.
809. *A grammar of assent* 7.1, p. 220; cf. 7.2, p. 238.
810. See Newman's letter to Pusey, 2 April 1866, in *Letters and diaries* vol. 22, p. 201.
811. See PPS 1.11, p. 97, where he does allow that feelings can be a starting point for prayer (PPS 1.19, p. 162).
812. PPS 3.7, p. 544. For forms as remedies against chaos, see PPS 1.20, p. 170; and 3.14, p. 607.
813. PPS 5.2, pp. 970–1.
814. PPS 7.13, p. 1528.
815. PPS 1.20, p. 166.
816. PPS 1.20, p. 167.
817. PPS 1.19, p. 163.
818. *Letters and diaries* vol. 6, pp. 46–7.
819. *Letters and diaries* vol. 4, p. 47.
820. p. 47. See also PPS 3.13, pp. 600–1; *Sermons bearing on subjects of the day* 18, esp. pp. 259–63 (on the lament Psalms).
821. PPS 6.22, p. 1382.

822. *Lectures on justification* 2, p. 41.
823. PPS 3.11, p. 577.
824. *A grammar of assent* 4.2, p. 79.
825. PPS 6.4, p. 1212.
826. PPS 6.17, p. 1337.
827. PPS 1.3, p. 26.
828. PPS 5.23, p. 1171.
829. PPS 1.3, pp. 28–9; cf. PPS 4.22, p. 940.
830. PPS 4.5, p. 781.
831. PPS 1.11, pp. 93–4.
832. PPS 3.23, pp. 697–8.
833. PPS 1.11, p. 94; cf. 7.15, p. 1536. It is only once we make prayer habitual that we avoid the common weakness of only praying *in extremis* (7.15, p. 1540).
834. PPS 1.11, p. 97.
835. PPS 7.15, p. 1537.
836. PPS 3.22, p. 694.
837. PPS 3.24, pp. 712–13.
838. *A grammar of assent* 1.1, pp. 7–8.
839. *A grammar of assent* 2, p. 13.
840. *A grammar of assent* 6.2, p. 191.
841. 'Liberalism', in *The dream of Gerontius and other poems*, p. 135.
842. PPS 1.1, p. 7. One is minded of the passage in his *Apologia* when Newman says that 'From the age of fifteen, dogma has been the fundamental principle of my religion: I know no other religion; I cannot enter into the idea of any other sort of religion; religion, as a mere sentiment, is to me a dream and a mockery. As well can there be filial love without the fact of a Supreme Being' (*Apologia,* p. 49).
843. Letter to Archbishop Manning, 24 November 1873, in *Letters and diaries* vol. 26, p. 390.
844. *Lectures on certain difficulties felt by Anglicans* 9, p. 225.
845. *Lectures on certain difficulties felt by Anglicans* 8, p. 190, repr. in *Apologia*.
846. See PPS 3.5, p. 527.
847. See for example his encomium to the splendours of patristic life and spirituality in *Lectures on justification* 13, pp. 383–6.
848. *Lectures on the prophetical office of the Church* 14, pp. 429–30.
849. *Sermons*, ed. cit. (1879), pp. 35–6.
850. *Poems*, p. 144.
851. Watson (1987, pp. 19–20) helpfully suggests a parallel with Newman here: both were realists, wanting to deal with life exactly as it was, scorning half-truths or imprecise utterances.
852. Wheeler (1990, p. 340) notes a number of important similarities between the two: both had similar English middle-class backgrounds; both loved music; both were very gifted intellectually; both were strongly influenced by Oxford, though in both cases their conversion to Rome alienated them from the university. For Hopkins' life see esp. White (1992), though White is harshly unsympathetic to the Catholicism of Hopkins' day.
853. He was also, for 30 years, the London-based consul-general for Hawaii, a poet and a High Churchman (White (1992) p. 18).
854. Wakefield (1993) p. 328.
855. *Journal and papers*, p. 165.
856. White (1992) p. 207.
857. He became devoted to Mary's Well at Ffynnon Fair, near St Beuno's, whose medieval Catholic associations and romantic ruins would have appealed; White (1992) pp. 241–3.
858. See *Journal and papers*, p. 258, and editorial comments on p. 440.
859. *Sermons* (1879) p. 17.
860. J. J. Feeney SJ, 'At St Beuno's', in *The Times Literary Supplement* 5000 (29 January 1999), pp. 13–14. Fr Feeney points out that a number of other comic verses written by Hopkins were destroyed by his great friend and fellow poet Robert Bridges.

861. *Sermons,* ed. cit. p. 83; cf. introd. to ed. cit., p. 9.

862. 'The wreck of the Deutschland' has inspired a great deal of comment. White (1992, p. 252) sees it as both a sea-disaster poem of a traditional Victorian kind, and a eulogy for modern Catholic exiles and martyrs. Wheeler (1990, p. 342) suggests that 'The wreck' articulates 'a theology of death which is grounded in Christ's own death and passion', and that it also reflects the influence of Ignatius' *Exercises* in Hopkins' ability to visualize meditatively the situations he writes about (p. 344). See also below.

863. *Sermons* (1879), p. 26.

864. For the influence of Scotus on Hopkins, see esp. Balthasar (*The glory of the Lord*, vol. 3), White (1992), esp. p. 100, and Devlin (introduction to *Sermons and spiritual writings*).

865. *Poems,* pp. 107–8.

866. The *felix culpa* theory: see *Spiritual writings,* p. 297; Devlin, Introduction, p. 109.

867. Balthasar vol. 3, p. 357.

868. Balthasar vol. 3, p. 358.

869. Balthasar vol. 3, p. 374.

870. Balthasar vol. 3, pp. 375–6. As he says, Hopkins is here close to the theology of St Bonaventure: 'God's utterance of himself in himself is God the expression, news of God' (Hopkins, *Sermons and spiritual writings,* quoted by Balthasar on p. 376).

871. Tyrrell, *Nova et vetera,* p. 296.

872. See the clear description in Watson (1987) pp. 31–2. White (1992, p. 200) curiously argues that both terms originate in a desire to disguise responsibility for what he feels, and perhaps to the long guilt-dominated years of the Jesuit novitiate. Balthasar argues that 'instress' is used by Hopkins for both the object and the subject: things express their instress, their deep, unique act, which establishes them, holds them together and holds them in tension, and there is required in the subject an answering stress, so that it can hold communion with the stress of things and experience them from within (pp. 365–6). See also Wakefield (1993) p. 330.

873. The intimate relationship between 'inscape' and 'instress' calls to mind Augustine's use of *forma* and *species* (though Augustine's use of them is not always consistent). In his *De vera religione, forma* is a precise word, always denoting the intelligible structure or identity of something, akin to Hopkins' 'inscape'. *Species* is a rather looser word; but it invariably denotes that which draws us towards something, whether the something is good or bad, and usually also denotes what it is in any given thing that has an impact on us. See the note by J. Pegon SJ in his edition of Augustine's *De vera religione: Oeuvres de Saint Augustin, VIII: La foi chrétienne* (Bibliothèque Augustinienne 8) (Paris: Desclée de Brouwer, 1951) pp. 486–8.

874. *Journal and papers,* pp. 151–2. There are many other descriptions of trees (see e.g. pp. 154–5).

875. *Sermons* (1880), pp. 90–1.

876. 'The wreck of the Deutschland' v. 13, in *Poems,* p. 122.

877. *Spiritual writings,* p. 135.

878. *Spiritual Writings,* p. 135.

879. *Poems,* p. 139.

880. 'The wreck of the Deutschland' v. 21, in *Poems,* p. 124. God's hands were 'unchancelling' because they had lifted the nuns from their convent chancel into the vocation of martyrs. Mackenzie, ed. cit. of *Poems,* p. 338.

881. The Methodist scholar Gordon Rupp ('A devotion of rapture in English Puritanism', in R. B. Knox (ed.), *Reformation, conformity and dissent: essays in honour of Geoffrey Nuttall* (London: Epworth, 1977, p. 116)) describes 'The wreck' as 'the finest exposition in non-theological English of what Luther meant by the "Righteousness of God"'

882. 'The wreck of the Deutschland' v. 29, in *Poems,* p. 126; on this section see Watson (1987) pp. 67–8.

883. 'The wreck of the Deutschland' v. 31.

884. v. 32, p. 127. 'Motionable mind': God calming human fears, embodying stability; 'bodes but bides': God decrees but bides his time; so Mackenzie, ed. cit. of *Poems,* p. 347; cf. Hopkins (1987) pp. 71–2.

885. 'Carrion comfort', in *Poems*, p. 183. Fr Devlin, in his introd. to *Sermons and devotional writings* (ed. cit., p. 118), suggests that the image of wrestling with God is 'somehow alien to Catholic spirituality'. The subject is too large to discuss here; but it is certainly true that relatively few Catholic spiritual writers use this language. But it is hard to think of any reason why they should not. Watson (1987, p. 113) has no doubts that this wrestling is what the poem is about; God is not just a wrestler but a thresher too, beating the life out of the poet like the beating-out of corn.

886. *Poems*, p. 93. Hopkins knows that patience is a tough virtue. In one of his last poems he says 'Patience, hard thing! the hard thing but to pray,/ But bid for, patience is!' (*Poems*, p. 185). See Watson (1987) pp. 119–21. Patience had been an indispensable, but deeply costly, virtue for Hopkins in surviving the demands of Jesuit formation and asceticism. There are surely echoes of George Herbert's spirituality in this poem, a point noted by Mackenzie (ed. cit. of *Poems*, p. 289).

887. See e.g. Part 1 v. 6, in *Poems*, p. 120.

888. 'The wreck of the Deutschland' v. 9, in *Poems*, p. 121. For Herbert see note 886.

889. v. 12, p. 122.

890. Quoted by Mackenzie, in *Poems*, p. 335.

891. 'Pilate' ll. 3–4, in *Poems*, p. 19. Many other poems refer to the experience: see e.g., 'A Voice from the World', ll. 45–6, in *Poems*, p. 49.

892. For the Victorian obsession with death, see Wheeler (1990) pp. 25–68: death was seen as either grim reaper or friend; euphemisms (notably those connected with sleep) for handling it became legion; and doubt in the face of what happens after death becomes increasingly apparent. Deathbed scenes are commonplace in nineteenth-century literature.

893. 'Spring and death', in *Poems*, pp. 17–18. The same point is made in 'The wreck of the Deutschland' v. 11, in *Poems*, pp. 121–2.

894. Balthasar vol. 3, p. 379.

895. *Devotional writings*, p. 154; see Balthasar vol. 3, p. 379.

896. *Devotional writings*, p. 155; partly quoted by Balthasar vol. 3, pp. 379–80.

897. *Devotional writings*, p. 155.

898. *Devotional writings*, p. 197. Balthasar (vol. 3, p. 383) argues that underlying this is Duns Scotus' Trinitarian theology: the 'great sacrifice' on which everything is founded is God's sacrifice of himself, which was God's first 'thought' of the world, to which we are summoned to respond.

899. *Poems*, pp. 89–90.

900. *Sermons* (1879), p. 48; cf. *Sermons* (1880) pp. 51–3.

901. *Devotional writings*, p. 263.

902. 'As kingfishers catch fire' v. 2, in *Poems*, p. 142.

903. 'That Nature is a Heraclitean Fire and of the comfort of the Resurrection', in *Poems*, p. 198, a poem that contrasts the infinite mutability of all that is with the ultimate fire from which all once came, in Heraclitus' (c.535–c.475 BCE) thought: Hopkins here interweaves Heraclitus with St Paul's teaching on resurrection ('we shall all be changed . . . ').

904. *Poems*, p. 186. See Mackenzie, p. 463.

905. *A basket of summer fruit* contains the dedication 'To the American Evangelists who lately visited England'; Bett (1950, p. 66) suggests that these must have been Moody and Sankey.

906. Bett (1950) p. 67.

907. For her life, see Dorling (1885); Bett (1950); and Maynard (1926).

908. She wrote, rather self-consciously, 'I was born beneath quiet hills, among green pastures, beside still waters. My first companion was a little stream' (*Two friends*, p. 1). She dedicated *Lacordaire* to her brother Alan.

909. Bett (1950) p. 18; Dorling (1885) p. 40. J. R. Watson (*The English hymn* (Oxford: Clarendon, 1997), p. 436) suggests that Dora's mother was 'tyrannical'.

910. Originally published in the *North British Review* (1862).

911. *Lacordaire*, p. 89.

912. For Woolman, see R. M. Jones, *The later periods of Quakerism* (London: Macmillan, 1921), vol. 1, pp. 67–8.

913. Her interest in mental illness led her to read widely in contemporary psychology, including

Maudsley's *Physiology and pathology of the mind* (Dorling (1885) p. 152). For her work in regard to the mentally ill, see pp. 143–55.

914. *Liber humanitatis* p. 137. She also cites, inter alia, Shelley, Herder, Hawthorne, Wordsworth, Sir Thomas Browne, Schiller, Kant, Newman, Goethe, J. S. Mill, George Eliot, Gibbon, George Herbert, Lamennais, Guyon, and de Tocqueville. For other sources see Bett (1950) pp. 39–40.

915. Her attitude to Mme Guyon was typically nuanced and original: whilst recognizing the exceptional nature of her personal experience, she praises her clarity and even her *rationality* ('her directions as a guide are clear, coherent, and eminently *rational*'), but notes the under-emphasis on the role of Christ and on our own status as sinners; 'also from their utter excision of natural feeling they seem to check the principle of warmth and expansion natural to all life' (*A basket of summer fruit*, pp. 31–2 and note).

916. She describes her mind, with characteristic self-deprecation, not as catholic, but as 'parasitical' (letter quoted in Dorling (1885) p. 70).

917. Bett (1950) pp. 16–23.

918. Constable, quoted in Dorling (1885) p. 161.

919. *Lacordaire*, p. 224.

920. *A basket of summer fruit*, p. 38.

921. p. 39.

922. pp. 40–1.

923. *John Woolman*, p. 11.

924. *The patience of hope*, p. 12.

925. p. 36.

926. *Lacordaire*, pp. 274 and 30 respectively.

927. p. 11. Cf. p. 90: 'Christianity had from the first presented itself to [Lacordaire] under its most stern, though most tender aspect, *as the immolation of man joined to that of God*' (her italics) – hence Lacordaire's commitment to a personal life of austerity.

928. *Lacordaire*, pp. 245–7.

929. p. 249.

930. p. 251.

931. *The power of prayer*, p. 7.

932. p. 8.

933. p. 17.

934. pp. 20–1.

935. p. 23.

936. p. 30.

937. p. 30.

938. pp. 46–7.

939. pp. 21–3.

940. p. 44.

941. Quoted in *John Woolman*, pp. 28–9.

942. p. 39.

943. pp. 48–9.

944. *The origin of species* 13, p. 433.

945. *Colloquia crucis* 2, pp. 48–9.

946. *Two friends*, p. 143.

947. *Two friends*, p. 143.

948. Letter to Professor Knight (1865), cited in Dorling (1885), pp. 87–8.

949. *Colloquia crucis* 1, p. 16.

950. *The power of prayer*, p. 25.

951. p. 32.

952. p. 36.

953. p. 37.

954. p. 38.

955. p. 39; italics Greenwell's.
956. *Colloquia crucis* 4, p. 91.
957. pp. 1–19.
958. pp. 2–3. Hence, as she points out elsewhere, we mean something very different when we speak of 'a good man' from what we mean when we speak of 'a good horse', On the comparative freedom of the will', in *Colloquia crucis*, p. 69).
959. p. 6.
960. p. 8.
961. p. 8.
962. p. 10.
963. p. 28.
964. p. 20. Note that elsewhere she notes that that freedom is limited ('a being, with infinite ends to attain, and but finite means at command, must work under continual check and pressure', and not to realize this 'is to miss the grandeur of that everyday tragedy, the conflict between will and circumstance', 'On the comparative freedom of the will', in *Colloquia crucis*, pp. 70–1).
965. p. 24.
966. p. 35.
967. p. 35.
968. p. 38.
969. p. 45.
970. *On the education of the imbecile*, p. 5.
971. p. 6.
972. p. 6.
973. p. 7.
974. *Colloquia crucis* 5, p. 107.
975. p. 8.
976. 'Folk-lore', in *Liber humanitatis*, pp. 145–6.
977. p. 148.
978. pp. 148–9.
979. pp. 149–50.
980. p. 150.
981. pp. 150–1.
982. p. 161.
983. p. 163.
984. p. 166.
985. *The patience of hope*, p. 92.
986. p. 94.
987. 'Our single women', in *Essays*, p. 16.
988. pp. 34–5.
989. pp. 58–9.
990. Quoted in Dorling (1885) p. 161.
991. *Great expectations* chapter 4, p. 54.
992. Cf. *Great expectations* chapter 38, where Pip describes Mrs Brandley and her daughter: 'The mother looked young, and the daughter looked old; the mother's complexion was pink, and the daughter's was yellow; the mother set up for frivolity, and the daughter for theology' (p. 318). Cf. also *Oliver Twist*: 'Dignity, and even holiness too, sometimes, are more questions of coat and waistcoat than some people imagine' (chapter 37, p. 322). And 'there are a good many ladies and gentlemen, claiming to be out-and-out Christians, between whom, and Mr Sikes' dog, there exist strong and singular points of resemblance' (*Oliver Twist* chapter 18, p. 182; both the dog and its owner were distinctly unattractive).
993. *Great expectations* chapter 7, p. 73.
994. *Little Dorrit* Book 1 chapter 3, p. 42.
995. *Little Dorrit* Book 2 chapter 10, pp. 520–1.

996. *Little Dorrit* Book 2 chapter 31, p. 753.

997. *Great expectations* 9, pp. 100–1.

998. p. 101.

999. In a letter of 21 December 1865 Eliot writes:
> I want to tell you that I was brought up in the Church of England, and never belonged to any other religious body. I care that this should be known, not at all on personal grounds, but because, as I have been, and perhaps shall be, depicting dissenters with much sympathy I would not have it supposed that the sympathy springs from any partiality of association. As to its origin historically, and *as a system of thought*, it is my conviction that the Church of England is the least morally dignified of all forms of Christianity i.e. all considerable forms dating from the Reformation; but as a portion of my earliest associations and most poetic memories, it would be more likely to tempt me into partiality than any form of dissent. (*Letters* vol. 4, pp. 213–14)

1000. *Letters* vol. 3, pp. 230–1.

1001. *The mill on the floss*, Book 7 chapter 4, p. 637.

1002. 'Evangelical teaching: Dr Cumming' in *Essays,* p. 161 (originally published in *Westminster Review* 64 (October 1855), pp. 436–62).

1003. *Adam Bede* chapter 18, p. 201.

1004. *Adam Bede* chapter 37, pp. 385–6.

1005. 'Janet's Repentance', in *Scenes of clerical life,* p. 319.

1006. *Middlemarch* chapter 61, p. 667.

1007. Bossuet had in 1688 written a *Histoire des variations des Églises protestantes.*

1008. *The mill on the floss* Book 4 chapter 1, pp. 363–4.

1009. *Romola* chapter 25, p. 234.

1010. *Romola* chapter 44, pp. 388–9.

1011. *Romola* chapter 59, p. 492.

1012. *Romola* chapter 61, p. 501.

1013. *Romola* chapter 71, p. 575.

1014. *Daniel Deronda* chapter 69, pp. 803–4.

1015. Feuerbach, *The essence of Christianity* (in the translation by Eliot herself), 1.2, p. 13. For the influence of Feuerbach on Eliot see esp. Willey (1964).

1016. *The essence of Christianity* 1.1, p. 5.

1017. Cf. Schelling's notion of God as a kind of self-developing principle of consciousness (Berlin (1999) p. 98).

1018. A. S. Byatt, introd. to *The mill on the floss,* p. 17.

1019. Quoted by A. S. Byatt, pp. 17–18.

1020. *Great expectations* chapter 56, p. 470. Angus Calder (introd. to ed. cit., pp. 27–8) says that 'fellowship' is the key virtue for Dickens, as for Dostoyevsky, William Morris, and William Temple.

1021. *Little Dorrit* Book 1 chapter 13, p. 166.

1022. *A tale of two cities* chapter 15, p. 403.

1023. *Romola,* Epilogue, pp. 582–3.

1024. *Adam Bede* chapter 50, p. 488. Romola's face is at its most radiantly beautiful when it is filled with loving sympathy and affection for her blind scholar-father (see chapter 5, p. 50). In *The mill on the floss* Eliot describes God as 'the Unseen Pity' (Book 7 chapter 5, p. 649). Cf. also *Daniel Deronda*: 'Want of sympathy condemns us to a corresponding stupidity' (chapter 48, p. 596).

1025. Letter of 8 May 1869 to Mrs Harriet Beecher Stowe, *Letters* vol. 5, p. 31.

1026. *Middlemarch* chapter 61, p. 668.

1027. *Essays,* pp. 186–7.

1028. See p. 188.

1029. See, e.g., 'Mr Gilfil's Love-story', in *Scenes of clerical life,* p. 244.

1030. See p. 177: 'While this poor little heart was being bruised with a weight too heavy for it, Nature was holding on her calm inexorable way, in unmoved and terrible beauty.'

1031. 'Janet's Repentance', in *Scenes of clerical life,* p. 322.

1032. *Adam Bede* chapter 1, p. 11. It is richly ironic that Adam himself ends up by 'running after some preacher' and marrying her!

1033. *Adam Bede* chapter 17, p. 183; cf. Feuerbach, *The essence of Christianity*, trans. G. Eliot: 'feeling is the organ of the divine . . . how couldst thou perceive the divine by feeling, if feeling were not itself divine in its nature?' (1.1, p. 9). Gill (1998, p. 156) notes that *Adam Bede* 'presents feeling as the most sensitive calibrator of moral discrimination'; and see Carroll, introd. to *Silas Marner* p. xxiv.

1034. *Oliver Twist* chapter 34, p. 307.

1035. 'The natural history of German life', in *Essays*, p. 269.

1036. See 'Janet's repentance', in *Scenes of clerical life*, p. 324: 'See to it, friend, before you pronounce a too hasty judgement, that your own moral sensibilities are not of a hoofed or clawed character. The keenest eye will not serve, unless you have the delicate fingers, with their subtle nerve filaments, which elude scientific lenses, and lose themselves in the invisible world of human sensations.'

1037. 'Janet's repentance', in *Scenes of clerical life*, p. 358. Cf. *Adam Bede*: 'All honour and reverence to the divine beauty of form! Let us cultivate it to the utmost . . . But let us love that other beauty too, which lies in no secret of proportion, but in the secret of deep human sympathy' (chapter 17, p. 180).

1038. *Adam Bede* chapter 15, p. 156. It is noticeable that at the end of the novel Dinah is unable to make the condemned Hetty feel anything similar. She has, as it were, to feel it for her.

1039. *Daniel Deronda* chapter 16, p. 178.

1040. p. 179; cf. chapter 41, p. 511: his 'conscience included sensibilities beyond the common, enlarged by his early habit of thinking himself imaginatively into the experience of others'.

1041. chapter 28, p. 324.

1042. chapter 32, p. 365.

1043. chapter 41, p. 514.

1044. 'My convictions as to the nature of the Deity are so held in equilibrio by the appearance of things in my glimmering apprehension that prayer, beyond that involved in culture, would be in my idea (though possibly I am quite wrong) a vain offering' (letter to Francis Watts, 3 August 1842, in *Letters* vol. 1, p. 143). It is possible here to sense echoes of Feuerbach's view of prayer: 'God is the nature of human feeling, unlimited, pure feeling, made objective. God is the optative of the human heart transformed into the *tempus finitum*, the certain, blissfull "IS" – the unrestricted omnipotence of feeling, prayer hearing itself' (*The essence of Christianity*, trans. G. Eliot, 12, p. 121). Thus 'in prayer, man forgets that there exists a limit to his wishes, and is happy in this forgetfulness' (p. 123).

1045. *Romola* chapter 47, p. 408.

1046. *A tale of two cities* Book 2 chapter 1, pp. 86–8 passim. Later Cruncher does his best to stop his poor wife from praying, and encourages his son to do the same. 'The devoutest person could have rendered no greater homage to the efficacy of an honest prayer than he did in this distrust of his wife. It was as if a professed unbeliever in ghosts should be frightened by a ghost story' (Book 2 chapter 14, p. 189).

1047. For the failure of *The wind in the willows* at first, see Prince (1994) p. 231. Grahame had written several earlier works, of which *The golden age* (1895) and *Dream days* (1898), both semi-autobiographical reflections on childhood, had been particularly well received.

1048. Kenneth Grahame, *The wind in the willows* (1908), pp. 1–2.

1049. For Grahame's life see the biographies by Green (1959) and Prince (1994).

1050. Quoted in Prince (1994) p. 336.

1051. Grahame's biographers both report that Wilhelm II had only two books with him on the royal yacht *Hohenzollern*: the Bible and *The golden age* (Green (1959) p. 291; Prince (1994) p. 231). *The golden age* was published in 1895 and was an immediate success.

1052. Grahame, *The golden age*, pp. 192–3.

BIBLIOGRAPHY
Primary Works

Andersen, Hans Christian, *The snow queen*, in *Hans Andersen's fairy tales: a selection*, trans. L. W. Kingsland (World's classics) (Oxford UP, 1959), pp. 228–72

Benson, Richard Meux SSJE, *Benedictus Dominus: a course of meditations* (London: Swift, n.d.)

Benson, Richard Meux SSJE, *The final Passover: a series of meditations upon the Passion of our Lord Jesus Christ* (London: Longmans, 1898)

Benson, Richard Meux SSJE, *The followers of the Lamb* (London: Longmans, 1900)

Benson, Richard Meux SSJE, *Letters*, ed. G. Congreve SSJE and W. H. Longridge SSJE (London: Mowbray, 1916)

Bodington, Charles, *Devotional life in the nineteenth century* (London: SPCK, 1905)

Books of devotion (London: Longmans, Green, 1908)

Booth, William, *In darkest England and the way out* (London: Salvation Army, 1890)

Bourne, Hugh: *A collection of hymns for camp meetings, revivals, &c., for the use of the Primitive Methodists* (Bemersley, nr Tunstall: Primitive Methodist Connexion, 1829) (includes *Large hymn book, for the use of the Primitive Methodists*, by Hugh Bourne); see also Ashworth, among Secondary Works below

Butler, Josephine, *Catharine of Siena: a biography* (London: Dyer, 1878)

Butler, Josephine, *Personal reminiscences of a great crusade* (London: Horace Marshall, 1896); see also Bell, among Secondary Works below

Butler, Samuel, *The way of all flesh* (London: Dent (Everyman), 1933)

Cobbett, William, *Rural rides* (1830; Harmondsworth: Penguin, 1967)

Darwin, Charles, *The origin of species* (1859; ed. J. W. Burrow, Harmondsworth: Penguin, 1968)

Dickens, Charles, *Great expectations* (1861; ed. Angus Calder, Harmondsworth: Penguin, 1965)

Dickens, Charles, *Little Dorrit* (1855–7; ed. Stephen Wall, Harmondsworth: Penguin, 1998)

Dickens, Charles, *Oliver Twist* (1837–9; ed. P. Fairclough, Harmondsworth: Penguin, 1966)

Dickens, Charles, *A tale of two cities* (1850; ed. George Woodcock, Harmondsworth: Penguin, 1970)

Eliot, George, Essays: Pinney, T. (ed.), *Essays of George Eliot* (London: Routledge & Kegan Paul, 1963)

Eliot, George, Journals: Harris, M., and Johnston, J. (eds), *The journals of George Eliot* (Cambridge UP, 1998)

Eliot, George, Letters: Haight, Gordon S. (ed.), *The George Eliot letters*, 9 vols (New Haven: Yale UP, 1954–78)

Eliot, George, *Scenes of clerical life* (1858; ed. D. Lodge, Harmondsworth: Penguin, 1973)

Eliot, George, *Adam Bede* (1859; ed. S. Gill, Harmondsworth: Penguin, 1980)

Eliot, George, *The mill on the floss* (1860; ed. A. S. Byatt, Harmondsworth: Penguin, 1979)

Eliot, George, *Silas Marner* (1861; ed. D. Carroll, Harmondsworth: Penguin, 1996)

Eliot, George, *Romola* (1862–3; ed. D. Barrett, Harmondsworth: Penguin, 1996)

Eliot, George, *Middlemarch* (1871; ed. W. J. Harvey, Harmondsworth: Penguin, 1965)

Eliot, George, *Daniel Deronda* (1876; ed. T. Cave, Harmondsworth: Penguin, 1995)

Faber, Frederick William, *All for Jesus, or, the easy ways of divine love*, 2nd edn (Baltimore: John Murphy, 1854)

Faber, Frederick William, *The Blessed Sacrament: or, the works and ways of God*, 3rd edn (London: Richardson, 1861)

Faber, Frederick William, *Growth in holiness, or, the progress of the spiritual life*, 3rd edn (London: Burns & Oates, 1932)

Faber, Frederick William, *Poems* (London: Burns & Oates, 1856)

Faber, Frederick William, *Hymns* (1861 edition) (London: Burns & Oates, 1880)

[Faber, Frederick William] Bowden, J. E., *The life and letters of Frederick William Faber DD* (London: Burns & Oates, n.d. [1869])

Feuerbach, Ludwig, *The essence of Christianity* (ET of *Das Wesen des Christentums* by Marian Evans, alias George Eliot) (1854; New York: Harper Torchbooks, 1957)

Gore, Charles, 'The Holy Spirit and inspiration' in Gore, C. (ed.), *Lux mundi: a series of studies in the religion of the Incarnation*, 15th edn (London: John Murray, 1904), pp. 230–66

Gosse, Edmund, *Father and son: a study of two temperaments* (1907; Harmondsworth: Penguin, 1949)

Grahame, Kenneth, *The golden age* (1895; 9th edn London: John Lane, The Bodley Head, 1898)

Grahame, Kenneth, *The wind in the willows* (1908; London: Methuen, 1961)

Greenwell, Dora, *A basket of summer fruit* (London: Dalby, Isbister, 1877)

Greenwell, Dora, *A present heaven* (Edinburgh: Thomas Constable, 1855)

Greenwell, Dora, *Camera obscura* (London: Dalby, Isbister, 1876)

Greenwell, Dora, *Carmina crucis* (Poems) (London: Bell & Daldy, 1869)

Greenwell, Dora, *Colloquia crucis* (London: Gibbings, 1899)

Greenwell, Dora, *Essays* (London: Alexander Strahan, 1866)

Greenwell, Dora, *John Woolman* (London: F. B. Kitto, 1871)

Greenwell, Dora, *Lacordaire* (London: Edmonston & Douglas, 1867)

Greenwell, Dora, *Liber humanitatis* (London: Dalby, Isbister, 1875)

Greenwell, Dora, *On the education of the imbecile* (in *North British Review* 97 (1868); repr. London: Strahan, 1869)

Greenwell, Dora, *Selected poems* (London: Allenson, 1906)

Greenwell, Dora, *The patience of hope* (Edinburgh: Thomas Constable, 1860)

Greenwell, Dora, *Two friends* (London: Gibbings, 1894)

Greenwell, Dora, see also Dorling, W., Bett, H., and Maynard, C. L. among Secondary Works below

Headlam, Stewart D., *Priestcraft and progress* (London: John Hodges, 1891)

Hopkins, Gerard Manley, *Poetical works*, ed. N. H. Mackenzie (Oxford: Clarendon, 1990)

Hopkins, Gerard Manley, *Sermons and devotional writings*, ed. C. Devlin SJ (London: Oxford UP, 1959)

Hopkins, Gerard Manley, *Journals and papers*, ed. H. House and G. Storey (London: Oxford UP, 1959)

Howitt, Mary, *Fireside verses* (London: Darton and Clark, n.d.)

Irving, Edward, *Collected writings*, ed. G. Carlyle, 5 vols (London: Alexander Strahan, 1864)

Jay, E. (ed.), *The Evangelical and Oxford Movements* (extracts from texts) (Cambridge UP, 1983)

Johnson, Dale A. (ed.), *Women in English religion 1700–1925* (Studies in women and religion 10) (New York: Edwin Mellen, 1983)

Keble, John, *The Christian year* (repr. from Oxford edition of 1914) (London: Society of SS Peter and Paul, 1976)

Keble, John, *Assize sermon on national apostasy* (Abingdon: Rocket, 1983)

Keble, John, *The Psalter in English verse* (London: Blackie, 1906)

Keble, John, *Sermons for the Christian year*, 11 vols (Oxford: Parker; London: Walter Smith, 1880–4)

Kingsley, Charles, *Alton Locke: tailor and poet* (Works, vol. 3) (London: Macmillan, 1881)

Kingsley, Charles, *Health and education* (London: Macmillan, 1879)

Kingsley, Charles, *The hermits* (Works, vol. 12) (London: Macmillan, 1879)

Kingsley, Charles, *Hypatia, or, new foes with an old face* (Works, vol. 4) (London: Macmillan, 1880)

Kingsley, Charles, *Miscellanies*, 2 vols, 2nd edn (London: Parker, 1860)

Kingsley, Charles, *The Roman and the Teuton* (Works, vol. 10) (London: Macmillan, 1879)

Kingsley, Charles, *The water babies* (Boots the Chemist illustrated edition) (London: Hodder and Stoughton, n.d.)

Kingsley, Charles, *Westminster sermons* (Works, vol. 27) (London: Macmillan, 1878)

Kingsley, Charles, *Charles Kingsley: his letters and memories of his life, edited by his wife*, 2 vols (London: Henry King, 1877)

Liddon, Henry Parry, *Life of Edward Bouverie Pusey*, 4th edn, 4 vols (London: Longmans, Green, 1894–8)

Liddon, Henry Parry, *Some elements of religion*, 6th edn (London: Longmans, Green, 1898)

Liddon, Henry Parry, *Christmas sermons* (*Christmastide at St Paul's*) (London: Rivingtons, 1889)

Manning, Henry Edward, *The love of Jesus to penitents* (Dublin: James Duffy, 1866)

Manning, Henry Edward, *The glories of the Sacred Heart* (London: Burns & Oates, 1876)

Manning, Henry Edward, *The pastoral office* (1883, privately printed)

Manning, Henry Edward, *Sermons on ecclesiastical subjects*, 4 vols (London: Burns & Oates, 1845–73)

Martineau, James, *The seat of authority in religion*, 4th edn (London: Longmans, 1898)

Martineau, James, *A study of religion: its sources and contents*, 2nd edn, 2 vols (Oxford: Clarendon, 1889)

Maurice, Frederick Denison, *The doctrine of sacrifice deduced from the scriptures* (Cambridge: Macmillan, 1854)

Maurice, Frederick Denison, *The Epistles of St John: a series of lectures on Christian ethics* (Cambridge: Macmillan, 1857)

Maurice, Frederick Denison, *The Gospel of St John: a series of discourses*, 2nd edn (London: Macmillan, 1894)

Maurice, Frederick Denison, *The kingdom of Christ*, 2nd edn (1842; ed. A. R. Vidler, 2 vols. London: SCM Press, 1958)

Maurice, Frederick Denison, *Lectures on the Apocalypse* (1860; 2nd edn London: Macmillan, 1885)

Maurice, Frederick Denison, *The Prayer-Book, considered especially in reference to the Romish system*, 2nd edn (London: Parker, 1852)

Maurice, Frederick Denison, *The religions of the world and their relations to Christianity* (1846; 6th edn London: Macmillan, 1886)

Maurice, Frederick Denison, *Theological essays*, 2nd edn (1853; London: James Clarke, 1957)

Meynell, Alice, *Poems*, complete edn (London: Burns Oates & Washbourne, 1923)

Meynell, Alice, *Prose and poetry* (London: Cape, 1947)

Moody, Clement, *Our cathedrals: are they to be reformed or abolished?* (letter to the Rt Hon Sir George Grey) (London: Longmans, 1856)

Mursell, Arthur, *James Phillippo Mursell: his life and work* (London: James Clarke, 1886)

Mursell, Arthur, *Lectures to working men* (delivered in the Free Trade Hall, Manchester), 5th series (Manchester: John Heywood, n.d. [c.1860]), vol. 2

Mursell, James Phillippo, *A sermon occasioned by the death of the late Reverend Robert Hall, M.A., preached at Harvey-Lane, Leicester, March 6, 1831* (London: Hamilton, Adams, n.d.)

Mursell, James Phillippo, *A discourse delivered in Bloomsbury Chapel, London, on the 63rd anniversary of the Baptist Missionary Society* (1855) (printed in A. Mursell, *James Phillippo Mursell*, pp. 207–60)

Mursell, James Phillippo, *Christian morals* (lecture to Leicester YMCA, 27 April 1856) (London: Arthur Hall, 1856

Mursell, James Phillippo, *The principles of Nonconformity* (lecture) (London: T. Ward, 1840)

Mursell, James Phillippo, *A zealous ministry, its character and worth* (address) (London: J. Heaton, 1857)

Mursell, James Phillippo, *Letters on education* (London: Hodder and Stoughton, 1871)

Neale, John Mason, *A commentary on the Psalms from primitive and mediaeval writers*, 4 vols, 4th edn (London: Joseph Masters, 1884)

Neale, John Mason, *Letters,* ed. Mary Sackville Lawson (London: Longmans, 1910)

Newman, John Henry, *The letters and diaries of John Henry Newman*, ed. Dessain et al. (Oxford: Clarendon, 1961–)

Newman, John Henry, *Apologia pro vita sua* (1873 edn; London: Longmans, Green, 1890)

Newman, John Henry, *The dream of Gerontius and other poems* (Oxford UP, 1914)

Newman, John Henry, *An essay in aid of a grammar of assent*, 6th edn (London: Longmans, Green, 1887)

Newman, John Henry, *An essay on the development of Christian doctrine*, 2nd edn (London: James Toovey, 1846)

Newman, John Henry, *The idea of a university* (London: Longmans, 1902)

Newman, John Henry, *Lectures on certain difficulties felt by Anglicans in submitting to the Catholic Church* (Dublin: Duffy, 1857)

Newman, John Henry, *Lectures on justification*, 2nd edn (London: Rivington, 1840)

Newman, John Henry, *Meditations and devotions*, 3rd edn (London: Longmans, 1894)

Newman, John Henry, *Parochial and plain sermons* (1891 edn; San Francisco: Ignatius, 1997) (cited in footnotes as PPS).

Newman, John Henry, *Essays critical and historical*, 2 vols (1828–46; republished 1871) (London: Basil Montague Pickering, 1872)

Newman, John Henry, *Lectures on the prophetical office of the church*, 2nd edn (London: Rivington, 1838)

Newman, John Henry, *Sermons bearing on subjects of the day* (London: Longmans, 1902)

The Nonconformist (London, 1841–) (weekly journal)

Oliphant, Margaret, *Salem Chapel* (1863; London: Dent, 1907)

Payne Knight, Richard, *An analytical inquiry into the principles of taste* (London: T. Payne, 1805)

Peacock, Thomas Love, *Nightmare Abbey*, in D. Garnett (ed.), *Thomas Love Peacock: the complete novels* (London: Rupert Hart-Davis, 1963), vol. 1, pp. 345–433

Pusey, Edward Bouverie, Preface to *Advice on hearing confession* by the Abbé Gaume (Oxford: Parker, 1878)

Pusey, Edward Bouverie, *The Councils of the Church* (Oxford: Parker, 1857)

Pusey, Edward Bouverie, *The Holy Eucharist a comfort to the penitent* (University Sermon, 1843)

Pusey, Edward Bouverie, *Lectures on Daniel the prophet*, 2nd edn (Oxford: Parker, 1868)

Pusey, Edward Bouverie, *Parochial and cathedral sermons* (London: Walter Smith, 1887)

Pusey, Edward Bouverie, *Parochial sermons*, 4 vols (London: Walter Smith, 1883)

Pusey, Edward Bouverie, *Spiritual letters*, ed. J. O. Johnston and W. C. E. Newbolt (London: Longmans, 1898)

Pusey, Edward Bouverie, *What is of faith as to everlasting punishment?* (Oxford: Parker, 1880)

[Robertson, Frederick William] Brooke, Stopford A., *Life and letters of Fred. W. Robertson MA*, 2 vols (London: Kegan Paul, Trench, 1882)

Romanes, George John, *Thoughts on religion*, ed. C. Gore (London: Longmans, 1895)

[Romanes, George John] *The life and letters of George John Romanes*, written and edited by his wife, 5th edn (London: Longmans, 1902)

Ryle, J. C., *Holiness* (London: James Clarke, 1952)

Shaw, Charles, *When I was a child* (first published 1892–3 in the *Staffordshire Sentinel*) (London: Caliban, 1977)

Shelley, Percy Bysshe, *Complete poetical works*, ed. T. Hutchinson and G. M. Matthews, 2nd edn (Oxford UP, 1970)

Shelley, Percy Bysshe, *A refutation of deism* (1814), in *Complete works*, ed. R. Ingpen and W. E. Peck (London: Benn, 1965) vol. 6, pp. 21–57

Shelley, Percy Bysshe, *On life*, in *Complete works*, ed. R. Ingpen and W. E. Peck (London: Benn, 1965) vol. 6, pp. 191–7

Shelley, Percy Bysshe, *On love*, in *Complete works*, ed. R. Ingpen and W. E. Peck (London: Benn, 1965) vol. 6, pp. 199–202

Shelley, Percy Bysshe, *Essay on Christianity*, in *Complete works*, ed. R. Ingpen and W. E. Peck (London: Benn, 1965) vol. 6, pp. 225–52

Simeon, Charles, *Horae homileticae*, 4th edn, 21 vols (London: Samuel Holdsworth, 1840) Pollard, A., *Let wisdom judge* (London: Inter-Varsity Fellowship, 1959)

Spurgeon, Charles, *Works* (Albany: Ages Software, 1997) (electronic reissue including all 63 volumes of the sermons); see also Carlile, J. C., and Bacon, E. W. among Secondary Works below

Taylor, Ann and Jane, *Hymns for infant minds* (1810), 44th edn (London: Jackson and Walford, 1858)

Tracts for the times, by members of the University of Oxford (London: Rivington, 1833–40)

Tyrrell, George, *Hard sayings* (London: Longmans, Green, 1900)

Tyrrell, George, *The inevitable question, and other chapters* (privately circulated, London, 1900)

Tyrrell, George, *The faith of the millions* (or *A more excellent way*), first series (London: Longmans, Green, 1901)

Tyrrell, George, *The faith of the millions*, second series (London: Longmans, Green, 1901)

Tyrrell, George, *Nova et vetera* (London: Longmans, 1897)

Tyrrell, George, *Through Scylla and Charybdis, or, The old theology and the new* (London: Longmans, Green, 1907)

Tyrrell, George, *Lex credendi* (London: Longmans, Green, 1907)

Tyrrell, George, *Essays on faith and immortality*, ed. M. D. Petre (London: Edward Arnold, 1914)

Tyrrell, George, *Autobiography and life*, ed. M. D. Petre, 2 vols (London: Edward Arnold, 1914)

Vaughan, R. A., *Hours with the mystics: a contribution to the history of religious opinion*, 5th edn, 2 vols (London: Gibbings, 1891)

Wilberforce, Samuel, introduction to *Eucharistica: meditations and prayers on the Most Holy Eucharist from Old English Divines* (London: James Burns, 1845)

Wordsworth, William, *Complete poetical works*, ed. T. Hutchinson, new edn rev. W. de Selincourt (Oxford UP, 1936)

Secondary Works

Allchin, A. M., *The silent rebellion: Anglican religious communities, 1845–1900* (London: SCM Press, 1958)

Ambler, R. W., *Ranters, revivalists and reformers: Primitive Methodist and rural society – South Lincolnshire, 1817–75* (Hull monographs in regional and local history 2) (Hull UP, 1989)

Ann Frances CSMV, 'William John Butler and the revival of the ascetic tradition', in W. J. Sheils, (ed.), *Monks, hermits and the ascetic tradition: papers read at the 1984 summer meeting and the 1985 winter meeting of the Ecclesiastical History Society* (Oxford: Blackwell, 1985), pp. 365–76

Ashworth, Jesse, *The life of the Venerable Hugh Bourne* (London: Toulson, 1888)

Aspinwall, B., 'Changing images of Roman Catholic religious orders in the nineteenth century', in W. J. Sheils (ed.), *Monks, hermits and the ascetic tradition: papers read at the 1984 summer meeting and the 1985 winter meeting of the Ecclesiastical History Society* (Oxford: Blackwell, 1985), pp. 351–64

Bacon, E. W., *Spurgeon: heir of the Puritans* (London: Allen and Unwin, 1967)

Balthasar, Hans Urs von, *The glory of the Lord: a theological aesthetics* (ET of *Herrlichkeit*) vol. 3, *Studies in theological styles: lay styles* (Edinburgh: T & T Clark, 1986)

Bebbington, D. W., *Evangelicalism in modern Britain: a history from the 1730s to the 1980s* (London: Routledge, 1989)

Bell, E. Moberly, *Josephine Butler: flame of fire* (London: Constable, 1962)

Berlin, Isaiah, *The roots of Romanticism* (London: Chatto & Windus, 1999)

Bett, Henry, *Dora Greenwell* (London: Epworth, 1950)

Bradley, Ian, *The call to seriousness: the Evangelical impact on the Victorians* (London: Cape, 1976)

Bradley, Ian, *Abide with me: the world of Victorian hymns* (London: SCM Press, 1997)

Briggs, Asa, *Victorian cities* (1963; Harmondsworth: Penguin, 1968)

Briggs, Asa, *A social history of England* (London: Weidenfeld & Nicolson, 1983)

Butler, Perry (ed.), *Pusey rediscovered* (London: SPCK, 1983)

Carlile, J. C., *C. H. Spurgeon: an interpretative biography* (London: Kingsgate, 1933)

Chadwick, Henry, 'Newman's significance for the Anglican Church', in D. Brown (ed.), *Newman: a man for our time* (London: SPCK, 1990), pp. 52–74

Chadwick, Owen, *The Victorian church* (An ecclesiastical history of England 5), 2 vols, London: Adam & Charles Black, 1966–70

Chadwick, Owen, *The secularization of the European mind in the nineteenth century* (Cambridge UP, 1975)

Chadwick, Owen, *Newman* (Past masters) (Oxford UP, 1983)

Chadwick, Owen, *The spirit of the Oxford Movement* (Cambridge UP, 1990)

Chandler, Michael, *The life and work of John Mason Neale, 1818–1866* (Leominster: Gracewing, 1995)

Chitty, Susan, *The beast and the monk: a life of Charles Kingsley* (London: Hodder and Stoughton, 1974)

Cohn-Sherbok, Dan, *The Jews of Canterbury, 1760–1931* (Canterbury: Yorick, 1984)

Crichton, James D., 'Popular devotion in Victorian England', in *The Month* 257 (1996), pp. 322–7

Cunningham, Valentine, *Everywhere spoken against: Dissent in the Victorian novel* (Oxford: Clarendon, 1975)

Dibble, Jeremy, *C. Hubert H. Parry: his life and music* (Oxford: Clarendon, 1992)

Digby, Anne, *The Poor Law in nineteenth-century England and Wales* (general series 104) (London: Historical Association, 1982)

Dixon, R., and Muthesius, S., *Victorian architecture* (London: Thames & Hudson, 1978)

Dorling, William, *Memoirs of Dora Greenwell* (London: James Clarke, 1885)

Edwards, David L., *Leaders of the Church of England 1828–1944* (London: Oxford UP, 1971)

Faber, Geoffrey, *Oxford apostles: a character study of the Oxford Movement* (1933; repr. London: Faber, 1974)

Fisher, Michael, *A vision of splendour: Gothic Revival in Staffordshire, 1840–1890* (Stafford: Michael Fisher, 1995)

Gill, Stephen, *Wordsworth and the Victorians* (Oxford: Clarendon, 1998)

Goldhawk, N. P., 'The Methodist people in the early Victorian age: spirituality and worship', in R. Davies, A. R. George, and G. Rupp (eds), *A history of the Methodist Church in Great Britain* 2 (London: Epworth, 1978), pp. 113–42

Gorce, Agnes de la, *Francis Thompson*; ET by H. F. Kynaston-Snell (London: Burns & Oates, 1933)

Gordon, James M., *Evangelical spirituality from the Wesleys to John Stott* (London: SPCK, 1991)

Green, Peter, *Kenneth Grahame, 1859–1932* (London: John Murray, 1959)

Haight, Gordon S., *George Eliot: a biography* (Oxford: Clarendon, 1968)

Hamer, Edna (Sr Dominic Savio CP), *Elizabeth Prout 1820–1864: a religious life for industrial England* (Downside Abbey, 1994) (review in *History* 82 (1997) pp. 167–8)

Hardy, Barbara, *The novels of George Eliot: a study in form* (London: Athlone, 1959)

Haynes, Barry, *Working-class life in Victorian Leicester: the Joseph Dare reports* (Leicester Libraries and Information Services, 1991)

Heimann, Mary, *Catholic devotion in Victorian England* (Oxford: Clarendon, 1995)

Heimann, Mary, 'Devotional stereotypes in English Catholicism, 1850–1914', in F. Tallett and N. Atkin (eds), *Catholicism in Britain and France since 1789* (London: Hambledon, 1996), pp. 13–26

Hennell, Michael, *John Venn and the Clapham Sect* (London: Lutterworth, 1958)

Hennell, Michael, *Sons of the prophets: Evangelical leaders of the Victorian church* (London: SPCK, 1979)

Imberg, Rune, *In quest of authority: the 'Tracts for the Times' and the development of the Tractarian leaders, 1833–1841* (Bibliotheca Historico-Ecclesiastica Lundensis 16) (Lund UP, 1987)

Jasper, R. C. D., 'The Prayer Book in the Victorian era', in A. Symondson (ed.), *The Victorian crisis of faith* (London: SPCK, 1970), pp. 107–22

Johnson, W. J., 'Piety among "The Society of People": the witness of Primitive Methodist local preachers in the North Midlands, 1812–1862', in W. J. Sheils and D. Wood (eds), *The ministry: clerical and lay* (Studies in Church history 26) (Oxford: Blackwell, 1989), pp. 343–56

Kendall, H. B., *The origin and history of the Primitive Methodist Church*, 2 vols (London: Edwin Dalton, 1905)

Kent, John, *Holding the fort: studies in Victorian revivalism* (London: Epworth, 1978)

Ker, Ian, *John Henry Newman: a biography* (Oxford UP, 1988)

Ker, Ian, *Healing the wound of humanity: the spirituality of John Henry Newman* (London: DLT, 1993)

Knight, Frances, *The nineteenth-century church and English society* (Cambridge UP, 1995)

McLeod, Hugh, *Class and religion in the late Victorian city* (London: Croom Helm, 1974)

McLeod, Hugh, *Religion and the working class in nineteenth-century Britain* (London: Macmillan, 1984)

McLeod, Hugh, *Religion and society in England, 1850–1914* (Basingstoke: Macmillan, 1996)

Maynard, Constance L., *Dora Greenwell: a prophet for our own times on the battleground of our faith* (London: Allenson, 1926)

Mitchell, Sheila, *Not disobedient: a history of United Baptist Church, Leicester* (Leicester, 1983)

Moran, Valentine G. SJ, 'George Tyrrell: theological journalist of genius', in *Downside Review* 103 (1985), pp. 161–203

Mumm, Susan, *Stolen daughters, virgin mothers: Anglican sisterhoods in Victorian Britain* (Leicester UP, 1999)

Newsome, David, 'Newman and Manning: spirituality and personal conflict', in P. Brooks (ed.), *Christian spirituality: essays in honour of Gordon Rupp* (London: SCM Press, 1975), pp. 285–306

Newsome, David, *The convert cardinals: John Henry Newman and Henry Edward Manning* (London: John Murray, 1993)

Nockles, Peter B., *The Oxford Movement in context: Anglican High Churchmanship 1760–1857* (Cambridge UP, 1994)

Norman, Edward, *Church and society in England 1770–1970* (Oxford: Clarendon, 1976)

Norman, Edward, *The English Catholic Church in the nineteenth century* (Oxford: Clarendon, 1984)

Norman, Edward, *The Victorian Christian Socialists* (Cambridge UP, 1987)

Paris, Bernard J., *Experiments in life: George Eliot's quest for values* (Detroit: Wayne State UP, 1965)

Pereiro, James, *Cardinal Manning: an intellectual biography* (Oxford: Clarendon, 1998)

Petre, M. D. (1912): see under Tyrrell, George, among Primary Works above

Prestige, G. L., *The life of Charles Gore, a great Englishman* (London: Heinemann, 1935)

Prickett, Stephen, *Victorian fantasy* (Hassocks: Harvester, 1979)

Prickett, Stephen, 'Church and university in the life of John Keble', in G. Rowell (ed.), *The English religious tradition and the genius of Anglicanism* (Wantage: Ikon, 1992), pp. 195–210

Prickett, Stephen, *Romanticism and religion: the tradition of Coleridge and Wordsworth in the Victorian church* (Cambridge UP, 1976)

Prince, Alison, *Kenneth Grahame: an innocent in the wild wood* (London: Allison and Busby, 1994)

Reardon, Bernard M. G., *From Coleridge to Gore: a century of religious thought in Britain* (London: Longmans, 1971)

Rose, J. K. M., *Ann and Jane Taylor as writers of improving verse for children in the early nineteenth century* (Leicester University MPhil thesis, 1991)

Rowell, Geoffrey, *The vision glorious: themes and personalities of the Catholic revival in Anglicanism* (Oxford UP, 1983)

Ryan, Robert M., *The Romantic Reformation: religious politics in English literature, 1789–1824* (Cambridge UP, 1997)

Sagovsky, Nicholas, *On God's side: a life of George Tyrrell* (Oxford: Clarendon, 1990)

Sandall, Robert, *The history of the Salvation Army*, 2 vols (London: Nelson, 1947)

Sharp, John, 'The influence of St Alphonsus Liguori in nineteenth-century Britain', in *Downside Review* 100 (1983), pp. 60–76

Strachan, C. G., *The Pentecostal theology of Edward Irving* (London: DLT, 1973)

Temple Patterson, A., *Radical Leicester: a history of Leicester 1780–1850* (Leicester University College, 1954)

Valenze, Deborah M. *Prophetic sons and daughters: female preaching and popular religion in industrial England* (Princeton UP, 1986) (review in *Journal of Ecclesiastical History* 38(1987), pp. 505–6)

Vidler, Alec, *The theology of F. D. Maurice* (London: SCM Press, 1948)

Wakefield, Gordon S., 'God and some English poets: 3. Gerard Manley Hopkins', in *Expository Times* 104 (1993) pp. 328–32

Walsh, J., Haydon, C., and Taylor, S. (eds), *The Church of England c.1689–c.1833: from toleration to Tractarianism* (Cambridge UP, 1993)

Ward, Benedicta, 'A Tractarian inheritance: the religious life in a patristic perspective', in Rowell, G. (ed.), *Tradition renewed* (London: DLT, 1986), pp. 215–24

Watson, J. R., *The poetry of Gerard Manley Hopkins* (Harmondsworth: Penguin, 1987)

Watts, Michael R., *The dissenters, 2: the expansion of Evangelical Nonconformity* (Oxford: Clarendon, 1995)

Wheeler, Michael, *Death and the future life in Victorian literature and theology* (Cambridge UP, 1990)

White, Norman, *Hopkins: a literary biography* (Oxford: Clarendon, 1992)

Wickham, E. R., *Church and people in an industrial city* (London: Lutterworth, 1957)

Wilkinson, John T., *Hugh Bourne, 1772–1852* (London: Epworth, 1952)

Willey, Basil, *Nineteenth century studies* (London: Chatto and Windus, 1964)

Wilson, Linda, '"She succeeds with cloudless brow ..." How active was the spirituality of Nonconformist women in the home during the period 1825–75?' in R. N. Swanson (ed.), *Gender and Christian religion* (Studies in Church history 34) (Woodbridge: Boydell, 1998), pp. 347–61

Withey, Donald A., *John Henry Newman: the Liturgy and the Breviary – their influence on his life as an Anglican* (London: Sheed and Ward, 1992)

Wolffe, J. (ed.), *Religion in Victorian Britain, V: culture and empire* (Manchester UP, 1997)

Yates, W. N., '"Bells and smells": London, Brighton and South Coast religion reconsidered', in *Southern History: a review of the history of southern England* 5 (1983), pp. 122–53

3

Losing Our Absolute

Spirituality in the Twentieth Century

INTRODUCTION

In his novel *The rainbow*, published (though almost immediately suppressed) in 1915, D. H. Lawrence describes a visit to Lincoln Cathedral by a newly-wed couple, Anna and Will Brangwen. Will is someone for whom Christian faith is intuitively true, and supremely embodied in the glory and beauty of a cathedral; Anna had too strong a sense of a greater Beyond, not susceptible of being contained within a church, to be able to believe as Will did. The visit to Lincoln has momentous consequences for both of them:

> They went home again, both of them altered. She had some new reverence for that which he wanted, he felt that his cathedrals would never again be to him as they had been. Before, he had thought them absolute. But now he saw them crouching under the sky, with still the dark, mysterious world of reality inside, but as a world within a world, a sort of side show, whereas before they had been as a world to him within a chaos: a reality, an order, an absolute, within a meaningless confusion.
>
> He had felt, before, that could he but go through the great door and look down the gloom towards the far-off, concluding wonder of the altar, that then, with the windows suspended around like tablets of jewels emanating their own glory, then he had arrived. Here the satisfaction he had yearned after came near, towards this, the porch of the great Unknown, all reality gathered, and there, the altar was the mystic door, through which all and everything must move on to eternity.
>
> But now, somehow, sadly and disillusioned, he realised that the doorway was no doorway. It was too narrow, it was false. Outside the cathedral were many flying spirits that could never be sifted through the jewelled gloom. He had lost his absolute . . .
>
> There was life outside the church. There was much that the church did not include. He thought of God, and of the whole blue rotonda of the day. That was something great and free. He thought of the ruins of the Grecian worship, and it seemed, a temple was never perfectly a temple, till it was ruined and mixed up with the winds and the sky and the herbs.
>
> Still he loved the church. As a symbol, he loved it. He tended it for what

it tried to represent, rather than for that which it did represent. Still he loved it. The little church across his garden-wall drew him, he gave it loving attention. But he went to take charge of it, to preserve it. It was as an old, sacred thing to him. He looked after the stone and the woodwork, mending the organ and restoring a piece of broken carving, repairing the church furniture. Later, he became choir-master also. [But] his life was shifting its centre.[1]

'He had lost his absolute.' The experience that Lawrence so vividly articulates would be that of many (perhaps even most) people in twentieth-century England. For many, the Church would indeed become 'a sort of side show', its domestic preoccupations and internal wranglings at best a timid echo of what had already taken place in the real world, and at worst a mildly intriguing irrelevance. For some, as for Will Brangwen, the church remained valuable, lovable even, but as a piece of 'heritage' to be preserved (a very English response to the problem of what to do with absolutes), not as a unique repository of truth to be revered. True, there were some who found with W. H. Auden that the

> hair-raising things
> that Hitler and Stalin were doing
> forced me to think about God.[2]

Yet for most the old certainties were dying, and the hair-raising things that Hitler and Stalin did only helped to bury them. The experience of war; the spiritual impoverishment that accompanied unprecedented technological change;[3] the seemingly inexorable decline in religious belief and adherence, together with an enduring spiritual hunger, which in turn led to the growth of a 'spirituality' relatively disconnected from ecclesial life or concerns – all these central features of the last century in the second Christian millennium reflect the consequences of 'losing our absolute'. And yet we shall find that, far from manifesting nothing more than Matthew Arnold's 'melancholy, long, withdrawing roar', Christian spirituality exhibited a vitality and (at its best) a continuing capacity to transform and renew both individuals and society which was all the more remarkable given the gloomy context in which it found itself. It is that context which needs examination first.

It is both impossible to estimate, and impossible to ignore, the impact on the spiritual life of the two world wars which dominated the first half of the twentieth century. The huge loss of life, together with the perceived ineffectiveness of organized religion, posed an unprecedented challenge to those seeking to offer an enduring spirituality. How they addressed that challenge will concern us later; but a further point needs making now. The horrendous slaughter in the trenches; the genocidal campaigns of Hitler and Stalin against the Jews and other innocent minorities; and the unspeakable barbarities inflicted by soldiers of supposedly civilized countries with long histories of religious adherence and cultural refinement – these terrible realities raised doubts not only about the existence of God, but also about the survival of humanity. And they underlined among other things two crucial (though all too easily forgotten) truths: first, that a spirituality which failed to address the human capacity for evil with the utmost seriousness was at best a vapid pipedream, and at worst a dangerous delusion; secondly, that the accumulated effect of centuries of sophistication, culture, learning, technological progress and indeed Christian teaching did not prevent the nations of Europe from descending into barbarism of the most horrendous kind.[4]

The changes that affected every aspect of English life during the twentieth century are no less important than the impact of two world wars. In 1900, Britain was arguably the greatest power in the world; and the brief Edwardian era saw the zenith of its imperial achievement.[5] One of the classic embodiments of Edwardian grandeur was the composer Edward Elgar, whose music articulates the greatness of imperial Britain as well as, in one crucial respect, its weakness. The musicologist Neville Cardus acutely points out the key flaw in Elgar's most famous choral work, his setting of Newman's *The dream of Gerontius*:

> At one point only does Elgar fail in *Gerontius* . . . He can do nothing much with the Demons . . . His devils . . . are even more gentlemanly than Milton's Lucifer is noble.[6]

It was just this gentlemanly inability to comprehend the seriousness of evil which was to compromise (at least among middle-class Christians) so much of Christianity's response to the horrors the twentieth century were to bring. Some, albeit with the benefit of hindsight, were aware that, beneath all that Edwardian pomp, darker uncertainties were at work. In 1934 T. S. Eliot made the point eloquently:

> When your fathers fixed the place of GOD,
> And settled all the inconvenient saints,
> Apostles, martyrs, in a kind of Whipsnade,
> Then they could set about imperial expansion
> Accompanied by industrial development.
> Exporting iron, coal and cotton goods
> And intellectual enlightenment
> And everything, including capital
> And several versions of the Word of GOD:
> The British race assured of a mission
> Performed it, but left much at home unsure.[7]

For the truth was that, beneath the comfortable exterior of Edwardian England, seismic changes were at work. Unemployment and poverty were increasing. Women were actively seeking the vote (and in 1918 obtained it). In 1906, the Conservatives were swept from power by the Liberals; and five years later, the Parliament Act definitively weakened the power of the hereditary grandees in the House of Lords.[8] Within the churches, the solid Protestant middle classes were becoming increasingly sceptical.[9]

The First World War accelerated all these processes. In 1926 the then Prime Minister, Stanley Baldwin, acknowledged that 'there is nothing the country needs so much as another Wesley or Whitefield' to provide moral and spiritual leadership.[10] He had little doubt that many of those among his contemporaries who were joining the burgeoning Labour Party would fifty years earlier have entered the ordained ministry, or been active Nonconformists.[11] He made these remarks in the year of the General Strike, which abruptly reminded the comfortable in English society of the appalling poverty besetting the underclass. In the 1930s, the gap between rich and poor widened further, as it would continue to do for much of the rest of the century.[12] The Second World War brought with it tighter belts for almost everyone and serious privation for many, a privation which continued during the years of rationing that followed.

And by the middle of the century England was already a very different place from the stately realm of Queen Victoria. The empire was being dismantled, while other imperial régimes (notably Soviet and American) were taking its place. The old class system was a much weaker, more adaptable thing after the wars than before them. Prosperity gradually increased;[13] and the National Health Service and increasing home ownership transformed most people's living standards.[14] Until the end of the First World War, many working-class women with children were virtually immured in their homes; only after that did the increasing availability of the pram transform people's lives.[15] And their lives were getting longer: almost everyone alive in England in 1980 had a better chance of seeing their next birthday than their forebears had in 1900.[16] More leisure, improved educational opportunities, and above all the ever-increasing *choices* available to people in almost every area of their lives, changed the fabric of existence for most people in England to a hitherto almost unimaginable degree.[17]

But was it for the better? The great violinist Yehudi Menuhin said that

> If I had to sum up the twentieth century, I would say that it raised the greatest hopes ever conceived by humanity, and destroyed all illusions and ideals.[18]

And in 1929 the Roman Catholic Christopher Dawson wrote prophetically:

> To-day, to the average European, and still more to the average American, Progress consists in the spread of the new urban-mechanical civilization: it means more cinemas, motor-cars for all, wireless installations, more elaborate methods of killing people, purchase on the hire system, preserved foods and picture papers.[19]

Dawson's critique was of a predominantly urbanized civilization which had lost touch with nature;[20] and in this respect at least he was not far from the world of D. H. Lawrence's novels. The following decades would see a different pattern: in post-1945 Britain, large cities began to decline while more people lived in semi-urban or suburban places. In the cities themselves, the gap between rich and poor widened further during the years of Margaret Thatcher's leadership. Life in late-twentieth-century England was unquestionably more comfortable than it had been when Edward VII was king.[21] But it was not necessarily happier. Thus (for example) technological sophistication made housework easier; it did not automatically make it more interesting.[22] W. H. Auden sardonically suggested that growing wealth did not change everything:

> In the Hungry Thirties
> boys used to sell their bodies
> for a square meal.
>
> In the Affluent Sixties
> they still did:
> to meet Hire-Purchase Payments.[23]

And the famous remark of the American feminist Betty Friedan in 1963 will have resonated with many on this side of the Atlantic too:

> It was a strange stirring, a sense of dissatisfaction, a yearning that women suffered in the middle of the twentieth century in the United States. Each suburban wife struggled with it alone. As she made the beds, shopped for groceries, matched slip cover material, ate peanut butter sandwiches, chauffeured Cub Scouts and Brownies, lay beside her husband at night, she was afraid to ask even of herself the silent question, 'Is this all?'[24]

By the 1970s, the sharp increase in the gap between rich and poor became apparent, and unemployment grew alarmingly.[25] The 1960s and 1970s also saw many taboos being broken, as 'permissiveness' increased and the nuclear family (itself effectively a creation of the 1950s) began to disintegrate.[26] True, England was becoming a more pluralist society, as immigration from Asia, Africa and the Caribbean brought new forms of cultural and religious expression to most of its cities: redundant Anglican and Nonconformist churches were more likely to become Black Pentecostal worship centres, or Sikh or Hindu temples, than furniture warehouses. And yet, as global communications improved and overseas travel became cheaper, England became in some respects more introverted, xenophobic even, its relationship with continental Europe often only lukewarm and attitudes to the Afro-Caribbean immigrants who had helped rejuvenate the British economy frequently hostile. It was as though the horrors of world war, and the growing possibility of nuclear catastrophe, together with the progressive despoliation of the planet through environmental neglect, were best addressed with a kind of myopia, a pervasive drawing-down of the blinds and turning inwards. One of the results was that 'spirituality', of almost every variety, thrived. But some of it thrived only by making a determined effort to drive evil and suffering firmly underground. In 1971 the American sociologist Peter L. Berger noted that

> modern society has banished the night from consciousness, as far as this is possible. The treatment of death in modern society, especially in America, is the sharpest manifestation of this.[27]

We shall return later to this preference for a homogenized, 'tranquillizer-spirituality'. First, though, something needs to be said about the impact of all this on the churches. Certainly the exponential growth of material wealth and consumer prosperity did nothing to arrest the decline of mainstream Christian denominations, almost all of which lost members as the century progressed – though there are some grounds for arguing that this decline was not nearly as rapid nor as comprehensive as late-Victorian secularists had predicted.[28] Even so, the pace and process of secularization left the churches in a dilemma. Should the gospel, the Christian 'absolute' once delivered to the saints, be repackaged, or even rewritten, or left in unapologetic archaism to become part of the nation's growing fondness for 'heritage'? Examples of all these responses will appear in the pages that follow; but Peter Berger's comment on the matter is worth noting now:

> The devilry of modernity has its own magic: the theologian who sups with *it* will find his spoon getting shorter and shorter – until that last supper in which he is left alone at the table, with no spoon at all and with an empty plate. The devil, one may guess, will by then have gone away to more interesting company.[29]

This is a variant on the remark of W. R. Inge, the 'gloomy Dean' of St Paul's Cathedral London, that those who marry the spirit of the age find themselves widowers in the next. On the other hand, taking refuge in a fortress-religion set over against the world may not be an option either. Helen Butcher, who was brought up in a poor area of inner-city Birmingham, recalls the tragic death of her young brother Tommy and the inadequacy of the local vicar's spiritual response:

> The Vicar from St Barnabas's, Mr Dugmore, came to console my mother . . . He told her that everything God did was for the best, and was quickly shown the door . . . I have seen her sink to her knees, tears streaming down her face, head raised, hands clenched together, arms upstretched, begging God to tell her what she had done that He had punished her so?[30]

The poet Stevie Smith, who oscillated between agnosticism and High Church Anglicanism, put the point in almost Lawrentian manner in her poem 'How do you see?' – 'better the fresh air', she writes, than the spurious world of religion. For

> the consolations of religion are so beautiful,
> But not when you look close.[31]

Furthermore, 'the consolations of religion' were themselves becoming less accessible. As the whirlwind of change helped to precipitate a positive tornado of liturgical revision across the churches, the distinguished Methodist theologian Gordon Wakefield observed in 1968 that 'any "books of devotion" had best be loose-leaf' if they were not to be out of date almost before they appeared.[32] The old ruminant intimacy with sacred texts that could be memorized and recalled at will was almost gone; and the loss was a grievous one.

Not everyone, however, found this dilemma depressing. In 1929 the great Methodist scholar W. R. Maltby wrote:

> God's wind and weather are always at work to search out the perishable elements in our structure, and time and again, when we longed only for finality and repose, we are required to rise and rebuild, or strengthen, or repair.[33]

Thirty years later, the reforms of the Second Vatican Council and the Roman Catholic policy of *aggiornamento* undoubtedly gave new impetus and boldness to the English

Catholic church (though they did nothing to stem its numerical decline). But something else, less public but no less significant, is worth noting here. As regular churchgoing declined, a great deal of what might be called 'implicit spirituality' was left in its wake. The social historian Asa Briggs points out that in 1954 a survey in Derby showed that, while 30% of the population were going to the cinema once a week, only 12% went to church on the previous Sunday; but very few people admitted to having no religion and almost every home possessed a Bible.[34] People still had recourse to religious practices *in extremis*: thus Robert Graves, an avowed agnostic, admits that when he came across a dead German sergeant-major on the Western Front during the First World War, he found that 'I needed a charm to get myself past this sinister figure. The simplest way, I found, was to cross myself.'[35]

And implicit spirituality went much deeper than momentary crises. Roger Edrington's survey of working-class men in urban Birmingham during 1984, which will be explored further below, suggests a society in which nearly everyone found organized religion irrelevant, yet a large majority still prayed (some of whom did not even believe in God!).[36] Even at the end of the twentieth century, relatively large numbers of people still came to church each week, and even larger numbers for rites of passage, and the great festivals of Christmas and Easter, though the hitherto inseparable link between believing and belonging could no longer be taken for granted.[37] There was an enormous market for 'spirituality', understood as a search for meaning with reference to enduring but invisible realities such as wholeness, compassion, justice, and self-fulfilment. Some of these more secular and amorphous manifestations of spirituality will require more attention below. All of them bear witness to an unprecedented development: 'spirituality' and 'religion' were beginning to be prised apart; and it would take all the energies and intelligence of religious people if the growing fascination with all things spiritual were not to leave them high and dry.

SPIRITUALITY AND THE CHURCH OF ENGLAND

Introduction

The twentieth century saw a steady (and, in the last decades, increasing) rate of decline in membership of the Church of England.[38] The 1950s saw some modest growth; but decline set in with a vengeance after 1960.[39] The impact of world war and the scepticism it evoked; the fact that, with ever-increasing social mobility, too many church buildings were in the wrong places or required costly remodelling to be of much use;[40] the extent to which consumerism replaced churchgoing as the favoured use of ever-increasing leisure time; and the growing perception that the churches were either irretrievably self-absorbed or irretrievably irrelevant or both – all these sapped the vitality and vision of twentieth-century English Anglicanism.

And yet the history of the Church of England during the century is in many respects one of amazing diversity and vitality as it sought to respond to these challenges.[41] It is still common to think of it as offering unequivocal and somewhat somnolent support to the status quo, in both war and peace. But this is misleading: the passing of the

Parliament Act in 1911, which allowed the House of Commons to override the Lords' veto, could not have taken place without the support of the bishops, led by the Archbishop of Canterbury, Randall Davidson.[42] And some wartime padres like Geoffrey Studdert-Kennedy had little time for canonizing an unthinking xenophobia. He wrote these prophetic words in 1923:

> Nationalism – which . . . is one of the outstanding features of European history during the nineteenth century – has its terrible side . . . The nations that are grown up like mushrooms all over Europe during the last century are really toadstools; and, unless their very nature can be changed, will poison and not purify the life of mankind . . . I think it would be true to say that three-quarters of what we call patriotism was herd-instinct and fear combined, though the rest may be the sublimest heroism. At any rate, it is perfectly certain that, if we don't look out, this patriotism . . . will be the very death of us, however beautiful it may be in itself.[43]

There were other signs of new life. The Parish and People Movement (founded at Birmingham in 1949) changed the face of Anglican worship by making the sung Eucharist the principal Sunday service in most parish churches.[44] The Anglo-Catholic movement enjoyed something of a golden age after the First World War:[45] it too played a part in fostering the centrality of eucharistic worship; but it also encouraged a passionate commitment to social justice and community involvement, notably in some of the poorest urban areas in the country.[46] And the movement fostered a new interest in spirituality long before the subject became fashionable among leisured consumers: in 1931 Mark Carpenter-Garnier, Anglican Bishop of Colombo, wrote in his Introduction to F. P. Harton's *The elements of the spiritual life* words that could as easily have introduced a book written in the 1990s:

> a new interest is being shown in prayer . . . there are many who can no longer be content with a formal and conventional religion. If they are to possess a religion at all, it must be one of personal experience.[47]

Nor were these the only sources of life in twentieth-century Anglicanism. Major new cathedrals were built (notably at Coventry, Liverpool and Guildford); there was a theological inventiveness that found expression in people as diverse as John Robinson, C. S. Lewis and Austin Farrer; broadcasting enabled Christian teaching to be communicated to far larger audiences; the renewal of liturgy resulted in the appearance of *The Alternative Service Book 1980*; relationships with other churches improved dramatically; bishops like William Temple, George Bell, David Jenkins, John Robinson, David Sheppard and others exerted a genuinely national influence, as did church reports such as *The family in contemporary society* (1958) and *Faith in the city* (1985). The Evangelical movement, at its lowest ebb in the 1920s when Anglo-Catholicism was dominant, recovered after the Second World War; and Anglican Evangelicalism in particular became more actively concerned with social and political issues, less narrowly focused on individual salvation.[48] Indeed in many respects it became the dominant movement within the Church of England once the ordination of women as priests divided Anglo-Catholicism in the late 1980s.

Devotion to God as Creator

In the exploration of Anglican spirituality that follows, the work of a number of writers will be drawn on. The variety and quality of what was produced attests both to the vitality of Anglicanism and to the ever-increasing appetite for spirituality as the century progressed.[49] It also attests to the universal recognition that, in the face of both world war and scientific secularism, the days of a comfortable piety (if they ever existed) were over. Studdert-Kennedy again caught the mood:

> Religion leaves a million questions unanswered and apparently unanswerable. Its purpose and object is not to make a man certain and cocksure about everything, but to make him certain about those things of which he must be certain if he is to live a human life at all.[50]

We shall return later to his and others' responses to the immediate reality of war. The question is: what kind of spirituality could do justice both to the integrity of scripture and Anglican tradition, and to the urgent questions and uncertainties of contemporaries? We may begin our reflections by exploring how the three persons of the Trinity elicited from different spiritual writers a rich theology of the spiritual life. In 1924 William Temple explored the implications of belief in God as Creator:

> to be conscious of absolute value and the absolute obligation which it imposes is plainly a direct awareness of something ultimate in the universe . . . It is a consciousness of the very object of the Creative Will; it is thus of itself a knowledge of God.[51]

And who is God? God is Spirit. For Temple, that means that

> God is not the totality of things – the All; nor is He an immanent principle to which all things conform; He is Spirit – active energy, alive and purposive, but free from the temporal and spatial limitations which are characteristic of matter.[52]

So the only possible explanation of the universe is a theistic one: that there exists an absolute Will, by and through which all things came to be. This insistence on the primacy of the divine will leads Temple to argue that it is within our conscience above all that we experience God, rather than in particular religious experiences or awareness of God.[53] Mysticism is thus unrepresentative of true religious experience:

> for religion is not departmental; it takes life as a whole for its sphere; and 'religious experience' is not an affair of isolated moments, it is a whole experience of life and the world, permeated through and through with religion.[54]

This is a characteristically Anglican approach. Temple goes on to point out that any religious experience involves a measure of interpretation: 'we never experience a mere "This".'[55] And it must vindicate itself against the charge of being merely an illusion. Temple maintains that 'it is doubtful if any man can go through life without ever feeling reverence for something which is morally so high above him as to be out of his reach, or awe before the great Reality on which he is utterly dependent', even if he explains this sense away in some manner.[56]

The strength of such an approach is its resistance to the idea of some separate 'spiritual' compartment, cut off from the mind and the will, and indeed from the rest of human life. But 'the great Reality' needs fleshing out if it is to inspire and attract; and one of the most compelling articulations of a God who could do this was provided by W. H. Vanstone in *Love's endeavour, love's expense* (1977), a theology of the spiritual life that was rooted in his experience as a parish priest, and in particular in watching two schoolboys giving all their love and attention to creating a model of a tract of countryside. From this he learned three vital lessons:

> The first was that, in such activity, there was both working and waiting. One could say that the activity of creating included the passivity of waiting – of waiting upon one's workmanship to see what emerged from it, and to see if that which emerged was 'right'. The second, which followed from the first, was that, in such activity, the creator gave to, or built into, his workmanship a certain power over himself . . . a power to affect himself, to have value, significance or importance for himself. The third, which followed from the second, was that in such activity disproportion between creator and workmanship, or between creator and material, was overcome by the gift of value. That which in itself was nothing was transformed, in the creative process, into a thing of value: as the work of a creator, it received a new status in relation to the creator.[57]

This leads Vanstone to recognize the overwhelming primacy and power of unconditional, disinterested love.[58] Such love must involve a genuine giving-up of control, and must risk rejection: 'the love of God must wait for the recognition of those who have power to recognise'.[59] For God's love to be fulfilled, we must *recognize* who it is that is loving us.[60] Hence 'the Church is what man is and does when he recognises what is happening in the being of the universe'.[61]

Devotion to Christ

Our response to such a God, then, is an act of recognition and of adoration.[62] For Evangelicals in particular, such an act is rooted supremely in what God did for us in Christ. John Stott sets out the key characteristics of the relationship of the Christian who has been 'justified by [Christ], redeemed for him and reconciled to him':[63] boldness, love and joy – all of which are public as well as private spiritual virtues: 'the Christian community is a community of celebration'.[64] Later he sets out spiritual principles for the life of the Christian: self-denial, or dying to self;[65] and, contrasted with it, self-affirmation:[66] 'we are God's heirs, looking forward with confidence to the glory which will one day be revealed. Becoming a Christian is a transforming experience. By changing us, it also changes our self-image.'[67]

F. P. Harton, rooted in Catholic theology, goes further, arguing for a *union* with God through Christ which, although far short of any absorption into the divine essence, nonetheless does involve a participation in the divine nature.[68] Why? Because God has adopted us as children.[69] Harton maintains that the divine adoption is unlike human adoption in that it is no legal formality: it actually makes us God's children. 'There is here no imputation of sonship, but actual sonship. We *are* the sons of God . . . because we are made one with Him Who is from all eternity [God's] Son.'[70] He distinguishes this sharply from Protestant doctrines of an imputed sonship: it is not as though God *declares* us to be God's children by looking on us in Christ; it is that we actually *become* children of God, as the branches are part of the vine, by virtue of our participation in the life of Christ.[71]

William Temple has some illuminating insights on what it means to live in and for Christ. Reflecting on the story of Jesus' encounter with the Samaritan woman in the fourth chapter of John's Gospel, he notes the 'wholesome development of faith' that takes place 'from a state of dependence on authority to an assurance arising out of experience'.[72] He contrasts this with the unquestioning obedience demanded by Communism and Fascism. Faith means rather

> trusting [God] as a man trusts his friend – rather as a child trusts his father. But we are not left to form what conception we can of the God whom we are to trust. He has made Himself apparent to us in the Son *whom he hath sent.*[73]

And our devotion to that Son may lead us to some difficult choices, as Temple points out in relation to the story of the anointing at Bethany:

> To the worldly mind the acts of devotion are always foolish. God does not require our costly gifts for His honour; better spend on good works what is lavished on worship; so men often say. And there is a lurking truth. For what men spend on acts of worship is spent on what they share, and the gift may therefore be infected with self-interest . . . Yet it is true also that where lavish expenditure expresses the overflowing of a heart's devotion, it is unspeakably precious. For love is the best thing that there is, and what represents its best moments shares that preciousness. *The poor at all times ye have with you, but me ye have not at all times.* The Lord would soon be taken away from Mary; and it is only at moments of vivid insight that any of us perceive His presence. At those times, there is a fervour in our love for the present Lord that will not often be found in our kindly attitude towards the poor. That may be genuine enough; and what we do for them is done to Him (Matt. 25.40); but it lacks the completeness of the love which is adoration. As the best thing is love itself, not the benefits which it confers, there must be no censure of its lavishness as disproportionate.[74]

For Temple, love is utterly primary, preceding obedience. 'Devotion is prior to obedience itself. I *cannot* obey unless I love; and if I am to love, I must be with Him whom I desire to love. Personal companionship with Christ is the first requirement, as it was for the disciples in Palestine.'[75]

Temple's Christ-centred spirituality is a striking synthesis of Catholic and Protestant theology, though it lacks here the prophetic fire of Frank Weston, whose memorable words at the 1923 Anglo-Catholic Congress inspired a generation of Catholic Anglicans:

> You must walk with Christ mystically present in you, through the streets of
> this country, and find the same Christ in the people of your cities and
> villages . . . It is folly, it is madness to suppose that you can worship Jesus in
> the sacrament and Jesus on the throne of glory, when you are sweating
> Him in the bodies and souls of His children . . . Go out into the highways
> and hedges, and look for Jesus in the ragged and the naked, in the
> oppressed and the sweated, in those who have lost hope, and in those who
> are struggling to make good. Look for Jesus in them; and when you have
> found Him gird yourself with the towel of fellowship and wash His Feet in
> the persons of His brethren.[76]

Devotion to the Holy Spirit

Something more of the rich diversity of contemporary Anglican spirituality can be
seen with reference to the person and doctrine of the Holy Spirit. Angela Tilby, reflecting on the opening chapter of Genesis, suggests that two theological languages meet
there: the first is that of the divine creation, the second that which articulates the
watery chaos which existed before that creation. The second language

> reminds us that what we are being formed out of here and now, as we
> continue to develop, is something unknown to us, something nevertheless
> which God's Spirit moves over and breathes upon, something which has
> the potential for a richer, deeper life than we could ever envisage with only
> our conscious minds and desires . . . The dark truth that is also part of us is
> not rejected. It is where the Spirit of God hovers, troubling our memory
> with discoveries yet to be made.[77]

Recalling Jesus' words to Nicodemus about the Spirit blowing where it wills,
William Temple insists that everything which helps promotes love, joy and peace
among human beings has its source in the divine love.[78] And, in a powerful passage, he
evokes a Spirit that is never the mere servant of religion:

> When we pray 'Come, Holy Ghost, our souls inspire,' we had better know
> what we are about. He will not carry us to easy triumphs and gratifying
> successes; more probably He will set us to some task for God in the full
> intention that we shall fail, so that others, learning wisdom by our failure,
> may carry the good cause forward. He may take us through loneliness,
> desertion by friends, apparent desertion even by God; that was the way
> Christ went to the Father. He may drive us into the wilderness to be
> tempted of the devil . . . We cannot call upon the 'Creator Spirit, by whose
> aid the world's foundations first were laid' in order to use omnipotence for
> the supply of our futile pleasures or the success of our futile plans. If we
> invoke Him, we must be ready for the glorious pain of being caught by His
> power out of our petty orbit into the eternal purposes of the Almighty.[79]

This is invigorating and bold writing, reminiscent of the words T. S. Eliot places on
the lips of Temple's predecessor Thomas Becket in *Murder in the Cathedral*:

> Unbar the doors! throw open the doors!
> I will not have the house of prayer, the church of Christ,
> The sanctuary, turned into a fortress.
> The Church shall protect her own, in her own way, not
> As oak and stone; stone and oak decay,
> Give no stay, but the Church shall endure.
> The Church shall be open, even to our enemies. Open the door![80]

The point is further developed by John V. Taylor in a study of the work of the Holy Spirit.[81] He argues that the Spirit works by creating the necessity for choice on the part of creatures, luring and leading them to ever higher degrees of recognition, consciousness and personhood, which in turn involves elements of risk and of suffering in God's continuing work of creation.[82] Our first responsibility is that of

> humbly watching in any situation in which we find ourselves in order to learn what God is trying to do there, and then doing it with him.[83]

To recover the God who is Spirit is to recover a God far bigger than our comfortable tranquillizer-God, and one who is in no way restricted to the sacraments of the church and in no way dependent on human response.[84] And to live in the Spirit is 'to be agonizingly aware of the contrast between what is and what should be'.[85]

Spiritual formation and growth

This typically Anglican refusal to restrict the action of God to religion and religious structures also informs Anglican understanding of spiritual formation and growth. Writing in 1935, Gabriel Hebert argues passionately for taking seriously the secular dimensions of most people's lives, instead of simply adding on a new religious dimension to them. He wonders whether Confirmation preparation has become a bit too much of the latter: 'ought we not perhaps to be working out a different technique of preparation for Confirmation, beginning with [young people's] actual interests, [their] home, [their] football club, [their] work, and showing [them] how it is just *these* that are to be laid on God's altar and redeemed?'[86]

Similarly, William Temple argues that true holiness demands, not ritual separation from the world of the profane, but the rigorous separation of what is righteous from what is sinful, of love from selfishness.[87] This is why, as Angela Tilby underlines,

> Christianity must learn about personal growth, and why it must not stop there. If we absorb the lessons of our inner journey we will realise that we are made to contribute to the whole human environment, and that we can and must do this, if we are to live.[88]

John Robinson, author of *Honest to God*, goes further, following the American Protestant theologian Paul Tillich in abandoning the fundamental notion of holiness as separation from anything at all, and instead seeing it as the secular experienced *at depth*:

> For Christianity . . . the holy is the 'depth' of the common, just as the 'secular' is not a (godless) section of life but the world (God's world, for

which Christ died) cut off and alienated from its true depth. The purpose of worship is not to retire from the secular into the department of the religious, let alone to escape from 'this world' into 'the other world', but to open oneself to the meeting of the Christ in the common.[89]

One of the difficulties that this view presents is that it risks making Christian life almost indistinguishable from that of others, and in the process removing from the notion of holiness or spiritual growth any sense of cost and of 'otherness'. The Evangelical John Stott, recalling that in scripture holiness is accessible only for those willing to take up and live by the cross of Christ, wonders 'if the real test of our hunger for holiness is our willingness to experience any degree of suffering if only thereby God will make us holy'.[90]

Spirituality and the Church
But there is a more important point still. One of the great achievements of twentieth-century Anglo-Catholic spirituality was its recovery of a strongly corporate view of the spiritual life. Gabriel Hebert argued powerfully for an ecclesiology rooted in the primitive church, believing that in his day

> there has arisen all over Christendom a movement of return, going back on the notion of a purely individual piety, and seeking to learn again more fully the meaning of the Church.[91]

He criticizes both Protestant and Catholic individualism: even mysticism he regards as 'manifestly for an *élite*, for the religiously gifted, for the few choice souls'.[92] Such spirituality risks leaving 'ordinary people' out in the cold.[93] The Incarnation demands a pattern of piety which consecrates 'the schoolboy's football and the shopkeeper's profits'. 'If the modern world regards Christianity as the special concern of the religiously-minded, and therefore leaves it on one side, it is because Christians themselves have set the example.'[94] Hence too

> we lose hold of the essence of Christianity if we interpret it simply as a way of holiness, having for its end the salvation and the perfection of the individual soul. Personal religion, so interpreted, becomes a way of escape from the body by meditation and contemplation. But Christianity is the redemption of the body, and of common life, by the Divine action in the Incarnation.[95]

Ascetic spirituality
This is not to say that Anglican spirituality scorns any emphasis on the individual. For F. P. Harton, the presence of the Spirit, and the consequent work of divine grace, confers upon us a divinely-given *potential*: it is up to us to decide whether to respond to the work of grace, and so to actualize that potential. If we don't, there will be little difference between the Christian and the non-Christian.[96] 'The whole purpose of Christian asceticism is to render the soul more and more responsive to the grace within it until at last it reaches perfection by way of ever-deepening surrender to the will of God.'[97] Properly understood, then, Christian asceticism is not the repression of

the natural, but its right direction; and Harton combines a positive evaluation of the physical with a vigilant emphasis on the reality of evil.[98] John Macquarrie goes further, arguing for asceticism as a way of looking at the whole of Christian life – a disciplined and demanding perspective that allows us to go deeper, beneath the comfortable surface of life: for him, it is precisely a structured asceticism that 'new age' spiritualities tend to lack.[99]

Within this context it is worth briefly noting how Harton understands mortification of the senses, a traditional dimension of Catholic spirituality. For him this is not a gloomy rejection of all things sensual, but a concern for simplicity of life and the ability to concentrate on what matters most in life:

> A multitude of sense-impressions are constantly clamouring for admission to the soul, but only those to which we pay attention actually find their way within. In the normal course of events our selection of sense impressions is more or less fortuitous. The untrained listener at an orchestral concert hears a great deal of noise going on, but is quite incapable of distinguishing between the trombone part and that of the French horn, though if there should be 'a tune' he recognises it and is happy: out of, say, sixteen sets of noises he has heard, by good fortune, part of one. With the trained musician the case is different: he will be able to keep clear in his mind the lines of the various instruments, or, if he will, follow the movement of a hidden part – say the viola – in its setting as though it had no competitors. Really to listen to music one needs to mortify one's sense of hearing and hear what one needs to hear.[100]

He applies this principle to a willingness to accept as though from the hand of God the adversities of daily life. This does not lead Harton to regard suffering as God's will. But he does want to stress that our attitude to adversity is

> one of the great tests of true spirituality. There are many people who 'seem to be religious' who nevertheless are constantly complaining over the slightest discomforts, rendering all about them unhappy by their minor selfishnesses; such people are lovers of self and not of God, and for that reason their religion, tried by the touchstone of mortification, is vain.[101]

But any mortification not rooted in 'an ardent love of Jesus crucified' is spurious – the more so if it is an excessive one.[102] 'Mortification in all its forms is the irresistible outcome of the love of Jesus.'[103]

Spirituality and suffering

This introduces us to the crucial issue of suffering and the reality of evil. Geoffrey Studdert-Kennedy argues that 'what Christ came to teach us is not the explanation of evil, but that He came to destroy it, and we ought to do the same'. He vigorously controverts the assumption that innocent suffering must be the will of God.[104] John Stott also has a strong awareness of the reality of evil: he too believes it is to be fought against, and to be overcome by good.[105] Jesus taught the universal extent of human evil, and its inward origin.[106] Hence the central paradox of human nature: our dignity and our depravity: 'we are capable both of the loftiest nobility and of the basest cruelty'.[107] Similarly, Reginald Somerset Ward sees all sickness as 'a battle between the normal forces of health and life and the attacking forces of decay and death. All sickness is an effort on the part of healthy elements against their foes.'[108] It is this effort, this battling against the forces of evil or death or dis-ease, which suffering elicits from us, that gives it any positive value it possesses.[109]

But there is more to be said. Pondering the implications of recent discovery about the human gene, Angela Tilby points out that

> If we simply imitate the blind ruthlessness of our genes we are more likely to end up in prison or in a psychiatric ward than in fulfilment. Human beings have knowledge of the death that awaits them, and need to learn to die in order to be whole. This is the great insight of Christian teaching, the gift that Christ brought into the world in his own person. We are not machines but wounded beings who need the lessons of our humiliations.[110]

William Temple seeks to explore the nature of evil, noting the fact that the Lamb of God came, in the words of the liturgy, to take away the 'sin' (not 'sins') of the world:

> for there is only one sin, and it is characteristic of the whole world. It is the self-will which prefers 'my' way to God's – which puts 'me' in the centre where only God is in place. It pervades the universe. It accounts for the cruelty of the jungle, where each animal follows its own appetite, unheeding and unable to heed any general good.[111]

And, in *Honest to God*, John Robinson cites the eighth chapter of St Paul's Letter to the Romans as a key starting point for a spirituality of suffering: 'the deepest groans of suffering of which the Apostle has been speaking, so far from separating us from the source of our being in the love of God are in fact pointers to it'.[112]

But it is Vanstone who offers perhaps the most significant Anglican exploration of this subject. For him, it is the self-emptying (in Greek, *kenosis*) of God in taking human flesh which must be the starting point. That self-emptying is total: it is not as though there is an unlimited amount of divine energy left over.[113] This leads him to a rich Trinitarian theology:

> Trinitarian theology asserts that God's love for His creation is not the love that is born of 'emptiness.' It is not analogous to the love with which a woman, deprived of children, may love a dog or a doll. It is the love which overflows from fullness. Its analogue is the love of a family who, united in mutual love, take an orphan into the home. They do so not of need but in the pure spontaneity of their own triumphant love. Nevertheless, in the weeks that follow, the family, once complete in itself, comes to need the newcomer. Without him the circle is now incomplete: . . . upon his response depends the triumph or the tragedy of the family's love. In spontaneous love, the family has surrendered its own fulfilment and placed it, precariously, in the orphan's hands. Love has surrendered its triumphant

self-sufficiency and created its own need . . . Of such a nature is the Kenosis of God – the self-emptying of Him Who is already in every way fulfilled.[114]

Now it follows that if God is 'wholly . . . spent and drained in that sublime self-giving which is the ground and source and origin of the universe,' his control over creation is always *precarious*.[115] Writing of the terrible tragedy of Aberfan, where an unsafe coal-heap slipped and destroyed a school full of children in October 1966, Vanstone says:

> We do not believe, of the children who died at Aberfan, that God willed their death as a means to some greater good . . . We believe that, at the moment when the mountain of Aberfan slipped, 'something went wrong': the step of creative risk was the step of disaster: the creative process passed out of control . . . Our preaching on the Sunday after the tragedy was not of a God Who, from the top of the mountain, caused or permitted, for His own inscrutable reasons, its disruption and descent; but of One Who received, at the foot of the mountain, its appalling impact, and Who, in the extremity of endeavour, will find yet new resource to restore and to redeem.[116]

Hence

> If the creation is the work of love, its 'security' lies not in its conformity to some predetermined plan but in the unsparing love which will not abandon a single fragment of it, and man's assurance must be the assurance not that all that happens is determined by God's plan but that all that happens is encompassed by His love.[117]

This kind of approach lends a particular dignity to a spirituality of waiting, a key theme for Vanstone, and one already signalled by T. S. Eliot, both in 'East Coker' and in words given to the crowd in *Murder in the Cathedral*:[118]

> For us, the poor, there is no action,
> But only to wait and to witness.[119]

For Vanstone, Jesus was not so much *betrayed* as *handed over*; and, whereas throughout the first part of the synoptic Gospels Jesus is almost invariably the subject of active verbs (he taught, he called, he spoke, etc.), from Gethsemane onwards he is almost invariably either the object of active verbs or the subject of passive ones.[120] It is precisely in and through his being-done-to that his most powerfully creative work was done.[121] This has prophetic implications for a society which tends to set action far above passivity: hence the negative connotations of being a patient, and of waiting, and the corrosive and common sin of impatience.[122] Instead we need to recover the profound significance of a God who waits on us, and the creative spiritual value of waiting – on God, on one another, on creation itself.[123]

The theology and practice of prayer
It remains to explore briefly some of the principal Anglican contributions to the

nature and practice of prayer. Almost all who reflected on the subject were acutely aware of the challenge: the Anglican Benedictine Bede Frost began his substantial study of prayer by quoting another Anglican religious who had said in 1930: 'it is generally recognised that our people to-day hardly pray at all'.[124] In his poem 'Faith healing', Philip Larkin brilliantly caricatures the spurious faith-healer asking people 'what's wrong?' and directing God in prayer about 'this eye, that knee' – but to no avail:

> What's wrong! Moustached in flowered frocks they shake:
> By now, all's wrong. In everyone there sleeps
> A sense of life lived according to love.
> To some it means the difference they could make
> By loving others, but across most it sweeps
> As all they might have done had they been loved.
> That nothing cures. An immense slackening ache,
> As when, thawing, the rigid landscape weeps,
> Spreads slowly through them.[125]

'All they might have done had they been loved.' This is the point at which the best contemporary Anglican exploration of prayer begins, for prayer is a response to the divine love; it is therefore the language, or energy, of a relationship; and its fundamental character is not *petition* but *communion*. No one catches this character more acutely than William Temple. For him, prayer is merely a making-explicit of a communion with God which can take many forms: science 'in its greatest phases is an intercourse of the mind of man with the Mind expressed in the universe'; and 'communion with the Eternal' in one form or another 'is probably not quite unknown to any human being'.[126] The key feature of prayer is its fundamentally relational character: one can have an aesthetic experience of, say, music without feeling any better disposed towards anyone: it is a sub-personal experience,[127] for

> nothing at all occurs to call our social qualities into play, nor is there any place for the action of our wills. In prayer the exact contrary is the fact. Not as mere appreciative intelligences do we pray, but as children who want to be with their Father, as friends who must mark off certain times to enjoy the company of their Friend. This Father is the composer of the music of the spheres; this Friend is the author of the tremendous drama of history. To enter into His mind is to be on the high places to which art aspires; but it is to be there in company.[128]

Furthermore, because God is more than the source of truth and beauty and is also the source of goodness, communion with God will always involve something more than an experience of beauty alone. 'Correspondence with His impulse therefore involves righteousness of will. This is one reason why prayer is a harder way of ascent to the spiritual heights than philosophy or art; it is also one reason why the achievement, if attained, is nobler. A completer humanity is carried to the lofty regions.'[129]

True prayer, then, will involve our entire lives. John Macquarrie, defining prayer as both 'passionate thinking' and 'compassionate thinking', makes the point that, in an age in which paradoxically both fragmentation and globalization are increasing, prayer allows us to hold things together – to 'think big'.[130] When someone asked Bishop Ian Ramsey how he would teach a miner to pray, he replied that he would try to find out the miner's enthusiasm, for his children or his car: 'enthusiasm is so often the gateway to adoration!' he said.[131] And William Temple links prayer and conduct thus:

> The proper relation in thought between prayer and conduct is not that conduct is supremely important and prayer may help it, but that prayer is supremely important and conduct tests it.[132]

But the really important point here is to see that prayer is relational, involving communion with God; and for Temple it is in this context that we must set the paradox of all Christian prayer: 'we are to be sure that God will grant our prayers; and when He does not, we are to go on praying'.[133] Why? Because the very task of perseverance deepens our trust in God: 'scarcely anything deepens and purifies faith in God for His own sake as surely as perseverance in prayer despite long disappointment'.[134] And the highest requirement for Christian prayer is that given to his disciples by Jesus at the Last Supper: to abide in his presence, for then all that we ask will come to pass for us.[135] 'Most of our prayers would be the better if they were completely free from any element of clamour or demand, and had more of the quality of a consultation in which we lay the needs of ourselves and of others before our Father that He may supply them as His loving wisdom suggests.'[136]

The weakness here is that not all prayer arises out of situations in which clamour and demand can be so easily set aside in favour of 'consultation'. There are occasions when Anglican spirituality breathes the air of the Oxbridge common room rather than the city street; and the fact that almost all the writers cited here are male may be no coincidence; few of them come close to Angela Tilby's discovery of a way of praying which became 'a container for desperation', a way of seeking meaning (and, eventually, healing) in the midst of a broken marriage.[137] John Robinson is acutely aware of the weaknesses of an academic approach to this subject, preferring Dag Hammarskjöld's dictum that 'In our era, the road to holiness necessarily passes through the world of action.' For Robinson, the key word is 'through. God is to be met in, with and under, not apart from, response to the world, the neighbour.'[138] Thus prayer is concerned with a 'being there at depth', not with specific religious practices; though it is a pity that he cannot conceive of those practices, rightly directed, helping us to 'be there at depth'.[139]

This leads us to the question of how God answers prayer, a question which preoccupied twentieth-century writers to a far greater extent than earlier ones as science progressively undermined the notion of there being specific (and otherwise unexplained) areas of life in which God could be believed to intervene. Part of the difficulty here, as Temple acutely observes, is in our reluctance to contemplate answers to prayer that do not suit us:

> Here we have a searching test of our prayer-life. Is it fruitful – in the effectiveness of our intercessions or our own growth in grace? If not, it is

because we are not praying in His name; and that, again, is because we are not abiding in Him nor His sayings in us. If we really so abide, we shall not only desire His will to be done rather than what would have been our own, but we shall know what it is. So often we get far enough to prefer His will to ours in principle; but we are not in communion with Him close enough to avoid insisting upon our judgement of what His will must be – like Peter at Caesarea Philippi or at the feet-washing. We will follow Him . . . But surely He does not mean to go *that* way . . . It leads to certain failure. It leads to a Cross.[140]

The point is put differently by Charles Gore, in a thoughtful manual he wrote for church members. He argues that petitionary prayer does not involve any attempt to change God's mind. Rather 'there are multitudes of things which God means for us, and through us for our brethren, which will never be ours or theirs unless we pray for them'.[141] Indeed, as he well puts it, 'prayer is a method of liberating the hand of God to do what He would do, but cannot do unless we correspond with His will'.[142]

But this still leaves open the question of how, if at all, God answers prayer. Two perceptive approaches are worth citing here. In *Soundings*, a collection of theological essays published in the 1960s by a group of liberal Cambridge academics, John Burnaby is suspicious of those who claim wonderful 'answers to prayer': 'the thoughtful Christian is likely to find here a grave abuse of prayer'.[143] Rather, since God redeemed the world not through 'an act of overriding omnipotence, but through the freely willed self-devotion of a man', we must conceive of prayer as presupposing an active desire to embrace and further the purposes of God (which means being honest in sharing our own desires with God too).[144] And when we do desire God's purposes, we do more than allow God to change us, because of

the nature of charity as a birth of the divine in the human. Wherever a human will suffers itself to be invaded by the will of God, it cannot remain a passive prisoner, but must take service with its divine captor. Or, to use a better metaphor, the life that is released in the soul that has consented to the wooing of God's grace is no longer a life *of* the soul, but the life and power of its union with God. And by that union the universal working of the love of God has increase. My prayer is not good for God's work in the world because it is good for me; it is good for me because it is good for God's work in the world . . . It is not easy to believe that prayer is either always or ever 'answered' in the way desired. It is possible – indeed necessary – to believe that true Christian prayer is always the service of God.[145]

The other approach is that of Peter Baelz. He defines petitionary prayer as 'the confluence of divine providence with human faith. Activity and passivity combine. Prayer is both a resting in God and a wrestling with God.'[146] Communion with God also always involves co-operation with God: 'the situation in which we find ourselves when we turn to prayer is the point at which our co-operation is required'.[147] Hence

we are not treating petition and answer in any mechanical way; we are setting the prayer in the context of a relationship between man and God which is all-embracing, and we are affirming that within the particularity of this context, at this particular juncture of events here and now, this particular prayer is a significant factor in shaping what follows after.[148]

He follows Gore (and Aquinas) in suggesting that perhaps our prayer allows or persuades God to do something which he might not have done, or not have been able to do, had we not prayed.[149] And furthermore

> In prayer we refuse to accept as ultimate what appear to be the fixed conditions of the world, because we believe that these conditions are not ultimate. They have a temporary validity within the purpose of God, but they are in the end subordinate to his love. We do not yet know what love can or cannot achieve. Our faith prompts us to pray, in Kierkegaard's phrase, even 'for the impossible.' Prayer 'is a form of expectation.' It is the growing point in the divine–human encounter. It is participation in new creation.[150]

Hence for Baelz all prayer has a future-oriented nature: it is 'in part an anticipation of the *parousia*, an adherence in the present to that which it is believed and hoped will be realized in the future'.[151]

This brings us to intercessory prayer, to which much of the above also applies. Thus Reginald Somerset Ward says that 'you cannot explain intercession except on the principle that God needs our co-operation to accomplish His work'.[152] We must simply ask 'the best' for those for whom we pray, as Christ did in his great prayer for his disciples in John 17.[153] John Macquarrie suggests that

> intercessory prayer provides, as it were, openings into the dense texture of the human situation through which can come the creative and healing power of the reality we call God . . . Prayer, as petition and intercession, helps to make the human reality porous to the divine reality, and not only that part of it actively engaged in prayer.[154]

John Austin Baker suggests that intercession best makes sense in terms of the power of God working through human capacity to be open to non-physical reality:

> Prayer is not telepathy; but at the natural level it may use this openness. For if our weak human affections can link up through the seemingly impassable obstacles and separations, why should not the power of God's love, which at all times is immediately present to each one of us, penetrate the self . . . prompting to this or that action? . . . It is to the openness of the human self to the power of divine love mediated through the activity of prayer that we may most reasonably attribute those cases of healing, guidance and inspiration, for many of which the evidence is so strong . . . The nub of the matter is that our love for the person prayed for is united with God's love for that same person, and communicated to them by God for their good.[155]

He makes the point that in any petitionary prayer there are at least three people involved – the one praying, the person being prayed for, and God; 'and what happens as a result will emerge from the interplay of all of them'.[156] But that is no excuse for leaving it all to God: love does not work like that: it works in specifics, actual needs and hopes.[157] And fundamental to prayer, in that case, must be a real closeness to those for whom we pray: 'if we want to be able to help others in this way, then we have to take trouble to be "in touch" with them.' If we pray for distant concerns, we must stand ready to be drawn into a deeper relationship with them than we had hitherto, so that the prayer both expresses and incarnates our sense of communion.[158]

Vanstone places intercession within his basic understanding of creation as a precarious, unconditional act of love: intercessors are often in the position of powerlessly looking on while someone else suffers. But that looking-on is never neutral: it is part of God's (often equally powerless) waiting on his creatures, longing to pour out upon them his infinite love, yet constrained both by his own nature and by the nature of the world he has made. Yet Vanstone's main point here is that as intercessors we are witnesses to *God's* precarious struggle to heal and sustain his creation, which is why 'the intercession of the Church expresses our understanding of how costly a thing we are asking when we say "Thy will be done."'[159]

John Taylor speaks of intercession as an exercise in awareness:

> True intercession places another person more firmly in the arms of the divine love which will never infringe that person's freedom, but which works through bestowals of awareness and recognition, through evocation and response, through the offer of choice and glimpse of possibility.[160]

Spirituality and priesthood

Anglican spirituality in the twentieth century is imaginative, intelligent and animated by a serious concern to address the issues and questions of the day. One significant weakness is worth pointing out in conclusion. Most of those who contributed significantly to this subject were ordained.[161] This may account for the relative lack of any real interest in lament, already noted: it certainly shapes the perspective and content of what they have to say. One compensation is some profound reflections on prayer and priesthood;[162] of these, the Anglo-Catholic Martin Thornton is perhaps the best. He insisted on the priest holding together the traditional disciplines of prayer and learning, yet 'in a secular world embraced and loved rather than defied or ignored'.[163] And he continues

> One calls in a plumber because he understands plumbing, not because of his wide experience of life, and one is coached by a golf professional *because* he is *not* a week-end amateur. One is suspicious of a doctor who has read no medical book for twenty years and knows nothing of modern drugs, and I suspect that intelligent modern Christians are getting suspicious of clergy who are for ever engaged in something other than prayer, learning and such-like professional occupations . . . It is precisely by *not* being busily activist that we may really learn to serve and love those who have to be. It is *because* the priest has time for prayer, study and reflection

that his guidance of those in the world's hurly-burly is likely to be worth having.[164]

Thornton goes on to warn of the risks of a narrow clericalism in which the priest's pattern of daily office and prayer is entirely separated from anything the active layperson can share in:

> a priest who conscientiously visits the sick in a bustling hospital, who is constantly among his people in crowded council houses, who acts as factory chaplain, and then retires to a well-run clergy-house furnished with medieval images, a secluded oratory, the reserved Sacrament, and French Oratorian piety, is surely *not* 'mixing with his people' as adult members of the Church.[165]

ROMAN CATHOLIC SPIRITUALITY

Introduction

Despite the Modernist crisis already described in the previous chapter, and its own exposure to the massive changes in society and attitude that the twentieth century brought, there is a sense in which the Roman Catholic Church in England entered the post-Victorian era with vigour and confidence.[166] The soaring grandeur of the 15th Duke of Norfolk's churches at Arundel and Norwich, both of which later became cathedrals, was exceeded only by Edward Lutyens' plan for the Metropolitan Cathedral at Liverpool, even though only the crypt of the latter was actually built. By 1920 the Roman Catholic population in England numbered over 2,000,000, with nearly 4,000 priests;[167] perhaps more significant still, lay Catholics took an increasingly prominent role in the life of both Church and nation in a manner unthinkable a century earlier: the careers of G. K. Chesterton, Hilaire Belloc, Graham Greene and Evelyn Waugh reflect a new confidence among middle-class Catholics, especially as most literary Catholics of this kind were converts.[168] After the Second World War, the influence of the American Thomas Merton's account of his spiritual autobiography in *The seven storey mountain*, published in England in 1949 in an abridged form by Evelyn Waugh, was considerable, even though Merton disliked England, and Waugh had quietly to expurgate extensive Anglophobic passages from the original. Here, for example, is Merton's acidulous view of the Church of England:

> Prayer is attractive enough when it is considered in a context of good food, and sunny joyous country churches, and the green English countryside. And, as a matter of fact, the Church of England means all this. It is a class religion, the cult of a special society and group, not even of a whole nation, but of the ruling minority in a nation. That is the principal basis for its rather strong coherence up to now. There is certainly not much doctrinal unity, much less a mystical bond between people many of whom have even ceased to believe in grace or Sacraments . . . The Church of England depends, for its existence, almost entirely on the solidarity and conser-

vatism of the English ruling class. Its strength is not in anything supernatural, but in the strong social and racial instincts which bind the members
of this caste together; and the English cling to their Church the way they
cling to their King and to their old schools: because of a big, vague, sweet
complex of subjective dispositions regarding the English countryside, old
castles and cottages, games of cricket in the long summer afternoons,
tea-parties on the Thames, croquet, roast-beef, pipe-smoking, the Christmas panto, *Punch* and the London *Times* and all those other things the
mere thought of which produces a kind of a warm and inexpressible ache
in the English heart.[169]

The passage is revealing not only of Merton's unhappy stay in England but of how
outsiders, and perhaps many Catholics, viewed the established church. By 1961
perhaps 10% of the entire nation could be said to be practising Catholics.[170] And the
spiritual leadership of John Heenan, and even more of Basil Hume (successively Arch-
bishops of Westminster), as well as the visit of Pope John Paul II in 1982, did a great
deal to raise its profile. Even so, its numbers too dropped alarmingly during the last
four decades of the century, despite (or perhaps because of) the wind of change
induced by the Second Vatican Council on the one hand, and the firm conservatism
of John Paul II on the other.

The Second Vatican Council

The influence of Vatican II, as it came to be known, on English spirituality was significant. In 1980, the National Pastoral Congress saw an unprecedented assembly of lay
and ordained English Roman Catholics calling for the renewal of the Church in the
spirit of the Second Vatican Council. In their response, *The Easter People*, the Catholic
bishops articulated a new understanding of holiness that was grounded not in rejection of the world but in the fullness of the Christian life within it:

> Many find the word 'holiness' off-putting since it sounds rarefied and
> more suited to monasteries and convents than to homes and workplaces or
> to the often humdrum routine or pressures of modern life. Others find the
> idea of the spiritual life an inordinately complicated one of special devo-
> tions and practices, of the acquisition of virtues, of complex levels of
> prayer and of ascending scales of perfection. Yet holiness or perfection is
> none of these things.[171]

Rather, it is the fruit of God's grace, given to all Christians in baptism. Thus, as the
Vatican Council document *Lumen gentium* had made clear, there is only one vision of
holiness:

> Each of us, priest or lay person, bishop, religious or deacon, hears the same
> call from God. We walk with Christ along different paths to the same
> destiny of eternal glory. In the family, in the seminary or presbytery, on the
> factory floor, in the office-building or school-room or farmer's field, it is
> Christ's way we follow in the circumstances of our daily life ... Our life as
> Christians is a growing into the likeness of Christ who died and rose again

to a new kind of existence. It is for each one of us a life-long process, making us other Christs while at the same time forming us into Christ; leading us through our membership of the Church to build up the Body of Christ.[172]

Friedrich von Hügel (1852–1925)

In the exploration of Roman Catholic spirituality that follows we shall draw on the work of four important figures, two lay and two ordained. Friedrich von Hügel was a walking ecumenical movement.[173] Born in Florence, the son of an Austrian baron and a Scottish Roman Catholic mother, he was almost entirely self-educated. He settled in England in 1867, marrying an aristocratic Englishwoman in 1873, and dying (after suffering persistent ill-health) in 1925.[174]

Von Hügel's life, though admittedly exceptional in its cosmopolitan character, does reflect something vital about English Roman Catholicism in the twentieth century: its European and (to some extent) universal perspective. Immigrants from Poland and other Catholic countries during and after the Second World War helped to develop this, as did the work of the Catholic Institute for International Relations.[175] It is instructive (and reflects the vitality of French Catholicism at the time) that one of the most influential and enduringly popular books of prayers to be published in England in the twentieth century was Michel Quoist's *Prayers of life*, which (unlike most Anglican equivalents) came not from a university or a quiet country retreat but from the working-class French seaport of Le Havre.[176]

Von Hügel's self-education equipped him with formidable intellectual foundations, and reflected the rich eclecticism of the best Catholic writing of his day. He was deeply influenced by Modernist thinkers such as George Tyrrell and Alfred Loisy, rather than by Newman (whom he considered puritanical).[177] His indebtedness to continental philosophers and theologians such as Troeltsch, Leibniz, Kant, Schopenhauer and Spinoza is apparent in his work, as is his love for earlier writers like St Augustine.[178] His writing reflects his generous, deeply ecumenical character; but it must be said that his style makes his work ponderous and frequently tedious to read.[179] He was in great demand as a spiritual director in the 1920s, and his spiritual letters are full of pastoral wisdom. From the point of view of spirituality, his most important major work was his first, *The mystical element of religion as studied in Saint Catherine of Genoa and her friends*, which first appeared in 1908.[180]

Near the beginning of his *Mystical element*, von Hügel suggested that there were essentially three elements in humanity's approach to religion. The first is 'sense and memory, the child's means of apprehending Religion', in which it is seen as 'a Fact and Thing' – not questioned, but trusted in and accepted.[181] The second element is 'question and argument, the youth's mode of approaching Religion.' This reflects 'the reasoning, argumentative, abstractive side of human nature', and envisages religion as 'Thought, System, a Philosophy'.[182] The third element is 'intuition, feeling, and volitional requirements and evidences, the Mature Man's special approaches to Faith'. This is the mystical approach:

here religion is rather felt than seen or reasoned about, is loved and lived rather than analysed, is action and power, rather than either external fact or intellectual verification.[183]

These three elements invariably interweave, even though they represent different chronological stages; and their co-existence always causes tension, of either a fruitful or dangerous kind.[184] Thus the transition from childlike acceptance and trust to mature questioning is tricky, but if fruitful will fuse the external and the intellectual. If not, the individual will settle either for superstition or for rationalism and indifference.[185] But the resulting fusion must then be appropriated more deeply into the will, as the third element is brought into play: if this goes wrong, fanaticism is the result.[186]

Von Hügel's schema is marred by dated attitudes to gender: he believed that women tended towards superstition or fanaticism, where men inclined to be too intellectual (though, as we shall see, it was a woman whom he chose as exemplary of the schema as a whole).[187] And his subsequent application of his schema to the New Testament and Christian history is decidedly questionable.[188] But his analysis led him to draw some fruitful conclusions. He maintained that many religious people wilfully refuse to move beyond the first element, that of trust, because 'the religious temper longs for simplification', and people react against a religion that obliges them to address awkward questions.[189] Yet differentiation and complexity are unavoidable within religion, which creates an inevitable tension, since 'man has an ineradicable and . . . profoundly fruitful thirst for Unity'.[190]

Even more problematic is the fact that religions tend towards exclusiveness, because they demand unconditional surrender of the self.[191] It is only when we realize that for Christians this surrender is to a *person*, not to a *structure*, that it becomes compatible with inner freedom.[192] Indeed von Hügel's emphasis on personhood is the key to his spiritual theology: for only by a progressive letting-go of our own character and 'lower' selves, in order to allow ourselves to be remade in the likeness of Christ, do we achieve the fullness of the religious life. Only then do childlike trust, institutional integrity, intellectual clarity, and deep inner serenity and intimacy with God, become mutually compatible.[193]

In his extended study of the life and spirituality of St Catherine of Genoa, von Hügel seeks to present someone who in an original manner fuses the three elements; and the choice of a lay married woman is a striking one.[194] He notes 'the richness and variety of her life at any one moment', the way in which she combines intensity of feeling with 'a rich balanced doctrine and . . . a quite heroic objectivity', and the way she combines an intense inner spiritual life with active and effective care of the poor.[195] She was profoundly sympathetic towards animals and plants, and is described as being exceptionally sentient, with a heightened sense of touch.[196] Yet she is not exemplary: she has no sense of humour, 'a serious drawback', though she is impulsive and affectionate.[197] But above all she is a whole person, with 'the infinitely winning qualities of a simple veracity'; she is fully alive, entirely at one with herself; 'a living, closely knit, ever-increasing spiritual organism, if there ever was one'.[198]

Such a person will be profoundly attractive;[199] but she will have had to overcome the pervasive evil of self-idolatry, an evil the mystical tradition has (in von Hügel's view) tended to undervalue, in order to achieve this degree of fulfilment.[200] Von Hügel draws two more crucial conclusions from his study: first, that only a spirituality able to embrace question and conflict can be considered authentic: it is precisely through her embodiment and integration of all the 'elements' of religion that St Catherine attains wholeness, and then only through an appropriate and socially aware asceticism;[201] and, secondly, that religion can only ever be one ingredient in our complete 'spirit-life':

> the soul cannot attain to its fullest possible spiritual development, without the vigorous specific action and differentiation of forces and functions of a not directly religious character, which will have to energize, each according to its own intrinsic nature, within the ever ampler, and ever more closely-knit, organization of the complete life of the soul.[202]

This second point is fundamental for von Hügel. Thus he wrote in 1898, to George Tyrrell SJ:

> As the body can live only by inhalation and exhalation . . . so the soul can live, to be fully normal in normal circumstances, only by a double process: occupation with the concrete and then abstraction from it, and this alternately, on and on. If it has not the latter it will grow empty and hazy, if it has not the former, it will grow earthly and heavy. Humanity at large is under *the strict obligation* . . . to practise *both these activities*.[203]

And he criticized Pusey for having been far too narrowly religious, and incapable of taking any interest in anything that was not explicitly religious.[204] In *The life of prayer* he compares Newman unfavourably with the abbé Huvelin: the latter's sense of the love of God in all things was more Franciscan, more world-affirming, and hence more joyful, than Newman's narrowly religious melancholy.[205] Hence von Hügel's enthusiasm for science (he was a keen amateur geologist), which at its best

> will . . . help to give depth and mystery, drama and pathos, a rich spirituality, to the whole experience and conception of the soul and of life, of the world and of God.[206]

Von Hügel's thoughtful and integrated theology of the spiritual life leads him to some profound reflections on suffering. It is not only by the attainment of our own personal wholeness, but by our sharing in something far bigger than we are – the Church – that we discover a means of responding creatively to the terrible challenge suffering presents. In the first place, this means our participation in the life of Christ:

> with Him, and alone with Him and those who still learn and live from and by Him, there is the union of the clearest, keenest sense of all the mysterious depth and breadth and length and height of human sadness, suffering, and sin, *and*, in spite of this and through this and at the end of this, a note of conquest and of triumphant joy.[207]

Hence 'it is . . . not the smoother, easier times and circumstances' in people's lives, but 'the unshrinking, full acceptance' of the hardest trials, that helps to lead us to the deepest possible trust in the love of God.[208] And the people who achieve such trust do so not by by-passing the trials but by embracing them.[209] This is not at all to say that suffering is of itself creative, but that

> wherever there is the fullest, deepest, interiority of human character and influence, *there* can ever be found profound trials and sufferings which have been thus utilized and transfigured.[210]

It is in this context that von Hügel's stress on ecclesiology matters: it is the Church which confers upon its members a sense of mutual interdependence which sustains us in our suffering:

> I wonder whether you realise a deep, great fact? That souls – all human souls – are deeply interconnected? That (I mean) we can, not only pray for each other, but *suffer* for each other?[211]

Much of this rich interplay of the individual and the corporate, the religious and the secular, informs von Hügel's attitude to prayer. He suggests three fundamental theological principles for Christian prayer. The first is the fact that God 'is a stupendously rich Reality', inexhaustibly so. The second is the fact that God created all things, and is to be found in all things, including 'innocent Nature as well as in all Supernature'. This point is particularly important, because it should lead us to see God as much in (say) coral insects as in heavenly truths:

> Such an inclusive and yet discriminating position brings also much help to our prayer. For in prayer, also, it brings a tension, to the verge of strain; and a *détente*, to the verge of relaxation. In both these movements of the soul God can, and God should, be envisaged – in the *détente*, the God of nature, the source of all that is wholesome and homely; and in the tension, the God of supernature, the source of all that is ardent and heroic. We thus escape dullness, monotony and the like – these subtle dangers of the spiritual life.[212]

The third principle is the fact that that 'the decisive preparation for prayer lies not in the prayer itself, but in the life prior to the prayer'.[213]

The spirituality of Friedrich von Hügel exerted a considerable influence on later Christians, and deservedly so; his balanced and penetrating analysis reflects immense pastoral sensitivity and wisdom as well as great learning. Only his orotund style limits his accessibility. Yet even this is sometimes dispensed with. In a letter of 1920 he offered a correspondent three attractive, secular and typically complementary images of the spiritual journey. The first is mountaineering: mountaineers climb with a 'quiet, regular, short step' which appears slow on the level but sustains them when they ascend steeply; and they stop and wait patiently when thick mist prevents their seeing where to go, only moving on again when it clears. The second is sailing: anyone engaged on a long sea journey must first set out their cabins prudently, choosing only stout and durable objects and arranging them in such a way that they will not break when storms come. The third is camel-driving: when desert sandstorms strike, camel-drivers dismount and fall prostrate face downwards on the sand, covering their heads with their cloaks, and wait for as many hours as necessary before proceeding on their journeys. And 'God is in the storms as in the calm!'[214]

John Chapman (1865–1933)

Unlike Friedrich von Hügel, Dom John Chapman OSB came from impeccably English stock. His father was an Anglican priest; he was educated privately and at Christ Church Oxford, and after training at Cuddesdon was ordained deacon in 1889 to serve his title at St Pancras in London, before increasing uncertainty as to the authority and theological integrity of the Church of England led to his being received into the Roman Church in 1890.[215] After first briefly trying his vocation with the Jesuits, he became a Benedictine and was ordained priest in 1895. In 1913 he was sent as superior to Caldey to help the monastic community there, newly-converted *en masse* from the Church of England, to become a Roman Catholic one: in 1914 he transferred to Downside. After serving as an army chaplain during the war he eventually returned to Downside as prior and in 1929 was elected its fourth abbot.[216]

Chapman was to become an outstandingly respected spiritual guide and counsellor; and his letters are a remarkable compendium of spiritual wisdom. (He wrote disarmingly: 'I rarely write letters. But, when I do, they frequently turn out to be very long indeed'.[217]) They reflect long and patient study and prayer, and intimate knowledge of a wide range of theologians; but above all they breathe the air of Benedictine *lectio divina* and meditation, by means of which extensive learning is appropriated and thoroughly digested.[218]

The influence of the French Catholic school of spirituality, with its stress on a loving and unconditional *abandon* to the will of God, is apparent in Chapman's approach to the spiritual life. In a letter written from Caldey in 1914, he tells a layperson that, when circumstances do not fit one's hopes,

> the only thing is to accept all the circumstances of one's life, and all the effects they seem to produce upon one, and use them as means of annihilating one's own will, cheerfully and willingly. There is no other recipe for prayer, I think.[219]

He maintains that we cope with feelings of anxiety by use of this French spiritual virtue of *abandon*: recognizing that such feelings come from the lower part of the soul, above which is the 'ground' of the soul in which prayer takes place: 'simplicity consists in keeping the whole soul subject to this ground (*fundus*) or apex; and this sovereign point (or hidden ground – whichever metaphor you like) must be continually united to God's Will'. Then

> If the soul turns to prayer, it *feels* the division: there is (1) worry and anxiety and trouble and bewilderment, and there is (2) also an unfelt, yet real, acquiescence in being anxious, troubled and bewildered, and a consciousness that the *real* self is at peace, while the anxiety and worry is unreal.[220]

This emphasis on praying at the still centre of the soul is a major theme for Chapman. He tells a Benedictine nun apparently suffering from spiritual aridity that

> The only thing that matters is the 'fine point' of the soul, and you have to learn to live by that, and not by any feelings, even of the most spiritual kind. Our Lord will strip you of all this spirituality, until you not only are sure you have no 'spiritual life', but also know that you ought not even to wish for it! It must be enough for you to be exactly in the state in which God puts you, – that is, in the state in which you find yourself.[221]

Chapman isn't sure, and doesn't care, whether this 'point' of the soul is the highest, or deepest: what matters is to stay there, and to want what God wants: 'the right intention' is crucial.[222] And we shall advance in the practice of spirituality by the gradual increase of the habit of living in the spirit, not in the flesh – that is, identifying our real self with the 'point of the soul', not with all the emotions and imaginations which trouble us. The real 'I' is the will which gives itself to God.[223]

This emphasis on submission to the will of God, or rather of being united with God's will, recurs frequently in his letters.[224] It can lead him almost to an overriding acceptance of divine Providence: 'we are *always* in touch with God; everything that happens is His arrangement, His Providence, and a means of grace, a push on to Heaven'. But it is clear that he means by this that God is always at work in whatever happens to us, not necessarily that he causes it.[225] Everything depends on what we do with what is given to us.[226]

This stress on obedience to the divine will can also lead Chapman to an unquestioning reverence for ecclesiastical authority, though he envisages that as a healthy antidote to doing whatever we happen to feel like.[227] And this is the crucial point; he wants to foster a spiritual life that is not self-indulgent, or introspective; so he tells a woman religious

> *Don't look into your soul*, but look at God . . . There is a danger of 'devout people' living for themselves instead of living for others.[228]

This informs his attitude to prayer. The test of true prayer is not what we happen to feel while we are praying, but the effect it has on our (and other people's) lives afterwards. He tells a layperson that

> the more time you can reasonably give to being alone with God, the easier it becomes to enjoy it (I don't mean pleasure, but the feeling that it is worth doing – that you are not simply lazy and wasting time). The test is not whether you feel anything at the time, but whether *afterwards* you feel (quite illogically) better, and more determined to serve God. The one thing you should gain by quiet prayer (just remaining with God, and making a number of aspirations to keep your imagination from wandering) is to feel the rest of the day that you want God's Will and nothing else.[229]

Far from leading to passivity, this receptivity towards God will lead to an enhanced energy in everything else.[230] And hence 'the one real proof that you have the *right kind of prayer for you*, is not that it always goes easily and always succeeds, but that it really does you good and changes your life'.[231] Hence too the sobering truth that prayer is often very hard work indeed:

[prayer] in the sense of union with God, [is] the most crucifying thing there is. One must do it for God's sake; but one will not get any satisfaction out of it, in the sense of feeling 'I am good at prayer', 'I have an infallible method.' That would be disastrous, since what we want to learn is precisely our own weakness, powerlessness, unworthiness. Nor ought one to expect 'a sense of the reality of the supernatural' . . . And one should wish for no prayer, except precisely the prayer that God gives us – probably very distracted and unsatisfactory in every way!

On the other hand, the only way to pray is to pray; and the way to pray well is to pray much. If one has no time for this, then one must at least pray regularly. But the less one prays, the worse it goes. And if circumstances do not permit even regularity, then one must put up with the fact that when one does try to pray, one can't pray – and our prayer will probably consist of telling this to God . . . You simply have to begin wherever you find yourself.[232]

Chapman's spirituality represents an attractive English version of the French Catholic tradition exemplified by St Vincent de Paul and Jean-Pierre de Caussade. He has little time for feelings in prayer ('*Feelings*: Protestants depend upon them. They are useful for beginners. They are not to be depended upon').[233] But there is a sanity and a large-heartedness which permeates his extensive correspondence. Witness his comment to a religious superior:

> When I am told, for example, that Sister X has beautiful visions, but does not keep her rule, I am inclined to reply that, without the visions, she might keep it even less, and might lose all heart.[234]

Gerald Vann (1906–63)

Our third Roman Catholic figure was another priest and scholar and, like Chapman, one with a deep pastoral heart. Vann entered the Dominican Order when he was still in his teens (in 1923), and spent most of his busy life teaching and lecturing successively in England and Scotland. It is perhaps not surprising to find the influence of St Thomas Aquinas, also a Dominican, looming large in his works, many of which originated as sermons and addresses given in London or elsewhere. His most famous work, *The divine pity*, which appeared in 1945, is subtitled 'a study in the social implications of the Beatitudes', and forms the foundation for the exploration that follows.

Like so many others, Vann stresses the importance for the spiritual life of our status as God's children: indeed we are at once adults and children,

> and it is the child-aspect which makes virtue christian, and which gives to the christian who is possessed of it the freedom and gaiety, the trustingness, the complete absence of self-righteousness and of calculating worry, and consequently the freshness and simplicity, that you find so prominent in the personality of the saint.[235]

In fact it is sin that destroys the child in us, leading us to replace a freely-willed and mature obedience to God, which alone makes life possible, with 'the pride of attempted autonomy'.[236] To be deprived of this childlikeness is to live the life of

Mammon, and that is to be in hell: 'for hell, like heaven, in the most important sense is not so much where you go as what you become', which is to be bereft of God.[237]

What does it mean to be God's children? First, it means seeking to foster 'a childlike trust in Providence, and so to be freed from fear'.[238] This is what Jesus means by poverty of spirit, the first Beatitude, which is the virtue that enables us to distinguish servile fear from childlike awe: 'beyond the completely servile fear of the slave there is the fear of the loving but as yet unreasoning child . . . beyond this again there is the fear, wholly identified now with loving awe, which is proper to the lover.'[239] Hence to grow in wisdom is to move, not simply from fear to love (for God is always to be approached with awe), but

> from the servile fear of the slave . . . to the loving reverence of the son . . .
> and in the end to the purely selfless fear of the lover, the fear of hurting
> what you love.[240]

So 'the first prayer is the prayer of awe of the Unknown, the prayer of the little child in the face of mystery and infinity, the prayer of Thomas the Apostle abashed by the response to his lack of faith: "My Lord and My God."'[241] And true, godly fear is 'the first stage in complete docility to the impulses of the Spirit'.[242]

Secondly, being God's children means recognizing that all we are given is God's, and God's free gift. In *The pain of Christ and the sorrow of God*, Vann reflects on the Prodigal's decision: to regard his father's gifts to him *as though they were his own*, and then to take them to a far country and inevitably squander them uselessly.[243] Rather we must see that we are stewards, not owners, of all we have and are; and Vann stresses the rich paradoxical nature of what this entails:

> You are only a steward of all that you have and all that you are; a steward for
> God and His family. But you are meant to be more than stewards of
> God's things: you are meant to be lovers as well. If you hurt anything of the
> things that God has made – by lust, or tyranny, or blindness, or by
> using things in any way as mere means to your pleasure or profit – you hurt
> yourself and all the world, because to that extent you continue to destroy
> the unity of the family. But if you love, and therefore can serve as well as
> use, can reverence as well as master; if you are a contemplative and have
> learnt to see and love instead of grabbing, and if your love is worship of
> God and not of yourself . . . then you return to the integrity of God's
> family, and, having nothing, you are at peace, because you have nothing to
> lose, and at the same time you possess all things, for yours is the
> kingdom.[244]

This is a succinct articulation of the monastic understanding of poverty of spirit. And Vann anchors it in the nature of our *desires*: 'the desire to have is deep in us: but it is really a misunderstanding if we think of it thus instead of as a desire to *be*. The heart is an infinite capacity and thirst for *being*: and we are never at rest until it is filled.'[245] 'It is what we want, what we will, that is fundamental to spirituality; and what we should seek is the will to give oneself readily to the things which concern the worship of God.'[246] Thus 'happiness is not, essentially, something we have but something we are.'[247] And we experience it when we try to see the divine beauty, not only in obviously beautiful or holy things, but in the poor and the ugly, 'in the waifs and strays of the world, in the dull and colourless moments as well as in the moments of great joy.'[248]

It is important to stress that in Vann's view our status as God's children should lead, not to a self-regarding introspection, but to a turning *outward*, from self to God; for the Beatitudes 'tell us, all of them, that the way to be happy is to search for something else' – here is a healthy antidote to too much self-absorbed spirituality.[249] This is not a prescription for frenetic activism; rather

> to be outward-turning in this sense means only that we fix our eyes on something other than our own self, we cease to be self-centred. It does not mean an absence of recollection . . . the one essential thing, quite simply, is that we should look at God, not for ever at ourselves.[250]

Vann carefully holds together here the necessarily introspective character of serious spiritual growth with a healthy refusal to allow that to become self-centred. Later he emphasizes that the outward-turning towards God necessarily includes an outward-turning towards one's neighbour.[251] The Church is a family, but an inclusive one: 'we have a right to a house, a home; but it must be, not a fortress from which all are excluded, but a home where all can find a welcome'.[252] He argues that true Christian mysticism 'can never be content with a solitary absorption in God on the mountaintop, unaware of the poor misguided worldlings who people the plains below; for the Word was made flesh and dwelt among us'.[253] Vann regards baptism as more than incorporation into the life of God; it is also to play a part in the conflict between good and evil. Writing in 1945, he tells people to

> think of the world of nature as involved in the grip of evil on the universe, and therefore as needing, in degree, the healing and restoring power of the Spirit: and then you will see the significance of baptism for the world as a whole.[254]

Baptism turns every Christian into a mediator; and confirmation, following from it, is 'the sacrament of social action'.[255]

And so to the second Beatitude ('blessed are the meek'), which prompts Vann to offer what is virtually a prospectus for the entire spiritual life, and worth quoting at length:

> If you study the mythologies and folk-lore of the peoples of the world . . . you find the same theme constantly recurring: the hero must make his long journey through the darkness of the sea or the night, he must slay the dragon or the serpent, he must come through death to the new life, the new birth. And in the christian story which is the fulfilment of these secular dreams of humanity . . . you find the same theme in its highest form in the sacrificial death of the Word who was made flesh and dwelt amongst us that we might be re-born to be the sons of God. But this is not simply a vicarious redemption in which we have no part: what was done in

and by Christ must be done also in a different fashion in and by ourselves; in us too the dragon must be slain, and we too must pass through death to the new life. What is the dragon? The power of evil, the mystery of iniquity under whose bondage we are as long as we are living not in God but in sin. And what is the death? The death of the false self, the self set up in rebellion against God, the self which seeks to be self-sufficient. How then are we to be re-born and become whole? By finding our true centre which is in God, finding God in all things, and the desire of God in all desires, and so beginning to live the life of worship instead of the life of self-worship . . . We find God through making for ourselves the long sea-journey – in the company and in the power of Him who made it for us first; we find God through overcoming, again in His power, the dark evil within us; we find God by realizing in the first place our need of God as a child realizes its need of a father, we find Him by learning to see the reality of sin and therefore to repent and be meek and humble of heart.[256]

Vann here draws together some of the classic themes of Christian spirituality: our nature as forgiven sinners, our status as adopted children; but he makes the spiritual life into an adventure of un-selfing as we seek God in all things. And that makes true meekness not some abject grovelling, but something subversive: it is

the strength that can turn all energies to service of God and the world instead of the self; it means the strength of the Baptist, defying kings and leading peoples, but knowing when the Christ comes that 'He must increase, I must decrease.'[257]

This is compelling spiritual writing, at once thoughtful, integrated and exhilarating. For Vann, true Christian piety is not 'soft sentimental escapism', but our duty (which is what the word 'piety' literally means), our response to what God has done for us – the duty of love and obedience and gratitude, owed by the child to its parents. True piety certainly involves the duty we owe to our families and our country; but it must not be restricted to these. Writing in 1945 Vann has these prophetic remarks to make in a footnote of *The divine pity*:

The *patria* is still the land where we were born, the soil on which we depend and which is specially ours, the culture and traditions in which we share; it is still to our own country that we owe the greatest debt, and to which *pietas* properly refers. But as the world becomes, in some ways, more and more a unity, so the scope of *pietas* is enlarged: we owe, in degree, a debt to all the countries from which we benefit materially or culturally, and ultimately to the whole world; and . . . we cannot think of political progress except in terms of the good of the world as a whole.[258]

It follows that true piety will involve suffering, not least in the costly willingness to leave self behind. Vann insists on the virtue of compassion, shared suffering, embodied in the example of Simon of Cyrene: 'to take up a cross thus for and with another is to turn it into a tree of life. There are things you will never know, never understand, except through suffering, and especially through suffering *with* another'.[259] Hence

> When I share in the suffering of someone I love, that actual sharing is the expression of something deeper, something permanent: the will-to-share, which is what we call love. And so in the mystery of redemption: the actual sharing is done through the humanity of Christ, but that actual sharing is the expression of the deeper and permanent mystery in the Godhead, the will-to-share, i.e., the will to be a *companion*.[260]

It follows that prayer and action for social justice are of the essence of the Christian spiritual life.[261] And compassion (or, as Vann calls it, the divine pity) is *the* defining Christian quality because it is at the furthest possible remove from a me-centred perspective.[262] 'Pity essentially depends on clarity of vision: you become most fully merciful when you become clean of heart.'[263] Pity enlarges the heart.[264] Hence the simplest of all prayers of compassion is beyond even lament or intercession: it is simply a statement of what is, of human need, as with the Virgin's laconic declaration: 'They have no wine.'[265] Here is Vann's noble and sober reflection on it:

> The prayer of sorrow turns into the prayer of pity: 'They have no wine.' The beauty of the world is ravaged, the purity sullied, the joy quenched, the harmony destroyed: it is in part my fault, and at least I must pray my sorrow, that to some extent I may undo the evil, and the earth to some extent may be restored. We can never return to the earthly paradise; there are some things that can never be changed however long the world goes on; but at least I can take the pain that is given me or the pain I choose and turn them into loving sorrow and into the prayer of sorrow and so increase a little the renewed sanctification and blessing, and the joy, of the world.[266]

Mary is our exemplar here: she has the gift of the highest wisdom which is the fruit of intimate experience of God, and which issues in the divine pity:

> Mary the Mother, Mary the Bride: the first is the epitome of all human experience, the mother of sorrows, the queen of the seven swords; the epitome of all that ordering of things, but ordering sweetly, which is motherhood; the epitome of all the care and responsibility and pity of the bearer for the born. But the second title is the key to the depth and the stillness and the wonder: is what turns experience into gentleness, understanding into pity, governance into sweetness, responsibility into compassion, sorrow into joy. In the eyes of the mother is the understanding of 'the beginning, and ending, and midst of the times'; but they are also and for ever the eyes of the girl, the bride, who says 'He that is mighty hath done great things in me.' To be like Mary you must have wisdom and be able to say 'I understand'; but to be able to say that you must first say with her 'Teach me.'[267]

But St Peter is our exemplar too. Vann cites Jesus' prediction of Peter's martyrdom to underlie the creative spiritual value of patience when we are no longer in control:

'Another shall gird thee.' We need patience to meet the special trials, the weakness and powerlessness, of old age; but we need patience, also, to meet the similar trials that may come upon us at any age: the sorrow of seeing our labours destroyed and we unable to prevent it . . . the hardness of having to watch others reap what we have sown . . . of having to realize that we have tried for so many years to be good christians and yet have made so little observable progress: all these things can give us a sense of powerlessness and therefore of impatience and perhaps a sort of despair. Then we have to draw ourselves back to the thought of the eternal present, the thought of the loving providence of the divine wisdom which disposes all things sweetly; we have to try to teach ourselves all over again to care and not to care, to learn to prepare for the future by making what use we can of each present moment as it comes, and leaving the rest, without worry, to the mercy of God.[268]

This marvellous passage also articulates all Vann's favourite themes: 'to care and not to care', the eternal present, the stress on abandonment to the present moment (reflecting the French school of Caussade and others), the echo of the Advent antiphon *O sapientia*, and above all the divine pity. 'The Gospel life of Peter begins with the summons to follow his Master; and it is with the same summons, Follow me, that his life in the Gospel ends.'[269] Peter is the exemplar of the spiritual life, whose letting-go of control leads to a far deeper freedom – the fallible fisherman who through the agency of the divine pity becomes the rock on which is founded the universal Church.

With Peter, we are to remember that all we receive is pure grace; and this is the secret of prayer.[270] For Vann, all prayer is by definition a reaching-out to the entire universe: 'we cannot pray as christians at all unless in our prayer the travail of all creation is at least implicitly expressed.'[271] Yet at the heart of prayer is that childlike wonder which we noted as the start of these reflections on Vann's thought. In that prayer

you are not asking anything: you are *quiet*, you are just *being with*, and there is love and wonder in your heart. So this prayer is indeed a beginning of beatitude; for the heart is filled and is content simply to be – and its being is all adoration. You find some hint of this utterly serene but utterly humble sense of infinity in some of the greatest music: in some of Bach or of César Franck, for example, or of the Beethoven of the last quartets, or again in Wolf's *Ganymed* . . . You find it expressed in the words of the apostle Thomas, abashed at his unbelief: My Lord and my God.[272]

This prayer is no comfortable avoidance of the sorrows of the world: 'your love of God still includes your love of your family', which is the whole human world.[273] Positively, however, it brings us to the prayer of gratitude, and here Gerald Vann's theme of the divine pity reaches its most profound and moving articulation:

There are problems which only the heart's knowledge, piercing to the heart of things where God's pity abides, can solve; and to solve them is to be grateful to God, for the solution is the pity. And this prayer, too, at its highest and best is part of the wordless prayer of wonder and adoration, for

the deepest wonder is aroused not simply by Beauty in itself, but by Beauty
stooping to comfort ugliness because of the pity which is love.[274]

Donald Nicholl (1923–97)

We conclude our exploration of twentieth-century Roman Catholic spirituality with
another layperson. Donald Nicholl was a Yorkshireman, born into an Anglican
family; he became a Roman Catholic in 1946, and in the following year married
Dorothy Tordoff, who had herself become a Catholic too: they had five children.
Nicholl was a university lecturer, first in medieval history, until he switched 'almost
overnight' to the study of twentieth-century Russian thought and immersed himself
in the work of Dostoyevsky and St Seraphim of Sarov.[275] He taught successively at
Edinburgh, Keele and the University of California before in 1981 being appointed
rector of the Ecumenical Institute of Tantur, near Jerusalem. He retired four years
later, and died of cancer in 1997. Nicholl was a person of unusually wide-ranging
interests and reading; he translated Dante's *Monarchia*, as well as a life of Edith Stein:
both were significant influences on him. His best and most influential book, *Holiness*,
first appeared in 1981.

And it is the nature and pursuit of holiness which lies at the heart of Nicholl's exploration of spirituality. But we need to begin somewhere else. In an address he gave in
1997, he describes how he was influenced by the French writer Sertillanges, who
insisted in his *La vie intellectuelle* (1940) that those who seek the truth through intellectual study need to spend as much time as possible in the open air.[276] In other words,
as Nicholl went on to argue, personal spirituality and lifestyle are inseparable from
authentic intellectual research;[277] and he has harsh words to say about what he calls
that *déformation professionelle* which separates academics from the 'real' world.[278]
Nicholl himself abandoned the rigorous and exclusive pursuit of medieval historical
research in order to combine university teaching with informal seminars on *The
brothers Karamazov* in a street café.[279]

So it is not surprising to find that Nicholl takes a thoroughly practical approach to
the subject of holiness. It is also a thoroughly scriptural one, even though it is
deepened by his wide pastoral experience, love of literature, and study of other great
world faiths. He says that 'the ultimate test of transparency – indeed, of spirituality in
general – is money; that is, whether we are straight about money'.[280] And he quotes a
student who asks the Buddhist monk Thich Nhat Hanh how Vietnamese monks
meditate; he replies, 'In our monastery no one is allowed to meditate until he has
spent at least three years learning how to serve tea to the older monks.'[281] We are far
from any narrowly intellectual search for holiness here; on the contrary, we must start
somewhere else:

> if only you work away at the rotten areas of yourself on which the light of
> Christ has been shed, then the burden of Christ will prove so light as to be
> no burden at all.[282]

So holiness begins with where we are, and with who we are. We must not be in a
hurry: for the busyness of so many western middle-class people is, in his view, a kind of
greed: 'greed generates hurry by leading us to try to push in more than there is really

room or time for'.[283] Teachers from all world faiths have regarded an ordered day as essential for holiness.[284] And we must be deeply committed to love of neighbour. Nicholl quotes Gandhi: 'If you don't find God in the very next person you meet it is a waste of time looking for him further.'[285]

Holiness is, then, practical, relational, unhurried, integrating. This is not to say that there should be no spiritual or religious practices marked off from everyday life: Nicholl regrets Protestantism's lack of interest in holy places, or things, or people, that stand over against society and its values.[286] Rather it is to say that holiness is the fruit of a rightly-directed life, a life that is oriented towards some transforming end or goal that is larger than you are. Once we have identified such an end, and allowed our lives to be shaped by it, even our small and spontaneous actions become creative:

> an action, if it is to be perfect, has to be spontaneous. It can only come about in a human being as a result of unremitting training directed towards some other end, beyond the immediate one.[287]

In reality, it is not so much a matter of our identifying an appropriate end or goal in our lives, as of that goal identifying us; and this is what the Bible means by vocation. Here too Nicholl has important things to say. First, true vocation is never a narrowly individual affair:

> Only by responding to one's unique, exclusive call from the Holy One can one move towards an inclusive, all-embracing relationship with all other creatures.[288]

Such a relationship is in itself the key test of the authenticity of a sense of vocation. Nicholl learned through experience that 'what you *are* always comes out; what you project rarely comes off'.[289] Secondly, true vocation will often cut across any plans we might have had for our lives: Nicholl suggests that Jesus' words to St Peter at the end of the Gospel of John ('Truly, I say to you . . . another will gird you and carry you where you do not wish to go') provide 'the classic meaning of call, or vocation'.[290]

The important point here is the letting-go of our own control over our lives and our plans. For Nicholl, the reason suffering offers a unique spiritual opportunity is because when it happens the initiative and *control* are taken from us: 'so long as our lives are in our own hands we will never really give up the very thing we need above all to give up if we are to be changed.'[291] Nicholl recalls the Orthodox custom of bride-groom and bride placing martyrs' crowns on each other's heads at their marriage, testifying to the fact that from now on neither can live according to their own will.[292] And he notes Edith Stein's key point: that sufferers can make some sense of their suffering by allowing it to draw them into the lives of other sufferers.[293] Our highest gift to another is our presence: 'presence, total presence of one to another, is what is ultimate'.[294] This is the essence of intercession: 'whenever we pray on behalf of others, we in some measure put ourselves in their place'.[295]

FREE CHURCH SPIRITUALITY

Introduction

In 1912 Peter (P. T.) Forsyth, Principal of the Congregationalist College at Hackney in London and one of the outstanding figures in twentieth-century Nonconformity, warned his fellow-Christians that 'spirituality may be made to cover anything from inspiration to eccentricity,' and he asked them: 'where is our last resort – to *Authority* or *Subjectivity?*'[296] He went on to point out that the tension between the revealed word of God in scripture and a free, unfettered Holy Spirit went to the heart of the theology of Dissent, so that the Free Churches were in a particularly strong position to address the dilemma he posed. And later in the same work he wrote:

> The greatest problem before Independency is how to regain its place in the great world Church; and to do it, not by the ineffective way of mere sympathy, which may begin and end in sentiment, but by some way which shall make the Church a real and respected power for the practical purpose of God with society. And that we shall never do simply in the name of a Christian charity, nor in that of a Christian liberty, which alone will but make us a refuge of cranks; but only in the name of the only Authority which creates a liberty we can never force.[297]

Forsyth's analysis of both problem and opportunity was acute; and he devoted his considerable energies to encouraging Nonconformity, with its distinctive fusion of Word and Spirit, authority and freedom, to respond to the challenge before it.[298] Furthermore he was followed by a number of outstanding Nonconformist thinkers, preachers and leaders, who similarly sought both to address the issues of the day, and in so doing to stamp a new identity and confidence on English Dissent. By the last decades of the century, however, it was clear that, whatever their success with the first of these objectives, they had failed with the second. Despite the occasional appearance of a Forsyth or a Donald Soper, mainstream English Nonconformity declined steadily through the century.[299]

Even so, it is important to recall the pervasive influence of the Free Churches in poor working-class areas during the last decades of the nineteenth and early decades of the twentieth centuries.[300] And Free Church preaching, with its vigorous combination of biblical proclamation and passionate engagement with the issues of the day, exerted an incalculable influence during the inter-war and immediate post-war eras: great figures like Leslie Weatherhead at the City Temple, W. E. Sangster at Central Hall Westminster, and Donald Soper at Kingsway Hall and Hyde Park Corner, will have touched and challenged thousands in a way few if any Anglican or Roman Catholic preachers achieved. Furthermore Nonconformist scholarship was immensely influential, not least in the historical study of Christian spirituality: the works of Raymond George, R. Newton Flew, and Gordon Wakefield stand alongside the German Friedrich Heiler's *Prayer* (1923) and Kenneth Kirk's *The vision of God* (1931) as ground-breaking attempts to ponder the spiritual traditions of Christianity with a view to appropriating their transforming power for today.[301] And, as we shall see, the spirituality of twentieth-century Dissent exhibited a vigour and vitality that belied the statisticians' report of a movement in deep and possibly terminal decline.

Spirituality and theology

We may begin by returning to Forsyth's 1912 book *Faith, freedom and the future*. He begins in characteristically vigorous style:

> It is in remarkable contrast with the manner of our own time that in the New Testament we find little said about spirituality and much about the Holy Ghost. Today we seem to have in some cases not so much as heard of a Holy Ghost.[302]

Yet without the work of the Holy Spirit in proclaiming, and helping individuals to appropriate for themselves, Christ's redeeming death and resurrection, the Christian Gospel would never have been heard.[303] Forsyth stresses the perils of a spirituality divorced from right (that is, biblically grounded) doctrinal beliefs: 'the subjectivity of the age feels itself comparatively independent of objective reality':[304] Spirit comes to be completely detached from Word. But 'Christianity is not spirituality apart from evangelical faith in the facts.'[305]

Forsyth's work represents a determined attempt to hold spirituality and doctrine together; and it was not his fault if subsequent generations saw them drift yet further and further apart. He himself had little doubt about where the fault lay: in an earlier work, he castigated his own age for its proneness to melancholy and apathy, a proneness paradoxically heightened by prosperity, which 'brings leanness of soul and meanness of ideal'.[306] He points out the problem: a prosperous culture needs, but eschews, a specific set of beliefs and values which alone will give it roots: 'our culture is wider than our actual creed . . . We go far, but do we go deep?'[307] And for him the answer lay not in some bland fusion of religious doctrines, but a whole-hearted return to the spirituality of scripture:

> We do need more reverence in our prayer, more beauty in our praise, less dread of tried and consecrated form. But still more do we want the breath-less awe, and the stammering tongue, and the solemn wonder, and the passionate gratitude, which are the true note of grace, and the worship of a soul plucked from the burning and snatched by a miracle from the abyss.[308]

That is well said. The problem, for Forsyth and even more for his successors, was that 'tried and consecrated forms' and 'the worship of a soul plucked from the burning' reflected a distinctive Protestant spirituality which would sit uneasily with the values and aspirations of a pluralist society unwilling to attach ultimate primacy to any one religious worldview.

The holy life

Forsyth's vigorously traditional Protestant understanding of the spiritual life is rooted in his central conviction that that life is entirely dependent upon our first being justified by God. The acceptance of Christ as saviour, and the gift of his justifying grace and unconditional forgiveness, do not obliterate our sins; but they do effect a total change in us, for thereafter 'within the Christian man there is a new spirit, a new taste, bias, conscience, terror, and affection'.[309] At the Last Judgement the key question will not be: how many are your sins? but: 'on which side have you stood and striven, under which King have you served or died?'[310] It is justification, not sanctification, that admits us to heaven: 'we enter heaven by a decisive change, and not merely by a progressive purification. And this is the very marrow of Protestant divinity and Evangelical faith.'[311] He is eloquent in describing the heart of Christ's work:

> Christ came not to *say* something, but to *do* something. His revelation was action more than instruction. He revealed by redeeming. The thing He did was not simply to make us aware of God's disposition in an impressive way. It was not to *declare* forgiveness. It was certainly not to *explain* forgiveness. And it was not even to *bestow* forgiveness. It was to *effect* forgiveness, to set up the relation of forgiveness both in God and man.[312]

For Forsyth, it follows that sanctification, the process whereby we are made holy, 'is not a perfection added to justification. It is the spirit of it drawn out, that perfection which is all there latent (and to God's eye patent) in justifying faith.'[313] For Forsyth, being justified is like becoming an adult: it may happen overnight, or take years; but it is invariably a decisive and unrepeatable change; and, even though it is by no means the final change to take place, it is the pledge and prerequisite of all that lies ahead.[314]

And what lies ahead is growth in holiness. We are to be holy because God is holy; and his holiness is rooted in his nature as Father.[315] This matters, because holiness is not some abstract or objective quality we simply acquire by virtue of being saved. It is the fruit of God's love, and of our relationship with him. Above all, it is the fruit of God's grace at work in us. For John Oman, that grace cannot be restricted simply to priestly or ecclesial channels.[316] Nor can it be conceived of as some irresistible force, in a Calvinist sense: rather it can be understood only in the context of personal relationships; and even conversion has to be seen, not as an overriding of human freewill, but as 'an awakening to our true relation both to God and man'.[317] Furthermore, it is within the secular that this relationship must be worked out:

> The test of a true faith is the extent to which its religion is secular, the extent to which its special religious experiences are tested by the experiences of every day. In the life of Jesus nothing is more conspicuous than His meagre interest in specially sacred doings, and His profound interest in the most ordinary doings of the secular life. In His parables, there are few figures from the special religious life of a specially religious time: the Pharisee praying with himself in the temple, the Priest and the Levite turning aside on the road to Jericho – self-approving and little approved men, solitary to their heart's core. But what a varied secular procession: kings and slaves, and bailiffs and debtors, and farmers and fisher-folk, and housewives and children, and all at their secular occupations, with more feasting than fasting, and more marriages than funerals![318]

In exploring the nature of holiness, Maltby too stresses the concrete and even secular nature of the language Jesus used, and thus of the scope and context of holiness itself.

Jesus gave us the name 'Father' which of itself invites to childlike and intimate relations. He encourages men to trust the analogy as far as it will go, assuring them that if they are childlike in their approach to God, they will find the divine response. He does not speak of 'Fatherhood.' If this was because there was no such word in Aramaic, we may still be thankful. But there is a deeper reason. In all His thinking He is actual and concrete.[319]

This is not to lose sight of the Old Testament perception that holiness was highly infectious, even tangible. In his exploration of holiness, Sangster points to the presence of this notion in the New Testament and links it with the concept of personality:

Believing Peter to be indwelt by God, people in Jerusalem 'carried out the sick into the streets, and laid them on beds and couches, that, as Peter came by, at the least his shadow might overshadow some of them' (Acts 5.15). But who will deny that a spiritual truth was struggling for expression even in the primitive idea of holiness by infection? All personality has a radiation. The radiations of those in whom God dwells are mighty beyond measurement. Much experience lies behind the common assertion that 'religion is caught, not taught.' In that sense of the word, holiness is felt to be an infection still.[320]

So the more we grow in holiness, the more infectious, or *attractive*, we become, for we draw others through us to Christ, as the first disciples did. And this infectious radiance of God's loving personality which makes us holy derives from our willingness to 'see ourselves in Christ':

Nobody really sees himself until he sees himself in Christ. Christ is a mirror. He reflects a perfect likeness of the image which falls on Him. A man can look at himself in the mirror which is Christ and say with truth: 'That is the man I am.' To a sensitised conscience, the revelation can be appalling, and we might be grateful to God that He saves us from seeing all the truth at a glance. But we must be more grateful that He allows us to see the truth about ourselves at all – and see it where alone it can be seen: *in Him*.[321]

This is classic Protestant divinity. We look on ourselves in Christ and see the terrible truth about the way we really are. But God in his infinite love also looks on us in Christ and sees, not the painful reality of how we are now, but the unimaginable perfection of what in Christ he can make us become.[322] So perfection is a goal, ultimately unrealizable fully in this world, yet indispensable as the defining aim and end of our lives; and in seeking it, we grow in the life of holiness. Thus Newton Flew can say that

holiness is not only (as Newman said) necessary for future blessedness. It is essential to the vitality and advance of the Christian message in this world.[323]

And he longs for the day when

sanctity, and no mere average standard of goodness, is enthroned as the practical ideal in all the sections of Christendom . . . It is essential for the individual Christian that the goal set before him should be not merely conversion, not merely a life of service, but perfection.[324]

Christian perfection

The use of the language of perfection in Nonconformist spirituality reflects its importance in the work of John Wesley.[325] In his study of Wesley's doctrine of Christian perfection, Sangster argues that the term itself must be dropped because of its ambiguity: 'perfect love' would be preferable, implying as it does a relational dimension.[326] And this cannot be reduced to mere feelings, which are inevitably transitory:[327] God's love can be stern precisely because it is *not* limited to feelings.[328] Nonetheless, perfect love must be more than mere duty: for the problem with duty is that 'right at its heart there is a holy egoism'.[329] By contrast, when seen as 'perfect love'

> Christian morality is not a list of things to be left undone. It is an active, vital principle, positive, rich, pulsating with eager life. It touches other life on all sides. It enters into a hundred relationships and glows with the gladness of fraternity.[330]

Both Forsyth and Flew go further here, though both agree with Sangster that 'perfection' is not sinlessness. Indeed, as Forsyth says, with characteristic vigour,

> it is doubtful if real holiness is quite possible to people who have no 'nature' in them, no passion, no flavour of the good brown earth. Take away that elemental rage from below and you make faith a blanched and inept thing. You have no more than quietist piety.[331]

For him, perfection is wholeness, not sinlessness:[332] it is 'the essential call and badge of all Christians', not just of some élite group.[333] When the New Testament speaks of the perfect, 'it means not the complete but the spiritually adult; not the fully sanctified but the duly justified'.[334] 'We are only perfect in [Christ] as we are in a condition to grow in Him.'[335]

So 'perfection' is the fruit of the decisive change wrought in us by Christ; but it is not a static or finished state; rather it is a goal, a dynamic by which we grow ever more fully in the life of Christ. Flew argues that the ideal of perfection in itself inspires people to seek more than they otherwise would:

> There is a spiritual law, discernible in the supreme creative achievements of art or literature, that nothing enduring is brought forth save by one whose aim is illimitable and whose standard is perfection. An artist is an artist because he attempts more than he can ever do . . . So, too, in religion the ultimate aim of the soul must be in its very nature illimitable . . . A man keeps his passion of discovery and adventure only because he knows that there is an impossible infinity of achievement before him. The moment he believes that his art is final in its accomplishment, or his truth perfect in its grasp, he ceases to be a man of science or an artist.[336]

He cites 2 Corinthians 3.18, with its reference to beholding the glory of God as if in a mirror, as indicating that St Paul was proclaiming 'an ideal life of communion with God which was at once the ultimate goal, and fragmentarily, but yet actually, could be lived in the world. The vision was in a mirror, but it was a real knowledge of One who would some day be seen face to face.'[337]

For Flew, the ideal of perfection is never merely individual;[338] and Sangster makes the same point:

> the contention that the work of the Church should be confined to developing the spiritual life of people in their separateness, merely as a preparation for the life to come, can be set out persuasively and devotionally, but it is, nevertheless, false.[339]

This is not only to emphasize a human desire to make the world better: rather it is to long to see God's will be done for the world:

> *this* world is not the end of our striving, or the whole purpose of our existence, but a Christian social order could be used by God to shape men to spirituality as clearly as Christian men are being used by God to challenge and shape the social order to His will. Because man is both individual and social in his nature, God's redemption compasses both, and there is no satisfying view of holiness which will ignore either.[340]

Hence for Sangster it is crucial to see both sin and holiness in the widest possible perspective: sin includes structural as well as personal evil, and perfection becomes far more than 'private' spiritual virtues.[341] And

> holiness is potent and mighty . . . It rebukes sin. It creates the appetite for itself. It blasts doubt and fosters faith. No man is quite the same after contact with a saint. He may fly from him, and even, in the obduracy of his sinning, hug his sin the tighter, but always, uneasily, he remembers.[342]

So true Christian holiness (or 'perfect love') gives the Christian life a goal and a dynamic it otherwise lacks;[343] and at its heart is, as Flew puts it, 'a process of repeated surrenders' rooted in Christ's act of free surrender made in his dying, and articulated supremely in the Letter to the Hebrews.[344] As we become progressively more Christlike, so we progressively reflect the radiance of his perfect love. In short, we become holy.

The theology and practice of prayer

Free Church thinkers differed in their understanding of prayer. The influential American Baptist Harry Emerson Fosdick argued that prayer was as natural to human beings as breathing and eating.[345] Leslie Weatherhead disagreed. For him it did not come naturally at all:

> Prayer is not instinctive like eating. I wish it were, and that one really hungered for God. If I give up food, I am driven to eat; the less I eat the more I want to, but the less I pray the less I want to.[346]

That is why prayer is hard work. Weatherhead confesses

> I have always found prayer difficult. So often it seems like a fruitless game of hide-and-seek where we seek and God hides. I know God is very patient with me. Without that patience I should be lost. But frankly, I have to be patient with Him. With no other friend would I go on seeking with such scant, conscious response. Yet I cannot leave prayer alone for long. My need drives me to Him. And I have a feeling that He has His own reasons for hiding Himself, and that finally all my seeking will prove infinitely worth while.[347]

Neville Ward stressed that the subject of prayer 'never comes alive to guilt but it does to curiosity and interest'.[348] The crucial thing is to see it in the context of the community of faith: it is primarily a corporate, not a personal (still less a private) activity.[349]

Weatherhead was deeply interested in the relationship between spirituality and psychology, and argued that prayer is based on natural laws, particularly on what Jung called the 'collective unconscious'.[350] This approach is in marked contrast to that of the Presbyterian H. H. Farmer. In his Gifford Lectures of 1950, Farmer emphasizes the capacity of true worship (or prayer: he uses the former term to include the latter) to unself the worshipper, freeing him or her of egocentricity.[351] This is partly the consequence of the worshipper's perception of God's essential *worth* (hence worth-ship), by comparison with which her or his own goodness is utterly inconsequential.[352] But it is also the consequence of the Christian belief in God as Father, which heightens our sense of the irreducibly personal dimension of all worship.[353]

Both the otherness and the personal nature of God are essential for true worship.[354] Together, they make possible the worshipper's awareness, supremely in the Eucharist, of being *loved* – that is, in Farmer's description, of being given all and of being asked to give all in return.[355] This awareness of being loved by God is at once intellectual and emotional, and not quite like anything else: Farmer speaks (not very helpfully) of 'a feeling-tone, pervading the whole awareness, which is akin to awe, but which is really *sui generis* and can only be described as the feeling-tone which accompanies, and is appropriate to, the living encounter with God.'[356] Evangelicals can make use of the traditional language of bride and bridegroom to convey the tone of the relationship more vividly.[357]

Forsyth goes even further than Farmer in stressing the fact that prayer is outrageously supernatural:

> There is nothing so abnormal, so unworldly, so supernatural, in human life as prayer, nothing that is more of an instinct, it is true, but also nothing that is less rational among all the things that keep above the level of the silly. The whole Christian life in so far as it is lived from the Cross and by the Cross is rationally an extravagance.[358]

He goes on to suggest that

> every life is a draft upon the unseen. If you are not praying towards God you are towards something else. You pray as your face is set – towards

Jerusalem or Babylon. The very egotism of craving life is prayer. The great difference is the object of it.[359]

If this is so, rightly-directed prayer ought to be distinctive, exciting even. Forsyth attacks the dullness of much Christian prayer:

What a reflection on our faith that so much piety should be humdrum, and deadly dull! Private prayer, when it is real action, is the greatest forge of personality.[360]

For Forsyth, 'prayer is for the religious life what original research is for science – by it we get direct contact with reality.'[361] He has no time for the Catholic belief that in prayer we are organically united with God: it is *communion*, not union, to which we are called.[362] Rather, prayer is energy;[363] and precisely because it is energy, it possesses a transforming power:

If the kingdom of God not only got over the murder of Christ, but made it its great lever, there is nothing that it cannot get over, and nothing it cannot turn to eternal blessing and to the glory of the holy name.[364]

And yet the paradox is that its power is rooted in selflessness: 'nothing is more striking in Christ's life than His combination of selflessness and power'.[365] Forsyth locates our prayer within the eternal prayer of Father and Son, thereby giving even private prayer an irreducibly corporate character:

all along Christ is being darkly formed within us as we pray; and our converse with God goes on rising to become an element of the intercourse of the Father and the Son, whom we overhear, as it were, at converse in us. Yet this does not insulate us from our kind; for other people are then no more alien to us, but near in a Lord who is to them what He is to us. Private prayer may thus become more really common prayer than public prayer is.[366]

For in Christ's eternal intercession to the Father, 'our best prayer, broken, soiled, and feeble as it is, is caught up and made prayer indeed and power with God'.[367] Thus

the real power of prayer in history is not a fusillade of praying units of whom Christ is the chief, but it is the corporate action of a Saviour-Intercessor and His community, a volume and energy of prayer organized in a Holy Spirit and in the Church the Spirit creates.[368]

'In prayer,' then, 'we do not so much work as interwork.'[369]

For Forsyth, prayer involves the whole of ourselves; and we must pray as we are, for otherwise 'you are praying in court-dress. You are trying to pray as you imagine one *should* pray to God, i.e. as another person than you are, and in other circumstances.'[370] It is vital to recall also, as Neville Ward points out, that you are praying to a God whose nature is also personal; and

the personal category withdraws God from our familiarity and domination. Persons are centres of freedom and endless surprise. Even the person, whom after years of companionship and love we think we know, can surprise, disappoint and shock us.[371]

Why do we pray? For Olive Wyon the answer is utterly simple. We pray not primarily in order to be made into better people; we pray in order that God's will may be done:

> *Thy will be done, on earth.* This prayer implies that God has fitted us exactly for the doing of His will; each of us is a delicate, highly skilled instrument, formed for one purpose only: the doing of His will, here and now, in this world. Yet how often we miss this truth; and this means that we miss the way in life; we are dissatisfied and restless. At the time we feel that there is something that eludes us. Is it because, at bottom, we are afraid of God? afraid to commit ourselves entirely to Him? . . . Yet . . . once this surrender has been made, there will come a growing desire, even a hunger and thirst, that the will of God may be wholly fulfilled in and through us.[372]

This too is classic Protestant divinity. Prayer is conformity with the will of God, not an aspiration after ontological union; and yet that surrender to God's will ignites all that is deepest and best within us. Wyon says that 'the heart of prayer is the spirit of obedience'.[373] But far from reducing us to grovelling slaves, such a spirit sets us free from 'that miserable morass of self-occupation which we call a "sense of inferiority"' because it instils in us the knowledge that God has created us for himself, to do his will.[374] Such obedience thus frees us from the perils of self-absorption.[375] It is in this sense that the Methodist Neville Ward can commend the Rosary, with its plea to Mary to 'pray for us sinners': for this

> is a reminder that Christ has abolished our loneliness, that we pray (even if alone or in an empty church) within the fabulous community of faith, live within it, owe more than we know to it, and particularly rely on the prayers of others, the whole communion of saints, of which the Blessed Virgin Mary is the representative figure.[376]

Nonconformists recognize that prayer is difficult, not least because set forms of prayer do not come naturally to them. Leslie Weatherhead says that 'perhaps reluctantly we are compelled to admit that to *pray* well demands as much practice and self-discipline as to *play* well on an instrument, and that we have not done much about it'.[377] For Forsyth, the way to cultivate the unceasing prayer commended in scripture is simply to pray more often. 'To learn to pray with freedom, force yourself to pray. The great liberty begins in necessity. Do not say, "I cannot pray. I am not in the spirit." Pray till you are in the spirit.'[378] You do not only learn to pray by praying: you learn to *want* to pray by praying. And the ultimate fruit of prayer is the enjoyment of God, a point made by the Methodist J. A. Chapman, whose theology reflects a mystical *attrait*:

> [Through prayer] we come to a living companionship with God, in which the child enjoys the Father, as the Father enjoys the child. This is what

religion finally is, the enjoyment of God. Such enjoyment has many avenues and sacraments. But it is prayer which makes us sensitive to them. I always find myself more sensitive to beauty after prayer.[379]

In the splendid final chapter of his book *The soul of prayer*, Forsyth explores the theme of importunate prayer (a theme which, as we have seen, is more frequently found in Protestant than in Catholic spirituality, though it is relatively rare in both). For Forsyth, 'prayer is not really a power till it is importunate. And it cannot be importunate unless it is felt to have a real effect on the Will of God.'[380] He accepts that all prayer must ultimately be submissive to the will of God; but not too quickly. 'Let us submit when we *must*, but let us keep the submission in reserve rather than in action, as a ground tone rather than the sole effort. Prayer with us has largely ceased to be *wrestling*. But is that not the dominant scriptural idea? . . . And is not our subdued note often but superinduced and unreal?'[381]

The reason prayer is wrestling with God is because it is an encounter between two wills: 'till one will or the other give way'. St Paul strove importunately with God, only submitting to God's will at the end of the struggle.[382] And the prayer of the Lord's Prayer ('thy will be done') can make sense only insofar as it is a passionate alignment of our wills with God's, not a limp submission.[383] God's will may be unalterable; but its practical outworking can be affected by our prayers.[384] This leads Forsyth to argue that in some circumstances wrestling with God, resisting God, may be doing what God wants:

> Prayer is wrestling with God. And it is better to fall thus into the hands of God than of man – even than your own. It is a resistance that God loves. It is quite foreign to a godless, self-willed defiant resistance . . . It is prayer in the solidarity of the Kingdom. It is a continuation of Christ's prayer, which in Gethsemane was a wrestle, an *agonia* with the Father. But if so, it is God pleading with God, God dealing with God – as the true atonement must be. And when God yields it is not to an outside influence He yields, but to Himself.[385]

The crucial point is that it is *not* God's will that we should compliantly accept whatever fate throws at us. Thus

> is it God's will that we should lie down and let the disease have its way? Why, a whole profession exists to say no . . . Resistance to this ordinance of God's is the doctor's business and the doctor's ally. And why? Because God ordained disease for the purpose of being resisted; He ordained the resistance, that from the conflict man might come out the stronger, and more full of resource and dominion over nature.[386]

Certainly 'obedience is the chief end. But obedience is not mere submission, mere resignation. It is not always acquiescence, even in prayer. We obey God as much when we urge our suit, and make a *real* petition of it, as when we accept His decision; as much when we try to change His will as when we bow to it.'[387] So when we suffer, we pray for the removal of pain, pray passionately, and then with exhaustion, sick from hope deferred and prayer's failure. But there is a higher prayer than that. It is a greater thing to pray for pain's conversion than for its removal. It is more of grace to pray that God would make a sacrament of it . . . It is not always easy for the sufferer, if he remain clear-eyed, to see that it is God's will. It may have been caused by an evil mind, or a light fool, or some stupid greed. But, now it is there, a certain treatment of it is God's will; and that is to capture and exploit it for Him. It is to make it serve the soul and glorify God. It is to consecrate its elements and make it sacramental. It is to convert it into prayer.[388]

In the book's magisterial peroration, which deserves extended quotation, Forsyth sets out the heart of Free Church piety – vigorous, biblical, honest, and full-blooded – and in the process delivers a broadside against the respectable spirituality of the established Church. For him, any form of pious submissiveness must

fall into the ecclesiastical type of religion, drawn from an age whose first virtue was submission to outward superiors. We shall come to canonize decorum and subduedness in life and worship (as the Episcopal Church with its monarchical ideas of religion has done). We shall think more of order than of effort, more of law than of life, more of fashion than of faith, of good form than of great power. But was subduedness *the* mark of the New Testament men? Our religion may gain some beauty in this way, but it loses vigour. It may gain style, but it loses power. It is good form, but mere aesthetic piety. It may consecrate manners, but it impoverishes the mind . . . And so we decline to a state of things in which we have no shocking sins – yes, and no splendid souls; when all souls are dully correct, as like as shillings, but as thin, and as cheap.

All our forms and views of religion have their test in prayer. Lose the importunity of prayer, reduce it to soliloquy, or even to colloquy, with God, lose the real conflict of will and will, lose the habit of wrestling and the hope of prevailing with God, make it mere walking with God in friendly talk; and, precious as that is, yet you tend to lose the reality of prayer at last. In principle you make it mere conversation instead of the soul's great action. You lose the food of character, the renewal of will. You may have beautiful prayers – but as ineffectual as beauty so often is, and as fleeting. And so in the end you lose the reality of religion. Redemption turns down into mere revelation, faith to assent, and devotion to a phase of culture. For you lose the *power* of the Cross and so of the soul.

Resist God, in the sense of rejecting God, and you will not be able to resist any evil. But resist God in the sense of closing with God, cling to Him with all your strength, not your weakness only, with your active and not only your passive faith, and He will give you strength. Cast yourself into His arms not to be caressed but to wrestle with Him. He loves that holy war. He may be too many for you, and lift you from your feet. But it will be to lift you from earth, and set you in the heavenly places which are theirs who fight the good fight and lay hold of God as their eternal life.[389]

Spiritual direction and Dissent

Finally, a word needs to be said about spiritual direction in the Nonconformist tradition. The Quaker writer J. Rendel Harris maintains that we may deduce the reality of divine guidance in our lives 'from the fact that we have been led; and we have none of us adequately recognized the amount of the raw material of theology that we already possess in our previous leadings'.[390] He warns against an over-eagerness to declare what is of the Spirit and what isn't, and reminds his readers that sometimes God is calling upon them to wait upon him, rather than leap to a decision.[391] Nor will the authentic call of God always conform to our rational expectations.[392] It will frequently be mediated through what may appear unlikely sources:[393]

> The problem of personal guidance is one in the study of which we constantly find ourselves walking softly, because of a sense that we are on the borders of a world other than our own, more intelligent, more sympathetic, and more populous. We loosen our shoestrings in advance, because we expect to hear presently the intimation that we have crossed into holy ground. Into holy ground, but not into forbidden territory, where trespassers are prosecuted, and where they set traps for them; both worlds are ours, and it is only because the Church has caricatured the next world by its out-of-date maps that we are afraid of making excursions thereto.[394]

At the very end of the twentieth century, Gordon Wakefield answers the question 'How can I still hold on to faith?' with the words 'my faith is not mine to lose'. As a cradle Christian, his faith was a gift entrusted to him by others: to abandon it is to abandon them. 'The Christian life for us is at once an adventure, a glorious anticipation of life in the Kingdom of God and a sojourn in a barren wilderness.'[395] Free Church explorers of the spiritual life, such as those cited here, catch this rich biblical paradox and articulate it with courage and honesty. One of its implications is that there must be room for doubt: writing exactly seventy years earlier than Wakefield, W. R. Maltby said that 'if we are to be religious we must have the chance of being irreligious'.[396] Absolute certainty is no longer available to us. The greatness of twentieth-century Nonconformity consists in the fact that, faced with this uncomfortable truth, it chose not to take refuge in a dull apathy or a bland and studied attempt to keep all one's options open; instead it chose to bring all that uncertainty, together with that sense of adventure, and lay both at the feet of God in the passionate conviction that there alone could a way forward be found. In this perspective Christian spirituality becomes not a cosy escape from the hard issues of scepticism and faith, but precisely and uniquely the means to engage with them.

PENTECOSTAL AND BLACK SPIRITUALITY

Pentecostal spirituality

The early Pentecostal movement in England

One of the most distinctive features of English spirituality in the twentieth century is the growth of the Pentecostal movement – effectively the only branch of Christianity to exhibit sustained growth in the country during this period. The origins of Pentecostalism are still a matter of dispute, not only because scholars disagree with one another but because an essentially oral, musical and experiential movement is less susceptible to neat academic assessment.[397] What is relevant for our purposes is the remarkable story of Alexander Boddy (1854–1930), a kind of precursor of modern English Pentecostalism. Boddy was an Anglican priest, born in County Durham, and originally a lawyer who had travelled widely and written travel books before ordination.[398] He began his ministry in 1884 as curate, and later vicar, of All Saints Sunderland, remaining there until 1922. He was deeply influenced by the Welsh Revival of 1904–5 as well as by the extraordinary events in Azusa Street, Los Angeles, which effectively mark the beginnings of modern Pentecostalism.[399] In 1907 he persuaded T. B. Barratt, a Pentecostal Methodist minister working in Oslo, to come to his church in Sunderland. Boddy himself describes what happened one afternoon in Sunderland shortly after this:

> One Sunday four of us were led together to pray at 9.30 p.m. in the Vicarage and we continued until nearly one in the morning. We had had a blessed day of worship and witness. The window blinds were not drawn down. I was opposite the window and so looked out at the church. A wonderful light suddenly filled the room and lingered over the church roof. One brother fell to the floor very suddenly, crying with tremendous vehemence, 'It is the Lord, there is no deception, brothers, it is the Lord Himself.' This continued on and on, the light lingering over the roof of the church, an emblem it seemed of blessing that was to be connected with this place. Only one saw the Lord, we three saw the light only. Then a brother kneeling at my right hand fell to the floor suddenly and cried in wonderful tones of awe, 'It's the blood, Oh, it's the blood.'[400]

Dramatic events of this kind soon attracted publicity, and incurred first the opposition and later the support of the local bishop.[401] But by the end of the First World War, Boddy had lost his spiritual confidence, and the movement faded in England.[402] The modern Pentecostal movement reached England, primarily from the United States, in the early 1960s.[403] By the end of that decade there were numerous small (mostly West Indian) free churches, of which the largest were Pentecostal in theology and practice.[404] Many of their members were immigrants who had hitherto been members of mainstream Christian denominations, but found their English equivalents either excessively formal or actively hostile.[405] The movement as a whole was and remained fissiparous in character, and had a number of similarities with the house church movement.[406] It exerted a considerable influence on members of other mainstream denominations, including Roman Catholicism;[407] and it was further (if briefly) invigorated by the 'Toronto Blessing' movement, which began in 1995.[408]

The main features of Pentecostal spirituality

The principal features of Pentecostal spirituality remain, broadly speaking, those that characterized the remarkable and pioneering Pentecostal church in Azusa Street, Los Angeles, founded by the Black American William Seymour (1870–1922): oral (that is, not prescribed or formalized) liturgy; a pattern of worship strongly characterized by music, the sharing of personal testimonies, the use of the body (such as in dance), and ecstatic phenomena such as speaking in tongues; a strong reverence for biblical authority; a consistent emphasis on the ministry of healing; and a pervasive stress on praise.[409] Inevitably some adaptation took place when Pentecostal spirituality was imported into the other mainstream churches. But the Catholic Simon Tugwell summarizes its importance thus:

> Christianity plus [in the sense of adding more doctrines to the traditional *depositum fidei*] is . . . no longer Christianity. But mystical movements, like Pentecostalism, arise precisely in protest against Christianity *minus*. In so far as they seek to bring people to an authentic experience of the 'new creation' in Christ, and so to get beyond a tepid and worldly christianity, that has lost its purpose, they are surely sound and even necessary to the church.[410]

And he told his fellow-Christians that 'it is time we woke up to the fact that people want more from the church than bingo and dances: they want God'.[411]

Pentecostal spirituality generally presupposes (at least in the principal Pentecostal churches) a clear sense of separation from 'the world': in this sense they seek to return to the biblical understanding of holiness as consecration, or being set apart, and advocate a Christian lifestyle that is sharply contrasted with contemporary society.[412] The writer of a catechetical handbook for one of the principal English Pentecostal churches tells fellow-members that 'We are to be separate from the world, [but] not too separate.'[413] The same writer also commends what might be described as 'positive thinking' as one significant way of living 'over against' society:

> Why is it vital to our spiritual health to saturate our minds with positive thoughts? In our daily contacts with other human beings we are likely to hear much that is negative. Some people will lament over the general condition of national and international affairs; others will complain to us about actions and/or attitudes of mutual friends or acquaintances: and still others may come to us to criticize us. Even in the Church we are subjected to much unpleasant conversation about programs and people. Therefore, we need to give much thought to what is of good report, virtuous, and praiseworthy simply to offset this flow of negative input. Furthermore, since it is true that what is in our minds and hearts will determine what comes out of our own mouths (see Matthew 15.18, 19), we will for this reason want to make our thoughts as wholesome and uplifting as possible.[414]

The importance of praise

This extract gives a vital clue to the essential character of Pentecostal spirituality. It is rooted in praise, the affirmation of God's mighty victory over evil in the cross of Christ, and the active anticipation of the coming of his kingdom.[415] Such praise, which finds its principal expression in music, is far more than simply a cheerful optimism, or an escape from a world filled with racism and personal hardship. Rather it is strongly eschatological: in praise, Pentecostals follow the author of the Book of Revelation in anticipating *as though it were happening now* God's ultimate victory over the forces of evil. It is a defiant, celebratory form of spirituality which seeks not only to thank God for existing blessings or look forward to new ones, but to lift God's future into the present and thereby help to bring it about: to dream impossible dreams and subvert the dull certainties of secular life or the perceived complacency of many Christian traditions.[416] 'Praying in tongues is a weapon of war against the devil, and against our passions, precisely because it is a prayer of praise, a prayer of peace.'[417] And praise reminds us that God is always beyond our control, never to be domesticated or reduced to dull human definitions; and A. M. Allchin has suggested that

> The practice of singing in tongues . . . might bring us to a new understanding of the ineffability of God, and of the properly apophatic nature of all theological language.[418]

Prayer and healing

But there is another element too. Pentecostals believe in praying and praising with both body and soul: hence the emphasis on dance and movement in liturgy. This charismatic, physical and uninhibited spirituality was undoubtedly stimulated by the free and counter-cultural spirit of England in the 1960s.[419] But it was also underpinned by a firmly corporate sense of solidarity in the midst of suffering: thus the Pentecostal practice of administering the laying-on of hands and praying for healing was never simply concerned with the well-being of a single individual: it recognized that 'the one for whom the prayer is said represents in his or her sick body the suffering world.'[420]

Black spirituality

Many of the central characteristics of Pentecostal spirituality reflect its inseparable relationship with Black Christian culture and experience. Asian and Afro-Caribbean immigrants who came to England during the second half of the twentieth century brought with them a long history of exploitation and suffering, together with a rich spiritual tradition to which the mainstream Christian churches were (at best) slow to respond and (at worst) positively hostile. The Black Christian tradition was rooted in African history, culture and religion; but it was also centred on a passionate belief in Jesus as both fellow-sufferer and liberator, and in the Holy Spirit as bestowing upon Christians an anticipatory experience of freedom and hope.[421] Some Black Christians found it possible to give expression to their spirituality in mainstream (i.e. non-Pentecostal) churches, which adopted a less rigorously separatist ethical code. An Anglican priest in Birmingham suggested that what they sought were

four things of infinite value: a real community that upheld you, a wide united
family not bereft of the wisdom of old people . . . a religion which was part of
a living culture, and a climate which was loving and undemanding.[422]

A Black evangelical theologian distinguishes three essential characteristics of Black
spirituality: first, the impossibility of dislocating prayer from the social context in
which it is practised; secondly, the crucial importance of defiant hope:

> when young black men are locked away in prison and in a cycle of crimi-
> nality with little or no chance of reformation, praying people must step in
> to give them a chance. When unemployment benefits or underemploy-
> ment are offered to us as a favour for which we must be thankful, we
> praying people must bring into being industries and jobs of our own.

The third characteristic is that 'prayer cannot be left unescorted . . . Prayer is not
passive: it is resistance of the highest order. It feeds the soul with a robust determination to see things change for the better.'[423]

For Black Christians, as for all Pentecostals, music was a central ingredient of any
authentic spiritual life:

> Our music opens up for the soul a direct link with God. You feel the Spirit
> moving within you through the music. Once it happened in our church
> . . . you feel a bond, you feel it swelling . . . if only every week were like this
> in church . . . It's not just the music; you're deep and intense through
> 'spiritual' music with God at the core of your being.

In the Black Christian spiritual tradition, prayer is more often free and spontaneous,
involving the whole person in an intimate dialogue or wrestling with God, and
supremely centred on worship rather than a private and personal discipline.[424] Corporate
prayer is just that: the prayer of an individual is surrounded and affirmed by the spontaneous and ejaculatory prayer of fellow worshippers.[425] The emphasis on the power and
presence of the Holy Spirit also encourages an interest in visions and dreams as means of
divine revelation and encounter;[426] but it also encourages the visualizing of another way
of living, in sharp contrast to that of 'the world'.[427] The experience of sickness and death
elicits from many Black Christians a profound spiritual sense of solidarity with the
person suffering, which finds expression in shared prayer and singing, Bible reading and
testimonies, and the laying-on of hands.[428] Above all, though, the proleptic celebration of
God's future, the defiance of present evil or suffering by joyfully anticipating all that is to
come, resonates through every aspect of Black Christian spirituality:

> When the battle is over, I shall wear a crown!
> I shall wear a crown! I shall wear a crown!
> When the battle is over, I shall wear a crown
> In the new Jerusalem!
>
> Such a fun to see!
> Satan lo-ose!
> Satan is a Loser Man.

> A Loser Man, a Loser Man.
> Satan is a Loser Man.
> A Loser Man all the time!
> Jesus is a Winner Man.[429]

SPIRITUALITY AND THE RELIGIOUS LIFE

Introduction

The twentieth century saw some of the leading monastic communities in England decline, as did the churches to which they belonged. But it also saw the flourishing of an astonishing diversity of experiments in community life; and even if many of these were short-lived, they often exerted a profound influence well beyond their walls.[430] Indeed, it could be said that the most important contribution made by Christian communities, whether formally religious or not, was in incarnating a pattern of spiritual life in which what was held in common took precedence over the concerns of the individual. The revival of concern for daily common prayer, which took place in the last decades of the century, was greatly indebted to the rich spirituality of monasticism, even though it also drew inspiration from the prayer of lay Christians in the early centuries of the church's life.[431]

The relationship between religious communities and the wider Church was always a fluid, open-ended one, and never more so than in the twentieth century. Many of the founders and spiritual guides of new monastic communities were not themselves living the religious life, though they were deeply influenced by it.[432] Some communities, such as the Ashram Community founded in Sheffield by the Methodist minister John Vincent in 1967, were for lay people with a particular commitment to prayer and political involvement.[433] Others, such as the informal community established by Philip and Sally Toynbee at Chepstow, reflect some of the characteristic concerns of such projects in the later twentieth century:

> Our community was established . . . with the purpose of exploring a way of
> life which would be ecologically sound and which would lead to self-devel-
> opment through shared experience.[434]

The Community of the Resurrection at Mirfield, founded in 1892 by Charles Gore, numbered among its members Fr Trevor Huddleston, later Bishop of Stepney and Archbishop of the Indian Ocean.[435] In *Naught for your comfort*, he gave expression to his own understanding of the letting-go which is at the heart of the monastic life, and which at one point caused him to leave his beloved South Africa and return to Yorkshire in obedience to his superior:

> For me, detachment is only real if it involves loving; loving to the fullest
> extent of one's nature – but recognising at the same time that such love is
> set in the context of a supernatural love of God. Then, when the moment
> of surrender, of parting, comes, one has a worth-while offering to make: an
> offering which is the love and affection of all the years, for all those one has
> known; it has some meaning, like the precious ointment poured out on
> the feet of Christ. And it is costly too.[436]

This was no empty rhetoric. But then the spirituality in which Huddleston was nurtured, and to which he gave such prophetic expression, was (like much Christian Socialist spirituality) rooted in the Incarnation. He wrote of his work with young Black Africans:

> One of the objects dearest to my heart is that of trying to open up to African boys and girls a wider and a fuller life. It seems to me that that is part of the meaning of the Christian faith itself, springing from a belief in the fact that God became man and, if He was prepared to pour His fullness into human nature, then human nature itself must be capable of such richness, must be made to receive it.[437]

Other religious communities drew their inspiration from earlier figures. The Anglican Society of St Francis effectively began at Cerne Abbas in Dorset in the 1920s, and reflects both a new interest in St Francis and Franciscan spirituality and an enthusiasm for developing new patterns of ministry and spiritual life dedicated to the service of the poor. The female equivalent, the Community of St Francis, originated in 1905 at South Petherton in Somerset. Both male and female Franciscans increased significantly in numbers during the twentieth century, and combined active ministry in deprived urban areas with centres set aside for the contemplative and monastic life.[438] The Franciscan tradition, together with that of the Carmelites, succeeded in articulating a vision of human and spiritual life which subverted the material assumptions of a capitalist society. Hence Mother Mary Clare SLG, of the Anglican Carmelite community at Fairacres, Oxford, can speak of contemplative prayer in the monastic tradition as reflecting a new nomadic spirit which rejects the material lures of 'a broken-down and over-ripe civilisation' and instead seeks a new statement of the purpose of human nature itself.[439]

The solitary life

The twentieth century also saw a recovery of the solitary life which had played so important a part in earlier Christian spirituality.[440] A number of enclosed and semi-eremitical communities were founded, many of which endured.[441] Many individuals, usually with mature experience of family or community life, embraced rules of life agreed with a spiritual director or other authority, and committed themselves to a life of simplicity which might also involve a ministry of writing or spiritual guidance.[442] Clergy, living either alone or in small communities, lived adapted forms of a monastic rule in the heart of inner-city areas.[443] And many laypeople unable to live a wholly or even partly enclosed life found inspiration from the tradition of monastic spirituality in fashioning a disciplined life under some form of rule and direction.[444]

Lay communities

Some twentieth-century communities combined a rule of life with a broad inclusiveness in regard to theology and prayer.[445] The lay women's community at St Julian's, on the edge of the small village of Coolham in Sussex, exemplifies the way such a combination can lead to profound spiritual insight in regard to the nature of relationships:

It became clear to us . . . that almost all the members of the Community were lacking at some point in a sense of security, a belief in their own value as persons . . . This insecurity is because so many of us suffer from a sense of non-value. It may be apparent at a surface level: more often it is hidden behind what appears to be an almost aggressive self-confidence, a façade behind which we take refuge. Also it may lead to an attempt to compensate for this by finding the longed-for sense of value in work well done, in human gifts, on the level of service to each other or to the guests. Sometimes we have tried to bolster each other up in this way, by praising achievements and work which contributed to the well-being of the house. But we had to see that, even when the appreciation was genuine, it did not touch the heart of the matter because it was a distraction from the true answer, which was to begin to find, each one of us, a sense of our own intrinsic worth, the value of beings made in the image of God and loved for ourselves, those selves including both our failings and our gifts. How this can be achieved still remains a mystery to us. We only know that the support of the Community seems to make it possible and that when it happens it is usually sudden and heralds a new beginning.[446]

Communities of this kind, as well as more formal monastic communities, played a hidden but vital role in fostering Christian unity by their witness to the primacy of prayer and spiritual values in promoting such unity.[447] They also played a major part in encouraging the growth of the retreat movement, which was a significant dimension of English spirituality in the twentieth century, even if it tended to appeal more to the leisured than to the poor.[448]

The contribution of monastic writers and spiritual guides to twentieth-century English spirituality has been enormous. The works of the Benedictine Maria Boulding, of the Jesuit Gerard W. Hughes, and of the anonymous Carthusian whose novice conferences have opened the door into this most austere and beautiful of Christian monastic traditions, have all been influential.[449] Among those who have reflected on the continuing importance of the monastic tradition itself were Dom Odo Brooke OSB, a Benedictine of Farnborough Abbey, who was an authority on the medieval tradition and especially on William of Saint-Thierry and Aelred of Rievaulx.[450]

Monastic spirituality: Dom Odo Brooke OSB (1909–71)

Drawing deeply on the experiential theology of these medieval spiritual writers, Brooke argued that 'the Christian Revelation is not completely understood until it is seen as lived in the individual soul in its ascent to God'.[451] Hence the importance of psychology in helping us to explore how the individual can appropriate that revelation personally; hence too the need to see theology itself as a discipline inseparable from prayer – a 'kneeling theology', as Brooke's fellow Benedictine Jean Leclercq put it.[452] And Brooke concludes that

This new perspective will respond to the needs of contemporary man to see the Christian message, not as extraneous to him, but as a fulfilment of his inward aspirations. The revelation of the Trinity must be seen, not only as the revelation of God, but also as the revelation of man who finds the meaning of his existence in a communion of persons, which is ultimately a communion with the Persons of the Trinity.[453]

Brooke develops this theme in a further article.[454] Again drawing on medieval monastic thought, he defines revelation succinctly as 'the meaning of history recognized through the faith of the believer'.[455] And (again mining the tradition of medieval monasticism) he argues that true spiritual knowledge is never simply the sum of rational processes, nor even (as with, say, Polanyi) a profound synthesis of the intellectual with the experiential. Rather it is, as in the Thomist tradition, *connatural*: 'to know God connaturally means to know God through becoming like him'.[456] And the means by which we become like God is in itself irreducibly personal: 'knowledge through connaturality in personal relationships is not based simply on a particular affinity of nature but on an intersubjective communion of persons'.[457] In this context, any authentic human relationship becomes a point of access to an authentic relationship with God.[458]

It is within this context that Dom Odo sees the enduring significance of the religious life. He suggests that the practice of Christianity may be set within one of two complementary perspectives – the incarnational and the eschatological:

> This contrast could be exemplified in the life of the monk and the life of the married person. Both the monk and the married person are involved in the transformation of *this* world through the risen Christ into the *new* world of the future. But the life of the monk visibly signifies the transformation of this world from 'beyond' the human condition and the life of the married visibly signifies the transformation of this world from 'within' the human condition. The monk is committed to this world no less than the married person. But he is committed to the world in another way.[459]

Brooke explains that 'other way' of the monastic life thus:

> We know that the new world in the future will be a communion of persons in a new kind of existence. They will be united in a new kind of way because they will be living together in the immediate presence of the Mystery of God. The monastic community anticipates this communion of persons united in a new kind of way through living together in the presence of the mystery of God . . . [which is] given in a life of prayer. But unlike the future eschatological community the presence of the divine mystery is given not immediately but through the mediation of a sign. Therefore the monastic community is a provisional anticipation of that future community, a sign pointing to the new world.[460]

In this context, the monastic community is a prophetic one, helping to restore to a technologically dominated society a renewed 'sense of the whole':

> Integration is given in a forward and not in a backward movement. We should not attempt to regress to the original primitive childhood state . . .

We should move on towards a more total experience. The human person should recapture the sense of the whole without losing his sense of identity. The human race should recapture the more symbolic, intuitive, consciousness without surrendering its rational, scientific, technological achievement. An authentic monasticism would point towards this integration.[461]

CASE STUDIES

Evelyn Underhill and the recovery of mysticism

Introduction: W. R. Inge and Cuthbert Butler

The close of the Victorian era and the first decades of the twentieth century saw a new interest in mysticism. The likeliest explanation for this lies in the development of psychology as a major intellectual discipline. The philosophical psychology of writers like Henri Bergson (who deeply influenced Evelyn Underhill) and William James undoubtedly helped to foster a new preoccupation with consciousness and the self.[462] And it would not be surprising if the rapid movement from Edwardian grandeur to imperial decline and the shadow of the Great War elicited a longing for a new interiority, not just as escape but as resource in an increasingly uncertain world.

The interest in mysticism was not restricted to the Christian tradition;[463] but it was with the recovery of that tradition in the search for a spirituality strong and deep enough to address contemporary life that we will be concerned here. William Ralph Inge (1860–1954), Dean of St Paul's in London from 1911 to 1934, was a key figure in this regard; and his Bampton Lectures on Christian mysticism (1899) signalled that new interest. His mystical thought is firmly Platonic;[464] and in some of his later work (he was an immensely prolific writer) he explored the English spiritual tradition and its relevance for his own age.[465]

In his 1905 St Margaret's Lectures, Inge distinguishes several kinds of mystical state. The first is the devotional life; the second, the intellectual life,

> when the religious philosopher . . . seems to behold what he sought in a blank trance which imposes silence on all the faculties, even the restless discursive intellect, and unites the thinker for a few moments with the primal source of all thought, the ineffable One.[466]

The third state is that of the nature-poet, absorbed in Platonic admiration of Beauty.[467] The fourth is that of the scientist studying nature:

> The scientific imagination creates a religion – not the old religion of nature, which peopled the world with Dryads . . . but a pure, humble, disinterested reverence and worship for the vastness and splendour and majesty of the universe.[468]

Inge here strikingly anticipates later scientific apologists such as Richard Dawkins.[469] Finally, Inge suggests a fifth mystical state: the mysticism of the active person. Inge's exemplar for this is the wildly idiosyncratic Charles Gordon of

Khartoum, who saw God everywhere.[470] Here Inge makes the interesting point that the active person, who wants to leave his or her mark on the world, will have different religious symbols from the scholar or poet who wants above all to *understand* the world, not to *change* it.[471] And this matters because mysticism, being concerned about the *immediate* experience of God, is necessarily concerned both with the symbols and language of such experience and with reaching beyond them.

Not everyone approved of the new interest in mysticism. Richard Meux Benson SSJE, founder of the Anglican Cowley Fathers, warned in a letter of 1906 that 'people can study mysticism just because they look upon it as a thing of the past'.[472] But Inge responds to this, and also to the psychological objection (that mysticism derives from neurosis) by suggesting that it is at least as important to study something by enquiring what it grows *towards* or *into* as it is to study it by enquiring where it comes from: things, after all, can transcend their origins.[473] Rather, as he perceptively notes, the *problem* for mysticism is the temptation to clutch at the fruition of spiritual union without being willing first to undergo the hard grind of disciplining the will and the intellect. But pleasant religious feelings are not often of much earthly (or even spiritual) use, as Inge sharply points out.[474]

In the final analysis Inge was too much a Platonist for his thought to address contemporary aspirations effectively; and his outlook on life was too relentlessly gloomy to become popular.[475] But he did stimulate a major interest in the recovery of the riches of the Christian mystical tradition in order to equip people with a spirituality for today. Another, arguably even more influential, figure in this regard was Dom Cuthbert Butler OSB (1858–1934), Abbot of Downside. Butler's classic *Western mysticism* (1922) is a study of the spirituality of Augustine of Hippo, Gregory the Great and Bernard of Clairvaux; and he sought to offer a presentation of what they themselves thought about mysticism, not as an academic treatise but in order to help with the formation of clergy and to explore mysticism as a religious experience.[476]

Butler is more alive to the limitations of thoroughgoing Platonism than Inge is.[477] He equates 'mysticism' with 'contemplation': the former owes its Christian origins to Pseudo-Dionysius, even though the word did not come to be used until modern times.[478] He defines it as 'an experimental perception of the presence of God in the soul, Who at all times is there';[479] and he cites a number of (Catholic) spiritual writers who describe it in their own words. Like Inge, Butler has no time for emotional and subjective spiritual experiences, characterized by 'highly-wrought religious emotions';[480] and he acknowledges that he himself has never had a direct mystical experience of the kind he sees described in the writings of those he studies.[481]

Underhill: introduction

Much of Butler's and Inge's work is directed towards the historical study of their subject and its implications for their own age; but their contribution towards a recovery of interest in the Christian spiritual tradition as a whole was enormous.[482] Together they help to provide the context for an exploration of the most important scholar of mysticism in the early twentieth century. Evelyn Underhill was born in 1875 in Wolverhampton, the only child of middle-class parents.[483] She studied at King's College for Women in London, becoming its first woman fellow. In 1907 she married a prosperous barrister, Hubert Stuart Moore. During the Great War she worked for Naval Intelligence;[484] and in 1921 she gave the Upton Lectures on the Philosophy of Religion at Manchester College, Oxford – the first woman to give a series of lectures on theology at Oxford. Much of her life was devoted to writing books, leading retreats, and giving spiritual direction.[485] She died on 15 June 1941.

In 1905, while in Venice, Underhill wrote a revealing letter to her future husband:

> last night a very smart professional palmist arrived here and proceeded to give a most absurd lecture with limelight illustrations of characteristic paws, in the hotel drawing-room. I learnt from it several curious things, chiefly that my affections are more sensual than platonic, that I have no self-confidence, [and] am inconstant, but literary.[486]

In 1932 she wrote

> I'm no intercessor myself – when I have the feel of God at all, I can think of nothing else – and when I haven't, I mostly fidget.[487]

This intriguing mixture of shyness, sensuality and love of all things literary combined with the capacity for undivided concentration on the reality of God is both characteristic and remarkable. It helped to make her a spiritual director of immense repute.[488] But Underhill's spirituality was not exclusively interior in perspective: she was a Socialist, in the late 1930s became a pacifist, and retained throughout her life a commitment to social justice.[489] Nor was she in any way narrowly religious in her interests and enthusiasms.[490] And her achievement was all the more remarkable for being attained without formal religious training or ecclesiastical support.[491]

In a letter of 1911, Underhill describes her early progress towards religious conviction:

> I wasn't brought up to religion really – except just in the formal way of course. So when the 'youthful crash' arrived it caught me fair and square, and for 8 or 9 years I really believed myself to be an atheist. Philosophy brought me round to an intelligent and irresponsible sort of theism which I enjoyed thoroughly but which did not last long. Gradually the net closed in on me and I was driven nearer and nearer to Christianity – half of me wishing it were true and half resisting violently all the time. In those days I used to frequent both English and Roman churches and wish I knew *what* their secret was. Finally I went to stay for a few days at a Convent of Perpetual Adoration. The day after I came away, a good deal shaken but unconvinced, I was 'converted' quite suddenly once and for all by an overpowering vision which had really no specific Christian elements, but yet convinced me that the Catholic Religion was true. It was so tightly bound up with (Roman) Catholicism, that I had no doubt, and have had none since (this happened between 4 and 5 years ago only), that that Church was my ultimate home. So strong is this conviction that to have any personal dealings with Anglicanism seems for me a kind of treachery. Unfortunately I allowed myself to be persuaded to wait a year before being

received; and meanwhile the Modernist storm broke, with the result that now, being myself 'Modernist' on many points, I can't get in without suppressions and evasions to which I can't quite bring myself. But I can't accept Anglicanism instead: it seems an integrally different thing. So here I am, going to Mass and so on of course, but entirely deprived of sacraments.[492]

It is worth noting Underhill's reference to an 'overpowering vision which had really no specific Christian elements' – we shall return to this later. This was to remain the situation for ten years. Much later, in 1931, she wrote to Dom John Chapman:

I have been for years now a practising Anglo-Catholic . . . and solidly believe in the Catholic status of the Anglican Church, as to orders and sacraments . . . It seems to me to be a respectable suburb of the city of God – but all the same, part of 'greater London'.[493]

Underhill was extremely well read, her interests ranging from Bengali mysticism to Kierkegaard, whom she studied at the very end of her life during the dark years of the Second World War.[494] She draws on an immense range of sources in her writings;[495] and she owed an immense debt to three contemporaries, each of whom in turn gave her spiritual direction: Reginald Somerset Ward, Abbot John Chapman of Downside (in 1935 Underhill wrote that Chapman 'knew more about *real* prayer than anyone I ever met'[496]), and above all Friedrich von Hügel.[497]

The nature of the spiritual life

We may begin our exploration of Underhill's spirituality with three significant observations she made at different points in her work. In her Upton Lectures of 1922 she offered an answer to the question of what lies at the heart of an authentic spiritual life:

God, in all His richness, immanent and transcendent: the whole response to the Eternal and Abiding of which any one man is capable, expressed in and through his this-worldly life.[498]

It follows that spirituality 'requires then an objective vision or certitude, something to aim at; and also a total integration of the self, its dedication to that aim. Both terms, vision and response, are essential to it'.[499] This is because, as she pointed out nine years later, human beings are 'twofold creatures', made for both outward action and inward transformation, for love of both God and neighbour; and we shall not be happy, in her view, if we settle only for one or the other.[500]

And the corollary of this is that real spiritual growth will be hard work. In 1934, in a Lent book she wrote for the diocese of London, she said

The spiritual life is a stern choice. It is not a consoling retreat from the difficulties of existence; but an invitation to enter fully into that difficult existence, and there apply the Charity of God and bear the cost.[501]

Thus to enter the world of contemplation 'means exchanging the lovely view [of, as it were, the high Alps] with the austere reality: penetrating the strange hill-country, slogging up stony tracks in heavy boots, bearing fatigue and risking fog and storm, helping fellow-climbers at one's own cost'.[502]

Underhill's own view of the spiritual life changed and developed over time; and we can identify some of the major developments by comparing two editions of her classic book *Mysticism*, which first appeared in 1911 and rapidly became popular. First, the early editions reflected her preoccupation with the esoteric world of hermeticism and magic, as well as with the currently fashionable philosophy of 'vitalism'. By the time of the twelfth edition, in 1930, this preoccupation is much diminished, to be replaced with an inchoate awareness of Freudian psychology.[503] The chapter entitled 'Mysticism and Magic' originally ended with a paragraph espousing an explicit mystical élitism which was omitted from later editions:

> Thus in spite of persistent efforts to the contrary, there will always be an inner and an outer Church: the inner Church of the mystics who *know*, the outer Church which, operating beneficently it is true, but – roughly speaking – upon the magical plane, only *knows about*. The New Testament is not without its reminders that this was bound to be the case (see, amongst other passages, Matt. 13.11, 1 Cor. 2.6 and 3.1).[504]

Secondly, her view of the Christian spiritual tradition became more nuanced in the sixteen years that separated the fifth edition (1914) from the twelfth edition (1930); and Underhill came to have a higher regard for writers whom previously she had not really considered as 'mystical' at all.[505] Her earlier reverence for the French quietist Madame Guyon is sharply diminished by 1930;[506] and St John of the Cross receives more positive treatment.[507] And mysticism itself, which in early editions she gushingly described as 'the most romantic thing in the universe', had by 1930 been downgraded to 'the most romantic of adventures'.[508]

But the most important and interesting development is in her attitude to Platonism. Where the early editions of *Mysticism* reflect an enthusiasm for Platonic ideas and Neoplatonic withdrawal from the material world, later ones show a marked shift in emphasis. Thus where in 1914 Underhill could write 'There is nothing of "social Christianity" in that supreme adventure whereby "God and the soul are made one thing"', by 1930 she has added 'even though no achievement of the soul truly takes place *in vacuo*, or leaves the universe of souls unchanged'.[509]

The nature of mysticism

This progressive development of her spirituality away from a Platonic escapism and towards a more affirmative and socially aware outlook is vital for understanding Underhill's thought. It helps us to grasp her developing sense of what exactly mysticism is. In her great eponymous work, she defines it as

> the expression of the innate tendency of the human spirit towards complete harmony with the transcendental order; whatever be the theological formula under which that order is understood.[510]

The theological inclusiveness is significant: she is envisaging a kind of 'higher' spiritual religion which mystics of all great world faiths share. In 1920, she says that 'the central fact [of the mystic's experience] is an overwhelming consciousness of God and of one's own soul', and adds that 'the overt recognition of that which orthodox Christians generally mean by a personal God is not essential'.[511] She goes on to infer a kind of interfaith élitism among mystics: the Hindu, Sufi and Christian mystic are far more like each other than any are like 'the average believer in their several creeds'.[512] For 'the claim of the mystical consciousness is to a closer reading of truth, to an apprehension of the divine unifying principle behind appearance'.[513] And this early élitism leaves little room for social awareness. Thus she explicitly says in 1925 that mysticism 'is in no way concerned with adding to, exploring, re-arranging, or improving anything in the visible universe'[514] – though later, as we shall see, she will acknowledge that the heightened energy and wisdom of the mystic can lead to some profound results. And, in some intriguing biblical exegesis, she speaks of Zacchaeus responding to the call of Jesus:

> this hasty descent to which he is summoned by God is simply a descent by love and desire in to [sic] that abyss of the Godhead which the intellect cannot understand.[515]

But she makes no mention of Zacchaeus' consequent decision to give away half of his possessions to the poor.

The élitism, even in the early works, is however more apparent than real. In 1925 she stresses that mystics are precisely those who are most fully in contact with the Real:

> their contemplation makes all that they do more real. Thus they show what Christian spirituality can be, and what a contribution it can make to the corporate life.[516]

And by this time she is also more fully aware of the risks of false or esoteric mysticism, and stresses the need for any mystic to be firmly rooted in the corporate life of the Church.[517] She also emphasizes that the difference between the mystic and the ordinary devout Christian is one of degree rather than of nature.[518]

The importance of mysticism

What exactly is the contribution that mysticism can make to the corporate life of Church and society? We may best approach this question by returning to what remained consistent throughout Underhill's spirituality: her undeviating emphasis on the reality of God. Thus she says

> We talk and write easily and freely about spiritual values and the spiritual life; but we remain fundamentally utilitarian, even pragmatic, at heart. We want spiritual things to work; and the standard we apply is our miserable little notion of how they ought to work. We always want to know whether they are helpful. Our philosophy and religion are orientated, not towards the awful vision of that principle before which Isaiah saw the seraphim veil their eyes; but merely towards the visible life of man and its needs. We may speak respectfully of Mary, and even study her psychology; but we feel that the really important thing is to encourage Martha to go on getting the lunch.[519]

She insists that this intrinsic and distinctively human capacity for what lies beyond us must be taken seriously: 'we cannot avoid our obligations by sending its best products to the convent, and its worst to the asylum'.[520] And the reason we keep trying to avoid our obligations is because serious attention to the reality of God is hugely demanding. At the very beginning of *Mysticism*, Underhill stresses that its primary concern is onto-logical, with the transformation of the subject by reference to its apprehension of the metaphysical Object. And the subject must be our entire personality, not just one bit of us.[521]

In short, mysticism changes us. In her Upton Lectures, Underhill seeks to integrate the new insights of psychology with the Christian spiritual tradition by identifying three key ways in which we realize 'our limited personal relations with [the] transcen-dent Other':[522] first, in our profound sense of security, of being 'safely held in a cosmos of which, despite all contrary appearance, peace is the very heart';[523] secondly, in the awareness of an 'intimate and reciprocal communion of a person with a Person';[524] thirdly, in the awareness of Spirit as 'an inflowing power, a veritable accession of vitality'.[525] These correspond to the Persons of the Trinity.[526] We experience a sense of there being more to life than blind chance; we begin to glimpse the possibilities of rela-tionship with that which exists outside us; and we experience within ourselves the power we need to respond to these possibilities.

Underhill thus adumbrates here a Trinitarian mysticism entirely compatible with modern psychology. And the reason why it was important to relate spirituality to psy-chology was in order to avoid the otherwise real danger of splitting off the spiritual from the everyday; for when that happens, spirituality becomes like the cultivation of a conservatory in a wilderness: 'whilst we are inside everything seems all right . . . But emerging from its doors, we find ourselves meeting the cold glances of those who deal in other kinds of reality.'[527] 'The setting apart of spiritual experience in a special com-partment, the keeping of it under glass, is daily becoming less possible' as we become increasingly aware of the interpenetration of spirituality, psychology and other disci-plines.[528] Hence in becoming more spiritual we do not change worlds: we change temper and attitude within our one world.[529]

In the Upton Lectures, this integrated view is then developed historically. Previous centuries, the saints, and the spiritual tradition, must no more be closed off from the present than the spiritual must be closed off from the psychological:[530] here too a con-servatory-style privatization must be avoided. For only then do we get a real sense of the role of the spiritual:

> The more we study the past, the more clearly we recognize that there are
> no 'ages of faith' . . . The spiritual man or woman is always fundamentally
> the same kind of man or woman; always reaching out with the same faith
> and love towards the heart of the same universe, though telling that faith
> and love in various tongues. He is far less the child of his time, than the
> transformer of it.[531]

She then proceeds to explore exactly how the spiritual person is an agent of social transformation: 'reconstruction of character and re-orientation of attention must precede reconstruction of society'.[532] This may well mean a temporary withdrawal from society in order to return to it renewed;[533] and Jesus gives us the clue as to how this happens in his answer to the rich young man:

> Jesus replies in effect, 'Put aside all lesser interests, strip off unrealities, and come, give yourself the chance of catching the infection of holiness from Me.'[534]

Thus the 'full living of the spiritual life' will imply

> at least these three characters. First, single-mindedness: to mean only God. Second, the full integration of the contemplative and active sides of existence, lifted up, harmonized, and completely consecrated to those interests which the self recognizes as Divine. Third, the power of reproducing this life; incorporating it in a group.[535]

We have come a long way here from any narrowly otherworldly understanding of mysticism. To be fair to Underhill, there are hints of this world-transforming view even in the original version of *Mysticism*. Thus she maintains in it that the great mystics experience (and communicate to others) 'an amazing, a superabundant vitality': St Paul goes out and founds the Church; St Joan of Arc leads the armies of France; St Francis and St Ignatius change the spiritual history of Europe.[536] So too, those who seek to make their own the mystical way even while living *in seculo* will receive a renewed vitality, for

> the spiritual life is not a special career, involving abstraction from the world of things. It is a part of every man's life; and until he has realised it he is not a complete human being.[537]

The key fruit of a deep focusing on the inner, mystical life is that of spiritual asceticism in general:

> The man who makes a success of his life, in any department, is he who has chosen one from amongst these claims and interests, and devoted to it his energetic powers of heart and will; 'unifying' himself about it, and from within it resisting all counter claims. He has one objective, one centre; has killed out the lesser ones, and simplified himself.[538]

This simplification is that of the ascetic, whom Inge accurately describes as 'the athlete of religion'.[539] It involves more stress on *being* than on *having*: 'you are enslaved by the verb "to have": all your reactions to life consist in corporate or individual demands, appetites, wants. That "love of life" of which we sometimes speak is mostly cupboard-love.'[540]

Growth in the spiritual life

This brings us to the question of exactly how we are to seek the fruits of authentic mystical experience. Underhill suggests that such experience is really an intensification of our normal experience, a moment in which we lose ourselves entirely in absorption in what is taking place.[541] The fundamental qualification for attaining, or deepening it, is a journey to the centre of our being:

At this very moment your thoughts are buzzing like a swarm of bees. The reduction of this fevered complex to a unity appears to be a task beyond all human power. Yet the situation is not as hopeless for you as it seems. All this [furious and inattentive busyness] is only happening upon the periphery of the mind, where it touches and reacts to the world of appearance. At the centre there is a stillness which even you are not able to break. There, the rhythm of your duration is one with the rhythm of the Universal Life. There, your essential self exists: the permanent being which persists through and behind the flow and change of your conscious states. You have been snatched to that centre once or twice. Turn your consciousness inward to it deliberately. Retreat to that point whence all the various lines of your activities flow, and to which at last they must return . . . The thing may sound absurd to you, but you can do it if you will: standing back, as it were, from the vague and purposeless reactions in which most men fritter their vital energies. Then you can survey with a certain calm, a certain detachment, your universe and the possibilities of life within it: can discern too, if you be at all inclined to mystical adventure, the stages of the road along which you must pass on your way towards harmony with the Real.[542]

The trouble is that all too often we treat this central 'spiritual principle' 'as the busy citizen treats his national monuments. It is there, it is important, a possession which adds dignity to his existence; but he never has time to go in'.[543]

It follows that the principal resources we need for this process are recollection, self-adjustment, and contemplative attention. Recollection is basically an exercise in total concentration: as you focus your entire mind on any given object, it begins slowly to exert 'unsuspected meaning, beauty, power'.[544] Surprisingly, she maintains that it matters little what the object is.[545] Once you have, by regular recollection, established a deep communion with this object, you can then turn 'this purified and universalized gaze back upon yourself' and 'observe your own being in a fresh relation with things'.[546] This is the key first stage of the contemplative life:

> It is not much more of an achievement than that first proud effort in which the baby stands upright for a moment and then relapses to the more natural and convenient crawl; but it holds within it the same earnest of future development.[547]

The second stage is self-adjustment: 'the deliberate rearrangement of your ideas, energies, and desires in harmony with that which you have seen'.[548] It is essentially self-simplification.[549] Taken together, these two steps form the essential basis for contemplation:

> You are not to confuse [contemplation] with pretty fancies about nature, such as all imaginative persons enjoy; still less, with a self-conscious and deliberate humanitarianism. It is a veritable condition of awareness, a direct perception, not an opinion or an idea. For those who attain it, the span of the senses is extended. These live in a world which is lit with an intenser light.[550]

This process of contemplation is capable of virtually limitless development as the mystic probes ever more deeply into the heart of Reality itself. The process is not an intellectual one: 'as it is not by the methods of the laboratory that we learn to know life, so it is not by the methods of the intellect that we learn to know God'.[551] Underhill quotes the *Cloud of unknowing* approvingly, with its insistence on love rather than thought as the way to God.[552]

Christian worship

At this point a major dilemma about Underhill's spirituality presents itself. This approach to contemplation is strongly Greek, lacking any substantial Christian content altogether. Underhill wants us to see what actually *is*, to encounter Reality itself.[553] She writes about union with God in a far more explicitly Christian manner:

> What does union with God mean? Not a nice feeling which we enjoy in devout moments. This may or may not be a by-product of union with God; probably not. It can never be its substance. Union with God means such an entire self-giving to the Divine Charity, such identification with its interests, that the whole of our human nature is transformed in God, irradiated by His absolute light, His sanctifying grace. Thus it is woven up into the organ of His creative activity, His redeeming purpose; conformed to the pattern of Christ, heart, soul, mind and strength. Each time this happens, it means that one more creature has achieved its destiny; and each soul in whom the life of the Spirit is born, sets out towards that goal.[554]

The difficulty is determining exactly how the process of contemplative attention she describes leads to our becoming 'conformed to the pattern of Christ'. She does acknowledge this difficulty: in a letter of 1932 she says that 'I come to Christ through God, whereas quite obviously lots of people come to God through Christ.'[555] And it is really only in her magnificent exploration of Christian worship, in a major book entitled simply *Worship*, that this problem is resolved. Underhill defines worship as 'the response of the creature to the Eternal': it is 'always a subject–object relationship'.[556] She argues that the 'primitive subconsciousness' which is a part of all of us is 'nowhere more active than in the practices of our religion' – which could be why worship excites such strong emotions among worshippers.[557] But worship will only work if we bring to it what we also bring to (say) great works of art: 'attention, surrender, sympathetic emotion', a point she makes in her Upton Lectures.[558] In a powerful passage in *Worship*, she warns that all worship tends to

> decline from adoration to demand, and from the supernatural to the ethical . . . And only in so far as it is released from this petty subjectivism, can it hope to grow up into any knowledge of the massive realities of that spiritual universe in which we live and move. It is the mood of deep admiration, the meek acknowledgment of mystery, the humble adoring gaze, which makes us capable of this revelation.[559]

Worship thus demands a fundamental un-selfing: hence the importance of adoration, which 'obliterates all thoughts of self' and which 'ought then to be the first point, both in public worship and in the private devotional life which supports that public worship and makes it real'.[560] 'Our little human affairs are reduced to their proper proportion when seen over against the spaceless Majesty and Beauty of God.'[561] Hence

> There is nothing paddock-like or parochial, nothing individualistic or subjective, in the genuine worship of the Church. The scene is set within the great landscape of Eternity, and includes in the upward sweep of adoration the invisible things of Him Who is invisible; so that all our various rites and methods are lost in the blaze of that light.[562]

But adoration is not all there is to worship; and thus far we have not really advanced towards a resolution of our dilemma other than by enlarging the perspective from personal contemplation to liturgical adoration. In *Worship*, however, Underhill goes on to identify four key ingredients of authentic worship: ritual, symbol, sacrament and sacrifice.[563] All of these, like human beings themselves, have a twofold character, at once inward and outward; all of them are irreducibly social, lifting us out of ourselves and into the rhythm of the worshipping community as it seeks God's transforming presence.[564] But it is with the last of these that we approach the heart of the matter. True, sacrifice is not exclusively a Christian phenomenon: it has deep primitive roots, 'and indeed always carries with it a reminiscence of the jungle. But its full meaning is disclosed in the absolute oblation of the Cross.'[565] Underhill considers the three forms of sacrifice in the Old Testament – oblation, communion and atonement – noting that the purpose of each was not simply ritual but *restoration*, an attempt to bring about a profound change in the relationship between humans and their Creator.[566] She stresses that all three forms of sacrifice are indispensable for authentic worship:[567] without oblation, for example, 'devotion soon becomes petty and even cosy, [and] turns back from self-oblation to self-consolation'.[568] And then she plays her trump card:

> Perhaps the most significant development in human religion has been the movement of the idea of sacrifice from propitiation to love.[569]

'The most significant development in human religion' – it is an awesome claim. But Underhill is emphatic: no worship is sufficient if it excludes the notion of costly, disinterested, anti-utilitarian offering.[570] For worship is directed to self-loss, not self-fulfilment.[571] And what she has in mind here is memorably articulated by a later Dominican scholar, himself a student of the relationship between psychology and spirituality. In 1952 Victor White OP wrote

> while sacrifice is indispensable, it is also impossible to the conscious ego – to you and me . . . it can be possible only to a greater power within us, the power which men have called God. Jung has said that no matter how much he and his patients contribute to an analysis, they can at best only prepare the way, remove the obstacles, to healing. Healing itself, he says, always comes in some wholly unexpected way from the unknown . . . like a miracle. For when the sacrifice is made, it is given back transformed and transforming. But sacrifice there must be, whether or not expressed in

external ordinances; and psychology has strangely confirmed what theology has always maintained, that sacrifice can only be complete and perfect when it is the free and whole self-oblation of a dying man, who must also be the dying God.[572]

For Underhill herself, all the rich diversity of Christian worship

> is conditioned by a concrete fact; the stooping down of the Absolute to disclose Himself within the narrow human radius, the historical incarnation of the Eternal Logos within time. The primary declaration of Christianity is not 'This Do' but 'This Happened' – indeed, is happening still, since the path of incarnation remains open, and Christ lives and acts in His Body, the Church, and gives Himself in its sacraments.[573]

Conclusion

Like Inge and Butler, Evelyn Underhill's exploration of mysticism is unquestionably open to the criticism that, notwithstanding later adjustments, its pervasive Platonism exposes it to the risk of lacking a clear Christian and biblical character, and as a result to the further hazard of being less an engagement with the world than a flight from it.[574] There is a marked lack of ethical application in much of her writing, and relatively little concern to consider exactly *how* the mystic might help bring about the transformation of creation for which she so deeply longs. Yet that does not derogate from her major achievement. Her presentation of a spirituality that integrates the great riches of the Christian spiritual tradition with the insights of modern psychology was not achieved without experiment. But that it was achieved at all is in itself eloquent testimony to Underhill's enduring importance. As she draws to the close of her magnificent Upton Lectures of 1922, she says

> Spirituality, as we have seen all along, must not be a lovely fluid notion or a merely self-regarding education; but an education for action, for the insertion of eternal values into the time-world.[575]

And, writing in the darkest hours of the Second World War, only months before her own death, Underhill sets out her understanding of the heart of Christian prayer in a manner at once profound and prophetic:

> in these first words [of the Lord's Prayer], the praying soul accepts once for all its true status as a member of the whole family of man. Our Father. It can never again enter into prayer as a ring-fenced individual, intent on a private relation with God; for this is a violation of the law of Charity. Its prayer must overflow the boundaries of selfhood to include the life, the needs of the race; accepting as a corollary of its filial relation with God a brotherly relation with all other souls however diverse, and at every point replacing 'mine' by 'ours'. This wide spreading love, this refusal of private advantage is the very condition of Christian prayer; for that prayer is an instrument of redemptive action, not merely of personal achievement. Here my enemy prays by my side, since the world of prayer has no frontiers; and in so doing he ceases to be my enemy, because we meet in God.[576]

G. K. Chesterton and the recovery of wonder

Spirituality and journalism

The growth of journalism and the mass media is one of the many significant features of twentieth-century English life.[577] At the end of the First World War, national daily newspapers were selling 3 million copies; by the beginning of the Second, their sales were over 10 million.[578] The introduction of radio not only allowed Winston Churchill to maintain national morale during the darkest days of war; it also offered a new opportunity to communicate spiritual values which able apologists like C. S. Lewis were to take up. In 1946 there were only 15,000 television licence-holders; by 1956 there were over 5 million; and the subsequent proliferation of television channels, not to mention the introduction of mobile telephones and the internet towards the end of the century, transformed the nature of society's communications.[579] The vast influence of television, videos and the internet did little good for the practice of religion; but it did not necessarily damage people's inherent beliefs or spiritual values. In short, it was good for *believing* but bad for *belonging*.[580]

It is tempting to conclude from these developments that their greatest impact, in particular on a relatively diffuse subject like spirituality, is likely to be at the end of the twentieth century, when the pace of change in journalism and the mass media was increasing rapidly. But there are good reasons for believing that the opposite is the case: that the most significant contribution made by journalism to English spirituality was made at the dawn of the twentieth century; and for three reasons. First, journalism was a more leisurely (though certainly not leisured) occupation then than it subsequently became, allowing people to probe more deeply beneath the surface of issues; secondly, at that time good writing and good journalism were, if not synonymous, certainly eminently compatible; thirdly, the existence in Edwardian times of what John Gross calls an atmosphere of 'confident give-and-take' enabled the best kind of adversarial journalism – involving wit and acuity of mind but also the ability to 'corner one's meaning' (as George Bernard Shaw put it) – to flourish.[581] It is significant that perhaps the finest exponent of this kind of journalism, G. K. Chesterton, described journalists as 'the priests of the modern world'.[582]

Chesterton: introduction

Gilbert Keith Chesterton was born in Kensington in 1874, and baptized into the Church of England;[583] he was received into the Roman Catholic Church in 1922. He described his father as 'serene, humorous and full of hobbies'.[584] His influence on his son must have been significant: much later, Chesterton was to celebrate that inner freedom to play and imagine, which allows us to conceive of a world as it ought to be.[585] He was educated at home and at St Paul's School, London.[586] From 1892 he spent three years at Slade School of Art and University College London. In 1901 he married Frances Blogg, to whom he had once written: 'You are a very stupid person. I don't believe you have the least idea how nice you are';[587] the marriage, though childless, was a close and happy one. In 1916 Gilbert replaced his brother Cecil as editor of *New Witness*, and in 1925 became editor of his own *G.K.'s Weekly*. A great deal of his output appeared in the form of newspaper articles, and his thought as a whole cannot be appreciated without taking them into account. Chesterton travelled widely, and had an extremely wide circle of friends. He died in 1936.

Chesterton was a person almost impossible to dislike, not least because of his ability to retain a sense of the childlike throughout his life.[588] He once said 'I believe in prolonging childhood';[589] and his fellow Catholic Ronald Knox wrote of him as someone who 'grew up from manhood into boyhood'.[590] His first and best biographer, Maisie Ward, went further: 'for most people,' she wrote, 'intensity of thought is much more difficult than action. With him it was the opposite. He used his mind unceasingly, his body as little as possible.'[591] This is not to say that Chesterton was mild or eirenic in his views: he said of himself that 'I could be a journalist [rather than a novelist] because I could not help being a controversialist.'[592] But it is to say that differences of opinion were very rarely accompanied by personal animosity. He once wrote of his most famous intellectual sparring-partner George Bernard Shaw:

> I can testify that I have never read a reply by Bernard Shaw that did not leave me in a better and not a worse temper or frame of mind; which did not seem to come out of inexhaustible fountains of fair-mindedness and intellectual geniality; which did not savour somehow of that native largeness which the philosopher attributed to the Magnanimous Man. It is necessary to disagree with him as much as I do, in order to admire him as much as I do; and I am proud of him as a foe even more than as a friend.[593]

And Maisie Ward writes of his entering the 'last years of his life having made no enemies in the exceedingly sensitive literary world to which he primarily belonged'.[594]

Chesterton's written output was huge; and some of it was either ephemeral or opinionated or over-written or all three at once. Some of his historical work is marred by a golden and eventually tedious nostalgia for an imagined medieval 'Merry England'; but even these are full of apposite and sometimes profound reflections.[595] Many of his theological works were the result of controversies in which he became involved: two in particular – *Heretics* (1905) and the even more popular *Orthodoxy* (1908) – arose from a long-running battle with Robert Blatchford, the scientific determinist who edited the *Clarion* newspaper.[596] It was precisely through the experience of engaging in this controversy that Chesterton's own conversion to Roman Catholicism was nurtured. Later works, notably *The everlasting man* (1925), reveal a more measured, less rampantly rhetorical, tone that underpins his Christian apologetic.

Spirituality and orthodoxy

Chesterton's spirituality is drawn from a traditional Christian and Catholic orthodoxy. 'The Christian ideal', he wrote, 'has not been tried and found wanting. It has been found difficult; and left untried.'[597] He wants to recover belief in a God who is both robustly 'other' and incarnate in our midst – and with it a belief in the dignity (indeed the *holiness*) of the individual as the primary agent of social justice and change. He has little time for psychological introspection, and none at all for what he takes to be the Buddhist (or Swinburnian) notion of a 'God within':

That external vigilance which has always been the mark of Christianity (the command that we should *watch* and pray) has expressed itself both in typical western orthodoxy and in typical western politics: but both depend on the idea of a divinity transcendent, different from ourselves, a deity that disappears. Certainly the most sagacious creeds may suggest that we should pursue God into deeper and deeper rings of the labyrinth of our own ego. But only we of Christendom have said that we should hunt God like an eagle upon the mountains; and we have killed all monsters in the chase.[598]

This is typical Chesterton: robust, uncomprehending even, in his antipathy to any kind of introspection; yet able to convey a sense of Christianity as attractive and exciting whilst rooted in a clear and objective transcendentalism. Without that, he believed, we go mad. Thus 'the mere pursuit of health always leads to something unhealthy'.[599] God must be seen as a creator, separate from his creation: 'a woman loses a child even in having a child. All creation is separation. Birth is as solemn a parting as death.'[600] Nor is this empty rhetoric: it is closely linked to the opening verses of Genesis. His famous defence of orthodoxy reflects this strongly objective view of religious truth; but it also reflects his love of paradox: 'for orthodox theology has specially insisted that Christ was not a being apart from God and man, like an elf, nor yet a being half human and half not, like a centaur, but both things at once and both things thoroughly, very man and very God.'[601] 'Christianity got over the difficulty of combining furious opposites by keeping them both, and keeping them both furious.'[602] Thus

> it *is* true that the historic Church has at once emphasised celibacy and emphasised the family; has at once (if one may put it so) been fiercely for having children and fiercely for not having children. It has kept them side by side like two strong colours, red and white, like the red and white upon the shield of St George. It has always had a healthy hatred of pink . . . And sometimes this pure gentleness and this pure fierceness met and justified their juncture; the paradox of all the prophets was fulfilled, and, in the soul of St Louis, the lion lay down with the lamb. But remember that this text is too lightly interpreted. It is constantly assured . . . that when the lion lies down with the lamb the lion becomes lamb-like. But that is brutal annexation and imperialism on the part of the lamb. That is simply the lamb absorbing the lion instead of the lion eating the lamb. The real problem is – Can the lion lie down with the lamb and still retain his royal ferocity? *That* is the problem the Church attempted; *that* is the miracle she achieved.[603]

This is splendid Christian apologetic, articulating the heart of what theologians call the sacramental view of the world without recourse to dull jargon. This is where journalistic skills assist the imaginative presentation of religious truth. Sometimes Chesterton can rise to poetic and spiritual reflection of great beauty:

On the third day the friends of Christ coming at daybreak to the place found the grave empty and the stone rolled away. In varying ways they realised the new wonder; but even they hardly realised that the world had died in the night. What they were looking at was the first day of a new creation, with a new heaven and a new earth; and in a semblance of the gardener God walked again in the garden, in the cool not of the evening but the dawn.[604]

Sometimes, however, the vigour of Chesterton's polemic elicits from the reader a lurking suspicion that he does not really understand what he criticizes, as when he says (in *The Blatchford controversies*): 'Christianity, which is a very mystical religion, has nevertheless been the religion of the most practical section of mankind. It has far more paradoxes than the Eastern philosophies, but it also builds far better roads.'[605]

The importance of wonder

The question is: what contribution does Chesterton make to spirituality? The first, and perhaps most substantial, answer is: in his emphasis on wonder. Few people had a greater capacity for seeing the miraculous in the heart of the everyday. In his early *Notebook* Chesterton wrote

> The mountains praise thee, O Lord!
> But what if a mountain said,
>   'I praise thee;
> But put a pine-tree halfway up on the left;
> It would be much more effective, believe me.'

> It is time that the religion of prayer gave
>   place to the religion of praise.[606]

What is latent here, and made explicit later, is another key Chesterton virtue: the ability to celebrate not just the *everyday* but the *particular*, the specific, the individual. Hence (as we shall see) his emphasis on Incarnation. Hence too Chesterton's interest (again doubtless honed by long experience of journalism) in precision, both of language and of truth. In his biography of St Francis he tries to explain the mystic's understanding of praise:

> When we say that a poet praises the whole creation, we commonly mean only that he praises the whole cosmos. But this sort of poet does really praise creation, in the sense of the act of creation. He praises the passage or transition from nonentity to entity; there falls here also the shadow of that archetypal image of the bridge, which has given to the priest his archaic and mysterious name. The mystic who passes through the moment when there is nothing but God does in some sense behold the beginningless beginnings in which there was really nothing else. He not only appreciates everything but the nothing of which everything was made.[607]

This sense of astonishment at the existence of anything at all goes very deep in Chesterton. Marshall McLuhan correctly noted that 'to him existence has a value utterly inexpressible, and absolutely superior to any arguments for optimism or pessimism'.[608] Maisie Ward cites one of Chesterton's last radio broadcasts:

> What has really happened during the last seven days and nights? Seven times we have been dissolved into darkness as we shall be dissolved into dust; our very selves, as far as we know, have been wiped out of the world of living things; and seven times we have been raised alive like Lazarus, and found all our limbs and senses unaltered, with the coming of the day . . . A great many people are at this moment paying rather too much attention to the spice of life, and rather too little attention to life.[609]

This may feel overwritten to some; but it is hard to dislike someone who can (in the same broadcast) say this of himself:

> It is much more important to remember that I have been intensely and imaginatively happy in the queerest because the quietest places. I have been filled with life from within in a cold waiting-room, in a deserted railway-junction. I have been completely alive sitting on an iron seat under an ugly lamp-post at a third-rate watering place. In short, I have experienced the mere excitement of existence in places that would commonly be called as dull as ditchwater. And, by the way, is ditchwater dull? Naturalists with microscopes have told me that it teems with quiet fun.[610]

For Chesterton, the sense of wonder is integral to our nature as human beings. In his autobiography Chesterton said that when young he 'hung on to the remains of religion by one thin thread of thanks'; and then famously wrote:

> At the back of our brains, so to speak, there was a forgotten blaze or burst of astonishment at our own existence. The object of the artistic and spiritual life was to dig for this submerged sunrise of wonder; so that a man sitting in a chair might suddenly understand that he was actually alive, and be happy.[611]

It is important to note that in his view this sense of wonder is far more than mere childlike astonishment. It has significant social implications; for 'unless we can make daybreak and daily bread and the creative secrets of labour interesting in themselves, there will fall on all our civilisations a fatigue which is the one disease from which all civilisations do not recover. So died the great Pagan Civilisation; of bread and circuses and forgetfulness of the household gods.'[612] Furthermore,

> In order that men should resist injustice, something more is necessary than that they should think injustice unpleasant. They must think injustice *absurd*; above all, they must think it startling.[613]

The key is our capacity to see the holiness of the individual:

> What dullness there is in our life arises mostly from its rapidity: people pass us too quickly to show us their interesting side. By the end of the week we have talked to a hundred bores; whereas, if we had stuck to one of them,

we might have found ourselves talking to a new friend, or a humorist, or a murderer, or a man who had seen a ghost. I do not believe that there are any ordinary people. That is, I do not believe that there are any people whose lives are really humdrum or whose characters are really colourless. But the trouble is that one can so quickly see them all in a lump, like a land surveyor, and it would take so long to see them one by one as they really are, like a great novelist . . . People talk much of the quarrel between science and religion; but the deepest difference is that the individual is so much bigger than the average, that the inside of life is much larger than the outside.[614]

By 'the inside' Chesterton is thinking not of the complexities of the psyche but of what 'ordinary' people really think and see. So the test of any spirituality will be its capacity to help us cope with the people next door, a point he makes in *Heretics*:

The best way that a man could test his readiness to encounter the common variety of mankind would be to climb down a chimney into any house at random, and get on as well as possible with the people inside. And that is essentially what each one of us did on the day that he was born.

Chesterton goes on to draw out the implications of this in what appears to be a vigorous defence of the family, but in reality reflects a number of other aspects of Chesterton's thought as well:

This is, indeed, the sublime and special romance of the family. It is romantic because . . . it is arbitrary. It is romantic because it is there. So long as you have groups of men chosen rationally, you have some special or sectarian atmosphere. It is when you have groups of men chosen irrationally that you have men . . . The supreme adventure is not falling in love. The supreme adventure is being born. There we do walk suddenly into a splendid and startling trap. There we do see something of which we have not dreamed before. Our father and mother do lie in wait for us and leap out on us, like brigands from a bush. Our uncle is a surprise. Our aunt is, in the beautiful common expression, a bolt from the blue. When we step into the family, by the act of being born, we do step into a world which is incalculable, into a world which has its own strange laws, into a world which could do without us, into a world that we have not made. In other words, when we step into the family we step into a fairy-tale.[615]

The romance of fairy-tale

This extract introduces us to three other distinctive aspects of Chesterton's spiritual world-view. The first is his love of fairy-tale, precisely *because* it challenges our assumptions about the everyday. Thus, in an article for *The illustrated London news*, he quotes an unnamed critic:

'Inhuman monsters do not really exist, except in fairy-tales'! There are plenty of inhuman monsters in the modern world; inhuman monsters control commerce and rule continents. The only real difference between fairy-tale and modern fact is this: that in fairy-tale the monsters are *fought*. That is one of the very many superiorities of fairy-tales.[616]

Love of romance and fairy-tale is of course linked with Chesterton's hearty appetite for all things transcendental, an appetite all the more attractive for being entirely devoid of undue solemnity: 'angels can fly because they can take themselves lightly'.[617] Or: 'it is easy to be heavy; hard to be light. Satan fell by the force of gravity.'[618]

Asceticism

The next distinctive aspect of Chesterton's spiritual worldview is his emphasis on asceticism, in the sense of learning to live creatively within limits and with what is *given*, learning to go narrower in order to go deeper in life.[619] In his poem *The world state* he sharply underlined how much easier it is to love everyone in general than to love one's neighbour in particular:

> Oh, how I love Humanity,
> With love so pure and pringlish,
> And how I hate the horrid French,
> Who never will be English!
>
> The International Idea,
> The largest and the clearest,
> Is welding all the nations now,
> Except the one that's nearest.
>
> This compromise has long been known,
> This scheme of partial pardons,
> In ethical societies
> And small suburban gardens –
>
> The villas and the chapels where
> I learned with little labour
> The way to love my fellow-man
> And hate my next-door neighbour.[620]

In *Orthodoxy* Chesterton wrote that 'every act of will is an act of self-limitation . . . In that sense every act is an act of self-sacrifice. When you choose anything, you reject everything else.'[621] And in *St Francis of Assisi* he stresses that true asceticism is a life of unconditional gratitude for the gift of life itself: the ascetic

> will be always throwing things away into a bottomless pit of unfathomable thanks. Men who think they are too modern to understand this are in fact too mean to understand it; we are most of us too mean to practise it. We are not generous enough to be ascetics; one might almost say not genial enough to be ascetics . . . The whole point about St Francis of Assisi is that he certainly was ascetical and he certainly was not gloomy.[622]

Hence St Francis was no forerunner of the Romantics: 'the whole point of him was that the secret of recovering the natural pleasures lay in regarding them in the light of a supernatural pleasure'.[623] And the Franciscan Third Order was designed 'to assist ordinary men to be ordinary with extraordinary exultation'.[624]

Spirituality and incarnation

The next and most important ingredient of Chesterton's spiritual worldview is his emphasis on Incarnation, the theological coping-stone for his love of the holy in the midst of the ordinary. He expresses it vividly in a poem he wrote for what was easily his favourite festival, Christmas:

> This world is wild as an old wives' tale,
> And strange the plain things are,
> The earth is enough and the air is enough
> For our wonder and our war;
> But our rest is as far as the fire-drake swings
> And our peace is put in impossible things
> Where clashed and thundered unthinkable wings
> Round an incredible star.
>
> To an open house in the evening
> Home shall men come,
> To an older place than Eden
> And a taller town than Rome.
> To the end of the way of the wandering star,
> To the things that cannot be and that are,
> To the place where God was homeless
> And all men are at home.[625]

Underlying the Incarnation for Chesterton was a healthy evaluation of the physical. In his book on Aquinas he underlines this:

> It was a very special idea of St Thomas that Man is to be studied in his whole manhood; that a man is not a man without his body, just as he is not a man without his soul. A corpse is not a man; but also a ghost is not a man. The earlier school of Augustine and even of Anselm had rather neglected this, treating the soul as the only necessary treasure, wrapped for a time in a negligible napkin.[626]

This is a false spirituality for Chesterton: true orthodoxy demands a right valuing of the physical as well as of the spiritual. Hence

> St Thomas wanted to recover what was in essence the body of Christ itself . . . And he wanted the body, and all its senses, because he believed, rightly or wrongly, that it was a Christian thing. It might be a humbler or homelier thing than the Platonic mind; that is why it was Christian. St Thomas was, if you will, taking the lower road when he walked in the steps of Aristotle. So was God, when He worked in the workshop of Joseph.[627]

Chesterton compared Christianity favourably with those religions and philosophies which concentrated on ages and developments and forgot the immediate and the particular (so he can speak of St Francis loving not Christianity but Christ, not humanity but human beings[628]) and in his early *Notebook* he wrote:

> We must certainly be in a novel. What I like about this novelist is that he takes such trouble about his minor characters.[629]

Christianity is rooted in a *story*, not in a *theory*; and in a story anything can happen; it is exciting because it is also dangerous.[630] And the logic of this is incarnation:

> Christianity is the only religion on earth that has felt that omnipotence made God incomplete. Christianity alone has felt that God, to be wholly God, must have been a rebel as well as a king.[631]

Hence, again, the irreducible dignity and beauty of the everyday, expressed with definitive simplicity in Chesterton's most famous poem, *The donkey*:

> When fishes flew and forests walked
> And figs grew upon thorn,
> Some moment when the moon was blood
> Then surely I was born.
>
> With monstrous head and sickening cry
> And ears like errant wings,
> The devil's walking parody
> On all four-footed things.
>
> The tattered outlaw of the earth,
> Of ancient crooked will;
> Starve, scourge, deride me: I am dumb,
> I keep my secret still.
>
> Fools! For I also had my hour;
> One far fierce hour and sweet:
> There was a shout about my ears,
> And palms before my feet.[632]

The attractiveness of Christianity

At the beginning of *Orthodoxy*, Chesterton poses the key question for him: 'how can we contrive to be at once astonished at the world and yet at home in it?'[633] 'Nearly all people I have ever met in this western society in which I live would agree to the general proposition that we need this life of practical romance; the combination of something that is strange with something that is secure. We need so to view the world as to combine an idea of wonder and an idea of welcome.'[634] To do this requires no special mystical insights; rather a pervasive capacity to see the strange and the supernatural in the everyday. 'Oddities only strike ordinary people. Oddities do not strike odd people. This is why ordinary people have a much more exciting time.'[635] And much in the universe is odd, indeed mysterious, accessible more to poetry than to logic:

> To accept everything is an exercise, to understand everything a strain. The poet only desires exaltation and expansion, a world to stretch himself in. The poet only asks to get his head into the heavens. It is the logician who seeks to get the heavens into his head. And it is his head that splits.[636]

Hence it follows that 'the madman is not the man who has lost his reason. The madman is the man who has lost everything except his reason.'[637] But Chesterton is then led to argue that a world that is merely the result of blind determinism is a thin, dull kind of world, a point later apologists for science would vigorously challenge.[638] Chesterton can allow room for doubt in a Christian view of the universe; but he is unfair in denying that to scientists: 'materialists and madmen never have doubts'.[639] He is certainly nearer the mark in pointing out that science has nothing to contribute to morality. But his primary concern is to argue that reason and science are inadequate without something else – mysticism:

> Mysticism keeps men sane. As long as you have mystery you have health; when you destroy mystery you create morbidity. The ordinary man has always been sane because the ordinary man has always been a mystic. He has permitted the twilight. He has always one foot in earth and the other in fairyland. He has always left himself free to doubt his gods; but (unlike the agnostic of to-day) free also to believe in them. He has always cared more for truth than for consistency. If he saw two truths that seemed to contradict each other, he would take the two truths and the contradiction along with them. His spiritual sight is stereoscopic, like his physical sight: he sees two pictures at once and yet sees all the better for that . . . It is exactly this balance of apparent contradictions that has been the whole buoyancy of the healthy man. The whole secret of mysticism is this: that man can understand everything by the help of what he does not understand. The morbid logician seeks to make everything lucid, and succeeds in making everything mysterious. The mystic allows one thing to be mysterious, and everything else becomes lucid.[640]

And not only lucid – it becomes attractive. Thus Chesterton unlocks the key to the mysticism of St Francis:

> A man will not roll in the snow for a stream of tendency by which all things fulfil the law of their being. He will not go without food in the name of something, not ourselves, that makes for righteousness. He will do things like this, or pretty nearly like this, under quite a different impulse. He will do these things when he is in love . . . The reader cannot even begin to see the sense of a story that may well seem to him a very wild one, until he understands that to this great mystic his religion was not a thing like a theory but a thing like a love-affair.[641]

For Chesterton, mysticism too involved a contemplative awe as well as a clear-sighted concern for what was objectively *out there*, not an introspective self-exploration. He points this out at the end of his study of Aquinas:

That *strangeness* of things, which is the light in all poetry, and indeed in all art, is really connected with their otherness; or what is called their objectivity. What is subjective must be stale; it is exactly what is objective that is in this imaginative manner strange. In this the great contemplative is the complete contrary of that false contemplative, the mystic who looks only into his own soul, the selfish artist who shrinks from the world and lives only in his own mind. According to St Thomas, the mind acts freely of itself, but its freedom exactly consists in finding a way out to liberty and the light of day; to reality and the land of the living . . . All their romance and glamour, so to speak, lies in the fact that they are real things; things *not* to be found by staring inwards at the mind . . . According to Aquinas, the object becomes a part of the mind; nay, according to Aquinas, the mind actually becomes the object. But, as one commentator acutely puts it, it only becomes the object and does not create the object. In other words, the object *is* an object; it can and does exist outside the mind, or in the absence of the mind. And *therefore* it enlarges the mind of which it becomes a part. The mind conquers a new province like an emperor; but only because the mind has answered the bell like a servant.[642]

Conclusion

The weaknesses in Chesterton's thought are too obvious to need much elaboration: the (often forced) paradoxes, the (sometimes extravagant) reverence for tradition, and the neo-medievalism, can easily pall; while elsewhere in his work the occasional hints of antisemitism, together with the distinctly ambivalent attitude to women's suffrage, are less easily justified.[643] Chesterton did insist on the reality of sin and evil: 'there are many who will smile at the saying; but it is profoundly true to say that the glad good news brought by the Gospel was the news of original sin.'[644] But, for all his genuine commitment to social justice, his political and social theories were far too jejune to address a world threatened by totalitarian and systemic evil.[645] His longing to communicate sometimes led him to simplify complex issues not really susceptible to the journalist's bold synoptic approach.[646]

Yet such criticism is too easy. Like Daniel Defoe, Chesterton looked at the spiritual life from a lay perspective quite different from that of the professional theologian or cleric. He found in Christianity something of enduring – and, more important, of *surprising* – worth; and then devoted his considerable energies to understanding and promoting it. He did this with a journalist's enthusiasm to communicate, but also with a journalist's insistence on clarity and precision. That earned him criticism from many religious people whose own attempts to convey the heart of their faith were vastly less compelling than his were. There is something of Chesterton in what C. S. Lewis memorably wrote about Spenser: 'he makes imaginable inner realities so vast and simple that they ordinarily escape us'.[647] He defended journalism against the charge that it is always undertaken in a hurry by pointing out that the same is true of fighting battles, and engaging in commerce;[648] and perhaps one crucial ingredient of a mature spirituality is the provision of resources that will enable us to cope when we must do the same. And he saw in the heart of Christian faith a bold contradiction which could still impart both meaning and energy to life in a troubled age:

Buddhism is centripetal, but Christianity is centrifugal: it breaks out. For the circle is perfect and infinite in its nature; but it is fixed for ever in its size; it can never be larger or smaller. But the cross, though it has at its heart a collision and a contradiction, can extend its four arms for ever without altering its shape. Because it has a paradox in its centre it can grow without changing. The circle returns upon itself and is bound. The cross opens its arms to the four winds; it is a signpost for free travellers.[649]

C. S. Lewis, Charles Williams, Dorothy L. Sayers and the recovery of tradition

Introduction

Chesterton had a great love of tradition. In *Orthodoxy*, he said that

tradition is only democracy extended through time. It is trusting to a consensus of common human voices rather than to some isolated or arbitrary record . . . Tradition means giving votes to the most obscure of all classes, our ancestors. It is the democracy of the dead.[650]

His love for tradition was instinctive, rooted in his character and nature, though by no means uncritical. Among those he influenced was an Ulster-born scholar called Clive Staples Lewis, known to his contemporaries as Jack and to his numerous disciples as C. S. Lewis;[651] and there are a number of similarities between the two men.[652] But where Chesterton was primarily a journalist, Lewis was an academic; and his love of the English literary tradition found expression in three substantial and scholarly works of a quite different temper from Chesterton.[653] Lewis was educated at English boarding schools before going up in 1917 to Oxford, where he remained for most of the rest of his life (though in 1954 he was elected to an English chair at Cambridge). In 1929 he became a Christian, famously describing himself as 'perhaps . . . the most dejected and reluctant convert in all England'.[654] In 1956 he married a divorced American, Joy Davidson, who died of cancer four years later; Lewis' *A grief observed* (1961) was to be one of the most influential books he wrote. He died on 22 November 1963.

C. S. Lewis was strongly influenced by three other writers with a fondness for literature and romance. The first was George MacDonald, whose book *Phantastes* Lewis first picked up at a railway station bookstall.[655] The second was J. R. R. Tolkien, a contemporary at Oxford, whose *The Lord of the Rings* was to become as popular as Lewis' Narnia stories and science fiction novels.[656] The third was Charles Williams (1886–1945), whose novel *The place of the lion* fascinated Lewis.[657]

Williams was born in London, the son of a foreign correspondence clerk. After education at St Albans and University College London, he entered the publishing business. Williams was also influenced by Chesterton, and like him had a deep love of English myth and tradition.[658] But he was also close to a range of esoteric and mystical writers such as A. E. Waite, whose interest in hermeticism and the occult had also influenced Evelyn Underhill. More significantly for our purposes, Williams was also influenced by Pseudo-Dionysius;[659] and he sought to hold together the 'negative theology' associated with Pseudo-Dionysius with the 'cataphatic' or affirmative theology of the mainstream tradition.[660]

One of Charles Williams' paramount interests was the work of Dante; and in this regard he in turn exerted an immense influence on Dorothy Leigh Sayers (1893–1957), scholar and playwright, but perhaps best known both as the author of successful crime fiction and as the translator of Dante's *Divine comedy*. Sayers was brought up in an East Anglian parish of which her father was incumbent.[661] After being educated at home she went to Somerville College Oxford in 1912. Her first detective story, *Whose body?*, was written in 1923. Her theological study *The mind of the Maker* (1941) explores the doctrine of the Trinity, in particular seeking to show how human creativity testifies to its truth.[662] Arguably her most famous work, a series of radio plays entitled *The man born to be king*, was broadcast in 1941 and published in 1943.

The journey into reality

Like Chesterton, each of these three writers reflects a concern to recover a healthy sense of wonder in the face both of the natural and the supernatural orders of reality. In a very early poem, 'Hymn in contemplation of sudden death' (1916), Dorothy Sayers writes:

> For every fair and useless thing
> That bids men pause from labouring
> To look and find the larkspur blue
> And marigolds of a different hue . . .
>
> For all things merry, quaint and strange . . .[663]

At the same time Sayers wanted to stress an unflinchingly realist Christianity:

> There will always be a few voices raised to protest against the introduction of 'reality' into religion; but I feel that the great obstacle in the path of Christianity today is that to so many it has become unreal, shadowy, 'a tale that is told.'[664]

Hence for her the power of Dante, whose every line 'is the record of an intimate personal experience; few men have ever . . . interpreted the universe so consistently in terms of their own self-exploring.'[665] She noted that in his *Paradiso*

> we find affirmed with the utmost clarity and consistency the fundamental Christian proposition that the journey to God is the journey into reality. To know all things in God is to know them as they really are.[666]

And she expressed vividly what it meant to reject this:

> If we refuse assent to reality: if we rebel against the nature of things and choose to think that what we at the moment want is the centre of the universe to which everything else ought to accommodate itself, the first effect on us will be that the whole universe will seem to be filled with an implacable and inexplicable hostility. We shall begin to feel that every-thing has a down on us, and that, being so badly treated, we have a just grievance against things in general. That is the knowledge of good and evil and the fall into illusion.[667]

Sayers condemned 'the nostalgia of childhood . . . the rejection of adult responsibility and the denial of all value to growth and time', which she saw as a common form of
escapism.[668] Above all, she wants to recover a whole Christianity, and like Chesterton
is virulently opposed to a boring one:

> Perhaps we are not following Christ all the way or in quite the right spirit.
> We are apt, for example, to be a little sparing of the psalms and the
> hosannas. We are chary of wielding the scourge of small cords, lest we
> should offend somebody or interfere with trade . . . Somehow or other, and
> with the best intentions, we have shown the world the typical Christian in
> the likeness of a crashing and rather ill-natured bore – and this is the Name
> of One who assuredly never bored a soul in those thirty-three years during
> which He passed through the world like a flame. Let us, in Heaven's name,
> drag out the Divine Drama from under the dreadful accumulation of
> slipshod thinking and trashy sentiment heaped upon it, and set it on an
> open stage to startle the world into some sort of vigorous reaction . . .[669]

Charles Williams similarly sought to combine both a pervasive awareness of spiritual reality and a positive evaluation of the physical, and especially of the body:

> The great world and energy of the body have been either deprecated or
> devotionalized; and by devotionalized I mean turned into a pale imitation
> of 'substance' [in Julian of Norwich's use of the term], of spirit; thus losing
> their own powers and privileges without, in general, gaining any others.[670]

This reverence for the physical is rooted in the medieval view of the Incarnation as the
culmination of God's plan for creation: 'the Incarnation is the point of creation, and
the divine "reason" for it.'[671]

We shall see below how Williams sought to relate the natural to the supernatural in a
Platonic and patristic manner. First it is worth noting Dorothy Sayers' stress on the
creativity of the word:

> Every word is a unique event: there is nothing exactly like it in the
> universe. Every word is an encounter in history: a meeting-place of images,
> each of which comes – like those Kings of Orient, who are shown assem-
> bling at the birthplace of the Word – bearing gifts, and attended by a long
> and glittering train of associates. Every word sits, like the city of Venice in
> her prime, at the meeting-place of east and west, land and sea, past and
> present, taking in and sending forth rich ladings, and functioning in the
> market-place of exchange. We can never permanently empty a word of all
> meanings save one: we can at most choose to restrict ourselves temporarily
> to a particular meaning in the context of a particular argument. We can
> never define one word or sentence in terms of another: we can at most find
> analogies between one unique event and another. For as a word is a unique
> event, so a sentence is a unique series of such events, and a work of art is a
> unique universe whose history bears no relation, except by analogy, to that
> of another. That is why it is impossible, in commenting or 'explaining' any
> work of art, to substitute the explanation for the work.[672]

This is a profoundly symbolist view of reality: everything, even the humble word, points to something greater beyond it. As C. S. Lewis puts it, 'the world which we mistake for reality is the flat outline of that which elsewhere veritably is in all the round of its unimaginable dimensions'.[673] For Sayers, what is needed to unlock it is the art of *contemplation*: 'the best that the interpreter can do is to contemplate the image with an open and a humble mind in the hope that it may communicate to him something of the reality which it images'.[674] In her view, Dante is supremely the poet of the 'Affirmative Way' – that is, the poet who articulates a rich image-based theology in which the ultimate divine reality can be apprehended, albeit to a limited degree, through particular images that reveal him. All God's creatures are images of him;[675] Christ, incarnate, uniquely images God, and through the sacraments continues to do so; and in the doctrine of the Trinity the unique image that is Christ takes its place within the Godhead:

> it is because of this eternal presence of the Image within the Godhead that it is possible to pursue the Way of Affirmation to the very confrontation of the soul with the immediate presence of God.[676]

C. S. Lewis puts the same point in a different way with reference to the medieval worldview:

> In modern, that is, in evolutionary, thought Man stands at the top of a stair whose foot is lost in obscurity; in this [medieval world-view], he stands at the bottom of a stair whose top is invisible with light.[677]

Charles Williams replaces Dante's (and originally Plato's) symbolic theology, in which the higher reality (lying above and behind the image) invariably draws the lower towards itself, with a more mutual dynamic: as Sayers herself puts it, 'we draw one another up by a continual exchange, passing one another, as it were, by turns upon the ladder of ascent, the higher always giving a hand to whoever is at the moment the lower'.[678]

Coinherence

This brings us to Williams' concept of coinherence. It has its origins in the patristic doctrine of the coinherence of the divine persons of the Trinity in each other.[679] The crucial point, for Williams as for the church fathers, is that 'co-inherence depends on individuality, as much as individuality on co-inherence'.[680] This interweaving of the individual and the corporate brings Williams to see cities as the natural focus for human fulfilment:

> The unexclusive life of the City . . . is everywhere vicarious life, up to the level of each capacity. It is as much the instinct of a gentleman as the climax of the saints. The 'bear one another's burdens' runs through all.[681]

To bear one another's burdens 'is not the reward of sanctity; it is a way of sanctity, but also it is the only way of bearable life'.[682] Hence Williams' stress on the concept of *exchange*, God's with ours through the Incarnation and ours with our neighbours by this bearing of one another's burdens, so that the whole Church becomes a reflection of the eternal mutual coinherence of the Trinity:[683]

So great a business of exchange and substitution fills the phrase 'bear ye one another's burdens' with a much fuller meaning than is generally ascribed to it. But that fuller meaning is no less practical than the usual meanings of being sympathetic and doing exterior acts 'of kindness and love.' It is very proper that they should be done. But that is because we ought to be 'members one of another' – *membra*, limbs, not members of the same society. Christians are not members of a club; they are 'members' of the Church, which is not a club.[684]

For Williams, this is the thrust of the great post-Communion prayer in the Prayer Book ('. . . that we are very members incorporate in the mystical body of thy Son, which is the blessed company of all faithful people . . . that we may continue in that holy fellowship, and do all such good works as thou hast prepared for us to walk in'). Williams comments:

> The 'good works which thou hast prepared for us to walk in' are those that belong to 'that holy fellowship'; they are therefore those peculiarly of exchange and substitution. They are prepared and they are there; we have only to walk in them. A little carrying of the burden, a little allowing our burden to be carried; a work as slow, as quiet, even as dull as by agreement to take up or give up a worry or a pain – a compact of substitution between friends – this is the beginning of the practice. The doctrine will grow in us of itself.[685]

In *The figure of Beatrice* Williams acknowledges that we can never know exactly how this coinherence works in practice:

> how body enters body, dimension supports dimension . . . we cannot tell; therefore we should more expressly long to understand the union of our nature with God's, that is, the Incarnation. This is at the root of that even physical co-inherence which is on this earth incapable of its full capacity.[686]

It is vital to note that Williams had in mind a doctrine with immediate practical implications. He applied his notion of coinherence to the Christian understanding of marriage, deploring the Church's preference for concentrating on the morals of marriage rather than on a healthy doctrine of love.[687] And Williams wrote more eloquently about love than about anything else, and specifically about the transforming power of romantic love as it found expression in Dante:

> Things intolerable outside a state of love become blessed within: laughter and love convert for a moment the dark habitations within the soul to renewed gardens in Eden. The primal knowledge is restored, and something like pardon restores something like innocence. The 'new life' exists. It cannot continue to exist permanently without faith and labour. Nothing that comes down from heaven can. But it renews nature if only for a moment; it flashes for a moment into the lover the life he was meant to possess instead of his own by the exposition in her [i.e. in his beloved] of the life she was meant to possess instead of her own.[688]

Hence one of the collects he composed for a marriage in 1938:

> Almighty and most merciful God, who by the glorious Incarnation and Atonement of Christ Jesus hast made men capable of eternal life: Increase among us the knowledge of the exchanges of Thy love, and from the common agony of our lives redeem us to the universal joy of Thy only City: through the fructiferous mediation of the same Jesus Christ our Lord and Saviour.[689]

The language may be overblown, but the principle is vital. By learning to live a life of deep mutual communion with others, a real and manifest bearing of one another's burdens, we not only discover our own deepest individuality: we also come to experience, through the Incarnation, an ever-deeper union of our own natures with that of God.

Images of God

There is a subversive dimension to this rich Platonic spirituality, and C. S. Lewis points it out. It is only in our play, 'our moments of permitted festivity', that we experience something of the life of Heaven. For the Christian, what seems least important here may in reality be supremely precious; for

> in this world everything is upside down. That which, if it could be prolonged here, would be a truancy, is likest that which in a better country is the End of ends. Joy is the serious business of Heaven.[690]

Interestingly, Dorothy Sayers manages to point to a spirituality of work by arguing that that too can express our identity as creatures made in the divine image. She writes a good deal about this;[691] human beings create, like God, not because they must but because they want to; *homo faber* 'cannot fulfil his true nature if he is prevented from making things for the love of the job; he is made in the image of the Maker, and he must himself create or become something less than a man'.[692]

One of the other implications of this kind of spirituality is a strong affirmation of the ubiquitous presence of God. C. S. Lewis shares Sayers' concern with contemplative attention:

> We may ignore, but we can nowhere evade, the presence of God. The world is crowded with Him. He walks everywhere *incognito*. And the *incognito* is not always hard to penetrate. The real labour is to remember, to attend. In fact, to come awake. Still more, to remain awake.[693]

This is not always easy. In *The Screwtape letters*, Lewis says

> Our [i.e. the devil's] cause is never more in danger than when a human, no longer desiring, but still intending, to do our Enemy's [God's] will, looks round upon a universe from which every trace of Him seems to have vanished, and asks why he has been forsaken, and still obeys.[694]

The theology of the image lends a particular dignity to human beings; and in a wartime sermon called 'The weight of glory' C. S. Lewis explores this from a different perspective. He suggests that the most obvious characteristic of the child (as indeed of the dog, or horse) is the desire to be praised.[695] Praise thus rapidly becomes flattery:

> but I thought I could detect a moment – a very, very short moment – before this happened, during which the satisfaction of having pleased those whom I rightly loved and rightly feared was pure.[696]

This longing to be affirmed and acknowledged is part of what it means to be human beings: it forms part of what Lewis calls our 'inconsolable secret'.[697] In this context, the promise of glory is crucial: for glory 'means good report with God, acceptance by God, response, acknowledgement, and welcome into the heart of things'.[698] It is this to which we can look forward. But there is a snag: our neighbour is destined for that as well. This leads Lewis to his lyrical conclusion:

> It is a serious thing to live in a society of possible gods and goddesses, to remember that the dullest and most uninteresting person you can talk to may one day be a creature which, if you saw it now, you would be strongly tempted to worship, or else a horror and a corruption such as you now meet, if at all, only in a nightmare. All day long we are, in some degree, helping each other to one or other of these destinations. It is in the light of these overwhelming possibilities, it is with the awe and the circumspection proper to them, that we should conduct all our dealings with one another, all friendships, all loves, all play, all politics. There are no *ordinary* people. You have never talked to a mere mortal. Nations, cultures, arts, civilisations – these are mortal, and their life is to ours as the life of a gnat. But it is immortals whom we joke with, work with, marry, snub, and exploit – immortal horrors or everlasting splendours. This does not mean that we are to be perpetually solemn. We must play. But our merriment must be of that kind (and it is, in fact, the merriest kind) which exists between people who have, from the outset, taken each other seriously . . . Next to the Blessed Sacrament itself, your neighbour is the holiest object presented to your senses. If he is your Christian neighbour he is holy in almost the same way, for in him Christ *vere latitat* – the glorifier and the glorified, Glory Himself – is truly hidden.[699]

Prayer

This brings us finally to the subject of prayer. In Lewis' *The Screwtape letters*, the Devil encourages a narrowly spiritual view of prayer. He tells Wormwood to make sure that the new Christian's prayers for his mother

> are always very 'spiritual', [i.e.] that he is always concerned with the state of her soul and never with her rheumatism . . . since his ideas about her soul will be very crude and often erroneous, he will, in some degree, be praying for an imaginary person, and it will be your task to make that imaginary person daily less and less like the real mother – the sharp-tongued old lady at the breakfast table. In time, you may get the cleavage so wide that no thought or feeling from his prayers for the imagined mother will ever flow

over into his treatment of the real one. I have had patients of my own so well in hand that they could be turned at a moment's notice from impassioned prayer for a wife's or son's 'soul' to beating or insulting the real wife or son without a qualm.[700]

This is a subtle and shrewd reflection on why so much prayer has so little effect. Lewis goes on to use Screwtape to point out a number of other important points about prayer: that structure and outward patterns of prayer matter, that the use and position of the body matters too.[701] And he warns of an over-reliance on feelings in prayer: the Devil wants Wormwood to keep Christians

> watching their own minds and trying to produce *feelings* there by the action of their own wills. When they meant to ask Him for charity, let them, instead start trying to manufacture charitable feelings for themselves and not notice that this is what they are doing. When they mean to pray for courage, let them really be trying to feel brave. When they say they are praying for forgiveness, let them be trying to feel forgiven. Teach them to estimate the value of each prayer by their success in producing the desired feeling.[702]

Screwtape wants Christians to pray to things rather than to God himself, and thus not to realize that it is only when thoughts and images are recognized as subjective and limited that true prayer can take place.[703]

In an appendix to his book *Miracles*, C. S. Lewis explores the question of how God can answer prayer. He argues that, being outside time, God sees everything in an eternal present; and that it is quite compatible with human freedom for God both to be able to foresee in advance what we shall request and to adjust the pattern of his creation in response to our prayers, if he so chooses. Rather than arguing for actions on God's part that are outright miracles, directly interfering with the course of the natural world, Lewis argues that *everything* that happens is providential: 'providence and Natural causation are not alternatives; both determine every event because both are one'.[704]

Spirituality and suffering

But this of course begs the question of why we suffer, and how we should respond when we do. Lewis writes movingly about the experience of waiting for medical results – what he calls

> the horrible by-products of anxiety; the incessant, circular movement of the thoughts, even the Pagan temptation to keep watch for irrational omens. And one prays; but mainly such prayers as are themselves a form of anguish.[705]

We should not feel guilty at such anxieties: 'the prayer in Gethsemane shows that the preceding anxiety is equally God's will and equally part of our human destiny'.[706] Lewis points out how Christ's Passion articulates universal experience: the prayer of anguish not granted; rejection by friends and religious groups, by the state and the people; and finally by God. With regard to this final dereliction, Lewis invokes the notion of creation as separation:

> If God will create, He will make something to be, and yet to be not Himself. To be created is, in some sense, to be ejected or separated. Can it be that the more perfect the creature is, the further this separation must at some point be pushed? . . . The 'hiddenness' of God perhaps presses most painfully on those who are in another way nearest to Him, and therefore God Himself, made man, will of all men be by God most forsaken?[707]

In several of her works, Dorothy Sayers reflects a similarly sensitive spirituality of suffering. In *He that should come* she has Balthazar, one of the Magi, say:

> If [God] is beside me, bearing the weight of His own creation;
> If I may hear His voice among the voices of the vanquished,
> If I may feel His hand touch mine in the darkness,
> If I may look upon the hidden face of God
> And read in the eyes of God
> That He is acquainted with grief.[708]

In *The devil to pay* she has someone say: 'There is no waste with God; He cancels nothing / But redeems all.'[709] And, in the most famous of her plays, *The man born to be King*, she has Jesus say in Gethsemane, quoting the Psalms:

> Out of the deep, O Lord, out of the deep . . . the deep waters . . . all thy waves have gone over me . . . It is the waiting that is so hard.[710]

Olive Wyon and the recovery of unity

Spirituality and ecumenism

The numerous attempts at organic Christian unity in England during the second half of the twentieth century nearly all ended in failure: the one striking success in this regard, the establishment of the United Reformed Church in 1972, did nothing to stem the numerical haemorrhage which continued apace in the new body.[711] But the movement towards Christian unity was one of the most positive responses to the horror of war and the rise of militant nationalism, even if its origins are to be found in the missionary endeavours of the Church.[712]

One of the issues raised in ecumenical spirituality was the question whether it was possible to attain a profound unity and harmony at a depth below that of mutually incompatible doctrinal formulations – a point Donald Nicholl explores with regard to the relationship between Christianity and other world faiths.[713] In 1964 Michael Ramsey suggested that

> In a depth below doctrinal thought and structure, heart speaks to heart. May there not be . . . a similar apartness in the realm of thought and nearness in the depth of religious meaning in the case of some of the cleavages about faith, justification, and the sacraments?[714]

Ramsey was influenced by Fr Herbert Kelly (1860-1950), founder of the Society of the Sacred Mission, an order of celibate priests within the Church of England.[715] Kelly (who also influenced William Temple) was committed to ecumenism, and above all to the reality of a God who was always above and beyond ecclesial formulations or individual spiritual experiences. At the early conferences organized by the Student Christian Movement, Kelly would enquire

> What does God *do*? Does God do anything? or is 'God' only a name for our ideals? There used to be a thing called theology, and it was about God. Now we have a thing called psychology of religion, and it's all about your nice feelings.[716]

And Ramsey commented, in 1960

> This is Kelly in a nutshell. The weight of his influence was this distinction between the Living God and man's thoughts about him, man's feelings derived from him . . . When once the conviction of the Living God is on top and felt to be greater than theological systems about him, then it is possible, without in the least wanting to disparage or disavow your own theological system, to find yourself in living contact with Christians of any and every kind.[717]

The recovery of unity: William Temple

Ramsey's question raises the issue of exactly what Christian unity ought to be, and hence of what spiritual path or paths might be expected to lead to it. Three different but complementary responses are worth outlining here. The first is that of one of Ramsey's predecessors as Archbishop of Canterbury, William Temple. Reflecting on chapter 17 of St John's Gospel, Temple says that

> the unity of the Church is precious not only for its utility in strengthening the Church as an evangelistic agent. It is itself in principle the consummation to which all history moves. The purpose of God in creation was, and is, to fashion a fellowship of free spirits knit together by a love in all its members which answers to the manifested love of God . . . The unity of the Church is something much more than unity of ecclesiastical structure, though it cannot be complete without this. It is the love of God in Christ possessing the hearts of men so as to unite them in itself – as the Father and the Son are united in that love of Each for Each which is the Holy Spirit . . . For His prayer is not only *that they may be one*; it is *that they may be one as we*. Before the loftiness of that hope and calling our little experience of unity and fellowship is humbled to the dust.[718]

It is to that far deeper intimacy that exists in the heart of the Trinity that Christians are called as they seek visible unity. Consequently, in Temple's view, the path towards that unity will be spiritual and personal, not institutional:

> Once again we are reminded how transcendent is that theme which alone deserves the name of Christian unity. We meet in committees and

construct our schemes of union; in face of the hideous fact of Christian divisions we are driven to this; but how paltry are our efforts compared with the call of God! The way to the union of Christendom does not lie through committee-rooms, though there is a task of formulation to be done there. It lies through personal union with the Lord so deep and real as to be comparable with His union with the Father.[719]

The recovery of unity: Lesslie Newbigin

A second response to the question of the nature of Christian unity and the means by which it might be attained is offered by the distinguished ecumenist Lesslie Newbigin, in a study of the nature of the Church.[720] He argues that the Church *experiences* the reality of the Holy Spirit in the lives of its members: hence St Paul's concern to draw Christians on from a preference for the more spectacular gifts of the Spirit to a deeper sense of the Spirit's 'more normal and abiding fruits.'[721] Newbigin calls for the traditional Catholic–Protestant tension about the work of the Holy Spirit to be enlarged by the inclusion of a Pentecostal perspective which stresses our experience of the Spirit's presence:[722]

> The apostle asked the converts of Apollos one question: 'Did ye receive the Holy Spirit when you believed?' and got a plain answer. His modern successors are more inclined to ask either 'Did you believe exactly what we teach?' or 'Were the hands that were laid on you our hands?', and – if the answer is satisfactory – to assure the converts that they have received the Holy Spirit even if they don't know it.[723]

It is only when we take seriously the reality of our own experience of the Spirit's presence and power that we begin to be able to understand exactly how the Spirit works in Church and world today.[724] This still leaves room for the Church's discernment of true and false spirits;[725] but 'we must take simply and seriously the truth that the Church is a communion in the Holy Spirit, and that He is no cypher, no abstract noun, but living Lord'.[726] For

> the supreme gift of the Spirit is not the spectacular power by which an individual may gain pre-eminence, but the humble and self-effacing love by which the body is built up and knit together.[727]

Newbigin underlines the tension in New Testament understanding of the Spirit's presence: it 'is both a real possession and a foretaste, an earnest of what is in store' – we are risen with Christ, yet await the resurrection.[728] We have to *live* this tension, not just state it;[729] and this brings us to the spiritual heart of the matter:

> *I live, yet not I; Christ lives in me* . . . The fundamental fact is death in order to live. The sinful, self-sufficient self must die to make room for Christ. But what is the new life which follows? It is not my old life resuscitated. It is Christ's life in me. Yet we cannot simply say that and leave it. *I* still live. Why is this? It is partly a matter of the paradox of having and yet not having . . . the paradox of the overlap of the ages. But it is more than this,

for even in the age to come the *I* will not simply be obliterated. Christ's life in me will still be also my life in Christ. What is to be obliterated is the self which is centred in itself, in order to make room for the self which is centred in Christ . . . The Church is called to be a union of men with Christ in the love of the Father whereby their separate beings are made one with that perfect mutual interpenetration in love, that perfect community which is the glory of God.[730]

The recovery of unity: Olive Wyon

Newbigin offers here a fine theological exploration of the inner spiritual nature of Christian unity. A third exploration of this theme, and one that leads us more explicitly to the subject of prayer, is provided by one of the most impressive contributors to the nascent spirituality of ecumenism in England: the Nonconformist scholar Olive Wyon (1881–1966).[731]

Wyon's approach to the spirituality of ecumenism can best be seen by beginning with her understanding of vocation. She resists the idea that God calls only the leisured and the privileged.[732] And this has implications for prayer: if we have no confidence in ourselves, we are likely to lack confidence in God. The opposite is also true: if we refuse to acknowledge the evil within ourselves, we shall be unable to pray. It was this refusal which, in Wyon's view, gave Hitler his opportunity:

> A great many of the people who followed Hitler were not abnormal. Most of them indeed were what everyone would call perfectly normal. But they did not know themselves, and they refused to see the evil in their own hearts.[733]

So a first requirement for prayer is a sense of God's active presence with us.[734] Too much prayer appears to presuppose a distant God, when Jesus shows us that God is near.[735] Wyon asks

> How is it . . . that our public worship is often so listless and dull? and our private prayers so thin and unsatisfying? Can it be that we have forgotten that God wants our worship? not as the homage of an inferior but as the love of the child in the Father's House.[736]

We can concentrate too much on *technique* rather than on practising the presence of God: 'a good deal of bewilderment about prayer is due to the fact that we are thinking more about *prayer* than about God.'[737]

The life of prayer, then, is not won by technique but by love. Wyon calls intercession 'a great mystery; no intellectual argument ever fully explains it to the mind. But to the heart that loves, it is a necessity.'[738] And in it

> we become aware of the desire of God, of the prayer of God, energizing in us, and we are drawn to intercede by the love of God Himself. For the love of God is like a stream which is ever flowing from God, and back to God again, drawing the world up to Himself.[739]

So intercession should begin with 'a definite "act" of union with this stream of God's love and power,' consciously seeking to unite our wills and hearts with that love:[740] one way to do that effectively is seriously to pray for those we do not like.[741] Good intercession involves *energy*, the energy

> with which God wills the salvation of mankind: this means that we must begin our intercession with worship, with an act of loving response to the One who is the whole meaning of life. One of the reasons for failure in this kind of prayer is our 'practical' habit of beginning with a list of names, or objects, which can be so deadly dull and uninspiring.[742]

It follows that good intercession will be hard work:

> In intercession our response to this divine effort [the groanings of the Spirit which cannot be uttered] will be our own effort to *care*, first of all, and then to overcome our disinclination to pray . . . The remembrance that the desire of God is a willed concentration will help us to be steadfast in joining our prayers to that divine movement.[743]

We may well find ourselves called to intercede for specific purposes or people; vocation applies to intercession as to everything else.[744] And it leads to new forms of outward service, for

> intercession is indeed a basic principle of human living: it expresses that corporate sense of community which is the real nature of human life; and it expresses that instinct to give to the point of sacrifice which is one of the deepest elements in our nature, fulfilled once for all by Christ on the Cross . . . Prayer, however personal and solitary, is never an individualistic activity.[745]

It is here that the ecumenical implications of Wyon's view of intercession become clear. Wyon believed that the world was 'waiting for a "revelation" of God in community. The Church is called to be this living community, in which all the barriers between man and man, class and class, race and race, are down for ever.'[746] And this process begins in prayer. She cites the Week of Prayer for Christian Unity in 1939 in Lyons, drawing hundreds of Protestants and Catholics together in prayer:

> as our desire for unity within the Church of Christ increases, so also shall we be moved to an ever more urgent desire for the righting of human wrongs . . . We are called to pray, and to work, for a new social and international order, informed by a spiritual purpose, in which every human being shall have full freedom to use all his gifts and faculties in the service of God.[747]

Alas, that ecumenical prayer in 1939 did not prevent the outbreak of world war a few months later. But Wyon is clear that prayer without corresponding love in action will be worthless: 'want of love to our fellow men and women is the root cause of all our failure in life and in prayer'.[748] And there is a far more important point still: for Wyon, the practice of true Christian prayer is *in itself* a subversive act, a challenge to contemporary totalitarian ideology; for to pray is to incarnate our nature and status as God's children, and thus to challenge totalitarians who live as though they were gods.[749] It is also to articulate our fundamental union one with another: thus when we pray the Our Father, we do so 'as members of the whole Family of God; and so . . . we are released from our self-centredness';[750] and our eucharistic worship similarly reinforces our sense of mutual interdependence, allowing us also to offer to God all our uncertainties and half-formed prayers and longings so that God can redeem them.[751]

Austin Farrer and the recovery of theology

Living the mystery

Among the twentieth-century figures responsible for holding theology and spirituality together at a time when they were in danger of moving further and further apart, Austin Farrer is prominent. He spent almost the whole of his working life as an academic and priest at Oxford University, culminating in his appointment as Warden of Keble College in 1960, where he remained until he died in 1968. He was a philosophical and biblical theologian whose works include substantial academic studies alongside devotional reflections and a collection of outstanding sermons.[752]

In his Bampton Lectures for 1948, subsequently published as *The glass of vision*, Farrer argued that the task of metaphysics 'is not with problems but with mysteries, and mysteries are not to be solved, but (always inadequately) to be described'.[753] The way to reconcile theology and spirituality is to recognize the irreducible mystery that lies at the heart of both; for 'the moving of . . . any men's minds by divine direction is . . . a profound and invisible mystery, as is the whole relation of the creature to the creator';[754] and the evidence of faith, never easily discernible, is paradoxically to be found in everything, but supremely in the connections between things.[755] We should therefore beware of too precise or propositional a defining of theological truth:

> a theme which stands out as clearly as any other in [St Mark's] passion narrative is that no man knows what to do with the divine when it falls into his hands: we are reminded of the Philistines in uneasy possession of the Ark of the Covenant.[756]

Farrer's is a faith which always allows room for doubt: and hence assurance is not my certainty of salvation, but God's assurance of me.[757] God is never at our disposal: 'it is part of the irony of the burial of Christ's body that men seek to wrap in the decency of funeral respect the flesh which God will immediately clothe with the radiance of glory, that mortality may be swallowed up in life'.[758]

Ultimately, then, the mystery at the heart of the Christian religion cannot be proved; it can only be lived. '*Solvitur immolando*, says the saint, about the paradox of the logicians. It is solved by sacrifice.'[759] And this points to the connection, not just between theology and spirituality, but between prayer and action:

> You can live your religion if you like; you can know the reality of God if you like; for God will rejoice to assist and infinitely over-reward whatever effort you will make. *Resolution* is the crucial point. That is the link by

which religious contemplation passes into practical action. From your prayers form simple resolutions – not, like the absurd resolutions of New Year's Day, resolutions for the next twelve months; but resolutions for the next twelve hours. Make them few enough to be practicable, and obey them for the sake of God himself. If you break them, repeat and renew them. What does God ask of me? is a part of every sincere prayer. By resolutions kept, men turn religious fantasy into the substance of living. By resolutions broken, men learn their weakness and are driven back on God. By resolutions renewed and kept they learn to live by him who says: 'my strength is made perfect in weakness' and 'my grace is sufficient for thee.'[760]

This of course is where poetry comes in; for Farrer, poetry as metaphor presents truth in a way that makes connections beyond the capacity of literal prose.[761] Metaphor *describes* reality; scientific language *analyses* it.[762]

Life in Christ

The fact that the heart of the divine is mystery does not mean there is nothing to be said about it. 'God is God, an infinite intensity of personal life.'[763] Hence the creative work of God finds its supreme expression in something personal: the life, teaching, death and resurrection of Jesus; and Jesus remains utterly central to Farrer's view of the spiritual life. And thus it follows that

the dead are not raised: immortalized men are not galvanized corpses. What is called the resurrection of the dead is a remaking of their life, in a stuff and in a fashion which are known to God alone. If we are made, we can be remade: he who created can create anew. Jesus Christ experimented with creation when he threw himself and all the world's hopes into nothingness, by the death on the cross.[764]

Now from this it follows that 'creation and crucifixion are the two poles of our faith, and each of them is God'.[765] Or, to put it another way,

Christ's life, and death, and resurrection, show us this, that through all our existence, and all the circumstances of it, God is drawing us up from destruction to everlasting life. And progress in the Christian way should mean this, that we learn more and more to experience our life as the saving work of God.[766]

But how do we do this? Farrer argues that 'when the supernatural occurs, something in the existing world is supernaturalized, for example, the manhood of Jesus Christ by union with the deity, or, to take a legendary instance, Balaam's ass by being enabled to speak.'[767] In our knowledge of our own existence there is some knowledge of God involved; 'it is because God's infinity is shadowed forth in finite existence that the knowledge of God as absolute being is natural knowledge to a finite mind.'[768] 'The idea of the supernatural is of a finite agent exceeding his natural power by higher assistance.'[769] Hence the finite does not exclude the infinite: in fact 'every mystery of religion, indeed one may say the very possibility of any spiritual religion, presupposes that it does not.'[770] Rather the mind must be thought of as placed between two presences: the simple presence of the infinite, and the changing and various presence of the finite. It has a natural tendency to become aware of both presences; but it cannot become aware of the infinite except by symbolizing it in terms of the finite.[771]

So spiritual perception works thus. First the mind appreciates some aspect of finite existence. Then 'there is a sublimer act, by which the finite act is itself appreciated as a symbol of the infinite'.[772] Prayer works similarly: just as physical contact is nothing godlike, yet through it supernatural power may be transmitted, so acts of prayer allow God to work supernaturally through the natural 'touching' of minds that takes place between the person praying and the person being prayed for.[773] 'It is not the touching, it is what the touching is made to convey – supernatural charity.'[774]

This intimate and delicate relationship between the natural and the supernatural is above all expressed in images, a theme which has a major role to play in Farrer's spiritual theology.[775] Human beings 'cannot conceive [of the word of God] except in images: and these images must be divinely given to him, if he is to know a supernatural divine act.'[776] We cannot just choose our own. Hence the role of revelation alongside reason in Christian theology: the choice, use and combination of the particular images employed by Christ is a matter of pure revelation: it 'must be simply a supernatural work: otherwise Christianity is an illusion.'[777]

It is important to recall here Farrer's insistence on the ultimate mystery and unpredictability of the divine; God is never susceptible of being domesticated. In a fine sermon on God's presence, Farrer recalls a colleague describing to him the Orthodox understanding of holiness, using an exceptionally vivid and contemporary image:

> The best way to describe it . . . is to call it a sort of spiritual air-raid drill. The divine presence is the point of explosive danger, and the moment of sacramental consecration is the moment of detonation. The ordinary citizens are protected by a solid stone screen, or rather wall, fencing them off from the altar, and they keep their heads well down to be on the safe side. Then there are the special anti-bomb personnel, the ministers equipped with special protective uniform, and specially trained, who enter the terrible enclosure with fear and wariness and go to the very point of danger. When the incident has been successfully neutralized, the deacon comes out and gives the all-clear to the congregation who get up and move about.[778]

This of course has strong Old Testament roots; and we might affect to despise its primitive fierceness. But it has something vital to teach us: that 'no people can think too highly of the holiness, the majesty of God, and what troubled [Old Testament worshippers] still troubles us: how we can live in immediate contact with God's holiness and not be destroyed by it.'[779]

In the New Testament, this notion of holiness is developed. Now *we* become the holy of holies: 'we are all priests and God is lodged in us; the New Testament says, in our actual bodies.'[780] But he dwells in us because he first dwells in Christ (here too Farrer's spirituality is firmly Christ-centred). And yet

Christ and the saints do not stand like the old Jewish priesthood as a screen between the holiness of God and us. We cannot push the duty of being worthy of God's indwelling off on to them. God in his mercy treats us all as one: one body of Christ in which the holiness of Christ, the single-minded devotion of Christ, is found. We are all bound together in that glorious body: Christ's self-sacrifice for us, and his continual prayers for us, hallow us and spread holiness upon us. In like manner the saints pray for us, and we pray for one another. In this whole body of the holy Church God resides.[781]

This stress on our incorporation into the communion of saints is another characteristic theme.[782] And our primary response to this reality is *repentance*, for we have nothing intrinsically good within ourselves other than what God can work within us.[783]

The mirror of the divine

We may, of course, not always experience the divine presence directly; and Farrer explores the issue of how precisely we experience God at the beginning of his first Bampton lecture.[784] Acknowledging his own failure to recognize within his experience the personalism advocated by Martin Buber and his followers (i.e. the direct personal sense of an encounter or colloquy with God), he describes himself as having been helped by Spinoza to find God in the secondary causes of life rather than necessarily directly:

> I would no longer attempt, with the psalmist, 'to set God before my face.' I would see him as the underlying cause of my thinking, especially of those thoughts in which I tried to think of him. I would dare to hope that sometimes my thought would become diaphanous, so that there should be some perception of the divine cause shining through the created effect, as a deep pool, settling into a clear tranquillity, permits us to see the spring in the bottom of it from which its waters rise. I would dare to hope that through a second cause the First Cause might be felt, when the second cause in question was itself a spirit, made in the image of the divine Spirit, and perpetually welling up out of his creative act.
>
> Such things, I say, I dared to hope for, and I will not say that my hope was in any way remarkably fulfilled, but I will say that by so viewing my attempted work of prayer, I was rid of the frustration which had baffled me before.[785]

In other words: a direct personal *experience* of God is not a *sine qua non* of authentic Christian spirituality. We may instead perceive or become aware of God as the source from which all our blessings flow. Thus later he says 'we can love a God whom we know by faith alone':[786] the veil that separates us from him is not blank, however impenetrable: 'it is painted with the image of God, and God himself painted it, and made it indelible with his blood'.[787] In a sermon, Farrer develops the analogy of gazing into the deep pool towards the spring that is God himself. We can only do this because

God reveals himself, not because we can see God by our own efforts; when we look deeply and closely, we see ourselves, but we see ourselves as Christ, and everything is transformed:

> What is this pool? Is it not the magic mirror spoken of by St James, into which a man looking beholds the face of his new birth, the image of Christ which he is to be by grace, not the image of what sin grafted on nature has made him? Here is the mirror-image which forms the face that looks upon it, instead of being formed by that face. O my God, to think that I may thus look into myself, and see not that cursed reflection of my own vanity which haunts me, but the likeness of Christ which thou hast predestined me to wear! Can it be indeed that if I will faithfully meditate and be still, if I will give my thoughts to thee to shape and govern, thou wilt prefigure Christ in them?[788]

The image of the mirror reflecting back Christ to us (as in 2 Corinthians 3.18) is another of Farrer's favourites, and he returns to it often.[789] The key point is that religion is the mirror-opposite, literally, of self-love: we look at the mirror and see, not ourselves, but Christ transfigured in us, and we in him. Hence the saint is not someone who 'is fully himself' but someone who 'has solved the problem of sincerity in the sole possible way by turning to God, the great I AM, and accepting the self his creator designed for him', a self that

> is not found by looking for it. We do not ask of God, 'What sort of person did you mean me to be?' – we say to him 'Lord, what wilt thou have me to do?'[790]

Farrer's spirituality is here a healthy antidote to the contemporary longing for self-fulfilment, or the notion that spiritual progress means becoming more and more fully what I want to be. Hence to go to church when we don't feel like it is to be driven back on the new life of our baptisms, a point he makes with power and eloquence:

> I must dig away the stony rubbish, and let out afresh the fountain of living waters, which God has opened there . . . We are loyal to the form for the honour of God, because he is gracious, because his mercy endures for ever, because there is nothing better that a man can do, than glorify him. But the keeping of the form drives us back upon the Spirit; and the Spirit fills the form with life. Then God walks in his temple, and the house is peopled with cherubim.[791]

'Religion is not self-improvement, or decent conduct or emotional worship. Religion is fidelity' – not just (or even primarily) our fidelity, but God's.[792] Christ 'came to take away the cold religion of duty, and to substitute the religion of delight. We are to do our duty – yes, but we are to delight in it.'[793]

For Farrer, to be spiritual is to see things as God sees them, to see them for what they are.[794] We ordinary mortals are stuck half way between heaven and earth when we pray, in a condition of frustration; the truly spiritual person is 'out and away: what God loves is lovely to him; he's up and after it'.[795] Again, Christ is both paradigm and saviour:

It was by being outside himself – by being ecstatic in the literal sense of that word that Jesus brought the life of the Blessed Trinity into our world; for it is in ecstasy and in mutual indwelling that the marvellous life of the Godhead consists, God our Father goes out of himself to be all in his Son – this is the first ecstasy: and the Son goes out of himself to live by that very indwelling of the Father in him – that is the second ecstasy. There is a third ecstasy when there is a creation, and God comes out of himself to be all and everywhere and all things in his creatures. It is the fourth ecstasy, when the creatures of God go out of themselves to be in the God who indwells them. But this ecstasy the creatures of God scarcely achieve, until the Son of God takes on the form of a creature, and lives therein the ecstatic life; and when he died on the cross, he gave it to us for a legacy . . . Ah, how much more he longs to give, than we to claim.[796]

Here too the Christ-centred nature of Farrer's spiritual theology is all-important. We die in order to live, unconditionally – not just in the sense of living by taking risks, but in the absolute and astonishing sense of being crucified with Christ:

Worldly wisdom says, 'Take reasonable risks,' but Christ says, 'Come and be hanged'; and that is no sort of worldly wisdom.[797]

This is, of course, much easier said than done. Farrer is acutely aware of how easily we take refuge in illusion – if only I were somewhere else, I could do this or that:

This is the great deception of the devil, to stop us loving, praying, working, now. It may be God's will you should fight your way out of your misfortunes; it cannot be his will that you should make them a reason to put off living as a child of God . . . No one is free but he who embraces the will of God, and shares in the great energy of love which makes and rules the world. Once we have seen that the will of God, here and now, is our bread and our happiness, what a light, what a liberty, shines on our path.[798]

This raises the question of the relationship between grace and freedom; and here too Farrer's thought is pervasively Christ-centred. He argues that providence and creation are inseparable:[799] God has made things the way they are, and this necessarily involves the risk of their suffering: infinite providence went to the making of the bird, as it did to the making of the mouse the bird eats. Again, it is only in Christ, in his cross and resurrection, that we see the ultimate end of creation – we could not infer it from what we see around us.[800] We must pray: 'Make me open to each thing and person in their turn, that I may not only love them, but be directed through the providences which speak in them.'[801] And thus

My believing in providence means that whatever happens it will be all right; not that one thing will happen rather than another.[802]

And grace is 'Jesus Christ entering us, Jesus Christ under the skin, the sacrifice of Jesus and the resurrection of Jesus spreading and fulfilling themselves in us.'[803] Grace is what causes us to reach out to God: 'before we touch the cross, Christ has shouldered it; before we shape a prayer, Christ has prayed it.'[804] And in Christ's radical freedom we see paradoxically someone utterly transparent to God: we see God himself in action. So with us: when we are most completely transparent to God's will, we are most completely free to be ourselves.[805] But that freedom was bought at terrible cost; and so is ours. 'The body you receive in this sacrament accomplished its purpose by nailing to a tree. You are to become this body, you are to be nailed; nailed to Christ's sacrificial will. The nails that hold you are God's commandments, your rules of life, prayers, confessions, communions regularly observed.'[806] This leads Farrer to a vigorous denunciation of the contemporary insistence on rights:

> The error of the unmerciful servant in Christ's parable is that he asserts his rights. He has a right to the recovery of his debt, and a right to the assistance of the law. He insists on having what is due to him, and he gets his due – he gets the prison and the torment. Perhaps hell is for those who ask for it; to those who claim their rights God gives their deserts, the rest he handles not in accordance with their merits but in accordance with his mercy. We all think we have rights – rights to so much pleasure and ease, rights to be let alone, rights to spend most of our money on ourselves, rights to receive apologies, rights to get our own back, rights to neglect other people's cares and concerns unless we have a fancy to meddle with them. Having rights is damnation; salvation is the receiving of Christ's body and blood, as paupers existing on the dying charity of the Son of God. We are not our own; we are bought with a price.[807]

This brings us to the mystery of the divine love. Farrer emphasizes the transforming effect of God's love in a typically arresting and thought-provoking way:

> Many truths of religion will bear endless meditation, but this above all; we can recall it as often as we pray, that God holds our love for him incomparably more dear than we hold the love of those who are dearest to us . . . By making a friend of a child we extend to him what belongs properly to our equal and by making friends of us our Father and our God extends to us by a stretch incomparably wider what belongs uniquely to his co-equal Son. If God's love for us were all the love there was, then divine love would never have been. It is only because divine love has a natural object that it overflows to embrace an adopted object. We are the children of God by adoption, the eternal Son of God is Son by nature.[808]

But how are we to love God, whom we have not seen, and perhaps not directly experienced?

> If we are to love God, we must feel him in the whole substance of our life: we cannot love disembodied ghosts, and the whole world pressing in on us is the body, or better, let us say, the hand, through which God upholds, directs, checks and caresses us.[809]

If we can only love God through the blessings we receive we become like Job, baffled and angry when these are taken away. 'Without Christ's revelation of redemptive suffering, and everlasting life, we should lack the voice which interprets to us the action of God's mysterious hands.'[810]

Spirituality and the Eucharist

And it is supremely in the Eucharist that we experience this revelation and make it our own. It is perhaps here that Farrer's thoughtful and searching divinity achieves its highest articulation.[811] In one of his eucharistic meditations, he says: 'Love shares flesh and blood with us in this present world, that the eyes which look us through at last may find in us a better substance than our vanity.'[812] This is what he writes for Trinity Sunday:

> Belief in the Trinity is not a distant speculation; the Trinity is that blessed family into which we are adopted. God has asked us into his house, he has spread his table before us, he has set out bread and wine. We are made one body with the Son of God, and in him converse with the Eternal Father, through the indwelling of the Holy Ghost.[813]

And (for Trinity 4):

> The gift of the Holy Ghost closes the last gap between the life of God and ours. Our Father and Maker certainly underlies and sustains our existence at every point, and yet an impenetrable veil hides him from us. The veil has no thickness, and yet we cannot see through it; his life is his, and our life is ours. The Son of God steps through the veil, clothed in our nature; he becomes one of us, he takes his place beside us in this very sacrament. Nevertheless the more Jesus Christ is revealed as a man, the more distinct he is from us, for each of us is another man. But the Holy Ghost is given by the Father and the Son to be our very soul. When we allow the love of God to move in us, we can no longer distinguish ours and his; he becomes us, he lives us. It is the firstfruits of the Spirit, the beginning of our being made divine.[814]

This process is costly; and Farrer commends the practice of sacramental confession in order to assist it. Here too, what we receive is Christ himself:

> To feed us with his body, he gives us bread and wine. To inform us with his mind, he gives us the Scriptures. To confront our sins, and to speak our pardon, he uses a man of flesh and blood . . . And I wish I could convey to those who do not know by experience, how much happiness, and what life-giving power, resides in this sacrament. But whether you find Christ in his priest, or somehow in your heart, do not neglect confession or go without the assurance of forgiveness; it is the everlasting spring of renewal, the miracle that does not fail.[815]

Elsewhere Farrer makes it clear that one person's dis-ease or sinfulness affects everyone else's too. Reflecting on the woman with the haemorrhage who touches Christ's hem, he notes that Jesus could not have felt her touch: fingers on a hem swinging loose make no impress.[816] It was Christ's spirit 'which felt the touch of faith'.[817] Similarly, my spiritual disease affects, even disquiets, my neighbours, even though they don't know the source of the disturbance. 'I contribute my mite to the sum of sadness, the impersonal mist by which we darken each, and which we take to be the air of the world.'[818] It isn't: it is the sum total of our dis-ease. 'Let me then, like the woman in her impurity, reach for the hem of Christ's garment, that I may touch heavenly virtue, and the river of death which runs from me may be stayed.'[819] And to touch Christ in this way is to participate in the healing of others:

> When I touch Jesus Christ, I touch him who touches all; when his virtue comes into me, there runs in me that which clears all eyes and enlivens all hearts. While my hand supports and caresses my own head my feeling is a circuit returned upon itself, but when I stretch out my hand and touch Christ, the circuit of affection runs through all creatures, and especially through those who love him.[820]

The theology and practice of prayer

Something needs to be said in conclusion about Farrer's understanding of prayer. 'To pray is to confront the will of God.'[821] Farrer quotes St Vincent de Paul, who asked some young peasant girls:

> 'What do you do when you pray?' . . . 'Father,' a girl replied, 'I listen to God.' – 'You could not do better,' he said, 'only would it not be more correct to say, you listen for God? You put yourself in his presence, and you take up an attitude of devout attention. That is all you can do. But God will make you aware, as it pleases him, of what he means you to know concerning his will.'[822]

In prayer, we bring to God all our desires – the bad ones, to repent of them; the good ones, to have them stretched and exercised by laying them before him; and the indifferent ones. Of the latter Farrer says

> Do not leave them wholly out, when you come to God, for they are most of you; but talk to God about the things that really concern you, even though they are neither directly to be repented of, nor directly to be made into prayers; but let them find their place, and learn their true proportion, in relation to God's holy will.[823]

On unanswered prayer, Farrer has a musical analogy that articulates exactly God's answer to Job:

> Suppose a musical composer were conducting his own newly written symphony; and suppose the little man who does the drums were suddenly to put up his hand, and ask to have the score altered – he hadn't a sufficiently interesting part. What could the composer do, but explain to him the structure of the piece? And what answer can our prayers or wishes discover, other than this – to be told to study the way the world goes, and why?[824]

There is a visual element in Farrer's understanding of prayer, as in his spiritual theology.[825] 'The plainest thing I can say is that to look at our Lord just means to talk to him in all seriousness about himself':[826] *this* is Christian contemplation, pithily articulated. Good prayer means learning to see clearly what is really there:

> Above all, we are blind: blindfold in our prejudice, blinkered by our preoccupations, drugged in our self regard: we do not see the glory of God. And above all, God longs to open our eyes. Here at least we know what the cure is. All we have to do is to practise looking through the eyes of Christ: and this is the contemplative art of prayer, when, invoking his aid, we turn over quietly what we know of God or have just read in the Scriptures, and try to see our lives and our neighbours in the light of it, and, what we have seen, to love and to adore.[827]

Elsewhere, Farrer touches the heart of the Christian view of creation:

> Every woman and every man, and I dare say every beast and every blade of grass, is the work of an almighty hand, which has poured into it an intensity of life, and an individuality of being, and a variety of perfections above what the angels of God can ever hope fully to grasp. We go about most of our time with our eyes glued to the floor, or looking up only to take in a dull façade of things, unable to penetrate and seize the living being in which the Creator himself is expressed. It takes the violent passion of love to break down the dull custom of incomprehension, the blindness of the eyes and the hardness of the heart.[828]

In view of all this, it is no surprise to be reminded by Farrer that true prayer is hard work; and both work and prayer are 'the constant object of the devil's attack', which is why we give so little effort to either.[829] 'No one will ever pray, to call it prayer, who does not keep some time inviolable for the purpose, however plausible the devil may be that day with his suggestions of doing something else' – just as no one will ever work who does not keep regular hours set apart for just that.[830] And the cost of prayer is underlined in a fine meditation on fasting:

> Why have men always fasted? Originally, perhaps, to move the pity of heaven by a sort of hunger-strike; to show that their prayers were in earnest. But it is as necessary now as ever it was that we should show our prayers to be in earnest. God bestows himself on those who desire him. What then is the evidence that we desire him? Not words alone, feeling still less. Nothing but action can give seriousness to our desire for God. We are in earnest if for God's sake we displease ourselves. If we abstain from needless indulgence, much more, if we find the weak point in our service of God, and attack it with resolution. Resolutions are no good, unless we are prepared to find them broken, and to renew them, every day. It is no fast if it is easy. Displease yourself, and have fellowship with Christ. For he pleased not himself, and his prayers were heard. And for what did he pray? He prayed for, and obtained, our salvation.[831]

Intercession too has to do with confronting the will of God; for it takes place when our minds flow into others' minds by means of God's will: 'we place our hearts at the disposal of God's will, to spread that influence which he has placed in us in support of our friends' happiness or virtue.'[832] And God can use our prayers for others, because when we do pray for others we come so close to God's own will that we allow it to work through us.[833] Intercession is 'an identification of ourselves with what God is working, and has been at work upon from the beginning.'[834] And it too is a serious business:

> It is not much use . . . praying for people [who are in some kind of trouble or need] if your prayer consists in telling God to make them good Christians. We should do better, if we were telling God all the good and delightful qualities he has put into our friend, and were thanking him for them with all sincerity. When you have blessed God for your friend, you can go on to pray for his blessing by God. This is the sort of prayer that breaks down barriers.[835]

Once again, the Eucharist offers the best of all opportunities for intercessory prayer: 'Let us not offer this holy sacrifice without praying for some other man, as though we were that man himself. It is an excellent thing, indeed, often to say all the prayers of the eucharist in the place and person of another man saying them; being that man in God's sight, so far as we know how.'[836]

Conclusion

There are occasional moments when Farrer's long years in the academic milieu suggest a slight constriction of his perspective – as when he follows Plato in taking for granted a hierarchy in human activity, so that the contemplation of philosophical truth is by definition a 'higher' act than picking fruit.[837] But that in no way makes his spirituality world-denying:

> Does our religion identify God's will with the existing set-up either in nature or in society? Emphatically *no*. Christ came to transform the world, not to conform to it, and the transformation was to be physical as well as moral.[838]

Elsewhere he recalled Amos complaining about religion as being 'nothing but a nuisance. Men offered sacrifice instead of making restitution. He would find much of the same folly among us, when prayers for peace and justice are made a substitute for action.'[839] Farrer's reflections on the spiritual life spring from an extraordinary combination of intellectual precision with deep and attentive prayer. It is divinity in the best sense of the word – and *Christian* divinity too, rooted in the person and nature of Christ as revealed to us in scripture. Perhaps (dare one say it?) it is also *Anglican* divinity of an exemplary kind, uniting head and heart in a spirituality of uncompromising integrity in which every sentence, and almost every word, has something significant to tell us – and something that will not only *teach* us, but *form* us as well. Take his reflections on the nature of thanksgiving:

We may think that we worship God because he is infinitely greater than we; but that is not why we worship God. The eternal Son is the perfect worshipper of the eternal Father, and he is not less than the Father, he is equal with him. He has a better reason than we have for thankful adoration; the Father has given him more than he has given to us; he has given him as much as he has himself. The Son thanks the Father for pouring into him the whole divine life, and he has the whole divine life in which to live out his thanks. We should do well, if we could thank God for all we are, with all we are. He thanks God for all he is with all that God is, for he also is God. Into his perfect worship of the Father Christ takes us up, by making us living parts of his worshipping body.[840]

And here is Farrer on the use of the Bible for prayer, in a passage that is surely the quintessence of Anglican divinity:

We can find the heart and substance of the work of God, which is Christ, by praying the scenes of the Gospel. Set Jesus before you in any one of the great scenes of his life. He stands in the waters of Jordan and accepts his calling to so strange a work. He conquers temptation in the wilderness. He calls disciples to share his calling . . . Above all, there are the scenes of his passion, and his glorious resurrection. Take any such scene, with the written word to help you – and – this is the great point – do not begin preaching yourself a sermon on your duty as resulting from what you read but do your best to go into the mind and heart of Jesus as he is there presented, and there occupied. See what his attitude is, what is the set of his will and the movement of his love towards his Father or his fellow men: and identify yourself, let yourself go with it. That requires no self-consciousness, no separate and special doing. We identify ourselves with what we adore; the heart that can love Christ is in Christ's keeping.[841]

Michael Ramsey and the recovery of glory

Introduction

Few church leaders in the modern era had the time to make a significant and enduring contribution to the spiritual life of their contemporaries: ironically, their workload increased as the number of their flock decreased. But one or two unquestionably did: P. T. Forsyth, William Temple, Basil Hume and a few others succeeded in holding together the spiritual and the institutional in a remarkable way. Another to do so was for a while a pupil at Repton School, where Temple had once been headmaster (1911–14), and where another future archbishop of Canterbury, Geoffrey Fisher, was also headmaster. His name was Arthur Michael Ramsey.[842]

In 1956 Ramsey wrote this about the great nineteenth-century theologian F. D. Maurice:

[Maurice] was able to be a pioneer precisely because he refused to succumb to the modernisms of his time, and because he drank deeply from a theology learnt from the Greek Fathers, from the Catholic order, from St John, and from the Gospel of God. He enabled others to build because he chose himself to 'dig.' And the English church can again lead the way in the problems which confront it only if it digs down to its own foundations, which are the Gospel of God, the sacramental life, and the soundest learning that its clergy and laity can possess.[843]

Most of that could as well be said of Ramsey himself. Like Maurice, his theology was firmly rooted in biblical and patristic scholarship and devotion; like Maurice also, he was deeply concerned about the major issues of his day. He was actively involved in politics while at Cambridge, where he was also drawn both to Anglo-Catholic worship and to William Temple's brand of intelligent and socially committed Anglicanism.[844] By temperament shy and ungainly, Ramsey became successively Regius Professor of Divinity at Cambridge (1950–2), Bishop of Durham (1952–6), Archbishop of York (1956–61) and Archbishop of Canterbury (1961–74). Among his books are two of particular significance for spirituality: *The glory of God and the Transfiguration of Christ*, and a late work, *Be still and know*, which exemplifies Ramsey's pithy, precise but profoundly spiritual mind.

The life of Christ and the life of the Church

There is a pervasively corporate tone to Ramsey's spirituality: the Church has an essential part to play.[845] And that part becomes clear only when it is itself seen in the light of the person, teaching, death and resurrection of Jesus. The central conviction of his *The Gospel and the Catholic Church* is that 'the meaning of the Christian Church becomes most clear when it is studied in terms of the Death and Resurrection of Jesus Christ'.[846] The relevance of the apostolic Church consisted precisely in its pointing to the death of the Messiah,

> and to the deeper issues of sin and judgement – sin in which the Christians had shared, judgement under which they stood together with the rest of mankind. In all this the Church was scandalous and unintelligible to men, but by all this and by nothing else it was relevant to their deepest needs.[847]

'And by nothing else' – the claim is bold, counter-cultural even, yet underpinned by Ramsey's conviction that Christ's death is precisely death to the self; and 'the death to the self *qua* self, first in Christ and thence in the disciples, is the ground and essence of the Church'.[848] But this death, which happened *outside* the disciples, has to become an event *within* them.[849] And the best commentary on what that means, and how that happens, will be 'found in the saints whose hidden life has been the response to the fact of their Baptism'.[850]

We thus have the lineaments of Ramsey's understanding of the spiritual life: the truth of Jesus Christ, as it is lived and embodied in the Church and appropriated in the life of individuals through participation in the sacraments and a willingness to die to self. It follows that for Ramsey individualism 'has no place in Christianity, and Christianity verily means its extinction'.[851] Indeed Ramsey goes further: for the Christian to 'cling to the immediacy of his own experience of Christ, and so, in the very midst of the Body of Christ, to be ensnared into an individualism and self-satisfaction which belie the truth about the one Body' is dangerous.[852] In fact Ramsey is suspicious of a spirituality which emphasizes our present experience of Christ but 'ignores the importance, for belief and conduct, of the historical coming of Jesus in the flesh and the historical society which links them to that coming':[853] this is to play into the hands of a narrow subjectivism, a 'glory to me' rather than 'glory to God' religion, a danger emphasized in Ramsey's view by the First Letter of St John.[854]

It also follows that the springboard for the spiritual life of Christians is baptism, through which we become God's children.[855] And baptism is no turning from the world: rather it is a turning *to* it with mind and heart renewed.[856] And it is that because it is itself rooted in the mystery of the Resurrection, an event of cosmic significance. The Resurrection of Jesus is a re-creation: the light that shines out of darkness, the glory of God in the face of Christ (2 Corinthians 4.5–6), reproduces and recreates anew the light at the dawn of all creation: 'a new world has dawned, and the Christians belong to it already.'[857]

Resurrection and glory

This is the context, both cosmic and corporate, in which we are to understand the spiritual life. And two rich theological themes will be seen to predominate in Ramsey's understanding of it: resurrection and glory. Both, however, are far from any easy triumphalism, for both emerge from suffering. Ramsey notes that in the Eucharist the *Sanctus* ('Holy, holy, holy . . .') of the liturgy 'immediately precedes the eucharistic action in which the glory of the Cross of Christ is set forth'.[858]

Ramsey notes how in the New Testament the Greek word *doxa* (which originally denoted human reputation or opinion) comes to denote the glory of the person of Christ, whose divinity is revealed in both his transfiguration and his crucifixion.[859] St Paul speaks of 'the glory of God in the face of Jesus Christ';[860] for St John, it is in the mutual self-giving of Father and Son that the deepest meaning of 'glory' lies – not in something they award themselves, or simply possess intrinsically.[861] Thus 'the glory seen in the works of Jesus is a glory whose secret the Passion ultimately discloses'.[862] This mutual self-giving finds its culmination in what Ramsey prefers to call the 'prayer of consecration' (rather than the priestly prayer) of Christ in John 17, where the mutual self-giving of Father and Son is extended to incorporate the disciples too within the same dynamic – and also all those who through them will come to believe.[863] 'It is by the humiliation of the Son's winning of glory in the toils of history that the eternal glory of the divine self-giving is most signally disclosed.'[864]

Nowhere in scripture is that 'eternal glory of the divine self-giving' more vividly set forth than in the story of the Transfiguration, another of Ramsey's favourite themes.[865] He notes that the Greek word translated as 'transfigured' denotes a profound change of form;[866] the disciples who are present when this happens to Jesus are given a foretaste of what at the end of time will become manifest to all the citizens of heaven.[867] He also notes that it was while praying that Jesus was transfigured:[868] 'we do not know that it is a prayer of agony and conflict like the prayer in Gethsemane, but we know that it is a prayer near to the radiance of God and the prayer of one who has chosen the way of death'.[869] In short, Jesus carried his troubles and conflicts with him to the mountain-top:

It was the transfiguration of the whole Christ, from his first obedience in childhood right through to the final obedience of Gethsemane and Calvary. The disciples could not grasp this at the time, but the writings of the apostolic age were to show that the link between the suffering and the glory came to be understood as belonging to the heart of the Christian message.[870]

The transfiguration of suffering occurs in Christian life when people respond to suffering with courage and 'an outgoing love and sympathy'.[871] When this happens,

> circumstances are transfigured. Something blocks your path, some fact of life or person or obstacle which is utterly thwarting and frustrating... But when it is seen in a larger context, and that context is Jesus crucified and risen, it is in a new orbit of relationships and while it remains, it remains differently. A phrase of St Paul in 2 Corinthians 4 seems to interpret the experience, when he contrasts our 'light affliction' with the 'exceeding weight of glory', the one belonging to time and the other to eternity. Such is the transforming of circumstances, not by their abolition but by the lifting of them into the orbit of a crucified and risen Jesus.[872]

Again, this cosmic context is characteristic of Ramsey's spirituality. And, just as Jesus is transformed at the Transfiguration, so must we be; as St Paul says, we respond to the self-giving generosity of God by *presenting* our bodies as a living sacrifice, by refusing to be *conformed* to this world, and by being *transformed* towards Christ by the gift of a new mind:[873]

> Through the transforming and the receiving of a new mind it becomes possible to discern what is the will of God and what are those things describable as good and perfect. Here indeed is a searching analysis of the transforming of human lives.[874]

How does this transformation take place? We have seen that for Ramsey the eternal glory of God is supremely manifested on the Cross, 'whereby the Father glorifies the Son, and the Son the Father. And, as with the Name, so with the Glory, it is to be found *within* the Christians' – for these words speak both of a redemptive action *and of an indwelling power*.[875] And that indwelling power is primarily appropriated in and through the sacraments of the Church: baptism first (as we have seen), then the Eucharist. By eating the bread and drinking the cup Christians are brought within the death of Christ: it becomes something *within* them, not simply external to them.[876] 'By sharing in the broken body and in the blood outpoured, the disciples will find interpreted both the crucifixion and the whole divine creation whose secrets the crucifixion unlocks.'[877]

Ramsey stresses the sacrificial dimension of the Eucharist:

> God in Christ offers; the Church His Body beholds the offering in all its costliness, and is drawn into it. The sacrifice is the action of God in Christ and in His Body.[878]

Here too the emphasis is on how we may appropriate in our own lives what the Prayer Book calls the 'fruits of our redemption'. Ramsey makes the same point about priesthood: it too must be an event *within* Christians, not simply some external rank or privilege conferred upon them.[879]

The prayer of the Church

Ramsey locates all Christian prayer, including the divine office, within a eucharistic framework; for all prayer forms links between one Eucharist and the next.[880] In fact Ramsey goes further:

> The Christian does not share in the Liturgy in order to live aright; he lives aright in order to share in the Liturgy. For the Liturgy is not an exercise of piety divorced from common life, it is rather the bringing of all common life into the sacrifice of Christ.[881]

And our natural response to that sacrifice is the offering of praise. In his exploration of glory, Ramsey stresses that human response to the divine glory is, in scripture, the act of giving glory back to God.[882] 'When men glorify Yahveh they do not add to His glory. They acknowledge it, submit to it, set their affections upon it, seek its greater manifestation, pray and give praise for it.'[883] And God's glory in creating the world and delivering his chosen people through the Exodus is not forgotten in the New Testament:

> In a truly catholic worship the joyful access of Christians to a Father and the thankfulness of Christians to a Saviour are interpenetrated by the adoration offered by the creature to the Creator. Herein is the blending of action and passivity, of movement and rest, which belongs to the tradition of the worship of the Catholic Church.[884]

To pray, then, is first and foremost to be in the presence of God;[885] but it is also to seek conformity with the divine will, which must include prayer for the coming of the Kingdom, for the conversion of both persons and society.[886] Hence to intercede 'is to bear others on the heart in God's presence'.[887] Prayer is a form of converse, listening as well as speaking; and meditative prayer has a key role in helping to remind us of this.[888]

It is not surprising to find that for Ramsey prayer is never individual or private: the prayer of the Holy Spirit links the prayer of Jesus and the prayer of Christians who make Jesus' prayer their own. This is what is meant by the 'fellowship' of the Holy Spirit: it means a participation in, a sharing of the Spirit's life.[889] As we have seen, prayer finds supreme expression in the Eucharist, in corporate worship:

> It is greatly to be desired that those who care specially for liturgy, and plan it, would give more care to the relation between liturgy and personal prayer and meditation. If every spare moment within and around the liturgy is filled with music and activity much is lost in the linking of liturgy to the meditative and contemplative aspects of the Christian life.[890]

In his exploration of prayer, Ramsey constantly interweaves the themes of suffering and glory. In *Be still and know* he again comments on John 17, arguing that Jesus prays that he may give glory to the Father 'by showing in the crucifixion the self-giving love which is the secret of glory from eternity'.[891] But here, perhaps more than anywhere else, it is vital to see that by becoming incorporated in Christ's life and making our own its self-giving love, we also open ourselves to all who suffer and draw them too into our prayer; and hence

> the prayer with beautiful buildings and lovely music must be a prayer which also speaks from the places where men and women work, or lack work, and are sad and hungry, suffer and die. To be near to the love of God is to be near, as Jesus showed, to the darkness of the world. That is the 'place of prayer.'[892]

This emphasis on the secular context of prayer is strengthened by the corporate nature of Ramsey's spirituality. He commends the Orthodox understanding of the communion of saints: in their liturgy,

> while the claims of sanctity are uncompromising for God is holy, there is no rigid frontier between saints in glory, saints who are being cleansed in Paradise [= Purgatory] and saints now struggling with their sins. To Western ideas, where praying *for* the departed and praying *to* the saints are somewhat separate, this Eastern language is striking. In the family of Jesus all pray for all and all ask for the prayers of all amidst the unique glory of Jesus.[893]

This in turn enlarges the perspective of our intercession: 'if . . . our prayer is shaped by the giving of glory to God in the quest of his will and his kingdom, then we may be lifted out of ourselves in the company of those who in Paradise and heaven seek that glory and reflect it.'[894] Furthermore,

> Our prayer looks towards the weak as well as towards the strong, and if we are faithful it will reach both ways since the glory of Christ is always one with the agony of his compassion. Such is the meaning of 'I believe in the Communion of Saints.'[895]

Conclusion

Michael Ramsey shares with Anglo-Catholics like Gabriel Hebert a strong emphasis on the transforming power of Christian worship: the liturgy is the key to the transformation of society as well as that of individuals.[896] But he draws from Protestant sources too. His studies of Luther and Calvin are judicious;[897] he helps to dispel the common illusion that all Protestants are individualists, and notes Calvin's emphasis on the significance of the ordained ministry as integral to the life and being of the Church.[898] Though firmly liberal in political terms, he criticized liberal theology for neglecting the transcendence of God and the dawn of a new creation in the redeeming work of Christ in its enthusiasm for secular ideas of progress. 'It is the message of the Bible, in all its richness, that the people of our generation need.' Above all, however, he stresses the uniquely Anglican formulation:

The meaning of the church of England [may] be stated thus: 'Here is the one Gospel of God; inevitably it includes the scriptures and the salvation of the individual; as inevitably the order and the sacramental life of the Body of Christ, and the freedom of thought wherewith Christ has made men free.' Translated into practice this means that the parish priest has a heavy responsibility; he must preach the Gospel and expound the scriptures, and he must also proclaim the corporate life of the Church and the spiritual meaning of its order. In every parish the Prayer-Book entitles the laity to hear the Gospel preached, and the scriptures expounded, and also to receive the full sacramental teaching of the historic Church including the ministry of Confession and Absolution for those who desire it. For the Anglican church is committed not to a vague position wherein the Evangelical and the Catholic views are alternatives, but to the scriptural faith wherein both elements are of one.[899]

If this sounds churchy, Ramsey reminds his readers of the Bible's own corrective in commenting on another of his favourite scriptural texts (the Letter to the Hebrews):

In the old sin offerings, the body of the animal was not eaten but was utterly destroyed outside the encampment. So, too, Jesus utterly rejected was put to death outside the city. Go out to him, that is the summons to Christians, go out to him and share his reproach and rejection.[900]

THEMATIC SPIRITUALITY

In order to do justice to the increasingly pluralist nature of English society in the twentieth century, some account needs to be given of a few of the principal themes which shaped the spirituality of the age, and which cannot be covered within denominational boundaries, or indeed in terms of the more traditional kinds of spiritual discourse within the context of the Church. In the second half of the twentieth century, 'spirituality' came to be used to refer to anything which was believed to nurture or comfort the human spirit, from aromatherapy to the possession of a pet.

If we are to remain broadly faithful to the notion of spirituality adumbrated in the first chapter of volume 1 of this work, we need to define the term with reference to those enduring spiritual realities which all the great world faiths (and other ideologies too) have identified as indispensable for human fulfilment: love, healing, forgiveness, justice, peace, and the search for mature and caring relationships. In short, it may be possible to conceive of 'spirituality' without religion; but it is impossible to conceive of it without morality, unless it is to be evacuated of almost any meaning at all. Even within these very broad parameters, space forbids the examination of more than a small number of these; but even this brief overview may serve to illustrate the unprecedented diversity of contemporary life, and point to some of the directions in which English spirituality was moving as the second Christian millennium moved to its close.

Spirituality and social justice

Spirituality and politics

Some of the principal figures and themes in the Christian Socialist movement of the nineteenth century, and the Anglo-Catholic movement of the early twentieth, have already been explored. The importance of fostering a spiritual life which could address the pressing social and political issues of the day increased as the twentieth century progressed – if 'progressed' is the right word: two world wars, the looming threat of nuclear and environmental catastrophe, the seemingly inexorable increase in the gap between rich and poor, the oppression of (or discrimination against) individuals because of their race, sexual orientation, or gender – all these helped to fuel the desire for a spirituality that both affirmed the holiness of this world, and equipped people to try to change that world.

Anglican socialists

Among the notable contributors to this process in England were several Anglican priests, most of whom combined traditional Christian theology with radical political commitment.[901] Stewart Headlam (1847–1924), Conrad Noel (1869–1942), Alan Ecclestone (1904–92) and Kenneth Leech (born 1939) all reflect a spirituality which rejected any separation of the spiritual from the political.[902] Conrad Noel condemns 'that false spirituality which despises material things and the needs of [people's] bodies and which divorces religion from socialism'.[903] He insists on depicting Jesus as a prophetic revolutionary:

> In contrast to the modern watered conception of Jesus, the 'Gentle Jesu, meek and mild', there stands out the Church's conception of the real historical Jesus, as suggested in her choice of a lesson at Christmastide with which she introduces his birth. 'Every battle of the warrior is with confused noise, and garments rolled in blood.'[904]

Stewart Headlam makes the point that the establishment of a just (for him this means a socialist) society is the first vital step (but only the first one) on the road to a truly spiritual one, for it is of little use to talk of prayer and holiness to people who are starving:

> One main reason why the Christian Religion longs for the accomplishment of Socialism is in order to give to all time and freedom from anxiety so that they may be able to think out first principles, and have the opportunity for living full and free lives, in which, among other things, Worship and Theology will play their own part.[905]

Only the removal of poverty and the satisfaction of basic material needs allows for the fostering of an authentic spiritual life.[906] For Headlam, 'Easter-day . . . has not only to do with life after death, it has to do with life *here*; it tells us that there is a great power at work, conquering all kinds of death everywhere; *renewing life* everywhere.'[907] Later in the century, the influence of liberation theology from South America and elsewhere would cause people to question the whole basis of a spirituality that is produced in a context of leisure and affluence. The Church of England report *Faith in the city*, which appeared in 1985, reflects the perspectives of liberation theology in calling for a pattern of training for clergy which assimilates academic study with systematic spiritual reflection on experience:

> What matters is whether [the clergy] have developed habits of reflection and social awareness such that they can draw creatively on their resources of theology and spirituality in the face of new realities and engage in a diaiogue with those of other faiths or none.[908]

Kenneth Leech makes the important point here that spiritual maturity is not the same as psychological maturity: rather the former is 'a theological goal which will bring us into collision with prevailing values, and will therefore bring threats to our adjustment and our peace of mind. It will also bring us into collision with much that passes for Christianity and for spirituality in our society.'[909] He criticizes the churches for their failure to meet the new spiritual hunger of the late 1960s, identifying three central components of this hunger: disenchantment with conventional religions, a desire for transcendence or 'deeper ways of experiencing reality', and a concern for peace and justice.[910] The key, in his view, is to hold the latter two together: 'true spirituality is not a leisure-time activity, a diversion from life. It is essentially subversive, and the test of its genuineness is practical.'[911] *Faith in the city* explicitly rejected the notion of a narrowly individualist Christianity: 'everything tells against the notion that there is a 'soul', quite independent of social and economic conditions, to which an entirely personal gospel may be addressed.'[912]

With characteristic acuteness, Alan Ecclestone analyses the situation in *Yes to God*:

> It is the case today that many sincere and honest christians have no conception of the extent to which the spirituality of the christian church is written off by those in every nation who care most for social justice and the fashioning of humaner life for all mankind. The Yes to God that is needed most is that which most humbly acknowledges first of all a pride, a lust for power, a cynicism, an insensitiveness to human suffering which went far to alienate the oppressed of the earth from the Church of Jesus Christ, and which, we may believe, made much of its spirituality stink in the nostrils of the Lord God of all the earth. Without such penitence, it may be said, the Yes to God stands in danger of being foolishly complacent.[913]

And he continues

> Prayer is paying attention, taking all the trouble in the world to pay attention, to the condition of the other person and other persons without limit. It means, no less, paying attention to the assumptions of our own lives, of our position in society, of the social class we belong to, and whose standards of life we would otherwise scarcely notice. It has been the manifest failure of christians in the past to take seriously the question of class, to appreciate class-consciousness, to note the consequences of class distinctions, which has gone far to render their spirituality poor and mean. What God affirms, humanity cannot afford to neglect.[914]

Spirituality and the sacraments

For all these writers, an authentic spirituality will be rooted in the sacraments, not least because they confer an irreducibly corporate dimension to the Christian life. For Headlam, the Mass unites any given group of Christians with the rest of Christendom, 'destroying our English isolation, making for Internationalism'.[915] The Mass is 'the great service of emancipation: freedom, expansion, self-expression, individuality, that is what the Lord's Supper bears witness to, and that is what Socialism aims at'.[916] For Conrad Noel,

> the celebration of the Mass is not merely a rending of the veil, so that we may perceive the inner divine reality of the outward and visible signs, but actually a transubstantiation, or more accurately a transformation, of the material of the Sacrament.[917]

Both Headlam and Noel also stress the importance of the sabbath, as standing for a healthy balance in human life between work and play. Headlam, who also stressed the virtue of a strong and disciplined family life, declared that 'the Christian Sunday properly spent is like Beauty, a kind of extra wayside Sacrament, an outward and visible sign of the well-ordered life which Christ desiderates.'[918] Conrad Noel notes the significance of the Levitical jubilee legislation, emphasizing the nature of the biblical sabbatical year as 'recreation, or more precisely re-creation'.[919]

Spirituality and sexuality

Later in the twentieth century, those concerned with spirituality and social justice addressed a number of issues more specifically. The relationship of spirituality and sexuality touches on the question of sexual orientation, and was explored sensitively by several writers.[920] Kenneth Leech makes the important point that the relationship between orientation and practice that arises in Christian views of homosexuality is precisely the relationship most emphasized in modern understandings of spirituality, which stress that faith must be manifested in works.[921] Michael Vasey proposed a positive Christian understanding of homosexuality;[922] he suggested that the scriptural concept of the covenant may offer a distinctively Christian approach to gay relationships;[923] and he explored the nature of desire in scripture, suggesting ways in which gay people may be able to contribute to 'rescuing desire, gentleness and intimacy from its limitation to the domestic sphere and restoring it to the public realm from which it has been driven'.[924] Those living with, and seeking to make some sense of, HIV and AIDS have also explored ways in which our attempts to respond to these terrible visitants may lead us to a deeper sense of mutual interdependence and indwelling, and perhaps a more honest embrace of the intimate relationship of love and death.[925] One person who died of AIDS in 1990 movingly reflected on the therapeutic power of the prayer of lament:

> Of course, there have been hard times. I have gone through a lot of loneliness and despair and anger and grief of all sorts. But I know and have experienced that when I get rid of all the emotional rubbish and my anger, when I am able to shout, 'Oh my God, this is awful, I have been aban-

doned and I am on my own,' then fear subsides and hope and faith emerge.[926]

Vasey also argued for the importance of recovering a positive Christian theology of friendship, rooted in scripture and the Christian tradition and recognizing the positive value of affectionate and intimate friendships between people of the same sex.[927]

Spiritual direction and social justice

This introduces the subject of spiritual direction, an area which grew in significance in the later decades of the twentieth century.[928] It is a subject to which Kenneth Leech has made a significant contribution.[929] He warns against the dangers of making it over-professional, or too close to psychotherapy;[930] direction is about growth, not problem-solving; and it is rooted in everyday life, not centred upon a neutral 'clinic'. He defines spiritual direction as 'a relationship of friendship in Christ between two people by which one is enabled, through the personal encounter, to discern more clearly the will of God for one's life, and to grow in discipleship and in the life of grace'.[931] Good spiritual direction will not be over-dependent on techniques, still less on individual directors, and will help challenge false spiritualities such as anti-materialism and fundamentalism.[932] And it can help give 'spiritual depth to Christian social action'.[933] Leech situates the practice of spiritual direction within the whole life of the church, and in particular within its sacramental life: spiritual direction should help people to *experience* the fullness of sacramental life.[934]

Peter Selby stresses the need for a spiritual guide who 'is still in touch with the emptiness as well as the glory, the doubt as well as the certainty, that characterize any attempt to grow in spiritual understanding'.[935] Selby also warns of the dangers of a privatized, technique-based, relaxation-oriented spiritual direction, and emphasizes that any authentic life of prayer will be inescapably corporate: 'our praying, no less than our action, has . . . a function in relation to the lives of other people at least as important as its function in our own.'[936] Rather 'we learn to pray in relation to the drama of human history which determines so much of what we individually experience'.[937]

Spirituality and racial justice [938]

The issue of racism came explicitly to public attention in the 1960s, notably with the first Race Relations Act of 1965. Kenneth Leech explored the issue in an important and disturbing book written in 1988;[939] in it, he set the issue against the ever-increasing disparity between rich and poor that marked British society during the last decades of the twentieth century.[940] He argues that 'liturgy is absolutely central to the struggle against racism', because it is there that our deepest commitments and longings are expressed in symbolic and sacramental forms.[941] The incorporation of Black spirituals with their 'sublimated outrage' into mainstream white worship, prayer at places associated with the National Front and racial violence, and small groups of praying Christians focusing on this issue, are among the responses he commends as helpful.[942] The rich tradition of Black spirituality in Afro-Caribbean, Asian and North American contexts remains a source of prophetic inspiration to those seeking both to combat racism and foster a genuinely multi-cultural spirituality in England.[943]

Spirituality and the environment

A growing concern for the environment can be found in later twentieth-century writings on spirituality, unsurprisingly linked with growing evidence of the human race's capacity for destroying it. In his study of the French author Péguy's work, Alan Ecclestone speaks of the need to recover a sense of earth to nourish our prayer: 'we have lacked the sap of the earth to give life to our dealings with Heaven'.[944] In part, he believes, this is because access to nature, and leisure to contemplate it, has until recently been the preserve of the wealthy.[945]

'New Age' spirituality has been pervasively concerned with the relationship between the human spirit and that of the earth and cosmos. It is no new thing: indeed it traces its origins to pre-Christian pagan and Druidic religion; and the characteristically post-modern preference for fashioning an eclectic spirituality drawn from a wide range of sources is, as we have seen, typical of much lay piety through the centuries.[946] It thus reflects a strong preference for ancient rites and sacred places: thus Glastonbury is a significant centre for spiritual seekers both Christian and 'alternative' alike.[947]

A more thoroughgoing basis for an ecological spirituality is offered by the Gaia hypothesis, which (though based on earlier insights) was first fully adumbrated by James Lovelock in the 1970s.[948] Lovelock, a scientist and Fellow of the Royal Society, argued that the entire earth is a single superorganism, to which he gave the name Gaia (after the Greek goddess of the earth).[949] On such a view, human fulfilment is achieved by recognition of our inseparability from the whole of creation around us and by playing our part as stewards of that creation, in the process losing an obsession with self in a manner not dissimilar from Buddhist thought:

> It may be that the destiny of mankind is to become tamed, so that the fierce, destructive, and greedy forces of tribalism and nationalism are fused into a compulsive urge to belong to the commonwealth of all creatures which constitutes Gaia. It might seem to be a surrender, but I suspect that the rewards, in the form of an increased sense of well-being and fulfilment, in knowing ourselves to be a dynamic part of a far greater entity, would be worth the loss of tribal freedom.[950]

In his exploration of different philosophical and theological models for thinking about the earth, Stephen Clark proposes a different approach, based on a purified and (in some respects) biblically-based nationalism. Recognizing that 'the land we care for is a land imbued with memories', he proceeds to argue that caring for that *particular* land or region need not be a bad thing provided that it allows for a rich diversity: 'loving the land we live in, in a proper way, involves respecting the variety of things and working with them to achieve a life that never simply stops'.[951] Hence

> Good nationalists are ones who do not claim too much, and who are ready to allow on the global level that diversity and gradual change that is a necessity within their neighbourhood . . . 'Nationalism' is not the belief that 'my nation' is the best and brightest, destined to destroy or convert all others . . . nationalism is rather the belief . . . that things are best managed when they are managed by the people closest to the problem.[952]

And he calls for a spirituality rooted in the biblical principle of the sabbath as the crown of creation. For Clark, that principle allows for an appreciation of the wonder and beauty, not merely the usefulness, of the world around us and of our fellow-creatures within it. It reminds us also that the vision of the new Jerusalem is always calling us onwards, inviting us to imagine and work towards a better world. Above all, though, 'the Sabbath is a moment when we are released to realize that everything is an end, not merely a means', for 'beauty is to be worshipped, and cannot be possessed'.[953]

Prayer and social justice

Those committed to exploring the relationship of spirituality and social justice see prayer as a primary element in that relationship. Conrad Noel notes the corporate context of the prayer Christ himself taught his disciples: 'all through it is not "me" but "us", not individualistic but collective; the needs and difficulties of the group are in contemplation.'[954] And Kenneth Leech went further in arguing that 'Christian prayer is inseparable from resistance and struggle.'[955] It is future-oriented, disturbing the chaos of the present in anticipation of what God will do to change the way things are. But what does this mean in practice? In *A staircase for silence*, Alan Ecclestone notes the crucial link between prayer and the way we pay attention to the world around us:

> it is not so much the gift of tongues that we now need as the gift of ears, not so much the proclamation of our beliefs as the willingness to listen to the ways in which we ourselves are being addressed, not so much the assertion of our knowledge but the silent admission that we are ready to learn.[956]

He begins his book *Yes to God* by suggesting that 'to pray is to seek to be enlightened';[957] 'it is so difficult a thing because it attempts so much'.[958] And he proceeds to set out exactly what it does attempt: an open-hearted and unconditional embracing of the world and its needs. We are very far indeed here from the perspectives of an Anglo-Saxon monk:

> Prayer seeks the elucidation of what being so engaged with the Yes of God to man both asks of us and gives. The prior condition of rich generous praying is an openness of heart and mind, an absence of defensive rigidity in dealing with experience, an avoidance of preconceived distinction between the spiritual life and life subject to and stamped by all the pressures of the world. Such prayer at no time is detached from living in the world, for how we pray depends to no small extent upon the way we are already acting in it. A spirituality that is not so open is being starved of its necessary food, and unwilling to adventure its gifts in acts of faith. The prayer of openness to full engagement with God's world is so demanding, so completely testing of the willingness of every man and woman to commit themselves in faith, so utterly a venture into the unknown, that it is not surprising that spiritualities have, as often as not, contrived to become inturned, legalistic, miserly and unexpectant. All too often a narrowly ecclesiastical or clerical version of the good life and prayer has in the past drawn to itself the energy and devotion that should have entered into the common life of humanity.[959]

This kind of prayer will frequently take place on the margins of experience; it will involve terrible risks, like the prophets of the Old Testament wrestling with God.[960] But its scope will be nothing less than the fullest range of human and creaturely experience.

Ecclestone explores what this might mean in practice in an essay called simply 'On Praying'.[961] Here he suggests that 'to pray is to make the most of our moments of perception'.[962] We should therefore begin with those moments when we use the language of prayer involuntarily. The first of these are moments of gladness, when we say things like 'Thank God!' He suggests that 'to have lived through a day and yet not be able to be thankful for one moment of it is to be living a death-in-life . . . Without such growth in sensitive awareness of, and thankful response to, the events of potential enrichment, we do in fact die spiritually.'[963] The second set of occasions are moments of need. The Syro-Phoenician woman's cry 'Lord, help me!' is the model for this kind of brief and anguished prayer, and it reflects our instinctive sense of dependence on what Ecclestone calls 'You whoever you are'.[964] The third set of occasions are moments of exhaustion, which is when texts we have learned by heart (if we are fortunate enough to have done so) acquire a deep ruminant value.[965]

More generally, Ecclestone suggests that all prayer consists of one of four kinds of activity: consuming ('our prayer is akin to a deliberate act of chewing over the material of daily experience in order that it may become nourishingly part of ourselves');[966] paying attention;[967] making connections ('we are to grow in a perception of the inter-relatedness of all things');[968] and resisting, for 'all living involves a degree of wrestling'.[969] But there must also be room in our prayer for wonder, though not simply in the sense of a passive acceptance of the *status quo*: rather we need, again and again, 'to be jolted out of our assumptions about the nature of things, and to be compelled to see them in terms "passing strange."'[970]

Ecclestone constantly stresses the inseparability of our prayer from the rest of our lives. Thus for example good communication with God presupposes good communication within the Christian community as a whole:

> An advertisement in *The Times* appeared as follows: 'Research shows that the average married couple have only 16 minutes of meaningful conversation together each week. How often does your husband talk to you? Is he more involved in hobbies, the telly, his work? Research writer, preparing thesis, is keen to hear case histories.' If communication in the basic community of life dwindles to such meagre proportions, if the communication within the parish churches gets absorbed in matters of finance . . . what chance is there that the common personal prayer of the people involved will grow rich by virtue of that which every member supplies?[971]

But there is a more important point still: if we are to grow spiritually at all, we must reflect deeply on the astonishing implications of the fact that we are ourselves unconditionally loved, a point Ecclestone makes with moving eloquence:

> It is one of the most moving experiences of life to watch a bewildered frightened human being, starved of friendship and hardly daring to be

expectant of it, blossom out into a happy, trustful and confident personal life as the result of being . . . welcomed and received. It is of the essence of the Gospel that we are so received in Christ, that His Yes to men is pronounced in such directly personal terms. Human beings like Nathanael and Philip, Nicodemus and Zaccheus, the woman of Samaria and the man born blind, are pictured as those faced abruptly by a personal intervention to which they respond with something like a gulp of astonishment. It is not simply that they had never been addressed like this before, though that was noticed and felt, but that they realised that it was the singularity of their life and being that was being marked . . . We in our learning to say Yes to God are required to approach each other as apprentices to the mystery of personal recognition, to take infinite trouble to grow into it, and to know within ourselves the transfiguring outcome of being sought out and known in this way. The light in which the reality of human life is thus seen is the presence itself, the Shekinah that has approached and filled the area of meeting with its revealing splendour. Before ever words are spoken, and beyond any words that may be uttered, those included in it know that they are loved.[972]

Spirituality and other faiths

Finally it is important to note briefly the relationship between Christian spirituality and the growing encounter with other world faiths, both within England as immigration grew and beyond it. As long ago as 1922, Evelyn Underhill proposed a nuanced approach to this subject:

> The pupil should be led to see his own religion as a part of the universal tendency of life to God. This need not involve any reduction of the claims made on him by his own church or creed; but the emphasis should always be on the likeness rather than the differences of the great religions of the world.[973]

During the darkest days of the Second World War (in 1940), Canon Peter Green of Salford spoke out passionately against antisemitism both in Germany and within England itself: 'how would it be,' he enquired, 'in these bad days of racial hates and wrongs, if we made a practice of looking for a Jew's virtues instead of for his faults?'[974] And he went on to commend specifically Jewish family life, love for children, civic responsibility, respect for human nature, and capacity for gratitude in response to life – all spiritual virtues from which Christians had much to learn.[975]

Nearly fifty years later, the Catholic Donald Nicholl reflected sadly on the way modern capitalism had eroded some of the profound spiritual riches of the great world faiths, supremely in its effective abolition of the balance between sacred and secular time (the disappearance of the sabbath, or holy or play day), and in its equally comprehensive abolition of any sense of distance or perspective in modern life.[976] Elsewhere he argued that the academic study of comparative religion is far different from a true spiritual encounter between people of different faiths, in which comparisons based simply on propositional truths are anathema. By contrast those seeking a spiritual encounter will stress that spirituality which Nicholl, following the German Klaus Klostermaier, defines as 'the real life of the mind'.[977]

True practitioners of this much deeper *scientia cordis* will experience a profound mutual *rapprochement* between the great world religions at a much deeper level than credal doctrines.[978] This *rapprochement* was extensively articulated by other Catholic explorers of interfaith spirituality, among them Thomas Merton, William Johnston, and Bede Griffiths.[979] Such an approach runs the risk of a loose syncretism; but Andrew Wingate, in a moving description of Christians and Muslims praying together, argues the opposite:

> Prayer is not the time for proselytization, but for meeting before God and receiving from God. It is not a time for expressing doctrinal statements and pinning people to them, but for laying ourselves open before God. If it is the Spirit in whom we meet, then even outwardly exclusive words may do no harm, for integrity and empathy mark the situation. If it is not, no amount of carefully chosen words can make an inclusive prayer.[980]

Spirituality and feminism

Introduction

It is undeniable that the twentieth century witnessed major developments in the opportunities available to women, both within and outside the churches, though even at the century's end religious institutions (whose members tended to be overwhelmingly female) remained dominated by men;[981] and it was only in the twentieth century that the number of canonized women saints rose above 20% of the total – and most of them were virgins and martyrs rather than married women with children.[982] The inequality of the sexes in western society by no means disappeared; what did disappear was the willingness of women passively to accept it.

In the context of spirituality, some women abandoned institutional religion altogether, opting to withdraw into a private spiritual world isolated from patriarchal control, or seeking meaning and fulfilment in literature, art, pagan traditions, or new kinds of community.[983] Others, however, sought change from within established institutions; and it is important to note the number and significance of twentieth-century women scholars of mysticism even within England.[984] What is undeniable is that feminism, in the sense of a movement or movements concerned to affirm the experience, dignity and equality of women, was no transient affair, nor was it something restricted to liberal and affluent western societies: across the world, the role and position of women was changing irreversibly; and the impact of this on the nature and development of spirituality was immense.[985]

Spirituality and language

In the first place, feminism led to significant changes in religious language and imagery.[986] Numerous feminist or gender-sensitive liturgies were produced even before inclusive language came to be generally accepted (which only happened in the last decade of the century).[987] Janet Morley suggests that using gender-inclusive language in liturgy and spiritual texts does more than merely allow women to worship:

> I have found that to examine how and why the feminine has been omitted
> from our ways of addressing God is to discover also what else has been left
> out. To release ourselves from the habit of always using certain predictable
> (and perhaps scarcely-noticed) formulae for the beginning of a prayer, may
> free the imagination to explore the unimaginable ways in which God
> reaches us.[988]

And Sara Maitland points out that 'the word "man" does not simply summon up, at
the conceptual level, an undifferentiated person with male biological characteristics,
but is actually value-laden in ways that Christians should think about very carefully.[989]

Ursula King, stressing the greater weight that tends to be given to experience in
feminist spirituality (by comparison with the more conceptual or 'objective' approach
favoured by many men), argued that religious language

> as found in prayers, songs, devotions, utterances of prophets and seers, and
> in the accounts of saints and mystics of all religions, is closer to its experi-
> ential source. It is thus more open to female imagery and experience than
> the language of systematised theological doctrine which is always closely
> controlled by reasoning rather than spontaneity.[990]

She notes the theory that male spiritual writers tend to prefer hierarchical images, such
as those of ascent, whereas female ones prefer images of inwardness such as the rooms
of a mansion;[991] and she notes the ways in which feminist thinking questions traditional symbols such as the understanding of God as powerful and masculine.[992] This
approach led many, both female and male, to look afresh at the spiritual tradition of
Christianity and question dominant (and almost invariably male) interpretations of
it.[993] Within the Roman Catholic tradition, Lavinia Byrne argued that the Church's
Divine Office, and especially the intercessions provided for daily prayer within it, did
not resonate with many women:

> The activities suggested there as ways of helping the Kingdom of God
> grow within seem to rely upon images of strife and of construction engi-
> neering, and imply that the Kingdom is about numbers and noise rather
> than attitudes and values.[994]

The articulation of anger and resentment, through gender-sensitive liturgy or the
rich and multivalent imagery of the Psalms, forms a vital dimension of women's spirituality.[995]

Spirituality and motherhood

But the use of more sensitive and appropriate language and imagery was only one of
the ways in which women helped to transform the pattern and texture of English spirituality in the twentieth century. Many women sought to develop a much more
ecologically affirming spirituality, drawing on a wide variety of sources (from the
theology of Teilhard de Chardin to the *Benedicite*) in doing so.[996] Some argued that
bodiliness and physicality played, or ought to play, a greater role in women's spiritual-

ity than in that of men.[997] It is, after all, unarguable that women's bodies create and cradle life in a way men's do not; and King goes so far as to suggest that

> it is easier for a man to lose himself in abstract thought and become separated from the sources of life; for women life itself is more organically interconnected. In traditional religious thought this has often been negatively evaluated when women have been described as being 'material,' more 'physical', more 'flesh' than men.[998]

King points out that we speak of 'mothering' to denote an extended process of birth and nurture, whereas 'fathering' still tends to denote a specific sexual act and nothing more.[999] The experience of birth-giving has some profound insights to offer to the spiritual life, and vice versa, even though it would be the crudest of stereotypes to suggest that this alone is constitutive of women's spirituality.[1000] Una Kroll argues for the primacy of the womb, and the periodicity of women's bodies, as pointing to a distinctive form of

> participation in God's birthing creativity, not necessarily through physical parenthood but also by becoming parents to ideas, books, businesses, religious communities and other enterprises.[1001]

Margaret Hebblethwaite offers a profound exploration of the theme of motherhood, including a range of thoughtful analogies between the nurture of a child and God's nurturing of us.[1002] She suggests that every child born incarnates the motherly love of God: 'can it be that God's love is so powerful, so restless and explosive that all the billions of people who have ever lived have not exhausted her drive to express it again and again? Can it be that God finds us as endearing to look at, in all our adult gaucheness, as we find little children . . . ?'[1003] To think of God as mother is to visualize ourselves within God's womb: 'there could not be a closer image of warmth, security and protection'.[1004] It is to experience at the most intimate level the love of God for us: Una Kroll, in proposing a close relationship between sexual and spiritual ecstasy, says that

> Ecstasy has given zest to my life. I could not have known what it was like if I had not been taught by God to love myself and so to begin to love others as myself.[1005]

But it is also to acknowledge something of the terrible cost to God of human suffering and unfaithfulness: Hebblethwaite vividly describes the shattering exhaustion and anxieties that motherhood brings, and which are rarely comprehensible to those who have never experienced them.[1006] Here surely really *is* a powerful analogy with God – as is the terrible experience of losing a child, an experience God herself has already made uniquely her own.[1007]

Women were not alone in conceiving of God as mother: Studdert-Kennedy explored the theme at length in a book published in 1928: 'women began the work of the world, and have done most of it ever since. Father was predatory, mother was creative'.[1008] And the human capacity for war underlines the fatal consequences of subordinating the feminine. 'Men will be more – not less than men – if they ever abandon war and take to universal love.'[1009] In Christ, we see the warrior and the woman blended to perfection.[1010] And Reginald Somerset Ward saw in human motherhood 'the shadow of the love of God the Holy Ghost', the parallel being the dove hovering, and the love of the Holy Spirit as offering shelter and protection.[1011]

Spirituality and peace-making: Greenham Common

More generally, but no less significantly, women argued for a far more integrating spirituality, with greater emphasis on connectedness, healing, wholeness, and a pervasive harmony between body and soul.[1012] This might find expression in dance or physical exercise;[1013] but above all it presupposes that women take time and care to foster a healthier self-image; for only once women feel more confident in themselves as they are can they engage in the search for a more whole society; and the constant emphasis in traditional spirituality on self-denial carries little weight for those who have never been encouraged to have much sense of self to deny.[1014] The discovery of an inner harmony through dance or spiritual growth is not an end in itself: indeed some women have argued that women in general are more naturally collaborative than men, more instinctively inclined to co-operate and seek an outer harmony rather than settle for a lonely autonomy.[1015]

Hence Ursula King can write:

> At its heart feminism is grounded in and empowered by an act of faith. One could describe this as a vision quest carried by the faith in the possibility of another reality, a hope which goes far beyond current social and empirical evidence.[1016]

Feminist spirituality, then, rejects any separation between inner and outer worlds: 'today, in feminism as elsewhere, spirituality is not an exclusive exploration of interiority and inwardness, but closely interwoven with all other dimensions of human experience, including social and political life.'[1017] 'Women's spirituality must be developed as a deep inner resource which shapes and sustains outward action.'[1018]

One practical manifestation of this kind of spirituality is an emphasis on peace-making.[1019] During the 1980s groups of women formed a peace camp at Greenham Common in Berkshire in order to protest against the possible deployment of cruise missiles by the United States and United Kingdom. Despite strong opposition both locally and nationally, the women's camp continued for many years, even after the closure of the American military camp there; the women celebrated not just peace but the future and fullness of life on earth.[1020] One woman who came to join the camp in December 1982 from Dublin wrote a moving evocation of the spiritual values that both impelled her to go and transformed her when she got there:

> I hadn't planned to come. I knew about it but I had excuses. Wanting to play some part, I went along to Trinity where the Irish women were preparing for the weekend. I listened to them speak of why they were going, of their fears and hopes and anxieties, of their inspiration. And for the first time what was to happen many times that weekend happened: from somewhere a spirit rose and flowing through my veins drowned out

all other words and thoughts. With a certainty unusual to me I simply knew I had to go. And so I went, for a hundred different reasons, for the earth, for the children, for the Greenham women, for peace and for the Spirit that had overtaken me. I knew nothing except that nuclear war was wrong and here was a chance for me to say no . . .

There was nobody giving orders or telling us what to do. We'd each had a message from the Greenham women, to bring a hymn to express why we were here and that was all . . . Sometime during that day we joined hands and began to sing. Hand in hand in hand, for nine miles we formed a living chain to lock in the horrors of war, to stand between them and our world and to say: we will meet your violence with a loving embrace, for it is the surest way of defusing it. How strong I felt when I joined my voice to the waves of voices shouting Freedom and when the echoes from so far away drifted across the base to my ears. I took my seeds and wrapped them in mud and with all the love and strength I felt threw them inside the fence: Take root and grow. Tell them that life will prevail and that in the midst of ugliness beauty can flourish.[1021]

'I joined my voice to the waves of voices shouting Freedom' – this reflects part of the fundamental concern of feminist spirituality to give a voice to those who have no voice: not just to other women, but to all who have been excluded from a patriarchal society.[1022]

Spirituality and home-making

Not all women were in a position to seek spiritual meaning through political protest. Others found it not through peace-making but through home-making.[1023] By 1950 vital changes in women's lifestyle had taken place in the UK: middle-class women had lost their domestic servants; and working-class housewives found themselves responsible for looking after the whole house.[1024] The relationship of the woman with her home can be a highly personal, even intimate one, capable of reflecting their spiritual values and aspirations.[1025] Thus fireplaces could become focuses for photographs and ornaments with symbolic associations, a family gathering-place expressing and holding a range of emotions and values.[1026] In some of the soulless 'new towns' of post-war Britain, many women ignored the open-plan designs of the architects and used net or lace curtains to close off the stark world outside and create warm inner spaces expressive of intimacy and love.[1027] Where the identities of most men were expressed and often developed through their occupations, women had to seek an identity elsewhere – in their relationships (as wives, mothers, daughters and friends), but also in their ability to create meaning and identity out of the often impersonal straitjacket imposed on them by the (usually male) designers of huge housing estates.[1028]

The implications of this for English spirituality may appear small; but women writers envisaged God not only as mother but also as home-maker. Lavinia Byrne said that

> I find that God is the God who brings together every thread of my experience because it was she who first knit me into being. This God is not a God who drops stitches or despairs of her task.[1029]

And elsewhere she writes

> God the homemaker lays a different kind of table, one around which people come to talk and laugh and share, to taste and to see that the Lord is good. God the homemaker puts the kettle on and draws up the chairs. God the homemaker wants to hear about the real problems and questions that exercise us, about the people we love and the people we fear. How is the presence of this God to be mediated in our midst?[1030]

Spirituality and war

Introduction

'War,' said Dean Inge, 'is a manifest evil'; but that did not prevent his contemporaries from engaging in the two bloodiest examples of that evil in human history.[1031] We have already noted briefly the impact of the twentieth century's two world wars. Both were responsible for the deaths of hundreds of thousands of soldiers and civilians, though the Second (which saw the massive bombing of British and European cities) saw far more civilian casualties than the first.[1032] And the culture of war affected everyone in innumerable indirect ways. Virtually every man born between 1880 and 1940 was eligible for military service, which gave three generations immediate experience of military life and discipline.[1033] The fear, or even hatred, of foreigners, and the corresponding predilection for facile jingoism, persisted long after the world wars were over, even though the experience of war itself did lead some (for example, the poets of the First World War) to oppose unthinking nationalism of this kind.[1034] The nostalgia for an irrecoverable (and usually idealized) pre-war past persisted too. Rose Macaulay describes a decidedly aristocratic example of that nostalgia:

> Richie, himself trapped into barbarism for three long, unbelievable years [during the Second World War], shrank back from it, reacted towards gentleness, towards bland tolerance, towards an excessive civility . . . In this pursuit he was impelled sometimes beyond his reasoning self, to grasp at the rich, trailing panoplies, the swinging censers, of churches from whose creeds and uses he was alien, because at least they embodied some continuance, some tradition; while cities and buildings, lovely emblems of history, fell shattered, or lost shape and line in a sprawl of common mass newness, while pastoral beauty was overrun and spoilt, while ancient communities were engulfed in the gaping maw of the beast of prey, and Europe dissolved into wavering anonymities, bitter of tongue, servile of deed, faint of heart . . . during all this frightening evanescence and dissolution the historic churches kept their strange courses . . . linking the dim past with the disrupted present and intimidating future, frail, tough chain of legend, myth, and mystery, stronghold of reaction and preserved values.[1035]

The longing for spiritual continuities and past certainties endured.[1036] But the Church had been badly damaged by war too, its national influence massively reduced.[1037] Evelyn Underhill wrote in 1922 that

> all who worked among our soldiers at the front were struck by the paradox of the immense amount of natural religion existing among them, combined with almost total alienation from religious institutions.[1038]

Many of the war poets explored with vigour and power the perceived failure of the churches to address the evil of war without equivocation.[1039] In 'A tear song', Wilfred Owen suggests that God accepts the human love and courage of the soldiers, but rejects the easy formalism of ordered institutional religion, here exemplified by cathedral evensong: God looks for our tears, not our formal prayers.[1040] The spirituality of the First World War poets has been explored elsewhere;[1041] we must be content here with some brief reflections on the subject.

The prayer of lament

First, the experience of war dispelled from most people any lingering belief in an omnipotent God who could intervene to right society's wrongs. In 'Spiritual isolation', Isaac Rosenberg (1890–1918), whose working-class upbringing was utterly different from that of Owen or Sassoon, offers a modern equivalent to the experience of Job:

> My Maker shunneth me.
> Even as a wretch stricken with leprosy
> So hold I pestilent supremacy.
> Yea! He hath fled as far as the uttermost star.[1042]

In the process, prayer and blasphemy, beseeching a living God and denouncing a dead one, became almost indistinguishably intertwined; indeed the decline in religious observance did not at all imply a decline in the practice of prayer, to which large numbers of unbelievers had recourse *in extremis*.[1043] This is Wilfred Owen:

> 'Oh! Jesus Christ! I'm hit,' he said; and died.
> Whether he vainly cursed or prayed indeed,
>   The Bullets chirped – In vain, vain, vain!
>   Machine-guns chuckled – Tut-tut! Tut-tut!
> And the Big Gun guffawed.[1044]

In a letter to his mother (dated 18 February 1918), Owen prefaced this poem with the words 'There is a point where prayer is indistinguishable from blasphemy. There is also a point where blasphemy is indistinguishable from prayer. As in this first verse . . .'[1045]

Some Christians sought to help people cope spiritually with the experience of war, though much of their efforts carried something of a *de haut en bas* tone.[1046] Charles Gore (1853–1932), Bishop successively of Worcester, Birmingham and Oxford, wrote a manual for church members during the First World War, in which he noted how people often turn to God in prayer at such times:

How many men during this war, who had long given up praying, have flung themselves on their knees and prayed, 'O merciful God, I pray Thee to keep my Tom safe! Truly it is a most welcome return to prayer.[1047]

There are, in Gore's view, higher forms of prayer than this (as there might well appear to be at a comfortable distance from the trenches); but nonetheless 'we should never cease to pray thus fervently and thus particularly for the things that we particularly need'.[1048]

But arguably the person who did most to articulate an authentic spiritual response to the experience of war without rejecting Christian faith was Geoffrey Studdert-Kennedy (1883–1929), who was an Anglican chaplain to the forces from 1916 to 1919 and came to be known affectionately as 'Woodbine Willie'.[1049] In 'The suffering God' we are given a good illustration of his spirituality:

> Are there no tears in the heart of the Eternal?
>   Is there no pain to pierce the soul of God?
> Then must He be a fiend of Hell infernal,
>   Beating the earth to pieces with His rod . . .
> Father, if He, the Christ, were Thy Revealer,
>   Truly the First Begotten of the Lord,
> Then must Thou be a Suff'rer and a Healer,
>   Pierced to the heart by the sorrow of the sword.
> Then must it mean, not only that Thy sorrow
>   Smote Thee that once upon the lonely tree,
> But that to-day, to-night, and on the morrow,
>   Still will not come, O Gallant God, to Thee . . .
> Not to the work of sordid selfish saving
>   Of our own souls to dwell with Him on high,
> But to the soldier's splendid selfless braving,
>   Eager to fight for Righteousness and die.[1050]

For Studdert-Kennedy, a suffering God shares in our suffering and redeems it from within, and thereby makes the soldiers' sacrifice both glorious and redemptive too.[1051] Only a God who has undergone at Calvary what people are now having to undergo in trenches is credible for him at all.[1052] Indeed Studdert-Kennedy explicitly denounces the notion of an omnipotent deity:

> And I hate the God of Power on His hellish heavenly throne,
> Looking down on rape and murder, hearing little children moan . . .
> And Thou hast no other splendour but the splendour of the Cross.
> For in Christ I see the martyrs and the beauty of their pain,
> And in Him I hear the promise that my dead shall rise again.
> High and lifted up, I see Him on the eternal Calvary,
> And two piercèd hands are stretching east and west o'er land and sea.
> On my knees I fall and worship that great Cross that shines above,
> For the very God of Heaven is not Power, but Power of Love.[1053]

He makes the point even more vividly in his 'Missing – believed killed: on reading a mother's letter', with its terrible conclusion:

> She only asked to keep one thing,
> the joy-light in his eyes:
> God has not even let her know
> Where his dead body lies.
>
> O Grave, where is thy victory?
> O Death, where is thy sting?
> Thy victory is ev'rywhere,
> Thy sting's in ev'rything.[1054]

In 'Tragedy', he attempts theodicy, quoting the advice of Job's wife to her tormented husband:

> I know. It is not easy to explain
> Why should there be such agony to bear?
> Why should the whole wide world be full of pain?
> But then, why should her hair
> Be like the sudden sunshine after rain?
>
> Turn cynic if you will. Curse God and die.
> You've ample reason for it. There's enough
> Of bitterness, God knows, to answer why.
> The road of life is rough,
> But then there is the glory of the sky.[1055]

And in 'The psychologist' he criticizes alternatives: the psychologist can *analyse* a saint, but cannot *make* one.[1056] It is only in our willingness honestly to hold together the horror of so many people's experience with prayer to the only kind of God who is credible in the light of that experience that we may ourselves find meaning and hope.

Others, of course, found even that response far too positive, and directed their laments towards those more immediately responsible for the horror of war. There is a moving lament in Isaac Rosenberg's 'Dead man's dump'. Rosenberg describes earth waiting for the dead soldiers and possessing them. Then he says

> What fierce imaginings their dark souls lit?
> Earth! have they gone into you!
> Somewhere they must have gone,
> And flung on your hard back
> Is their soul's sack
> Emptied of God-ancestralled essences.
> Who hurled them out? Who hurled?[1057]

There is no immortality beyond the grave. Their souls' 'sacks', emptied of God-ancestralled essences, have been 'hurled out' by generals and politicians blithely unaware of their souls' uniqueness. There is no hope of resurrection here.[1058] The non-combatant poet F. S. Flint wrote a moving 'Lament' in which he underlines the fact that war takes precisely the nation's youngest men and kills them:

> The young men of the world
> Are condemned to death.
> They have been called up to die
> For the crime of their fathers . . .
>
> The young men of the world
> No longer possess the road:
> The road possesses them.
> They no longer inherit the earth:
> The earth inherits them.
> They are no longer the masters of fire:
> Fire is their master;
> They serve him, he destroys them.
> They no longer rule the waters:
> The genius of the seas
> Has invented a new monster,
> And they fly from its teeth.
> They no longer breathe freely:
> The genius of the air
> Has contrived a new terror
> That rends them into pieces . . .
>
> Weep, weep, o women,
> And old men break your hearts.[1059]

It is worth noting here the evocations of biblical and Greek ideas about inheriting the earth and mastering fire. For Flint, war represents precisely a reversal of all that is most noble and spiritual in human life. For Edmund Blunden, it represents a reversal of religious faith. This is his sharp subversion of the wisdom of Psalm 37:

> I have been young, and now am not too old;
> And I have seen the righteous forsaken,
> His health, his honour and his quality taken.
>   This is not what we were formerly told.
>
> I have seen a green country, useful to the race,
> Knocked silly with guns and mines, its villages vanished,
> Even the last rat and last kestrel banished –
>   God bless us all, this was peculiar grace.[1060]

Women, spirituality and war

Women's poetry articulates the full range of responses to what Vera Brittain called 'the aching grief of England's war'.[1061] The Scottish writer Naomi Mitchison, whose daughter died at childbirth in 1940, lays her sorrow alongside that of millions whose loved ones have perished in war as a result of what she describes as the 'Satanic possession' of individuals like Himmler and Franco.[1062] Audrey Hewlett declares that 'Christ's great Cross is trampled in the dust' in her evocation of October 1940;[1063] while Juliette de Bairacli-Levy writes movingly of her dead husband's

dogs, restless, restless, with tortured ears
Listening for his swift, light tread upon the path.[1064]

In her poem 'Easter 1942', Maud Cherrill cries out

O God, O God, through all the blood and strife,
To broken hearts and tired eyes dull with tears
Grant but to catch one glimpse of a new life
    Beyond these years.[1065]

And Patricia Ledward, mourning the death of the poet Timothy Corsellis at the age of
20 in 1941, writes:

Play on, O Harlem band, O swing your blues!
Rend every stone with your terrible, lamenting cry:
Those who would sing of life, and hope, and joy,
Are driven out to hunt, to kill, to die.[1066]

Conclusion

But passionate eloquence is not the only authentic spiritual response to war. Local war
memorials, inscriptions on gravestones, letters of condolence, and rituals of remembrance may strike many as beyond the confines of the spiritual.[1067] But they may assist
the grieving process of those who struggle to make some sense of the appalling horror
of two world wars. And the gentle sentimentality of popular wartime songs and music
may help bring meaning and healing as much as the more sophisticated reflections
considered above. Fred E. Weatherly, one of the most prolific of such song-writers,
illustrates the point; and this, one of his most popular songs, was set to music of
utterly appropriate lyricism by Eric Coates.[1068] There is no attempt to explain, and still
less to offer some form of consolation, religious or other. Yet its unabashed emotionalism has its own integrity:

Oh the green hills of Somerset
Go rolling to the shore.
'Twas there we said that we'd get wed
When spring came round once more
'Twas there we kissed and said goodbye
Beside the kirkyard wall
And the song the blackbird sang to us
was the sweetest song of all.
    Green hills of Somerset,
    Green hills of Somerset,
    When shall we walk by you,
    Green hills, once more?

Oh the green hills of Somerset
Go rolling to the sea.
And still today the violets
Are blooming there for me,

Where shadows kiss the waving grass
Beside the kirkyard wall.
But the song the blackbird sings to me
Is the saddest song of all.
    Green hills of Somerset,
    Green hills of Somerset,
    No more we walk by you,
    Green hills no more.

Spirituality and the Arts

Introduction

The relationship between spirituality and the arts in twentieth-century England is a large and complex one; and we can do little more here than point to some of the rich themes and possibilities it opens up. Even a brief exploration is bound to be subjective; and to restrict the scope by focusing only on artists concerned with explicitly religious themes would involve an unacceptable reduction of what the term 'spiritual' can encompass. In what follows, reference will be made to the work of the artists Cecil Collins (1908–89) and Stanley Spencer (1891–1959), and the composers John Tavener (b.1944) and Jonathan Harvey (b.1939); but we shall also have recourse to the thought of the philosopher and novelist Iris Murdoch and to a number of others, in particular with regard to the relationship between spirituality and architecture. First, however, a few words about the four artists already mentioned seems appropriate.

Cecil Collins had a profoundly spiritual understanding of art, though he did not regard art as having a moral dimension.[1069] Rather, 'the purpose of Art is to worship and praise life through wonder and magic'.[1070] And God 'is the Good that includes all good. God is the Poetry that includes all poetry, the Beauty that includes all Beauty.'[1071] He cited with approval the French Thomist Jacques Maritain's observation that the modern world 'is ruining the leisure of the soul.'[1072] The influence of William Blake is palpable in his writings, as it is also in the work of Stanley Spencer, whose quasi-pantheistic faith, though heavily indebted to Christian iconography and tradition, affirmed the religious nature of all creation, and in particular of English landscapes familiar to the artist.[1073]

The influence of Blake (and indeed of Cecil Collins) is apparent in the work of John Tavener, who was received into the Orthodox Church in 1977.[1074] He adopted a particularly intransigent attitude towards progress in both music and religion.[1075] On music, he declared roundly that 'all non-traditional music seemed to me contrived, concerned with satisfying the ego, and to have nothing, absolutely nothing, to do with the sacred.'[1076] Thus he dismisses Beethoven's *Missa Solemnis* as 'just an excuse for an expansive exercise in anguished self-expression: Beethoven's "ego" railing against God.'[1077] His near-contemporary Jonathan Harvey has been profoundly influenced by Anglican Christianity (including Evelyn Underhill's *Mysticism*), both western and eastern mystical traditions, and perhaps supremely by the Tibetan Mahayana tradition of Buddhism.[1078] His writings and musical works reflect a particular and lifelong interest in the nature of the 'spiritual'.[1079]

Spirituality and the vision of the beautiful

How do artists help us to see the spiritual in the midst of the everyday, and to grow as attentive spiritual beings? Cecil Collins reflects on this theme in his *The vision of the fool*. The 'greatest Fool in history' was Christ; but the Fool has been rejected by society because today everything is judged by its usefulness.[1080] The artist is a Fool, 'and Art is a cosmic folly by which purity of consciousness can be attained':[1081] the fool thus awakens the fool in others;[1082] and April Fools' Day is

> a day that should be kept and celebrated religiously and universally. A holy day, when no work is done. A day given over to the divine fantasy of holy gaiety. A day of the giving away in unending foolish non-rational generosity, of gifts clothed in the marvels of the imagination . . . This would be the one day in the year during which all human beings could dissolve the cruel monotony of the utilitarian principle of work and respectability, that with the plausible teeth of its mechanism, tries to destroy the mysterious wonders of life.[1083]

This is an anti-scientific view; for Collins, 'science has desacramentalized matter'.[1084] Stanley Spencer takes a still more sensual approach. His pantheism, and perhaps the influence of Blake, caused him to maintain that 'there are a vast series of spiritual qualities of feeling that can only be found in a house and not in a church'.[1085] Hence his domestic paintings, many of them involving nudes, and the Lawrentian celebration of physicality which is characteristic of much of his work.[1086] There is also a good deal of self-absorption: so that the *Christ in the wilderness* series, painted in 1939 while he was living alone, show a number of biblical scenes with a strong overtone of self-portraiture.[1087] Even so, there is something haunting and beautiful about *Consider the lilies*, one of this series, with a chubby, bearded and tousled Jesus on his hands and knees staring in fascination at the lilies: the sense of wonder at the presence of the divine in the heart of the everyday is palpable.[1088] Thus many of his paintings reveal Christ in the Berkshire village of Cookham, and subsidiary figures are (as in much medieval art) given faces well known to Spencer.[1089]

There is something characteristically Western and individualist about this unabashed celebration of the artist's own persona and personal surroundings; and it points to a crucial issue in late twentieth-century English spirituality, to be explored more fully below – is the spiritual life fundamentally about the *fulfilment* of the self, or about its *denial*? Iris Murdoch (a prime exemplar of someone whose thought was profoundly spiritual and moral without being religious) argues for the latter. She stesses the importance of holding together the great transcendental realities of goodness and beauty, as in Plato's philosophy; and she stresses the potential moral and spiritual value of the artistic vision:

> the idea of a patient, loving regard, directed upon a person, a thing, a situation, presents the will not as unimpeded movement but as something very much more like 'obedience'.[1090]

But this requires a degree of unselfing. 'Virtue is *au fond* the same in the artist as in the good man in that it is a selfless attention to nature: something which is easy to name but very hard to achieve.'[1091] Something similar may be said of prayer, which for Murdoch 'is properly not petition, but simply an attention to God which is a form of love'.[1092] Focusing our attention in this way is profoundly creative ('that God, attended to, is a powerful source of (often good) energy is a psychological fact'[1093]). This kind of unself-ing attention is an important spiritual, aesthetic and psychological as well as a moral virtue:

> we take a self-forgetful pleasure in the sheer alien pointless independent existence of animals, birds, stone and trees. 'Not how the world is, but that it is, is the mystical'.[1094]

Such attention is not, of course, some kind of objective or dispassionate observation from a safe distance, a point that is as important for the artist as for the spiritual pilgrim seeking the divine. In his study of the art and sculpture of the great Italian artist Alberto Giacometti (1901–66), famous for his skeletal and miniaturized figures, David Sylvester notes that

> experiments in perception show that in normal vision the mind corrects the retinal image so that distant things are not perceived small but life-size and distant. Giacometti's peculiar tendency is to see in a way that is free of the normal conceptual adjustments and reacts to what is strictly visible. This is not, however, an impartial, unselective way of seeing. On the contrary, it singles things out with great emphasis.[1095]

Giacometti was interested in the mutuality of our attention, i.e. in the fact that the object of our gaze is also looking at us:

> face to face with a Giacometti image, the spectator finds himself as if involved in a reciprocal relationship . . . The confrontation seems to say that the reality of a person is only established through his relation to another but that this relation reveals the solitude of each, the untraversable distance between them, recognises that this other is no projection or extension of oneself or creature subject to oneself but a being separate from oneself.[1096]

Spirituality and the vision of the eternal

Approaches such as this leave effectively intact the traditional western subject–object split, which other twentieth-century artists seek to subvert. In a lecture on the rela-tionship of spirituality and music, the distinguished singer Janet Baker compared musical performers to priests, mediating between composer and listener.[1097] Such mediation is by definition unselfish if it is to be authentic; and there is a sense in which everyone is called to it, to be a bridge-builder, *pontifex*, between one reality and another.[1098] This is a strikingly modest articulation of the role of performer. John Tavener, however, goes much further still. He describes his own massive work *Ultimos ritos* (1972) as being really 'about crucifixion and burial of the self'.[1099] The artist or composer is no more than a mouthpiece or channel through which the divine may choose to manifest itself, provided the self is willing to get out of the way, so to speak.

Hence his vigorous anathematizing of all western individuality in regard to music. In the end, all authentic music or art is simply a manifestation of the eternal, of what has always been there:

> I regard metaphysics as a fountainhead through which all music must flow, and I think the key word is 'flow'. As St Irenaeus of Lyons said, 'God will always have something more to teach man, and man will always have something more to learn from God.'[1100]

This does insert music into the heart of the meaning of life itself: 'in the end, the glory of music is inseparable from the superabundance of life'.[1101] Furthermore, as Jonathan Harvey points out, aesthetic and spiritual pleasure are of a different order from material pleasure: the former are inclusive, at no-one's expense, whilst the latter invariably means someone else doing without.[1102] But Harvey also notes that 'music that is so stripped of polyphonic and harmonic elaboration that it takes second place to the symbolic significance may prove inaccessible to those unsympathetic to that significance'.[1103]

Jonathan Harvey's own exploration of the relationship between spirituality and the self is a fascinating one. He contrasts what he calls the 'linear' music of past centuries with the 'global' music of the twentieth century. Linear music

> is concerned with composing against what has happened already, what has been established as a pattern, so that is a vivid force in the now, in the present. The now is always informed by a tension against what has just happened, a breaking up of what has just happened and breaking out of it in some way, either by violent contrast or by slight contrast or by near similarity or by exact repetition. It all makes a meaningful interval and a meaningful statement with its own colour and tension.[1104]

By contrast, 'global' music

> is to do with eternity; it is more to do with spirituality, it is more to do with seeing everything as a whole, as a unity, from above, and it doesn't have the tension of the detail . . . we start with a general feeling for eternity and unity, we arrive at the specific individuality in detail, and that detail is informed and made more vivid by what was preliminary to it; whereas the current paradigm is to work from detail to a kind of abstraction – a law, which really reduces the detail ultimately to being less interesting than its explanation. This isn't real knowledge; it is knowledge about things, not knowledge of things in all their vividness.[1105]

Elsewhere Harvey argues that more listeners to serious music will be attracted 'if they see that music is dealing with matters which concern them philosophically and spiritually'.[1106] He wants to break down the inherited western subject–object split, so that 'knowledge about' is replaced by a far deeper 'knowledge of'.[1107] And the belief that music can help foster that profound inner and outer unity and at-oneness that is close to Buddhist *nirvana* is characteristic of Harvey.[1108] This does not, however, reduce it to a static Tavener-like declamation of absolute truth: for Harvey, music has to do with ambiguity as well as with unity. Indeed the ambiguity is part of the adventurousness of music:

> I take no joy in composing if I set out in broad daylight knowing exactly what I want: I feel cheated of the adventure that makes music art. Instead each new work must grope out into some dark region, in which the imagination and the unconscious can operate together.[1109]

There are important analogies with the spiritual journey here, not least as it is articulated in the Bible: Abraham, after all, 'set out, not knowing where he was going' (Hebrews 11.8); and the composer must do the same. But does this run the risk of turning the composer (or the spiritual pilgrim) into a Galahad-like hero? Not for Harvey, for the greatest potential of music lies in its capacity to help us to penetrate behind language, behind the subject–object split, and introduce us into 'a world prior to the dictates of the constitution of the speaking subject' – that is, into (or as close as we can attain to) pure awareness itself.[1110] For Harvey, this is the awareness that existed before the Fall, before we needed language to particularize and separate.[1111]

This approach is arguably incompatible with Orthodox Christianity, for which the creative work of the Word is inseparable from the Godhead, so that the notion of a 'pure awareness' (other than as the characteristic experience of the preliterate child) before and above the existence of words is illusory. But Harvey, deeply influenced by Buddhist spirituality, wants to argue for a spiritual reality that transcends and heals all differentiation in a rich and harmonious unity; and he believes Jesus himself helped to bring this about, for he 'heals the rift between post-Renaissance individuality and spiritual community'.[1112]

Music and suffering humanity

And the reason this matters is because the consequence of separation and fragmentation is suffering, which for Harvey constitutes the most fundamental question that life throws at us.[1113] In his view, the purpose of music

> is . . . to reveal the nature of suffering and to heal. The one big question of existence. And the nature of suffering is connected with the separation of self and other, the narrow ego which is set up as an illusory existent, the belief that I am separated and therefore in a relationship of duality and even of conflict with the world: even physical suffering is subtly connected with this. So these are things which music, as it were, represents a statement about. This is the purpose of music.[1114]

Harvey believes that fragmentation and alienation are in part the consequence of a male-dominated view of reality, which we urgently need to subvert:

> Humankind is a tiny speck in a vast complex of galaxy clusters, and even on Earth we are only a minuscule proportion of the planet's evolution, a product, seemingly, of genetic randomness. We are unable to access truth because of our concept-making mind, through which the world impinges, and our observation of objects changes the objects as we observe them.

The crisis of alienation and isolation that such a worldview has precipitated is essentially a masculine crisis, created by men in a patriarchal system using characteristically male modes of analysis. The world we see, that we acknowledge, is the world we create: and it is largely a male one. To understand that we are *part* of a world that is *creating itself*, however, is a feminine understanding: an understanding based in wholeness, community, intuition, connection, healing, emotion, ambiguity. The reunion of masculine and feminine is the still obscure revolution of paradigms that we secretly long for.[1115]

Jonathan Harvey's spirituality is a striking synthesis of Buddhist teaching with western mysticism; and in a century which witnessed the most horrific violence imaginable between nations, ethnic groupings, and other fragmented parts of humanity, its relevance is clear. This is his conclusion:

I am not my body. I am not my mind. I am not the whole collection of my body and my mind, since the parts do not make a new whole, except for convenience of reference. Neither am I outside my body mind as some 'soul.' Me and my other do not exist from their own side except by conventional imputation. They cannot be found. All turbulence, all suffering, arises from erroneously imputing real (as opposed to conventional) existence to 'I' and to 'the other.' When this is deeply understood – and that is normally thought to take years of practice – compassion is felt. *Seeing through* suffering, *seeing through* our unliberated state of *samsara*, as an ignorant and tragically unnecessary condition for living beings, is 'compassionate wisdom.' *Music is a picture of 'wisdom.'*[1116]

Spirituality and architecture: sacred space

To move from this exalted exploration of the transcendental power of music to the relationship between spirituality and architecture, and specifically to the spiritual role and potential of the church building as it was articulated in the twentieth century, may appear too abrupt a transition. In reality many of the same issues arise here too. The Anglican bishop David Stancliffe positively stresses the biblical notion of creation as separation in his exploration of the spiritual role of the religious building.[1117] For Christians, Jesus *is* the Temple, ordering our chaos, cleansing the Jewish Temple because it had become dis-ordered. Hence churches have a special role and power at moments of separation, such as rites of passage. And he proposes a theological rationale for the relationship between the divine and the material: God is present in, but not restricted to, a sacred place. *Presence*, not *containment*, is the properly sacramental view. Inevitably, this leaves sacred buildings separated from the rest of creation, standing over against it, in a manner far from Harvey's vision of unity and oneness.[1118]

Positively, however, this view allows sacred buildings to be seen as not only *sacred* but *safe* space, where 'the sparrow finds a home, and the swallow a nest for herself', as the Psalmist puts it.[1119] Evelyn Underhill emphasizes this, arguing for the value of such buildings as repositories and transmitters of past stories, giving identity and meaning to those who inhabit them, especially in an age of spiritual homelessness.[1120] And

W. H. Vanstone develops this point, arguing that a sacred building should be understood in terms of an offering of love, a response to the unconditional love of God. Its beauty is not to be determined by utilitarian criteria, for

> love has been expended upon it and expressed in the care of it. In that love and care the building has been offered to God. That the building is little used, and in that sense unnecessary, is irrelevant. That a similar building stands at no great distance away is also irrelevant. The presentation of such facts as if they were decisive is often, and understandably, resented. Attachment to a Church building is by no means to be dismissed as sentimentality: it may well contain a profound, though possibly inarticulate, understanding of what that building is. In the last analysis, the only justification for the destruction of an offering is that it may become the basis or material of a richer, more lasting or more appropriate offering.[1121]

Alan Ecclestone, with characteristic power, articulates a vision of how sacred buildings may inspire and enlarge our spirituality:

> Much of the difficulty that most people experience in their efforts to pray springs from a kind of confinement, a too narrow restriction of their attention, of whose character they are hardly aware. Protesting that their faith is concerned with the whole of life, they fail to see that they have grown accustomed to approaching prayer through certain specialised channels. Worship means certain liturgical forms, the exposition of the Word means discourses upon the Scriptures, and the furnishing of churches and places of prayer becomes so traditionally ecclesiastical, that something like an enclave has been created for praying before we begin. Too rarely indeed does a church or cathedral, apart from quite genuine appeals for the relief of the victims of war and disaster, make clear to any beholder how or why it is at all concerned with all aspects of human life . . . Today we are rather worse off than the men of the Middle Ages for whom the artist carved in stone and wood or painted upon walls and glass the great images of their faith in terms congruent with their outlook upon the world. To the assembled people he could say 'this is your life,' the story in which you have a part. Every child today grows up surrounded by a wealth of pictures and models of a quite different world, of life conceived of in quite different ways. These things are there in his home and schools; they are rarely there in the parish church. The world he knows is stocked with marvels; the church he enters is apparently indifferent to them.[1122]

The idealizing of the past: 'Celtic' spirituality

The role and purpose of the sacred building returns us to an issue raised by John Tavener: is spirituality a matter of re-presenting the timeless truths of the past, making the creative artist into a mouthpiece for the divine rather than an originator? Such an uncritical approach to tradition might have its own integrity; but in the second half of the twentieth century it was vulnerable to exploitation by the purveyors of a particular view of the 'heritage' of the past, for whom 'the invention of tradition turned out to be a highly profitable marketing enterprise'.[1123]

The fondness for neo-Tudor architecture and period detail, the love of all things chintzy and rural (as though the two were somehow synonymous), had its impact on English spirituality, for example in encouraging a particular view of all things Celtic as being somehow the quintessence of an undemanding and leisured tranquillity, as though St Columba and his contemporaries were the equivalent of eighteenth-century gentlemen, gazing out placidly on Capability Brown landscapes.[1124] Such an approach may simply imply a longing to escape from the urbanized world of the twentieth century, or a retreat to the imagined greatness of earlier ages in British history.[1125] It is a poor substitute for the bold relationship between religion and the arts envisaged by people like Walter Hussey.[1126] Nor is it of much use to the poor, for whom restoring the past has little interest by comparison with building a better future.[1127] Stevie Smith's astringent poem 'The past' is worth recalling:

> People who are always praising the past
> And especially the times of faith as best
> Ought to go and live in the Middle Ages
> And be burnt at the stake as witches and sages.[1128]

The fascination with all things Celtic that arose during the closing decades of the twentieth century is not only a recent phenomenon: one scholar has pointed out that such an attitude to the Celts can be traced back to the time of Bede, and represents a form of English nostalgia, celebrating the imagined purity and beauty of ancient Scottish or Irish spirituality in a way that would never be found among inhabitants of Glasgow or Galway.[1129] In fairness, Christianity has frequently exhibited a fondness for idealizing a supposed golden age, perhaps especially for the pristine perfection of the apostolic Christian community; in a religion rooted in history, this is hardly surprising. But what is characteristically English may be said to be the way in which particular features of early 'Celtic' piety – such as a love of nature, or a predilection for solitude – are isolated from their contexts. In reality there is very little evidence to suggest that such things are any more 'Celtic' than Anglo-Saxon or European, and that if they were indeed to be found among (say) early Irish or Scottish Christians, they were only ingredients in a piety that certainly included a severe attention to sin, penance and the reality of evil.

Spirituality and psychology

Introduction

In view of the rapid development of psychology during the twentieth century, it is not surprising to find a new concern among spiritual writers for the self, and a new interest in charting its inner nature and dynamic. But the growth of psychology was not the only reason for this. A turning-inwards, away from the horrors of war and the unpredictable impact of increasing change, is perhaps to be expected; and the fact that people were living longer, had more leisure time, and thus more opportunity to study themselves, accelerated this tendency.[1130] It was, of course, by no means an unmixed blessing. Millions who lived in poverty had no time to become anxious about their inner landscapes; and not all purveyors of wisdom about it were to be trusted anyway. In the midst of the growing clamour for therapy and inner well-being and the spiralling levels of anxiety, observers could be forgiven for wondering what had happened to what used simply to be described as 'being unhappy'.[1131] And Peter Selby made a trenchant point when he wrote that

> if the human potential movement has potential only for those humans who engage in it, it were better it did not exist.[1132]

Nonetheless, the increasing abundance of knowledge about the inner workings of the psyche unquestionably allowed explorers of the spiritual life to examine more deeply the nature and workings of the self, and to learn from those who had made that examination their life's work. The writer Philip Toynbee praised Franz Kafka:

> The reason why Kafka remains such a central figure for our age is that he was one of the first and bravest explorers of our inner wilderness . . . More truly a saint than many of those who have used religious faith only as a means of escaping, or denying, the wilderness within.[1133]

Toynbee, who in later life was a practising lay Anglican, wrote a 'spiritual autobiography', *Part of a journey* (1977–9), which will be cited below and which explores with moving honesty his own personal journey. Another such explorer is Harry Williams (b. 1919), who explicitly uses the phrase 'a theology of the self' in what was arguably his most influential book, *The true wilderness*.[1134] Williams is an Anglican priest who became a monk of the Community of the Resurrection at Mirfield. In his autobiography he describes how he came to reject any form of religion that was dispensed, so to speak, from some external authority:

> The confirmation itself [at Cranleigh School] by the Bishop of Guildford (Dr Macmillan) didn't make much impression on me. He spoke to the parents afterwards and advised them to give their sons a book called *A Religion of your Own*. I can't remember who the author was. What was clear to me on reading it was that its title was a misnomer. It presented you with a prefabricated religion and rule of life which you could make your own only by buying the package deal.[1135]

Williams went on to offer radical reinterpretations of fundamental Christian doctrines in terms of inner personal experience. Thus in *Poverty, chastity, obedience*, Williams reinterprets the traditional monastic virtues in terms of self-awareness and psychology.[1136] In *True resurrection* he does the same with Easter: thus the resurrection of the body 'means my body being raised up to its own life. It means mind and body no longer making war on each other in a bid for domination, but recognizing that they are both equally me.'[1137] And (on miracle)

> The essence of miracle is not that it is dramatic, nor that it interferes with the natural world regarded as an external structure which works according to its own laws. Miracle is not what we invoke when science appears to have failed. The essence of miracle is our discovery of what we are.[1138]

Resurrection is basically a miracle of self-discovery.[1139] And the Holy Spirit 'is our-selves in the depths of what we are . . . theologically, the Spirit is called God in me.'[1140] Gethsemane means facing the enemies within.[1141] This approach attracted a good deal of fierce criticism from orthodox sources.[1142] But Williams was not simply in tune with the times. It could be argued that his work represents an important stage in the evolution of a more self-aware spirituality, and one that pays attention to the pioneer-ing work of psychologists and others.

The influence of Jung

Among those others one person in particular has exerted a profound influence on twentieth-century English spirituality: Carl Jung.[1143] For Jung, the 'self' meant the total personality: both the conscious, reflecting element of the personality, which he called the 'ego', and the unconscious element, which in Jung's opinion included both personal memories and inherited archetypal attributes common to all human beings.[1144] Thus by exploring the self, notably (though not only) by attending to one's dreams and unconscious processes, the person begins to become more fully aware of how all human nature works – and, in Jung's view, of the presence of the God who is at work within the self.[1145]

The impact of Jung has been extensive: thus his interest in the diversity of personal-ity types led to a new awareness that what is appropriate for one person's spiritual journey might not be for another.[1146] It has led some to a wholesale psychologizing of spirituality, as in Harry Williams' view of repentance: for him it is

> discovering something about yourself, something positive, not negative. It means realizing that you have potentialities of which you have been so far unaware . . . discovering that you have more to you than you dreamt or knew, becoming bored with being only a quarter of what you are and therefore taking the risk of surrendering to the whole, and thus finding more abundant life.[1147]

Others have taken a more nuanced view. The Dominican scholar Victor White, in his fine post-war study of psychology and theology *God and the unconscious* (to which Jung wrote a Foreword), argued that the two disciplines were complementary, but not to be confused. Thus for the theologian sin is an evil that people *do*, something active, whereas for many psychologists it is an evil that people *suffer*:

> it is a sickness, and as such something essentially involuntary . . . some-thing that *happens to* us, not something we *do* . . . We may say that while the sacrament of penance deals with certain evil results of human *freedom*, psychotherapy deals with certain results of human *compulsions*.[1148]

One deals with *misdeeds*, the other with *misfortunes*. The crucial difference consists in the theologian's active awareness of the reality and culpability of sin. And even Satan cannot *make* people sin: it is ultimately their own free choice.[1149] Psychology can help us understand why we sin, and psychiatry diagnose when sin is the result of sickness; but theology demands a clear-eyed recognition that much sin is the consequence of human evil, and spirituality must reckon with that too.

One of the aspects of Jung's thought which most influenced explorers of spirituality was his notion of the shadow: those elements of our personality which we have, freely or unconsciously, chosen to reject, at least during the first part of our lives, but which make their influence felt and demands honest recognition if we are to grow as people throughout our lives.[1150] Thus, as one Jungian priest put it, 'to face and own our own shadow is the road to self-realization'.[1151] And self-realization, or, in Jung's term, 'individuation', is for Christians a process assisted and perfected by grace: it is the search for what patristic theologians called our own lost likeness to God.[1152]

The implications of this for our understanding of spirituality are considerable; and there is space to give just one example. Laurens van der Post, another twentieth-century writer who was deeply indebted to Jung, speaks in his works of his pervasive sense of there being an other self within him, alongside his (so to speak) normal self, an 'other voice' that took over from time to time.[1153] He offers a moving illustration of how psychological insight can help human beings not only to *grow*, but even to *survive*. Believing his own life to have been irrevocably changed by his spontaneous offer of a cup of coffee to two Japanese men in Pretoria in 1926 (which led to his own profound exploration of Japanese culture and language), he describes how that single action almost certainly saved his life when he was arrested by the Japanese during the Second World War. While in prison he concludes from this experience the need

> to be aware of the importance of the small in life . . . Creation, it seemed to me, was even more active in the apparently humble, often despised, rejected and insignificant detail of the immediate life of the individual, than on the melodramatic and grandiloquent stage on which the establishments and authorities of the world sought it. No life, however humble . . . was ever without universal importance if it truly followed its own natural gift, even if it was only to plough a straight furrow and plant potatoes well. Out of sight of heart and mind of their world, as prisoners were naturally disposed to think, and even in their dreams, unconvinced that saving intervention from without was possible, it had a decisive element of reassurance for me and in due course for all. Whatever chance remained of survival, it proclaimed, depended on a creative attention and positive response to the daily trifles of imprisonment, living an imperilled 'now' as if it were a safe and assured 'forever.'[1154]

This is a fine example of how honest introspection can be subversive, allowing someone struggling to survive to discover spiritual resources within. The philosopher Gillian Rose, a secular Jew who was baptized as a Christian before dying of cancer, makes a similar point when she writes about how she felt on hearing of her poor prognosis following an operation:

> 'Control' in this context has two distinct meanings, both equally crucial. In the first place, 'control', as you would expect, means priority and ability to manage, not to force, the compliance of others, to determine what others think or do. In the second, more elusive sense – a sense which, nev-

ertheless, saves my life and which, once achieved, may induce the relin-
quishing of 'control' in the first sense – 'control' means that when
something untoward happens, some trauma or damage, whether inflicted
by the commissions or omissions of others, or some cosmic force, one
makes the initially unwelcome event one's own inner occupation. You
work to adopt the most loveless, forlorn, aggressive child as your own, and
do not leave her to develop into an even more vengeful monster, who constantly wishes you ill. In ill-health as in unhappy love, this is the hardest
work: it requires taking in before letting be.[1155]

This surely is close to the heart of any authentic spirituality: this is what Rose calls
'love's work', the immensely difficult process of seeking creatively to respond to what
we do not choose.

Reality and illusion

The difference, in this context, between creativity and compliance introduces us to
another important twentieth-century figure whose work is relevant to English spirituality: the child psychiatrist Donald Winnicott.

Winnicott, who died in 1971, drew attention to the formative importance of the
way the mother introduces the child to the interface between reality and illusion, and
helps it to recognize the creative value of both.[1156] The ability to do this is crucial for
the development of a richly imaginative inner life.[1157] In Winnicott's view, mental
(schizoid) illness consists *either* in being so out of touch with the external world that
you cannot perceive reality, *or* so firmly anchored in objective reality that you are out
of touch with the subjective world.[1158] The risk is that we settle for what he calls *com-
pliant* living, refusing ever to challenge either our inherited predispositions or the
hand life deals us, instead of the *creative* living we are capable of attaining.[1159] The
crucial issue is how we handle the interface of reality and illusion; and in Winnicott's
view it is in playing that the child learns to do this best. Religion, the arts, and other
'intermediate' areas of experience can help adults to do this by offering safe places for
us to experiment until a proper balance is attained.[1160] Kenneth Leech noted that

> it is in the *integration* of the inner and outer worlds that true spirituality is
> clearly distinguished from false.[1161]

Prayer and self-fulfilment

A psychological approach to spirituality tends to lead to a downgrading of 'external'
truth, such as religious doctrines, in favour of authentic personal experience. Philip
Toynbee castigates both western and eastern religious traditions in this regard:

> Faced with the Inexpressible the West has tried to describe it in absurdly
> concrete terms: the whole traditional theology is a case of the misplaced
> concrete. Faced with the Inexpressible the fault of the East has been to play
> about with paradox and negation.[1162]

For Toynbee, the important thing is not the theological, but the spiritual:

When Jason asked me what I believed, I said that what had begun as a half-frivolous hypothesis – let's see how things would look if we think of man as a spiritual being – had become the best illumination of any that I'd ever tried. In this light the whole of human life becomes – not intelligible, but alive with meaning; many-dimensional; vividly-coloured. All the old problems have been changed into a single great luminous mystery.[1163]

And the ultimate aim is self-fulfilment:

To be fully extended according to one's own unique nature and capacities – that's the only thing that matters. And the beauty of it is that since every human soul is unique the light that it sees and the light that it shines have never been seen or shone before. Each of us may see, and reflect, a glimmer of the same Great Light, but every glimmer is a little different from all the others. This is the great wonder of the Equality of Souls.[1164]

Toynbee boldly rejects the notion that this downgrading of doctrine makes God vague: 'one current idea which seems to me false and dangerous – that the more liberal-minded a faith becomes the more attenuated and ineffable must be its conception of God'.[1165] We may judge the validity of his claim by looking at how Harry Williams understands prayer. It is not surprising to find him describe it in terms of the self:

prayer is the means by which we become aware of the final me. Prayer is going down deep into myself to the place where I can find the final me. Prayer is anything which puts me in touch with the final me.[1166]

Positively, this leads Williams to emphasize the importance of honesty in prayer: we must bring before God the whole of what we feel or think, without evasion.[1167] And in part this preoccupation with the self is a means to an end. Intercession requires a recognition of my identification with others, which is only possible once we have learned to accept ourselves, for only then are we able 'to share their hurt so that it is felt to lie on our own shoulders as well as theirs'.[1168] Thus for Williams

prayer begins as the opening of my heart and mind to God's love for me. And it never ceases to be that however wide, and indeed universal, the implications and demands of that love are discovered to be. When, on the other hand, christian public political action begins to be divorced from the tender intimate love which gave it birth, it begins to become a power-game and as such no less a denial of God's love than the evil it opposes. Causes begin to matter more than people and the Son of God is on the way to being crucified afresh in the name of righteousness and by campaigns and committees. For how can I love my neighbour as myself unless I am deeply aware of what I am, that I am being loved into fullness of life by the Father of us all?[1169]

And yet doubts remain, above all the lingering suspicion that a spiritual journey which begins with self-exploration is very likely to end there. Reflecting on the nature of priesthood in 1935, Peter Green makes a distinction firmly at odds with the self-exploration of Harry Williams. Comparing the oil lamp with the electric light, Green points out that where the first will be exhausted eventually because its energy is drawn entirely from within, the second can go on for ever because it draws on energy from outside. Where the first is comparable to St Paul's 'life according to the flesh', the second is comparable to his 'life according to the Spirit' – a God-centred, not me-centred spirituality.[1170] 'What the world needs is not you, not me, but God.'[1171]

A much more radical approach to spirituality and the self in the last decades of the twentieth century has been the recovery of interest in the Ignatian tradition. St Ignatius of Loyola's own *Spiritual exercises* and *Constitutions*, designed to equip people for an active apostolic form of the religious life and summoning them to an unequivocal openness to the will of God, articulated an imaginative pattern of spirituality which was firmly linked with love and service of one's neighbour: 'love', as St Ignatius put it, 'consists in a mutual sharing of goods'.[1172] This approach has become the subject of extensive adaptation and exploration as individuals become increasingly interested in a pattern of spirituality which integrates prayer and action and is both flexible and demanding.[1173]

Spirituality and the world of work

Another manifestation of what might be called a psychological approach to spirituality is the interest in self-help and the development of the individual's potential in relation to the work place.[1174] The recognition that people will work better if they are happier, and the consequent interest in encouraging them to develop a broad-based 'portfolio' approach to an increasingly diversified career;[1175] the use of psychological profiling, varying kinds of therapies and forms of relaxation (including retreats) – all these testify not only to a prosperous society in search of meaning and inner fulfilment, but also to a concern for gentler, more affective values to set alongside the harsh acquisitiveness of unfettered capitalism. Those values are sought from a wide variety of sources, Christian and others, which in turn illustrates the fact that, in a highly educated society, people are far less likely to take any given source of wisdom 'on trust'.

Spirituality and ageing

One last example of the fruitful interchange between psychology and spirituality is worth considering: the experience of ageing, an experience more and more people encountered as life expectancy increased. The Methodist Neville Ward suggests that this experience offers fresh opportunities, chances to ponder religious truth which may have been avoided during earlier, busier stages of life: and then, 'finding a new orientation of the self is a matter of life and death . . . in the sense that people must attend to the question what it is all for and what they are for or else run the risk of retreating into a shrinking existence of nostalgias and compensations'.[1176]

Yet this is costly. In her study of prayer, the Roman Catholic Maria Boulding OSB points out the difficulty of accepting that one may never achieve one's most cherished goals:

It is a very painful realization, and much may depend on what I do with it. I can rebel and refuse to face it, which leads to resentment and a flirtation with unreality. I can acquiesce in a cynical and disillusioned way, which leads to loss of the vision and checks growth. Or I can accept it very lovingly in faith.

At a greater depth than before I am being asked to accept the reality of the human condition. God's Son accepted it in his incarnation more deeply and lovingly than I shall ever be able to, but my acceptance is within his. He did the Father's perfect work within his limited humanity, and all humanity's limitations are shot through with glory in consequence. God has chosen, freely chosen, to work creatively within my limitations too. When I accept them I am consenting to go along with his vision, not acquiescing in some kind of regretful decision on his part to make the best of a bad job.[1177]

In a profound article on the spirituality of old age, the Orthodox Metropolitan Anthony of Sourozh argues that 'it is given to us to live and relive our past until we have solved the problems which emerge'.[1178] We must relive past and unresolved experiences in the light of all subsequent experience; and only then, if appropriate, can we renounce them and let them go.[1179] Unresolved feelings of guilt towards someone who has died can be resolved by asking the dead person to forgive us.[1180] 'Ask yourself about your immediate circle of relatives, friends, acquaintances, ask yourself – am I at peace with each of them? If you are not, find that peace.'[1181] For Metropolitan Anthony, old age brings a greater emphasis on receptivity: but 'there is a difference between being passive and being contemplative . . . We need to learn to be contemplative, and look at events steadily with all the experience of life, with all the detachment which can be possessed only when we do not rush into action.'[1182] And 'to be able to receive graciously, gratefully, joyfully is an art which we do not always possess.'[1183]

Spirituality may be able to contribute to a positive attitude towards ageing and the elderly not only by articulating an inclusive vision of 'spiritual care' but also by helping to shape the values and meanings which are attached to particular stages of life.[1184] It can remind society not to judge people solely or even primarily by what they do, or by how much they can contribute, and instead to value them simply for who they are. It can run counter to a narrowly utilitarian worldview and give old age a rich and positive meaning in its own right. And it can do this by reminding everyone that the real, the enduring spiritual values in life – such as forgiveness, healing, justice, wholeness and peace-making – need not diminish with biological ageing. A spirituality of ageing can remind society of the subversive potential of human beings to draw forth and share meaning, identity and purpose even from what appears to be the least propitious dimensions of creaturely existence.

Spirituality and the secular quest

The persistence of spirituality

We may conclude with some reflections on how spirituality addresses, and is addressed by, the progressive secularity of contemporary society. There is some evidence to suggest that declining patterns of churchgoing, and even of formal belief in God, were not matched by a commensurate decline in people's spirituality: people continued to believe even when they were no longer interested in belonging to religious organizations.[1185] The fragmentation of life associated with postmodernism undoubtedly encouraged this: people became consumers rather than producers, in a society dominated by information technology rather than industry; and they lived more of their lives in discrete compartments, each sealed off from the others. In such a society personal spiritual fulfilment came to take precedence over corporate religion.[1186]

Some argued that this was not surprising: the persistence of a spiritual dimension to life in a secular age was only to be expected. In 1934 T. S. Eliot wrote eloquently of the increasing irrelevance of the Church in people's lives.[1187] Yet, as he went on to point out, the world does not change: the struggle between good and evil continues; and the need for a spiritual dimension to life remains.[1188] To neglect churches and shrines, and to neglect the desert that is in the heart of each person we meet, is to risk neglecting that struggle.[1189] We are, or ought to be, modern Nehemiahs, alert and vigilant: 'therefore some must labour, and others must hold the spears'.[1190] And he famously suggests that authentic religious experience will not easily relinquish its hold upon us, despite our persistent preference for living in illusion:

> Peace, and be at peace with your thoughts and visions.
> These things had to come to you and you to accept them,
> This is your share of the eternal burden,
> The perpetual glory. This is one moment,
> But know that another
> Shall pierce you with a sudden painful joy
> When the figure of God's purpose is made complete.
> You shall forget these things, toiling in the household,
> You shall remember them, droning by the fire,
> When age and forgetfulness sweeten memory
> Only like a dream that has often been told
> And often been changed in the telling. They will seem unreal.
> Human kind cannot bear very much reality.[1191]

Much of the evidence for the persistence of spirituality in a secular age is inevitably anecdotal: we do not know how typical was the labourer from Preston, born at the end of the nineteenth century, who 'abandoned church going as a married man but did not repudiate Christian teaching. The family always said a prayer before meals when he was at home.'[1192]

But some of the evidence is firmer. The American Roger Edrington carried out some research among 50 working-class men in the Erdington district of Birmingham in 1984.[1193] Scarcely any of them went to church or were interested in whether there was a life after death;[1194] and ten of them said they were atheists. Yet 72% of them admitted to praying, either regularly or occasionally; of the ten atheists, four prayed, even though they did not believe in God;[1195] and of the 12 agnostics, 4 never prayed at all, 6 prayed sometimes, and two prayed every night before going to bed.[1196] Furthermore approximately 60% believed they had had some kind of spiritual or religious experience.[1197] Those who did pray seemed to regard it as quite straightforward, like shopping: 'I just do the standard praying if I want something.'[1198] It was strictly private: most had never spoken to anyone, even their wives, about their prayer; and some felt the lavatory was the most appropriate (because most private) place for it.[1199] One person said

> I always get a feeling that I'm not just saying it to myself and I'm not the only person who's just hearing it. I believe that God does hear me. I feel quite good about it afterwards.[1200]

Another, still in shock after the death of his wife ('the biggest shock of me life'), went on to say, amid tears: 'I've lost complete confidence in Jesus since he took me wife and son.' He still prays a little prayer every night 'just before I drop off. But is it worth it?'[1201] And another, on whether God answers prayer, responded

> Has he heard me? . . . Well, if he's got a bit of spare time. He's a pretty busy man, isn't he, sort of thing. He can't listen to millions, can he? As I say, in a spare minute sort of thing like, I hope he listens to me prayer like sort of thing. I say the prayer over and over again in case he doesn't hear. He's a very busy man. I suppose he can listen to everybody really.[1202]

It would be foolish to make too much of one small survey. But it does argue for the persistence of an explicitly spiritual dimension to life long after any credal convictions or churchgoing habits had disappeared.[1203] We might not be surprised to find some of those interviewed admitting it was when they were *in extremis* that they turned to prayer, like the ex-soldier who said he prayed

> because I remember when . . . this captain of the Gurkha Rifles carried me across this paddy field and the Japs were shelling over him. I always remember, 'Oh God! Oh God!' That's what comes out of your mouth. He's got to be there for you to do that, that's my opinion.[1204]

Yet the way people respond in moments of crisis may well lead to a deeper spiritual commitment thereafter, and the persistence of the instinct for prayer is something that pastors and others would do well to take seriously.[1205]

The practice of prayer in a secular age

Surveys of this kind raise difficult questions about what it means to pray in a secular society, a subject explored by D. Z. Phillips, a philosopher of religion, in a notable study published in 1965. Phillips rejects the notion of prayer as mere talking to oneself, on the grounds that it is quite unlike the way people otherwise talk to themselves.[1206] Instead Phillips uses the analogy of the teacher–pupil relationship. The pupil tells the teacher things the latter knows already; but that does not lessen the value of the pupil articulating what she or he knows:

the analogy has obvious limitations, but it is sufficient to show that prayer is not pointless *simply* because it is uninformative. God is told nothing, but in the telling, the person who confesses is told something about the state of his soul.[1207]

Similarly the practice of paying attention, not simply in the sense of striving or concentrating but in the deeper sense of giving one's whole being to a particular object, is fundamental to prayer.[1208] For knowledge of God is not knowledge *about* something, not a knowledge that can be increased by much learning: 'deepening one's knowledge of the divine is not a matter of increasing intelligibility'.[1209] Indeed prayer is by definition talking to someone whom one does not understand; and the confession of one's inadequacy is central to the understanding of oneself arrived at through prayer.[1210] This is because the experience of oneself as having been *forgiven* is fundamental to the way we apprehend God: it is the sense of having been both forgiven and accepted which makes prayer both possible and therapeutic. 'Being able to see that one is forgiven by God entails being able to live with oneself. In coming to know God, one comes to know oneself.'[1211] It is precisely through prayer and worship that we discover what the meaning of life is: we cannot find it out for ourselves.[1212]

Phillips believes that thanksgiving is also vital to prayer: 'by thanksgiving, the believer recognizes that life has hope; he is rescued from despair'.[1213] It is this which alone can give meaning to suffering; and here Phillips quotes Simone Weil: 'The extreme greatness of Christianity lies in the fact that it does not seek a supernatural remedy for suffering but a supernatural use for it.'[1214] Similarly we don't expect petitionary prayer to cause immediate changes in what happens: 'the prayer of petition is best understood, not as an attempt at influencing the way things go, but as an expression of, and a request for, devotion to God *through* the way things go.'[1215]

Yet the central dilemma remains: how can prayer be valid once its theological and credal framework is either loosened or removed altogether? The difficulty about the separation of spirituality from theology, as John Macquarrie noted in 1972, was that the result could only be chaotic: an uncontrolled vitality, bearing witness to humanity's enduring need for the spiritual, yet lacking any criteria for 'testing the spirits'.[1216] Religious experience, however defined, suffers from the same difficulty: hence the importance of C. C. J. Webb's point, in a lecture on religious experience delivered in 1944, that such experience should not be seen or interpreted as though it were private: 'religion is so obviously a function of the community'.[1217] Hence too the need for revelation ultimately to be submitted to the scrutiny of reason, a point Webb makes as well.[1218]

Princess Diana and the 'religion of the heart'

These observations are worth bearing in mind as we consider one of the most interesting manifestations of the persistence of the spiritual in people's lives in late twentieth-century England: the reaction to the death in August 1997 of Diana, Princess of Wales. That reaction was particularly strong among women and members of minority groups, whose presence at places of mourning following Diana's death was noteworthy.[1219] The spirituality that came to be associated with Diana herself, as well as with the reaction to her death, had a number of striking features.

First, it involved a search for personal authenticity and self-fulfilment. Diana is quoted as saying, in 1993:

> From now on I am going to own myself and be true to myself. I no longer want to live someone else's idea of what and who I should be. I am going to be me.[1220]

Yet, unlike some manifestations of the theology of self-awareness explored above, Diana's spirituality was not entirely self-centred: it did involve real humanitarian concern for others, concern that was rooted not in justice or politics but in a profound compassion.[1221]

Secondly, this kind of spirituality involved an extensive and eclectic choice of ideological and other resources in classic postmodernist style. Diana herself drew upon advisers, astrologers, clairvoyants, gym trainers, homeopaths, hypnotherapists, osteopaths, masseurs, New Age therapists, soothsayers, tarot card readers, psychotherapists: almost everyone (one feels) except conventional clerics.[1222] Perhaps inevitably, this led to what some might feel to be a degree of credulity: thus Diana herself seemed to have believed in a 'spirit world' to which all dead people go, and with which she could commune.[1223]

Thirdly, such spirituality stresses images of 'the heart', feelings, self-expression, instincts, intuitions, me-centredness – as opposed to principles, religious teachings, doctrines and ideas.[1224] In this regard it has much in common with the results of Edrington's research in Birmingham, as well as with some of what was explored above in terms of the relationship of spirituality and psychology. God became a spirit within;[1225] and, as Linda Woodhead pointed out, Diana's 'religion of the heart' found its ontological basis not in the divine so much as in the human.[1226]

Fourthly, such spirituality is entirely compatible with an apolitical consumerism; and one commentator shrewdly described it as 'spiritual shopping'.[1227] It demands no clear commitment to any particular tradition, and although it issues in a pervasive compassion it need not address other more difficult ethical principles.

Two profound responses to this kind of spirituality are worth quoting. Linda Woodhead, directly addressing the Diana phenomenon, makes a telling point:

> Where Charles favoured a religion based on a mix of Prayer Book Anglicanism and the books of Laurens van der Post, Diana depended on nothing more than intuition, feeling, and a sense of spiritual connection with others. The latter, of course, are qualities to which anyone can lay claim, irrespective of class, education, or gender. Historically, they have proved particularly congenial to women who have always played a preponderant role in the mystical, affective strands of religion, probably because of their exclusion from institutions of learning and clerical power.[1228]

The second response dates from nearly half a century before Diana's untimely death. In his study of Jungian psychology, the Dominican Victor White notes Jung's point that '*whenever* the Spirit of God is excluded from human consideration, an unconscious substitute takes its place'.[1229] And White concludes:

could it be that gods and demons, heavens and hell, are ineradicable from the nooks and crannies of the human mind, and that if the human mind is deprived of its heaven above and its hell beneath, then it must make its heaven and corresponding hell on earth?[1230]

Hence the concentration camps, and 'the new disease of unconscious religion which becomes epidemic when man is filched of his gods'.[1231] White notes the propensity of clergy and moralists to bewail the decline of marriage and our loss of a sense of the sanctity of sexuality and the home:

> There is an undeniable but superficial sense in which that is true. But the deeper levels revealed in the analyst's consulting room show that these catastrophes are more often to be attributed to the fact that unconsciously marriage has been regarded as *too* sacred rather than otherwise, and hence required to bear a weight too heavy for it, and which in other days carried *it*. Sex is expected to provide a mystical union, the partner a divinity, the home a heaven – each, in short, is required to provide a substitute for religion and to be saddled with a task to which each is of its nature unequal.[1232]

In short, we may pay a high price for cutting spirituality adrift from its intellectual and theological moorings, and from its corporate context in the life of the people of God, even if doing so opens up a wide range of new horizons and perspectives in which people can find spiritual meaning in life.

Spirituality, health and education

The increasingly pluralist nature of English society in the late twentieth century, together with the persistent interest in 'spirituality', has encouraged those involved in health and education to look for ways of incorporating a spiritual dimension into their work without restricting that dimension to any particular religious tradition. Space prohibits any extended reflection on this subject; and, perhaps unsurprisingly, definitions of what is meant by 'spiritual' or 'spirituality' in this context tend to be vague. One Department of Education report defines 'spirituality' as the valuing of the non-material aspects of life, and intimations of an enduring reality'.[1233]

David Stoter, an Anglican hospital chaplain, linked spirituality with wholeness and integration, and argued that the spiritual dimension of life 'enables the search for meaning in life and provides a common bond between individuals'.[1234] The distinction between 'religious' and 'spiritual' needs allows those involved in health and education to help people find meaning, purpose and direction without necessarily having recourse to religious commitment or practices; and it makes the carer's role at least in part into that of an interpreter or 'go-between', helping people to make sense of what they are experiencing.[1235] This very inclusiveness allows for the opening up of rich areas of human experience hitherto little acknowledged in either health care or educational curricula; and the twenty-first century may see departments of 'spiritual care' or 'spiritual nurture' burgeoning in both of these areas.[1236]

The notion of care is in itself profoundly spiritual; as Sheila Cassidy has memorably put it, real care is prophetic:

It is a lavishing of precious resources, our precious ointment on the handi-
capped, the insane, the rejected and the dying that most clearly reveals the
love of Christ in our times. It is this gratuitous caring, this unilateral declaration of love which proclaims the gospel more powerfully than bishops
and theologians.[1237]

And such care, refusing as it does to separate the physical from the spiritual (let
alone the spiritual from the religious), encouraged many to see the importance of
physical health (both personal and environmental) in the fostering of any mature
spirituality.[1238]

Spirituality and science: Michael Polanyi and Richard Dawkins

We may conclude with two brief studies of how scientists have suggested ways of
filling the spiritual vacuum created by the absence of formal religious belief. The distinguished physical chemist Michael Polanyi explores D. Z. Phillips' point about the
difference between knowledge *about* and knowledge *of* something or someone.
Polanyi suggests that the distinction is false: authentic personal knowledge of
anything is no detached, Olympian objectivity: rather

> it commits us, passionately and far beyond our comprehension, to a vision
> of reality. Of this responsibility we cannot divest ourselves by setting up
> objective criteria of verifiability – or falsifiability, or testability, or what you
> will. For we live in it as in the garment of our own skin. Like love, to which
> it is akin, this commitment is a 'shirt of flame', blazing with passion and,
> also like love, consumed by devotion to a universal demand. Such is the
> true sense of objectivity in science.[1239]

Hence Polanyi can claim that 'a scientific theory which calls attention to its own
beauty, and partly relies on it for claiming to represent empirical reality, is akin to a
work of art which calls attention to its own beauty as a token of artistic reality. It is also
akin to the mystical contemplation of nature.'[1240] We *participate* in what we know.[1241]
And we *communicate* what we know to others.[1242] Polanyi has a far richer doctrine of
the way we know things than, say, William Temple, who sees science and mathematics
as involving only a discursive, analytical knowledge;[1243] and he thus suggests that
rigorous scientific enquiry has its own, intrinsically spiritual, character.

This understanding of knowledge allows Polanyi to speak of *contemplation*, or
indwelling, among scientists: 'astronomic observations are made by dwelling in astronomic theory, and it is this internal enjoyment of astronomy which makes the
astronomer interested in the stars.' Similarly for mathematics. Thus

> a true understanding of science and mathematics includes the capacity for
> a contemplative experience of them, and the teaching of these sciences
> must aim at imparting this capacity to the pupil. The task of inducing an
> intelligent contemplation of music and dramatic art aims likewise at
> enabling a person to surrender himself to works of art. This is neither to
> observe nor to handle them, but to live in them.[1244]

Polanyi suggests that the excitement the scientist experiences in meeting new challenges is not purely intellectual; rather it is akin to that experienced by the animal when it plays:

> Animals at play seek excitement, and even when they have outgrown the playful stage they need activity. Human beings develop this desire for tension in a variety of forms. Man is one of the few animals who continues to play throughout adult life. Men have also at all times gone out in search of adventure and enjoyed tales of adventure . . . Our gigantic modern amusement industry betokens the popular forms of this desire; but our craving for mental dissatisfaction enters also into the highest forms of man's spontaneous originality.[1245]

And it is precisely this breaking-out of existing constraints by living in and beyond them which is the scientific equivalent of ecstatic vision.[1246] 'Contemplation dissolves the screen, stops our movement through experience and pours us straight into experience; we cease to handle things and become immersed in them. Contemplation has no ulterior intention or ulterior meaning; in it we cease to deal with things and become absorbed in the inherent quality of our experience, for its own sake.'[1247] Polanyi compares this process with Christian mysticism, which he understands as the willingness to go beyond intellectual understanding and achieve contemplative communion with God through love. Here too what is needed is not objective observation, but passionate contemplation, which itself involves a breaking-out from existing mental constraints into a new level of experience and being. 'Proximity to God is not an observation, for it overwhelms and pervades the worshipper. An observer must be relatively detached from that which he observes, and religious experience transforms the worshipper.'[1248] Unlike scientific or artistic contemplation, however, Christian mysticism is always straining after something yet further away – the ultimately unattainable fullness of the divine:

> Christian worship sustains, as it were, an eternal, never to be consummated hunch: a heuristic vision which is accepted for the sake of its unresolvable tension. It is like an obsession with a problem known to be insoluble, which yet follows, against reason, unswervingly, the heuristic command: 'Look at the unknown!' Christianity sedulously fosters, and in a sense permanently satisfies, man's craving for mental dissatisfaction by offering him the comfort of a crucified God.[1249]

Like the mystic, the scientist is always both contemplating truth and dwelling within it, and yet also always breaking out from our objective detachment towards new truth as yet undiscovered and unexplored. 'Religion, considered as an act of worship, is an indwelling rather than an affirmation. God cannot be observed, any more than truth or beauty can be observed.'[1250] And religious doubt, like scientific doubt, can spur us on to discover yet deeper levels of religious truth and experience: in this sense Polanyi can say that 'an era of great religious discoveries may lie before us'.[1251]

In *Unweaving the rainbow*, the formidable scientific polemicist Richard Dawkins emphasizes that science in itself evokes profound and continuing wonder from those who study it with attention, thereby removing the need for the kind of spurious wonder evoked (in his view) by religion or astrology. At times he comes close to spirituality in the language he uses: 'the feeling of awed wonder that science can give us is one of the highest experiences of which the human psyche is capable.'[1252] And his central credo is clear-cut:

> I believe that an orderly universe, one indifferent to human preoccupations, in which everything has an explanation even if we still have a long way to go before we find it, is a more beautiful, more wonderful place than a universe tricked out with capricious, *ad hoc* magic.[1253]

Dawkins' starting-point is the wonder of our actual existence. In a chapter appositely entitled 'The anaesthetic of familiarity', he writes

> We are going to die, and that makes us the lucky ones. Most people are never going to die because they are never going to be born. The potential people who could have been here in my place but who will in fact never see the light of day outnumber the sand grains of Arabia.[1254]

This fundamental, almost Chestertonian, sense of the gratuitousness and wonder of being alive should affect all we do and are. 'What is the use of bringing a baby into the world if the only thing it does with its life is just work to go on living?'[1255] Hence Dawkins argues that 'without losing lucidity, indeed with added lucidity, we need to reclaim for real science that style of awed wonder that moved mystics like Blake.'[1256] This leads Dawkins, after an extensive exploration of particular scientific truths which are likely to evoke such wonder, to criticize religions and others who seek to encourage us to recover a sense of the childlike in our attitude to the world around us:

> An active readiness to be deceived can be called childish because it is common – and defensible – among children. I suspect that its persistence in adults stems from a hankering after, indeed a pining for, the lost securities and comforts of childhood . . . The adult world may seem a cold and empty place, with no fairies and no Father Christmas, no Toyland or Narnia, no Happy Hunting Ground where mourned pets go, and no angels – guardian or garden variety. But there are also no devils, no hellfire, no wicked witches, no ghosts, no haunted houses, no daemonic possession, no bogeymen or ogres.[1257]

Dawkins further warns of the dangers of a combination of childish gullibility 'coupled with its opposite – stubborn persistence in a belief, once acquired'.[1258] And he warns of the dangers of a pseudo-mysticism, such as that of Teilhard de Chardin, which uses the language of science with no real content, and cites Sir Peter Medawar's criticisms of Teilhard, and indeed of

> the notorious fondness of mystics for 'energy' and 'vibrations', technical terms misused to create the illusion of scientific content where there is no content of any kind.[1259]

CONCLUSION: THE STAR MAKER

In 1937, with the shadows of war falling again across Europe, Olaf Stapledon (1886–1950) wrote a remarkable science fiction novel which he called *Star Maker*. He tried explicitly 'to construct an imaginative sketch of the dread but vital whole of things' (the adjectives are not empty rhetoric but a sharp awareness of the threat that faced humanity as he wrote), and in particular to suggest a vision of the 'spiritual life' which might help make sense of human experience as a whole.[1260] His story begins with reflections on the meaninglessness of so much modern existence: 'we were always hurrying from one little urgent task to another, but the upshot was insubstantial'.[1261] The narrator then undergoes a cosmic journey which introduces him, in a manner not dissimilar to Swift's Gulliver, to a range of societies, allowing Stapledon to offer a critique of some forms of introverted spirituality.[1262] The book ends with the narrator, back home with his family, contemplating the future of the world:

> Sitting there on the heather, on our planetary grain, I shrank from the abysses that opened up on every side, and in the future. The silent darkness, the featureless unknown, were more dread than all the terrors that imagination had mustered. Peering, the mind could see nothing sure, nothing in all human experience to be grasped as certain, except uncertainty itself; nothing but obscurity gendered by a thick haze of theories. Man's science was a mere mist of numbers; his philosophy but a fog of words . . .
>
> And yet? I singled out our window. We had been happy together! We had found, or we had created, our little treasure of community. This was the one rock in all the welter of experience . . .
>
> And the future? Black with the rising storm of this world's madness, though shot through with flashes of a new and violent hope, the hope of a sane, a reasonable, a happier world. Between our time and that future, what horror lay in store? Oppressors would not meekly give way. And we two, accustomed only to security and mildness, were fit only for a kindly world; wherein, none being tormented, none turns desperate. We were adapted only to fair weather, for the practice of the friendly but not too difficult, not heroical virtues, in a society both secure and just. Instead, we found ourselves in an age of titanic conflict . . . when grave choices must be made in crisis after crisis, and no simple or familiar principles were adequate . . .
>
> How to face such an age? How to muster courage, being capable only of homely virtues? How to do this, yet preserve the mind's integrity, never to let the struggle destroy in one's own heart what one tried to serve in the world, the spirit's integrity.
>
> Two lights for guidance. The first, our little glowing atom of community, with all that it signifies. The second, the cold light of the stars . . . Strange that in this light, in which even the dearest love is frostily assessed . . . the human crisis does not lose but gains significance. Strange, that it seems more, not less, urgent to play some part in this struggle.[1263]

Stapledon matters for two reasons. First, he points to the two perspectives within which any authentic vision of the spiritual life must be set. The hearth, and the stars: on the one hand, the intimacy of human communities and relationships; on the other, the awesome grandeur of a universe still far beyond human knowledge or control – and, caught between them, a fragile humanity acutely conscious of its incapacity for the challenges it faces. The two perspectives belong together: humanity's capacity to find meaning and purpose in the first will determine, and will be determined by, what significance it attaches to its responsibilities for the second.

But Stapledon matters for a more important reason too. Like the great oracular prophecies of Isaiah, stirring up the easy apathy or bitter hopelessness of the Jewish people in exile and kindling within them a vision of hope for the future, Stapledon tried to do the same for his own generation. Sixty years later, at the end of the twentieth century, the situation was not self-evidently better. Although world war or nuclear holocaust appeared less likely, nations still waged war; environmental catastrophe still loomed threateningly; and the capacity of human beings for self-absorbed isolationism while millions lived in entirely avoidable poverty or suffering remained undiminished.

Yet, on New Year's Eve 1999, an unprecedented universal celebration took place, as societies of every conceivable culture and religion welcomed the dawn of the third millennium since the birth of the founder of Christianity. The celebration was fleeting, and betokened no spectacular religious revival. But it did offer a sudden startling glimpse of a different kind of world; and it underlined the scope for a new Stapledon to dream of how things could be. Such prophetic dreaming is the best possible test of the enduring vitality of a spiritual tradition; and the achievement of English spirituality in adapting and renewing itself in the face of countless changes bodes well for its future. Meanwhile the prophet Habakkuk's vision, at once practical and transcendental, defiantly hopeful in the face of a daunting future, may speak to a new age as it spoke to an older one, reminding both of the Star Maker's endless capacity for renewal and surprise:

> Though the fig tree does not blossom,
>   and no fruit is on the vines;
> though the produce of the olive fails
>   and the fields yield no food;
> though the flock is cut off from the fold
>   and there is no herd in the stalls,
> yet I will rejoice in the LORD;
>   I will exult in the God of my salvation.[1264]

NOTES

1. From Chapter 7 ('The Cathedral') of D. H. Lawrence, *The rainbow*, pp. 193–4.

2. 'A thanksgiving', in *Thank you, fog: last poems by W. H. Auden* (London: Faber, 1974), p. 39.

3. Dean Inge wrote in 1948 that 'there is no close parallel in history to the systematic undermining of the social order which we see about us' (*The end of an age and other essays* (London: Putnam, 1948), p. 12).

4. The remarks of George Steiner on the Holocaust and the rise of Nazism are relevant here: 'It is more than arguable that the genius for speculative abstraction, for aesthetic formalism, for disinterested inquiry immune to the roughage of common needs and pursuits which have marked European intellectual, artistic, scientific eminence, disabled our humanity. Where sensibility and understanding are schooled to respond most intensely to the cry in the poem, to the agony in the painting or to the absolute in the philosophic proposition or scientific axiom, the cry in the street may go unheard.' ('Remembering the future', in *Theology* (November/December 1990) p. 439).

5. See Clarke (1996), esp. p. 3; for a vivid description of Edwardian England see Tuchman (1980) pp. 3–14. Edwardian England was ruled by landed gentry: there were 45 people in Great Britain who owned over 100,000 acres each; and out of a population of 44,500,000, there were 2,500 landowners who owned more than 3,000 acres apiece and had landed incomes of over £3,000 (Tuchman, pp. 26–7). Between 18 and 20 million people had incomes of less than £160 p.a. (p. 27). The death of Queen Victoria, just after the turn of the century (24 January 1901) felt to many like the end of an era (p. 58). Within months Lord Salisbury had gone too; queen, Prime Minister and century departed almost together (p. 59). The funeral of Edward VII in 1910 was an occasion of extraordinary imperial grandeur (see Tuchman's wonderful description in her *August 1914*, also published as *The guns of August* (London: Constable, 1962), pp. 13–26).

6. Neville Cardus, *Ten composers* (London: Cape, 1945), p. 135. The whole of Cardus' nuanced essay on Elgar (pp. 123–38) is worth reading as an exploration of the guiding spirit of Edwardian England.

7. Eliot, 'Choruses from *The Rock*' (1934), in *Poems and plays*, pp. 151–2.

8. See Tuchman (1980), esp. pp. 353–401, for a succinct summary.

9. Adrian Hastings expresses this well: 'What was new in the Edwardian age was less the Church's loss of the working class because the poor had never really belonged to it, than the unmistakable decline in Christian belief of the middle class . . . The core religion of England had long been lay, Protestant, middle-class and scriptural . . . That would no longer do. Evolution and historical criticism, by the Edwardian age, had punctured it quite irredeemably. While pockets of active resistance remained . . . the main stream of the bourgeoisie was now flowing uncontrollably towards an agnosticism surfaced over for some with soft undogmatic pieties nourished, for want of better, upon sunsets and daffodils' (1986, p. 41).

10. Baldwin (1926) p. 195.

11. p. 196.

12. Hastings (1986, p. 244) points out the huge regional variations in unemployment: in 1934 it stood at 67% in Jarrow, and only 3% in High Wycombe.

13. During the long Conservative government of 1951–64, average earnings rose by 110% (Hastings (1986) p. 413).

14. William Beveridge's report *Social insurance and allied services* appeared in 1942, paving the way for the National Health Service. For home ownership, see Clarke (1996) pp. 144–5.

15. See Ravetz (1995) p. 194.

16. Clarke (1996) p. 40.

17. As Grace Davie points out (1994, pp. 199–200) people applied their unprecedented freedom of choice to religion, either by adopting an eclectic mix of different elements from different religions, or by pursuing fragmentation to its logical conclusion – 'selecting one particular fragment of what is on offer and expanding this to form a complete world view'.

18. Quoted in Eric Hobsbawm, *Age of extremes: the short twentieth century, 1914–1991* (London: Michael Joseph, 1994), p. 2.

19. Dawson (1929) p. 6.

20. See e.g. Dawson (1929) p. 69.

21. By 1922 there were 1 million telephones in the UK; by 1938, 3 million (Clarke (1996) p. 178). In real terms consumer expenditure rose by 45% between 1952 and 1964: the largest items were food, drink and tobacco (p. 254). There was an unparalleled consumer boom between 1955 and 1960: the proportion of those using refrigerators rose from 6 to 16%, washing machines from 25 to 44%, and car owners from 18 to 32% (Briggs (1983) p. 303). Harold Macmillan's 'You've never had it so good' slogan was coined for the 1959 election, which he won.

22. See Rosalind Miles (1989) p. 282, and Wilson (1980) p. 13.

23. 'Economics', in *Thank you, fog: last poems* (London: Faber, 1974), p. 31.

24. Betty Friedan, *The feminine mystique* (1963), quoted in Miles (1981) p. 274.

25. Before 1970, the highest unemployment figure attained since the Second World War was 555,000 in 1968; by 1972 it was 870,000, by 1977 1,455,000, and by 1981 3 million.

26. After the Second World War, there was a divorce bulge as well as a baby boom: in 1947–8 over 100,000 divorces went through (Clarke (1996) p. 165). The 1969 Divorce Reform Act made irretrievable breakdown the only grounds for divorce by either party; it also provided for mandatory divorce after five years at the request of any one party. The historian Lawrence Stone wrote these words at the end of his important study of the history of marriage:

> All the historian can say with confidence is that the metamorphosis of a largely non-separating and non-divorcing society, such as England from the Middle Ages to the mid-nineteenth century, into a separating and divorcing one in the late twentieth, is perhaps the most profound and far-reaching social change to have occurred in the last five hundred years. A gigantic moral, religious, and legal revolution has accompanied and made possible the shift from a system of marriage prematurely terminated by death to a system of marriage prematurely terminated by choice. It is an open question whether individuals and societies can adapt more easily to conditions caused by a free exercise of the will than to conditions caused by the inexorable accident of fate (*The road to divorce: England 1530–1987* (Oxford UP, 1990), p. 422).

Some attempts have been made to encourage a spirituality which will foster family and home life, though most are only tentative: see e.g. the Church of England's report *Something to celebrate: valuing families in church and society* (London: Church House Publishing, 1995), esp. pp. 162–4.

27. Berger (1971) p. 95.

28. Clarke (1996, p. 160) notes that organized religion (esp. the Church of England) held its ground far more than many late-Victorian writers on a crisis of faith could have predicted. Roberts' survey of the experience of working-class women from Lancashire shows that almost all of them were brought up with at least some degree of Christian teaching (1984, p. 170). Even so, the only traditional denomination actually to grow numerically during the twentieth century was Roman Catholicism (Clarke, p. 161), and as the twentieth century advanced it too was caught in the grip of serious decline. Only the Pentecostals, the house churches, and some of the other great world faiths (such as Buddhism) continued to buck the trend. Adrian Hastings (1986, p. 37) stresses the importance of not underestimating the influence of religion in England at the start of the twentieth century: there is widespread evidence of great pastoral vigour and congregational vitality. Even so, there is also evidence of a levelling-off; and the large majority of working-class townsfolk, at least in the north, did not go to church, and probably never did – at least, not since the Industrial Revolution, despite the valiant efforts of the Primitive Methodists and the Anglo-Catholics (p. 37; but see the remarks of Elizabeth Roberts (1984) pp. 4–5).

29. Berger (1971) p. 37.

30. Helen Butcher, *The treacle stick: Ladywood, Aston and Erdington, 1917–1942* (Warwick:

Quercus, 1999), pp. 15–16.

31. 'How do you see?', in Stevie Smith, *Poems* (1978) p. 242.

32. Wakefield (1968) p. 10.

33. 1929, pp. 10–11. Maltby goes on to note that 'We live in an atmosphere of question and debate, and the questions often survive the answers, even when the answers have been good, and return to haunt the mind with vague uncertainties' (1929, pp. 37–8). And he points out that the vast increases in our understanding of the universe make it correspondingly harder to believe in a *personal* God (1929, p. 52; see also p. 39).

34. Briggs (1983) p. 292.

35. Graves, *Goodbye to all that* (1929) p. 223.

36. See below, Edrington (1987) and Hollenweger (1989) pp. 279–81.

37. See the excellent study by Grace Davie (1994) on this theme.

38. In the 25 years before the First World War there were over 500,000 Anglican baptisms annually. The figure went below that for the first time in 1916; after 1922 it never reached it again until after the Second World War. In 1932 it fell below 400,000 (Hastings (1986) p. 254).

39. In 1960, 191,000 people were confirmed in the Church of England (34.2 per thousand of population); in 1970 there were 113,000 (19.7 per thousand). Ordination figures decreased from 636 in 1963 to 437 in 1970 and 273 in 1976. Between 1969 and 1984 the Church of England declared 1,086 churches redundant. 'It is not exaggerated to conclude that between 1960 and 1985 the Church of England as a going concern was effectively reduced to not much more than half its previous size' (Hastings (1986) p. 603).

40. For this subject see Robin Gill, *A vision for growth* (London: SPCK, 1994). Gill argues that there were two main reasons for the decline of the Church of England in the twentieth century, and both were strategic. The first was that during the nineteenth century too many churches were built (1994, p. 46); the second, that nearly all of them were built in what turned out to be the wrong places: in inner-city areas, where the population would later decline. This is not at all to blame the Victorian pioneers of church building: society simply changed too quickly for any strategy rooted in buildings to have any chance of enduring success. Gill goes on to point out that these factors had several consequences: many people became more attached to a church building than to Christianity (not always for the wrong reasons: it might, for example, embody the whole reality of 'community' in a given area), so that if their church had to close, they ceased worshipping altogether. Furthermore, many people found themselves personally responsible for debts on their church building, and became very bitter and disillusioned if the building had to close (p. 53). Gill may underestimate the scale of decline of any sense of 'belonging' in twentieth-century England; but his observations are important nonetheless.

41. In 1994 the sociologist Grace Davie noted that 'curiously, and in a rather paradoxical way, the Church of England still does meet the spiritual needs of a substantial proportion of English people, despite their reluctance to attend its services' (1994, pp. 16–17).

42. Clarke (1996) pp. 65–6.

43. 1923, pp. 118–19.

44. See Hastings (1986) pp. 442–3.

45. For a succinct summary, see Hastings (1986), esp. pp. 77–83 and 442–3. The Anglo-Catholic Congress of 1923, presided over by Bishop Frank Weston of Zanzibar, was a high point: for a week thousands of delegates (perhaps 16,000) overflowed the Albert Hall, having begun with solemn high mass at St Paul's (Hastings (1986) p. 199). This was the great age of Anglo-Catholic foundations like Mirfield and Kelham; and many leading bishops were celibate Anglo-Catholics (e.g. Gore, Lang, Frere and Garbett).

46. For this, see further below under 'Spirituality and social justice'.

47. Introduction to Harton (1932). For Harton himself, see the Glossary to this chapter.

48. The National Evangelical Anglican Congress at Keele in 1967 was a major milestone for Anglican Evangelicalism: attended by over 1,000 people, it saw a new Evangelicalism con-

cerned to engage with social issues rather than withdraw into an introspective individualism. Dudley-Smith (1999, p. 10) notes that a key issue for the twentieth-century English Evangelical movement was the place of the mind, and issues raised by academic theology. For a thorough exploration of the subject, see Bebbington (1989) pp. 181–270.

49. For a brief description of the authors cited, see the Glossary to this chapter.
50. Studdert-Kennedy (1923) p. 33.
51. Temple (1924) p. 35.
52. Temple (1955) p. 64.
53. Temple (1924) p. 36.
54. Temple (1924) p. 37. Cf. Studdert-Kennedy (1925, p. 26), who warns of the danger of science compartmentalizing life by making specialized study increasingly inevitable; but religious people do the same thing by allowing their faith to become just one other ingredient of their lives, and 'failing to find any religious significance in the vast revolution taking place before their eyes' (p. 28). 'This organized religion is revolting, it is death to the spiritual life' (p. 63) – here he refers to a church simply or primarily concerned with its own self-preservation. Christology is crucial here: 'we cannot believe that God is like Christ, so we make Christ like God to compensate' (p. 79). Elsewhere he refers to 'that cheap and shallow "pure spirituality" which looks upon the body as the enemy of the soul, and talks as though it were true that because man does not live by bread alone, he therefore does not need bread at all' (1928, p. 136). 'A religious department of life is a contradiction in terms, for the very essence of religion is that it is the relation of the living part to the living whole' (1923, p. 23).
55. Temple (1924) p. 38.
56. p. 39.
57. Vanstone (1977) pp. 32–3.
58. Vanstone (1977) pp. 40–1; cf. William Temple: 'what we find [in Jesus' answer to the Baptist's question about whether he really is the Messiah] is power in complete subordination to love; and that is something like a definition of the Kingdom of God' (1955, p. xxviii).
59. Vanstone (1977) p. 95.
60. p. 96.
61. p. 99.
62. John V. Taylor wrote in 1972 out of a conviction 'that nothing is more needed by humanity today, and by the church in particular, than the recovery of a sense of "beyond-ness" in the whole of life to revive the springs of wonder and adoration. And, oddly enough to our distorted view, our retrieval of mystery is dependent on our reinstatement of the body, with its rhythms and dreams and ways of knowing' (1972, p. 45; cf. p. 222 'our need is not for more wonders but for more wonder').
63. Stott (1986) p. 238.
64. p. 239.
65. pp. 259–61.
66. pp. 261–5.
67. p. 263.
68. Harton says that 'even the soul most advanced in the spiritual life . . . does not become God. The divine nature is ultimate and infinite, human nature ever remains derivative and finite, man is still God's creature . . . and we must keep this sense of fundamental creatureliness ever before us. Union with God presupposes the continuous union of two beings, not the absorption of one into the other' (1932, p. 10). Note though that in 1937 Harton can speak of 'the truth of our deification': 'God gives us participation in His nature, not in His being' (1937, p. 17). 'This deification consists primarily in the uniting of two beings who are and ever remain distinct, God and the human soul' (p. 18).
69. Harton (1937) pp. 12–13.
70. Harton (1932) p. 11.
71. In his later *Life in Christ*, Harton does not distinguish so sharply between the human and divine adoption: both effect a transformation in our status (1937, pp. 12–13). And by being

adopted, we are given a share or participation in the divine being (1937, p. 16). In any case the old distinction between Catholic and Protestant notions of imparted or imputed righteousness may not significantly affect the life of prayer: Anglican Evangelicals speak with equal intimacy and directness about our status as God's children (see, among many examples, Baughen (1996) pp. 78–80).

72. Temple (1955) p. 70.
73. p. 85.
74. pp. 190–1.
75. p. 238.
76. Weston, quoted in Harton (1932) p. 59.
77. Tilby (1989) p. 20.
78. Temple (1955) p. 49.
79. pp. 288–9.
80. Eliot, *Murder in the Cathedral* Act II, in *Poems and plays* (1969) p. 273.
81. *The go-between God* (1972).
82. Taylor (1972) pp. 33–5.
83. p. 39.
84. pp. 48, 59 and p. 69: 'the prophets and apostles were obsessed by divine revelation or the lack of it; we are obsessed by human response or the lack of it.' Cf. p. 100: 'natural man seems to grow up with a desperate need to be approved of.'
85. p. 96. This eschatological approach to Christian life is shared by the Anglo-Catholic Eric Mascall in his thinking about the Church (1953, pp. 24–5).
86. Hebert (1935) p. 194.
87. Temple (1955) p. 318.
88. Tilby (1989) p. 35.
89. Robinson (1963) p. 87.
90. Stott (1986) p. 298.
91. Hebert (1935) pp. 125–6.
92. p. 142.
93. p. 143.
94. p. 144.
95. (1935, p. 158). In a valuable exploration of the nature of Christian belonging, Peter Selby insists that in the Bible participation in the true Israel transcended ethnicity: 'The Church . . . is not an ethnic community: it is required to think inwards from the outside. It is required to assume always that the stranger may be an angel of God, bearing some new word or some new gift. It is to think this way not because its members are naturally more hospitable or less defensive than other people are, but because it has certain memories and certain longings: it is to remember that it is a community of those whose memory is of being a family constituted of outsiders, adopted in a great and continuing act of inclusion' (Selby (1991) p. 43).
96. Harton (1932) pp. 18–19.
97. p. 19.
98. See Harton (1932) p. 16. He notes that St Paul's conception of the Christian as an athlete in training 'underlies the whole theory of asceticism' (p. 66). See also pp. 101 and 103. Harton does, however, have relatively little room for a positive evaluation of the emotions; thus anger is more or less completely dismissed as a bad thing, and the examples given trivial (the man raving for an hour because his breakfast coffee is cold (1932, p. 144)).
99. Macquarrie (1972) pp. 16–18. Gabriel Hebert also stresses the fundamental spiritual truth, anchored in the Eucharist, that 'the whole life of Christians is a sacrificial life' (1935, pp. 80–1).
100. Harton (1932) p. 173.
101. p. 181.
102. p. 187.
103. p. 187.

104. Studdert-Kennedy (1923) p. 130.

105. Stott (1986) p. 280.

106. Stott (1992) pp. 372–3.

107. Stott (1992) p. 374.

108. Ward, cited in Morgan (1963) p. 96.

109. See Morgan (1963) p. 97.

110. Tilby (1989) p. 46.

111. Temple (1955) p. 24.

112. Robinson (1953) p. 60.

113. Vanstone (1977) p. 60 (the notion of the divine self-emptying originates in St Paul, Philippians 2.5–7). Cf. Studdert-Kennedy: 'The Father Whom we worship is revealed in Christ crucified as well as in Christ risen, and Christ ascending, and in that revelation there is no sign of what I call, for lack of a better term, "easy omnipotence"' (1923, p. 48).

114. Vanstone (1977) pp. 68–9.

115. p. 62.

116. p. 65.

117. p. 66.

118. See Vanstone (1977) pp. 427 and 49, and Vanstone (1982).

119. Eliot, *Murder in the Cathedral* Act I, in *Poems and plays*, p. 240. See also 'East Coker', in *Poems and plays*, esp. p. 180; and (for a study of 'East Coker' as a poem about interior transformation) Gordon (1988) pp. 102–14.

120. See e.g. Vanstone (1982) p. 20. Vanstone is anticipated here by the Methodist J. Alexander Findlay, who stresses the passivity of Jesus (*The way, the truth and the life* (London: Hodder and Stoughton, 1940), p. 105) and the importance of Jesus' being handed over (p. 15).

121. 'The passion phase was the "greatest" phase of Jesus' life' (Vanstone (1982) p. 75).

122. Vanstone (1982) chapters 3 and 4.

123. Chapters 6 and 7. Cf. Simon Tugwell (1980, p. 45): 'Blessed are those who are not in too much of a hurry to get things done, and know how to wait, helpless, nailed to their cross. Against all the odds, it is truly they who will inherit the earth.'

124. Quoted in Frost (1935) p. 3 n. 1. Hence Frost's book. He argues that the recovery of Catholic faith and practice has unfortunately not been accompanied by a recovery of a serious commitment to mental prayer.

125. Larkin, 'Faith Healing', in *Poems*, p. 126.

126. Temple (1924) p. 41.

127. p. 43.

128. p. 43. Other writers stress the theological principle of prayer being grounded in our adoption as God's children; see e.g. Baelz (1968) p. 10; Frost (1935) pp. 21–2.

129. Temple (1924) p. 44.

130. Macquarrie (1972) p. 33.

131. From David L. Edwards, *Ian Ramsey* (1973), p. 67; also quoted in Wilkinson (1978) p. 120.

132. Temple (1924) p. 45. Hence too 'it is only the man who loves God with all his being who will be able to love his neighbour as himself' (p. 46). Cf. Temple (1955) pp. 91–2: 'Nothing is more precious in the spiritual life than that communion with God which is enjoyed when the soul reposes upon God in utter self-abandonment, and God exercises His moulding power upon the soul thus resting, plastic, in His hands.'

133. Temple (1955) p. 304.

134. p. 304.

135. p. 305, commenting on John 15.7.

136. pp. 316–17.

137. Tilby (1987) p. 56. Of the writers cited here, only Studdert-Kennedy finds room for the prayer of lament (see pp. 480–6 below). By contrast, John Burnaby is critical of the Psalms of lament: 'the type of *Klage-lied*, of complaint or expostulation, to which not less than a quarter of the psalms belong, is animated by a temper which even the most reckless allegorizing can

scarcely baptize into Christianity' (1962, p. 236). Eric Mascall takes a more temperate (and much more pastoral) view: 'I do not think that any one who has shared in the offices of the religious communities, and has reflected on the function that the appeal for the help of God with which they open has exercised in the building up of lives dedicated to God, will reject, as Professor Burnaby does, the *Deus in adjutorium meum intende; Domine, ad adjuvandum me festina* as merely the cry of "self-conscious 'saints' crying to God for vengeance upon their enemies"' (*Up and down in Adria* (London: Faith Press, 1963), p. 99).

138. Robinson (1967) p. 120.

139. Robinson (1963, p. 99) follows Dietrich Bonhoeffer in speaking of 'a non-religious under-standing of prayer':
> to open oneself to another *unconditionally* in love *is* to be with him in the presence of God, and that is the heart of intercession. To pray for another is to expose both oneself and him to the common ground of our being; it is to see one's concern for him in terms of *ultimate* concern, to let *God* into the relationship. Intercession is to *be with* another at that depth, whether in silence or compassion or action.

140. Temple (1955) pp. 263–4; my italics. Cf. p. 76.

141. Gore (1916) p. 129.

142. p. 130. This is very close to Aquinas' dictum: 'we do not pray in order to change God's plan, but in order to obtain by our prayers those things which God planned to bring about by means of prayers, in order . . . that our prayers should entitle us to receive what almighty God planned from all eternity to give us' (*Summa theologiae* 2a2ae.83.2; see Brian Davies OP, *The thought of Thomas Aquinas* (Oxford: Clarendon, 1992), p. 180). The Methodist Neville Ward makes a similar point (1967, p. 85): 'there is no reason to think that God will do *on his own* what he purposes to do *with man*. If man will not end war, then, though we pray forever, God will not end it *for man*.'

143. Burnaby (1962) p. 225. He was the author of one of the finest studies of St Augustine in English: *Amor Dei* (London, 1938).

144. Burnaby (1962) pp. 230 and 234–5.

145. p. 233. Eric Mascall, in a critique of *Soundings* entitled *Up and down in Adria* (London: Faith Press, 1963), p. 98, suggests that Burnaby should have gone further in insisting that 'the specific characteristic of *Christian* prayer is not that it is the prayer of human wills which have become one with the will of God, but that it is the prayer of the risen and ascended God-man Jesus Christ being prayed by him in and through his members' – hence the importance of the Eucharist.

146. Baelz , in *Soundings*, p. 101.

147. p. 102.

148. pp. 115–16.

149. C. S. Lewis makes a similar point in *The Screwtape letters* (1955), pp. 138–9.

150. Baelz, in *Soundings*, p. 118.

151. p. 99.

152. Ward, in Morgan (1963) p. 132; cf. Burnaby: 'we cannot "explain" intercession by telepathy, any more than we can "explain" prayer for ourselves by autosuggestion; for the heart of all Christian prayer is faith in *God* (1962, p. 227).

153. Ward, in Morgan (1963) p. 134. Characteristically Ward stresses the enormous *power* waiting to be unleashed through intercessory prayer: 'if we were but awake to the tremendous powers which lie dormant in our souls for want of the life which will let them loose from their slumber, we should be so quickly able to transform this world of ours with all its misery and suffering' (p. 137).

154. Macquarrie (1972) pp. 27–8.

155. Baker (1970) pp. 384–5.

156. p. 386.

157. p. 386.

158. p. 389.

159. Vanstone (1977) p. 111. Evangelicals present intercession as a spiritual battle against the powers of evil: see Baughen (1996) pp. 92–7.
160. Taylor (1972) p. 234, though this approach still leaves open the question of what more God can do for someone that God is not already doing short of infringing their free will.
161. And therefore, by definition for most of the century, male. This subject will be discussed more fully below. Graham Neville makes the point ('Lay theology: the case of Dorothy L. Sayers', in *Theology* 102 (1999) p. 347) that Anglican lay theological writers in the twentieth century, like C. S. Lewis and Dorothy Sayers, tended to be ignored by professional theologians; and hence their importance was in the field of apologetic rather than the development of theology.
162. See, e.g., Green (1935) and Frost (1933).
163. Thornton (1965) p. 141.
164. pp. 141–2.
165. pp. 142–3.
166. For twentieth-century English Roman Catholicism see Hastings 1986 (with bibliographies).
167. Hastings (1986) p. 134.
168. For Chesterton, see below, pp. 425–36.
169. Merton, *The seven storey mountain* pp. 65–6. The original was published in 1948. In his preface to the English version (*Elected silence*), Waugh claimed to be making only minor abridgements. But this was not true.
170. Hastings (1986) p. 475.
171. *The Easter People*, para. 190.
172. *The Easter People*, paras. 192–4.
173. Steere (1964, p. 1) describes him as 'in himself a kind of European ecumenical movement'.
174. For von Hügel's life, see Bedoyère (1951).
175. Originally launched in 1940 as the Sword of the Spirit; renamed in 1965.
176. *Prayers of life* were first translated into English in 1963.
177. See Bedoyère (1951) p. 32. Bedoyère covers von Hügel's relations with the Modernists in great detail.
178. He cites, among other explicit sources, Huvelin and Troeltsch in the Preface to the 2nd edition of *The mystical element* (p. vii); for his indebtedness to continental philosophers, see p. xxix. He told a correspondent in 1919 that Augustine's *Confessions* taught him more than any other book after the Gospels and the Psalms (1964, p. 80).
179. See the remarks of Bedoyère (1951, p. xiii).
180. It is not surprising, in view of its great length and turgid style, that von Hügel had difficulty in getting it published (Bedoyère (1951) p. 222); but it deservedly led to the establishment of his scholarly reputation and honorary doctorates from St Andrews and Oxford (p. 227). A second edition appeared in 1923.
181. von Hügel (1923) vol. 1, p. 51.
182. Vol. 1, p. 52.
183. Vol. 1, p. 53.
184. Vol. 1, p. 53, and vol. 2, p. 387.
185. Vol. 1, pp. 54–5.
186. Vol. 1, p. 55.
187. Vol. 1, p. 58.
188. Vol. 1, pp. 58–65.
189. Vol. 1, p. 65.
190. Vol. 2, p. 148; see also vol. 2, pp. 150–2.
191. Vol. 1, pp. 70–2.
192. See vol. 1, p. 72.
193. See vol. 1, p. 77.
194. See vol. 1, pp. 87 and 248.
195. Vol. 1, pp. 112, 119 and 142.
196. Vol. 1, pp. 163 and 178.
197. Vol. 1, p. 223.

198. Vol. 1, pp. 224 and 229.
199. Vol. 1, p. 245.
200. See vol. 2, p. 293, and more generally (on mysticism and evil) pp. 290–308.
201. See vol. 2, p. 120 and (on asceticism) pp. 343 and 355, where he says that authentic asceticism will always be 'corrected by social Christianity'. No solo mysticism will do.
202. Vol. 2, p. 393.
203. 1964, pp. 41–2.
204. 1974, p. 73 (letter of 1918).
205. 1964, p. 122.
206. 1923, vol. 1, p. 45. See vol. 2, pp. 367–86, esp. p. 377, where he emphasizes the importance of scientific method as an antidote to his otherwise thoroughgoing stress on the personal element in religion as primary.
207. Vol. 1, p. 27.
208. Vol. 2, pp. 291–2.
209. p. 292.
210. p. 292. In 1916 he wrote that it is the 'apparent sterility of suffering' which misleads: suffering is not in any way a good thing; but God 'can, and will, and does give concomitant opportunities and graces and growths to the sufferer, if and when the latter is humble, watchful and prayerful in such utilisations' (1964, p. 68).
211. 1964, p. 78 (letter of 1919).
212. 1964, pp. 103–4.
213. 1964, p. 110.
214. 1964, pp. 85–6.
215. His problem with Anglicanism appears in a letter of 1914: 'In Anglicanism everyone can choose even what they "believe" (if that *is* belief)' (*Letters*, p. 129).
216. Biographical details from Dom Roger Hudleston's memoir, in Chapman (1935) pp. 1–30.
217. Chapman (1935) p. 62.
218. He cites mainstream authorities like Aquinas and St John of the Cross frequently, though he is highly critical of St Teresa, whom he sometimes regards as dangerously misleading (see, e.g., pp. 268 and 271–3: 'St Teresa pleases all the people (like myself, once upon a time, who prefer Christianity to Buddhism) – who want to use their faculties, and meditate in a warm room, by the fire, instead of going up the mountain into the snow' (with St John of the Cross) (p. 273). He is particularly influenced by the French school, with its emphasis on *abandon* to the divine providence and will: St François de Sales (who 'has lasted out all others with me', p. 170), de Caussade (especially his letters), St Vincent de Paul, St Thérèse of Lisieux et al. He also cites the English mystics, esp. the *Cloud* and Rolle's *Fire of love* (p. 135; cf. pp. 149–50 and 264). He had a particular love for St Matthew's Gospel and the letters of St Paul (e.g. Ephesians and Colossians (p. 149)). He commends Chesterton's *Orthodoxy* (pp. 206 and 208). His letters to a Jesuit (pp. 191–284) reveal a balanced, sane and thoughtful view on scholastic philosophy and theology, the relationship of reason and revelation, the value of modern philosophy (see, e.g., his comments on Kant, Hegel etc., pp. 198 and 210, and Fichte, p. 201, and his strictures on writers of manuals of scholastic philosophy, p. 237).
219. p. 33.
220. pp. 42–3.
221. p. 160.
222. p. 175.
223. p. 175.
224. See, e.g., pp. 94–6, and p. 100, where he speaks of 'pure prayer – prayer of the will – pure intention without words'.
225. p. 100.
226. 'It is an enormous advantage to be a Christian, a Catholic; to know, to see. To have explicit faith. To have a Church next door. To have a good Mother. To have a cross Master. To have only one leg. To have the prayer of union. All are graces' (p. 221).

227. 'We want the authority of the Church given to our Superiors, and the approbation of the Church given to our manner of life. Otherwise we are only playing at being Religious; doing what we choose to do, because we like it' (in a letter to a religious superior, pp. 129–30).
228. pp. 176–7.
229. p. 36.
230. p. 36. Elsewhere Chapman makes this point again: in prayer, the will often works almost imperceptibly:
    When the will works, without the imagination and emotions, its action is almost impercep-tible and quite quiet. There is usually no *pleasure*; only the satisfaction that all is right, and that one is occupied with what is the best of all occupations. I believe the effects are much greater, afterwards, than when there is some consolation, and some effort in the prayer (p. 130).
231. p. 135; cf. pp. 75 and 78.
232. pp. 52–3.
233. p. 99.
234. p. 124.
235. Vann (1956) p. 23.
236. p. 28; for the importance of obedience see p. 17.
237. p. 29.
238. p. 31.
239. pp. 35–6.
240. p. 37. Vann has no time for a guilt-inducing spirituality: 'how terrible it is when people allow their confession to be a cause of endless worry to them, when its whole purpose is to bring them back to God and His peace' (p. 87; cf. p. 89).
241. p. 38.
242. p. 39.
243. Vann (1947) pp. 27–8.
244. Vann (1956) p. 33.
245. p. 33. Here as elsewhere Vann's Thomist formation is evident.
246. p. 40.
247. p. 94.
248. p. 30.
249. p. 21.
250. p. 38.
251. p. 82.
252. p. 122.
253. Vann (1950) p. 27.
254. Vann (1956) p. 45. Cf. the remark of another twentieth-century English Catholic writer, Fr Hugh Lavery, who says that Baptism gives us a new *nationality*: now we are 'naturalized into Christ', citizens of a new commonwealth (Lavery (1982ii) p. 26).
255. Vann (1956) pp. 64–5; and see p. 88, for a similarly outward-looking view of the sacrament of penance. The same applies to Vann's approach to marriage. For him, marriage is the normal means for that outward-turning love which is the theme of Vann's study of the Beatitudes. It is the search for that unity which is at once interior and outward-directed. Marriage
    must be for the world a visible demonstration of the religion of love; and that it will be, first of all, by its own unity and peace; but the unity and peace must turn outward, must radiate love and light and the homage of service, so that the home may be, not only something that others can admire, but a hearth to which they can always come and be welcome, sit, and be warm (1956, p. 163).
256. pp. 49–50.
257. p. 52.
258. p. 55. Cf. Vann (1950) pp. 20–1: 'patriotism . . . is a virtue: not nationalism, not enmity or pride or aggressiveness in regard to other nations, but a reverence and gratitude for the gifts

that have come down to us'.

259. Vann (1956) p. 77; cf. 1947, p. 53: 'we are a family: we suffer *because* of one another, and also, unconsciously, we suffer *for* one another' – even for and with the animal creation.

260. Vann (1947) p. 81; cf. p. 91. Note the corporate nature of the spiritual life in regard to suffering, a central feature of Vann's spirituality: see also 1956, p. 131: 'your suffering is meant to be redemptive, but not for yourself merely, but for the world ... There are mysteries of substitution which we cannot fathom but which the saints have sensed'.

261. Vann (1956) pp. 94–102.

262. p. 120.

263. p. 128.

264. p. 129.

265. pp. 110 and 136.

266. p. 136.

267. p. 179. In *The seven swords*, Vann stresses the spiritual importance of the Church's teaching on the virginity of Mary; it is precisely as mother and maiden that Mary has something unique to offer us, as someone who holds together both the letting-go inherent in motherhood and the spontaneity and purity of heart that are the fruits of virginity (1950, pp. 7–8). 'As in Mary the Mother there is, unsullied by possessiveness, the mother's pride and joy in her Child, so in Mary the Maiden there is, unsullied by any self-regardingness, the girl's awe and joy in a Beauty and a Love whose infinite loveliness she can only adore', p. 10.

268. pp. 140–1.

269. p. 141.

270. For a fine articulation of this, see the article by Vann's fellow Dominican Herbert McCabe (in *Doctrine and life*, August 1970, repr. in *God matters* (London: Mowbray, 1987), pp. 215–25).

271. Vann (1956) p. 186.

272. p. 157.

273. p. 158.

274. p. 158.

275. See Adrian Hastings' biographical reflection at the beginning of Nicholl (1997), esp. p. xiv.

276. Nicholl (1997) p. 3.

277. p. 6.

278. See 'Is there a *locus classicus* for theology?' (1982, repr. in 1997 chapter 4; cf. 1998 p. 48). Theology should be done in community, with both women and men, and without children being excluded; and even then all of us must stand ready to face dis-location, as the people of Israel did.

279. See 'The Karamazov brothers as teachers of religion' (1979, repr. in 1997 chapter 5).

280. 1998, p. 210.

281. Quoted in 1981, p. 27. Cf. the remark of the Indian sage Vinoba Bhave: 'since I help to fill the buckets, why should I not help to empty them?' (quoted on p. 126).

282. 1998, p. 145.

283. 1981, p. 72.

284. 1981, p. 104. Rather, we should learn to sense and advert to the distinctive 'feel' of the morning/afternoon/evening etc.

285. Quoted in 1981, p. 25.

286. 1998, p. 219.

287. 1998, p. 45. A person's smallest deeds can have a profound impact on her or his subsequent life, or those of others (1997, p. 99; cf. 1998, p. 19, and 1998, p. 185 on the effects of the spoken word).

288. 1981, p. 42.

289. 1981, p. 54.

290. 1997, p. 2.

291. 1981, p. 134. The supreme moment of loss of control is birth (p. 135) – we don't choose to be born: we have to accept that it has happened.

292. 'From now on each of them is a martyr, a witness to the mystery of suffering in marriage' (1981, p. 132).
293. 1997, p. 133.
294. 1998, p. 234.
295. 1981, p. 152.
296. Forsyth (1912) pp. vii and viii respectively. For Forsyth see W. L. Bradley, *P. T. Forsyth: the man and his work* (London, 1952).
297. Forsyth (1912) p. 306.
298. He saw Congregationalism as ideally suited to address the challenge; see pp. 333–7.
299. For Congregationalism, see Daniel Jenkins, *Congregationalism: a restatement* (London: Faber, 1954). He concedes (p. 66) that the denomination had to some extent become restricted to the *petite bourgeoisie*, and was certainly identified as such. He also concedes (p. 145) that Congregationalism had been less successful than Anglicanism at providing a coherent and satisfying form of spiritual discipline for its members. Adrian Hastings (1986, p. 118) suggests that the Selly Oak colleges at Birmingham (of which the first was founded by George Cadbury in 1903, and the federation formed in 1919) exemplify twentieth-century Nonconformity: practical, social, but with little doctrinal undergirding and thus little sense of enduring definition. By the 1930s Nonconformity no longer represented a significant political constituency, other than in Scotland and Wales. 'The young man of left wing inspiration and Free Church background was now most likely to be an agnostic' (Hastings (1986) p. 267). Congregationalist membership declined by 20% in the 1960s; Methodist membership declined by 24% in 15 years between 1960 and 1975 (Hastings (1986) p. 552). By 1984 its membership had declined to 458,206, a decrease of 11% in 7 years (p. 603). The United Reformed Church (formed by the fusion of the English Congregational and Presbyterian Churches in 1973) began with a membership of 192,000: by 1984 it had 132,000, a decrease of just over 30%. As the mainstream Free Churches declined, they became more liberal (though there is no evidence to suggest that they would have declined less had they become more conservative instead).
300. For a vivid example of that influence, see Arnold Bennett's depiction of chapel-going and chapel society in *Anna of the five towns* (1902), esp. chapter 5 ('The revival'). The impact of Sunday schools on children's spiritual formation must have been significant as well.
301. For George, Newton Flew and Wakefield, see the Glossary and Bibliography to this chapter. Heiler's *Das Gebet* (translated into English in 1932 as *Prayer*) exerted a profound influence on the developing study of biblical spirituality, as did Kenneth Kirk's *The vision of God* with regard to the spirituality of the patristic age.
302. Forsyth (1912) p. 1.
303. p. 11.
304. p. 2.
305. p. 39.
306. Forsyth (1897) p. 69.
307. p. 69.
308. p. 74.
309. p. 109.
310. p. 110.
311. p. 111.
312. p. 19.
313. p. 127.
314. p. 133.
315. The divine Father is the holy. And the Holy Father's first care is holiness.' (Forsyth (1897) p. 4).
316. Oman (1917) pp. 54–5.
317. p. 64.
318. p. 67. A similar point, about the discovery of God in the midst of the everyday, is made by the Methodist J. A. Chapman (1934, p. 95).

319. Maltby (1929) p. 57.

320. Sangster (1954) p. 30.

321. Sangster (1957) p. 67. On the importance of living in the truth, without illusion, see Neville Ward (1967) p. 51.

322. Sangster discusses the once-vexed question of whether holiness, like righteousness, was 'imputed' or 'imparted' to us by God. He describes Forsyth as a moderate modern representative of the 'imputation' school – human beings, as radically sinful, can never attain or achieve holiness in themselves; so it can only be imputed to them, in the form of Christ's holiness (1954, p. 186). Others, like Wesley, argue that it can be imparted, even in an instant (pp. 186–7). For Sangster, though, the difference is largely one of emphasis (p. 189).

323. Flew (1934) p. xiv.

324. pp. 397–8.

325. See above, chapter 1.

326. Sangster (1943) p. 147. Like Sangster, the Salvationist Samuel Logan Brengle also sees holiness as 'pure love' (1896, pp. ix–x). And he goes on to say (p. 2) that

> [holiness] is a state in which God is loved and trusted with a perfect heart. But though the heart may be perfect, the head may be very imperfect, and through the imperfections of his head – of his memory, his judgment, his reason – the holy man may make many mistakes. Yet God looks at the sincerity of his purpose, at the love and faith of his heart – not at the imperfections of the head – and calls him a holy man. Holiness is not absolute perfection, which belongs to God only . . . But it is Christian perfection – such perfection and obedience of the heart as a poor fallen creature, aided by almighty power and boundless grace, can give.

327. Sangster (1943) pp. 150–1.

328. p. 151.

329. p. 153.

330. p. 154.

331. Forsyth (1897) pp. 103–4.

332. pp. 110–11. One or two Nonconformists go further in declaring that Christians can achieve, or by grace be led into, a state of sinlessness here on earth. The Salvationist Samuel Brengle maintains that the sanctified person is no longer tempted in the ordinary way people are – e.g. to drink, or wealth (1896, pp. 18–19). Satan will continue to tempt such a person, but the person will have no difficulty in rejecting these temptations, as Christ did after his baptism (pp. 19–20).

333. Forsyth (1897) p. 119.

334. p. 132.

335. p. 138; cf. Sangster: 'the emphasis of the New Testament is not on perfection but on *growth*' (1954, p. 39). It is worth comparing this with that of the Anglo-Catholic Bede Frost OSB, who says that 'perfection consists in the loving union of the will with God, a union . . . made possible by a right use of His gifts' (1935, p. 27).

336. Flew (1934) pp. 6–7.

337. p. 51. Flew is clear that this communion with God is in no sense a deification (p. 62).

338. p. 25; cf. p. 84.

339. Sangster (1943) p. 182.

340. pp. 182–3. Cf. (on the overriding importance of seeking and doing God's will) Neville Ward (1967) p. 82.

341. Sangster (1943) pp. 183–4.

342. p. 193. This persistence of sin does not contradict Neville Ward's point (1967, p. 45), quoting Baudelaire, that sin is essentially *boring*: we become caught in a cycle of habitual sin.

343. Sangster (1943) pp. 193–4.

344. Flew (1934) pp. 414–15.

345. Fosdick (1915) p. 18.

346. Weatherhead (1965) p. 151. For Weatherhead see J. Travell, *Doctor of souls: a biography of Dr Leslie Dixon Weatherhead* (Cambridge: Lutterworth, 1999).
347. Weatherhead (1958) p. 18.
348. Ward (1967) pp. 11–12.
349. Chapter 1.
350. Weatherhead (1951) pp. 236–51, esp. p. 243.
351. Farmer (1954) pp. 53–4.
352. p. 55.
353. pp. 57–8.
354. p. 60.
355. p. 63; for the Eucharist see also pp. 178–9.
356. p. 79. It is likely that he has in mind here the German Friedrich Schleiermacher's notion of absolute dependence on God, which he goes on to explore in detail (pp. 116–25).
357. See, e.g., Baughen (1996) pp. 83–9.
358. Forsyth (1916) p. 59.
359. p. 60.
360. p. 77. Cf. Neville Ward (1967, p. 17): 'as long as prayer is something one feels one ought to do it remains a formidable bore'.
361. Forsyth (1916) p. 78.
362. See Forsyth (1916) p. 19.
363. p. 12; cf. p. 79.
364. p. 36.
365. p. 41.
366. p. 24. Cf. p. 39: 'The atmosphere of prayer is communion. Common prayer is the inevitable fruit of a gospel like Christ's.' And the most seemingly private prayer can and should be rooted in the well-being of the whole community (p. 40).
367. p. 45.
368. p. 55.
369. p. 57.
370. p. 66.
371. Ward (1967) p. 28.
372. Wyon (1943) p. 23. For Wyon, see below, pp. 444–9.
373. p. 30.
374. p. 30.
375. p. 32.
376. Ward (1971) p. xii.
377. Weatherhead (1958) p. 3; cf. Wyon (1962) p. 61: 'the practice of prayer consists in a balanced use of discipline and freedom. Discipline comes first.'
378. Forsyth (1916) p. 62.
379. Chapman (1934) pp. 124–5. For Chapman see Wakefield (1999) pp. 68–9.
380. Forsyth (1916) p. 81.
381. p. 82. Cf. Neville Ward: 'it is true that we are nearest to God when we are loving him, but we are certainly very close when we are fighting him' (1967, p. 145).
382. Forsyth (1916) p. 83.
383. p. 84.
384. See p. 86.
385. p. 87; Wakefield (1995, pp. 73–4) notes the influence of Ritschl on Forsyth here.
386. Forsyth (1916) p. 89.
387. p. 90.
388. p. 42.
389. pp. 91–2.
390. Harris (1905) p. 5.
391. pp. 30–1 and 42.

392. p. 43.
393. p. 53.
394. pp. 64–5.
395. Wakefield (1999) p. 23.
396. Maltby (1929) p. 39.
397. Harvey Cox (1995), in a vivid if rather anecdotal account of Pentecostal origins and spirituality, describes the impact on late-nineteenth-century America of the 'World's Parliament of Religions' which was a part of the Great Columbian Exposition at Chicago in 1893, which presaged a golden millennial age of spiritual renewal. He makes the point that both that and Azusa Street (see below) 'looked backward into history in order to gaze forward into the future', the Exposition to classical Greece and Rome, and Azusa Street to apostolic Christianity (p. 29).

The origins of modern Pentecostalism are shrouded in dispute and uncertainty; not many contemporary records were kept, or accounts written; the two most famous early leaders, Charles F. Parham and William Joseph Seymour, famously fell out with one another; there are issues of racism and gender as well as of place. For brief recent accounts, see Cox (1995, chapter 2), Suurmond (1994, pp. 1ff.), Cecil M. Robeck Jr., 'Pentecostal origins from a global perspective' (in Hunter and Hocken (1993) pp. 166–80), and the responses by Japie J. Lapoorta and James R. Goff Jr. in the same collection. This much seems clear:

(1) Seymour, a black American, had attended Parham's Bible schools in Houston, Texas in early 1906, before moving to Los Angeles. He had learned from Parham the doctrine that speaking in tongues was the 'Bible evidence' of baptism in the Spirit in keeping with the apostolic experience of Acts 2.4 (Robeck (1993) p. 173).

(2) Seymour established a home Bible study group in Los Angeles, on North Bonnie Brae Street: when, in April 1906, members of the group began to speak in tongues, word spread rapidly, and the rapidly increasing congregation moved to an old Methodist church property on Azusa Street on 15 April (Robeck (1993) pp. 173–4) (now demolished; see Cox (1995) pp. 64–5). Cox (1995, pp. 51–2) points out the ironies: Los Angeles, named after Our Lady Queen of the Angels, was fast becoming a city of spectacular consumption and racism: 'it provides the perfect starting point for the story of a religious movement that exemplifies the tangled interaction of religion and culture in the contemporary world.'

(3) Seymour's thriving new church had these features:
- it was racially integrated from the start (extraordinarily rare at the time), and perhaps the only such church which had an Afro-American pastor;
- worship there included dancing, embracing as well as speaking in tongues;
- people were welcome to speak, testify, read scripture, sing, or manifest some charism, much as Seymour himself was;
- crucially, Seymour's doctrine stressed the priesthood of all believers and an emphasis on an ethical component – not just speaking in tongues. For Seymour, the fruits of the Spirit in a transformed spiritual and moral life were just as much evidence of the Spirit's work as speaking in tongues was (Robeck (1993) p. 178). It is here that he parted company with Parham, for whom tongues remained the indispensable Bible evidence of authenticity (pp. 178–9).

(4) Parham's subsequent arrest on charges of homosexuality, charges which were never proved, and the collapse of his reputation, inevitably left Seymour as the principal Pentecostal founder/leader in subsequent historiography.

What is undeniable is that modern Pentecostalism thrived among the poor, the uneducated and the minority racial groupings, though it is arguable that its ministry has become increasingly middle-class (see Quebedeaux (1975) p. 219). Charismatic renewal has, however, always been predominantly middle-class in nature (p. 220).
398. Hollenweger (1997) p. 343; Quebedeaux (1975) p. 71. For Boddy's life and work, see Harper (1965, chapter 4), Quebedeaux (1975, pp. 71–7) and Kay (1990, pp. 17–42).
399. See note 397.

400. Boddy, extract from *The latter rain evangel*, cited in Kay (1990) p. 21.
401. Harper (1965) p. 39.
402. Harper suggests (1965, pp. 45–6) that lack of leadership (and opposition from Christian leaders) caused the Pentecostal movement to flag in Britain. Hollenweger (1997, p. 344) suggests it was in part because Boddy was from an upper-class background, whereas most of the early Pentecostals were from much poorer backgrounds.
403. The modern charismatic movement began in California in 1959, but unlike the original Pentecostal movement did not involve a break with mainstream churches. It was strikingly at odds with the mood of the sixties, but thrived nonetheless. The visits to England of prominent Pentecostalists such as David Du Plessis and Dennis Bennett helped to establish it here (Quebedeaux (1975) pp. 87–93). It was opposed by Evangelicals like John Stott; in 1964 Michael Harper resigned his curacy at All Souls Langham Place and in 1964 founded the Fountain Trust as an ecumenical charismatic institution (this was dissolved in 1978) (Quebedeaux (1975) p. 89; for the Fountain Trust and Harper's work, see Quebedeaux (1975) pp. 149–52 and Hocken (1997) pp. 115–22).
404. The largest were the New Testament Church of God and the Church of God of Prophecy, both in origin North American Pentecostal churches. For a good brief summary, see Root (1979).
405. Wilkinson (1993) pp. 78–9. Root suggests (1979, p. 4) that most Black-led churches in England are in the Church of God tradition, which sees speaking in tongues or baptism in the Spirit as a 'third experience' subsequent to conversion and sanctification; whereas the Holiness tradition emphasizes only conversion and sanctification, and the Elim or Assemblies of God Pentecostal tradition replaced sanctification by baptism in the Spirit as a 'second experience' (the Elim Pentecostal Church was founded by a Welshman in Ireland in 1915; see Kay (1990) for a full account: the British Assemblies of God were formed in 1924). L. Lovett (in Burgess and McGee (1988) p. 77, art. 'Black Holiness-Pentecostalism') argues that Black Holiness Pentecostalism is a movement in several denominations, professing belief in Spirit baptism accompanied by various signs, including speaking in tongues; participants believe that the baptism in the Holy Spirit is a normative post-conversion experience available to all Christians to enable them to become more effective witnesses. In 1975 the largest of the Black-led churches in England was the New Testament Church of God, with 4,466 members and about 20,000 attenders in 1975 (Root (1979) p. 4). Some of the Pentecostal churches are international, and although their English leadership and membership is largely Black some have White international leaders (p. 5).
406. For this see Walker (1998) (for history); Forster (1986) (for vivid accounts of individual house church movements). In general, the house churches strongly emphasize eldership, Christian discipling, rejection of the mainstream churches, strong biblically-based ethical teaching, subordination of women to men, and an active eschatological expectancy.
407. Simon Tugwell OP (1972) gives a brief historical summary of this (pp. 35–9; see also Quebedeaux (1975) pp. 93–100). Catholic Pentecostalism may be said to have begun in the USA in 1967; but earlier signs of its proper place in Catholic teaching and theology are Leo XIII's encyclical *Divinum illud munus* (1897) as well as works by Bede Jarrett, Gerald Vann et al.
408. See Walker (1998). The reasons why Black-led Pentecostal churches have grown are not hard to identify: Root suggests, inter alia, racism in mainstream churches; a sense of communal and shared identity as exiles in a strange land; a desire to retain the cultural and spiritual forms of expression they had known in the West Indies (1979, pp. 6–7); and the fact that they often thrive in run-down urban areas where mainstream churches are failing (p. 9). Furthermore their ministry is local, part-time, and closely identified with their membership.
409. Hollenweger (1997), esp. pp. 18–19 and 196; R. P. Spittler (art. 'Spirituality, Pentecostal and Charismatic', in Burgess and McGee (1988) pp. 804–9); Suurmond (1994) pp. 19–21 and 85; and see note 397 above.
410. Tugwell (1972) pp. 87–8.
411. p. 13.

412. Root (1979) pp. 13–14; Suurmond (1994) p. 153 (speaking from personal experience).
413. Sunday School Lessons (Adult Book), Church of God World-Wide Mission (Pentecostal), September–December 1985, p. 19; cf. p. 32.
414. pp. 8–9.
415. Dennis Bennett, the Episcopalian priest whose ministry at Van Nuys, Los Angeles, caused a furore once he espoused Pentecostal teaching, maintained that 'the key to [receiving the Holy Spirit in one's life] is *praise*. It is in praising God that we enable Him to respond to us' (quoted in Harper (1965) p. 66; and see Bennett's own autobiographical account *Nine o'clock in the morning* (Eastbourne: Kingsway, 1974)). Spencer (1990, p. 14) suggests that Black Afro-American spirituals 'lyricized an inward liberation'; that the Exodus event was their theological anchor (p. 18); and he notes the significant element of *anticipation* in their lyrics (p. 19).
416. For the importance of music in Pentecostal spirituality, see Cox (1995) chapter 8, where he explores the relationship between Pentecostal music and jazz; Hollenweger (1989ii and 1997); and Spencer (1990).
417. Tugwell (1972) p. 72; see also p. 62.
418. A. M. Allchin, *Participation in God* (London: DLT, 1988), p. 67.
419. See Bebbington (1989) p. 232 and Goldingay (1996).
420. Suurmond (1994) p. 25. For the relationship of prayer to healing in charismatic spirituality, see Hollenweger (1989i). For some useful insights about the wider social significance of charismatic healing, see Goldingay (1996) pp. 182–3.
421. See the excellent study by Wilkinson (1993), esp. pp. 13–14.
422. 'West Indies in Britain', quoted in Wilkinson (1993) p. 79.
423. Experience of a young Black Anglican, quoted in Wilkinson (1993) p. 106.
424. See Wilkinson (1993) pp. 106–7.
425. Worrall (1987) p. 10.
426. Wilkinson (1993) p. 111.
427. Worrall (1987) p. 12.
428. Wilkinson (1993) pp. 112–13.
429. Quoted in Kerridge (1995), pp. 153 and 157.
430. For an overall survey, see Anson (1964).
431. See Perham (1993); George Guiver, *Company of voices* (London: SPCK, 1988); Robert Taft, *The Liturgy of the Hours in east and west* (St John's Collegeville Liturgical Press, 1986).
432. Allchin (1976) p. 476 (citing the example of Fr Gilbert Shaw, a married priest who exerted a profound influence for many years as spiritual guide to the (Carmelite) Anglican Community of the Sisters of the Love of God at Fairacres, Oxford (for whom see R. D. Hacking, *Such a long journey* (Oxford: Mowbray, 1988)).
433. See Newton (1994) pp. 101–3. Vincent describes them as 'a community of disciples of Jesus Christ which seeks to provoke new calls from the Gospel, enable new ventures of faith, support new enterprises in service, experiment with new ways of action, have as much as possible in common, pioneer action in politics, discover and stand beside those in need, provide alternative models for the churches' (quoted on p. 102).
434. Quoted in Toynbee (1981) p. 28.
435. For the Community of the Resurrection, see Wilkinson (1992), and see also pp. 409–11 above.
436. *Naught for your comfort* (London: Collins, 1956), p. 16.
437. Huddleston (1956) p. 150. For his view of the religious life, see further Wilkinson (1992) p. 311.
438. See John R. H. Moorman, *The Franciscans in England* (London: Mowbray, 1974), chapter 10. The contemplative Community of St Clare at Freeland in Oxfordshire, the experiment in the solitary life undertaken by Brother Ramon SSF (a prolific writer on the spiritual life) at Glasshampton in Worcestershire, and the growth of a Franciscan Third Order among lay people living 'in the world' reflect the way Franciscan spirituality has managed to hold

together the active and the contemplative within a single tradition.

439. See Mother Mary Clare SLG, *Prayer: encountering the depths* (Fairacres Publications 31) (Oxford: Community of the Sisters of the Love of God, 1973), p. 4.

440. See A. M. Allchin, *Solitude and communion: papers on the hermit life given at St David's* (Oxford: Fairacres, 1977), esp. the article by Mother Mary Clare SLG; and also Peter Anson, *The call of the desert: the solitary life in the Christian church* (London: SPCK, 1964), pp. 216–20.

441. A good example was the (Anglican) Servants of the Will of God, founded at Crawley Down in Sussex in 1939 (see Anson (1964) p. 217).

442. A good example was Fr William Sirr, who joined the Society of the Divine Compassion (an Anglican Franciscan order) in 1902, acting as its Superior from 1906 until 1912. In 1915 William went to join SSJE at Cowley, seeking a more enclosed life. He went to Glasshampton in 1918, where he lived at first as a hermit. In 1919 he set about establishing a monastic community there, and for 12 years lived the monastic life in a broadly Cistercian form. But it was not easy for new arrivals to live the full and very strict monastic life with a highly experienced and austere monk aspiring to a Cistercian-style ideal; hence for most of 18 years he lived there alone. He remained at Glasshampton until ill health obliged him to leave in 1936. He died in 1937. See Curtis (1978): Curtis stresses that Fr William's primary *attrait* was always towards the Cistercian rather than the Benedictine spirit (p. 46), and that for many years prior to going to Glasshampton he longed for a more solitary life of prayer and reparation.

443. A good example is that of Fr George Potter in south London: see his autobiography *Father Potter of Peckham* and his account of the Brotherhood of the Holy Cross (London: Hodder and Stoughton, 1955).

444. See (in general) Esther de Waal, *Seeking God: the way of St Benedict* (London: Collins, 1984); and the writings of Brother Ramon SSF, who lived for many years as a hermit.

445. For a general overview of Christian lay communities in England in the first half of the twentieth century, see Hardy (2000), pp. 163–202.

446. M. I. Potts, *St Julian's: an experiment in two continents* (London: SCM Press, 1968) (from the chapter on 'Reality').

447. Allchin (1976) p. 482 (and p. 478 on the special role of Anglican religious communities in fostering ecumenism).

448. See John Townroe, 'Retreat', in C. Jones et al. (eds.), *The study of spirituality* (London: SPCK, 1986), pp. 578–81.

449. See esp. Maria Boulding OSB, *Marked for life: prayer in the Easter Christ* (London: SPCK, 1979), and *The coming of God* (London: SPCK, 1982); Gerard W. Hughes SJ, *God of surprises* (London: DLT, 1985); A Carthusian, *The way of silent love;* (London: DLT, 1993), *The wound of love: a Carthusian miscellany* (London: DLT, 1994), *The call of silent love* (London: DLT, 1995); *Interior prayer* (London: DLT, 1996); *From Advent to Pentecost* (London: DLT, 1999).

450. See the essays in Brooke (1980).

451. Brooke, 'Towards an integral theology' (originally published in 1964, repr. in Brooke (1980) p. 228).

452. Brooke (1980) p. 228 and p. 231 n. 13.

453. p. 229.

454. 'Towards a theology of connatural knowledge', originally published in 1967; repr. in Brooke (1980) pp. 232–49.

455. p. 232.

456. p. 234.

457. p. 236.

458. Hence the importance of spiritual friendship for Aelred of Rievaulx: Brooke (1980) pp. 236–7, and see above, pp. 411–13.

459. Brooke (1980) p. 253 (original text has 'man' for 'person').

460. p. 253.

461. pp. 254–5.

462. See esp. *Mysticism*; and *Letters*, p. 146: 'I'm still drunk with Bergson, who sharpened one's mind and swept one off one's feet both at once. Those lectures have been a real, great experience' (1913).

463. The London publishers G. Bell and Sons produced the Quest series during the war years, which comprised studies of the mystics including Buddhist, Islamic and Jewish ones, as well as Underhill's book on Ruysbroeck (Greene (1991) p. 62).

464. Thus, e.g., he unquestioningly declares that 'the ultimate values which have been revealed to us are Goodness or Love, Truth, and Beauty' (*Mysticism in religion*, p. 71); and see p. 97 for his lyrical encomium of Plato himself; and also his *The Platonic tradition in English religious thought* (1926). He does admit that 'no direct Hellenic influence can be traced in our Lord's teaching' (1926, p. 27).

465. The first of Inge's 1905 St Margaret's lectures (published as *Studies of English mystics*) is on this theme. He points to the paradox involved in the fact that, though by virtue of our nature we are to be like God, nonetheless 'the self-centred life is spiritual death' (1906, p. 2). Hence the need to listen to those who have had profound spiritual experiences themselves (p. 3); though if these experiences are to help us they must resonate with something in our own lives (p. 20).

466. Inge (1906) pp. 7–8. In his view, this was the goal of Plotinus and Spinoza.

467. p. 8.

468. p. 9.

469. See below, pp. 506–8.

470. Inge (1906) p. 11. For Gordon's strange mix of mysticism, compassion and longing for death, see Anthony Nutting, *Gordon: martyr and misfit* (London: Constable, 1966), esp. pp. 83–90 and 191–2.

471. Inge (1906) pp. 12–13.

472. Benson, *Letters* p. 326.

473. Inge (1906) p. 24.

474. pp. 30–1.

475. See, e.g., his distinctly gloomy reflections on contemporary society on pp. 136–41.

476. See Butler (1922), Preface p. vii, and p. 1. He cites Inge with approval (p. 18). See also Rowan Williams, 'Butler's *Western mysticism*: towards an assessment', in *Downside Review* 102 (1984), pp. 197–215.

477. Thus he warns against exaggerating the Neoplatonic element in Augustine's early treatises (p. 57).

478. Butler (1922) p. 3.

479. p. 302.

480. p. 298.

481. p. 299.

482. There is space only to note their common interest in the Greek patristic idea of deification. Butler suggests that it was thanks to the popularity of the Latin translation of Pseudo-Dionysius that 'deification' came into vogue in the West soon after St Bernard, long after it had become habitual in the East as a means of describing union with God in this life (1922, p. 159). Inge (*Mysticism in religion*, pp. 44–5 and 1899, p. 357) suggests that the notion of deification reflects the much looser use of the Greek word *theos* by comparison with the English *God* in classical times; hence the Church found the word in common currency. He also points out (1899, p. 358) that the notion grew in Christianity as apocalyptic faded. In an appendix to his Bampton Lectures (1899, pp. 356–68), Inge considers the three main Christian views of deification, arguing that all are ultimately aspects of the one truth.

483. For Underhill's life, see Greene (1991) and Loades (1997).

484. See Charles Williams, introd. to *The letters of Evelyn Underhill*, p. 14.

485. She was a prolific writer, producing 39 books and over 350 articles (Greene (1991) p. 2). More importantly, she was a substantial scholar, editing a number of original texts which included (from the British Museum MS) Marguerite Porete's *Mirror of simple souls* (Greene, p. 63). Her first book, *A bar-lamb's ballad-book* (1902) was a volume of humorous verse. She wrote novels,

mostly with elaborate spiritual themes. Her spiritual books include extended studies of Ruys-broeck (1915) and Jacopone da Todi (1919). Her two most influential and substantial works were *Mysticism* (1911) and *Worship* (1937).

486. *Letters*, p. 55.

487. *Letters*, p. 205.

488. From the mid-1920s onwards, Underhill began to work as a retreat director, giving increasing numbers of retreats (though note that her letters are full of spiritual direction from much earlier: see, e.g., the letter of 16 January 1908, in *Letters*, pp. 71–4).

489. Her pacifism was influenced by Aldous Huxley's pamphlet 'What are you going to do about it?' (Greene (1991) p. 134). Loades (1997, p. 8) suggests that, in the light of Underhill's later pacifism, the 1914 preface to *Practical mysticism* makes very uncomfortable reading, extolling as it does the militarist spirituality of General Gordon, Florence Nightingale and St Joan of Arc (see p. 14).

490. Greene (1991, p. 44) notes her playfulness and love of cats, qualities that seem to have endured (see also Charles Williams, introd. to *Letters*, p. 29). She also enjoyed bookbinding (Charles Williams, introd. to *Letters*, p. 10) and archaeology (p. 30). Williams also stresses (p. 11) her enduring love of Europe. For a few years from 1940 she was a member of an occult group (Williams, pp. 12–13). She appears to have had a gift for friendship, and had a number of very close friends (esp. female).

491. See Greene (1991) pp. 7–8.

492. *Letters*, pp. 125–6.

493. *Letters*, p. 195.

494. *Letters*, p. 309.

495. In early adulthood she considered herself a Modernist and for some time read Tyrrell and Maud Petre (*Letters*, p. 65) – hence her decision not to join the Roman Church once it vigor-ously proscribed Modernist teaching. (On the other hand, as Greene suggests (p. 30), it could have been precisely her long experience in the 'borderland' which helped to deepen and give perspective to her spirituality). The philosophy of Henri Bergson was very influential in her early work (see esp. *Mysticism*). She did not warm to Newman, speaking once of his 'spiritual selfishness' (cited in Greene (1991) p. 101; see also *Letters*, p. 275, 11 July 1939). In a letter of 26 February 1936 she says that Pusey 'strikes me as much bigger spiritually than Newman, though not so brilliant' (*Letters*, p. 338). She frequently quotes approvingly from Quaker sources, perhaps esp. George Fox and John Woolman. Her studies of more recent French mystical writers are well worth reading: see, e.g., 'Mysticism in modern France' in *The essen-tials of mysticism* (1920) pp. 199–245, which includes studies of St Thérèse of Lisieux, Lucie-Christine and Charles Péguy. She also frequently cites St Elizabeth of the Trinity (1880–1906). Among many other writers she cites, Wittgenstein (1927, p. 34), Friedrich Heiler (on prayer) (*Letters*, p. 171) and Rudolf Otto (*The idea of the holy*) are worth noting. In later life she became influenced by Orthodoxy, esp. its liturgy, and joined the Fellowship of SS Alban and Sergius (see *Letters*, p. 243, 8 February 1935). The influence of Augustine is palpable at times: see, e.g., her 'Thoughts on prayer and the divine immanence' (1931; repr. in *Collected papers*, esp. p. 92).

496. *Letters*, p. 247.

497. In a letter of 16 September 1911 Underhill wrote: 'I forget whether I told you that I have become the friend (or rather, disciple and adorer) of Von Hügel. He is the most wonderful personality I have ever known – so saintly, so truthful, sane and tolerant. I feel very safe and happy sitting in his shadow, and he has been most awfully kind to me' (*Letters*, p. 129). See also Charles Williams, introd. to *Letters*, p. 26; Greene (1991) pp. 78ff. The correspondence between Underhill and von Hügel does not appear to have survived (Williams, p. 46).

498. Underhill (1922) p. 149.

499. p. 149.

500. See 'The inside of life' (1931), repr. in 1946, esp. pp. 96 and 104.

501. *The school of charity*, p. 6.

502. 'What is mysticism?' (1936), repr. in 1946, p. 118.
503. A paragraph on hermetic philosophy is omitted from chapter 2.4 (p. 316 in 1914 edn, para. beginning 'This same belief'). The 1930 edition incorporates some awareness of Freudian psychology (see p. 288, where a para. on Freud's interpretation of dreams is added), though no mention is made of Freud in the 1930 index despite his appearance in the text. In chapter 1.2, 'Mysticism and Vitalism', Underhill downgrades the significance of Rudolph Eucken in 1930, by which time her awareness of the severe limitations of 'Vitalism' is clear. Thus in 1914 Eucken's thought is described as 'the nearest approach, perhaps, which any modern thinker has made to a constructive mysticism' (1914, p. 31). And at the same place she describes Vitalism as 'the first great contribution of the twentieth century to the history of man's quest of reality. A true "child of its time," it is everywhere in the air ... ' (1914, pp. 30–1). The reference to Eucken on p. 148 of 1914 has been replaced by a reference to Boehme in 1930 (p. 123). In 1914 she says that Vitalism 'is likely to be useful in our present attempt towards an understanding of mysticism' (p. 33); in 1930 this has become 'may be useful ... ' (p. 28) (italics mine). Material included in 1914 in praise of Vitalism is omitted in 1930. In 1914 she describes Vitalism as 'this majestic dream of Time and Motion' (p. 38) – omitted in 1930. In 1914 she writes 'The mystics, again, declare themselves to know the divinely real, free, and active "World of Becoming" which Vitalistic philosophy expounds to us' (p. 42) – the italicized words are omitted in 1930.

　　The chapter on mysticism and magic (1.7) is significantly adjusted in 1930, downgrading her evaluation of the latter. Whole sections are omitted in the later edition; subtle qualifications are added (thus, e.g., 'rituals and sacraments . . . must have . . . a magical character' (1914, p. 197) becomes in 1930 (p. 163) 'a certain magical character' (italics added). 'Thus in 1914 she says 'Few recognize that the whole business of the true magician is not with vulgar marvels, but with transcendental matters' (pp. 181–2); this is omitted in 1930. In 1914 she writes of 'magic, in its perfect and uncorrupted form' (p. 182): in 1930 the words 'perfect and' are omitted. A large section on Eliphas Lévi, whom she describes as 'probably the sanest and certainly the most readable occult philosopher of the nineteenth century' (p. 184) is almost completely omitted in 1930.

　　In 1914 she says this about the Latin Mass:
　　Did the Catholic Church choose to acknowledge a law long known to the adepts of magic, she has here an explanation of that instinct which has caused her to cling so strenuously to a Latin liturgy, much of whose amazing and truly magic power would evaporate were it translated into the vulgar tongue (p. 190).
　　This is omitted in 1930 (see p. 158).
504. Mysticism (1914 edn, p. 199).
505. In 1914 she describes Bunyan as 'the last and least mystical of a long series of minds' (p. 155); in 1930 (p. 130) the italicized words are omitted! In the Appendix to both editions ('A historical sketch'), 1930 relocates Origen with St Clement of Alexandria (p. 455) instead of with St Macarius of Egypt (1914, p. 546). John Cassian is added in 1930 (p. 546): he doesn't appear in 1914. Similarly SS Romuald, Peter Damian, Bruno, Anselm, Hildegard of Bingen and Joachim of Fiore are added in 1930 (pp. 458 and 460) to the medieval section. The discussion of St Bernard is notably more positive in 1930 (see p. 459 and compare with 1914, p. 547). A number of early Franciscans are added in 1930 (p. 461). In 1914 Walter Hilton is described as 'pre-eminently a lover, not a metaphysician; a devout and gentle spirit anxious to share his certitudes with other men' (p. 555). In 1930 this is changed to 'pre-eminently a spiritual director, the practical teacher of interior ways, not a metaphysician' (p. 466). More significantly still, in 1914 Underhill says that the influence of St Augustine 'was nothing in comparison with that exercised by . . . Dionysius the Areopagite' (1914, p. 545); in 1930 she is changing her view entirely, saying that 'second only to that of St Augustine was the influence exercised by . . . Dionysius the Areopagite' (1930, p. 456). In 1930 she is more positive still about the Quaker George Fox (cf. 1930, p. 469, with 1914, p. 558), and adds Isaac Penington and John Woolman (1930, p. 470). In 1930 her treatment of the seventeenth-century French school is

far more nuanced, including Pierre de Bérulle and Benedict Canfield (p. 470). Caussade is added in 1930 (p. 472). Her description of William Blake is as positive in 1930 as in 1914; but she omits in 1930 her description of him as 'a determined and outspoken foe of conventional Christianity' (1914, p. 562; cf. 1930, p. 473). Blake concludes her historical appendix. The 1930 Bibliography has some new editions of standard spiritual texts. It also includes St Anselm, Blosius, St Bridget of Sweden, Cassian, St Catherine dei Ricci, St Jeanne Françoise de Chantal, St Elizabeth of Schönau, Gerard Groote, Gerson, Joachim of Flora, Lucie-Christine, Ramon Lull, St Maria Maddelena dei Pazzi, Marie de l'Incarnation, Nicholas of Cusa, Origen, Isaac Penington, St Peter of Alcantara, Rabi`a, Peter Sterry and John Woolman. The secondary section is extensively revised and updated in 1930.

506. There are notably fewer references to Guyon in 1930 than in 1914. Thus she appears with Rolle, Suso, and St Teresa in the 1914 edn of chapter 1.4 (p. 109) ('The characteristics of mysticism'), but has disappeared by 1930 (p. 91). The 1930 edition is harsher on her: thus 1914 has 'Madame Guyon's rather unbalanced, diffuse, and sentimental character lacks the richness and dignity . . . of St Catherine's mind' (pp. 220–1), 1930 has 'Madame Guyon's unbalanced, diffuse, and sentimental character entirely lacks the richness and dignity . . . of St Catherine's mind' (pp. 182–3). At the same point, 1930 describes Guyon as 'an ideal "laboratory specimen" for the religious psychologist' (p. 183), a phrase not in 1914. In the chapter on 'Voices and visions' (2.5), an analysis of St Teresa of Avila added in 1930 replaces the analysis of Guyon in 1914 (1914, p. 329; 1930, p. 274). The same thing takes place later in the same chapter: a para. starting 'So, too, Madame Guyon' (1914, p. 327) is replaced in 1930 with another starting 'So, too, St Teresa' (1930, p. 281). In 1930 she is described as 'a devout but somewhat self-occupied soul' (p. 385), a description not present in 1914. In chapter 2.9 ('The Dark Night of the Soul'), a text from Guyon in 1914 (p. 466) is replaced with one from Caussade (p. 390). In the concluding historical appendix, 1914 describes Guyon as 'one of the most interesting personalities of the time . . . an instance of considerable mystical genius linked with a feeble surface intelligence' (p. 560); in 1930 this is changed to 'an example of the unfortunate results of an alliance of mystical tendencies with a feeble surface intelligence' (p. 472).

507. References to him increase in 1930: see, e.g., chapter 1.5 ('Mysticism and theology'), where he is absent in 1914 (pp. 115 and 116) and is present in the same passages in 1930 (pp. 96 and 97).

508. Cf. 1914, p. 91 with 1930, p. 76.

509. 1914, p. 359; 1930, p. 300. Where 1914 has 'the superb words of Plotinus' (referring to 'the flight of the Alone to the Alone') (p. 98), in 1930 she has simply 'in the words of Plotinus' (p. 82). A reference to the 'love of Ideal Beauty' in 1914 becomes 'the thirst for Perfection' in 1930 (1914, p. 242; 1930 p. 201). In the chapter on 'The Illumination of the Self' (2.4), 1914 has:

> It will be observed that . . . the claim of the mystic is not yet to supreme communion, to that 'flight of the Alone to the Alone' which is the Plotinian image for the utmost bliss of the emancipated soul. A vision, and a knowledge, which is the result of conscious harmony with the divine World of Becoming, is the ideal held out: not self-mergence in the Principle of Life, but willing and harmonious revolution about Him, that 'in dancing we may know what is done' (1914, pp. 281–2).

1930 has:

> It will be observed that . . . the claim of the mystic is not yet to supreme communion; the 'Spiritual Marriage' of the Christian mystic, or that 'flight of the Alone to the Alone' which is the Plotinian image for the utmost bliss of the emancipated soul. He has now got through preliminaries; detached himself from his chief entanglements; re-oriented his instinctive life. The result is a new and solid certitude about God, and his own soul's relation to God: an 'enlightenment' in which he is adjusted to new standards of conduct and thought (1930, p. 234).

Note the reference to the spiritual marriage added in 1930; and the reference to 'conduct and thought' as well as to mystical experience. In the historical Appendix, a sentence extolling Plotinus ('These things . . . merely served Plotinus on his mystical side as a means of expressing as much of his own sublime experience as he chose to tell the world' (1914, p. 544)) is omitted in 1930. Finally, it is worth noting that in her 1920 essay 'The mysticism of Plotinus', repr. in that year's *The essentials of mysticism*, she can refer to the Plotinian doctrine of man as having become 'in due course the classical doctrine of Christian mysticism . . . Man, like the rest of Creation, has come forth from God and will only find happiness and full life when his true being is re-united, first with the Divine Mind, and ultimately with the One' (1920, pp. 124–5), though this essay is by no means uncritical, acknowledging Plotinus' undervaluing of the human and entire lack of interest in the social dimension of Christianity; see 1920, pp. 130–1.

510. *Mysticism* p. xiv. In *The mystics of the Church* she defines it as 'the direct intuition or experience of God' (1925, p. 9).
511. *Essential mysticism,* pp. 9 and 10.
512. p. 11; so too, 'an identical consciousness of close communion with God is obtained by the non-sacramental Quakers in their silence and by the sacramental Catholics in the Eucharist' (p. 28).
513. p. 14.
514. *The mystics of the Church,* p. 81.
515. p. 86.
516. 1925, p. 12.
517. p. 16.
518. p. 25.
519. 'The philosophy of contemplation', in *The essentials of mysticism* (1995) p. 98.
520. p. 100.
521. *Mysticism* (1914) p. viii; 'Life as prayer', repr. in 1946, pp. 62–3.
522. 1922, p. 6.
523. p. 6.
524. p. 7.
525. p. 10.
526. p. 11.
527. 1922, p. 19.
528. pp. 19–20.
529. p. 25.
530. 1922, p. 32.
531. p. 37.
532. pp. 41–2.
533. cf. 1922, p. 55.
534. p. 44.
535. p. 50.
536. *Mysticism* (1930) pp. 429–31; cf. *The essentials of mysticism* (1920) p. 39. She does acknowledge that in the final analysis the influence of the mystics on the life of the Church and world is literally incalculable: we just don't know (1920, p. 43).
537. 1914, p. 14.
538. p. 89.
539. *The end of an age and other essays* (London: Putnam, 1948), p. 70.
540. 1914, p. 91.
541. p. 53.
542. pp. 59–60.
543. p. 64.
544. p. 75.
545. pp. 119–20; and cf. p. 126, where she refers to Julian's contemplation of a hazelnut (though Julian was not focusing on the hazelnut in anything like the way Underhill appears to suggest).

546. p. 76.
547. p. 77.
548. p. 100.
549. p. 101.
550. p. 123.
551. p. 140.
552. pp. 140–1.
553. See also the eloquent passage on contemplation in *Mysticism* (1930) pp. 301–2.
554. *The school of charity*, p. 49.
555. *Letters*, p. 205. Cf. 'Left to myself [I] would just go off on God alone' (*Letters*, p. 234, 21 June 1934). But elsewhere she does celebrate 'the open-air element [in Christ's prayer-life], which always seems to me so central to the Gospels and so sadly ignored by the over-Churchy' (letter of 23 January 1937, in *Letters*, p. 255).
556. 1937, p. 3; cf. p. 61, where she defines Christian worship as 'the total adoring response of man to the one Eternal God self-revealed in time'.
557. 1937, pp. 6–7.
558. 1922, p. 137.
559. 1937, p. 17.
560. Article 'Worship' (1929), repr. in 1946, p. 70. The Methodist Neville Ward, who was influenced by Underhill, makes a similar point (1967, pp. 26–38).
561. p. 78.
562. 1937, pp. 142–3.
563. 1937, p. 20.
564. pp. 22–3.
565. p. 50; cf. p. 47: 'worship, the response of the human creature to the Divine, is summed up in sacrifice; the action which expresses more fully than any other his deep if uncomprehended relation to God.'
566. This notion of transformation is fundamental to Underhill's view of worship. It is always irreducibly corporate, social and transforming, directed to the sanctification of life – see 1937, p. 77. For the relationship of atonement and mysticism, see her essay on the subject in *The essentials of mysticism* (1920) pp. 44–63, esp. p. 53: 'the true business of an atoner is a constructive one. He is called upon to heal a disharmony; bridge a gap between two things which, though separate, desire to be one.'
567. 1937, p. 51.
568. p. 67.
569. p. 52.
570. p. 70.
571. p. 81.
572. White (1952) pp. 232–3.
573. 1937, p. 68.
574. See the remarks of Terry Tastard (1991, esp. pp. 429–30).
575. 1922, p. 224.
576. *Abba* (1940), pp. 18–19.
577. For an introduction to the relationship of spirituality and the media, see the articles in *The Way* 31 (1991), entitled 'Media and communication'.
578. Clarke (1996) p. 116.
579. See Clarke (1996) p. 250.
580. See Grace Davie (1994), esp. pp. 112–14.
581. Shaw wrote to William Archer in 1894 saying that he suspected him 'of not having precisely cornered your own meaning, judging from your very loose expression of it' (*The collected letters of George Bernard Shaw*, ed. Dan H. Laurence (London: Max Reinhardt), vol. 1, p. 469). For John Gross' point, see Conlon (1987) p. 261.

582. *The illustrated London news* 1906, in *Complete Works* (hereafter *CW*) vol. 27, p. 221.

583. *Autobiography*, p. 9.

584. p. 10.

585. 1937, pp. 107–8; cf. (on the value of play and of hobbies) 1937, pp. 42–5.

586. Maisie Ward stresses the positive impact on Chesterton of being educated chiefly at home, not at boarding schools (1945, p. 24). She also quotes the High Master at St Paul's describing Gilbert to his mother: 'Six foot of genius. Cherish him, Mrs Chesterton, cherish him' (1945, p. 42).

587. Quoted Ward (1945) p. 77. One of Chesterton's friends commented that Gilbert 'passed from the care of his mother to the care of his wife' (quoted on pp. 109–10).

588. A characteristic he shared with C. S. Lewis, neither of whom had children of their own.

589. Chesterton (1937) p. 53.

590. Quoted in Conlon (1987) p. 47.

591. Ward (1945) p. 379.

592. 1937, p. 289.

593. 1937, pp. 227–8.

594. Ward (1945) p. 515.

595. Note, for example, Chesterton's entirely accurate remark in his study of Aquinas: 'this medieval period was rather specially the period of communal or corporate thinking, and in some matters it was really rather larger than the individualistic modern thinking' (1933, p. 447).

596. *Orthodoxy* in particular has won plaudits from all quarters; the Catholic scholar Étienne Gilson hailed it as 'the best piece of apologetic the century had produced', and was even more extravagantly enamoured of Chesterton's *St Thomas Aquinas* (see Dooley's Foreword to *Orthodoxy*, ed. cit., p. 34; Wyndham Lewis, 'Diamonds of the gayest', in Conlon (1987) p. 149; but see also Alfred Noyes' penetrating observations on this ('The centrality of Chesterton', in Conlon (1987) p. 131).

597. 1910, p. 61.

598. 1908, p. 339.

599. p. 280; cf. 1923, p. 38 and *The illustrated London news* (1906), in *CW* vol. 27, pp. 228–9.

600. 1908, p. 281.

601. p. 296.

602. p. 299; cf. p. 352.

603. pp. 302–3.

604. 1925, p. 345.

605. 1904, p. 382. Cf. the wonderful passage in *Orthodoxy* (1908, p. 335) where he compares Christianity and Buddhism. It is clear that Chesterton does not really understand Buddhism; yet even so his scorn of an easy or muddled syncretism is superbly articulated.

606. *Notebook*, quoted in Ward (1945) p. 58.

607. 1923, pp. 74–5. The Latin word for priest, *pontifex*, means 'bridge-builder'.

608. 'G. K. Chesterton: a practical mystic', in Conlon (1987) p. 1. Maisie Ward (1945, p. 15) traces Chesterton's sense of wonder and joy to reading George Macdonald's story *The princess and the goblin*.

609. Quoted in Ward (1945) p. 547. Cf. *Orthodoxy*, p. 267: 'Men spoke much in my boyhood of restricted or ruined men of genius: and it was common to say that many a man was a Great Might-Have-Been. To me it is a more solid and startling fact that any man in the street is a Great-Might-Not-Have-Been' (1908, p. 267).

610. Quoted in Ward (1945) pp. 545–6.

611. 1937, pp. 94–5.

612. From an article in *The Listener*, quoted in Ward (1945) p. 547.

613. *The illustrated London news* (1906), in *CW* vol. 27, p. 140.

614. *The illustrated London news* (1908), in *CW* vol. 28, pp. 204–5.

615. 1905, pp. 142–3.

616. *The illustrated London news* (1906), in *CW* vol. 27, pp. 119–20. Cf. also 'The fairy-tale means extraordinary things as seen by ordinary people' whereas the secular philosophy of the coldly rational means 'ordinary things as seen by extraordinary people' (*The illustrated London news* (1905), in *CW* vol. 27, p. 72). Cf. also 'Fairyland is nothing but the sunny country of common sense' (1908, p. 252). And, in a poem called *The sword of surprise*:

> Sunder me from my bones, O sword of God,
> Till they stand stark and strange as do the trees;
> That I whose heart goes up with the soaring woods
> May marvel as much at these.
> Sunder me from my blood that in the dark
> I hear that red ancestral river run,
> Like branching buried floods that find the sea
> But never see the sun.
>
> Give me miraculous eyes to see my eyes,
> Those rolling mirrors made alive in me,
> Terrible crystal more incredible
> Than all the things they see.
>
> Sunder me from my soul, that I may see
> The sins like streaming wounds, the life's brave beat:
> Till I shall save myself, as I would save
> A stranger in the street. (*Collected poems*, pp. 65–6)

This is Chesterton's equivalent of the medieval *nosce teipsum* etc. But it too implies a degree of naïveté: 'education precisely consists in the realisation of a permanent simplicity that abides behind all civilisations, the life that is more than meat, the body that is more than raiment' (*Illustrated London news* (1905), in *CW* vol. 27, p. 71).

617. 1908, p. 325.

618. p. 326. Cf. pp. 325–6, and *The illustrated London news* (1906), in *CW* vol. 27, p. 206: 'it is the test of a good religion whether you can joke about it'.

619. See esp. 1905, p. 61; 1908, p. 350; and 1937, pp. 32 and 109.

620. *Collected poems*, p. 16. Cf. *Heretics*, p. 61.

621. 1908, p. 243.

622. 1923, p. 77.

623. p. 70; cf. 'Modern people think the supernatural so improbable that they want to see it [hence unhealthy interest in spiritualism]. I think it so probable that I leave it alone. Spirits are not worth all this fuss; I know that, for I am one myself' (*The illustrated London news* (1906), in *CW* vol. 27, pp. 166–7.

624. 1923, p. 95.

625. *The house of Christmas*, vv. 4–5, in *Collected poems*, p. 141.

626. 1933, pp. 433–4.

627. p. 437.

628. 1923, pp. 29–30; cf. p. 82, where he notes St Francis' ability to love trees rather than the wood.

629. Quoted in Ward (1945) p. 60.

630. 1908, p. 341; cf. 1925, pp. 378–9.

631. 1908, p. 343.

632. *Collected poems*, p. 325.

633. 1908, p. 212.

634. p. 213.

635. p. 218.

636. p. 220.

637. p. 222.

638. p. 226.

639. p. 227.

640. pp. 230–1; cf. 1904, p. 384.

641. 1923, pp. 29–30.

642. 1933, p. 541.

643. On Chesterton's antisemitism, W. H. Auden is probably correct in laying the real blame on Hilaire Belloc and on Chesterton's brother; see his remarks in Conlon (1987) p. 262.

644. 1923, p. 39. Cf. 1908, pp. 217 and 321; and 1937, p. 329, where he says that the principal reason he joined the Roman Catholic Church was 'to get rid of my sins'.

645. As John Gross points out, 'he belonged to the world before totalitarianism' (in Conlon (1987) p. 257). See also Ward (1945) p. 49. But it is well worth noting that Chesterton was no uncritical chauvinist. In *What's wrong with the world* he wrote: 'imperialism in its common patriotic pretensions appears to me both weak and perilous. It is the attempt of a European country to create a kind of sham Europe which it can dominate, instead of the real Europe, which it can only share. It is a love of living with one's inferiors (1910, p. 91). And note his remark on Mussolini's Fascism, which 'appeals to an appetite for authority, without very clearly giving the authority for the appetite' (quoted in Ward (1945) p. 492).

646. John Raymond acutely observes that 'like all good publicists, he was a great simplifier' ('Jeekaycee', in Conlon (1987) p. 159).

647. C. S. Lewis, *The allegory of love* (London: Oxford UP, 1936), pp. 358–9.

648. p. 302.

649. 1908, p. 231; cf. 1925, pp. 265–8.

650. 1908, pp. 250–1; cf. *The illustrated London news* (1908), in *CW* vol. 28, p. 23.

651. During his year of military service (1917–18) Lewis read a volume of Chesterton's essays (Wilson (1990) p. 55). *The everlasting man* had a profound influence on Lewis in the period of his movement towards Christianity (Wilson, p. 108).

652. Apart from the curious fact of both becoming known by their initials and not their first names, both had childless marriages yet a great love of children and children's stories; both were prolific writers (and later broadcasters) who enjoyed controversy; both became doughty apologists for Christianity having first been sceptics; both were drawn to romance (and especially medieval) literature and culture; both were in many respects conservative and strongly Anglophile. For Lewis see the excellent biography by A. N. Wilson (1990).

653. *The allegory of love* (1936), *The discarded image* (published posthumously in 1964) and *English literature in the sixteenth century excluding drama* (1954), part of the Oxford History of English Literature.

654. See his autobiography *Surprised by joy* (1955), p. 182.

655. Wilson (1990) p. 45. Wilson acutely describes MacDonald as representing for Lewis 'the missing link between Spenser's *Faerie Queene* and the writings of Freud and Jung (1990, p. 46).

656. For Tolkien's influence on Lewis, see Wilson (1990).

657. See Wilson (1990) pp. 149–50.

658. For Charles Williams' life, see Ridler's introd. to Williams (1958), esp. p. liv.

659. See Ridler, introd. to Williams (1958), p. xxxix.

660. For Pseudo-Dionysius, see also C. S. Lewis, *The discarded image* (Cambridge UP, 1967), pp. 70–5. The importance of a dialectical holding-together of contrary principles appears pervasive for Williams. Thus he says in an essay that 'The trouble about Shakespeare is that he is both Christian and non-Christian, and it is fatal to call him either' (1958, p. 39).

661. For her life see Loades (1993) and Barbara Reynolds, *Dorothy L. Sayers: her life and soul* (London, 1993).

662. See Graham Neville's article 'Lay theology: the case of Dorothy L. Sayers' in *Theology* 102 (1999), p. 349. Neville argues that lay Anglican theological writers in the twentieth century, like C. S. Lewis and Dorothy Sayers, tended to be ignored by professional theologians; and hence their importance was in the field of apologetic rather than the development of theology. But Dorothy Sayers did make an important contribution to theology: emphasizing traditional Christian dogmas, and focusing on the fatherhood of God and the brotherhood of

Christians as the essence of Christianity (p. 348).

663. Cited in Loades (1993) p. 10.

664. Prologue to *He that should come*, cited in Loades (1993) p. 17.

665. Sayers, introd. to *Dante: The Divine Comedy 1 (Hell)* (Penguin Classics) (Harmondsworth: Penguin, 1949), p. 10.

666. Sayers, introd. to *Dante: The Divine Comedy 3 (Paradise)* (Penguin Classics) (Harmondsworth: Penguin, 1962), p. 16.

667. 'The meaning of heaven and hell' (1948) in 1954, p. 64. Hence in part the importance of Dante's *Inferno*: it reveals the corruptibility of us all. See Barbara Reynolds, 'Dorothy's Dante: a fiftieth anniversary tribute to Sayers' *Commedia*', in *The Times Literary Supplement* 5046 (17 December 1999), pp. 11–13, esp. p. 12.

668. 'On writing *the devil to pay*', in Loades (1993) p. 38.

669. *The dogma is the drama* (1938), cited in Loades (1993) p. 54.

670. Williams (1958) p. 69. Theologically this emphasis is rooted in his stress on the primacy of the Incarnation, and in particular on Duns Scotus' view of the latter as the crown and fulfilment of God's overall plan for creation (see 1958, p. 76).

671. Williams, 'Natural goodness' (1941), repr. in 1993, p. 36.

672. Sayers (1957) p. 183.

673. *The allegory of love* (London: Oxford UP, 1936, repr. 1958), p. 45.

674. Sayers (1957) p. 184. Elsewhere she points out how an author can make use of a universal image of enormous power without being aware of having done so ('Dante's imagery, 1: Symbolic', (1947) in 1954, pp. 18–20).

675. Sayers (1957) p. 187.

676. p. 188.

677. *The discarded image* (Cambridge UP, 1967), pp. 74–5.

678. Sayers (1957) p. 194. See also Dorothy Sayers' introd. to *The Divine Comedy: Paradise* (Harmondsworth: Penguin, 1962), p. 21. Charles Williams also seeks to universalize the theology of images, so that anyone can image the good and the divine (see Sayers (1957) pp. 199–200). Williams emphasizes the *reality* of the image in its own right: Dante is no vapid spiritualizer (see Williams (1943) p. 172).

679. See Williams (1943) p. 92 and n. 1. For a brief summary of the Trinitarian theology of the Cappadocian fathers (and especially of St Gregory of Nyssa, whose thought is particularly significant in this connection), see Thomas Hopko, 'The Trinity in the Cappadocians' (in McGinn et al. (eds), *Christian spirituality I: origins to the twelfth century* (World spirituality) (New York: Crossroad, 1985 and London: SCM Press, 1989), pp. 260–75, esp. pp. 271–4. A. M. Allchin notes (*Participation in God* (London: DLT, 1988), p. 6) that in biblical terms coinherence is rooted in the New Testament articulation of the inseparability of the human from the divine as a consequence of the Incarnation.

680. Williams (1943) p. 172. Dorothy Sayers quotes the scientist Julian Huxley: 'persons are individuals who transcend their merely organic individuality in conscious participation' (introduction to Dante's *The Divine Comedy: Paradise* (Harmondsworth: Penguin, 1962), p. 31).

681. 1958, p. 107; cf. 1943, p. 14.

682. Williams (1958) p. 109.

683. See e.g. Williams (1958) p. 149.

684. p. 151.

685. p. 154.

686. Williams (1943) p. 195.

687. Williams (1958) p. 156.

688. Williams, 'The theology of romantic love' (from *He came down from heaven*), repr. in 1993, pp. 77–8.

689. Williams (1958) p. 195.

690. Lewis (1963–4) pp. 89–90.

691. See, e.g., *The zeal of thy house*, Scene II, cited in Loades (1993) p. 55 – 'to labour is to pray'.

692. *A Christian basis for the post-war world*, cited in Loades (1993) p. 132. The consequence of the Fall was not so much to make work *difficult* as to make it *necessary*, an economic necessity, no longer something engaged in for its own sake. Economics is thus allowed to become the basis for human nature (pp. 132–3).

693. Lewis (1963–4) p. 72.

694. Lewis (1955) p. 47.

695. Lewis (1941) p. 95.

696. 1941, p. 96.

697. p. 98.

698. p. 98.

699. pp. 101–2.

700. Lewis (1955) pp. 21–2.

701. pp. 24–5.

702. pp. 25–6.

703. pp. 27–8.

704. Lewis (1947) p. 183; cf. 1963–4, p. 53. His argument is basically that of Aquinas; that God may well have decided in advance to make a particular event hang upon our prayer.

705. Lewis (1963–4) p. 39.

706. p. 40.

707. pp. 41–2.

708. Sayers, *He that should come*, Prologue, in Loades (1993) p. 22.

709. Sayers, *The devil to pay*, in Loades (1993) p. 46.

710. 'The King's Supper', Scene 3, in Sayers (1945) p. 254.

711. Hastings (1986) p. 603.

712. The Edinburgh Missionary Conference in 1910 could be said to mark the start of the modern ecumenical movement (Hastings (1986) p. 87). In the 1920s the second Viscount Halifax, the lay leader of Anglo-Catholicism, met with the abbé Portal and Cardinal Mercier to try to get *Apostolicae curae* revoked. The first conversation was in 1921, and was unofficial; in 1923 they were resumed with more of an official air (though Mercier never realized how unrepresentative Halifax was of Anglicanism) (Hastings (1986) pp. 208–9). Mercier died in 1926 and the conversations were terminated. Chadwick (1990, pp. 64–5) suggests that Nazism created a strong Christian-led longing for international peace and reconciliation, which helped foster a far more popular ecumenical movement, finding supreme expression in the World Council of Churches, which first met at Amsterdam in 1948. For the earlier movements towards unity, such as the establishment of the Student Christian Movement (SCM), see Hastings (1986) chapter 5. See also Wilkinson (1978) p. 200.

713. See above under 'Spirituality and social justice'.

714. Quoted in John Newton's study of ecumenical spirituality (1994, p. 2).

715. For Kelly see *S. S. M.: an idea still working* (Society of the Sacred Mission, 1980), and the bibliographical references cited there.

716. Cited on p. 24.

717. Cited on p. 24.

718. Temple (1955) pp. 319–20.

719. p. 327.

720. Newbigin, *The household of God* (1953).

721. p. 92.

722. pp. 93–4.

723. p. 95.

724. p. 95.

725. p. 97.

726. p. 98.

727. p. 104.

728. p. 115.
729. p. 116.
730. pp. 123–5.
731. For Wyon see the Glossary to this chapter.
732. Wyon (1943) p. 36.
733. 1962, p. 22.
734. 1943, p. 14; cf. 1962, p. 13: 'we pray, or we want to pray, because *God is*'.
735. 1943, p. 21.
736. 1943, p. 88.
737. 1962, p. 33.
738. Wyon (1943) p. 115.
739. p. 115.
740. pp. 115–16.
741. p. 117.
742. p. 116; for prayer as response, see Wyon (1962) chapter 4.
743. 1943, p. 117.
744. p. 118.
745. p. 119.
746. p. 121.
747. p. 122.
748. p. 49.
749. p. 17.
750. pp. 20–1. Cf. the reflections of two church leaders whose ecumenical ministry in Liverpool
      was very influential: David Sheppard and Derek Worlock, *Better together* (London: Hodder
      and Stoughton, 1988), pp. 275–6.
751. 1954, p. 62. Wyon argues that in intercession we become priests, 'transmitters of the redeem-
      ing transforming grace of God' (1954, p. 68). Like all priests, we must persevere in this prayer
      even when we appear to get no answer: we can recall, at such moments, Jesus' prayer for Judas.
      But intercession is priestly in another way too: 'the essence of intercession is vicarious offering'
      (1954, p. 70). Neville Ward (1967, p. 116) makes the further point that unity involves 'a
      sharing of each other's knowledge, and the fruit of savouring some strange tastes whose very
      strangeness can bring a new interest into our devotional life and even the possibility of finding
      helps to prayer for which we may have been vainly looking for years'. In other words: prayer
      for unity is *in itself* transforming.
752. For a complete list of his writings, see Farrer, *Reflective faith: essays in philosophical theology*, ed.
      Charles C. Conti (London: SPCK, 1972), pp. 227–34. His philosophical works include
      Finite and infinite (1943) and *Faith and speculation* (1967).
753. Farrer (1948) p. 63.
754. p. 113.
755. pp. 187–8.
756. p. 139.
757. See the sermon on assurance, 1991, pp. 5–8.
758. 1948, p. 144. The whole of this section, in which he explores the relationship between the
      anointing at Bethany and the end of Mark's Gospel, is fascinating: 1948, pp. 140–5.
759. Farrer (1991) p. 88.
760. p. 88.
761. See his essay 'Poetic truth', 1972, p. 26.
762. p. 29.
763. Farrer (1991) p. 19.
764. 1991, p. 3 – an immensely suggestive passage.
765. p. 10.
766. p. 152.
767. 1948, p. 12.

768. p. 93.
769. p. 14.
770. pp. 32–3.
771. p. 90.
772. p. 90. Elsewhere Farrer makes the point that the resurrection of Christ 'is neither contrary to the natural order, nor in accordance with the natural order: it is clean beyond the natural order; it is a next stage after nature has run her course' (1991, p. 140).
773. 1948, p. 27.
774. p. 28. This theme of touching recurs in his writing: whenever we pray, we touch God, and even when our touch is cold and formal, his is invariably warm and pulsing with life (1991, p. 203). At Christmas, 'Mary holds her finger out, and a divine hand closes on it. The maker of the world is born a begging child' (1991, p. 209).
775. In the Bampton Lectures he stresses the significance of 'certain dominant images' in Jesus' thought: the Kingdom of God, the Son of Man, the image of Israel, and, 'in the action of the supper, the infinitely complex and fertile image of sacrifice and communion, of expiation and covenant' (1948, p. 42). Hence 'we have to listen to the Spirit speaking divine things: and the way to appreciate his speech is to quicken our own minds with the life of the inspired images' (p. 44) – that is, those images just cited.
776. 1948, p. 108.
777. p. 109; cf. p. 110. Farrer distinguishes between 'master-images and subordinate images' both in the Old Testament prophets and the New Testament writings (p. 136). The master-images are given, *revealed*; not susceptible of being replaced, though they can and do constantly 'throw out fresh branches'.
778. 1991, p. 97.
779. p. 98.
780. p. 98.
781. p. 99. Note the distinctive blend of Reformed and Catholic theology here.
782. See 1952, p. 33: 'The prayer which saves the world is one with the existence of the man who prays. It is with such a prayer that the saints and Christ himself pray for men's happiness, prosperity, and peace, and by the virtue of this sacrament our prayer and theirs is one.'
783. 1952, p. 100.
784. 1948, pp. 7–8.
785. pp. 7–8.
786. p. 61.
787. p. 61.
788. 1991, p. 148.
789. 'The glass shows us no face of ours; it shows us the face of our glorious Lord. And the relation of looking-glass to gazer is reversed; instead of the mirror-image taking form from the gazer's face, the gazer's face takes form from the image, changed from glory to glory under the radiance of the Lord's Spirit' (1991, p. 156). Cf. also 'Only the day of judgement will strike the glass for ever from our hands, and leave us nowhere reflected but in the pupils of the eyes of God' (1991, p. 203).
790. 1970, p. 200.
791. 1991, p. 162.
792. p. 170.
793. p. 136.
794. p. 73.
795. p. 73.
796. p. 75.
797. p. 122. Elsewhere Farrer says that, to both Greeks and Israelites, wisdom was two things: 'knowing how to live, in the most profound and human sense – how to make of your life what your life was made for . . . [and] to know those truths about yourself, and about the realities surrounding you, which you must know if you are to respond appropriately to the demands of your situation, and so live truly well' (1970, p. 69).

798.   1958, p. 55.
799.   1989, p. 26.
800.   p. 30.
801.   p. 31.
802.   1991, p. 118.
803.   p. 21.
804.   p. 21.
805.   p. 138.
806.   1952, p. 24; for Lent 3.
807.   p. 59.
808.   1989, pp. 18–19.
809.   1991, p. 152.
810.   p. 152, cf. also 1952, p. 32.
811.   See especially the marvellous meditations in his *The crown of the year.*
812.   1952, p. 8.
813.   p. 37.
814.   p. 41.
815.   1970, p. 179.
816.   1958, pp. 36–7.
817.   p. 36.
818.   p. 37.
819.   p. 37.
820.   p. 39.
821.   1991, p. 105.
822.   1970, p. 200.
823.   1991, p. 106.
824.   p. 137.
825.   See esp. 1991, p. 110.
826.   1991, p. 157.
827.   p. 112.
828.   'Poetic truth', pp. 30–1. Cf. pp. 37–8: 'The chief impediment to religion in this age, I often think, is that no one ever looks at anything at all: not so as to contemplate it, to apprehend what it is to be that thing, and plumb, if he can, the deep fact of its individual existence.' Farrer elsewhere suggests that the thing which constitutes the special likeness which human beings have to God, and which animals do not share, is 'the power to get outside our skins, and see things impartially' (1973, p. 21).
829.   1973, p. 101.
830.   p. 101.
831.   1952, p. 22.
832.   1991, p. 107.
833.   p. 107.
834.   1970, p. 169.
835.   1991, p. 135.
836.   1952, p. 20.
837.   1948, pp. 19–23. Cf. also pp. 97–8, where he writes somewhat disparagingly of 'the unin-structed Hottentot', whose 'religion is not so high a wisdom' as that of the Christian philosopher.
838.   1991, p. 126.
839.   1973, p. 100.
840.   1952, p. 18.
841.   1970, p. 169.
842.   For Ramsey's life see the excellent study by Chadwick (1990).

843. 1956, p. 216. Chadwick points out (1990, p. 63) the significance of Maurice for Ramsey.

844. See Chadwick (1990) pp. 20–5.

845. This stress on the impossibility of being an individual Christian is a vital theme for Ramsey: see, e.g., 1956, pp. 36–7, where he argues that to become a Christian is precisely to join the Church, to become part of the body of Christ; and that similarly

> justification by faith is never a solitary relationship with a solitary Christ. The man who is justified is an individual, but the Christ who justifies is one with His people as His Body; and the act of faith, in releasing a man from self, brings him into dependence upon his neighbours in Christ. Faith and justification are inseparable from initiation into the one Body (1956, p. 37).

846. 1956, p. vi, from Preface to 1st edn.

847. 1956, p. 4.

848. p. 26.

849. p. 29.

850. p. 33. Ramsey stresses the importance of the Name and the Glory of God in scripture (p. 91). The Name of God is outwardly manifested as his glory, and in the Old Testament it rests upon Israel. In the New Testament, the Name is disclosed by the Son's life and death; and Christians, in becoming Christians, are 'brought "within" the Name' (p. 92): 'they are baptized into it, they confess it, praise it, love it, proclaim it, bear it, and in it they pray, give thanks, heal, suffer, die' (p. 92).

851. p. 38.

852. p. 43.

853. p. 56.

854. p. 75. In *Be still and know* (1982, p. 51) he notes how, in John 17, the unity of Christians 'is not just a fellowship amongst themselves but a unity in the Father and in the Son, in a way that resembles the Father being in the Son and the Son being in the Father.'

855. 'It is the emphatic teaching of the New Testament that men *become* sons of God through the action of the Holy Spirit who reproduces Christ's sonship in them' (1961, p. 32).

856. 1982, p. 56.

857. 1961, p. 33.

858. 1967, p. 13.

859. p. 28. In this book Ramsey suggests that the Greek word *doxa* came to represent both the Hebrew *kabod* (literally 'weight', and, in post-exilic writings (e.g. Isaiah 60), also 'radiance' or 'splendour') and the *shekinah* of Yahweh, which in the intertestamental period came to be used as 'a way of speaking about God such as conveys the truth of His omnipresence, accessibility and special activity within the created world without infringing the doctrine of His transcendence' (1967, p. 19). 'Hence conceptions which are distinct in Hebrew and Aramaic literature became, in the Septuagint, fused into a unified imagery of God's glory and God's dwelling or tabernacling with His people' (p. 20). This is the background, in Ramsey's view, for the association of glory in the New Testament with a *person*, and specifically with that person in whom God tabernacled among human beings.

860. 2 Corinthians 4.3–6; Ramsey (1967) p. 46.

861. 1967, p. 65.

862. p. 65.

863. pp. 76–7 and 79.

864. p. 86.

865. The theme is covered in detail in 1967, pp. 101–end.

866. *metamorphousthai* (1967, p. 114).

867. Ramsey points out that many New Testament texts incorporating references to *doxa* are eschatological, looking forward to the glory of the second coming (*parousia*) of Christ (1967, p. 36). Similarly the glory that indwells the Church is invisible, entirely distinct from ecclesiastical grandeur, and necessarily incomplete, because it points towards the infinitely greater glory of the *parousia* (pp. 88–9).

868. p. 112.
869. 1982, pp. 64–5.
870. Hence St Peter: 'If you are reproached with the name of Christ, you are blessed, because the Spirit of the glory and of God rests upon you' – a notable phrase, as Ramsey points out (1982, p. 65).
871. 1982, p. 66.
872. p. 67. In 1967 Ramsey makes the point at greater length: for Christians, both suffering, and knowledge, and the world itself, are transfigured through this mystery (p. 145). Transfiguration is not a pious hope for the future, but the active transformation of all things here and now, in and through the suffering and glory of the Son of God (pp. 146–7).
873. Romans 12.1–2.
874. 1982, p. 69.
875. 1956, pp. 92–3.
876. p. 101. This theme recurs elsewhere (see, e.g., p. 29).
877. p. 103.
878. p. 117.
879. See p. 115 and Ramsey's *The Christian priest today* (1972, revised edn 1985).
880. This stress on the primarily liturgical nature of New Testament prayer recurs in *The Gospel and the Catholic Church* (1956, p. 94). Thus the Lord's Prayer must be seen as liturgical: that is, 'it is the sharing by men in the one action of Christ, through their dying to their own egotisms as they are joined in one Body with His death and resurrection'. Ramsey resists Friedrich Heiler's distinction between prophetic and mystical prayer, preferring to see both as rooted in the redemptive action of Christ as it is given expression in corporate Christian worship. But, as Gordon Wakefield gently observes, it may be that Ramsey never 'felt on his pulse the ethos and the power of "prophetic prayer"' ('Michael Ramsey: a theological appraisal', in *Theology* 91 (1988), p. 462).
881. 1956, p. 119.
882. Heb. *kabed*, to glorify (1967, p. 92).
883. 1967, p. 92.
884. p. 97.
885. 1982, p. 73.
886. p. 75.
887. p. 74. 'Intercession thus becomes not the bombardment of God with requests so much as the bringing of our desires within the stream of God's own compassion'. Ramsey points out that in the Letter to the Hebrews the Greek word translated 'intercede' does not properly mean to speak, but to be present with (p. 54).
888. See p. 82.
889. pp. 77 and 113; cf. 1956, p. 93.
890. 1982, p. 78. For Ramsey, one way of making that link is by praying with the Psalms (p. 79; cf. 1967, p. 97). The Psalter was Christ's prayer-book: 'using the Psalter in the name of Christ the members of the Body make their own the prayer of the Head' (1967, p. 98).
891. 1982, p. 50.
892. pp. 13–14.
893. p. 116; the same point is made in 1956, p. 147.
894. 1982, p. 118.
895. p. 119.
896. Hence his disapproval of private Masses or non-communicating ones (see e.g. 1956, p. 173).
897. 1956, pp. 181–203.
898. pp. 187 and 194–5.
899. p. 209.
900. 1982, p. 59; cf. Hebrews 13.11–16.
901. The writings of Henry (R. H.) Tawney strongly influenced the writers cited here, especially his *The acquisitive society* (1921), the Labour manifesto *Secondary education for all* (1924),

Religion and the rise of capitalism (1926), *Labour and the nation* (1929) and *Equality* (1931), a passionate fusion of Christian and socialist thought. For a good brief modern summary of early Christian Socialism see Leech (1992) pp. 122–32 and Wilkinson (1998).

902. Another significant contributor to this area whom space precludes from further mention is Charles Marson (1859–1914), who spent much of his priestly ministry in rural Somerset; like Headlam, he was a doughty critic of social injustice and deeply committed to applying a radical Christianity to the ills he saw around him. For Marson see Reckitt, 'Charles Marson, 1859–1914, and the real disorders of the Church', in Reckitt (1968) pp. 89–134. His works (which are not cited here) include *God's co-operative society: suggestions on the strategy of the Church* (1914), consisting of essays and addresses; *The Psalms at work* (1894); *Charity organisation and Jesus Christ* (1896); and *Village silhouettes* (1914), reflecting his ministry in rural Somerset.

903. 1939, p. 215; original 'men's bodies'.

904. Noel (1937) p. 206.

905. Headlam (1907) p. 67.

906. See Headlam (1907) pp. 68–70.

907. Headlam (1878) p. 20.

908. *Faith in the city: a call for action by church and nation* (London: Church House Publishing, 1985), p. 119, para. 6.57. See also p. 63, para. 3.32.

909. Leech (1986) p. 6.

910. Leech (1977) p. 11.

911. Leech (1980) p. 79.

912. *Faith in the city: a call for action by church and nation* (London: Church House Publishing, 1985), p. 51. The report itself has little to say about spirituality; but it did spawn a number of reflections on urban spirituality (see, e.g., John and Angela Pearce, *Inner-city spirituality* (Grove spirituality series 21) (Bramcote, Nottingham: Grove Books, 1987); or publications of the Urban Theology Unit at Sheffield, such as *Hymns of the city*, compiled by John J. Vincent (Sheffield: Urban Theology Unit, 1989).

913. Ecclestone (1975) pp. 83–4.

914. pp. 84–5; original has 'What God affirms, men cannot afford to neglect'.

915. Headlam (1907) p. 21.

916. p. 54.

917. 1939, p. 217. Leech stresses that our whole lives are meant to be eucharistic; and we must do this in a selfish world, a world of waste and pollution and inequality (1980, p. 110).

918. Headlam (1907) p. 14. For his stress on family piety see Headlam (1878) p. 91.

919. Noel (1937) p. 78.

920. See Leech (1992) pp. 56–67, Vasey (1995) and Jim Cotter, *Good fruits: same-sex relationships and Christian faith*, 2nd edn (Exeter: Cairns, 1988). Cotter says that 'spiritual and sexual growth can happen only in relationship . . . and both kinds of growth demand courage' (p. 20). A number of official church reports explored the relationship of spirituality and sexuality, albeit briefly: see, e.g., the Church of England's *Issues in human sexuality* (London: Church House Publishing, 1991), p. 27, para. 3.20.

921. Leech (1992) p. 60.

922. 'The church . . . faces the dilemma that when it presents itself as the primary opposition to this public gay identity, it is opposing the form of homosexuality which is least easily identified with St Paul's strictures' (Vasey (1995) p. 140).

923. Vasey (1995) p. 233.

924. p. 232. He points to the importance of desire in some Old Testament texts such as Psalm 63: 'Human desire is primarily for God . . . Out of this innate vitality and desire springs the whole diverse range of human activity' (p. 64). In the Bible, human desires are met not only in sex but in other important activities such as the shared table (Psalm 41.9), shared worship (Psalm 42), and civic art and ritual (Psalm 68.24–7) (p. 65). See also Kenneth Leech, '"The carnality of grace": sexuality, spirituality and pastoral ministry', in Woodward (ed.) (1990) pp. 59–68.

925. See the essays and reflections in Woodward (ed.) (1990), esp. those of Andrew Henderson (p. 43) and Sara Maitland (pp. 94–5).

926. The reflections of Nigel Sheldrick, quoted in Woodward (ed.) (1990) p. 20. Not everyone can respond so positively, of course: see the reflections of Victoria in the same book (pp. 90–1).

927. Vasey (1995) pp. 72 and 91. He draws attention to the way Jesus encouraged intimate friendship, esp. in John (p. 121), where 'the disciple Jesus loved' has a special intimacy with Christ, esp. on Easter morning (p. 123); and he also notes Jesus' concern to *befriend* those normally regarded as beyond the pale (p. 123). See also J. Michael Clark, 'Gay spirituality' (in P. H. van Ness (ed.), *Spirituality and the secular quest* (World spirituality) (New York: Crossroad, 1996), pp. 335–55, esp. pp. 343–4. For another exploration of Christian friendship, see David Moss, 'Friendship: St Anselm, *theoria* and the convolution of sense' in J. Milbank et al. (eds), *Radical orthodoxy: a new theology* (London: Routledge, 1999), pp. 127–42.

928. For a good introduction, see *Approaches to spiritual direction* (Supplement to *The Way* 54 (1985)); David L. Fleming SJ (ed.), *The Christian ministry of spiritual direction* (consisting of articles from *Review for Religious*) (St Louis: Review for Religious, 1988); K. Fischer, *Women at the well: feminist perspectives on spiritual direction* (London: SPCK, 1989); G. Jeff, *Spiritual direction for every Christian* (London: SPCK, 1987).

929. He explored its history in *Soul friend* (1977).

930. See, e.g., Leech (1977) pp. 90–136 and Leech (1986) pp. 24–5 and 55–65.

931. Leech (1986) p. 48.

932. p. 51.

933. p. 52; and chapter 6, on the prophetic dimension of spiritual direction; cf. Leech (1977) chapter 6.

934. 1977, pp. 121–3.

935. Selby (1983) p. 3.

936. pp. 16 and 19.

937. p. 52.

938. See also under 'Pentecostal spirituality' above.

939. Leech, *Struggle in Babylon* (1988).

940. In 1982 the relative earnings of the low paid were lower than in 1886 when the data were first collected (Leech (1988) p. 13), a fact all the more appalling at a time when affluence for so many was increasing all the time.

941. Leech (1988) p. 185. He criticizes the Church of England's *Alternative Service Book 1980* for making no attempt at all to help articulate a more racially sensitive liturgy (p. 186).

942. Leech (1988) pp. 189–90.

943. See, for example, the Trinitarian spirituality of Ananias Mpunzi, 'Black theology as liberation theology', in Basil Moore (ed.), *Black theology: the South African voice* (London: Hurst, 1973), pp. 130–40), abbreviated version repr. in Alistair Kee (ed.), *A reader in political theology* (London: SCM Press, 1974), pp. 130–5).

944. Ecclestone (1977) p. 50.

945. p. 53.

946. For an excellent introduction to all the main aspects of New Age spirituality, see Sutcliffe and Bowman (2000). Sutcliffe persuasively argues (p. 31) that the sharp increase, in the late twentieth century, of people living alone has encouraged a search for meaning in new (and usually highly social) patterns of spirituality, such as the occult or paganism.

947. See Marion Bowman, 'More of the same? Christianity, vernacular religion and alternative spirituality in Glastonbury', in Sutcliffe and Bowman (2000) pp. 83–104.

948. See Lovelock (1995) (originally published in 1979), and (for a positive theological reflection on it) Celia Deane-Drummond, 'God and Gaia: myth or reality?' in *Theology* 95 (1992), pp. 277–85. Deane-Drummond warns against any attempt to give the Gaia theory a pseudo-mystical gloss (pp. 283–4), and points out the essentially pessimistic nature of that theory: nature is ultimately malevolent in its attitude to humankind (p. 281).

949. Lovelock (1995) p. vii.

950. p. 140.
951. Clark (1993) pp. 52 and 53.
952. pp. 54 and 156.
953. pp. 110–21. Clark is here defending the Greek view of nature as inviting our wonder, but condemning our insistence on possessing (and thus spoiling) what we see (see esp. p. 121).
954. Noel (1937) p. 342.
955. Leech (1980) p. 68.
956. Ecclestone (1977) p. 41.
957. Ecclestone (1975) p. 7.
958. p. 8.
959. pp. 12–13; original reads 'common life of men'.
960. pp. 25–6.
961. Ecclestone (1968), repr. in 1999 pp. 58–71.
962. p. 60.
963. pp. 60–1. Cf. *Yes to God* (1975) p. 94: 'too much of human life, including prayer, remains arrested at an adolescent stage'.
964. Ecclestone (1968/1999) p. 62.
965. p. 64.
966. p. 65.
967. For this see above.
968. Ecclestone (1968/1999) p. 66.
969. p. 66.
970. p. 79. He further commends finding space for play in our prayer (p. 81).
971. Ecclestone (1975) pp. 127–8.
972. p. 116.
973. Underhill (1922) p. 190.
974. Green (1940) pp. 52–3. For English antisemitism during wartime, see Calder (1969) pp. 498–500.
975. Green (1940) pp. 53–5.
976. See 'Spirit: a force for survival' (1994), repr. in Nicholl (1997) pp. 90–1.
977. 'Scientia cordis' (1975), repr. in 1997, chapter 13, p. 156.
978. p. 157.
979. See esp. Merton's *Asian Journal*, Johnston's *The mysticism of The cloud of unknowing*, and Bede Griffiths' *Return to the centre* and *A new vision of reality: western science, eastern mysticism and Christian faith*.
980. Andrew Wingate, *Encounter in the Spirit: Muslim–Christian dialogue in practice*, 2nd edn, (Geneva: WCC Publications, 1991), pp. 74–5.
981. See King (1993) p. 23; Davie (1994) pp. 118–21.
982. Byrne (1988) pp. 24–5; P. Sheldrake, *Spirituality and history* (London: SPCK, 1991), p. 70.
983. See Karen Armstrong (1986) pp. 301 and 302–7; King (1993) p. 111. Some feminists look to witchcraft for inspiration (such as feminist Wicca), or to a spirituality based on a renewed form of the ancient Goddess worship. See Dorothy A. Lee, 'Goddess religion and women's spirituality: a Christian feminist response', in *Theology* 102 (1999), pp. 19–28; and Susan Greenwood, 'Gender and power in magical practices', in Sutcliffe and Bowman (2000) pp. 137–54. Both Lee and Greenwood provide useful bibliographies.
984. King (1993, p. 95) notes this: e.g. Evelyn Underhill, Grace Warrack, Phyllis Hodgson, Geraldine Hodgson and Hope Emily Allen.
985. Ursula King (1993, p. 58) distinguishes 'feminine' (as denoting that which distinguishes women as women and reinforces their sense of being objects rather than subjects) from 'female' (as denoting 'the specific experience of women in conceiving and producing human life . . . and in everything that pertains to this at the biological and personal level') and 'feminist', which she suggests denotes above all the experience of contemporary women (albeit with historical antecedents) and 'entails the critical analysis of both feminine and

female experience but must proceed beyond these to the further criticism of the feminist experience itself'. See also King (1993) p. 15.

986. For a general introduction to this theme, see Purvis (1989) pp. 505–6.

987. These included Janet Morley and Hannah Ward (eds), *Celebrating women* (London: Movement for the Ordination of Women, 1986; new and extended edn, London: SPCK, 1995); Janet Morley, *All desires known* (London: Movement for the Ordination of Women, 1988); *Women included: a book of services and prayers (The St Hilda Community)* (London: SPCK, 1991).

988. *All desires known* (London: Movement for the Ordination of Women, 1988), p. 5.

989. Maitland (1983) p. 164.

990. King (1993) p. 43. For the argument that feminist theology gives more value to experience than does traditional male-dominated theology, see King (1993) p. 157 and Hebblethwaite (1984) p. 129.

991. King (1993) p. 102.

992. See King (1993) p. 171.

993. See, e.g., Don Cupitt, *Mysticism after modernity* (Oxford: Blackwell, 1998); Grace Jantzen, *Power, gender and Christian mysticism* (Cambridge UP, 1995); Margaret Miles, *The image and practice of holiness* (London: SCM Press, 1988); Philip Sheldrake, *Spirituality and history* (London: SPCK, 1991). On the use of images in contemporary spirituality, see *Images of God* (Supplement to *The Way* 26:4 (October 1986); *Imagination and images* (*The Way*, April 1984); P. Sheldrake, *Images of holiness* (London: SPCK, 1987).

994. 1988, p. 11. Instead she commends the Psalms as containing a rich variety of images, many of which 'can be reappropriated and feed God's life within the Christbearing woman' (p. 13).

995. See King (1993) pp. 12–31. Kathy Nairne and Gerrilyn Smith (*Dealing with depression*, London: Women's Press, 1984, p. 124) note that 'however it comes out, our anger is a sign of our vitality'. For the relevance of the imagery of the Psalms for women today, see Ulrike Bail, '"O God, hear my prayer": Psalm 55 and violence against women', in A. Brenner and C. R. Fontaine (eds), *Wisdom and Psalms: a feminist companion to the Bible,* second series (Sheffield Academic Press, 1998), pp. 242–63.

996. See, e.g., Maitland (1983) pp. 181–3.

997. See King (1993) pp. 70–1. This too was explored historically: see esp. the works of Caroline Walker Bynum, and in particular her *The resurrection of the body in western Christianity, 200–1336* (New York: Columbia UP, 1995).

998. King (1993) pp. 70–1.

999. p. 74.

1000. See p. 77.

1001. 'A womb-centred life', in Hurcombe (1987) p. 94. Kroll argues that menstruation reminds women of human dependence on God in a way denied to men, as a result of which men are more prone to illusions of omnipotence (p. 98); and also that the menopause allows women to come creatively to terms with loss in a way that many men never succeed in doing (p. 101).

1002. Hebblethwaite (1984). She suggests that the use of fantasies and the imagination in prayer can be profoundly creative, just as it is for women awaiting childbirth (1984, p. 26).

1003. pp. 14–15.

1004. p. 21.

1005. Kroll, 'A womb-centred life', in Hurcombe (1987) p. 102.

1006. See Hebblethwaite (1984) pp. 57–63.

1007. pp. 75–6.

1008. Studdert-Kennedy (1928) p. 59.

1009. p. 103.

1010. p. 152.

1011. Cited in Morgan (1963) p. 47.

1012. Ursula King quotes N. Chodorow: 'the basic feminine sense of self is connected to the world, the basic masculine sense of self is separate' (1993, p. 81). See also Purvis (1989) pp. 506–10.

1013. The St Hilda's Community (an inclusive group of women and men committed to the ordination of women who met regularly for worship in London before the Church of England's General Synod voted to ordain women) encouraged the use of liturgical dance: one of those who taught it said 'it was a revelation to me. Suddenly I felt properly joined to the earth after years, it seemed, of being caught in a spiritual limbo between heaven and earth. The contact with the floor, or with the ground out of doors, roots us in unity, harmony and healing' (*Women included: a book of services and prayers (The St Hilda Community)* (London: SPCK, 1991), p. 32). Lavinia Byrne celebrates bicycling as fostering this sense of harmony (1988, pp. 72 and 78–9).

1014. See esp. King (1993) p. 79 and p. 110: 'one cannot surrender a sense of self one has never possessed'; cf. also p. 191. King suggests (p. 81) that the boundaries of the female sense of 'self' are more permeable than those of the man.' Authors of a study of depression among women point out that 'depression can result from giving out for years while never getting much back for ourselves' (Kathy Nairne and Gerrilyn Smith, *Dealing with depression* (London: Women's Press, 1984), p. 51).

1015. See Lavinia Byrne (1988) p. 41. It is striking to note that it is a male theologian, Don Cupitt, who began one of his most famous books with the words 'Modern people increasingly demand autonomy . . . they want to live their own lives, which means making one's own rules' (*Taking leave of God* (London: SCM Press, 1980), p. ix).

1016. King (1993) p. 85.

1017. p. 86.

1018. p. 189. Cf. Lavinia Byrne: 'Jesus in the Gospels is at pains to remind the woman at the well of Samaria that the source of her own life and potential for growth lies within' (1988, p. 68).

1019. King (1993, p. 11) suggests that our relationship to nature and concern for peace are key dimensions of feminist spirituality.

1020. Miles (1981) p. 278.

1021. Cited in Barbara Harford and Sarah Hopkins, *Greenham Common: women at the wire* (London: Women's Press, 1984), pp. 91–2.

1022. See Purvis (1989) p. 503.

1023. Ravetz (1995, p. 187) argues that women are much more interested in interiors of houses than exteriors, a significant fact since most estate agents are male! Judy Attfield makes the same point (in Attfield and Kirkham (1995) p. 220).

1024. Ravetz (1995) p. 189. Rosalind Miles points out (1989, p. 282) that the proliferation of machines for housework has also helped to make it a solitary, boring activity. See also Kathy Nairne and Gerrilyn Smith, *Dealing with depression* (London: Women's Press, 1984), pp. 57–8.

1025. Ravetz (1995) p. 202.

1026. See Partington (1995), esp. p. 209. A woman might use any designed object to 'make meanings' which might be quite independent of the intended function of the object concerned (p. 210).

1027. See Judy Attfield, 'Inside Pram Town: a case study of Harlow house interiors, 1951–61' in Attfield and Kirkham (1995) pp. 219 and 222). Lace curtains etc. could be one of the few ways a housewife could express her pride in her work (since otherwise housework had no visible manifestation; it only 'showed' when it was not being done) (p. 234).

1028. See Attfield, p. 229.

1029. Byrne (1988) p. xii.

1030. p. 49.

1031. *The end of an age and other essays* (London: Putnam, 1948), p. 114.

1032. In just four months, from September 1940 to January 1941, 13,339 people were killed in London and 17,937 severely injured as a result of the bombing (Briggs (1983) p. 269).

1033. Clarke (1996) p. 232.

1034. Wilkinson (1978, p. 212) points out how anti-German feeling was far stronger at home during and after the First World War than among soldiers at the front.

1035. *The world my wilderness* (1950; London: Virago, 1983), pp. 149–50.

1036. Wilfred Owen, no friend of institutional Christianity, said 'How blind are men to twilight's mystic things' ('The little mermaid', in *Poems,* p. 25).

1037. See Fussell (1975) and especially Wilkinson (1978). Adrian Hastings (1986, pp. 47–8) argues that Christianity had already lost the intellectual battle before the First World War; 'what the war did was to shatter its social and political role as well: to unveil the truth to high and low alike of ecclesiastical near-irrelevance'. And see, among many other examples, Siegfried Sassoon's poem 'The Bishop of Byegumb', whose eponymous subject 'made me love Religion less and less'. (Sassoon, *The war poems,* p. 141; cf. 'They', p. 57; 'The Prince of Wounds', p. 19). Sassoon, reflecting on the failure of the churches to offer any convincing way of responding to the horrors of war, acknowledged: 'could *anyone* – from a fully informed religious understanding – have made a success of the subject?' (*The war poems,* p. 47). See also his ferocious 'Devotion to duty' (p. 142), in which he compares George V to King David pretending to grieve over the death of Uriah the Hittite. Robert Graves strongly criticizes the behaviour of the Anglican chaplains during the war, commending the RC ones far more (see *Goodbye to all that,* pp. 198–9, where he tells the story of a chaplain who, just before the Loos campaign, preached 'a violent sermon on the Battle against Sin, at which one old soldier behind me grumbled: "Christ, as if one bloody push wasn't enough to worry about at a time!"'; cf. p. 231). But Graves was not always objective: see the comments of Alan Wilkinson (1978, pp. 110–11).

1038. Underhill (1922) p. 122. Underhill's reference to 'all who worked' probably means the officer class, who (in many cases for the first time) found themselves confronted with direct experience of working-class culture and religion. Alan Wilkinson suggests that Roman Catholic chaplains may in general have exercised a more pastorally effective ministry among the combatants because the provision of sacramental confession and extreme unction, as well as the familiarity of easily memorable prayers such as the rosary, may have been more accessible at moments of crisis than the formal language of the Prayer Book (1978, pp. 132–3 and 144).

1039. See, among many others, Wilfred Owen's 'Unto what pinnacles' (*Poems,* p. 40), with its vigorous denunciation of any religious aspiration; and the same poet's 'Maundy Thursday' (*Poems,* p. 86). In 'Le Christianisme' (1917), Owen reflects on the lifelessness of the saints immured in bombed churches (*Poems,* p. 103; and see the comments of Jon Silkin (1987, p. 233)).

1040. Owen, *Poems,* pp. 119–20.

1041. See Gordon Mursell, *Out of the deep* (London: DLT, 1989), pp. 135–59.

1042. Rosenberg, 'Spiritual isolation' (printed in *Night and day,* 1912, and quoted in Silkin (1987, p. 266)). Silkin shows how Rosenberg challenged his own inherited notion of God as the lawgiver. In one poem, 'God', he went so far as to suggest that God's 'body lodged a rat where men nursed souls' (quoted Silkin (1987) p. 267). This God has to be rejected, and replaced perhaps by a weaker God (p. 270).

1043. See Calder (1969) p. 480. For some of the ways in which combatants had instinctive recourse to prayer *in extremis,* see Wilkinson pp. 147, 156 (on the power of singing), 157–8 (on the value of the Psalms), and 163 ('they wanted to believe that there was Someone outside themselves who would keep them and their families safe'). Wilkinson also notes (p. 195) the popularity of lucky coins and charms, pictures and crucifixes among combatants.

1044. Owen, *Poems,* p. 145.

1045. Quoted on p. 145.

1046. See Wilkinson (1986) pp. 459–62.

1047. Gore (1916) p. 134.

1048. p. 134. It is not surprising that the First World War saw an increase in prayer for the dead (Wilkinson (1978) p. 176).

1049. For Studdert-Kennedy see Wilkinson (1978) pp. 136–40; Mursell, *Out of the deep* (London: DLT, 1989) pp. 143–54, and 156); and William Purcell, *Woodbine Willie* (London, 1962).

1050. 1983, pp. 12–13. Cf. 'The comrade God' (1932) pp. 67–8.

1051. The notion of a noble self-sacrifice was of course not new: see Wilkinson (1986) pp. 459–60.

1052. See 'The comrade God', quoted above.

1053. 'High and lifted up', pp. 42–3.

1054. p. 80.

1055. 1983, p. 95.

1056. pp. 107–8.

1057. In Silkin (ed.) (1981) p. 211.

1058. 'If the body is treated thus, can there really be a soul, which is any better treated? The spiritual part of man dies with his body. The body is parted from life, not from a soul' (Silkin (1987) p. 288). Silkin (1987, p. 287) compares Owen's (universal) sense of pity with Rosenberg's (specific and individual) sense of tenderness for the dead. And for Rosenberg, human beings are *beautiful* too:

> Beauty is a great paradox –
> Music's secret soul creeping about the senses
> To wrestle with man's coarser nature.
> It is hard when beauty loses.
> (from 'The Amulet', in Silkin (ed.) (1981) p. 216).

1059. Cited in Silkin (ed.) (1981) pp. 147–8.

1060. 'Report on experience', vv. 1–2.

1061. Vera Brittain, 'September, 1939', in Powell (1999) p. 9.

1062. Mitchison, 'Clemency Ealasaid', in Powell (1999) p. 64.

1063. Hewlett, 'October, 1940', in Powell (1999) p. 82.

1064. de Bairacli-Levy, 'Killed in action', in Powell (1999) p. 121.

1065. Cherrill, 'Easter 1942', in Powell (1999) p. 157.

1066. Ledward, 'In memoriam', in Powell (1999) p. 140.

1067. See Wilkinson (1978) chapter 12.

1068. For Weatherley and Coates, see Coates' *Suite in four movements* (1953; repr. London: Thames Publishing, 1986), esp. pp. 117–20.

1069. See *The artist in society*, in 1994, p. 60.

1070. *The eternal presence*, in 1994, p. 65.

1071. p. 66.

1072. *The vision of the fool*, in 1994, pp. 72–3.

1073. Spencer seems to have drawn back from explicit commitment to Christianity, or indeed to any religion, just as he drew back from any long-term commitment to another human being (see Spencer (1980) p. 28). There are similarities between him and Kenneth Grahame, both of whom idealized landscapes familiar to them since childhood and imbued them with a brilliant if limited naturalistic creativity. Blake's influence on Spencer's often erotic emphasis on the divine presence in the heart of the material is palpable (see also p. 34).

1074. See Tavener (1999) p. 33.

1075. For his strictures on evolution see 1999, p. 83.

1076. pp. 35–6.

1077. p. 55. Tavener clearly finds this railing against God hard to take – see p. 56: 'we cannot just rage with our feeble egos against God'. It is not clear what view Tavener would take of the imprecatory Psalms.

1078. Harvey spent some years as a choirboy at the Anglican choir school at Tenbury. For Underhill's influence see Harvey (1999) p. 3; for the influence of the twentieth-century educationalist Rudolf Steiner, see Whittall (1999) p. 14 and Harvey (1999) p. 4; for the influence of Buddhism, see esp. Harvey (1999) pp. 5–6. Both Steiner and Buddhism emphasized the fundamental spiritual interconnectedness of all things.

1079. Unsurprisingly Harvey readily acknowledges the influence of continental contemporary composers with a particular interest in the spiritual dimension of music – among them Karlheinz Stockhausen and Olivier Messiaen.

1080. Collins (1994) p. 74.

1081. p. 76.

1082. p. 77.

1083. p. 78.

1084. *The artist in the new age*, in Collins (1994) p. 99.

1085. Tate Gallery Spencer Archive, 733.3.6, perhaps January 1938; quoted in 1980, p. 29.

1086. See e.g. *The temptation of St Anthony* (1945), 1980 pp. 209–10. For Spencer and D. H. Lawrence, see MacCarthy (1998) p. 3.

1087. See 1980, pp. 169ff.

1088. Painted in 1939; see 1980, p. 172. Spencer said, speaking of Moses encountering God in the burning bush, that 'I could see the richness that underlies the Bible in Cookham in the hedges in the yew trees' (quoted MacCarthy (1998) p. 7). In the wonderful series of war paintings he made at Burghclere, Spencer shows ordinary physical human beings thrown into extraordinary and horrifying situations, and hints at the ultimate triumph of love (perhaps especially sexual love) over the evil of war.

1089. Spencer's early *Two girls and a beehive* (1910) shows two local girls (whom Spencer knew) looking over a fence at a beehive, while the shadowy figure of Christ appears in the background from behind a bush (1980, pp. 38–9). This setting of Christ in Cookham would become a common theme of his painting. *The centurion's servant* (1914) reproduces a number of Cookham villagers praying at the bedside of the sick man (the artist and his family posed for these): the sick man is stretched languorously across the bed.

1090. Murdoch (1970) p. 40.

1091. p. 41.

1092. p. 55. Murdoch describes prayer as 'properly not petition, but simply an attention to God which is a form of love' (p. 55); 'Whatever one thinks of its theological context, it does seem that prayer can actually induce a better quality of consciousness and provide an energy for good action which would not otherwise be available' (p. 83).

1093. p. 56; cf. p. 83.

1094. p. 85.

1095. Sylvester (1994) p. 38.

1096. p. 46.

1097. Baker (1988) p. 2.

1098. p. 10.

1099. Tavener (1999) p. 16.

1100. 1999, p. 119. See also p. 73: 'from both a Christian and Platonic point of view . . . all music already exists. When God created the world he created everything.'

1101. p. 120.

1102. 'Aesthetic or spiritual pleasure must outweigh material pleasure. Material pleasure is at another's expense – if we have it, someone else can't. That leads to greed, causing envy, causing stress, causing an explosion. Aesthetic pleasure is at no-one's expense' (1992, p. 614).

1103. Harvey (1999) p. 71.

1104. Whittall (1999) p. 33.

1105. p. 33.

1106. Harvey (1992) p. 614.

1107. John V. Taylor uses this antithesis in regard to inter-faith dialogue: 'debates about inter-faith dialogue usually betray too static an idea of what a religion is. It suggests that what shapes men is the truth *about* God whereas in fact it is the truth *of* God . . . But I believe it is truer to think of a religion as a people's tradition of response to the reality the Holy Spirit has set before their eyes' (Taylor (1972) pp. 181–2). For an extended attempt to propose a way of transcending the subject–object split (with particular regard to the way we see the created world around us), see Sallie McFague, *Super, natural Christians* (Fortress Press, 1997).

1108. See Harvey (1999) p. 1. Music can help to heal realities which had hitherto been separated; and it can thus also help prepare us for death (p. 83). Compare the reaction of George Eliot in 1858: 'How music that stirs all one's devout emotions blends everything into harmony –

makes one feel part of one whole, which one loves all alike, losing the sense of a separate self' (cited in *The journals of George Eliot*, ed. M. Harris and J. Johnston (Cambridge UP, 1998), p. 308).

1109. Harvey (1999) p. 28.

1110. p. 39, quoting Julia Kristeva.

1111. p. 49.

1112. p. 53. Elsewhere he argues that 'the interplay between "self" and "whole" in music has a Buddhist flavour and is deeply fascinating' ('Madonna of Winter and Spring', in *Musical Times* 127 (1986), p. 432).

1113. See Whittall (1999) p. 19.

1114. Harvey (1999) p. 34. Harvey's two-act opera *Inquest of love* (1992) explores this theme at length; see Whittall (1999) pp. 70–1.

1115. Harvey (1999) pp. 37–8.

1116. pp. 84–5.

1117. He points out that the word 'temple' originally derives from *temno* (I cut): see his 'Monuments, myths and mission', in *Church Building* 55 (1999) pp. 10–11 and 56 (1999) pp. 10–11).

1118. Stancliffe notes the importance of the medieval rite of consecration, *separating* the Church from everything profane. Others take a different view. Michael Wilson ('Spirituality and management', in Halliburton (1995) pp. 52–65) underlines the inseparability of the sacred from the secular in the history and theology of cathedrals, as does Michael Kitchener ('Sacred and secular in cathedral institutions', pp. 30–9). The very size and fascination of the cathedral dwarfs any attempt to give it a narrowly ecclesiastical or diocesan remit (a point made by Halliburton himself in 'The cathedral and the city', p. 72; and cf. Keith Walker, 'Sacred visual art', pp. 43–51, esp. p. 46). It is interesting to note a woman writer, Angela Tilby, suggesting the importance of building bridges between cathedrals and modern science, emphasizing the importance of the unity and integrity of creation rather than the religious building standing over against 'the world' (in Platten and Lewis (1998) p. 168). The different approaches taken by men and women to this issue underline Harvey's emphasis on the importance of the integration of masculine and feminine dimensions in music and spirituality.

1119. Psalm 84.3.

1120. Underhill (1922) pp. 129, 144–6. See also the remarks of Christopher Lewis, in Platten and Lewis (1998) p. 154. Cf. also Philip Larkin's poem 'Church going', where he speaks of 'a serious house on serious earth . . . / In whose blent air all our compulsions meet,/ Are recognized, and robed as destinies' (*Poems*, p. 98).

1121. Vanstone (1977) p. 109.

1122. Ecclestone (1975) pp. 46–7.

1123. Woodham (1997) p. 213.

1124. As Woodham points out (pp. 211–12), an enterprising American company took the carefully-chosen English names 'Crabtree' and 'Evelyn' and successfully marketed 'heritage' quality products. The National Trust did the same thing. The 'marketing of retrospection' is exemplified by Laura Ashley, or Royal Doulton's 'Old Country Roses' bone china design, the world's best-selling tableware design (p. 217).

1125. See Woodham (1997) pp. 89–90.

1126. As successively Vicar of St Matthew's Northampton and Dean of Chichester, Hussey was responsible for commissioning many outstanding works of art and music (see, e.g., Humphrey Carpenter, *Benjamin Britten* (London: Faber, 1992), p. 187).

1127. See Jeremy Paxman, *The English* (London: Michael Joseph, 1998; repr. Penguin, 1999), p. 152.

1128. Stevie Smith (1978) p. 216.

1129. See Bradley (1999), esp. p. 202: 'at a time when the English are facing an identity crisis and suffering from guilt about their imperial past, this romanticisation of the inhabitants of the Celtic fringes and recovery of such mythical stereotypes as the Spiritual Gael and the Visionary Celt has proved very appealing.'

1130. Heelas (1999, p. 99) argues that New Age spirituality is predicated on the assumption that life is not working for large numbers of people: they aren't happy, or at least aren't satisfied. So they look *inwards* for meaning and purpose. In New Age movements, 'the Self is in control' (p. 101): no one is going to be dictated to.

1131. Many spiritual writers note the rise in levels of anxiety: see, e.g., Leslie Weatherhead (1958) p. 25 and n. 1.

1132. Selby (1983) p. 54.

1133. Toynbee (1981) p. 241.

1134. Williams (1965) p. 14.

1135. Williams (1982) p. 85.

1136. See, e.g., (1975) pp. 40 and 83.

1137. Williams (1972/1983) p. 33.

1138. p. 51.

1139. p. 52.

1140. Williams (1965) p. 32.

1141. p. 47.

1142. See esp. Williams' essay 'Theology and self-awareness', in *Soundings* (1962), and the critique of it by Eric Mascall in chapter 2 (eloquently entitled 'Pumping out the bilge') of his book *Up and down in Adria* (London: Faith Press, 1963). In particular, Mascall takes Williams to task for an uncritical approach to modern psychology, concentrating too much on Freudian insights.

1143. See esp. White (1952), a striking study of the relationship between Jung's psychology and traditional Thomist Catholic doctrine; and Bryant (1983). Bryant underlines the extent to which Jung sees the work and presence of God everywhere, not simply in some narrowly defined religious area of life (see, e.g., p. 39).

1144. See Bryant (1983) p. 39. Jung himself describes the concept of the self as 'the central point in my thinking and in my researches' (*Memories, dreams, reflections*, ed. A. Jaffé, ET by R. and C. Winston (London: Collins, 1967), p. 234).

1144. Bryant (1983) p. 41. Robert Segal ('Jung's psychologising of religion', in Sutcliffe and Bowman (2000) p. 65) emphasizes, against writers like Bryant, the fact that for Jung God existed *only* within the soul – and had no independent, objective existence outside it.

1146. See esp. Isabel Briggs Myers and Peter B. Myers, *Gifts differing* (Palo Alto, California: Consulting Psychologists Press, 1984). The Myers Briggs Type Indicator, based on Jung's book *Psychological types* (first English translation 1923), became immensely popular in spiritual, psychological and business circles in Europe and North America towards the end of the twentieth century.

1147. Williams (1965) pp. 81–2. Eric Mascall pounces on Williams' view of sin as psychological derangement rather than as renunciation of our dependence on God (*Up and down in Adria*, p. 40).

1148. White (1952) pp. 165–6.

1149. p. 184.

1150. See the exposition of Jung's ideas in Bryant (1983) chapter 5.

1151. Bryant (1983) p. 82.

1152. p. 91.

1153. See esp. his autobiographical work *Yet being someone other* (1983), and in particular his description of the moment he is arrested by the Japanese in Java (pp. 315–18).

1154. 1983, p. 318.

1155. Rose (1995) pp. 90–1.

1156. See, e.g., 1964, pp. 69 and 73, and 1971, p. 11. Winnicott was not a Christian, believing that the soul was a property of the psyche, and had no existence outside the functions of the brain: see Winnicott (1988) p. 52.

1157. See 1964, p. 105. The average good parent 'is helping the child to distinguish between the actual happenings and what goes on in the imagination. She is sorting out for the infant the actual from the enriching fantasy' (1964, p. 109). See also 1988, pp. 110–11.

1158. Winnicott (1971) pp. 66–7.

1159. 'We find either that individuals live creatively and feel that life is worth living or else that they cannot live creatively and are doubtful about the value of living. This variable in human beings is directly related to the quality and quantity of environmental provision at the beginning or in the early phases of each baby's living experience' (1971, p. 71).

1160. See 1971, p. 3. Winnicott and John Bowlby were pioneers of a progressive attitude towards children, abandoning old authoritarian models and encouraging child-centred love and attention. Their views chimed in with mothers in rebellion against old rule-based approaches that taught it was wrong to comfort your crying baby or to feed it on demand; and although they became unpopular with feminists, 'their appeal was not so much in terms of the return of women to the home – however much their masculine prejudices stamp their work – but of the flowering of love for children in a war-torn world' (Wilson (1980) p. 189).

1161. Leech (1977) p. 108.

1162. Toynbee (1981) p. 66.

1163. p. 112.

1164. p. 139.

1165. p. 246.

1166. Williams (1982) p. 354.

1167. Williams (1977) p. 43; cf. pp. 44–7.

1168. Williams (1982) p. 366; cf. 1977 p. 60.

1169. Williams (1977) Prologue.

1170. Green (1935) pp. 51–3.

1171. p. 57.

1172. Louis J. Puhl SJ, *The Spiritual Exercises of St Ignatius* (Chicago: Loyola UP, 1951), p. 101 (para. 231).

1173. See, among numerous other books, William Yeomans, 'Prayer' (an article on Ignatius' understanding of prayer), in *The way* 3 (1963), pp. 196–204; Philip Sheldrake, *Spirituality and history* (London: SPCK, 1991), for much valuable material on the context of St Ignatius; Gerard W. Hughes SJ, *God of surprises* (London: DLT, 1985), which is arguably the most influential recent exploration of the Ignatian tradition; and David Lonsdale SJ, *Eyes to see, ears to hear* (London: DLT, 1990), for a recent introduction to Ignatian spirituality. For an exploration of this subject in the light of liberation theology, see Juan Luis Segundo, *The Christ of the Ignatian Exercises* (Jesus of Nazareth Yesterday and Today, vol. 4), ET by J. Drury (London: Sheed and Ward, 1988).

1174. See (among many other books) Charles Handy, *The hungry spirit* (London: Hutchinson, 1997); Geoffrey Harding, *Lying down in church: stress in the city* (Worthing: Churchman, 1990); Elizabeth Puttick, 'Personal development: the spiritualisation and secularisation of the Human Potential Movement', in Sutcliffe and Bowman (2000) pp. 201–19.

1175. For this, see esp. Handy (1997) p. 118.

1176. Ward (1971) p. 102.

1177. Boulding (1979) p. 80.

1178. 1999, p. 30.

1179. p. 31.

1180. p. 32.

1181. p. 37.

1182. p. 33.

1183. p. 35. Ursula King ('Spirituality, ageing and gender', in Jewell (ed.) (1999) p. 149) makes the further point that women live longer than men, and will therefore have specific spiritual needs in old age that most men will not have.

1184. See Howes (1999) p. 99.

1185. See Davie (1994), esp. chapter 5 (e.g. her reflections on the response to the 1989 Hillsborough football tragedy, pp. 88–91).

1186. See esp. Davie (1994) (e.g. p. 192).

1187. See 'Choruses from *The rock*' (1934), in Eliot, pp. 147–8.

1188. Otherwise, as he puts it in 'The Dry Salvages', we may find we have 'had the experience but missed the meaning' (*Four Quartets* (1969) p. 186).

1189. pp. 148–9.

1190. p. 158.

1191. Eliot, *Murder in the Cathedral* II (1969) p. 271.

1192. Roberts (1984) p. 215 n. 16. Roberts describes people from similar backgrounds who were brought up to say their prayers morning and evening, and continued to do so throughout their lives (p. 15).

1193. See Edrington (1987). The men were aged between 18 and 84. The interviews took place in 1984. 56% of them described themselves as believers, though there was a wide variety of opinion as to what 'believing' meant (1987, p. 62).

1194. p. 113. The great majority did not worry whether there was a life after death or not (p. 98). Only 39% of believers believed there was (p. 100).

1195. p. 94.

1196. p. 95.

1197. p. 110.

1198. p. 95.

1199. p. 96; cf. p. 104, on personal religious experience, similarly felt to be strictly private.

1200. p. 97.

1201. p. 68.

1202. p. 98.

1203. Ursula King (in her article 'Spirituality, ageing, and gender', in Jewell (ed.) (1999) p. 148), makes a similar point. But we should also note that the sociologist Peter Berger was quoting the same statistic, drawn from research in Germany, back in 1967 (Berger (1971) p. 40: 68% believed in God, but 86% prayed!).

1204. p. 108.

1205. p. 174.

1206. Phillips acknowledges that there may be no one there when people who are praying think there is; but that does not turn their prayer into talking to themselves (1965, p. 31). Nor is prayer a conversation in the manner similar to conventional inter-personal encounters. (p. 50).

1207. p. 59.

1208. p. 71. Here, as so often, Phillips is dependent on Simone Weil.

1209. p. 60.

1210. p. 62.

1211. p. 63.

1212. p. 66.

1213. p. 97.

1214. p. 103. We don't thank God for what happens in our lives: we thank God for the fact of there being any life at all.

1215. pp. 120–1 (my italics).

1216. Macquarrie (1972) p. 2.

1217. Webb (1945) p. 39 (arguing against the philosopher Alfred Whitehead's assertion that 'religion is what the individual does with his solitariness'). Webb was Professor of the Philosophy of the Christian Religion at the University of Oxford.

1218. p. 41.

1219. See the introduction to Richards, Wilson and Woodhead (eds), *Diana: the making of a media saint* (London: Tauris, 1999), p. 8.

1220. Quoted in Heelas (1999) p. 98.

1221. Woodhead (1999) p. 129.

1222. See Heelas (1999) p. 98.

1223. p. 111, and Woodhead (1999) p. 132, where she notes that Diana's 'heaven' had no gates – anyone could get there.

1224. See Heelas (1999) p. 107.

1225. pp. 112–13; Woodhead (1999) p. 122.

1226. Woodhead (1991) p. 131.

1227. Heelas (1999) p. 114.

1228. Woodhead (1999) p. 129.

1229. Jung, *Der Geist der Psychologie*, quoted in White (1952) p. 17.

1230. White (1952) p. 17.

1231. p. 18.

1232. p. 19. Depth psychology has, in White's view, revealed the reality and importance of the divine as inescapable in the fashioning of human health and happiness (1952, p. 21).

1233. Quoted in Charles Handy, *The hungry spirit* (London: Hutchinson, 1997), p. 108.

1233. Stoter, *Spiritual aspects of health care* (London: Times Mirror International, 1995), p. 3. He offers a fuller definition of 'spiritual care' in health terms on p. 8.

1235. I am indebted for this point to James Woodward, *A study of the role of the acute health care chaplain in England* (unpub. DPhil thesis, Open University, 1998), esp. pp. 222–4 and 229.

1236. The NAHAT report *Spiritual care in the NHS: a guide for purchasers and providers* (Birmingham: NHS Confederation, 1996, pp. 8–9) explicitly calls for departments of spiritual care to be set up by NHS Trusts. See also (for spirituality and health care): Aldridge, D., 'Spirituality, healing and medicine', in *British journal of general practice* 41 (1991) pp. 425–7; Harrison, N. J., 'Spirituality and nursing practice', in *Journal of clinical nursing* 2 (1993) pp. 211–7; Labun, E., 'Spiritual care: an element in nursing planning', in *Journal of advanced nursing* 3 (1988), pp. 314–20; (for spirituality and education): Jill Robson and David Lonsdale (eds.), *Can spirituality be taught?* (Association of Centres of Adult Theological Education and British Council of Churches, n.d.); Thatcher, A., *Spirituality and the curriculum* (London: Cassell, 1999).

1237. Cassidy (1988) p. 2.

1238. Innumerable books and courses on varying kinds of physical and spiritual well-being appeared during the last decades of the twentieth century. Space permits brief mention only of one: the Alexander Technique (founded by F. M. Alexander, 1869–1955), whose careful attention to fundamental principles such as balance, awareness and direction proved helpful to many during the twentieth century as a whole: see esp. Michael Gelb, *Body learning: an introduction to the Alexander Technique* (London: Aurum, 1987).

1239. Polanyi (1958) p. 64.

1240. p. 133.

1241. Peter Forster notes the significance of this insight for prayer: when we pray, we participate in the continuing work of God in creating and sustaining all that is ('Providence and prayer', in Torrance, Thomas F., *Belief in science and in Christian life: the relevance of Michael Polanyi's thought for Christian faith and life* (Edinburgh: Handsel, 1980), p. 126.

1242. Polanyi tells the story of Clever Hans, the horse that was able to answer mathematical problems, written on a blackboard in front of him, by tapping with his hoofs the correct answers – until someone asked him a question to which the questioner did not know the answer. Then the horse tapped on without rhyme or reason. It turned out 'that all the severely sceptical experts had involuntarily and unknowingly signalled to the horse to stop tapping at the point where they – knowing the right answer – expected him to stop' (1958, p. 169).

1243. See Temple (1924) p. 29.

1244. Polanyi (1958) pp. 195–6. Note that for Polanyi, as Peter Forster observes, reality is not neutral: it 'speaks to man, "evoking" or "prompting" (to use Polanyi's own words) a response of commitment' ('Providence and prayer', in Torrance, Thomas F. (ed.), *Belief in science and in Christian life: the relevance of Michael Polanyi's thought for Christian faith and life* (Edinburgh: Handsel, 1980), p. 115.

1245. p. 196.
1246. p. 196.
1247. p. 197.
1248. p. 198.
1249. p. 199.
1250. p. 279.
1251. p. 285. Cf. Polanyi's approach with Dorothy Sayers reflecting on the passion ('and it is a passion') of the change-ringer, a passion that 'finds its satisfaction in mathematical completeness and mechanical perfection' (*The nine tailors*, cited in Loades (1993) p. 23). Harry Williams adumbrates a similar theory of knowledge as participation-in, rather than external knowledge-of, in *True resurrection* chapter 3 ('Resurrection and mind'). True knowledge leads to personal union with what is known (1972/1983, p. 79); and 'the writer can write authentically only of those experiences he himself undergoes' (p. 89). 'To grasp any human situation in its depth and subtlety [and] imagination is the *sine qua non* of knowing'. 'The way of knowing as communion is the natural way of nourishing our humanity. Because it is natural it is also spiritual' (p. 95, though this latter remark underlines Williams' tendency to move almost too easily from the physical to the spiritual, so keen is he to affirm their indissolubility). And he continues:

> The place where we feel most at home, the people we most deeply love, the works of genius which have most fired our imagination, these are instances of the Word being made flesh and dwelling among us, and thus creating us. Each of these instances confronts us with its own mystery. We cannot fully describe or explain any of them. It is in being themselves that they beckon us to communion with them and their final identity is intellectually elusive. (1972/1983 p. 96).

This leads Williams to reject the Church's insistence that they hold propositional truths as uniquely authoritative, and instead suggests that they be raised up as witnesses to mystery which can be known only by means of knowledge as communion (1972/1983, p. 99).
1252. Dawkins (1998) p. x.
1253. p. xi.
1254. p. 1. In other words, as he astringently points out, it is overwhelmingly more likely that we be dead than alive (p. 3).
1255. p. 5.
1256. p. 18.
1257. p. 142.
1258. p. 144.
1259. p. 185. Cf. p. 188: 'New Age cults of all kinds are swimming in bogus scientific language, regurgitated, half-understood (no, less than half) jargon.'
1260. See his own Preface (1937) pp. vii–viii.
1261. Stapledon (1937) p. 2.
1262. Thus (to take one example) he describes species of beings whose search for 'God' had led them to concentrate on inward meditation which in turn had made them 'insensitive to the suffering of their less-awakened fellows and careless of the communal enterprise of their kind' (1937, p. 119).
1263. pp. 328–9 and 333–4.
1264. Habakkuk 3.17–18 NRSV.

BIBLIOGRAPHY

Primary Works

Aldred, Joe (ed.), *Praying with power* (London: Continuum, 2000)

Anthony of Sourozh, Metropolitan (Anthony Bloom), 'The spirituality of old age', in Jewell, Albert (ed.), *Spirituality and ageing* (London: Jessica Kingsley, 1999), pp. 30–8 (also published as *The spirituality of ageing* (Christian Council on Ageing, Occasional Papers 4), 3rd edn (Derby: Epworth House, 1995)

Baelz, Peter, *Prayer and providence* (London: SCM Press, 1968)

Baker, John Austin, *The foolishness of God* (London: DLT, 1970)

Baldwin, Stanley, *On England* (London: Philip Allan, 1926)

Baughen, Michael, *The prayer principle* (Amersham: Candle Press, 1996) (originally published 1992 as *Getting through to God*)

Boulding, Maria, OSB, *The coming of God* (London: SPCK, 1982)

Boulding, Maria, OSB, *Marked for life: prayer in the Easter Christ* (London: SPCK, 1979)

Brengle, Samuel Logan, *Helps to holiness* (1896) (London: Salvationist Publishing, 1948)

Brooke, Rupert, *The poetical works*, ed. G. Keynes (London: Faber, 1970)

Burnaby, John, 'Christian prayer', in Vidler, A. R. (ed.), *Soundings: essays concerning Christian understanding* (Cambridge UP, 1962), pp. 219–38

Butler, Cuthbert, *Western mysticism* (London: Constable, 1922)

Byrne, Lavinia, *Women before God* (London: SPCK, 1988)

Cassidy, Sheila, *Sharing the darkness: the spirituality of caring* (London: DLT, 1988)

Chapman, J. Arundel, *The supernatural life* (London: Epworth, 1934)

Chapman, John: Hudleston, Dom Roger (ed.), *The spiritual letters of Dom John Chapman OSB* (London: Sheed and Ward, 1935)

Chesterton, G. K., *Autobiography* (London: Hutchinson, 1937)

Chesterton, G. K., *The Blatchford controversies* (1904), in D. Dooley (ed.), *The collected works of G. K. Chesterton*, vol. 1 (San Francisco: Ignatius, 1986), pp. 367–95

Chesterton, G. K., *Collected poems*, 12th edn (London: Methuen, 1950)

Chesterton, G. K., *The everlasting man*, in *The collected works of G. K. Chesterton*, vol. 2 (San Francisco: Ignatius, 1986), pp. 143–407

Chesterton, G. K., *Heretics* (1905), in D. Dooley (ed.), *The collected works of G. K. Chesterton*, vol. 1 (San Francisco: Ignatius, 1986), pp. 39–207

Chesterton, G. K., *The illustrated London news 1905–1907* (articles), in L. J. Clipper (ed.), *The collected works of G. K. Chesterton*, vol. 27 (San Francisco: Ignatius, 1986)

Chesterton, G. K., *The illustrated London news 1908–1910* (articles), in L. J. Clipper (ed.), *The collected works of G. K. Chesterton*, vol. 28 (San Francisco: Ignatius, 1987)

Chesterton, G. K., *Orthodoxy* (1908), in D. Dooley (ed.), *The collected works of G. K. Chesterton*, vol. 1 (San Francisco: Ignatius, 1986), pp. 211–366

Chesterton, G. K., *St Francis of Assisi* (1923), in *The collected works of G. K. Chesterton*, vol. 2 (San Francisco: Ignatius, 1986), pp. 25–133

Chesterton, G. K., *St Thomas Aquinas* (1933), in *The collected works of G. K. Chesterton*, vol. 2 (San Francisco: Ignatius, 1986), pp. 409–551

Chesterton, G. K., *What's wrong with the world* (1910), in *The collected works of G. K. Chesterton*, vol. 4 (San Francisco: Ignatius, 1987), pp. 33–224

Chesterton, G. K., see also Conlon, D. J.

Collins, Cecil, *The vision of the fool and other writings*, ed. Brian Keeble (Ipswich: Golgonooza, 1994)

Davies, John D., *Beginning now: contemporary experience of Creation and Fall* (London: Collins, 1971)

Dawkins, Richard, *Unweaving the rainbow: science, delusion and the appetite for wonder* (Harmondsworth: Penguin, 1998)

Dawson, Christopher, *Progress and religion: an historical enquiry* (London: Sheed and Ward, 1929)

Dix, Gregory, OSB, *The shape of the liturgy*, 2nd edn (Westminster: Dacre, 1945)

The Easter People: a message from the Roman Catholic bishops of England and Wales in light of the National Pastoral Congress, Liverpool 1980 (Slough: St Paul Publications, 1980)

Ecclestone, Alan, *Firing the clay* (ed. Jim Cotter) (Sheffield: Cairns, 1999)

Ecclestone, Alan, *A staircase for silence* (London: DLT, 1977)

Ecclestone, Alan, *Yes to God* (London: DLT, 1975)

Eliot, T. S., *Complete poems and plays* (London: Faber and Faber, 1969)

Farmer, Herbert H., *Revelation and religion: studies in the theological interpretation of religious types* (London: Nisbet, 1954)

Farrer, Austin, *The crown of the year: weekly paragraphs for the Holy Sacrament* (London: A. & C. Black (Dacre Press), 1952)

Farrer, Austin, *The glass of vision* (Bampton Lectures 1948) (London: A. & C. Black (Dacre Press), 1948)

Farrer, Austin, *Lord I believe: suggestions for turning the Creed into prayer* (1958) (Cambridge, MA: Cowley, 1989)

Farrer, Austin, 'Poetic truth', in *Reflective faith: essays in philosophical theology*, ed. C. C. Conti (London: SPCK, 1972), pp. 24–38

Farrer, Austin, Sermons: Conti, C. C. (ed.), *The end of man* (London: SPCK, 1973); Houlden, J. L. (ed.), *A celebration of faith* (London: Hodder and Stoughton, 1970); Houlden, J. L. (ed.), *Austin Farrer: the essential sermons* (London: SPCK, 1991)

Farrer, Austin, see also: Mascall and Box, *The Blessed Virgin Mary*

Flew, R. Newton, *The idea of perfection in Christian theology* (Oxford UP, 1934)

Forsyth, P. T., *God the holy Father* (1897) (London: Hodder and Stoughton, 1957)

Forsyth, P. T., *Faith, freedom, and the future* (London: Hodder and Stoughton, 1912)

Forsyth, P. T., *The soul of prayer* (London: Independent Press, 1916)

Fosdick, Harry Emerson, *The meaning of prayer* (London: SCM Press, 1917)

Frost, Bede, OSB, *The art of mental prayer*, rev. edn (London: Philip Allan, 1935)

Frost, Bede, OSB, *Priesthood and prayer* (London: Mowbray, 1933)

George, A. Raymond, *Communion with God in the New Testament* (London: Epworth, 1953)

Gore, Charles, *The religion of the Church: a manual of membership* (London: Mowbray, 1916)

Graves, Robert, *Goodbye to all that* (1929; Harmondsworth: Penguin, 1960)

Green, Peter, *The man of God* (London: Hodder and Stoughton, 1935)

Green, Peter, *The path of life* (London: Longmans, Green, 1940)

Harris, J. Rendel, *The guiding hand of God* (London: Thomas Law, 1905)

Harton, F. P., *The elements of the spiritual life: a study in ascetical theology* (London: SPCK, 1932)

Harton, F. P., *Life in Christ* (London: Mowbrays, 1937)

Harvey, Jonathan, 'Madonna of Winter and Spring', in *Musical Times* 127 (1986), pp. 432–4

Harvey, Jonathan, 'Sounding out the inner self', in *Musical Times* 133 (1992), pp. 613–15

Harvey, Jonathan, *In quest of Spirit: thoughts on music* (Berkeley: California UP, 1999)

Headlam, Stewart, *The Socialist's Church* (London, 1907)

Headlam, Stewart, *Priestcraft and progress* (London: John Hodges, 1878)

Hebert, A. G., *Liturgy and society: the function of the Church in the modern world* (London: Faber, 1935)

Hurcombe, Linda (ed.), *Sex and God: some varieties of women's religious experience* (London: Routledge and Kegan Paul, 1987)

Inge, William Ralph, *Christian mysticism* (London: Methuen, 1899)

Inge, William Ralph, *Mysticism in religion* (London: Hutchinson, n.d.)

Inge, William Ralph, *The Platonic tradition in English religious thought* (Hulsean Lectures 1925–6) (London: Longmans, 1926)

Inge, William Ralph, *Studies of English mystics* (St Margaret's Lectures 1905) (London: John Murray, 1906)

Interior prayer: Carthusian novice conferences (London: DLT, 1996)

The Jubilee book of the Benedictines of Nashdom, 1914–1964 (London: Faith Press, 1964)

King, Ursula, *Women and spirituality: voices of protest and promise*, 2nd edn (Basingstoke: Macmillan, 1993)

Larkin, Philip, *Collected poems*, ed. A. Thwaite (London: Marvell and Faber, 1988)

Lavery, Hugh, *Reflections on the Creed* (Slough: St Paul, 1982) (1982i)

Lavery, Hugh, *Sacraments* (London: DLT, 1982) (1982ii)

Lawrence, D. H., *The rainbow* (1915; ed. J. Hewitt, Dent: Everyman, 1993)

Leech, Kenneth, *The eye of the storm: spiritual resources for the pursuit of justice* (London: DLT, 1992)

Leech, Kenneth, *Soul friend: a study of spirituality* (London: Sheldon, 1977)

Leech, Kenneth, *Spirituality and pastoral care* (London: Sheldon, 1986)

Leech, Kenneth, *Struggle in Babylon: racism in the cities and churches of Britain* (London: Sheldon, 1988)

Leech, Kenneth, *True prayer* (London: Sheldon, 1980)

Lewis, C. S., *Prayer: letters to Malcolm* (1963–4; London: HarperCollins, 1998)

Lewis, C. S., *Miracles: a preliminary study* (1947; London: Collins, 1960)

Lewis, C. S., *The Screwtape letters* (1942; London: Collins, 1955)

Lewis, C. S., *The weight of glory* (1941; repr. in *Screwtape proposes a toast* (London: HarperCollins, 1998), pp. 87–102

Macquarrie, John, *Paths in spirituality* (London: SCM Press, 1972)

Maitland, Sara, *A map of the new country: women and Christianity* (London: Routledge and Kegan Paul, 1983)

Maltby, W. R., *The significance of Jesus* (Burwash Memorial Lectures 1928) (London: SCM Press, 1929)

Milbank, J., Pickstock, C. and Ward, G., *Radical orthodoxy: a new theology* (London: Routledge, 1999)

Murdoch, Iris, *The sovereignty of good* (London: Routledge and Kegan Paul, 1970)

Newbigin, Lesslie, *The household of God* (London: SCM Press, 1953)

Newton, John, *Heart speaks to heart: studies in ecumenical spirituality* (London: DLT, 1994)

Nicholl, Donald, *The beatitude of truth* (London: DLT, 1997)

Nicholl, Donald, *Holiness* (1981; 2nd edn, London: DLT, 1996)

Nicholl, Donald, *The testing of hearts: a pilgrim's journey*, revised edn (London: DLT, 1998)

Noel, Conrad, *Autobiography*, ed. S. Dark (London: Dent, 1945)

Noel, Conrad, *Jesus the heretic* (London: Religious Book Club, 1939)

Noel, Conrad, *The life of Jesus* (London: Dent, 1937)

Northcott, Hubert, CR, *Man, God, and prayer* (London: SPCK, 1954)

Oman, John, *Grace and personality* (Cambridge UP, 1917)

Owen, Wilfred, *Poems*, ed. Jon Stallworthy (London: Hogarth, 1985)

Phillips, D. Z., *The concept of prayer* (Oxford: Blackwell, 1965 and 1981)

Polanyi, Michael, *Personal knowledge: towards a post-critical philosophy* (London: Routledge and Kegan Paul, 1958)

Powell, Anne (ed.), *Shadows of war: British women's poetry of the Second World War* (Stroud: Sutton, 1999)

Ramsey, Michael, *Be still and know* (London: Collins, 1982)

Ramsey, Michael, *The gospel and the Catholic Church* (1936; 2nd edn, London: Longmans, Green, 1956)

Ramsey, Michael, *The glory of God and the transfiguration of Christ* (1949; rev. edn, London: DLT, 1967)

Ramsey, Michael, *Holy Spirit: a biblical study* (London: SPCK, 1977)

Ramsey, Michael, *The resurrection of Christ* (1945; rev. edn, London: Collins, 1961)

Ramsey, Michael, see also Chadwick, O.

Robinson, John A. T., *But that I can't believe!* (London: Collins, 1967)

Robinson, John A. T., *Honest to God* (London: SCM Press, 1963)

Rhymes, Douglas, *Prayer in the secular city* (London: Lutterworth, 1967)

Rose, Gillian, *Love's work* (London: Chatto and Windus, 1995)

Sangster, W. E., *The path to perfection* (London: Hodder and Stoughton, 1943)

Sangster, W. E., *The pure in heart* (London: Epworth, 1954)

Sangster, W. E., *The secret of radiant life* (London: Hodder and Stoughton, 1957)

Sangster, W. E., *Teach me to pray* (Nashville, Tenn.: Upper Room, 1959)

Sassoon, Siegfried, *The war poems* (London: Faber, 1983)

Sayers, Dorothy L., *Spiritual writings*, ed. Ann Loades (London: SPCK, 1993)

Sayers, Dorothy L., *The man born to be King* (London: Gollancz, 1945)

Sayers, Dorothy L., 'The poetry of the image in Dante and Charles Williams', in *Further papers on Dante* (London: Methuen, 1957)

Sayers, Dorothy L., *Introductory papers on Dante* (London: Methuen, 1954)

Selby, Peter, *Belonging* (London: SPCK, 1991)

Selby, Peter, *Liberating God* (London: SPCK, 1983)

Silkin, Jon (ed.), *The Penguin book of First World War poetry*, 2nd edn (Harmondsworth: Penguin, 1981)

Smith, Stevie, *Selected poems* (Harmondsworth: Penguin, 1978)

Spencer, Stanley: *Stanley Spencer RA* (London: Royal Academy of Arts, 1980) (exhibition catalogue)

Stapledon, Olaf, *Star maker* (London: Methuen, 1937)

Stott, John, *The contemporary Christian* (1992), in *The essential John Stott* (Leicester: Inter-Varsity, 1999), pp. 343–657

Stott, John, *The cross of Christ* (1986), in *The essential John Stott* (Leicester: Inter-Varsity, 1999), pp. 1–341

Studdert-Kennedy, Geoffrey, *The word and the work* (London: Longmans, Green, 1925)

Studdert-Kennedy, Geoffrey, *The new man in Christ*, ed. W. M. Ede (London: Hodder and Stoughton, 1932)

Studdert-Kennedy, Geoffrey, *The warrior, the woman and the Christ* (London: Hodder and Stoughton, 1928)

Studdert-Kennedy, Geoffrey, *The wicket gate, or plain bread* (London: Hodder and Stoughton, 1923)

Studdert-Kennedy, Geoffrey, *The unutterable beauty* (1927; London: Mowbray, 1983)

Tavener, John, *The music of silence: a composer's testament*, ed. Brian Keeble (London: Faber, 1999)

Taylor, John V., *The go-between God: the Holy Spirit and the Christian mission* (London: SCM Press, 1972)

Temple, William, *Christus veritas: an essay* (London: Macmillan, 1924)

Temple, William, *Readings in St John's Gospel* (London: Macmillan, 1955)

Thornton, Martin, *English spirituality: an outline of ascetical theology according to the English pastoral tradition* (London: SPCK, 1963; repr. Cambridge, MA: Cowley, 1986)

Thornton, Martin, *Pastoral theology: a reorientation* (London: SPCK, 1958)

Thornton, Martin, *The rock and the river* (London: Hodder and Stoughton, 1965)

Tilby, Angela, 'Bearing witness', in *Lay Christians: a variety of gifts* (Supplement no. 60 to *The Way*, August 1987, pp. 51–63)

Tilby, Angela, *Let there be light: praying with Genesis* (London: DLT, 1989)

Toynbee, Philip, *Part of a journey: an autobiographical journal, 1977–1979* (London: Collins, 1981)

Tugwell, Simon, OP, *Did you receive the Spirit?* (London: DLT, 1972)

Tugwell, Simon, OP, *Prayer*, 2 vols (Dublin: Veritas, 1974)

Tugwell, Simon, OP, *Reflections on the Beatitudes* (London: DLT, 1980)

Underhill, Evelyn, *Abba* (1940; Harrisburg, PA: Morehouse, 1982)

Underhill, Evelyn, *The essentials of mysticism and other essays* (London: Dent, 1920)

Underhill, Evelyn, *The essentials of mysticism and other essays* (Oxford: Oneworld, 1995) (extracts from *The essentials of mysticism* (1920), *Mixed pastures* (1933), and *The house of the soul* (1929))

Underhill, Evelyn, *The fruits of the Spirit* (1942; Harrisburg, PA: Morehouse, 1982)

Underhill, Evelyn, *The life of the Spirit and the life of to-day* (Upton Lectures 1921–2) (London: Methuen, 1922)

Underhill, Evelyn, *Man and the supernatural* (London: Methuen, 1927)

Underhill, Evelyn, *Mysticism: a study in the nature and development of man's spiritual consciousness*; 5th edn (London: Methuen, 1914); 12th edn (Oxford: Oneworld, 1993)

Underhill, Evelyn, *The mystics of the Church* (London: James Clarke, 1925)

Underhill, Evelyn, *Letters*, ed. C. Williams (1943; London: DLT, 1991)

Underhill, Evelyn, *Collected papers*, ed. L. Menzies (London: Longmans, Green, 1946)

Underhill, Evelyn, *Practical mysticism* (1914; Columbus, Ohio: Ariel, 1986)

Underhill, Evelyn, *The school of charity* and *The mystery of sacrifice* (London: Longmans, 1954)

Underhill, Evelyn, *Worship*, 2nd edn (London: Nisbet and Co., 1937)

Vann, Gerald, OP, *The divine pity: a study in the social implications of the Beatitudes* (1945; London: Collins, 1956)

Vann, Gerald, OP, *At the foot of the Cross: the seven lessons of Mary for the sorrowing heart* (1950; Manchester, New Hampshire: Sophia, 1998)

Vann, Gerald, OP, *The pain of Christ and the sorrow of God* (1947; New York: Alba, 1994)

Vanstone, W. H., *Love's endeavour, love's expense* (London: DLT, 1977)

Vanstone, W. H., *The stature of waiting* (London: DLT, 1982)

von Hügel, Friedrich, *The mystical element of religion as studied in Saint Catherine of Genoa and her friends*, 2 vols (1908; 2nd edn, London: Dent, 1923)

von Hügel, Friedrich, *Spiritual counsels and letters*, ed. D. V. Steere (London: DLT, 1964)

Wakefield, Gordon S., *Medicines for the heart* (Buxton: Church in the Marketplace, 1999) (sermons)

Wakefield, Gordon S., *The life of the Spirit today* (report of British Council of Churches Working Party on the Spiritual Life) (London: Epworth, 1968)

Ward, Neville, *Five for sorrow, ten for joy: a consideration of the rosary* (London: Epworth, 1971)

Ward, Neville, *The use of praying* (London: Epworth, 1967; new edn 1998)

Ward, Reginald Somerset, see also Morgan, E. R.

Weatherhead, Leslie D., *The Christian agnostic* (London: Hodder and Stoughton, 1965)

Weatherhead, Leslie D., *A private house of prayer* (London: Hodder and Stoughton, 1958)

Weatherhead, Leslie D., *Psychology, religion and healing* (London: Hodder and Stoughton, 1951; 2nd edn 1952/3)

Weatherhead, Leslie D., *Salute to a sufferer* (1962; London: Arthur James, 1986)

Webb, C. C. J., *Religious experience* (London: Oxford UP, 1945)

Williams, Charles, *Essential writings in spirituality and theology*, ed. C. Heeling (Cambridge, MA: Cowley, 1993)

Williams, Charles, *The figure of Beatrice: a study in Dante* (London: Faber, 1943)

Williams, Charles, *The image of the city and other essays* (London: Oxford UP, 1958)

Williams, Harry, *Becoming what I am* (London: DLT, 1977)

Williams, Harry, *Poverty, chastity and obedience: the true virtues* (London: Mitchell Beazley, 1975)

Williams, Harry, *Some day I'll find you: an autobiography* (London: Mitchell Beazley, 1982)

Williams, Harry, 'Theology and self-awareness', in A. R. Vidler (ed.), *Soundings: essays concerning Christian understanding* (Cambridge UP, 1962), pp. 67–102

Williams, Harry, *True resurrection* (1972; London: Collins, 1983)

Williams, Harry, *The true wilderness* (London: Constable, 1965)

Winnicott, D. W., *The child, the family, and the outside world* (Harmondsworth: Penguin, 1964)

Winnicott, D. W., *Human nature* (London: Free Association, 1988)

Winnicott, D. W., *Playing and reality* (London: Tavistock, 1971)

Wyon, Olive, *The altar fire* (London: SCM Press, 1954)

Wyon, Olive, *Prayer* (London: Collins, 1962)

Wyon, Olive, *The school of prayer* (London: SCM Press, 1943)

Secondary Works

Allchin, A. M., 'Monastic life and unity in Christ', in M. B. Pennington (ed.), *One yet two: monastic tradition east and west* (Cistercian Studies 29) (Kalamazoo, MI: Cistercian Publications, 1976), pp. 474–86

Anson, Peter, *The call of the desert* (London: SPCK, 1964)

Armstrong, Karen, *The gospel according to woman: Christianity's creation of the sex war in the West* (London: Elm Tree, 1986)

Baker, Janet, *Spirituality and music* (Eric Symes Abbott Memorial Lecture 3) (1988)

Bedoyère, Michael de la, *The life of Baron von Hügel* (London: Dent, 1951)

Berger, Peter L., *A rumour of angels* (Harmondsworth: Penguin, 1971)

Bradley, Ian, *Celtic Christianity: making myths and chasing dreams* (Edinburgh UP, 1999)

Brooke, Odo, OSB, *Studies in monastic theology* (Cistercian Studies 37) (Kalamazoo, MI: Cistercian Publications, 1980) (collected articles)

Bryant, Christopher, SSJE, *Jung and the Christian way* (London: DLT, 1983)

Burgess, Stanley M. and McGee, Gary B. (eds), *Dictionary of Pentecostal and Charismatic Movements* (Grand Rapids, MI: Zondervan, 1988)

Calder, Angus, *The people's war: Britain 1939–1945* (London: Jonathan Cape, 1969; repr. Pimlico, 1992)

Chadwick, Owen, *Michael Ramsey: a life* (Oxford: Clarendon, 1990)

Clark, Stephen R. L., *Thinking about the earth: philosophical and theological models for ecology* (London: Mowbray, 1993)

Clarke, Peter, *Hope and glory: Britain 1900–1990* (Penguin History of Britain) (Harmondsworth: Penguin, 1996)

Conlon, D. J. (ed.), *G. K. Chesterton: a half century of views* (Oxford UP, 1987)

Cox, Harvey, *Fire from heaven: the rise of Pentecostal spirituality and the reshaping of religion in the twenty-first century* (Reading, MA: Addison-Wesley, 1995)

Curtis, Geoffrey, CR, *William of Glasshampton*, 2nd edn (London: SPCK, 1978)

Davie, Grace, *Religion in Britain since 1945: believing without belonging* (Oxford: Blackwell, 1994)

Dudley-Smith, Timothy, *John Stott: the making of a leader* (Leicester: Inter-Varsity, 1999)

Edrington, Roger B., *Everyday men: living in a climate of unbelief* (Studies in the intercultural history of Christianity, 46) (Frankfurt-am-Main: Peter Lang, 1987)

Forster, Roger, *Ten new churches* (London: MARC Europe, 1986)

Fussell, Paul, *The Great War and modern memory* (New York and London: Oxford UP, 1975)

Goldingay, John, 'Charismatic spirituality: some theological reflections', in *Theology* 99 (1996), pp. 177–87

Gordon, Lyndall, *Eliot's new life* (Oxford UP, 1988)

Greene, Dana, *Evelyn Underhill: artist of the infinite life* (London: DLT, 1991; New York: Crossroad, 1990)

Halliburton, John (ed.), *Cathedrals and society: a theological appraisal* (Manchester: Tiltman Desktop Publishing, 1995)

Hardy, Dennis, *Utopian England: community experiments 1900–1945* (London: Spon, 2000)

Harper, Michael, *As at the beginning: the twentieth century Pentecostal revival* (London: Hodder and Stoughton, 1965)

Hastings, Adrian, *A history of English Christianity, 1920–1985* (London: Collins, 1986)

Hebblethwaite, Margaret, *Motherhood and God* (London: Geoffrey Chapman, 1984)

Heelas, Paul, 'Diana's self and the quest within', in J. Richards et al. (eds), *Diana: the making of a media saint* (London: Tauris, 1999), pp. 98–118

Hocken, Peter, *Streams of renewal: the origins and development of the charismatic movement in Great Britain*, rev. edn (Carlisle: Paternoster, 1997)

Holden, Pat (ed.), *Women's religious experience: cross-cultural perspectives* (Beckenham: Croom Helm, 1983)

Hollenweger, Walter J., 'Healing through prayer: superstition or forgotten Christian tradition?', in *Theology* 92 (1989), pp. 166–74 (1989i)

Hollenweger, Walter J., 'Music in the service of reconciliation', in *Theology* 92 (1989), pp. 276–86 (1989ii)

Hollenweger, Walter J., *Pentecostalism: origins and developments worldwide* (Peabody, MA: Hendrickson, 1997)

Howse, Kenneth, *Religion, spirituality and older people* (London: Centre for Policy on Ageing, 1999)

Hunter, Harold D. and Hocken, Peter D. (eds), *All together in one place: theological papers from the Brighton conference on world evangelization* (Sheffield: Sheffield Academic Press, 1993)

Kay, William K., *Inside story: a history of British Assemblies of God* (Mattersey, nr Doncaster: Mattersea Hall Publishing, 1990)

Kerridge, Roy, *The storm is passing over: a look at Black Churches in Britain* (London: Thames and Hudson, 1995)

Loades, Ann, *Evelyn Underhill* (Fount Christian thinkers) (London: HarperCollins, 1997)

Lovelock, James, *Gaia: a new look at life on earth* (1979; rev. edn Oxford UP, 1995)

MacCarthy, Fiona, *Stanley Spencer: an English vision* (London: Yale UP, 1998)

Mascall, E. L., *Corpus Christi* (London: Longmans, 1953)

Mascall, E. L. and Box, H. S. (eds), *The Blessed Virgin Mary: essays by Anglican writers* (London: DLT, 1963)

Miles, Rosalind, *The women's history of the world* (London: Collins Paladin, 1989)

Morgan, E. R., *Reginald Somerset Ward, 1881–1962: his life and letters* (London: Mowbray, 1963)

Packer, J. I., *Knowing God* (1973), 2nd edn (London: Hodder and Stoughton, 1993)

Partington, Angela, 'The designer housewife in the 1950s', in J. Attfield and P. Kirkham (eds), *A view from the interior: women and design* (London: Women's Press, 1989; repr. with new material 1995), pp. 206–14

Perham, Michael (ed.), *The renewal of common prayer: unity and diversity in Church of England worship* (London: SPCK and Church House Publishing, 1993)

Platten, S. and Lewis, C., *Flagships of the Spirit: cathedrals in society* (London: DLT, 1998)

Purvis, Sally B., 'Christian feminist spirituality', in L. Dupré and D. E. Saliers (eds), *Christian spirituality III: post-Reformation and modern* (World Spirituality) (New York: Crossroad, 1989), pp. 500–19

Ravetz, Alison, 'A view from the interior', in J. Attfield and P. Kirkham (eds), *A view from the interior: women and design* (London: Women's Press, 1989, repr. with new material 1995), pp. 187–205

Reckitt, Maurice B., *For Christ and the people: studies of four Socialist priests and prophets of the Church of England, 1870–1930* (London: SPCK, 1968)

Roberts, Elizabeth, *A woman's place: an oral history of working-class women, 1890–1940* (Oxford: Blackwell, 1984)

Quebedeaux, Richard A., *Charismatic renewal: the origins, development, and significance of Neo-Pentecostalism as a religious movement in the United States and Great Britain, 1901–74* (Oxford University DPhil thesis, 1975)

Root, John, *Encountering West Indian Pentecostalism: its ministry and worship* (Grove booklets on ministry and worship 66) (Bramcote, Notts.: Grove, 1979)

Silkin, Jon, *Out of battle: the poetry of the Great War*, 2nd edn (London: Routledge and Kegan Paul, 1987)

Spencer, Jon Michael, *Protest and praise: sacred music of black religion* (Minneapolis: Fortress, 1990)

Sutcliffe, S. and Bowman, M. (eds), *Beyond new age: exploring alternative spirituality* (Edinburgh UP, 2000)

Suurmond, Jean-Jacques, *Word and spirit at play: towards a charismatic theology* (London: SCM Press, 1994)

Sylvester, David, *Looking at Giacometti* (London: Chatto and Windus, 1994)

Tastard, Terry, 'Divine presence and human freedom: the spirituality of Evelyn Underhill reconsidered', in *Theology* 94 (1991), pp. 426–32

Townroe, John, 'Retreats', in Cheslyn Jones et al. (eds), *The study of spirituality* (London: SPCK, 1986), pp. 578–81

Tuchman, Barbara, *The proud tower: a portrait of the world before the War, 1890–1914* (1962; London: Macmillan, 1980)

van der Post, Laurens, *Yet being someone other* (London: Hogarth, 1983)

Vasey, Michael, *Strangers and friends: a new exploration of homosexuality and the Bible* (London: Hodder and Stoughton, 1995)

Wakefield, Gordon S., 'Forsyth on prayer', in T. Hart (ed.), *Justice the true and only mercy: essays on the life and theology of Peter Taylor Forsyth* (Edinburgh: T. and T. Clark, 1995), pp. 67–76

Wakefield, Gordon S., *Methodist spirituality* (London: Epworth, 1999)

Walker, Andrew, *Restoring the Kingdom: the radical Christianity of the house church movement*, 4th edn, (Guildford: Eagle, 1998)

Ward, Maisie, *Gilbert Keith Chesterton* (London: Sheed and Ward, 1945)

White, Victor, OP, *God and the unconscious*; (London: Harvill, 1952)

Whittall, Arnold, *Jonathan Harvey* (London: Faber, 1999)

Wilkinson, Alan, *Christian Socialism: Scott Holland to Tony Blair* (1998 Scott Holland Lectures) (London: SCM Press, 1998)

Wilkinson, Alan, *The Church of England and the First World War* (London: SPCK, 1978)

Wilkinson, Alan, 'The poetry of war', in *Theology* 89 (1986), pp. 459–70

Wilkinson, Alan, *The Community of the Resurrection: a centenary history* (London: SCM Press, 1992)

Wilkinson, John L., *Church in Black and White* (Windows on theology) (Bonn: Pahl-Rugenstein; Edinburgh: St Andrew, 1993)

Wilson, A. N., *C. S. Lewis: a biography* (London: Collins, 1990)

Wilson, Elizabeth, *Only halfway to Paradise: women in postwar Britain, 1945–1968* (London: Tavistock, 1980)

Woodham, Jonathan M., *Twentieth-century design* (Oxford history of art) (Oxford UP, 1997)

Woodhead, Linda, 'Diana and the religion of the heart', in J. Richards et al. (eds), *Diana: the making of a media saint* (London: Tauris, 1999), pp. 119–39

Woodward, James (ed.), *Embracing the chaos: theological responses to AIDS* (London: SPCK, 1990)

Worrall, B. G., 'Some reflections on Black-led churches in England', in *Theology* 90 (1987), pp. 5–14

GLOSSARY OF AUTHORS

This glossary includes those writers whose work is discussed in this chapter, and whose biographical details are not included in the section that deals with them.

Baelz, Peter (1923–2000)

Anglican priest and theologian; Regius Professor of Moral and Pastoral Theology, University of Oxford 1972–9; Dean of Durham 1980–8.

Baker, John Austin (1928–)

Anglican priest and theologian; Bishop of Salisbury 1982–93.

Byrne, Lavinia (1947–)

Roman Catholic theologian and broadcaster; for many years she was a member of the Institute of the Blessed Virgin Mary, a Roman Catholic religious order.

Chapman, J. Arundel (1885–1934)

Theological tutor at Didsbury College, Manchester 1924–30, and at Headingley College 1930–4. He was deeply influenced by von Hügel and a range of other Christian sources, and developed a theology with strongly mystical overtones. He committed suicide in June 1934.

Dawson, Christopher (1898–1970)

Roman Catholic historian and educational theorist; held chairs at Exeter, Liverpool and Harvard.

Ecclestone, Alan (1904–92)

Anglican priest; Ecclestone worked in industrial parishes in Cumbria and Sheffield and produced, in *Yes to God*, one of the finest books on spirituality to appear in English in the twentieth century. In 1948, disillusioned with Labour, he joined the Communist Party and remained for years an active member. Like many Christian Socialists he saw the Eucharist in strongly social terms, and (unlike some of them) he served his parishioners with what Alan Wilkinson (1998, p. 175) describes as 'Benedictine-like stability'.

Eliot, T(homas) S(tearns) (1888–1965)

Anglican layperson. Born at St Louis, Missouri; moved to England where he was baptized and confirmed in the Church of England in 1927, becoming both a devout traditional Anglican and a literary figure of international repute. Eliot's early poetical works, such as *Prufrock* (1917) and *The waste land* (1922), reflect his agnosticism. Later, in his Christian period, he was deeply influenced by Lancelot Andrewes, Dante, St John of the Cross and Julian of Norwich. *Murder in the Cathedral* (1935), a play about the death of Thomas Becket, was written for the Canterbury Festival, 1935. In *The ideal of a Christian society* (1939), Eliot offers a powerful critique of Fascism, largely as a form of paganism.

Flew, R. Newton (1886–1962)

Methodist minister. Flew was the first non-Anglican to win a DD by examination at Oxford University. Newton Flew represents the anti-charismatic strain in Methodism. His work *The idea of perfection* was produced in 1934: in it he acknowledges his indebtedness to von Hügel (Preface, p. ix). He clearly longed to restore to Dissent a coherent and thoroughly theological vision of Christian perfection, though the specifics of precisely how that vision would draw and transform people in the middle of the twentieth century is not really made clear.

P. T. (Peter) Forsyth (1848–1921)

Congregationalist minister. Principal of Hackney Congregational College from 1901 until his death in 1921; perhaps the greatest English theologian of the Edwardian era, and certainly the outstanding figure in early twentieth-century Congregationalism.

George, A(lfred) Raymond (1912–99)

Methodist minister, theologian and liturgical scholar.

Gore, Charles (1853–1932)

Anglican priest and theologian, and successively Bishop of Worcester, Birmingham and Oxford. Gore helped to found the Christian Social Union in 1889, and in the same year became prominent as a result of the controversy surrounding *Lux mundi*, a volume of essays he edited. In 1887 he founded what became the Community of the Resurrection at Mirfield, Yorkshire.

Green, Peter (1871–1961)

Anglican priest. Rector of St Philip's Salford for almost 50 years (until 1950), and 'in the true succession of the great parish priests of the Church of England' (obituary in *The Times*, 18 November 1961).

Harris, J(ames) Rendel (1852–1941)

Quaker textual critic and theologian: he became curator of manuscripts at the John Rylands Library, Manchester.

Harton, Frederick Percy (1889–1958)

Anglican priest; Dean of Wells. His *The elements of the spiritual life: a study in ascetical theology* (1932) was written in order to 'give to my brethren of the Anglican Communion what we do not at present possess, a comprehensive study of the Christian spiritual life' (Preface, p. v). He draws on the work of established Catholic writers like St Thomas Aquinas, St Francis de Sales and St Vincent de Paul.

Headlam, Stewart (1847–1924)

Anglican priest. Educated at Eton and Cambridge, he was strongly influenced by F. D. Maurice. He was ordained priest in 1872, becoming curate of Bethnal Green in east London in 1873, but his deeply felt political views later caused his bishop to refuse to license him; most of his ministry was devoted to social and educational reform. He vigorously defended the secularist Bradlaugh, to the consternation of his bishop; but he also vigorously defended the First World War, believing the allies to be engaged in a spiritual combat.

Hebert, (Arthur) Gabriel (1886–1963)

Anglican priest and religious of the Society of the Sacred Mission, Kelham. His *The Parish Communion* (1937) reflected the liturgical renewal movement within contemporary continental Catholicism, and significantly influenced the worshipping life of the Church of England. *Liturgy and society* (1935) argues for the role of the whole Church, articulated in its liturgy, as a source of peace and reconciliation for the whole church. Hebert was also strongly influenced by F. D. Maurice, whom he described as 'that seer and prophet of the future whose importance has never yet been fully recognized', (1935, p. 108).

King, Ursula (1938–)
Professor of Theology and Religious Studies at the University of Bristol; the author of many books on women, world religions and spirituality.

Leech, Kenneth (1939–)
Anglican priest; he was for six years Rector of St Matthew's, Bethnal Green, and has written substantial and influential studies of Christian spirituality which reflect both profound learning, Anglo-Catholic theology, and passionate social commitment.

Macquarrie, John (1919–)
Anglican priest. Lady Margaret Professor of Divinity, University of Oxford, 1970–86, and author of a number of influential theological works.

Maitland, Sara (1950–)
Roman Catholic (formerly Anglican) writer and theologian.

Micklem, Nathaniel (1888–1976)
Congregational minister. Principal of Mansfield College 1931–53. He was much influenced by Catholic as well as Anglican theology. He became one of the most influential expositors of contemporary understanding of Reformation theology.

Noel, Conrad (1869–1942)
Anglican priest. Noel became a passionate preacher of 'Catholic Socialism', becoming in 1908 full-time organizing secretary of the Church Socialist League. He was Vicar of Thaxted in Essex from 1910 until his death in 1942: here he preached a vigorously Christian Socialist Gospel (with lyrical medieval overtones) that combined a lasting belief in the Soviet Communist ideal with a love of fine liturgy and music. He aroused huge controversy by flying the Red Flag and the Sinn Fein flag, as well as by holding a procession of the Blessed Sacrament through the streets of the town and giving Benediction from the steps of the old Guildhall there.

Oman, John (1860–1939)
Presbyterian minister and theologian, he was Principal of Westminster College Cambridge from 1925 to 1935. Among his works were *The Church and the divine order* (1911) and *Grace and personality* (1917).

Phillips, D(ewi) Z(ephaniah) (1934–)
Welsh philosopher; he has written extensively on philosophical and theological subjects.

Polanyi, Michael (1891–1976)
Born in Budapest, he became a professor of physical chemistry and of social studies at the University of Manchester, and a Fellow of Merton College Oxford. He was a Fellow of the Royal Society. His books *Personal knowledge* and *The study of man* won him the Lecomte de Noüy Award, 1959.

Robinson, John A. T. (1919–83)
Anglican priest, New Testament scholar and Bishop of Woolwich 1959–69. His *Honest to God* (1963) sold nearly a million copies within three years and supremely articulated the theological mood of the 1960s. It contains some important reflections on spirituality.

Sangster, William Edwin (1900–59)
Methodist minister, Minister of Central Hall Westminster from 1939 to 1955. His works include *The path to perfection: an examination and restatement of John Wesley's doctrine of Christian perfection* (1943) – written 'during the period in which I forsook my home to share the life of bombed-out people in a public air-raid shelter' (Preface, p. 6); *The pure in heart: a study in Christian sanctity*

(1954), an extended study of the nature of Christian holiness; and *Teach me to pray* (with *How to form a prayer cell* and *How to live in Christ*).

Selby, Peter (1941–)
Anglican priest and theologian; Bishop of Worcester from 1997.

Stott, John (1921–)
Anglican priest. Stott exemplifies the dominant strand in Anglican Evangelicalism during the century: of middle-class background, educated at independent school and Cambridge, he reflects the extensive influence of the university Christian Unions. After firmly rejecting his father's insistence that he join the army, Stott was ordained a deacon at All Souls Langham Place, in London, which has remained the base for his increasingly influential ministry ever since. Stott chaired the second Evangelical Anglican Congress, at Nottingham in 1977, which accelerated the development of a more socially committed Evangelicalism.

Studdert-Kennedy, Geoffrey (1883–1929)
Anglican priest. The most famous Chaplain to the Forces during the First World War (which earned him the nickname 'Woodbine Willie'); priest, poet and author; he became active after the War on behalf of the Industrial Christian Fellowship (*The word and the work* (1925) is dedicated 'to the unemployed men and women of Great Britain'). His *The warrior, the woman and the Christ* (1928) shows a disquieting reverence for Mussolini (see e.g. pp. 104 and 106). His work shows the influence of G. K. Chesterton in its use of vivid populist language and imagery.

Taylor, John V. (1914–2001)
Anglican priest. Taylor worked for the Church Missionary Society from 1945–74. Bishop of Winchester 1975–85. His *The go-between God* (1972), a study of the Holy Spirit, has been immensely influential.

Temple, William (1881–1944)
Anglican priest and Archbishop of Canterbury 1942–4. Perhaps the most distinguished English Christian leader of the century, he was also a distinguished scholar, whose social thought in particular was enduringly influential (see e.g. *Christianity and social order*, 1942). In terms of spirituality, his *Readings in St John's Gospel* (first series 1938; second series 1939; complete edition 1945) is outstanding: a profound series of scriptural meditations.

Thornton, Martin (1915–86)
Anglican priest and scholar, whose contribution to a recovery of a balanced Catholic spirituality was outstanding. Perhaps his most famous work was *English spirituality: an outline of ascetical theology according to the English pastoral tradition* (1963). The full title is significant: this is not a general history of English spirituality, but a specific argument related to a particular tradition within it. His refusal to deal with Protestant spirituality in *English spirituality* is explained by his remark in *The rock and the river* (1965): 'a major inconsistency in modern Protestantism is that while it regards prayer as absolutely central to the Christian life, as the very heart of religion, it is nevertheless dismissed from theological thought to the position of a minor appendage' (p. 20). He argues that 'central to English Spirituality is the speculative-affective synthesis. There must be both intellectual and affective elements in healthy prayer' (1965, p. 79). For Thornton, 'ascetical' theology deals with the fundamental duties and disciplines of the Christian life; primarily, it is an approach to all branches of theology, a way of doing theology, and only secondarily is it a subject within theology. Thornton alas chooses to distinguish these two by referring to the first as '*ascetical* theology' and the second as 'ascetical-theology' (1963, pp. 20–1). This rather confusing and idiosyncratic terminology should not conceal the enduring power and importance of his spiritual legacy.

Tilby, Angela (1950–)
Anglican priest, theologian and broadcaster.

Toynbee, Philip (1916–81)
Writer, reviewer and journalist.

Vanstone, W(illiam) H(ubert) (1923–99)
Anglican priest, and parish priest of Kirkholt in Manchester diocese 1955–76. In *Love's endeavour, love's expense* (1977), his most famous book, Vanstone writes about his own sense of vocation: his father was an Anglican priest; and it was the direct personal encounter with poverty that precipitated the young Vanstone to follow his father's example (p. 5). But by the time he was ordained, in the 1950s, life on northern housing estates was no longer as grim as it had been while he was growing up in the 1930s: the previously vital ministry of the Church was no longer so important in a welfare-state society (pp. 7–8). When he moved to a new housing estate without a church, he was struck by the Church's irrelevance (p. 12). He recalls the precise moment at which he was suddenly made aware that it was precisely people's apparent lack of need for the church which paradoxically made it all the more necessary (pp. 15–16); that 'the importance of the Church lies in something other than its service to, or satisfaction of, the needs of man' (p. 16).

Vasey, Michael (1946–99)
Anglican priest, author and liturgist; tutor at St John's College, Durham, 1975–99.

Ward, Neville (1915–92)
Methodist minister and author. Among his books are *The use of praying* (1967), an outstanding exploration of the subject, and *Five for sorrow, ten for joy* (1971) – an exploration of the rosary. He was influenced by D. Z. Phillips' *The concept of prayer* (1965) as well as by a wide range of Christian traditions.

Ward, Reginald Somerset (1881–1962)
Son of an Anglican priest, he was himself ordained and became incumbent of Chiddingfold in Surrey before resigning in 1915 in order to concentrate on spiritual direction, settling at Farncombe in Surrey. Morgan (1963, p. 15) points out that 'a distaste for institutional forms of religion and formal occasions remained with him all his life'. Ward was a convinced pacifist who also wrote a life of Robespierre. Ward first became aware of a new reality in prayer, and 'an intense consciousness of our Lord', while a curate at Barnsbury in London (Morgan (1963) pp. 20–1). On reading St Teresa and Julian of Norwich he became aware that these experiences were mystical; and his letters of spiritual direction are full of profound wisdom. In his letters he recorded his conclusion that nearly all his spiritual experiences 'consisted of the revelation that God had done something in my life which showed He loved me' (Morgan (1963) p. 69).

Weatherhead, Leslie (1893–1976)
Methodist; minister of the City Temple in London 1936–59; President of the Methodist Conference 1955–6. Weatherhead exerted an immense influence as preacher and writer, and played an important part in reconciling religion with psychiatry. Weatherhead's own life was not free from anxieties and stress: in the introduction to his *A private house of prayer* he acknowledges the fears sown in his own heart during childhood (1958, p. 28). See J. Travell, *Doctor of souls: a biography of Leslie Dixon Weatherhead* (Cambridge: Lutterworth, 1999), and Wakefield (1999).

Williams, Harry (1919–)
Anglican priest; Fellow of Trinity College Cambridge 1951–69, and Dean from 1958 to 1969. He became a monk in the Community of the Resurrection at Mirfield in 1972. His books include *The true wilderness*, *True resurrection*, and the autobiographical *Some day I'll find you.*

Wyon, Olive (1881–1966)

Distinguished lay scholar, ecumenist and spiritual writer; born in London and brought up in a Non-conformist context. She was very close to the Community of Grandchamp, which began in 1931, consisting of lay women from the Reformed tradition who built up a centre for prayer and meditation using the Taizé office. Her *Living springs* (1963) was dedicated to the foundress. This stress on the communal dimension of prayer was crucial for Wyon. She became Principal of St Colm's Missionary College of the Church of Scotland in Edinburgh in 1951, but before that was actively involved in the World Council of Churches at Geneva. She wrote a number of books on prayer, and her writing is drawn from a rich variety of sources: one of her books, *The school of prayer*, is dedicated to Evelyn Underhill.

Index